P9-EDW-374

36: *British Novelists, 1890-1929: Modernists,* edited by Thomas F. Staley (1985)

37: *American Writers of the Early Republic,* edited by Emory Elliott (1985)

38: *Afro-American Writers After 1955: Dramatists and Prose Writers,* edited by Thadious M. Davis and Trudier Harris (1985)

39: *British Novelists, 1660-1800,* 2 parts, edited by Martin C. Battestin (1985)

40: *Poets of Great Britain and Ireland Since 1960,* 2 parts, edited by Vincent B. Sherry, Jr. (1985)

41: *Afro-American Poets Since 1955,* edited by Trudier Harris and Thadious M. Davis (1985)

42: *American Writers for Children Before 1900,* edited by Glenn E. Estes (1985)

43: *American Newspaper Journalists, 1690-1872,* edited by Perry J. Ashley (1986)

44: *American Screenwriters,* Second Series, edited by Randall Clark, Robert E. Morsberger, and Stephen O. Lesser (1986)

45: *American Poets, 1880-1945,* First Series, edited by Peter Quartermain (1986)

46: *American Literary Publishing Houses, 1900-1980: Trade and Paperback,* edited by Peter Dzwonkoski (1986)

47: *American Historians, 1866-1912,* edited by Clyde N. Wilson (1986)

48: *American Poets, 1880-1945,* Second Series, edited by Peter Quartermain (1986)

49: *American Literary Publishing Houses, 1638-1899,* 2 parts, edited by Peter Dzwonkoski (1986)

50: *Afro-American Writers Before the Harlem Renaissance,* edited by Trudier Harris (1986)

51: *Afro-American Writers from the Harlem Renaissance to 1940,* edited by Trudier Harris (1987)

52: *American Writers for Children Since 1960: Fiction,* edited by Glenn E. Estes (1986)

53: *Canadian Writers Since 1960,* First Series, edited by W. H. New (1986)

54: *American Poets, 1880-1945,* Third Series, 2 parts, edited by Peter Quartermain (1987)

55: *Victorian Prose Writers Before 1867,* edited by William B. Thesing (1987)

56: *German Fiction Writers, 1914-1945,* edited by James Hardin (1987)

57: *Victorian Prose Writers After 1867,* edited by William B. Thesing (1987)

58: *Jacobean and Caroline Dramatists,* edited by Fredson Bowers (1987)

59: *American Literary Critics and Scholars, 1800-1850,* edited by John W. Rathbun and Monica M. Grecu (1987)

60: *Canadian Writers Since 1960,* Second Series, edited by W. H. New (1987)

61: *American Writers for Children Since 1960: Poets, Illustrators, and Nonfiction Authors,* edited by Glenn E. Estes (1987)

62: *Elizabethan Dramatists,* edited by Fredson Bowers (1987)

63: *Modern American Critics, 1920-1955,* edited by Gregory S. Jay (1988)

64: *American Literary Critics and Scholars, 1850-1880,* edited by John W. Rathbun and Monica M. Grecu (1988)

65: *French Novelists, 1900-1930,* edited by Catharine Savage Brosman (1988)

66: *German Fiction Writers, 1885-1913,* 2 parts, edited by James Hardin (1988)

67: *Modern American Critics Since 1955,* edited by Gregory S. Jay (1988)

68: *Canadian Writers, 1920-1959,* First Series, edited by W. H. New (1988)

69: *Contemporary German Fiction Writers,* First Series, edited by Wolfgang D. Elfe and James Hardin (1988)

70: *British Mystery Writers, 1860-1919,* edited by Bernard Benstock and Thomas F. Staley (1988)

LIBRARY
ST. MICHAEL'S PREP SCHOOL
1042 STAR RD. - ORANGE, CA 92669

(Continued on back endsheets)

Dictionary of Literary Biography • Volume Eighty-three

French Novelists Since 1960

Dictionary of Literary Biography • Volume Eighty-three

French Novelists Since 1960

Edited by
Catharine Savage Brosman
Tulane University

8052

A Bruccoli Clark Layman Book
Gale Research Inc. • Book Tower • Detroit, Michigan 48226

Advisory Board for
DICTIONARY OF LITERARY BIOGRAPHY

Louis S. Auchincloss
John Baker
William Cagle
Jane Christensen
Patrick O'Connor
Peter S. Prescott

Matthew J. Bruccoli and Richard Layman, *Editorial Directors*
C. E. Frazer Clark, Jr., *Managing Editor*

Manufactured by Edwards Brothers, Inc.
Ann Arbor, Michigan
Printed in the United States of America

Copyright ©1989
GALE RESEARCH INC.

Library of Congress Cataloging-in-Publication Data

French novelists since 1960/edited by Catharine Savage Brosman.
     p.   cm.–(Dictionary of literary biography; v. 83)
     "A Bruccoli Clark Layman book."
     Includes index.
     ISBN 0-8103-4561-7
     1. French fiction–20th century–Dictionaries. 2. French fiction–20th century–Bio-bibliography. 3. Novelists. French–20th century–Biography–Dictionaries. I. Brosman, Catharine Savage, 1934- . II. Series.
PQ671.F69 1989
843'.914'09–dc19
[B]   89-1127
                                                              CIP

In memory: Edward Curtis Hill (1863-1958) and Phoebe Elliott Hill (1864-1952)

Contents

Plan of the Series

. . . Almost the most prodigious asset of a country, and perhaps its most precious possession, is its native literary product—when that product is fine and noble and enduring.

Mark Twain*

The advisory board, the editors, and the publisher of the *Dictionary of Literary Biography* are joined in endorsing Mark Twain's declaration. The literature of a nation provides an inexhaustible resource of permanent worth. We intend to make literature and its creators better understood and more accessible to students and the reading public, while satisfying the standards of teachers and scholars.

To meet these requirements, *literary biography* has been construed in terms of the author's achievement. The most important thing about a writer is his writing. Accordingly, the entries in *DLB* are career biographies, tracing the development of the author's canon and the evolution of his reputation.

The purpose of *DLB* is not only to provide reliable information in a convenient format but also to place the figures in the larger perspective of literary history and to offer appraisals of their accomplishments by qualified scholars.

The publication plan for *DLB* resulted from two years of preparation. The project was proposed to Bruccoli Clark by Frederick G. Ruffner, president of the Gale Research Company, in November 1975. After specimen entries were prepared and typeset, an advisory board was formed to refine the entry format and develop the series rationale. In meetings held during 1976, the publisher, series editors, and advisory board approved the scheme for a comprehensive biographical dictionary of persons who contributed to North American literature. Editorial work on the first volume began in January 1977, and it was published in 1978. In order to make *DLB* more than a reference tool and to compile volumes that individually have claim to status as literary history, it was decided to organize volumes by topic, period, or genre. Each of these freestanding volumes provides a biographical-bibliographical guide and overview for a particular area of literature. We are convinced that this organization—as opposed to a single alphabet method—constitutes a valuable innovation in the presentation of reference material. The volume plan necessarily requires many decisions for the placement and treatment of authors who might properly be included in two or three volumes. In some instances a major figure will be included in separate volumes, but with different entries emphasizing the aspect of his career appropriate to each volume. Ernest Hemingway, for example, is represented in *American Writers in Paris, 1920-1939* by an entry focusing on his expatriate apprenticeship; he is also in *American Novelists, 1910-1945* with an entry surveying his entire career. Each volume includes a cumulative index of subject authors and articles. Comprehensive indexes to the entire series are planned.

With volume ten in 1982 it was decided to enlarge the scope of *DLB*. By the end of 1986 twenty-one volumes treating British literature had been published, and volumes for Commonwealth and Modern European literature were in progress. The series has been further augmented by the *DLB Yearbooks* (since 1981) which update published entries and add new entries to keep the *DLB* current with contemporary activity. There have also been *DLB Documentary Series* volumes which provide biographical and critical source materials for figures whose work is judged to have particular interest for students. One of these companion volumes is entirely devoted to Tennessee Williams.

We define literature as the *intellectual commerce of a nation:* not merely as belles lettres but as that ample and complex process by which ideas are generated, shaped, and transmitted. *DLB* entries are not limited to "creative writers" but extend to other figures who in their time and in their way influenced the mind of a people. Thus the series encompasses historians, journalists, publishers, and screenwriters. By this means readers of *DLB* may be aided to perceive litera-

*From an unpublished section of Mark Twain's autobiography, copyright © by the Mark Twain Company.

ture not as cult scripture in the keeping of intellectual high priests but firmly positioned at the center of a nation's life.

DLB includes the major writers appropriate to each volume and those standing in the ranks immediately behind them. Scholarly and critical counsel has been sought in deciding which minor figures to include and how full their entries should be. Wherever possible, useful references are made to figures who do not warrant separate entries.

Each *DLB* volume has a volume editor responsible for planning the volume, selecting the figures for inclusion, and assigning the entries. Volume editors are also responsible for preparing, where appropriate, appendices surveying the major periodicals and literary and intellectual movements for their volumes, as well as lists of further readings. Work on the series as a whole is coordinated at the Bruccoli Clark Layman editorial center in Columbia, South Carolina, where the editorial staff is responsible for accuracy of the published volumes.

One feature that distinguishes *DLB* is the illustration policy–its concern with the iconography of literature. Just as an author is influenced by his surroundings, so is the reader's understanding of the author enhanced by a knowledge of his environment. Therefore *DLB* volumes include not only drawings, paintings, and photographs of authors, often depicting them at various stages in their careers, but also illustrations of their families and places where they lived. Title pages are regularly reproduced in facsimile along with dust jackets for modern authors. The dust jackets are a special feature of *DLB* because they often document better than anything else the way in which an author's work was perceived in its own time. Specimens of the writers' manuscripts are included when feasible.

Samuel Johnson rightly decreed that "The chief glory of every people arises from its authors." The purpose of the *Dictionary of Literary Biography* is to compile literary history in the surest way available to us–by accurate and comprehensive treatment of the lives and work of those who contributed to it.

The *DLB* Advisory Board

Foreword

DLB 83: French Novelists Since 1960 is the third of three volumes in the *DLB* series devoted to French fiction writers of the present century. The first volume, *DLB 65: 1900-1930*, treats novelists whose principal production appeared either before World War I or in the ten years or so following the war and who are thus associated chiefly with the early decades of the century, even if, like Roger Martin du Gard and François Mauriac, they continued publishing well after 1930. The second, *DLB 72: French Novelists 1930-1960*, spanning the second decade of the interwar period, World War II, and the following fifteen years, deals with what can accurately be called the generation of committed literature and French existentialism. With a few exceptions, the present volume features authors whose careers were established in the years just preceding 1960 or shortly thereafter, or whose most characteristic or most significant works date from this period. Among them are the New Novelists, whose remarkable literary innovations began to attract widespread attention in the late 1950s and 1960s, although in some cases their first work appeared earlier.

This chronological grouping of novelists whose careers often spanned more than one period was made on practical grounds more than on critical ones; the arrangement is not to be taken as an attempt to define literary schools and generations, although to some degree the authors classed together share aesthetic and other concerns, and among their works there are similarities characteristic of their historical periods.

What Jean-Paul Sartre saw as the acceleration of the pace of the historical process in the twentieth century has had as its parallel the rapid evolution of fictional form, as writers search for new forms, or at least attempt to shape old forms to changing realities. This is one of the hallmarks of modern French fiction and particularly of the writers in the present volume. Yet few critics in 1900 could have conceived of the variety and richness that the novel would display in France well before the end of the new century. A form that had been preeminently associated with the mi-

metic intentions of romanticism and realism–although certain of the symbolists had also adapted it to their ends–was to undergo, by mid century or shortly thereafter, modifications so sweeping and numerous as to test its identity, eroding its generic distinctiveness and making it, in the term of more than one critic, an *anti-roman*. By interior ironies, redefinition of its contours, and restatement of its subject matter, the novel form has been called into question and has taken on alternately the features of poetry, criticism, drama, autobiography, essay, history, documentary, and film. It has thus shown more of the remarkable resilience that had already made it the preferred genre of postclassical France. In the early decades of the century, even as the poet Paul Valéry was observing that he would not compose a novel because of the arbitrariness of the genre–that is, he could not deign to write a sentence such as "The marquise ordered her carriage and went out at five o'clock"–Marcel Proust, André Gide, and others were demonstrating how fictional structure could be like that of a great poem, or a great cathedral, or a piece of music, a puzzle, or a mathematical formula, with internal rigor and coherence as well as ornamental beauty. Some decades later, Claude Mauriac would show what a striking fiction *can* be composed on the motif "The marquise went out at five o'clock." From the early *roman*–the medieval term meaning a narrative, whether in prose or verse, in the vulgar or Romance tongue–through its late medieval, Renaissance, and numerous modern avatars, the romance or novel has proven itself to be both beloved of popular audiences and suitable for some of the loftiest and most ingenious expressions of sentiment and ideas of which the Western mind has proven itself capable. It is as if the very concept of story, with its linear structure corresponding to the temporal dimension of human experience, were singularly fitting for the rendering of this experience; even later fictions that are deliberately nonlinear and atemporal, by authors such as Claude Mauriac and Alain Robbe-Grillet, draw their identities from reference to the basic journey pattern that they are seeking to overturn.

Nor has any literary genre been more sensitive to the tremendous developments in the sciences as well as to the profound social and historical changes of the century. Even if analogies such as those critics once sought to establish between Albert Einstein and Proust–to take but one example–have proven shaky, post-Newtonian physics and its vast technological consequences have affected, it would seem, the contents of fiction and its form alike, if only in some writers' refusal to give their works a sense of closure, seeking instead the impression of expansion, as well as non-linearity, distortions brought about by observers, and other parallels to physical phenomena. Mathematics itself is reflected in certain fictional undertakings, as the essay on Georges Perec in this volume demonstrates. Philosophy, linguistics, and the social sciences have had an even greater impact; not only have individual writers been influenced by such figures as Friedrich Nietzsche, Sigmund Freud, Edmund Husserl, Henri Bergson, and, more recently, Ferdinand de Saussure, Claude Lévi-Strauss, and Jacques Lacan: twentieth-century psychology, psychiatry, anthropology, and sociology have claimed the novel as one of their fields of investigation as well as a privileged form of expression. Such characteristics as fictional polyvalence and ambiguity, multiple plots and narrators, and competing levels of reality within the text mirror the multiplication of modes of knowledge in the twentieth century. Most of all, the modern French novel has shared with the sciences an epistemological function, calling into question previous modes of knowledge, proposing new ones, and questioning, by its ironic self-interrogation, the very possibility and value of knowledge. As for the great historical upheavals of the twentieth century–wars, persecutions, economic crises, revolutions, colonial uprisings–they have left their mark on the content and form alike of modern French fiction, especially in the novels of the middle period, but even in more recent ones, which reflect, directly or indirectly, the sense of apocalypse that, for many, marked the 1930s and 1940s. Much of the work of Jean Cayrol, Marguerite Duras, Elie Wiesel, and others in this volume would be incomprehensible without reference to the horrors of World War II, which some of these writers experienced personally.

The desire to show the widest possible range of fictional types and experimentation, while giving full treatment to those authors who

are now considered the greatest modern French novelists, is the principle underlying *DLB 65*, *DLB 72*, and *DLB 83*. In the first two volumes, both historical importance and what now seems like lasting value are weighed. In the present volume, authors such as Michel Butor, Robbe-Grillet, and Claude Simon, whose names are familiar in many countries and who will certainly be considered years from now as major voices of their generation, are found side by side with less well known figures whose fame may be far from assured but whose fictional practice or vision has awakened considerable interest. Throughout these three volumes, authors representing various currents, such as the poetic novel, the working-class novel, the feminist novel, the ideological novel, and the experimental novel, are included in the selection. In this context the term *experimental* is not intended to denote any particular technique or content but merely a departure from previous norms; as Robbe-Grillet rightly observed, Gustave Flaubert wrote the "new novel" of 1857, Proust that of 1913. In addition, these volumes treat numerous other figures whose production does not fit entirely into the rough categories just mentioned. There is a wide range of aesthetic, ideological, and behavioral opposites: innovators and traditionalists, Communists and royalists, Catholics and atheists, feminists and misogynists, working-class writers and aristocrats, partisans of thought and partisans of action, activists and recluses, practitioners of the *roman-fleuve* and those of the terse narrative.

Readers will note, however, the predominant movement toward formal and ideological liberalism–that is, a loosening of forms and an ideological drift away from authoritarian nineteenth-century structures and standards toward a questioning of all inherited values. That these phenomena do not always appear together does not detract from their forcefulness in the modern French novel, which, it can be argued, has functioned more than once as an instrument of social change, while also reacting to change. On the one hand, for instance, a great literary innovator such as Proust was in most respects a social conservative; on the other, a literary traditionalist such as Martin du Gard questioned profoundly the society that preceded World War I. Similarly, while questioning social and literary structures that have marginalized women and others, a recent novelist, Marie Cardinal, has retained a somewhat traditional, linear organization in her fiction. Broadly speaking, while few of the formal innovators included in the present volume have been political activists, unlike their predecessors of the 1930s and 1940s, most have contested, even if indirectly, social structures and the assumptions about individual human beings and groups on which they are based.

Readers will observe in addition the significant place occupied in modern French fiction by foreign literary influences, particularly American writers and such novelists as Fyodor Dostoyevski and Franz Kafka, and by other arts–painting, the cinema–whose aesthetic principles often underlie the fictional experimentation. It is more than a curiosity, furthermore, that many French novelists have traveled widely or lived abroad. Among authors treated in the present volume, Butor and Robbe-Grillet have spent lengthy periods of time in the United States; Vladimir Volkoff, Monique Wittig, and Wiesel make their homes in the United States. There are also several foreigners, including Volkoff, Wiesel, and Romain Gary, who have made French their literary language, although they were born to others. This literary cosmopolitanism has been a major influence in the development of the modern French novel.

A further phenomenon to be noted is the importance of magazines, schools, and other connections among French novelists; despite, on the part of some writers, tendencies to iconoclasm and independence, occasionally to isolation, many, like their counterparts in previous centuries, have played important roles in literary groups, notably those of the *Nouvelle Revue Française* and *Tel Quel*. It would, however, be erroneous to assume that these groupings, with the exception of surrealism and a few others, represented some sort of orthodoxy and were more than loose associations. Literary friendships have been strikingly important, as the essays on Gide and Martin du Gard in *DLB 65* illustrate. Taken as a whole, the modern French novel illustrates in several ways what Julia Kristeva terms intertextuality–strictly, the presence of one text in another, for instance, by allusion or quotation; more loosely construed, any reference of a text (thematic or formal) to previous ones. For these novelists have been voracious readers as well as writers, and they have written for those who know the canon, even when they have rejected it: for example, Nathalie Sarraute's notion of character cannot be understood without reference to Honoré de Balzac. Reflected in the essays of all three volumes is a web of personal relationships among authors, not just the friendships referred

to above but also marriages and love affairs between writers that were central to their development; the most striking illustration is furnished by two authors in *DLB 72*, Louis Aragon and Elsa Triolet, in the joint publication of their *Œuvres romanesques croisées* (1964-1974). Another notable literary relationship, which affected the younger writer's work, is that between Claude Mauriac, who is discussed in the present volume, and his father, François, treated in *DLB 65*.

In the period after 1960 there are several main strains in French fiction, some of which overlap. One, but not the most important, is the continuation of the realistic or mimetic vein, illustrated in the novel of manners, which was characteristic of much nineteenth-century fiction, and in the social and political novels of such outstanding modern authors as Aragon and Martin du Gard. In the case of certain writers, among them Michel de Saint Pierre and Volkoff, realism is associated with conservatism in politics or other areas. It would be a mistake to assume that recent realists merely use the formulas of their predecessors; in most cases, they have renewed the mode by integrating into it either formal diversity, contemporary concerns, or other features that mark it as belonging to its age. A second strain is a new classicism, although it is not truly new, since the classical concern for beauty and concision of expression and truth of psychological analysis is not foreign to such other twentieth-century writers as Gide, François Mauriac, Raymond Radiguet, and Albert Camus, and even, paradoxically, the expansive modernist Proust. The renewed classicism of the post-1960 years, at times a reaction to opposite tendencies in fiction, is evident in the terse psychological narratives of Françoise Sagan and others.

A third strain is that of surrealism. Butor remarked that French writers whose formative years were spent when surrealism was a significant influence were indelibly marked by it, if in different ways. His own writing embodies his particular manner of going beyond this influence; the fiction of André Pieyre de Mandiargues and Julien Gracq, whose *Au château d'Argol* (*The Castle of Argol*, 1938) André Breton called the one genuine surrealist novel, shows surrealism's persistent vitality. A fourth strain is the mythological, sometimes connected to surrealism and visible in a wide range of writers, from Robbe-Grillet, who used the Oedipus story as an organizing principle for *Les Gommes* (*The Erasers*, 1953); through Butor, whose novels are structured as mythological quests and refer to such figures as Theseus; to Gracq, who made the Grail quest central in his work; to Michel Tournier and Mandiargues, whose fiction is permeated with myths from various cultures. Even the historical novels of Jules Roy, which re-create the past of French Algeria, include oblique references to sun myths, and, in a sense, produce their own myth. It seems clear that myth has assumed for many twentieth-century writers the function of an organizing principle, adopted perhaps as a reaction against rationalism and its nineteenth-century offshoot, positivism. It serves both to connect their works to premodern man, as the anthropologists have described him, and to express the troubled psyche of post-Freudian man.

The most important strain of recent fiction, one that is related to some of the elements discussed above, is the move away from the committed literature of the previous generation. In "Qu'est-ce que la littérature?" (*What Is Literature?*, 1947) Sartre, the model of the committed writer, called for a new fiction to fit the postwar understanding of social and psychological man and displayed his own innovations in *Le Sursis* (*The Reprieve*) in 1945. But his understanding of fiction as rooted in the political problems of the period and directed toward identifying, if not solving, these problems seemed, to many of those reaching artistic maturity in the 1950s and later, ill-fitted to their own time. It suited neither their postlapsarian, postcataclysmic sense of the well-deserved death of intellectual, cultural, and political beliefs of the past and a concurrent loss of meaning nor their changed understanding of writing, which had evolved under the influence of linguistics and other disciplines and was characterized by distrust of language and a preoccupation with structure. The results of this reaction were the spectacular formal experiments of Butor, Robbe-Grillet, Sarraute, Simon, and others, and, more generally, the widespread rejection of fictional formulas, especially notions of plot and character. No longer wedded to the formulas of realism, nor to an earlier aestheticism, these New Novelists denied that the world could be imitated in a book, that it was even knowable, and, at the extreme, saw in fiction a purely mental and arbitrary creation, self-generating and self-reflexive. This new fiction in turn created a new criticism to deal with it—in the essays of Roland Barthes and Jean Ricardou, for instance—which was then directed toward earlier fiction, creating thus a re-reading of the literary past well suited to the con-

temporary conviction that the literary fact, like others, has no absolute meaning, but only relative ones.

It should not be thought, however, that formalism has completely dominated French fiction since 1960. The realistic and classical psychological novels alluded to earlier have had both critical and popular success. And, despite distancing themselves from earlier novelists, some experimental writers have combined their formal innovations with a search for meaning, as they have redefined it, often in a context of anguish, which does not resemble the metaphysical and ethical *Angst* of the existentialists some years before but rather seems to reflect a loss of epistemological grounding. In Simon's *La Route des Flandres* (*The Flanders Road*, 1960), the phrase "How can one know?" punctuates and haunts the text. Butor observed that he wrote to become more intelligent. Others, having made clear their view that language does not reveal the world but instead creates it, have shown how this creative power can form as many versions of the world as there are minds. Among some authors, one can discern even a more traditional concern for the mechanisms of social institutions and for the self. Under siege from almost the beginning of the century, when Proust identified the multiple and contradictory selves that made up his characters, and more and more assailed in the works of Sartre and then those of Robbe-Grillet, the idea of a self has not entirely disappeared even among those who reject an earlier literary psychology, and several authors treated here, especially women, have been interested in the expanded possibilities of fictional techniques apparently less for the sake of technique than as models for developing their own voices and styles to express their particular concerns.

One further observation to be made on French literary life concerns the numerous and prestigious prizes for fiction, prizes that are mentioned time and again in the *DLB* essays. The announcements of the Goncourt, Médicis, Fémina, Renaudot, Interallié, and Académie Française awards are always major events of the literary year. Several novelists treated in these three volumes won the Nobel Prize for Literature: Romain Rolland (1915), Roger Martin du Gard (1937), André Gide (1947), François Mauriac (1952), Albert Camus (1957), Jean-Paul Sartre (who rejected the 1964 prize), Claude Simon (1985). The Irish novelist Samuel Beckett, who wrote a large part of his work in French and was the Nobel laureate in 1969, is treated in volumes 13 and 15 of the *DLB*.

Three practical observations need to be added. First, the *DLB* twentieth-century French novelists volumes do not include essays on writers whose work belongs to a Francophone literature outside of France; the development of fiction in Black Africa, North Africa, and the Antilles is separate and significant enough to deserve treatment by itself, and Quebec novelists are treated in the *DLB* volumes on Canadian writers. Nor are novelists dealt with here who are considered Swiss or Belgian. Second, the claim is not being made that these three *DLB*s are exhaustive. There are other novelists in France in this cen-

tury who, it might be argued, deserve a place in one of these three volumes. While some were omitted for practical reasons, including the difficulty of finding English-language specialists on their work, others were excluded because, in one way or another, their work did not seem as representative or as significant as that of others. Such decisions inevitably reflect editorial preferences. Third, the lists of references following each essay do not include several major general bibliographies; along with suggestions for further reading, these are given at the end of each volume.

—Catharine Savage Brosman

Acknowledgments

This book was produced by Bruccoli Clark Layman, Inc. Karen L. Rood is senior editor for the *Dictionary of Literary Biography* series. Margaret A. Van Antwerp was the in-house editor.

Production coordinator is Kimberly Casey. Art supervisor is Susan Todd. Penney L. Haughton is responsible for layout and graphics. Copyediting supervisor is Joan M. Prince. Typesetting supervisor is Kathleen M. Flanagan. William Adams, Laura Ingram, and Michael D. Senecal are editorial associates. The production staff includes Brandy H. Barefoot, Rowena Betts, Charles D. Brower, Joseph M. Bruccoli, Amanda Caulley, Teresa Chaney, Patricia Coate, Mary Colborn, Sarah A. Estes, Brian A. Glassman, Cynthia Hallman, Kathy S. Merlette, Sheri Beckett Neal, and Virginia Smith. Jean W. Ross is permissions editor.

Walter W. Ross and Jennifer Toth did the library research with the assistance of the reference staff at the Thomas Cooper Library of the University of South Carolina: Daniel Boice, Cathy Eckman, Gary Geer, Cathie Gottlieb, David L. Haggard, Jens Holley, Dennis Isbell, Jackie Kinder, Marcia Martin, Jean Rhyne, Beverly Steele, Ellen Tillett, Carol Tobin, and Virginia Weathers.

French Novelists Since 1960

Dictionary of Literary Biography

Hervé Bazin
(Jean Pierre Marie Hervé-Bazin)
(17 April 1911-)

Terence Dawson
National University of Singapore

BOOKS: *Parcelles,* as Jean Marbolivien (Paris: Editions de la Jeune Académie, 1933);

Visages, as Jean Marbolivien (Poitiers: Editions de l'Action Intellectuelle, 1934);

Jour, anonymous (Nice: Iles de Lérins/Journal des Poètes, 1947); revised in *Jour, suivi de A la poursuite d'Iris* (1971);

A la poursuite d'Iris (Nice: Iles de Lérins, 1948); revised in *Jour, suivi de A la poursuite d'Iris* (1971);

Vipère au poing (Paris: Grasset, 1948); translated by W. J. Strachan as *Grasping the Viper* (London: Secker & Warburg, 1950); republished as *Viper in the Fist* (New York: Prentice-Hall, 1951);

La Tête contre les murs (Paris: Grasset, 1949); translated by Strachan as *Head Against the Wall* (London: Secker & Warburg, 1952; New York: Prentice-Hall, 1952);

La Mort du petit cheval (Paris: Grasset, 1950);

Le Bureau des mariages (Paris: Grasset, 1951);

Lève-toi et marche (Paris: Grasset, 1952); translated by Herma Briffault as *Constance* (New York: Crown, 1955);

Allez vous rhabiller au bestiaire (Périgueux: Privately printed, 1953);

Humeurs (Paris: Grasset, 1953);

L'Huile sur le feu (Paris: Grasset, 1954);

Le Miracle privé (Carcassonne: Recherches Graphiques, 1955);

Qui j'ose aimer (Paris: Grasset, 1956); translated by Richard Howard as *A Tribe of Women* (London: Hamilton, 1958; New York: Simon & Schuster, 1958); republished as *An End to Passion* (New York: Hillman Books, 1960);

La Clope (Quebec: Institut Littéraire du Québec, 1959);

La Fin des asiles (Paris: Grasset, 1959);

Au nom du fils (Paris: Seuil, 1960); translated by Howard as *In the Name of the Son* (London: Secker & Warburg, 1962; New York: Simon & Schuster, 1962);

Chapeau bas (Paris: Seuil, 1963);

Plumons l'oiseau (Paris: Grasset, 1966);

Le Matrimoine (Paris: Seuil, 1967);

Les Bienheureux de la Désolation (Paris: Seuil, 1970); translated by Derek Coltman as *Tristan* (New York: Simon & Schuster, 1971; London: Hodder & Stoughton, 1972);

Jour, suivi de A la poursuite d'Iris (Paris: Seuil, 1971);

Cri de la chouette (Paris: Grasset, 1972);

Madame Ex (Paris: Seuil, 1975); translated by Philip Crant and Helen Platt (Columbia, S.C.: French Literature Publications, 1978);

Souvenirs d'un amnésique (Paris: Rombaldi, 1976);

Traits (Paris: Seuil, 1976);

Ce que je crois (Paris: Grasset, 1977);

Un Feu dévore un autre feu (Paris: Seuil, 1978);

L'Eglise verte (Paris: Seuil, 1981);

Qui est le prince? (Paris: Grasset, 1981);

Abécédaire (Paris: Grasset, 1984);

Le Démon de minuit (Paris: Grasset, 1988).

TELEVISION: *Qui j'ose aimer,* 11 February 1976.

OTHER: Pierre Demeuse, *La Nuit londonienne,*
   preface by Bazin (Brussels: Dutilleul, 1955);
Albertine Sarrazin, *Romans, lettres et poèmes,* pref-
   ace by Bazin (Paris: Jean-Jacques Pauvert,
   1967);
Jean-Pierre Desclozeaux, Picha, Puig-Rosado, and
   Siné, *Au secours!,* preface by Bazin (Paris:
   Calmann-Lévy, 1973);
Franck Innocent, *Peinture: Franck Innocent,* pref-
   ace by Bazin (Rouen: Editions BDS, 1973);
Roland Dorgelès, *Images,* preface by Bazin (Paris:
   Albin Michel, 1975);
"A Propos des prix littéraires: L'Académie Gon-
   court," afterword to *Le Défi des Goncourt,* by
   Jacques Robichon (Paris: Denoël, 1975);
   translated as "Literary Prizes: The Goncourt
   Prizes," *News from France,* 2 (16 November
   1976): 13-19;
Maurice Grevisse, *Le Bon Usage,* tenth edition, pref-
   ace by Bazin (Gembloux: J. Duculot, 1975);
Le Loiret rural de 1900 à 1930, preface by Bazin
   (Paris: Editions du Chêne, 1978);
"Le Grand Méchant doux," in *Autopsy,* by Bazin
   and others (Paris: Plasma, 1984).

PERIODICAL PUBLICATIONS: "Nid à rats," *Cor-
   respondances,* 1 (1954): 47-52, 87-94, 127-
   132, 168-170;
"Qui veut faire l'ange: Chapitre d'un futur
   roman de Hervé Bazin," *Lettres Francaises*
   (1-7 November 1956): 4;
"Ma Conception du roman," *Table Ronde,* 131 (No-
   vember 1958): 14-17;
"Une Nouvelle de Hervé Bazin, de l'Académie
   Goncourt: 'La Tire,'" *Nouvelles Littéraires* (9
   October 1958): 1, 2;
"Probité," *Stop,* 1 (Fourth Trimester 1960): 1-3;
"La Mansarde," *Œuvres Libres,* 200 (January
   1963): 71-80;
"Hervé Bazin fait le point," *Figaro Littéraire,* no.
   1177 (25 November-1 December 1968): 6-9.

Hervé Bazin is best known as the author of
Vipère au poing (1948; translated as *Grasping the
Viper,* 1950), a devastating account of the hatred
between a boy and his mother. He has written
twelve other novels, the most successful of which
are about the difficulties characteristic of family
life. He has also published three collections of
poems, short stories, and several works of nonfiction. In a poll conducted in 1956 by *Nouvelles
Littéraires,* he was voted the best novelist of the previous decade. The following year he was awarded
the Grand Prix de Littérature de Monaco and, in

Hervé Bazin (photograph copyright © Jerry Bauer)

1958, he was elected to the Académie Goncourt,
of which he became president in 1973. Since
1960 he has been president of the Association
des Ecrivains de l'Ouest. In 1967 he won the
Grand Prix de l'Humour Noir and in October
1974 the Grand Prix International de Poésie. He
has campaigned vigorously for world peace, for
which he was awarded the Lenin Peace Prize in
1979. He is one of the finest stylists and storytell-
ers of his time.

The first phase of Bazin's literary career is
marked by the violence of his iconoclasm; the second, by a reappraisal of the values to which he
had appeared to be hostile. There is less of a
change of heart here than there might seem.
Bazin writes passionately, but he is a conservative
at heart. His very revolt can be seen as a desire
to believe in the institutions on which he pours
scorn–notably, the family. His entire work is the
product of his early disappointments at home. He
has been called "le spécialiste des difficultés
familiales" (the specialist in family problems).
There can be no doubt that his own unhappy
childhood, the tensions in his first two marriages,
and the conflicts following his two divorces provided the material for his best works. Although

he has explored other subjects, it is as an autobiographical novelist that he will be remembered.

Jean Pierre Marie Hervé-Bazin was born at Angers on 17 April 1911. His family belonged to the landed gentry and included several writers. His great-uncle was René Bazin (1853-1932), whose works were held in considerable esteem during the first two decades of the twentieth century. His father, Jacques Hervé-Bazin, was a lawyer and a university professor of law who had married (Jeanne) Paule Guilloteaux in January 1909. In spite of the fact that theirs was a marriage of convenience, they had three children. The eldest, Ferdinand, was born in December 1909; Jean Pierre, the writer (who throughout his career has used the name Hervé Bazin), sixteen months later; the youngest, Pierre, in August 1912. Paule, who lacked any maternal instinct, soon entrusted their care to her mother-in-law. World War I further divided the family. Although his position exempted him from military service, Jacques Hervé-Bazin enlisted and won the Croix de Guerre. Wounded, he was discharged and offered a post as professor of law in Shanghai. He left for China alone, but three months after his departure his wife decided to follow him. Given that their marriage was already showing signs of strain, it is difficult to understand why she made this decision, especially since it entailed a grueling journey. What is clear is that her decision became the single most important event in her son's life.

His mother's absence marked Hervé Bazin deeply. He seems to have resented every moment of his upbringing. In 1919 he was sent to school in Angers. A few weeks later, while playing croquet, he received a blow on the head. As soon as he was able to return to school, his grandmother died. A telegram was sent to his parents, but they were unable to return from China for another six months. Greeting his mother at the station, Bazin clumsily stepped on her foot. She slapped him. He never forgave her. He had missed her when she was absent; he now took a violent antipathy to her presence.

It was decided that the children should be removed from school and taught at home by a tutor. After three tutors had come and gone, Bazin drew up a petition asking his father to send them all to boarding school. Although his father agreed, the three brothers were sent to different schools. Bazin did not take any better to boarding school than he had to home teaching. When he was twelve he was expelled from Sainte-Croix

for trying to run away to Paris. At his next school, Notre-Dame de Combrée, he was allowed to stay only three months. Then he was entrusted to a priest in a nearby town, but this program did not work, either. Finally, he was sent to his father's old tutor, the abbé Maire, who lived in the Vosges. He stayed only eighteen months. Bazin was obviously a difficult child.

Under such circumstances it is surprising that he passed the *baccalauréat,* finishing first in an open competition in the natural sciences. In July 1928 he went to the coast for the first time and fell in love with a girl called Noémie. But more problems were on their way. Bazin wanted to study literature at the Ecole de Journalisme in Lille. His father wanted him to study law. He was forced to capitulate. It was in 1928, during his year at the Faculté de Droit at Angers, that he published his first poem in a student magazine, *L'Alliance Universitaire et Scolaire.* When he withdrew from his first-year law exams, his family decided he should be sent to a military academy. Bazin ran away. Arriving home, he took his father's car, crashed it, and wandered for a week in a daze. He was found at a friend's house, in need of hospitalization. After his discharge from a psychiatric hospital his father persuaded him to work at a family bank in Châteaubriant. Bazin soon left with the excuse that he wanted to prepare for the management exams at the Banque de France in Saint-Nazaire. His real reason was to be closer to Noémie. But her father, on hearing about one of his pranks, put an abrupt end to their relationship. Bazin was distraught. He went to Paris. His father, furious, followed him there and ordered him to join the army. He did so but, by exaggerating his myopia, secured his discharge.

A post was found for him in an uncle's chemical plant, where he met Odette Danigo. Soon afterward, they were both dismissed. His family offered to give him an allowance so that he could study literature, on the condition that he abandon Odette. He accepted the money but continued seeing her. During this time he contributed several poems to small journals (among them *La Bohème* and *L'Œuvre Latine*) mostly under the pseudonym Jean Marbolivien. Many were republished in his first small volume of collected poems, *Parcelles* (Fragments, 1933); for this same body of verse he had won the Grand Prix de Poésie 1932 de l'Union Latine. He joined a group of poets who called themselves Le Cercle d'Hermès (The Circle of Hermes). He was also writing children's stories and reviews for newspapers, notably *L'Echo de Paris*, for which he interviewed, among others, Paul Claudel, Louis Aragon, and Paul Valéry. After meeting Valéry, Bazin sent him some of his poems. Valéry's comment was not encouraging: "Vous n'êtes pas fait pour la poésie, essayez donc la prose" (You are not made for poetry, try your hand at prose). Bazin eventually took his advice but never stopped trying to prove Valéry wrong.

Bazin was nothing if not headstrong. In 1934, against his parents' advice, he married Odette Danigo. They had a son, whom they named Jacques, after Bazin's father. The compliment did little to appease the indignant parent. Within two years Bazin and Odette separated. His life was becoming increasingly difficult. When his father died, Bazin was forced to do odd jobs, including selling scrap iron. Throughout the 1930s he suffered from more or less constant nervous exhaustion, for which he periodically needed to be hospitalized. Sometime after the fall of France in World War II, he joined the Cartier group of the Resistance and assumed the name Nicolas Donzance. In 1941 Bazin turned thirty. His early promise had come to nothing. He had almost abandoned writing, and his personal life was in disarray.

Then, unexpectedly, everything came together. In April 1945 he met Jacqueline Dussolier, who became his second wife in 1948, and began writing again with furious energy. He wrote three novels in quick succession but did not offer any of them to a publisher. He destroyed the manuscripts in 1950. Their importance stems from the fact that they were, in effect, the rough drafts of his subsequent successes. He was also writing poems, one after the other. He signed many of his postwar articles Nic Hervé-Bazin, as this was the name by which many of his friends still knew him. In 1946 he founded a literary review entitled *La Coquille*, which means both shell and misprint (with a hint of *coquin*, or mischievous). Only eight issues appeared, but the magazine put Bazin in touch with many other writers who met at his home on Saturday evenings. In 1947 his collection of poems, *Jour* (Day), published anonymously, won him the Prix Guillaume Apollinaire. Encouraged by this success, he started rewriting the novel which was to make him famous.

Jean Rezeau, a small boy, comes across a sleeping viper and strangles it. The narrator, who is Jean Rezeau grown up, likens the expression in the snake's eyes to the hatred which he sees, a few years later, in those of his mother. The boy, nicknamed Brasse-Bouillon, brings the snake home to show his family, but his parents are conspicuously absent. Such is the opening of *Vipère au poing*, which traces the events which follow the return of Jean's parents from China to La Belle Angerie, the family home. Jacques Rezeau is a university professor who will agree to anything as long as he can continue with his work in peace. Mme Paule Rezeau, whom Frédie, Jean's elder brother, dubs Folcoche (for *folle cochonne*, or demented pig), is entirely devoid of maternal affection. She is devious, hypocritical, and vindictive. She wants the children to be taught by a tutor. Various weak or unsuitable priests come and go. The tension mounts continually. One day she tries to force some bad fish down Frédie's throat. The children respond by trying to poison her. The novel climaxes in an improbable and farcical attempt to drown Paule, who survives only by virtue of her indomitable will. Subsequently, she overplays her hand, and Jean is able to gain his father's consent that he and his brothers be sent away to boarding school.

Vipère au poing is undoubtedly autobiographical. Some of the minor characters–the governess and the maid, who is deaf and dumb–are given the names of their real-life originals. And yet Bazin has time and again denied that his work is autobiographical: "Je ne suis pas Brasse-Bouillon" (I am not Brasse-Bouillon). There is no contradiction here. The important point is not whether the experiences of Brasse-Bouillon are modeled on Bazin's own, but whether the situations described constitute a satisfying fiction. Whether one approves or disapproves of the subject matter, Folcoche captures the imagination. The novel is not about Mme Paule Hervé-Bazin. It is about a fictional protagonist's violent feelings toward another fictional character.

The essentially fictional nature of the relationship between son and mother is emphasized by the parallels between them. Jean recognizes that he has all the faults which he sees in his mother. Folcoche admits that Jean resembles her more than he does either of his brothers. They mirror one another; they are essentially one. Folcoche is an image of a destructive mother in a man's imagination. By implication Jean's hatred of her is a hatred of an aspect of his own character. Thus, his campaign against her, which is described in military imagery, is a civil war. The ending of the novel is ambivalent. His partial victory is also a partial defeat, for it is that aspect of his character which he has inherited from Folcoche–his own aggressive, vindictive, and unforgiving nature–which triumphs at the end.

Although the novel focuses on Jean's hatred of his mother, it is not as one-sided as many critics have suggested. M. Rezeau comes in for his share of criticism. Jean has little respect for the way in which his father abdicates authority. The casual attitude Jean has toward Madeleine, a young peasant girl whom he seduces only to abandon, is an echo of his father's desire not to be bothered by anything with which he cannot cope. *Vipère au poing* is a scathing satire on French bourgeois manners. Everything against which Jean revolts is a consequence of the fundamental absence of love in his early life resulting from his parents' unhappy marriage. His rage stems from the intimation that he is the product of their inability to love.

Bazin has been accused of deliberately trying to shock the reading public. He is something of an enfant terrible, and the charge has stuck, although it is probably unfair. Bazin's first novel was rushed into print. He delivered the manuscript to Grasset on 19 January 1948. At 3:30 the following afternoon Jean Blanzat sent him a message asking him to telephone. The following day a second message invited him to sign the contract. The publishers moved with such haste because they were evidently gambling on a *succès de scandale*. On 23 May 1948 *Vipère au poing* was published. Reviews were mixed, but not one was indifferent. The novel was awarded the Prix des Lecteurs and missed winning the prestigious Prix Goncourt by only one vote. The celebrated Colette, who had written so eloquently on her mother Sido, was unwilling to let the latter prize go to a novel which culminated in attempted matricide. But she could not prevent the novel from becoming a best-seller. Like Vladimir Nabokov's *Lolita* a few years later, *Vipère au poing* owed its success more to its audacious subject matter than to its literary merits and became notorious for the wrong reasons. Critics argued fiercely about Bazin's attitude toward his subject; very little was said about the means by which he had achieved the vivid impression which the novel makes, though Bazin was already a master of style and effect.

The same day that *Vipère au poing* was published, his second child, Jean-Paul, was born. The name is again important, for it combines his own and his mother's–a small but significant gesture.

His professional and private life had taken a new turn. Restless as ever, within three months Bazin had begun another novel, *La Tête contre les murs* (1949; translated as *Head Against the Wall*, 1952). It is the story of Arthur Gérane, a young man who has spent four years living away from home, moving from job to job. The novel opens with him breaking into his family home, burning some of his father's papers for the fun of it, stealing a gun and some money, and making his escape in his father's car. He drives into a tree which has been felled across the road and is found concussed the following morning. His father, a judge, deems it best to have him confined to a psychiatric hospital. Arthur escapes, is caught again, and again runs away. The novel traces the bewildering and horrifying course of his experiences in various psychiatric institutions, vividly described as they were at the time. On one escapade in the Vosges, he meets Stéphanie, with whom he finds a kind of happiness. They marry, and it looks as if he is going to make a complete recovery. But catching sight of some gendarmes, he takes flight; he is caught and confined again. He escapes again, but when Stéphanie–who clearly loves him–suggests he give himself up, he is distraught. Trying to flee, he falls, never to recover. Several critics attacked this second novel for being so like Bazin's first, but there are important differences. *Vipère au poing* is a domestic drama told in the first person; *La Tête contre les murs* is not only a personal but also a social tragedy narrated in the third person. Their main protagonists have little in common. Brasse-Bouillon is constantly affirming his identity; Gérane is always evading his. If there is a link between them, it is that they are equally unable to respond to the love which is shown them, by Madeleine and Stéphanie respectively.

Bazin's next novel, *La Mort du petit cheval* (The Death of the Little Horse, 1950), takes up this same theme. It is a continuation of *Vipère au poing*. Brasse-Bouillon is attracted to a girl named Micou, but Folcoche forces their separation. He flees to Paris, where he struggles to make enough money to study literature. There he meets Paule Leconidec, who helps him, and falls in love with another girl named Monique, whom he marries despite his parents' opposition. When his father dies, his mother contrives that Marcel, her favorite son, inherit everything. Brasse-Bouillon and his older brother Frédie slip into the house one night and discover letters which reveal that Marcel is the son of an adulterous relationship. The tables are turned. The two brothers turn to each other, and the novel ends with Folcoche disappearing into the night. *La Mort du petit cheval* is a revised version of "Bleu," a novel which Bazin wrote about his relationship with Noémie but never published. It suffers from the faults of many sequels. The characters do not have the mythic qualities of the originals. Folcoche's adultery is unconvincing; so too is the conjugal felicity of the young couple. The novel lacks the intensity displayed in Bazin's previous works and occasionally verges on the sentimental. It was evident that Bazin needed to rethink his material. His adolescent experiences were not an inexhaustible well. That Bazin was a gifted writer was not in doubt. His epigrammatic phrases and powerful style were beginning to earn him considerable admiration. He knew how to tell a story. The question which now faced him was: Did he have a story to tell? He spent the next decade experimenting with different kinds of fiction, trying to find a new voice.

Unable to come up with an idea for a novel, Bazin collected eight of his short stories, some of which had appeared previously in magazines, under the title *Le Bureau des mariages* (The Marriage Bureau, 1951). They owe little to autobiographical experience and show his skill at bringing out a small psychological detail to good effect. Most depend on an ironic twist. For example, the title story is about a couple who are bored with their relationship. Secretly, each begins to correspond with a member of the opposite sex. They finally arrange to meet their correspondents, only to discover that they have been writing to one another. Perhaps the best of the collection is "La Raine et le crapaud" (The Frog and the Toad), which has a tenderness not evident in Bazin's earlier work.

The following year Bazin published a novel which showed a different side of his personality. *Lève-toi et marche* (1952; translated as *Constance*, 1955) is the story of Constance Orglaise, who is confined to a wheelchair; but such is her determination that no challenge seems too much for her. She adopts a child as crippled as herself and sets herself the task of making Claude walk. She tries to help others, undeterred by her many failures. She loves Serge, a young man who does not care for her, and is loved by Luc, for whom she has no affection. Slowly the paralysis gains on her. She finally accepts the extreme unction given by a priest and is kissed by Luc, but she dies without acknowledging either. *Lève-toi et marche* reveals

Bazin's major limitation: his novels are truly effective only when the plots have a foundation in fact. His first three novels drew heavily on his own adolescence; his fourth was inspired by a young American girl named Jamie Kofmann. By the time he wrote *Lève-toi et marche*, he had convinced himself that he needed to draw on other people's experiences but was not sure how to handle such a narrative. It is, moreover, too obviously an attempt to answer Camus's question from *La Peste* (*The Plague*, 1947): "Peut-on être un saint sans Dieu?" (Can there be a lay saint?). Much as one might admire the girl's courage, this is a disappointing novel.

Bazin turned again to journalism. In 1952 he became special reporter for *Paris-Presse* at the trial of Marie Besnard, who had been accused of poisoning her husband. The following year he published two collections of poems. *Allez vous rhabiller au bestiaire* (Go and Get Dressed in the Bestiary), which consists of seven poems about animals, was printed for private circulation only. *Humeurs* (Moods), published by Grasset, is a longer collection of poems which Bazin subsequently admitted were too disparate to be put together. In 1953 he became a staff member for Grasset, his publisher, where he worked until 1961. In 1954 he became literary reviewer for *Information*. He had begun a new novel, "Nid à rats" (Nest of Rats), several extracts of which were published from 1954 to 1963. But the work was never completed.

For his next completed novel he took up the theme of a short story published in 1952 as "Tête-de-Toile" (Head of Cloth) in the *Revue de Paris* and amplified it. The narrator of *L'Huile sur le feu* (Oil on the Fire, 1954) is a sixteen-year-old girl named Céline Colu. Her father, Bertrand Colu, had his face badly burned during the war and wears a balaclava helmet to hide the wound. Her mother no longer loves him. They both love her, and because she loves them both, she cannot choose which to live with. Several fires break out, one after another, and her father, known as Tête-de-Drap (Sheet-head), manifests considerable courage in fighting them. Céline discovers that her father is also responsible for lighting the fires and that he has been driven to this behavior as a result of his wife's disgust with his burned face. The dénouement is sadly predictable. Bertrand, smitten by guilt for having let an old woman die in one of the fires, throws himself into a blaze. The story is well told, but the novel is never more than a well-told story. Bazin was still looking for a subject commensurate with his talent.

The next turning point in Bazin's life came with *Qui j'ose aimer* (1956; translated as *A Tribe of Women*, 1958), which is about a group of women who live in a house called La Fouve. The narrator is Isa, who lives with her mother, Belle, and her retarded sister, Berthe. The fourth member of the household is Nathalie, a kind of governess. Belle, a young widow, returns after a short absence with Maurice Mélizet, a lawyer. The novel ostensibly traces Isa's reaction to him. Although reluctant to do so, she finally calls him papa. Belle falls prey to a disfiguring sickness and gradually wastes away. While she is dying Maurice becomes Isa's lover, but when Belle dies, Isa is smitten with guilt and refuses Maurice's advances. He leaves, and Isa, who is pregnant, decides to remain at La Fouve. A publisher's blurb describes the novel as "l'histoire de Phèdre inversée" (the story of Phaedra inverted).

Opinion was divided between those who thought Bazin had at last found a sufficiently complex subject and those who thought that the love between Maurice and Isa was not convincing enough to carry the novel. But this, surely, was Bazin's intention. For, in spite of the fact that Isa is the narrator, the novel is best considered from Maurice's point of view, for Belle's sickness coincides with, and thus symbolically reflects, Maurice's attentions to Isa. In other words, *Qui j'ose aimer* is not primarily about Isa but about a man torn between a mother and her daughter. Maurice's love is deliberately shown to be insubstantial. He is tainted by the same tendency as Brasse-Bouillon and Gérane: an inability to consolidate a relationship. *Qui j'ose aimer* did, however, consolidate Bazin's reputation. Largely owing to its success, Bazin won the *Nouvelles Littéraires* poll, the Grand Prix de Littérature de Monaco, and election to the Académie Goncourt.

Meanwhile, Bazin's personal life was in disarray. His second marriage, which had produced four children, Jean-Paul, Maryvonne, Catherine, and Dominique, was breaking up. In 1958 he met Monique Serre-Gray, but his wife Jacqueline refused to give him a divorce. This was the background against which he worked on two very different undertakings. The first was a result of the impact made by *La Tête contre les murs*: he was commissioned by the World Health Organization to write a series of articles on mental institutions. These began to appear in *France-Soir* in April 1959 under the title "Le Tour d'Europe de la Folie" (The Tour of Europe of Madness). They were published in revised form under the title *La Fin des asiles* (The End of Asylums) later the same year. He had also begun a novel.

Daniel Astin, a professor of literature living in Chelles (Bazin's hometown at the time of writing), is the narrator of the 1960 novel *Au nom du fils* (translated as *In the Name of the Son*, 1962). He has always had difficulties committing himself to another person. His wife, Gisèle, was killed by a bomb during the war. When he returns from the front, he finds Laure, his sister-in-law, looking after the children, the youngest of whom, named Bruno, Daniel suspects might not be his. The novel opens with him chasing Bruno. When he catches up with the boy, Bruno lets slip that he thinks Daniel loves him less than he loves his other children. Daniel determines to win the boy's confidence, a challenge to which he subordinates everything else. He gradually succeeds, and in doing so discovers love for the first time. But in one important respect, his love still falls short. All along he has taken Laure for granted. His proposal of marriage to her is almost insultingly casual. Like Bazin's other heroes, Daniel has a marked inability to declare his love for a woman.

Au nom du fils is a reminder that the love between a man and his child is as fitting a subject for a novel as the love between a man and a woman. The author does no preaching: he sees that Daniel's experience is unbalanced. And the novel contains many of Bazin's most eloquent passages. It had a very mixed reception. Some greeted it with derision. For example, Robert Kanters wrote: "Ce n'est plus une vipère que M. Bazin porte au poing, mais un plat de nouilles" (It is no longer a viper that M. Bazin holds in his fist, but a plate of noodles). Jean Anglade, however, described it as "un roman si français qu'on rougit à le lire" (a novel so French that one blushes when reading it). Certainly Bazin put as much of himself into this book as he had a decade earlier into his first success. Its new tone is all the more remarkable given the two personal catastrophes which interrupted its writing. On 23 December 1959, going to fetch his mother from her home for Christmas, Bazin was involved in a serious car accident and had to spend six weeks in the hospital. A few months later his mother, no longer able to live on her own, came to stay with him and Jacqueline and died a few weeks later. She left everything she was able to bequeath freely to her eldest grandson, Jacques, ignoring not only Bazin but also the children of his second marriage. He once expressed his feelings about his mother's action with telling succinctness: "On a beau être un porc-épic, ça fait mal tout de même" (Even a porcupine can be hurt). Bazin did not love his mother, but he deeply felt the absence of her maternal affection.

Hindered by his complicated personal life, Bazin was slowing down. Several years passed before the publication of *Chapeau bas* (Hats Off, 1963), a collection of short stories, the best of which had first appeared in 1958. "Souvenirs d'un amnésique" (Memoirs of an Amnesiac; later published as the title piece of Bazin's 1976 collection) is about a man who goes on a business trip to Montreal. When he fails to return, his wife carries on and builds up his business, a lumberyard. One day, many years later, she discovers her husband Henri, whom she can scarcely recognize, on the premises. He explains that his failure to return had been owing to a concussion and a loss of his memory. His wife is at first suspicious, but when she realizes that he has not returned to take everything from her, she accepts him. Three more years elapsed before *Plumons l'oiseau* (Let Us Pluck the Bird, 1966), which is an amusing attack on grammarians and what the French call "l'esprit de système" (which, as Bazin portrays it in this work, might best be defined as overly methodical thought). It is Bazin's only full-length humorous work.

In May 1967 Bazin finally obtained his divorce from his second wife and soon afterward married Monique Serre-Grey. His next novel explores marital life. Published in 1967, it has the extraordinary title, *Le Matrimoine* (The Matrimonk), which Bazin has explained thus: "J'appelle 'Matrimoine' tout ce qui dans le mariage relève normalement de la femme, comme ce qui tend de nos jours à passer de part de lion en part de lionne (LUI)" (By "Matrimoine" I mean everything which in a marriage normally concerns the wife, especially that which used to belong in the male preserve [HIM]). The novel is about the relationship between Abel and Mariette Bretaudeau, seen from Abel's point of view. There is no plot. The novel is composed of Abel's various reflections and reactions to a marriage kept together only by inertia and habit. It is punctuated by clichés whose value the reader must decide for himself. For example, Abel claims that "Le vrai médiocre est d'abord satisfait. Je ne suis pas satisfait" (The truly mediocre person is always satisfied. I am not satisfied)— in other words, that because he is dissatisfied, he

is not mediocre. Is this to be taken at face value? Or is this opinion precisely the kind which labels him as ordinary? Like many of Bazin's other works, this one is rooted in autobiographical experiences, although Mariette bears no more relation to Bazin's second wife than one of Picasso's portraits relates to a mistress/subject of whom he had tired. *Le Matrimoine* is a devastating portrait of a provincial marriage, given spice by the ambiguity of the author's intention. It was another bestseller. The first edition sold out in less than two weeks and was largely responsible for Bazin's being awarded the Grand Prix de l'Humour Noir in October 1967.

Having exorcised his spleen, he started work on another documentary-cum-novel for which he spent more than three years researching his material. Although called "un roman" (or novel), *Les Bienheureux de la Désolation* (1970; translated as *Tristan*, 1971) is effectively a documentary about the evacuation of Tristan de Cunha when the small colony which lived on these remote islands was threatened by the eruption of a volcano in October 1961. Bazin describes the frustrations of the exiles during their two-year stay in England and their decision to return to the islands. Its central characters are fictional, but there is no plot woven around them. Many critics described it as "un conte philosophique" (a philosophical story in the vein of Voltaire's *Candide*). This is precisely its weakness, for its reflections on the mixed blessings of civilization come to a conclusion which, because the novel is based on fact, is relevant only for a small community.

Although none of his works had made the same impact as his first, such was Bazin's reputation that, in June 1971, he was elected vice-president of the Académie Goncourt. Once again, success came at a time when he was struggling to find a subject for another novel. Not having one at hand, he contented himself with reworking and reordering the poems which he had published in 1947 and 1948. The new edition, *Jour, suivi de A la poursuite d'Iris* (Day, followed by In Pursuit of Iris, 1971), is a much more cohesive volume than either of the original ones. Bazin had always wanted to be recognized as a poet. Now, at last, he was. Later the same year his sixth and last child, Claude, was born—an event which coincided with Bazin's beginning a novel in which he hoped to put to rest the subject which had made him well known.

Cri de la chouette (Screech of the Barn Owl, 1972) is, in part, an attempt to bury Folcoche once and for all. It is a continuation of the Rezeau saga. Jean is now forty-eight years old. He is married to Bertille, whose daughter, Salomé, he treats as one of his own children. Folcoche arrives unexpectedly and finds herself falling prey to a rising passion for Salomé. She tries to raise Salomé against her family. When she fails, so too does her strength. She falls sick and dies. It is a disappointing plot but told with a conviction that makes it almost as powerful as the novel in which Folcoche first appears.

In 1973 Bazin succeeded Roland Dorgelès as president of the Académie Goncourt. It seemed that a new phase had begun in his life. Somewhat surprisingly, his next novel suggests that he still had not exorcised the image of a devouring mother which had haunted him so long. *Madame Ex* (1975; translated into English in 1978) traces a divorced woman's grasping and hypocritical dealings with her ex-husband and her attempts to make her children hate their father as much as she does. They divide into "mamiens" and "papiens" (mother's pets and father's pets), and the outcome is somewhat predictable: two of the children run away to stay with their father, while another, who is hostile to him, becomes pregnant. The woman is forced to capitulate, and the novel ends on a would-be happy note. Bazin's subject was topical in that the propriety of divorce was being hotly debated in France at the time. But because the novel has a third-person narrator, it lacks the emotional unity which makes *Vipère au poing* so memorable.

For many years Bazin had been composing maxims and epigrams in the form of short and pithy poems. In 1976 he published a collection of these as *Traits* (Rough Sketches). Although not always successful, they reveal Bazin's biting humor at its best. The following year he gave an extended answer to a question often put to him. *Ce que je crois* (What I Believe, 1977) is divided into eleven chapters, each of which neatly tackles an issue: God's existence, science, death, women, the young, the family, and so forth. Although it is a well-written work, it is riddled with clichés, such as his "ten commandments" on how to raise children and his canned history of civilization's major turning points.

That Bazin had lost his touch is evident in his next novel. *Un Feu dévore un autre feu* (One Fire Burns Out Another's Burning, 1978) is set in an improbable Central American country in the midst of an even less probable counterrevolution. Manuel Alcovar, a revolutionary, is attend-ing the wedding of his girlfriend Maria's sister. The entire wedding party is shot by the crew of an army tank, while Manuel and Maria escape to the French embassy. The cultural attaché hides them in his house. Manuel eventually falls sick and tries to leave. Maria follows him. They are picked up by an army patrol and shot. This is not the stuff of great fiction.

Bazin's next novel demonstrates his deep-rooted love of nature in the precision of his terminology and plasticity of his language. *L'Eglise verte* (The Green Cathedral, 1981) is the story of Actaeon and Artemis in reverse. Jean-Luc Godion, a retired teacher, and his daughter, Claude, often walk in the forest. One day they come across a young man bathing naked in a clearing. They watch him–Claude, who is a young divorcée, with interest. The young man is suspected of being responsible for some small thefts from farms bordering on the forest. A party of police goes in search of him, and finds him wounded. He refuses to disclose his name. Eventually, the real criminal is discovered, and the young man is cleared. But he does not want to enter into a relationship with Claude. The novel ends with her looking down at the clearing where she first saw the young man, asking her father whether it was all a dream. The novel has many beautiful passages; it is an obviously heartfelt hymn to nature. But it has no depth. Bazin is at his best when describing personal antipathy.

In 1981, with *Qui est le prince?* (Who is the Prince?), Bazin took up a form of fiction that had long interested him: writing for children. It is worth noting that Bazin's daughter Maryvonne has also written children's books (for example, *La Rose bleue* [The Blue Rose], 1977). Bazin's *Abécédaire* (ABC), a volume of reflections on various subjects presented alphabetically, appeared in 1984. Some are predictable–his entry for *paix* (peace), for example. But on the whole it is an entertaining work which reveals both his humor and his personal modesty. His entry for *mouche* (housefly) recalls the fact that his father's hobby was entomology. Jacques Hervé-Bazin named several new species of flies after his children. Bazin, in his seventies, writes: "Mais à treize ans, j'avais ma mouche! Ce qui restera de mon œuvre dans un siècle, je ne sais. Mais une mouche porte mon nom, une mouche vole pour moi jusqu'à la fin du monde!" (But at thirteen, I had my own fly! Of what will remain of my work in a hundred years time, I have no idea. But a fly bears my name; a fly will carry my name until the end of time!).

His most recent novel, *Le Démon de minuit* (The Midnight Demon, 1988), is about a seventy-year-old historian who collects shells. It opens with Gérard suffering a heart attack, from which he recovers and thereupon resolves to live the rest of his life as fully as he is able. His marriage has collapsed. He no longer loves Solange, his wife, who is having an affair with another man, and so he turns to Béatrice, a young woman with whom he has corresponded but whom he has never met, who once sent him an unusual snail shell. Their affair coincides with the death of his brother Séverin, a schoolteacher. He learns of this from Yveline, a young colleague of Séverin's with whom Gérard has also corresponded for several years. Gérard and Yveline meet at the funeral; she is forty-six years younger than he but has clearly grown to love him through his letters. They marry and have a child, but shortly after he suffers another heart attack. There is a possibility of his recovering, but if he did he would almost certainly be paralyzed. Yveline, knowing how much he would hate this, hopes he dies, for that way "il aura gagné! Il n'a jamais été vieux" (he will have won! He has never been old). His determination to uphold his right to love ("le droit à l'amour"), to live his life in the way he chooses to the very end, is the main theme, but the novel is also about the complexities of family life which arise when a man has a great-grandchild from his first marriage of the same age as a grandchild from his second, both of whom are older than the son he has by Yveline, his third wife. The family tree given at the outset prepares the reader for an exploration of all these interconnected threads. Instead, Bazin provides a dynastic novella, sometimes moving, but never absorbing.

Bazin is a consummate stylist. The honor was well deserved when, in 1975, he was invited to write a preface for the tenth edition of Maurice Grevisse's *Le Bon Usage*, the standard guide to correct French. He is a craftsman. But he lacks that something extra–imagination or vision–which is a prerequisite of great art. Bazin has achieved a wide readership. By 1985 fourteen million copies of his works had been sold in France and another thirteen million had been sold in translation. But in only three novels has he found a subject equal to his considerable talent: *Vipère au poing*, *Qui j'ose aimer*, and *Le Matrimoine*.

It remains to be seen whether he has another in preparation.

Interviews:
Christine Garnier, "Hervé Bazin," in her *L'Homme et son personnage* (Paris: Grasset, 1955), pp. 1-19;
Phillip A. Crant, "Un Entretien avec Hervé Bazin," *French Review*, 47 (Spring 1974): 253-260;
Henri Deligny, "Interview. Hervé Bazin: 'La Famille n'est pas plus bourgeoise que la respiration,'" *Monde de l'Education*, no. 25 (February 1977): 12-14;
Jean-Louis de Rambures, "Hervé Bazin," in his *Comment travaillent les écrivains* (Paris: Flammarion, 1978), pp. 27-33;
Rambures, "Le Rêve au poing," *Nouvelles Littéraires*, no. 2658 (27 October-2 November 1978): 5;
Annette Colin-Simard, "L'Homme en tant qu'homme est né en Afrique," *Jeune Afrique*, no. 931 (8 November 1978): 97-99.

Bibliography:
Keith Goesch, *Hervé Bazin*, Calepins de Bibliographie 7, volume 1 (Paris: Lettres Modernes/Minard, 1985).

References:
Jean Anglade, *Hervé Bazin* (Paris: Gallimard, 1962);
Pierre Cogny, *Sept Romanciers au-delà du roman* (Paris: Nizet, 1963), pp. 31-52;
Martin Dufossé, "Tradition et évolution dans les romans angevins d'Hervé Bazin," in *Les Angevins de la littérature*, edited by Georges Cesbron (Angers: Presses de l'Université, 1979), pp. 613-624;
Maurice Genevoix, "Hervé Bazin," *Biblio*, 24 (May-June 1956): 1-7;
Alphonse Leguil, "Grammaire et style narratifs chez Hervé Bazin (dans *Vipère au poing* et *Le Matrimoine*)," in *Les Angevins de la littérature*, edited by Cesbron (Angers: Presses de l'Université, 1979), pp. 625-667;
Catherine Macé et Marie-Paule Séité, *Hervé Bazin* (Saint-Brieuc: Presses Universitaires de Bretagne, 1971);
Pierre Moustiers, *Hervé Bazin, ou le romancier en mouvement* (Paris: Seuil, 1973);
Georges Raillard, "Hervé Bazin," in *Ecrivains d'aujourd'hui*, edited by Bernard Pingaud (Paris: Grasset, 1960), pp. 71-78.

Michel Butor
(14 September 1926-   )

F. C. St. Aubyn
University of Pittsburgh

SELECTED BOOKS: *Passage de Milan* (Paris: Editions de Minuit, 1954); chapters 11-12, translated by Donald Schier, *Carleton Miscellany*, 4 (Summer 1963): 121-132; chapters 7-10, translated by Guy Daniels, in *The Award Avant-Garde Reader,* edited by Gil Orlovitz (New York: Award Books, 1965), pp. 25-83;

L'Emploi du temps (Paris: Editions de Minuit, 1956); translated by Jean Stewart as *Passing Time* (New York: Simon & Schuster, 1960; London: Faber & Faber, 1961);

La Modification (Paris: Editions de Minuit, 1957); translated by Stewart as *Second Thoughts* (London: Faber & Faber, 1958); republished as *A Change of Heart* (New York: Simon & Schuster, 1959);

Le Génie du lieu (Paris: Gallimard, 1958); translated by Lydia Davis as *The Spirit of Mediterranean Places* (Marlboro, Vt.: Marlboro Press, 1986);

Degrés (Paris: Gallimard, 1960); translated by Richard Howard as *Degrees* (New York: Simon & Schuster, 1961; London: Methuen, 1962);

Répertoire: Etudes et conférences, 1948-1959 (Paris: Editions de Minuit, 1960); translated in part in *Inventory* (1968);

Histoire extraordinaire: Essai sur un rêve de Baudelaire (Paris: Gallimard, 1961); translated by Howard as *Histoire Extraordinaire: Essay on a Dream of Baudelaire's* (London: Cape, 1969);

Mobile: Etude pour une représentation des Etats-Unis (Paris: Gallimard, 1962); translated by Howard as *Mobile: Study for a Representation of the United States* (New York: Simon & Schuster, 1963);

Réseau aérien: Texte radiophonique (Paris: Gallimard, 1962);

Votre Faust, libretto by Butor, music by Henri Pousseur (Paris: Gallimard, 1962);

Description de San Marco (Paris: Gallimard, 1963); translated by Barbara Mason as *Description of San Marco* (Fredericton, N.B.: York Press, 1983);

Michel Butor, 1974 (photograph by Bill Jay)

Répertoire II: Etudes et conférences, 1959-1963 (Paris: Editions de Minuit, 1964); translated in part in *Inventory* (1968);

Essais sur les Modernes (Paris: Gallimard, 1964);

Hérold (Paris: Georges Fall, 1964);

Illustrations (Paris: Gallimard, 1964);

Litanie d'eau: Poème sur dix gravures de Gregory Masurovsky (Paris: La Hune, 1964);

Les Œuvres d'art imaginaires chez Proust (London: Athlone Press, University of London, 1964); translated by Remy Hall as "The Imaginary Works of Art in Proust," in *Inventory* (1968);

Dans les flammes: Chanson du moine à Madame Nhu (Stuttgart: Belser, 1965);

6 810 000 litres d'eau par seconde (Paris: Gallimard, 1965); translated by Elinor S. Miller as *Niagara* (Chicago: Regnery, 1969);

Dialogues des règnes (Paris: Brunidor, 1967);

Portrait de l'artiste en jeune singe: Capriccio (Paris: Gallimard, 1967);

Paysage de répons, suivi de Dialogues de règnes (Albeuve: Castella, 1968);

La Banlieue de l'aube à l'aurore: Mouvement brownien (Montpellier: Fata Morgana, 1968);

Essais sur "Les Essais" (Paris: Gallimard, 1968);

Répertoire III (Paris: Editions de Minuit, 1968); translated in part in *Inventory* (1968);

Inventory, translated by Howard and others, edited by Howard (New York: Simon & Schuster, 1968; London: Cape, 1970);

Essais sur le roman (Paris: Gallimard, 1969);

Illustrations II (Paris: Gallimard, 1969);

Les Mots dans la peinture (Geneva: Albert Skira, 1969); translated in part by Joy N. Humes as "Painting Words," *TriQuarterly*, no. 20 (Winter 1971): 98-112;

La Rose des vents: 32 Rhumbs pour Charles Fourier (Paris: Gallimard, 1970);

Dialogue avec 33 variations de Ludwig van Beethoven sur une valse de Diabelli (Paris: Gallimard, 1971);

Où, volume 2 of *Le Génie du lieu* (Paris: Gallimard, 1971);

Peverelli: Répertoire I 1957-1960 (Montpellier: Fata Morgana, 1972);

Rabelais, ou c'était pour rire, by Butor and Denis Hollier (Paris: Larousse, 1972);

Les Sept Femmes de Gilbert le mauvais (Autre Heptaèdre), illustrations by Cesare Peverelli (Montpellier: Fata Morgana, 1972);

Travaux d'approche: Eocène, Miocène, Pliocène (Paris: Gallimard, 1972);

Illustrations III (Paris: Gallimard, 1973);

Intervalle: Anecdote en expansion (Paris: Gallimard, 1973);

Répertoire IV (Paris: Editions de Minuit, 1974);

Matière de rêves (Paris: Gallimard, 1975);

Illustrations IV (Paris: Gallimard, 1976);

Second sous-sol, volume 2 of *Matière de rêves* (Paris: Gallimard, 1976);

Troisième dessous, volume 3 of *Matière de rêves* (Paris: Gallimard, 1977);

Boomerang, volume 3 of *Le Génie du lieu* (Paris: Gallimard, 1978); translated in part by Michael Spencer as *Letters from the Antipodes* (St. Lucia: University of Queensland Press; Athens: Ohio University Press, 1981);

Elseneur: suite dramatique (Yverdon, Switzerland: Henri Cronaz, 1979);

Envois (Paris: Gallimard, 1980);

Vanité: Conversation dans les Alpes-Maritimes (Paris: Balland, 1980);

Explorations (Lausanne: Editions de l'Aire, 1981);

Quadruple fond, volume 4 of *Matière de rêves* (Paris: Gallimard, 1981);

Brassée d'avril (Paris: Editions de la Différence, 1982);

Naufragés de l'Arche, photographs by Pierre Bérenger (Paris: Editions de la Différence, 1982);

Répertoire V (Paris: Editions de Minuit, 1982);

Exprès, volume 2 of *Envois* (Paris: Gallimard, 1983);

Problèmes de l'art contemporain à partir des travaux d'Henri Maccheroni, by Butor and Michel Sicard (Paris: Christian Bourgois, 1983);

Vieira da Silva: Peintures (Paris: L'Autre Musée, 1983);

Alechinsky dans le texte (Paris: Editions Galilée, 1984);

Avant-goût (Paris: Ubacs, 1984);

Herbier lunaire (Paris: Editions de la Différence, 1984);

Chantier (Gourdon: Dominique Bedou, 1985);

Improvisations sur Henri Michaux (Montpellier: Fata Morgana, 1985);

Mille et un plis, volume 5 of *Matière de rêves* (Paris: Gallimard, 1985);

L'Œil de Prague: Dialogue avec Charles Baudelaire autour des travaux de Jiri Kolar, suivi de Réponses et de Le Prague de Kafka par Jiri Kolar (Paris: Editions de la Différence, 1986);

Avant-goût II (Paris: Ubacs, 1987);

Le Retour du boomerang (Paris: Presses Universitaires de France, 1988).

TRANSLATIONS: György Lukács, *Brève Histoire de la littérature allemande (du XVIIIᵉ siècle à nos jours)*, translated by Butor and Lucien Goldmann (Paris: Nagel, 1949);

Aron Gurwitsch, *Théorie du champ de la conscience* (Paris: Desclée De Brouwer, 1957);

William Shakespeare, *Tout est bien qui finit bien*, in *Œuvres complètes*, volume 5 (Paris: Formes et Reflets, 1959);

Bernardino de Sahagún, *De l'origine des dieux* (Montpellier: Fata Morgana, 1981).

PERIODICAL PUBLICATIONS: "Hommage partiel à Max Ernst," *Vrille* (25 July 1945): n.p.;

"Petite Croisière préliminaire à une reconnaissance de l'archipel Joyce," *Vie Intellectuelle,* 16 (May 1948): 104-135;

"L'Alchimie et son langage," *Critique,* 9 (October 1953): 884-891;

"Istanbul," *Monde Nouveau,* no. 92 (September 1955): 118-123;

"Les Relations de parenté dans *L'Ours* de William Faulkner," *Lettres Nouvelles,* no. 38 (May 1956): 734-745;

"Poèmes anciens," *Lettres Nouvelles,* no. 68 (February 1959): 190-202;

"La Musique, art réaliste," *Esprit,* 28 (January 1960): 138-156;

"L'Appel des Rocheuses," text by Butor, photographs by Ansel Adams and Edward Weston, *Réalités,* no. 197 (June 1962): 76-83.

Michel Butor's enduring reputation may well rest on his four early novels, published from 1954 to 1960. Although he has not, since *Degrés* of 1960, published a work that resembles a novel in the generally accepted definition of the genre, he has produced what might be termed "semifictions," and he has continued to elaborate on the experimentation initiated by his novels in so many literary forms and to such an extent that he may be considered in the future as one of the most radical and persuasive innovators of the twentieth century.

The son of Emile and Anne Brajeux Butor, Michel Butor was born 14 September 1926 in Mons-en-Barœul, a suburb of the city of Lille, in the northeast corner of France near the Belgian border. His father was a railway official who was also an amateur artist, which might help explain Butor's later interest in both timetables and the arts. The family, which eventually included eight children of which Butor was the fourth, moved to Paris when he was three. In 1939 the family relocated in Evreux, west of Paris, where Butor studied at the Collège Saint-François-de-Sales, but the following year he was back in Paris at the Lycée Louis-le-Grand. Butor spent the year 1942-1943 studying philosophy, among other subjects; the following year he prepared for the Ecole Normale Supérieure. In 1945 he enrolled in the school of letters at the Sorbonne, but he soon shifted his focus to philosophy. That was also the year he published his first essay, at the age of nineteen, on the painter Max Ernst in the little magazine *Vrille*.

That brief effort was the forerunner of a long series of critical essays in which Butor took a new look at such earlier artists as the Germans Albrecht Dürer and Holbein the Younger, the Italian Caravaggio, the Japanese Hokusai, and such later artists as Monet and the Dutchman Mondrian. When not analyzing painting, Butor has collaborated with a host of contemporary artists, from Pierre Alechinsky to Victor Vasarely. Among his French collaborators are Jacques Hérold, Bernard Dufour, Camille Bryen; he has also worked with the Italian Cesare Peverelli who lives in Paris and with Ania Staritsky, a Russian who lived and worked in France.

From 1946 to 1949 Butor continued his studies and prepared his thesis, "Les Mathématiques et l'idée de nécessité" (Mathematics and the Idea of Necessity), with Gaston Bachelard as his director. He held various jobs in the Collège Philosophique while life in Paris gave him the opportunity to meet writers and artists and to attend his first international conference. Although he failed the *agrégation*, the examination necessary for entry into the teaching profession at the university level, he had already published in 1948 an article on James Joyce in *Vie Intellectuelle*, his first attempt at literary criticism. That essay has been translated into Spanish, Italian, German, Romanian, Czech, Polish, and Hungarian. Like the essay on Max Ernst, this piece on Joyce presaged an enormous quantity of criticism which includes work on the English poet John Donne as well as the American writers Henry James, Ezra Pound, William Faulkner, and William Styron. The Spaniard Cervantes as well as the Russians Dostoyevski and Tolstoy have served him as subjects, while he has examined dozens of French writers, from François Villon to Roland Barthes. A full evaluation of Butor as literary critic may well prove him to be one of the outstanding critical voices of the twentieth century.

In 1949 Butor collaborated with the structural sociologist Lucien Goldmann on a translation from German of a history of German literature by the Hungarian philosopher György Lukács. Butor's most notable translations since then have been: in 1957, *The Field of Consciousness* by the anthropologist Aron Gurwitsch; in 1959, Shakespeare's *All's Well That Ends Well*; and in 1981, a portion of Bernardino de Sahagún's *Historia general de las cosas de Nueva España*.

In 1950 Butor was named a teacher at the lycée where Mallarmé had taught in Sens, just southeast of Paris, but he soon accepted a position offered by the government as teacher of French in the Egyptian town of El Minya, some

150 miles south of Cairo. Thus began Butor's great love affair with travel and the experience of foreign cultures. He tells two amusing stories about his experiences in Egypt. As a writer he needed a table, but since none was to be had in El Minya he had to demonstrate the theory that "essence precedes existence" by showing the carpenter in detail what he was to build. Next Butor found himself trying to teach French from a text whose subject was the train when none of the Egyptian students had ever seen a train. Butor's sojourn in Egypt initiated his long career teaching outside of France. In Egypt, too, Butor began his first novel, *Passage de Milan* (Milan Passage, 1954).

Upon his return from Egypt, Butor obtained a two-year appointment, starting in 1951, as teacher of French at the University of Manchester in England. During those two years he completed *Passage de Milan* and traveled to Tunisia, Algeria, and Italy. In 1953 Butor was back in Paris, where *Critique* published his essay on the subject of alchemy and its language, his first article on literary and linguistic theory which was to be followed by a spate of theoretical works on the novel as research, the novel as a laboratory of the narrative, the relationship between poetry and prose, the use of personal pronouns, and many other topics.

Passage de Milan was published in 1954 by Editions de Minuit, which encouraged the radical experimentation of several of the writers who were soon to be known as the New Novelists. While the reviews were generally favorable, the book did not sell well and has yet to be translated into English in its entirety, although portions have appeared in the *Carleton Miscellany* (1963) and in *The Award Avant-Garde Reader* (1965). The title can mean both Milan Passage, the street where the novel is set, and Passage of the Kite, the savage bird of prey connected with the Egyptian studies of one of the characters. In the novel Butor uses the time-tested device of the apartment house. The idea may have been suggested by the Pension Vauquer in Balzac's novel *Le Père Goriot* (1834). Both Balzac's and Butor's apartment houses bring together types from all walks of life, and for both the top floor is the realm of the least affluent and least socially acceptable. But Butor's use of the apartment house is more complex than Balzac's. Butor's novel can be described as a vertical novel, for the important movement throughout is between floors. He is enormously successful in revealing the inner lives of many of his sixty-six characters through his frequent use of interior monologue. Although stream of consciousness appeared in French literature some fifty years before Joyce's *Ulysses* (1922), critics are certainly right in seeing Joyce's influence on *Passage de Milan,* given Butor's early and abiding interest in his works. Often Butor prefaces a monologue with the name of the character and by the sixth chapter he puts the characters' names in the margin. This scheme, which presages the many "scripts" to come, permits the reader to shift quickly from character to character.

The action of *Passage de Milan* takes place within twelve hours, from seven in the evening until seven in the morning, and is neatly divided into twelve chapters. The movement is from Friday evening to Saturday morning, from Venus to Saturn, from the evening star named for the goddess of love and beauty to the planet Saturn, the god of agriculture whose festival became an unrestrained orgy. Counting the ground floor, the apartment house has seven stories. Butor's subsequent novels show this same symmetrical and symbolic organization.

The vertical movement is reinforced by three motifs with mythological overtones, another characteristic of all of Butor's novels. On the highest level are images that have to do with the sky. At the beginning of the novel, one of the characters, the abbé Jean, observes the flight of an airplane or perhaps a hawk—it is not clear which, although the hawk is a figure that recurs throughout the text. The hawk, a free-soaring soul, not only symbolizes human aspirations and the hieratic prefiguration of things to come, but it is also intimately connected with Jean's work, for he is a specialist in Egyptian hieroglyphics. On the second level is the recurrent motif of church bells tolling the hour. Here is man's call to man on the most spiritual plane and yet a reminder that man is also earthbound, for the church and its bells are man-made. The bells sound the call of soul to immortal soul and at the same time relentlessly draw attention to the passing of time and the aging of the mortal body. On the lowest level, in the bowels of the earth, there are the subway trains that link the isolated group of apartment dwellers with the working, moving masses of Paris. The intermittent rumbles that shake the inhabitants of the building serve as reminders that human beings are inevitably earthbound, not only tied together in the isolation of family and home but joined as well to the rest of humanity. Thus the novel becomes an experiment in time and space and thus in simultaneity.

The concierge and his wife, with their names out of the Middle Ages, Godefroy and Elénore, and their ridiculous family name, Poulet (chicken), which contrasts with the symbolic use of birds elsewhere in the novel, occupy the ground floor. The first floor belongs to Madame Ralon and her two priest sons, Jean and Alexis, as well as their cook, Madame Tenant. This last name is the present participle of *tenir*, to hold, while the noun means figuratively a champion or defender. The irony is that Madame Ralon shared her vagabond husband with Madame Tenant so that his memory holds the two women together. On the second floor is the apartment of the middle-aged, unsuccessful bank employee, Frédéric Mogne, and his numerous household–father, mother-in-law, wife, and five children–with, on this particular evening, the eldest daughter and son-in-law as dinner guests. On the third floor lives the wealthy aesthete, Samuel Léonard, with his niece (who is perhaps his daughter) and two servants–an Egyptian boy Ahmed, to whom he has a homosexual attachment, and his cook, Madame Phyllis. The central action of the evening takes place on the fourth floor. Léon and Lydie Vertigues are giving a coming-out party for their daughter Angèle on her twentieth birthday, to which all the young people in the apartment house are invited. The Vertigues, newcomers to the upper bourgeoisie, also have a servant, the poor Gertrude. An artist, Martin de Vere, his wife and three children, plus a roomer, Gaston Mourre, occupy the fifth floor. The sixth floor provides sleeping quarters for the two Mogne sons, Vincent and Gérard; Madame Ralon's penniless nephew, Louis Lécuyer; and the servants of the various families in the building, as well as a subway employee, a saleswoman, and an old unemployed domestic, Elisabeth Mercadier.

Butor notes that "Tout immeuble est un entrepôt, avec ses étages et son trafic, les meubles qu'on emménage ou qu'on emporte, les humains qui ont là leur lieu d'attache, avec leurs parents et leurs possessions, et ceux qui ne reviendront plus" (Every apartment house is a warehouse, with its floors and traffic, the furniture that is moved in or out, the human beings who have their roots there, with their families and their possessions, and those who will no longer come back). Every mind, he goes on to say, is a warehouse, too: "toute tête est un entrepôt, où dorment des statues de dieux et de démons de toute taille et de tout âge, dont l'inventaire n'est jamais dressé" (every head is a warehouse where statues of gods and demons of every size and age sleep, whose inventory is never drawn up). What takes place within the apartment house is comparable to what takes place within the mind, the interior monologue, which provides the substance of the novel. In describing some Egyptian bas-reliefs in the Louvre, one of the characters notes that "L'artiste de Béni-Hassan fait passer d'une danseuse ou d'un guerrier à l'autre par la continuation d'un même mouvement, mais dans les grandes frises des lutteurs, chaque fois un noir et un rouge, il a mêlé les instants successifs de divers combats, de telle sorte que les séries de figures s'enlacent dans un immense contrepoint" (The artist of Béni-Hassan causes the eye to pass from one dancer or warrior to the other by the continuation of the same movement, but in the large friezes of wrestlers, each time a black and a red, he has mingled the successive views of different fights, in such a way that the series of figures are interlaced in an immense counterpoint). The story of *Passage de Milan* becomes "an immense counterpoint" as the lives and movements of the characters on one floor of the apartment house repeat those of characters on other floors.

The story opens with the abbé Jean looking out the window, witnessing the passage of what may be an airplane or a hawk although he interprets what he sees as the flight of the hieratic bird, the kite, the mythical bird of ancient Egypt, the god Horus, "the sun of death." The novel closes with the abbé Alexis saying a prayer over a corpse. The relations between the brothers are vaguely disturbing, with homosexual overtones revealed in Jean's dreams. The relationship between the two priests is echoed by the relationship between the two Mogne brothers, while the homosexual attachment of Samuel Léonard to his servant Ahmed is repeated by the attachment of Vincent to Ahmed. Jean's dreams also reveal that his Christian faith has been seriously undermined by his studies in Egyptology. The faith of his brother Alexis is shaky, too, for the reader feels that he has taken orders only because Jean has. The industrial age has supplanted the age of faith, the apartment house has replaced the church, since its basement with its vaults and paved floor is the crypt of a former church.

On the door of Alexis's room Louis notes "un plan de métro de Paris, un emploi du temps en damier et un calendrier" (a map of the Paris subway, a timetable in a checkered pattern, and a calendar). These three elements–impersonal, mathematical guides so essential to the organization of complex modern life–here suggest the mechanization and isolation of the contemporary world; in Butor's second novel, *L'Emploi du temps* (literally, Work Schedule, 1956; translated as *Passing Time*, 1960), they become basic figures. An unfinished painting by the artist on the fifth floor is described as resembling a timetable, illustrating the extent to which such formulae have influenced modern man's vision. The destruction of the painting by fire, which foreshadows the many sinister fires in *L'Emploi du temps*, is paralleled by the tragedy of Angèle, whose accidental death after the party is one of the last events in the novel and perhaps the most dramatic indication of the flawed nature of an apparently stable society.

Printed on the back cover of the novel is Butor's observation: "Les événements futurs projettent déjà leur ombre sur nous" (Future events already project their shadow on us). While Angèle's party is taking place, Samuel Léonard has invited eight friends, all of them writers, to his apartment just below. They are attempting one of Butor's most desired undertakings, a collective work. During their deliberations one man mentions the evocative power of certain words, another of Butor's preoccupations. A reference is made to an imaginary book, *The Suburbs of Trieste*, which seems to recall James Joyce's sojourn in that city. While the men are gravely if somewhat hollowly discussing the book on the third floor, Léonard's cook, Madame Phyllis, is attempting to read it on the sixth floor. Madame Tenant, a specialist in bizarre and touching stories, had passed on to her this little novel. Léonard and his friends are hoping to introduce into literature a new dimension, a projection into the future along the lines of science fiction, still another of Butor's interests. They would like to replace memory by a consciousness of the future, but one of the speakers has already noted that, "sacrifiant tout à l'avenir, on l'empêche de s'approcher" (by sacrificing everything to the future, one prevents it from arriving). The failure of Samuel Léonard and his friends to realize any of their plans echoes the tragedy of Angèle.

After her party Angèle is sitting alone in the living room dreaming of the future when one of her recent guests arrives, the son of influential friends of her father, a ne'er-do-well invited because of the connection. He has returned to steal something from the apartment, but when he is surprised by Angèle, he tries to kiss her. They are in turn surprised by Louis Lécuyer, who has come down from the sixth floor because he cannot get Angèle out of his mind. Louis throws a candlestick at the boy. Angèle slips and hits her head on the marble fireplace, dying instantly. Louis takes refuge in the basement, the former church, where he is discovered by Samuel Léonard who helps him flee France to a new life in Egypt.

If Butor attempted too much in *Passage de Milan*, he nevertheless demonstrated a profound understanding of the most divergent types. By observing and describing their relationships Butor revealed in part the tragedy of modern society. Haunted by myths and dreams, desires and ambitions, his characters meet without touching and part without communicating. The death of the innocent Angèle, combined with the flight of the innocent, penniless, and lovesick Louis and the unresolved problems of the other inhabitants of the apartment house, leaves the reader with the uncomfortable feeling of the uselessness and sadness of contemporary life.

In 1954, the year *Passage de Milan* appeared, Butor was assigned to the French lycée in Salonika, Greece, where he began his second novel. The following year he visited Crete, Delphi, Istanbul, and Smyrna. Upon his return to Paris he published his impressions of Istanbul in the September 1955 issue of *Monde Nouveau*. The article presaged the long series of essays Butor has published in book form in three volumes (to date) under the collective title *Le Génie du lieu* (The Spirit of Place, 1958, 1971, 1978), which refers both to the distinctive character of a place as well as the genie or spirit presiding over its destiny. In October 1955 Butor succeeded Roland Barthes at the Ecole Normale Supérieure in the job of preparing teachers for service abroad. *L'Emploi du temps* appeared in 1956, attracted a great deal of attention, and was awarded the Prix Félix Fénéon. The prize launched Butor's career as novelist and writer.

The maps, bus routes, and calendars which govern complicated urban life dominate *L'Emploi du temps*. A young Frenchman, Jacques Revel, whose last name is connected with the verb *révéler*, to reveal, since he is the one who will "reveal" the whole story by writing it, has come to Bleston, a large industrial city of the English Midlands, to work for a year translating correspondence in the office of an export firm. Able to make himself understood only with difficulty, he is overcome by the forbidding ugliness, wretched weather, and appallingly bad food. Lonely and lost, he asks directions of a man who turns out to be an African immigrant named Horace Buck.

Horace plays the role of the alien–menacing because he is so different–like the Egyptian boy Ahmed in *Passage de Milan*. Horace speaks English only a bit better than Jacques and hates the city of Bleston with even more vehemence. Butor probably took the name Buck from Uncle Buck in Faulkner's *The Bear:* his study of that work, published in *Lettres Nouvelles* (1956), dates from the same year as the novel; Horace is an expert player of an amusement-park game known as The Bear Hunt; and at one point in a drunken stupor he allows Jacques to guide him along "like a brown bear." Ironically enough, it is this uprooted black who eventually makes it possible for Jacques to exchange his miserable room with a view of a blank, brick wall in a hotel named ominously The Screw–the allusion to Henry James's novelette *The Turn of the Screw* is obvious both from the name of the hotel and its frightening, oppressive atmosphere–for a pleasant room with an agreeable view in a private home. Horace also becomes his first friend, a friend whom Jacques does not hesitate to call "my savior." Jacques also makes the acquaintance of James Jenkins, a coworker who introduces him to a woman named Ann Bailey.

In order to survive in the face of the hostile environment Jacques begins to keep a diary. As *Passage de Milan* is based on a twelve-hour time span, *L'Emploi du temps* is based on the twelve months of the year. Jacques starts his diary seven months after his arrival and ends it the day, the moment he leaves. That means there are five chapters, one for each month left of his year in Bleston, May through September, each divided into five parts, one for each weekday. The five chapters recall the five acts of classical French drama while their titles recall its development: "L'Entrée" (The Entrance), "Les Présages" (The Omens), "L'Accident" (The Accident), "Les Deux Sœurs" (The Two Sisters), and "L'Adieu" (The Farewell). Jacques tries to write on at least three different levels. Not only is he attempting to keep abreast of events as they occur and catch up on events of the seven months already elapsed, but at a certain point he begins to reread what he has written. As he rewrites what he is rereading he adds to the original event the new truth about it or himself that he has learned subsequently. Time inevitably becomes involved with

space as Jacques attempts to get acquainted with the great, sprawling city of Bleston. If *Passage de Milan* is a vertical novel, certainly *L'Emploi du temps* is a horizontal one. Butor even found it expedient to include a map of Bleston so the reader can follow more easily Jacques's peregrinations through the city.

The narration is an attempt in one mind to apprehend present reality in its constantly shifting but inescapable relationships with the past and the future. As Jacques wanders like a phantom through Bleston, exterior objects pass before his eyes and to some extent inform his consciousness. An amusement arcade where Horace Buck may have started a fire in May triggers Jacques's recollection of the innumerable fires which haunt the city of Bleston and of the ominous role Horace may have played in this one. During an apparently simple visit to a newsreel theater, Rome becomes confused in time and place with Crete, so that past time becomes confused not only with itself but also with the present as history and myth become life.

In a similar way a death in the past–perhaps an accident, perhaps a murder–becomes connected with a killing described in a mystery novel purchased by Jacques, significantly titled *Le Meurtre de Bleston* (The Murder of Bleston). These crimes are in turn confused with an attempted murder of which Jacques thinks his friend James Jenkins is guilty. Both the "real" and the "fictional" crimes are connected to Ann Bailey and her family and James Jenkins and his mother. Butor also ties them to the stained-glass windows in the Old Cathedral depicting the fratricide of Abel by Cain, as well as to the architecture of the New Cathedral, the series of tapestries in the city museum which recount the story of Theseus, and the diorama of Bleston in the University Museum of Natural History. Jacques, as he notes in his journal, is like Theseus threading his way through the labyrinth of Bleston while Ann Bailey (with her map) is like Ariadne with her thread. The comparison extends to his romantic life as his attentions, first directed to Ann, are diverted to her younger and more beautiful sister, Rose, whom Jacques designates as Phaedra, although in the end Jacques fails to win either one.

Among the many leitmotivs is the name Hamilton. Jacques arrives at and departs from Hamilton Station. On one of his first long walks he gets lost on the road that leads to the town of Hamilton. Most important, *Le Meurtre de Bleston* was written under the pseudonym of J. C. Hamil-

ton. The reader is tempted to find in the initials
J.C. an allusion to Jesus Christ because the novel
is in many ways a parable and an attempt is
made to murder Hamilton for the revelations he
has made. Through a series of coincidences
Jacques learns that J. C. Hamilton is George William Burton, whose identity he reveals to the Bailey and Jenkins families. As it turns out, he has
put the author George William Burton in double
jeopardy. The Bailey sisters have a cousin,
Henry, who loaned the book to a friend, Richard
Tenn. The novel describes Richard Tenn's house
inside and out in minute detail. In addition, the
murder is a fratricide. Richard Tenn's brother
had been killed in a suspicious automobile accident three years earlier. The author also makes
scathing remarks about the architecture of the
New Cathedral. After Jacques has revealed the author's identity to James Jenkins, it turns out that
James's grandfather was the sculptor for the New
Cathedral. When Burton is run down in the
street by a black Morris car, Jacques suspects
both Richard Tenn and James Jenkins. Tenn's
Morris is grey, leaving Jacques with the nagging
suspicion that James with his black Morris is the
guilty party. Nothing is proved. Jacques is nevertheless acutely aware of his own guilt in revealing
the identity of J. C. Hamilton.

Fire is one of the dominant elements of
Bleston. The stained-glass windows in the Old Cathedral depict Sodom and Gomorrah in flames,
and Jacques soon learns that the bishop's palace
at Bleston had been destroyed by fire. The stained-
glass windows depict the burning of the city of
Cain while the tapestries in the museum show Athens in flames. Jacques is so haunted by Bleston
that he feels it is the city that encourages him to
avenge himself by fire. When Rose announces
her engagement, he burns his map of Bleston,
dreams that the Burtons' maid serves the detective story soaked in flaming rum for dessert, and
destroys in flames a ticket to the local amusement
park. He sees a film titled *The Red Nights of Roma*
in which that city burns while the city of Petra
appears to be a burn left in the cliff of
Transjordania. He is almost overcome by the desire to burn his manuscript, but he restrains himself, for by this time he has been able to say to
the evil city of Bleston, "Nous sommes quittes"
(We are even).

Water is the other dominant element of
Bleston. Water images are found on almost every
page and water symbolism abounds. The city, on
the great sluggish River Slee, is plagued by end-

less fog and rain, pools and puddles. There is a
character named Brooks, for example, and
Jacques eventually lives on Dew Street. As
Jacques gets off the train in Bleston, the raindrops become a "myriade de petits miroirs" (myriad of little mirrors) in the station lights—an
image in which water, fire, and mirror imagery,
also prevalent in the novel, become fused.
Jacques remembers how frightful he looked in
the mirror after spending his first night in
Bleston. Near the end of the book he looks in
the mirror, splashes water on his face, and
watches the drops of water roll down his cheeks.
Because of the dark night his window looks like a
mirror. When Jacques finally conquers himself
and Bleston he realizes that the journal he has
kept, the white page, is a mirror to trap Bleston.
In the end he watches, through his own reflection in a window, "les innombrables gouttes
d'eau, miniscules miroirs sphériques, tomber
inlassablement dans Dew Street" (the innumerable drops of water, minuscule spherical mirrors
falling untiringly in Dew Street). With this figure
Butor gathers all the water-mirror figures and
takes the reader back to the "myriad of little mirrors" in the raindrops of the first page of the
book.

The connections established among the
stained-glass windows, the tapestries, the films,
the detective story, myths, the reality of Bleston,
and the numerous characters of the book make
of *L'Emploi du temps* a counterpoint of much
larger and more complicated proportions than
that attempted in *Passage de Milan*. In *L'Emploi du
temps* the novel becomes its own subject. Burton
as the author of detective stories provides Butor
with a mouthpiece for many of his ideas. In repeating Burton's remarks about his art Jacques notes
"l'apparition à l'intérieur du roman comme d'une
nouvelle dimension" (the appearance within the
novel of something like a new dimension). "A
new dimension" was exactly what Léonard and
his friends in *Passage de Milan* were hoping to
add to the novel and precisely what the New Novelists added to literature. *L'Emploi du temps* itself
is something of a detective novel in much the
same way as Alain Robbe-Grillet's early novels.
The use of the detective-novel form permits the
writer to reveal his intentions little by little. The
characters as well as the reader are held in suspense and learn what is necessary at the same
time and only when it is too late to alter events.
The novel as a sort of parody of the detective
story takes on the added dimension of irony

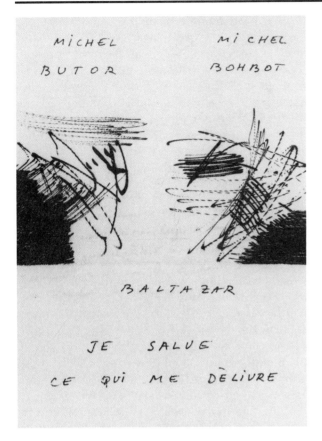
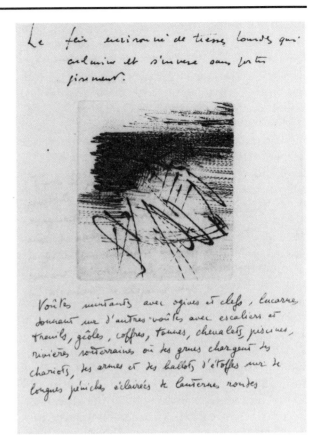

Title page and interior page from the unique copy of a handmade booklet by Butor, Michel Bohbot, and Julius Baltazar. Bohbot's writing appears at the top of each page, Butor's at the bottom. The illustrations are by Baltazar (The William J. Jones Collections of Rimbaud–Butor at Southwest Missouri State University).

since it both is and is not what it appears to be.

Jacques is restrained from burning his manuscript by the great number of sentences and pages written, the time necessary to put them all down, and the weight of the hours spent. But if writing, as Jacques notes early in the story of his time in Bleston, is a way of surviving, it is also a way of dying, for this pile of pages which took so much of his time to write is in part the cause of Jacques's loss of both Ann and Rose, his defeat in love at the very moment he conquers Bleston. He can only say, after his harrowing year, "je suis le survivant de moi-même" (I am the survivor of myself). His story is a "labyrinthe du temps et de la mémoire" (labyrinth of time and memory), covering only a year but a year in which the myths of the ages return to play themselves out in the life of a young man who has come the reader knows not from where and who is returning the reader knows not to what. With no past and a liberated future Jacques is everyman. His struggle is the struggle of all men to master themselves and their hostile environment. Much is lost in the attempt, but what is essential is gained. Never in

this novel is there a retrospective logic laid over the past to make of it something it never was. The truth is never revealed in its total nakedness: it is revealed only bit by bit, not consecutively and chronologically but piece by piece, like a three-dimensional jigsaw puzzle. Even after it is as complete as it will ever be there remains an unknown landscape which still covers mysteries never to be revealed.

In 1956 Butor accepted a teaching post at the Ecole Internationale in Geneva, Switzerland, a city in which he still teaches part time. He spent a month in Rome in 1957 in preparation for the writing of his next novel, *La Modification,* which was published that same year, awarded the Prix Théophraste Renaudot, and translated into English as *Second Thoughts* in 1958. With its appearance Butor's place among the New Novelists was recognized.

If *L'Emploi du temps* is the story of a life-and-death struggle with the city of Bleston, *La Modification* presents a love affair with the city of Rome. Jacques loses his loves because of his hatred of Bleston; Léon loses his love in a sense because of his love of Rome. Divided into three sections of three chapters each, *La Modification* exhibits the same mathematical precision as the previous novels while recounting in meticulous detail a train trip from Paris to Rome with great attention to the stations along the way.

Léon Delmont, head of the Paris office of an Italian typewriter firm, is making the trip, one he has made many times. But this time he is going unannounced to tell his mistress, Cécile, that he has found a job and a place for her to live in Paris and that he is prepared to leave his wife and four children in this last fling at life. By the end of the second section of the book Léon has changed his mind: he will not even see Cécile in Rome but will return to his wife Henriette in Paris. This is the only "modification" that takes place, not inherently a very interesting one. The way and how of the modification are the substance of the novel.

Butor again plays with names. Léon and his family reside in an apartment on the Place du Panthéon. The square, with its eighteenth-century mausoleum not unlike the Pantheon erected several centuries earlier in Rome, is located on the Mont Sainte-Geneviève, a place which suggests Léon's vaguely Italianate surname, Delmont. The Pantheon is the first of a series of relationships established between Paris and Rome. The second is the ruins of the Baths of Julian the Apostate, located just down the Boulevard Saint-Michel from the Rue Soufflot, which leads to the Pantheon. The Baths of Julian, the Roman emperor, are linked with the *Letters* of Julian, a book that Léon has read on one of his many trips between Paris and Rome. The book becomes a leitmotiv mentioned at least six times. Before he became emperor, Julian was sent to protect and govern the provinces of Gaul. While doing so he wintered in Paris, presumably living in what are now designated as his baths. After he became emperor he reverted to paganism, thus earning the epithet of apostate. The Baths of Julian, located near Léon's point of departure in Paris, correspond to the Baths of Diocletian located near his point of arrival, the railroad station, in Rome. Nominally a Catholic, Léon is something of an apostate, but his aversion to the papacy is mild compared to that of Cécile, just as Julian's edicts against the Christians were relatively tolerant compared to those of Diocletian. The museums of the Louvre and the Vatican are another parallel established between the two cities.

Léon's trip ought to be for him a liberation, a rejuvenation, a great cleansing of body and mind, a deliverance, since his liberty "s'appelle Cécile" (is called Cécile) and Rome is "le lieu de l'authenticité" (the place of authenticity). But during his all-night trip Léon is pursued in his dreams by a specter, the Grand Veneur, or Master of the Hounds, of the Forest of Fontainebleau. Strangely enough, this specter is a bogey not from his own youth, but from that of his wife. When the Grand Veneur first appears he asks "M'entendez-vous?" (Do you hear me?). His questions furnish other leitmotivs: "Qu'attendez-vous?" (What are you waiting for?), "Où êtes-vous?" (Where are you?), "Etes-vous fou?" (Are you crazy?), "Qui êtes-vous?" (Who are you?). Léon is also haunted by dreams of watery subterranean caverns like those experienced by the abbé Jean in *Passage de Milan*. In the dream the questions of the Grand Veneur become first those of the Stygian boatman: "Qu'attendez-vous?" "M'entendez-vous?" "Qui êtes-vous?"; next, those of an Italian customs officer: "Où êtes-vous, que faites-vous, que voulez-vous?" (Where are you, what are you doing, what do you want?); and finally, in a veritable paroxysm, those of an apparition that strangely and vaguely resembles Léon: "Qui êtes-vous?" "Où allez-vous?" "Que cherchez-vous?" "Qui aimez-vous?" "Que voulez-vous?" "Qu'attendez-vous?" "Que sentez-vous?" "Me voyez-vous?" "M'entendez-vous?" (Who are you? Where are you going? What are you hunting for? Whom do you love? What do you want? What are you waiting for? What do you feel? Do you see me? Do you hear me?). The answers to these questions, and others, constitute, as one critic put it, "a spiritual hunt."

In Léon's dreams he is assailed by a sibyl, a pope, the "King of Judgment," and a procession of all the Roman gods and emperors. He sees great flights of birds like those in the dreams of the abbé Jean in *Passage de Milan*. Here, they are ravens, the bird of ill omen. They form a crown for the Janus-like customs officer, double-faced because he presides over the French-Italian border, double-faced because Léon must choose between a past on one side of the border and a future on the other. The crown is composed of black feathers, each of which is edged with a border of flame, an image that is repeated in connection with Cécile's hair. In his dreams Léon also encounters a fatal horseman who has on his fists ravens with their wings outspread. And finally Léon witnesses a flight of ravens that rises above a farm he passes during his trip. Such is the nightmarish world in which Léon makes his existential choice.

The interpretation of such signs and symbols in Butor's novels is a delicate task. Léon in his compartment on the train speaks of a briefcase across from him on the rack above another passenger's head and notes that it is "comme une légende qui n'en est pas moins explicative, ou énigmatique, pour être une chose, une possession et non un mot" (like an inscription that is no less explanatory, or enigmatic, for being a thing, a possession, and not a word). If Butor has contributed to a "new realism" in French literature it is through his concept of the relationship of words with things. In the Louvre Léon is attracted by two paintings by a third-rate artist, Pannini, because they depict many imaginary views of ancient and modern Rome. He is intrigued because there appears to be no difference between the objects represented as real and those represented as painted, as if the artist had wanted to give "un équivalent absolu de la réalité" (an absolute equivalent of reality). Butor seems to be striving for this "absolute equivalent of reality" through words, a process which lies at the very heart of both Léon's choice and Butor's novel.

Léon's choice is an existential one and can constitute a liberation for him only if he learns to read the signs of this world and to distinguish between those things, those acts, those gestures, those sentiments that are painted and those that are real. The things one "sees" in the world are all appearances, like objects in a painting, and because they are only appearances they are all equal. Butor's task is to describe those appearances with words in such a way that they are neither more nor less explanatory nor enigmatic than they are in life. But he must describe them so that Léon's choice, while clearly announced but still unexpected, proves to be the only choice for him psychologically. To achieve this goal is to come as near to an absolute equivalent of reality in words as a writer can.

To these ideas must be added Butor's concept of sacrifice. During his trip Léon notes that the train is passing along "the Lamartinian lake," that is, Lac du Bourget, the lake of Alphonse de Lamartine's best-known poem, "Le Lac." Lamartine wrote the poem in memory of his love for a married woman who died shortly after their encounter on the shores of the lake. His heroine was in a sense sacrificed so that Lamartine might express himself and become a great poet. In Butor's novel the situation is similar, and, as the al-

lusion to Lamartine's lake suggests, someone must be sacrificed. In one of the scenes with the sibyl in her gloomy grotto she asks the "he" of these dreams, "T'imagines-tu que je ne sais pas que toi aussi tu vas à la recherche de ton père afin qu'il t'enseigne l'avenir de ta race?" (Do you imagine that I do not know that you too are going in search of your father so that he can inform you about the future of your race?). The "he" replies, "je ne veux que sortir de là, rentrer chez moi, reprendre le chemin que j'avais commencé" (I only want to get out of here, return home, and take up again the path I had begun). Léon is convinced that he would never reply as "he" had done, but he also knows that to learn about the future of his race, to take up his path again, he must return to Henriette and his children, the way of reality.

The reason for his choice is a complex one. Léon arrives at this reorganization of himself and his life, this metamorphosis, when he realizes that he truly loves Cécile only to the extent that she is for him the face of Rome and its voice, that he does not love her without Rome and outside Rome, that he loves her only because of Rome. With this realization comes the knowledge that he must analyze the myth that Rome is for him. Once he does so the "modification" takes place. He discovers that the fissure within himself is in communication with an immense historical fissure. He has nurtured "une croyance secrète à un retour à la *pax romana*, à une organisation impériale du monde autour d'une ville capitale" (a secret belief in a return to the *pax romana*, to an imperial organization of the world around a capital city) with "Rome au centre de la terre" (Rome at the center of the earth). The fact is that "le souvenir de l'Empire est maintenant une figure insuffisante pour désigner l'avenir" (the memory of the Empire is now an insufficient figure to denote the future of this world), an idea Butor will set forth at length in *Le Génie du lieu*. For Léon, then, Cécile must be sacrificed. That is why Léon says to himself, "je dois écrire un livre" (I must write a book), a book that will fill the void created by his discovery, since there is no other liberty represented by Cécile, a book that will "préparer, permettre, . . . à cette liberté future hors de notre portée, lui permettre, dans une mesure si infime soit-elle, de se constituer, de s'établir" (prepare, permit, . . . this future liberty beyond our reach, permit it in no matter how slight a measure, to take form, to establish itself). He will attempt to "faire revivre sur le mode de la lecture cet épisode crucial de votre aventure, le mouvement qui s'est produit dans votre esprit accompagnant le déplacement de votre corps d'une gare à l'autre à travers tous les paysages intermédiaires, vers ce livre futur et nécessaire" (make relive as an act of reading this crucial episode of your adventure, the movement which took place in your mind accompanying the displacement of your body from one station to another across all the intermediate landscapes, toward this future and necessary book). The book will take the form of the book he holds in his hand, a book he purchased in the Paris station and which he still has not read and whose title and author he still does not know upon his arrival in Rome.

Just as Samuel Léonard and his friends in *Passage de Milan* were attempting to write a book that would embody a new concept of the future, just as Jacques had to keep a diary in *L'Emploi du temps* in order to survive, so Léon will write his book which will be the book the reader has just completed. *La Modification* thus becomes the recital of its own genesis. The creation of the poem is not the subject of the poem but the poem itself for Mallarmé. Marcel Proust's creation of *A la recherche du temps perdu* (*Remembrance of Things Past*, 1913-1927) is not only a re-creation of the past in the present but also the very meaning of the narrator's life both past and future. Just as Roquentin in Jean-Paul Sartre's *La Nausée* will write a book in which he will arrive at accepting himself in the past, so Léon will write a book in which he will arrive at a knowledge of himself that will be his future liberation.

In *La Modification* Butor combines the interior monologue and the manipulation of time found in his earlier works. The most radical innovation is Butor's insistent use of the second-person plural pronoun, *vous,* except on rare occasions when the narrator in some of the dreams refers to someone in the third person. The device, Butor's experiment with the technique of stream of consciousness, disoriented readers and critics alike. One of the problems with the interior monologue is that most authors indicate the intrusion of the exterior world upon this interior discourse only frequently enough to give the reader certain necessary signposts to that world. Although interior discourse allows no time for the naming of exterior phenomena which present themselves to consciousness and which cause consciousness to be, these exterior phenomena nevertheless provide a continuous background

for the interior monologue. Naming forces the background of consciousness to become the foreground because it interrupts the monologue; the physical stimulus once put into words is no longer a stimulus but a description of the stimulus, which falsifies the whole process as much as not mentioning the exterior world at all. Narration in the second-person plural simplifies by one step, according to Butor, this attempt at a description of the flow of consciousness, because by the use of *vous* the author identifies the reader with the narrator, whereas *il* (he) would indicate someone who is neither the reader nor the narrator.

This story of a forty-five-year-old man trying to decide whether he will leave his wife and family for a younger woman is lifted out of its banality because the reader realizes when he finishes his difficult task that Butor has convinced him that it is he who must suffer the "modification" necessary to arrive at his own liberation, that only through an enormous effort at self-analysis can choice be made and creation realized. Although Butor moves smoothly from the specific to the general, from the individual to the universal, the relationship he establishes between the Rome of his hero and the Rome of the Roman Empire is too intellectual to be entirely convincing. And the constant use of the second person—an experiment that has not often been repeated or imitated—becomes fatiguing in the end; yet *La Modification* remains a novel rich in suggestion that well exemplifies Butor's concept of literature not as a luxury but as a living necessity.

In 1958 Butor published *Le Génie du lieu* (translated as *The Spirit of Mediterranean Places*, 1986) and married Marie-Jo Mas, a philosophy student he had encountered at the Ecole Internationale two years earlier. They honeymooned in Venice. The following year Butor began work on his fourth novel, *Degrés* (1960; translated as *Degrees*, 1961), and signed a long-term contract with the publishing house Gallimard. The Butors' first daughter, Cécile, was born in 1959, followed by Agnès (1960), Irène (1962), and Mathilde (1967). Editions de Minuit retained the rights to certain works by Butor, and it was they who published his first collection of essays, *Répertoire: Etudes et conférences, 1948-1959* (1960), which won the Prix de la Critique Littéraire. Beginning in January of that year Butor, on the first of his many visits to the United States, spent a semester as visiting professor at Bryn Mawr College in Pennsylvania. During the summer he taught at Middlebury College in Vermont.

Degrés was published by Gallimard. The title encompasses many meanings of the word *degrees*. The central situation concerns the various degrees of relationship in a Parisian lycée among thirty-one students and their eleven professors, and the students' academic degrees. Their studies inevitably involve the degrees of longitude and latitude, of heat, and of the circle; their private lives raise questions of degrees of drunkenness. In addition, several of the important characters come down with the grippe which ineluctably necessitates a thermometer.

More specifically the plot concerns a boy of fifteen, Pierre Eller, who has two professors who are also his uncles. One of the uncles shares Pierre's first name while his last name, Vernier, is the term given to a short scale made to slide along the divisions of a graduated instrument to indicate parts of divisions. The young Pierre's surname calls to mind the German *Elle*, ell or yardstick, while *Eller* or *Erle* in German is the alder tree. Alder in French is *aune*, but the *aune* is also a former measure of length roughly the equivalent of the English yard. To compound the situation, the popular name for the alder in French is *vergne* or *verne*, very close to Vernier, the name of the man who will attempt to take the measure of one day in time. The novel exhibits Butor's fondness for symmetry, for it is divided into three parts, one for each successive narrator. The parts are in turn divided into seven sections.

The three parts are in a sense variations on the same structure. In the first part the characters are taken up three by three, in the second two by two, and in the third one by one. In each of the triads of the first part, three characters are introduced in each of the seven sections, either two professors and one student or two students and one professor. Thus at the end of the first part ten students and all eleven of the professors have been introduced. In part two fourteen new students are presented, and in part three seven. In addition, the triads of part one are relatives but these family connections become more and more tenuous as the reader progresses through the seven sections. The characters in part one are also treated according to the relative proximity of their dwelling places. While family relationships still play a role in part two, the characters are taken up according to geography. Like the degrees of blood relationship in part one, the degrees of geographical proximity slowly become weaker and weaker through the seven sections. The seven characters introduced in the sections of part three are treated according to the relationships already established, those of blood or of geography.

Only this exterior form of the novel is reassuring, for the content is infinitely difficult, more exasperatingly difficult even than *La Modification*. Pierre Eller's uncle Pierre Vernier is the boy's professor of history and geography, that is, of history as time and geography as space. The uncle decides to write for his nephew some notes which he wants to be a true phenomenological description, in his own words, "une description littérale, sans intervention de mon imagination, un simple enregistrement de faits exacts" (a literal description, without the intervention of my imagination, a simple recording of exact events) so that the nephew might someday enjoy a total recall of Tuesday, 12 October 1954, his fifteenth birthday. *Degrés* is initially recounted in the first person by the uncle as he tells what happens and addresses himself to his nephew. But the uncle quickly realizes that he must consider all the space in which these events take place, that he must imagine a great many other events impossible to verify, that "Au milieu de ces quelques points bien solides, s'introduit un élément d'irrémédiable incertitude qu'il n'est possible d'atténuer qu'en multipliant les références, qu'en précisant de plus en plus les situations, qu'en éclairant les uns après les autres les champs de probabilités" (In the midst of these few solid points, an element of irremediable uncertainty is introduced which it is possible to attenuate only by multiplying the references, by fixing the situations more and more precisely, by clarifying the fields of possibilities one after the other). In the same way that it is impossible to represent the earth with precision without deforming it, so it is impossible to represent reality in language without employing a certain type of projection. But the representation of what is happening in the contemporary world and of universal history is constantly falsified by the ubiquitous Mercator projection. Finally the best the uncle can do is to choose as his point of departure the discovery and conquest of America.

To fix the enormous mass of information needed to illuminate only one day the uncle is forced not only to set up for himself a strict work schedule, an *emploi du temps*, but also to call upon his nephew for information which only he can supply. The minute the nephew takes an active part in the project he becomes "I" and the uncle becomes "you," thus reversing the pronominal system used in the narration to this point. As the uncle becomes increasingly involved, his teaching suffers and his social life comes to a halt. Eventually even the nephew realizes that his uncle is driven by some sort of demon; the uncle finally takes refuge in drink and falls ill, so ill that he has to give up his classes. A shift in viewpoint takes place at precisely the moment when the existential other, in the form of Eller's other uncle, Henri Jouret, begins to look upon Vernier and Eller, transforming the relationship from I-subject and you-object to us-object, and judging that relationship. The writing of the manuscript is taken over by Jouret, who is Eller's professor of Greek and Latin, the languages of the sources of Western civilization, and of French, the language in which the characters communicate. The third part of the novel is thus primarily written from another point of view according to which "I" becomes Jouret, "you" again becomes Eller, and "he" becomes Vernier. The final words of the book are Vernier's confused question, "Qui parle?" (Who's speaking?), a question the reader must ask himself frequently throughout the novel and a question which echoes the many others in Butor's previous novels. Vernier's relationships with his relatives, Eller's parents, so deteriorate that he has to move from the room he sublets in their apartment to a room in the apartment of Jouret. Because the nephew has become so nervous and tired his parents move him into his uncle's vacated room, a symbolic replacement of age by youth.

All of the subject matter–history, geography, literature, science, and mathematics–that the students study in class provides the mythological background for this novel, as do the boys' scout-troop activities and their extracurricular reading of cheap science-fiction magazines passed from hand to hand. Eller's friend Alain Mouron has a dream in which he is a chamois (his scout troup is called the Chamois) hunting for refuge in the cave that haunts so many of Butor's dreamers. In the end it is Michel Daval, who also has an uncle on the faculty, who accuses Eller of an abnormal relationship with Vernier, reveals to him that the other professors know that Eller is his uncle's informant, and precipitates the crisis which ends Eller's collaboration.

A tall North African whose face is covered by a mask of adhesive tape combines something of the roles of Ahmed in *Passage de Milan*, Horace Buck in *L'Emploi du temps*, and the Grand Veneur in *La Modification*. He haunts the Latin Quarter and is constantly observing the boys as

they go to and from school. His presence generates a leitmotiv mentioned at least eight times, and he becomes, along with the names of the various scout troops to which the boys belong, a part of the fauna of the novel. His eyes peering through the adhesive tape resemble those of a wolf so that when Eller learns that professors are accusing him of spying for his uncle, he suddenly feels himself turning into a wolf. When he notes that his uncle is becoming more and more possessed, he recognizes too that Vernier's look is more and more that of a wolf, that of the North African. When the North African finally speaks to Eller, making an indecent proposal, the boy is astonished to realize that he is thinking of his uncle. The North African is associated in the boys' minds with the werewolves they have encountered in their science fiction, while one of the students is named, inevitably, Frédéric Wolf.

Eller's classmate Daval has written and later gives him a note repeating the dialogue between two professors revealing Eller's guilty collaboration. Eller keeps the note for a long time in an empty match box and finally lays it on Vernier's pillow as an offering, the symbol of his forgiveness and of his childhood now lost forever.

In telling his story Butor has come dangerously close to enumeration in his attempt to reveal who was and is doing and studying what and where they are every minute. His narrative is saved because in the end one cares about the uncle and the nephew, the professor and the student as people. The uncle is obviously dying from his efforts. Does Butor mean that such a reproduction of reality in words is doomed to failure, that "ce vestige d'une conscience et d'une musique future" (this vestige of a consciousness and of a future music) is all that is possible? Or does he mean that it is inevitable that the older generation must die in its attempt to rear and educate the young? In an interview published in *French Review* (October 1962), Butor has said that he means both.

As in *L'Emploi du temps*, and *La Modification*, the book the reader has before him is the book the hero wrote or would write, and in creating it, Butor has allowed his reader to participate in the creative act, has shown the reader how a book is a way not only of dying but also of surviving, and that in his knowledge of time, imperfect though it may be, he will find his ultimate liberation. Butor's every novel retraces, as Sartre put it in speaking of Jean Genet, "l'histoire d'une libération." For Butor the liberation is one that affects the author and his characters as well as his readers.

With *Degrés* Butor published the last of what can properly be called novels according to the generally accepted definition of the genre. In 1961 his penetrating study of the poet Baudelaire, *Histoire extraordinaire* (translated, 1969), appeared, followed in 1962 by his most radical experiment, *Mobile* (translated, 1963), a nonfiction work in which he draws a critical but well-balanced historical view of contemporary America as the land of the free and not-so-free, in a form and format which disconcerted the critics and discouraged readers. Reviewers did not realize that the text was organized state by state according to the alphabet and faulted the book for its apparently disjointed references and its failure to progress in an orderly fashion to a logical conclusion. That year also saw publication of the radio script *Réseau aérien* (Aerial Network), about concurrent voyages east and west to the French island of New Caledonia in the South Pacific, as well as Butor's collaboration with the Belgian composer Henri Pousseur on the opera *Votre Faust* (Your Faust).

As R.-M. Albérès has pointed out in a 1964 article for *Revue de Paris*, all Butor's writing, whether explicitly fiction or not, is an attempt at interpretation, an "étude critique de la connaissance du réel" (critical study of the knowledge of the real). Like others of his generation, he has renounced the importance of generic distinctions, which can be more of an impediment than an aid to this enterprise of interpretation. The four novels of his early period include both compositional and content elements that belong to expository prose, such as dating, maps, quotations from histories, atlases, scientific texts, and so forth. Similarly, much of his work after *Degrés* bears some resemblance to fiction and might be called "semi-fiction." *Mobile*, although really *hors genre* (not belonging to any genre), shares many qualities of modern poetry–Butor's debt to William Carlos Williams has been shown–but also, by its scope, structure, and rich patterns of observations and mythic elements, creates a kind of cultural "fiction," that is, a fictitious America, with its individualized yet typical characters, its cultural geography, and its characteristic material features. In *Description de San Marco*, which can be viewed as a redoing of the famous passages on Venice and its cathedral in Proust's *A la recherche du temps perdu*, Butor imbeds fragments of overheard conversations, somewhat in the manner of

Proust himself and Nathalie Sarraute, into his observations on the city; these dialogues create the impression of fictional presences, in counterpoint to the observer's own.

Since 1962 Butor has traveled extensively and spent considerable time in the United States as well as Japan and Australia. His *Description de San Marco,* inspired by the Venetian basilica, came out in 1963 (and was translated as *Description of San Marco* in 1983), and in 1964 his first volume of art criticism, entitled *Illustrations*, was published; three additional volumes have appeared to date. In 1965 he produced a second book about America, an "étude stéréophonique" (stereophonic study), as he called it, about Niagara Falls entitled *6 810 000 litres d'eau par seconde* (translated as *Niagara*, 1969). He wrote a haunting semi-autobiographical fantasy titled *Portrait de l'artiste en jeune singe* (Portrait of the Artist as a Young Monkey) in 1967 and participated in the founding of the Writers Union during the 1968 Paris uprisings.

In 1970 Butor was named adjunct professor at the University of Nice and moved with his family to a house in that city overlooking the Mediterranean. Three years later the novelette *Intervalle: Anecdote en expansion* (Interval: Anecdote in Expansion) appeared. While the form is intriguing, the plot is precisely that of the 1946 film *Brief Encounter,* adapted from the play by Noël Coward and described by its director David Lean as "a bit trivial" in content. The expansion of the anecdote proceeds by Butor's use of three columns on most pages: the one on the left is reserved for the description of the contents of a waiting room in a train station and for the conversations between two travelers, a man and a woman who meet, dream of a life together, and then go their separate ways; the second consists for the most part of quotations from books by Butor and others; the third includes the revisions Butor had made of the text. One problem is that these manipulations overpower the "trivial content" and leave the reader with little that could be called a story. Nevertheless, the ingenious organization does offer a model for generating texts to come.

In 1973 Butor was also denied the title of University Professor in France. In spite of this refusal he was given an assistant professorship at Nice and named visiting professor in Geneva. In 1975 he gave up his post in Nice but continued to commute to Geneva to teach. That was also the year he published the first volume of his fascinating *Matière de rêves* (The Stuff of Dreams); the fifth volume appeared in 1985. In these texts, as in most dreams, the narrator undergoes traumatic metamorphoses, finds himself in compromising situations, and must run outrageous risks. Family members naturally have roles in these dreams, but they are joined by a great array of fictional characters from several literary traditions, as well as by historical artists and composers. Continuing his active and prolific poetic collaboration with different artists, Butor published a volume of poems in prose under the title *Brassée d'avril* (An Armful of April) in 1982 with illustrations by Vieira da Silva. The Butors currently reside in the little town of Gaillard in France, just across the border from Geneva, where he was granted a professorship in 1975.

The period of the New Novelists is now history and even the New New Novelists are being replaced by writers who have returned to more traditional forms, although their works invariably reveal the influence of Butor and his generation. The novel can never again be the same. Butor's works since *Mobile* have presented readers with various problems. His literary, art, and music criticism are addressed to an audience of specialists rather than to the reading public. His travel works, such as *Où* (1971; its untranslatable title is a play on the words *où*, where, and *ou*, or) and *Boomerang* (1978; translated in part as *Letter from the Antipodes*), are frequently so complex that they mystify readers. Finally, the poetry and poetic prose that Butor has written in collaboration with artists often appear in such rare, limited, and costly editions that these works are unavailable to a large audience. Nevertheless, with his experiments Butor remains one of the most radical innovators of his period; future readers may find his works a source of interest and pleasure. Certainly they are worth the effort.

Letters:

Cartes et lettres: Correspondance 1966-1979, by Butor and Christian Dotrement (Paris: Editions Galilée, 1986).

Bibliographies:

Margaret Church, Ronald Cummings, and John Feaster, "Five Modern French Novelists: A Bibliography: Butor," *Modern Fiction Studies*, 16 (Spring 1970): 85-86, 89;

Michael Spencer, "*Etat présent* of Butor Studies," *Australian Journal of French Studies*, 8, no. 1 (1971): 84-97;

Alain-Valery Aelberts and Jean-Jacques Auquier, "Bibliographie butorienne," *Revue Rêvée*, part 7 (Braine-le-Comte, Belgium: Editions Lettera Amorosa, 1975);

F. C. St. Aubyn, "Michel Butor: A Bibliography of His Works: 1945-1972 (with Addenda 1973-1975), Part I," *West Coast Review*, 12 (June 1977): 43-49; "Part II (1958-1962)," *West Coast Review*, 12 (January 1978): 33-40; "Part III (1963-1967)," *West Coast Review*, 13 (June 1978): 40-57; "Part IV (1968-1975)," *West Coast Review*, 13 (October 1978): 42-50;

Barbara Mason, *Michel Butor: A Checklist* (London: Grant & Cutler, 1979);

St. Aubyn, "Butor's Rare and Limited Editions: 1956-1983," *Review of Contemporary Fiction*, 5 (Fall 1985): 176-183;

St. Aubyn, *The William J. Jones Collections– Rimbaud, Butor–at Southwest Missouri State University* (Springfield: Southwest Missouri State University, 1986).

References:

R.-M. Albérès, *Michel Butor* (Paris: Editions Universitaires, 1964);

Albérès, "Michel Butor on le roman 'transcendental,' " *Revue de Paris,* 71st year (March 1964): 61-71;

Arc, special issue on Butor, no. 39 (1969);

François Aubral, *Michel Butor* (Paris: Seghers, 1973);

Catharine Savage Brosman, "Michel Butor and *Paterson,*" *Forum for Modern Languages Studies,* 7 (April 1971): 126-133;

Butor/Colloque de Cerisy (Paris: Union Générale d'Editions, 1974);

Cahiers du Centre d'Etudes et de Recherches Marxistes, special issue on Butor, no. 62 (1968);

Georges Charbonnier, *Entretiens avec Michel Butor* (Paris: Gallimard, 1967);

Lucien Dällenbach, *Le Livre et ses miroirs dans l'œuvre romanesque de Michel Butor* (Paris: Minard, 1972);

André Helbo, *Michel Butor, vers une littérature du signe* (Brussels: Editions Complexe, 1975);

Kentucky Romance Quarterly, special issue on Butor, 38, no. 1 (1985);

Bernard Lalande, *"La Modification": Analyse critique* (Paris: Hatier, 1972);

Michel Launay, *Résistances: Conversations aux Antipodes* (Paris: Presses Universitaires de France, 1983);

Jean-Marie Le Sidaner, *Voyageur à la roue* (Paris: Encre Editions, 1979);

Livres de France, special issue on Butor, no. 6 (June-July 1962);

Mary Lydon, *Perpetuum Mobile: A Study of the Novels and Aesthetics of Michel Butor* (Edmonton: University of Alberta Press, 1980);

Magazine Littéraire, special issue on Butor, 110 (March 1976);

Dean McWilliams, *The Narratives of Michel Butor: The Writer as Janus* (Athens: Ohio University Press, 1978);

Musique en jeu, special issue on Butor, 4 (1971);

Obliques, special issue on Butor (February 1975);

Œuvres et Critiques, special issue on Butor, 10, no. 2 (1985);

Lois Oppenheim, *Intentionality and Intersubjectivity: A Phenomenological Study of Butor's "La Modification"* (Lexington, Ky.: French Forum, 1980);

Georges Perros, *Lettres à Michel Butor,* 2 volumes (Rennes: Ubacs, 1982, 1983);

Patrice Quéréel, *"La Modification" de Butor* (Paris: Hachette, 1973);

Georges Raillard, *Butor* (Paris: Gallimard, 1968);

Review of Contemporary Fiction: Charles Bukowski-Michel Butor, 5 (Fall 1985);

Jean Roudaut, *Michel Butor ou Le Livre futur* (Paris: Gallimard, 1964);

Leon S. Roudiez, *Michel Butor* (New York: Columbia University Press, 1965);

F. C. St. Aubyn, "Entretien avec Michel Butor," *French Review,* 36 (October 1962): 12-22;

Madeleine Santschi, *Voyage avec Michel Butor* (Lausanne: Age d'Homme, 1982);

Michael C. Spencer, *Michel Butor* (New York: Twayne, 1974);

Spencer, *Site, citation et collaboration chez Michel Butor* (Sherbrooke, Que.: Naaman, 1986);

Skimao and Bernard Teulon-Nouailles, *Michel Butor* (Lyons: La Manufacture, 1988);

Texte en Main, special issue on Butor, no. 2 (1984);

Gisela Thiele, *Die Romane Michel Butors: Untersuchungen zur Struktur von "Passage de Milan," "L'Emploi du Temps," "La Modification," "Degrés"* (Heidelberg: Carl Winter Universitätsverlag, 1975);

Françoise Van Rossum-Guyon, *Critique du roman: Essai sur "La Modification" de Michel Butor* (Paris: Gallimard, 1970);

Jennifer Waelti-Walters, *Alchimie et littérature: A propos de "Portrait de l'artiste en jeune singe" de Michel Butor* (Paris: Denoël, 1975);

Waelti-Walters, *Michel Butor: A Study of His View of the World and A Panorama of His Work, 1954-1974* (Victoria, B.C.: Sono Nis Press, 1977);

Friedrich Wolfzettel, *Michel Butor und der Kollektivroman: Von "Passage de Milan" zu "Degrés"* (Heidelberg: Carl Winter Universitätsverlag, 1969);

World Literature Today, special issue on Butor, 56 (Spring 1982).

Marie Cardinal
(9 March 1929-)

Françoise Lionnet
Northwestern University

BOOKS: *Ecoutez la mer* (Paris: Julliard, 1962);
La Mule de corbillard (Paris: Julliard, 1963);
Guide junior de Paris, by Cardinal and Christiane Cardinal (Paris: Julliard, 1964);
La Souricière (Paris: Julliard, 1965);
Cet Eté-là, published with *Deux ou trois choses que je sais d'elle*, by Jean-Luc Godard (Paris: Julliard, 1967);
Mao, by Cardinal and Lucien Bodard (Paris: Gallimard, 1970);
La Clé sur la porte (Paris: Grasset, 1972);
Les Mots pour le dire (Paris: Grasset, 1975); translated by Pat Goodheart as *The Words to Say It* (Cambridge, Mass.: VanVactor & Goodheart, 1983);
Autrement dit, by Cardinal and Annie Leclerc (Paris: Grasset, 1977);
Une Vie pour deux (Paris: Grasset, 1978);
Au pays de mes racines, published with *Au pays de Moussia*, by Bénédicte Ronfard (Paris: Grasset, 1980);
Le Passé empiété (Paris: Grasset, 1983);
Les Grands Désordres (Paris: Grasset, 1987).

OTHER: Suzanne Horer and Jeanne Socquet, eds., *La Création étouffée*, includes an untitled essay by Cardinal (Paris: Pierre Horay, 1973), pp. 153-163;
Horer, *La Sexualité des femmes*, preface by Cardinal (Paris: Grasset, 1980);
La Médée d'Euripide, translated, with a preface, by Cardinal (Montreal: Editions Victor-Lévy Beaulieu, 1986; Paris: Grasset, 1987).

Marie Cardinal, 1986 (photograph copyright © Michel Dubreuil)

Marie Cardinal's writings since 1962 articulate the major intellectual concerns of contemporary France: psychoanalysis and language; the politics of decolonization; questions of female creativity and the sociocultural construction of gender. But her significance as a novelist rests on her ability to translate these concerns into a thematics and a narrative form which have broad appeal. She is, by all standards, a popular author. Her best-known works, *La Clé sur la porte* (Open-door Policy, 1972) and *Les Mots pour le dire* (1975; translated as *The Words to Say It*, 1983), have each sold 3,800,000 copies in Europe, and *Les Mots pour le dire* has been translated into eighteen languages. Cardinal has become, in the words of one American critic, "a leading spokeswoman for the female condition." An accomplished writer, Cardinal often interweaves present narrative with reminiscences about the fragrances, colors, faces, and sensations of her early Mediterranean world. Her experiences as a child of French colonialism in Algeria have allowed her to express the feelings of guilt, power-lessness, and dispossession common to those who suffer from the combined effects of patriarchy and imperialism, war and exile.

Her works constitute, in her own terms, "un seul livre" (a single book) and contain much information about the author's life in Algeria, France, and Quebec. But they do not form a body of strictly "autobiographical writing" because the persona, the "I" or the "she" of the works, is at once much more and far less than the living author. One might heed her warning: "J'ai besoin d'être la femme de chacun de mes livres . . . et comme j'espère écrire au moins vingt livres, on pourra dire que j'ai écrit vingt autobiographies . . ." (I need to be the woman of each one of my books . . . and since I hope to write at least twenty books, people will be able to say that I have written twenty autobiographies . . .). In this ironic comment on the problematic reception of her major novel, *Les Mots pour le dire*, which was alternatively labeled "novel," "essay," and "autobiographical testimony" on the best-seller lists, Cardinal summarizes the dilemmas faced by female writers confronted with critics who have continually tried to decode women's literature as "autobiographical," thus minimizing its importance and its scope. To fight against the stigma of such reductive labeling Cardinal produces carefully crafted works which transgress traditional notions of genre: "Je n'aime pas que les livres aient un genre défini, j'aime qu'ils soient à la fois roman, poésie, essai, recherche, histoire, philosophie" (I don't like books to belong to a definite genre, I like them to be at once fiction, poetry, essay, investigation, history, philosophy). Cardinal's success can be measured by the fact that she has achieved just such a blurring of traditional categories, thus emancipating herself and her readers from the cultural, social, and literary codings which can restrict appreciation of the multifaceted realities of life and literature, gender and genre. Her originality is to have done so while retaining a somewhat traditional and linear narrative style, unlike, for example, Hélène Cixous, Chantal Chawaf, and other proponents of a radically experimental form of *écriture féminine* (feminine writing). Such aesthetically experimental literature, while evoking admiration, rarely moves readers the way Cardinal's characters do: her women so resemble ourselves that reading about them can be a deeply emotional experience.

A *pied-noir* (Algerian-French), born and raised in Algiers, Cardinal hardly knew her French father; her parents were divorced in 1929, the year of her birth. Her mother harbored a deep and lasting resentment against this man who had irresponsibly caused their first daughter's death from tubercular meningitis because he had neglected treating his own tuberculosis. He died in 1946, during Cardinal's adolescence, and she always regretted not having known him better. *Le Passé empiété* (Infringement upon the Past, 1983) is about her mythical identification with this larger-than-life ghost whose life she imagines and reconstructs. Cardinal's mother was a *pied-noir* and belonged to a prominent bourgeois Catholic and colonial family whose history had been closely linked to the establishment and management of a "French" Algeria since the mid nineteenth century. The war of Algerian independence marked the end of that era, and in the 1960s her mother was "repatriated" to France, where she slowly sank into ill health and alcoholism, an episode which Cardinal has recounted in *Les Mots pour le dire*.

A thoroughly *pied-noir* writer, Cardinal describes Mediterranean nature with a lyricism and a sensuality which recall the Camus of *Noces* (Nuptials, 1939) and *L'Eté* (Summer, 1954). Profoundly attached to a country which she saw torn by war, she did not return to Algeria for more than fifteen years after independence was achieved. She has related her first encounters with independent Algeria in *Au pays de mes racines* (In the Country of my Roots, 1980), a journal-essay on biculturalism and colonialism. After obtaining a *licence* and a *diplôme d'études supérieures* in philosophy from the Université d'Alger and marrying Jean-Pierre Ronfard, she taught French language and literature in Greece, Portugal, and Austria for seven years while her husband held university jobs. She gave birth to three children in the space of four years: the first two born in Algiers, and the last in Lisbon, in the late 1950s. Unable to prepare for the *agrégation* (a competitive degree required of all French university professors), Cardinal lived and worked as a free-lance writer in Paris after relocating there with her family in the 1960s. Her husband eventually took a job in Montreal, where he now runs a theater. Currently Cardinal resides in Montreal, when she is not traveling, discussing her works, or defending "la cause des femmes" (women's causes). She spends summers in the south of France.

By her own admission, she is a writer who needs to be in touch with her public, participating in an average of 150 conferences and debates per year. She also teaches a fall seminar in the Continuing Education Division of the Université de Montréal. These contacts, she says, provide her with an important and necessary opportunity to interact with students and readers and not to become isolated as a writer. She receives a vast amount of mail from readers and has said that she is especially pleased by letters from those who feel that her writings have given voice to a generation of expatriates forced by economic, social, or political realities to leave Algeria and relocate in the industrialized nations of the world.

Cardinal's major themes are loss, abandonment, and the fear of death: symbolic loss of origin (loss of motherland, loss of identity), loss of love, loss of sanity, and the fear of suicide. However, she believes in the hypothetical possibility of personal liberation through language and emphasizes that it is thanks to the difficult process of verbalizing these fears, as in psychoanalysis, and through the creative efforts involved in living freely and imaginatively as a writer, that her protagonists are able to cope with the traumas of a difficult relationship with both "mother and motherland," as Marguerite Le Clézio put it in a 1981 article in the *Stanford French Review*.

Cardinal's first book, *Ecoutez la mer* (Listen to the Sea, 1962), is a love story about a German writer, Karl, living in Paris and a *pied-noir* expatriate, Maria, who is the narrator of the novel. As she begins to fall in love with Karl, Maria finds that she is rediscovering her own personal rhythms, the rhythms of the land she has left behind. Weaving present sensations and fearful memories from the past, Maria recounts her childhood to Karl, who in turn shares with her his experiences as a sixteen-year-old recruit in the German army fighting on the Russian front during World War II. This pairing of the main protagonists' early experiences of war and fear provides a shading of perceptions as Maria discovers what it means to face anguish and death. Her exchanges with Karl lift her out of a downward spiral of depression. It is by sharing the story of his fears as a young soldier that she gradually learns to get out of her own prison of painful memories: "Je ne bouge pas, je sens les larmes qui montent et qui débordent très vite. Karl me regarde, c'est ce qu'il voulait: me sortir de moi-même, me montrer que d'autres connaissent la peur, qu'on s'en sort" (I am motionless, I can feel the tears welling up and running down quickly. Karl looks at me, that's what he wanted: to pull me out of myself, to show me that others experi-

ence fear, that it is possible to make it). When the narrator leaves Paris, and Karl, to return to her family in Canada, her hallucinations and anguish return, and the book ends on the image of a little girl dancing to the tune of Arabic music under the white-hot sky of Algeria: "Je vois le ciel glorieux, la terre rouge des collines. Tout est beau. Je peux tout faire pour l'amour de cela. . . . Ma danse est une action de grâces pour le goût des figues mûres, pour la fraîcheur de la mer, pour la chaleur du soleil, pour le parfum des belles de nuit" (I see the glorious sky, the red earth on the hills. Everything is beautiful. I can do anything for the love of all this. . . . My dance is a gesture of thanksgiving for the taste of ripe figs, for the coolness of the sea, for the heat of the sun, for the smell of the cereus).

Cardinal's writing recalls Colette's love of nature and sensitivity to the descriptive nuances of language. Her interest in the emancipatory potential of the creative process and her belief in its importance for re-creating one's self and developing a sense of accomplishment are clear from her own statements about this first novel, which won the 1962 Prix International du Premier Roman: "Mon premier livre a été l'aube de ma naissance, de ma guérison. Je me suis aventurée dans ces premières pages blanches comme une femme perdue dans le désert trouverait la trace de l'eau" (My first book was the dawn of my rebirth, of my recovery. I ventured out on those white pages just like a woman lost in the desert who would suddenly have found a way to water). The process of writing becomes an attempt to replace the loss, to fill the void left by the existential realities of life. In this regard, Cardinal's feminist aesthetic of writing is radically opposed to the notion, examined by certain contemporary French theoretical thinkers (Jacques Derrida and Maurice Blanchot, for example), that writing is a form of death, or an illusory effort at staving off the inevitability of death. For Cardinal, to become able to articulate the specificity of women's experiences is an exhilarating process which propels writer and reader into a dialogical encounter and thus empowers both to take distance on a stifling tradition of misogynist literature.

Her second book, *La Mule de corbillard* (The Hearse Mule, 1963), is the story of a seventy-year-old woman who is profoundly attached to a small Mediterranean farm which she does not own but which her schoolteacher father has been tenant-farming ever since she was very young. Cardinal's talent for characterization emerges from this portrait of a woman who loses everything in turn: the man she loves, the farm which is her whole life, and the work of art she has created–a cathedral made of shells, a masterpiece which occupies her free time after her lover leaves. Madeleine Couturier (note the initials) derives her strength and resilience from her contact with nature: "Ma terre et moi, ça fait deux sœurs jumelles. On se comprend" (My land and I, we are twin sisters. We understand each other). The novel takes the form of a circular journey: the aging Mlle Couturier takes her daily walks around the vast domain planted with vineyards which belongs to Garcia, the man who repossessed her meager five hectares because wartime authorities demanded that he harvest a certain quantity of maize and castor-oil plants. The most convenient way to meet the quota was to use the land cared for by Couturier, who now nurses a profound and murderous hatred toward him, "une haine lente et dominatrice" (a slow and crushing hatred). Wishing to harness and control her powerful feelings, she bides her time, waiting for the day when she will be able to bury Garcia. Allegorical of the feudal conditions of colonialism, *La Mule de corbillard* was published to scattered critical acclaim for the precision of its decriptive style and the depth of emotions it portrays. It was made into a movie of the same title in 1985.

Her third novel, *La Souricière* (The Mousetrap, 1965), is the story of a mental breakdown which ends in suicide. The narrative–which has five chapters–is like a tragedy in five acts, moving inexorably toward its conclusion. A young Provençal woman, Camille (a name which recalls the heroine of Colette's *La Chatte* [*Saha the Cat*, 1933]), marries a Sorbonne professor fifteen years her senior and finds herself transplanted into Parisian domesticity. The effects of three successive pregnancies contribute to the erosion of Camille's sense of reality. She becomes obsessed with physical decay and death and falls into a catatonic stupor which is diagnosed as an aggravated case of postpartum depression, "un cas classique de mélancolie" (a classic case of melancholia). She becomes imprisoned in morbid images: "Elle a peur d'être obligée de subir la mort avec ce corps. Elle a peur d'assister à la putréfaction de sa chair, à sa liquéfaction et de rester enfermée dans une boîte plombée, avec des os, des lambeaux de viande pullulant de vers" (She is afraid she will be forced to endure death in this body. She is afraid of participating in the putrefaction of her flesh, in its liquefaction, afraid of re-

maining locked within an iron box, with her bones, her worm-infested shreds of meat). Images of death come to haunt her because she realizes that to give birth to a human being is also, in the long run, to give death ("Elle leur a donné la mort sans le faire exprès" [She has given them death without meaning to]).

Feeling abandoned by her husband, François, who has been offered an academic job in the United States, Camille turns to her new friend Alain for comfort. With his help, she begins to develop a new sense of self and greater confidence. But François returns after a two-year absence, only to arouse in Camille new feelings of inadequacy because he refuses to acknowledge that she has changed in any way. Camille discovers that while he was away he lived with another woman, who is pregnant with his child, although they have agreed not to see each other again. Shocked by the news, Camille begins to identify with the American woman and to experience vicariously her pregnancy: "Plus la grossesse avance, plus Camille s'active dans la maison. . . . Le ventre de Camille pèse. . . . Camille se remet à saigner du nez. Elle grossit" (The further the pregnancy advances, the more active Camille becomes in the house. . . . Camille's belly has become heavy. . . . Camille starts to have nosebleeds again. She is getting fat). In a last effort to regain a sense of sanity, Camille returns to Alain, who this time stands in judgment of her erratic behavior. Feeling abandoned by all, she takes her life. The novel ends on the wry comments of the omniscient narrator who announces a happy ending for François and his American lover: they get married shortly after Camille's funeral and "live happily ever after."

This early work clearly illustrates, as Marilyn Yalom has remarked in her *Maternity, Mortality, and the Literature of Madness* (1985), that Cardinal's "strength as a writer lies largely in her ability to render mental conditions through an evocation of feminine specificity in the flesh. . . . Madness and sanity, maternity, and death are firmly encased within the author/protagonist's skin and flesh, which in Cardinal's books become not only the focus of the narrative action but also the index of her spiritual journey."

Cet Eté-là (That Summer, 1967) is the journal of a season in the life of the author, the summer of 1966, during which she participated in the making of two movies: Jean-Luc Godard's *Deux ou trois choses que je sais d'elle* (*Two or Three Things I Know about Her*) and Robert Bresson's ad-

-22-

bruits qui balancent.

Cette fois, ça y était! J'avais conclu un marché avec un mort, un

marché passionnant et exigeant. Exigeant, car il n'était pas question *je ne devrais jamais céder à la tentation*

de m'octroyer les mots de ce mort après les avoir libérés de leur beau

~~corset~~. Passionnant car la métrique ~~apporte~~ au texte un élan que je *que je venais d'ecrire* *appui dont je devais tenir compte*

~~debais remplacer par~~ une écriture qui ne s'appuiera pas sur les *Je me suis efforcé de travailler avec particulierement*

sonorités des mots mais sur les rythmes des répliques et des

séquences.

C'est avec un immense respect pour Euripide que j'ai conclu ce *je voulais*

marché, ~~dans le but de~~ restituer Médée au public. Pas ma Médée, la

sienne, la Médée d'Euripide. *de cette tragédie, Médée et les comédiennes, parceque la cause qu'elles plaident et la vie que qu'elles plaident encore aujourd'hui!*

Ce sont les femmes qui m'ont donné cette hardiesse, la cause des *longtemps*

femmes. Il y a ~~tant d'années~~ qu'elles me motivent!

Nostalgie. Soudain me manquaient les lampes à abat-jours verts de

la bibliothèque de l'Université d'Alger, quand la nuit tombait avec un

peu de fraicheur, faisant descendre le parfum des glycines depuis les

jardins des hauteurs jusqu'au centre de la ville. Aussi, à Paris, la

salle de lecture de la Bibliothèque Nationale, les soirs où la pluie

s'acharnait en vain contre les verrières, là haut, très loin,

ailleurs, dehors . Lentes heures passées dans les livres. Protégée par

les volumes en murailles autour de moi, jusqu'au toit, jusqu'au ciel,

dans le cocon de la petite lumière, dans le silence habité par le

glissement des pages...Dans le phare enchanté où se réfugient les

lueurss millénaires des êtres humains...

Page from the revised typescript for Cardinal's preface to her 1986 translation of Euripides' Medea *(by permission of the author)* aptation of *Mouchette* by Georges Bernanos. In her preface to the 1979 edition Cardinal surveys her literary production of the early 1960s (*Ecoutez la mer*, *La Mule de corbillard*, and *La Souricière*) to bemoan the republication without her permission of these early works in the late 1970s (after *Les Mots pour le dire* had become a runaway best-seller). Because these were her first attempts at writing and contain the rough shape of many themes which are further developed in her later works, Cardinal has stated that she would have preferred having the opportunity to publish her first novels together in a single volume with an explanatory introduction. *La Souricière*, in particular, relates a story superficially similar to the one in *Les Mots pour le dire*, although the latter has more density and complexity. Indeed, when they first appeared Cardinal's early novels sold few copies. Flawed by an as yet imperfect control over the material, they are nonetheless moving works and provide insight into the maturation process of a talented writer.

With *La Clé sur la porte*, her fifth book, Cardinal came into her own and reached a wide readership. The book was at first a succès de scandale because of its frank portrayal of a certain generation of young people, "les contestataires," the critics of bourgeois, capitalist society who were known as the 1968 generation. The narrator is the forty-year-old mother of Grégoire (eighteen years old), Charlotte (sixteen), and Dorothée (fourteen). She decides to allow her children to live an experiment in freedom and responsibility, in contrast to her own strict and stifling upbringing. The children's friends come and go freely in their small Paris apartment, camping on the floor, sharing in a communal form of living which wreaks havoc in the mother's private life. Her own friends desert her, but she feels enriched by the presence of these teenagers whose life-style forces her to reexamine her own values: "Leur présence a bouleversé ma vie et j'en suis très heureuse. J'ai l'impression de vivre plus et mieux. Je ne suis plus du tout encombrée par les problèmes matériels secondaires. Je suis complètement soulagée des mondanités" (Their presence has transformed my life. I am very happy about it. I feel my life is fuller, better. I am completely relieved of any social obligations). Making every effort to be a liberated mother without becoming an overly permissive parent, she tries to be a friend as well as a guide. As the children tread the thin line between freedom and anarchy, the narrator analyzes with affection,

humor, and lucidity their internal motivations. She shares in their problems, which run the gamut from school (or work) to teenage pregnancy, drug addiction, and running away from home. Long sections of the book are devoted to summer vacations spent in the United States and Canada, especially, where her husband lives and works. More of a "conte philosophique" or philosophical essay on youth and freedom, and on the exploitation of youth by consumer society, this work is of historical and sociological interest for its personal insights into a period which caused profound changes in the educational system and the culture of contemporary France.

Perhaps her most powerful work to date, *Les Mots pour le dire* has received wide critical attention. It won the Prix Littré 1976, an award given annually for the best medical-arts book published in France. The remarkable story of a mental illness, it popularizes the subject of the psychiatric or "talking" cure. The narrator/protagonist, whose outward symptom is constant menstrual bleeding, undergoes a lengthy Freudian psychoanalysis in the course of which she comes to understand that her "illness" is none other than her progressive inability to cope with the lies of patriarchy, with the *dressage*, the relentless indoctrination into rigid codes of conduct that went on while she was growing up: "Jour après jour, depuis ma naissance, on avait fabriqué: mes gestes, mes attitudes, mon vocabulaire. On avait réprimé mes besoins, mes envies, mes élans, on les avait endigués, maquillés, emprisonnés" (Day after day, ever since my birth, I had been molded: my gestures, my attitudes, my vocabulary. My needs were repressed along with my wants, my spontaneity. They had been walled, masked, disguised, imprisoned). Turned into a puppet for the benefit of her bourgeois social class, "jeune femme modèle digne de ma mère" (model young wife and mother, worthy of my own mother), the narrator, in the course of her painful journey, aims at rediscovering the woman who had become effaced, "la femme oubliée, plus qu'oubliée, dissoute" (the forgotten woman, more than forgotten, disintegrated), the female self to whom she now attempts to give birth. Indeed the imagery she uses to describe the location of the psychoanalyst's office is particularly suited to the birthing metaphor: it is an island of surprising calm in the midst of Paris, at the end of a narrow cul-de-sac, "une ruelle en impasse." She escapes into the dark office, a womblike room, where she lies on the couch "recroque-

villée comme un foetus dans une matrice. . . .
Embryon gros de moi-même" (Curled up like a
fetus in the womb. . . . Embryo pregnant with myself).

The problem faced by the analysand is the
same dilemma that Cardinal the writer must confront: how to find her own "words to say it," how
not to let herself be silenced by her initial need
for constant reference to a rigid literary code
and pious reverence for the great masters
(Boileau's seventeenth-century *Art poétique* contains a famous dictum which every French child
learns in school: "Ce qui se conçoit bien s'énonce
clairement/Et les mots pour le dire viennent
aisément" [What one understands well, one can express clearly/And the words to say it can easily be
found]; hence the book's title). Cardinal brilliantly articulates the anxieties of female authorship in a culture which does not give women writers their due and thus aborts their attempts at
creating a tradition of their own.

In keeping with her desire to retrieve those
elements of female experience which have been repressed by culture, Cardinal focuses on menstrua-
tion, a phenomenon which is shrouded in ancient
taboos and thus has the potential for great metaphoric play. At the beginning of the novel the narrator is comatose, chemically tranquilized and sub-
missive. Her body, however, is hysterically alive.
The constant hemorrhaging becomes the disturbing sign of a feminine difference flowing out of
control, a difference which her gynecologist (who
is her uncle) blithely decides to erase by suggesting that she needs a hysterectomy. Hence her escape from the clinic and her decision to start analysis, thus narrowly avoiding a final, symbolic, and
radical amputation of femininity. The menstrual
blood, which had been a convenient way to avoid
facing her very real fear of death, soon stops,
and the narrator's journey through the maze of
her memory brings back to her consciousness the
origin of her fears: it is the unsavory revelation
by her mother of her unsuccessful attempts at
aborting the narrator because, in the aftermath
of their divorce, a pregnancy would only serve to
remind the mother of her hatred for her husband. Recalling this odious confession, and the
damage it did to her psyche, the narrator
conflates this experience with one of torture, as
countless individuals were tortured during the
long years of the Algerian war. Weaving together
the personal and the political, her individual history and the Algerian tragedy, Cardinal succeeds
in metaphorically linking her attacks of anxiety,

"la chose" (the thing), to her feelings of impotence in affairs of the state. Indeed, she says: "Il
me semble que la chose a pris racine en moi
d'une façon permanente, quand j'ai compris que
nous allions assassiner l'Algérie. Car l'Algérie,
c'était ma vraie mère" (It seems to me that the
thing took root in me permanently when I understood that we were about to assassinate Algeria.
For Algeria was my real mother).

Impeccably written, in a prose rich with delicate notations, *Les Mots pour le dire* is a profoundly moving story about a woman and her
country, about a daughter and her parents,
about femininity and madness. In the words of
one American reviewer, Cardinal describes "the
long psychoanalysis that not only relieved her of
mysterious miseries, but also converted her, to
her great surprise, into a successful author. Since
she follows chronologically the steps by which
she disinterred her memories and perceived the
connections between her condition and her loveless upbringing, the account comes to resemble a
detective story, causing the reader to await each
new clue with astonishment and curiosity."

Les Mots pour le dire bears witness to the efforts of a woman who finds the words needed to
express the physicality of women and the shadowy realities of war and censorship: "Les mots
pouvaient être des blessures ou des cicatrices de
blessures, ils pouvaient ressembler à une dent
gâtée dans un sourire de plaisir. . . . Les mots
pouvaient être des monstres, les S.S. de
l'inconscient, refoulant la pensée des vivants dans
les prisons de l'oubli" (Words could be wounds or
the scars from old wounds, they could look like a
rotten tooth in a smile of pleasure. . . . Words
could be monsters, the SS of the unconscious, re-
pressing the thoughts of the living into the prisons of oblivion). It is thus regrettable that the
English translation, published in 1983, has down-
played the political dimensions of the work by simply cutting out certain passages and framing the
text with a strictly Freudian preface and afterword by Bruno Bettelheim, whose sympathetic
comments tend nonetheless to filter the English
reader's understanding of the narrative through
a slightly deforming lens. Both *La Clé sur la porte*
and *Les Mots pour le dire* were made into movies,
the first starring Annie Girardot and the second,
Nicole Garcia.

Autrement dit (In Other Words, 1977), a series of conversations between Cardinal and her
friend Annie Leclerc, is an indispensable text for
anyone wishing to understand Cardinal's life and

artistic method. The author discusses her biography and her creative technique, her views on feminism, writing, and life, as well as her struggle to liberate language, to acquire the right–seldom granted to "serious" women writers–to use words which are forceful and expressive of physical realities.

Une Vie pour deux (One Life for Two, 1978), a work of dialectical tensions, is structurally quite complex. It takes place in Ireland, a country divided against itself, much as the narrator, Simone, feels divided between the "I" and the impossible "we" she forms with her husband of some twenty years, Jean-François, as well as between the "I" and a "she" reconstructed by the narrative: the young woman named Mary MacLaughlin whose dead body is found on the beach not far from the vacationing couple's summer cottage. Three tales become inextricably intertwined: Simone and Jean-François's daily life in Corvagh, Simone's memories of her past, and the imagined story of Mary MacLaughlin's life. The first person alternates both with a third-person account of Simone's and Jean-François's past and present life, and with the successive episodes of a novel within the novel entitled *Histoire de Mary MacLaughlin.*

The couple's life is completely changed by the discovery of the faceless, disfigured body. This discovery becomes the starting point for a series of reflections during which the couple interrogates themselves and the past, turning Mary into a persona around whom their own doubts, regrets, and obsessions become crystallized. Focusing on the theme of the woman who is overwhelmed by familial responsibilities to the point of losing all personal identity, Cardinal describes with affection and tenderness the naive young woman full of dreams and confidence that Simone was: "Je m'étais aventurée bravement dans la vie, portant les lourdes valises des principes, vêtue des légers vêtements de la naíveté et de la confiance enfantines. . . . Je n'ai pas cheminé longtemps. Vite sont accourus la fatigue et le froid" (I ventured bravely on the paths of life, carrying suitcases heavy with principles, lightly clothed in the naive trust of childhood. . . . I did not get very far. Fatigue and cold soon caught up with me).

In counterpoint to Simone's life, which appears in retrospect to have been full of joys and sorrows, pleasures and pains, the loneliness of Mary MacLaughlin's trajectory emerges in filigree. Raised in a large, poor, rural family, Mary

dreams of becoming a doctor. She moves to the city, studies hard, and passes exams. She becomes pregnant by a man who is already married and the father of two; she decides against having an abortion and has to abandon her studies. She immigrates to New York and works as a nurse to support herself and her son. Torn between the need to fulfill her dreams of a career and the necessity of working full-time in order to raise her son, Mary becomes progressively bitter and disenchanted: "Et pourquoi ne pourrait-elle pas avoir un enfant et être elle-même?. . . Pourquoi toujours ce choix: lui ou moi? Si je l'aime je ne peux pas m'aimer? Pourquoi? J'aime Sean. Je l'aime plus qu'aucune autre personne et je sais que je l'aimerai toujours, mais pourquoi me forcer à l'aimer plus que moi-même?" (Why couldn't she have a child and be herself? . . . Why always the same dilemma: he or I? If I love him, I can't love myself? Why? I love Sean. I love him more than anybody else, and I know that I will always love him, but why should I be forced to love him more than myself?). Faced with one of the most archaic and tragic conflicts of women's lives, Mary gives up–"un jour elle baissa les bras, elle abandonna" (One day she drops her arms, she lets go)–and returns to Ireland with her son who is now twelve years old. She has learned to dissimulate and to survive, but has lost all hope. It is not clear whether her death is a suicide. But by imagining Mary's life, and writing it down in a notebook, Simone and Jean-François together acquire a renewed understanding of each other's motivations: "A partir de ce jour, à cause du cahier qui est une œuvre commune–même si elle est seule à l'écrire–Jean-François et Simone ont commencé à former un couple" (From that day on, because of the notebook which is a joint effort–even if she is the only one who writes–Jean-François and Simone started becoming a couple). As Carolyn A. Durham has convincingly argued in a 1985 article for *Tulsa Studies in Women's Literature*, this novel shows Cardinal's dialectical worldview: she "consistently rejects the unity of the two in one as an illusion of the moment, left over from a conventional and misleading romanticism of the couple, in favor of a mobile relationship between the self and a multiplicity of others."

Au pays de mes racines is the journal of Cardinal's first return visit to her native land, of her attempts to understand the advantages and disadvantages of being a cultural *métis*: "Pourquoi vouloir retourner là-bas, pourquoi écrire ces pages sinon pour essayer de comprendre l'équilibre ou le déséquilibre que créent en moi l'alliance ou la guerre de deux cultures? . . . Je voudrais pouvoir être tranquillement bi-culturée sans que la névrose s'empare de ma personne bicéphale" (Why do I want to return there, why do I want to write these pages if not with the purpose of understanding the balance or imbalance created in me by my two allied or warring cultures? . . . I would like to be able to live a quietly bicultural life without my bicephalous person becoming caught up in neurosis). As a report on the conditions of life in Socialist Algeria, on the advances made by Algerian women, on the meaning of history, and on the author's newly found sense of peace at being reconciled with the past and with herself, this essay captures Cardinal's unique blend of lyrical vulnerabilities and political sensitivities.

The title of her 1983 novel, *Le Passé empiété*, provides the author with a metaphor for both her work's themes and the process of writing which is allegorized in this fast-paced, spellbinding narrative about the imagined life of her father. Adopting "a kind of literary transsexuality," as French reviewer Gérard-Humbert Goury has noted in the *Magazine Littéraire*, Cardinal infringes upon the past to reconstruct the life and loves of Jean-Maurice, the father she hardly knew, engaging in a dialogue so intimate that it moves from "he" to "I" as she attempts to wrestle with the personality of this male figure: "J'installe mon père dans ma personne comme on installe chez soi un bébé, un jeune animal, une nouvelle plante" (I install my father within my own person the way one welcomes a baby, a young animal, or a new plant into one's home).

The narrator describes herself as a "brodeuse," a woman who embroiders; "le passé empiété" is also the term used to refer to a particular type of embroidery stitching, with the leading thread going back and over the previous stitch. Having achieved fame thanks to her "embroideries," which are sold all over the world, the fifty-year-old protagonist buys her grown children a motorcycle. They have an accident and are severely hurt. After two years of treatment and rehabilitation, they are completely recovered. But the mother, still anguished and guilt-ridden, blames herself for being overly generous with her money and for indirectly causing the accident. To sort out her feelings, she decides to spend time alone at her brother's beach house. There, she becomes progressively entranced by the

phantasmagorical image of a rider, a father figure, an Agamemnon for whom she becomes Electra, an Agamemnon who is responsible for Iphigenia's death, as Jean-Maurice is responsible for his daughter Odette's meningitis. In keeping with her talent for rendering the physicality of human experiences, Cardinal completely merges the personality of the narrator with that of the father: "Il faut que je sois mon père pour l'exprimer. Il faut que je sois lui. Je, c'est lui et moi. Je désire être mon père, vivre dans sa peau et dans sa tête, sentir sa moustache pousser sous mon nez, aimer comme lui" (I must become my father in order to express him. I must be him. *I* is both him and me. I want to be my father, to live in his skin and in his head, to feel his mustache growing under my nose, to love in his own way). Reinterpreting her family myths, Cardinal observes with earthiness, humor, and compassion the couple formed by Jean-Maurice and Mimi during the affluent and carefree 1920s.

Soon it is the figure of Clytemnestra, Agamemnon's wife, who also invades the narrator's private space, and the mythical characters of Greek drama provide a backdrop for this narrative "tapestry" depicting the tragedy of families divided by death and vengeance. Behind the presence of Clytemnestra, it is both the narrator and her own mother who are evoked. The depth and violence of a mother's feelings; the pain of losing a child; the cancers of bitterness and silence, those twin weapons of women who, from time immemorial, have felt powerless in the face of social structures they had no part in building; the difficulty of psychologically separating oneself from one's parents and one's children: all these questions are raised by the last section of the narrative, which invites the reader to reflect upon the links between past and future, historical context and individual circumstances.

In her most recent novel, *Les Grands Désordres* (Great Upheavals, 1987), Cardinal focuses on a mother's desperate attempt to help her daughter, who has become addicted to heroin. Elsa Labbé, a child psychologist who has been widowed since age twenty-two, has suffered from the Algerian war. Her husband Jacques was killed while fighting for the French army in North Africa. She has raised her daughter, Laure, alone while studying and then practicing in Paris and has always led a well-ordered and rational middle-class existence.

Laure, now in her twenties, presents Elsa with the greatest crisis of her life. Forced to reexamine her priorities, she decides to take a leave of absence: "Pour aider sa fille, elle va entrer vingt-quatre heures sur vingt-quatre dans le désordre de Laure. Ce désordre deviendra son ordre. Ce sera son occupation à plein temps" (To help her daughter, she is going to enter Laure's disorderly life for twenty-four hours a day. This disorder will become her order. It will be her full-time occupation). Elsa takes her daughter away from Paris, to the south of France and to Morocco. Some of the most moving pages of the novel describe Elsa's realization that Laure's body—mutilated by needles—figures the abyss which now exists between them and which forces Elsa to embark on a nomadic search for a solution she feels powerless to find: "L'errance devint le propre de leurs vies.... Elsa est entrée, en même temps que dans l'errance géographique, dans une vertigineuse errance intellectuelle. Désormais, ses connaissances ressembleront à des sables mouvants . . ." (To wander/to err, such was now their predicament. . . . At the same time that she started her geographical wanderings, Elsa came face to face with a vertiginous intellectual uncertainty. From now on, her knowledge will be like quicksand . . .). Elsa discovers that her science is powerless to cure her daughter, as is her love. After three years Laure finally succeeds in helping herself, thanks to the love of another addict.

Meanwhile, Elsa's life has undergone such upheavals that—as a form of personal therapy—she decides to recount her experiences. But, unable to write with the distance she feels she needs, she hires a ghostwriter who can "translate" her experiences. (This is a role with which Cardinal herself is familiar, since she has been a ghostwriter for the author Lucien Bodard.) The ghostwriter's own narrative of his emerging love for Elsa frames the story of Elsa and Laure, thus introducing a new perspective on the ways that reading and interpreting someone else's experiences can become a powerful seduction, a seduction which ends up transforming both Elsa and the writer. Having learned to let go of her adult daughter and of the false values which used to imprison her, Elsa discovers the power of stories to transform and subjugate: a power with which Cardinal's own readers are by now familiar.

While implying that attempts to re-vision the past—the traditions that subtend the Western heritage as well as one's individual and personal history—are important gestures of rebirth and reconciliation, Cardinal would also seem to suggest that the process of self-discovery through a network of relationships is a fundamental mode of healing of the narrating self, and an important first step on the road to social change. Her essays and novels testify to her commitment to articulate radically new definitions of femininity, motherhood, and creativity, definitions which would be liberating for men and women, parents and children.

References:

Carolyn A. Durham, "Feminism and Formalism: Dialectical Structures in Marie Cardinal's *Une Vie pour deux*," *Tulsa Studies in Women's Literature*, 4 (Spring 1985): 83-99;

Durham, "Patterns of Influence: Simone de Beauvoir and Marie Cardinal," *French Review*, 60 (February 1987): 341-348;

Marguerite Le Clézio, "Mother and Motherland: The Daughter's Quest for Origins," *Stanford French Review*, 5 (Winter 1981): 381-389;

Françoise Lionnet, *Autobiographical Voices: Race, Gender, Self-Portraiture* (Ithaca & London: Cornell University Press, 1989);

Lionnet, "*Métissage*, Emancipation and Female Textuality in Two Francophone Writers," in *Life/Lines: Theorizing Women's Autobiography*, edited by Bella Brodzki and Celeste Schenck (Ithaca & London: Cornell University Press, 1988);

Elaine A. Martin, "Mothers, Madness, and the Middle Class in *The Bell Jar* and *Les Mots pour le dire*," *French-American Review*, 5 (Spring 1981): 24-47;

Martin, "Uncommon Women and Common Experience: Bruckner, Cardinal, Drewitz and Mallet-Joris," Ph.D. dissertation, Indiana University, 1983;

Judith Mayne, "Feminist Film Theory and Criticism," *Signs: Journal of Women in Culture and Society*, 11 (Autumn 1985): 81-100;

Trinh T. Minh-ha, "L'innécriture: feminisme et littérature," *French Forum*, 8 (January 1983): 45-63;

Marilyn Yalom, *Maternity, Mortality, and the Literature of Madness* (University Park & London: Pennsylvania State University Press, 1985).

Jean Cayrol

(6 June 1911-   )

Terence Dawson
National University of Singapore

BOOKS: *Les Poèmes du Pasteur Grimm* (Tunis: Editions des Mirages, 1935);

Le Hollandais volant (Marseilles: Cahiers du Sud, 1936);

Les Phénomènes célestes (Marseilles: Cahiers du Sud, 1939);

L'Age d'or (Paris: Magné/Brussels: Edition Universelle, 1939);

Le Dernier Homme (Brussels: Cahiers du "Journal des Poètes," 1940);

No Man's Land (Algiers: Fontaine, 1943);

Miroir de la Rédemption, précédé de Et nunc (Neuchâtel: Baconnière/Paris: Seuil, 1944);

Poèmes de la nuit et du brouillard, suivi de Larmes publiques (Paris: Seghers, 1946);

Passe-temps de l'homme et des oiseaux, suivi de Dans le meilleur des mondes (Neuchâtel: Baconnière/Paris: Seuil, 1947);

On vous parle, volume 1 of *Je vivrai l'amour des autres* (Neuchâtel: Baconnière/Paris: Seuil, 1947);

Les Premiers Jours, volume 2 of *Je vivrai l'amour des autres* (Neuchâtel: Baconnière/Paris: Seuil, 1947);

La Vie répond (Paris: GLM, 1948);

La Noire (Neuchâtel: Baconnière/Paris: Seuil, 1949);

La Couronne du chrétien (Neuchâtel: Baconnière, 1949);

Le Charnier natal (Lormont: Editions d'Art Vulc, 1950);

Le Feu qui prend, volume 3 of *Je vivrai l'amour des autres* (Neuchâtel: Baconnière/Paris: Seuil, 1950);

Lazare parmi nous (Neuchâtel: Baconnière/Paris: Seuil, 1950);

Les Mille et une nuits du chrétien (Paris: Editions Téqui, 1952);

Le Vent de la mémoire (Neuchâtel: Baconnière/Paris: Seuil, 1952);

Les Mots sont aussi des demeures (Neuchâtel: Baconnière/Paris: Seuil, 1952);

L'Espace d'une nuit (Neuchâtel: Baconnière/Paris: Seuil, 1954); translated by Gerard Hopkins as *All in a Night* (London: Faber, 1957);

Manessier (Paris: Georges Fall, 1955);

Pour tous les temps (Paris: Seuil, 1955);

Le Déménagement (Paris: Seuil, 1956);

La Gaffe (Paris: Seuil, 1957);

Les Corps étrangers (Paris: Seuil, 1959); translated by Richard Howard as *Foreign Bodies* (New York: Putnam's, 1960);

Les Pleins et les Déliés (Paris: Seuil, 1960);

Le Droit de regard, by Cayrol and Claude Durand (Paris: Seuil, 1963);

Le Froid du soleil (Paris: Seuil, 1963);

Muriel (Paris: Seuil, 1963);

Le Coup de grâce, by Cayrol and Durand (Paris: Seuil, 1965);

Midi Minuit (Paris: Seuil, 1966);

Je l'entends encore (Paris: Seuil, 1968);

De l'espace humain (Paris: Seuil, 1968);

Poésie-Journal (Paris: Seuil, 1969);

Histoire d'une prairie (Paris: Seuil, 1969);

N'oubliez pas que nous nous aimons (Paris: Seuil, 1971);

Histoire d'un désert (Paris: Seuil, 1972);

Histoire de la mer (Paris: Seuil, 1973);

Lectures (Paris: Seuil, 1973);

Kakemono Hôtel (Paris: Seuil, 1974);

Histoire de la forêt (Paris: Seuil, 1975);

Histoire d'une maison (Paris: Seuil, 1976);

Poésie-Journal, volume 2 (Paris: Seuil, 1977);

Les Enfants pillards (Paris: Seuil, 1978);

Histoire du ciel (Paris: Seuil, 1979);

Exposés au soleil (Paris: Seuil, 1980);

Poésie-Journal, volume 3 (Paris: Seuil, 1980);

L'Homme dans le rétroviseur (Paris: Seuil, 1981);

Il était une fois Jean Cayrol (Paris: Seuil, 1982);

Un Mot d'auteur (Paris: Seuil, 1983);

Qui suis-je? suivi de Une Mémoire toute fraîche (Paris: Seuil, 1984);

Poèmes clefs (Paris: Seuil, 1985);

Les Châtaignes (Paris: Seuil, 1986);

Des nuits plus blanches que nature (Paris: Seuil, 1987);

Œuvre poétique (Paris: Seuil, 1988).

MOTION PICTURES: *Nuit et brouillard*, dialogue by Cayrol, 1956;

On vous parle, screenplay by Cayrol and Claude Durand, 1960;

La Frontière, screenplay by Cayrol and Durand, 1961;

Madame se meurt, screenplay by Cayrol and Durand, 1961;

De tout pour faire un monde, screenplay by Cayrol and Durand, 1962;

Muriel, screenplay by Cayrol, 1963;

Le Coup de grâce, screenplay by Cayrol and Durand, 1965;

La Déesse, screenplay and direction by Cayrol, 1966.

TELEVISION: *Spécialité de la mer*, script by Cayrol and Claude Durand, 1960.

RADIO: *La Parole aux vivants*, script by Cayrol, 1950.

OTHER: "Le Coin de table," in *Ecrire 1: "Premières Œuvres" publiées sous la direction de Jean Cayrol* (Paris: Seuil, 1956);

Les Quatre Saisons, illustrations by Mitsumasa Anno, text by Cayrol (Paris: Hachette, 1977).

PERIODICAL PUBLICATIONS: *Ulysse*, by Cayrol and Jacques Dalléas, *Cahiers du Fleuve* (1934);

Ce n'est pas la mer, *Cahiers du Fleuve* (1935);

"Simulacre," *Biblio*, 31 (November 1963): 10-13.

Jean Cayrol is one of the most original writers of his generation. He has been enormously prolific, always innovative, and consistently well reviewed. His works include some twenty-five novels, several novellas and short stories, over fifteen volumes of poetry, screenplays, television scripts, and essays on a wide range of topics. His poetry has been praised by Max Jacob, Albert Béguin, and Claude Roy. His novels have been admired by Roland Barthes, Jean Ricardou, Philippe Sollers, Yves Bonnefoy, and Alain Bosquet. He was a well-respected editor at Editions du Seuil where, in 1956, he founded a successful collection of first works by new writers. He has enjoyed a place near the center of French literary life for more than half a century, while always retaining his own individual voice. He was elected to the Académie Goncourt in 1974.

Cayrol's work constitutes a sequence, a personal odyssey. Three phases can be discerned. The first is his period as a young poet, during which he wrote religious-symbolist poems which showed considerable promise but were at the same time somewhat forced. The second period covers his first twenty years as a novelist, which many regard as the time of his most significant work. During the period 1947-1968 he was considered one of France's leading novelists. His novels are regarded as precursors of the *nouveau roman*, the new novel which emerged in France in the 1950s. The third phase begins in the mid 1960s: it is marked by a disregard for realism and a corresponding enjoyment of fantasy for its own sake. It is in this period that Cayrol has revealed himself as a great comic novelist. Although critics have shown much less interest in his recent work, largely because it cannot be conveniently labeled, it represents some of the most accomplished writing of the last twenty years.

Cayrol has drawn much of his material from personal experience. It would be a mistake, however, to describe his work as autobiographical in the usual sense of this word. The experiences which his characters face reflect an inner world which is not strictly his own. The dilemmas at the heart of his fictions are of the kind every reader can recognize, because they reflect universal problems–how to come to terms with one's own past, how to overcome one's shortcomings, and how to meet the obligations of relationship. He has been called a Catholic novelist. But neither the experiences he describes nor the goals his characters attain are in any sense theological. By definition, a Catholic writer is one who has a plan, whereas Cayrol has constantly insisted that he writes without any notion of where his story is going to take him. He allows an idea to work within him and sees his task as exploring its unknown aspects. While his technique has many affinities with that of the various *nouveaux romanciers*, there is an all-important difference, well illustrated by a phrase used by Roland Barthes in his 1952 essay "Jean Cayrol et ses romans": "il y a un homme cayrolien" (there is a Cayrolian man). There is no Robbe-Grillet man. In contrast with the *nouveau roman*, Cayrol's work is humanistic. His novels are quests, and like all literature of quest, what is (or is not) discovered at the end represents something which the hero or heroine is unconsciously struggling to assimilate throughout. In this sense, the encounters which make up the novels are purposeful: their func-

Advertisement for Cayrol's volume of stories published in 1984, the year he won the Grand Prix National des Lettres

tion is to cause the main protagonist to come to terms with his conflicting experiences. Cayrol never preaches. He is an explorer of states of consciousness. It is left to the reader to decide on the value of each encounter.

Cayrol has always been reticent about his life. He has consistently evaded questions even about his date of birth. This is not a pose. Throughout his career he has given interviews in which he has discussed his work, including those elements in it which are of autobiographical origin. But he distinguishes between clarification of an element and its interpretation. What an episode means for him he regards as his affair. It concerns a reader only to the extent that it corresponds to something in his or her imagination.

Jean Raphaël Marie Noël Cayrol was born in Bordeaux on 6 June 1911 into a professional middle-class family. His parents were Antoine Cayrol, a doctor, and Marie Berrogain Cayrol.

Like many writers, he had a childhood marked by an early interest in literature. In 1927, at the age of sixteen, together with Jacques Dalléas, he founded a literary journal, *Abeilles et Pensées* (Bees and Thoughts). Fourteen numbers appeared, which is no small achievement for a teenager. While studying literature and law at the University of Bordeaux, he founded another journal, the *Cahiers du Fleuve* (Journal of the River), which attracted the attention of many critics and writers, and to which Max Jacob and Henry Daniel-Rops contributed. It was in the *Cahiers du Fleuve* that Cayrol published his first substantial works: *Ulysse* (1934), a dramatic dialogue in five "tableaux" which he wrote with Jacques Dalléas, and *Ce n'est pas la mer* (It Is Not the Sea, 1935), his first major collection of poems. Both were well reviewed.

On graduating in law, he decided to practice, using his parents' home. His first client shouted her business at him so loudly that his father intervened and asked her to leave. Cayrol maintains that it was this "incident burlesque" which put an end to his legal career. In 1937 he became a librarian at the Bordeaux chamber of commerce and wrote poetry in his spare time. His early collections of poems include *Les Poèmes du Pasteur Grimm* (The Poems of Pastor Grimm, 1935), *Le Hollandais volant* (The Flying Dutchman, 1936), *Les Phénomènes célestes* and *L'Age d'or* (Celestial Phenomena and The Golden Age, 1939), and *Le Dernier Homme* (The Last Man, 1940). While these works show undeniable talent, there is little to distinguish them from those of his contemporaries, Luc Estang, for example, or Patrice de la Tour du Pin. They are works of anguish, but of an anguish learned from literature, and not from life. Their importance for Cayrol is that they are also an apprenticeship in the use of language.

At the outbreak of World War II he enlisted in the navy, in which he had done his military service in 1934. When France fell to Germany, Cayrol wanted to go to London. Since he was unable to leave the country, his brother persuaded him to join the Resistance group led by Col. Gilbert Renault Rémy. In March 1942 he was arrested but released for want of evidence. Three months later he and his brother were arrested and taken to prison at Fresnes. Several of his literary friends, including Louis Aragon, Pierre Drieu La Rochelle, Pierre Emmanuel, and Albert Béguin–that is, men with widely differing political convictions–appealed on his behalf, but to no avail. In March 1943 the two brothers were sent to the concentration camp at Mauthausen, where Jean Cayrol remained until the Liberation.

The war was without doubt the single most important event in Cayrol's life. The world of the concentration camp–the *Nacht und Nebel* (night and fog)–and his brother's death there marked him deeply. He returned home but was never quite able to settle. He was haunted by his experiences, and perhaps most of all by the unanswered question: "Why have I been allowed to return from the dead?" Many of his works make reference to the war, or to an imaginary holocaust. The prison camps of Fresnes and Mauthausen are specifically mentioned in *Je l'entends encore* (I Can Still Hear It, 1968) and in *Histoire d'une maison* (The Story of a House, 1976). And yet, in contrast to other war novels, there is never any detail given. Cayrol does not describe any horrors. The concentration camps to

which he refers do not have any specific or historic value. They are a symbol of "what man has done to man." It is Cayrol's belief that many of those who returned from the war were unable to rediscover any sense of purpose. Much of his work is about man's acceptance of a correspondingly provisional life. *L'homme cayrolien* is a man unconsciously struggling to integrate, in his life, a meaning of which he has but the faintest intimation. For Cayrol, writing is a means by which to explore his own intimations.

At the instigation of Albert Béguin, a collection of Cayrol's poems, *Miroir de la Rédemption* (Mirror of the Redemption, 1944), many of which were written while he was in prison at Fresnes, was published in the series Cahiers du Rhône by Editions de la Baconnière in Neuchâtel, and by Editions du Seuil in Paris. When he returned to France after the war, Cayrol put his experiences into two further, and extraordinarily powerful, volumes of poems, *Poèmes de la nuit et du brouillard* (Poems of the Night and Fog, 1946) and *Passe-temps de l'homme et des oiseaux* (Pastime of Man and the Birds, 1947).

Poetry was no longer his only medium. Within a year of his release from concentration camp, Cayrol began writing a trilogy called *Je vivrai l'amour des autres* (I Shall Live the Life of Others). The serialization of the opening volume, *On vous parle* (Someone Is Speaking to You, 1947), in *Esprit*, a monthly journal, did much to attract attention to the almost simultaneous appearance in book form. *On vous parle* is a short novel composed of unnumbered chapters. Its anonymous narrator, a young man who has come down in the world, is haphazardly remembering elements and episodes from his life. He thinks in turn about his jacket, various friends and acquaintances, his own death, his adolescence spent pushing his grandmother about in a wheelchair, his arrest by the Gestapo while waiting in a queue outside a cinema, his return from the war, his disillusionment and attempted suicide. His recollections and fantasies become increasingly bleak. He is thrown out of the tiny room in which he lives, a room as sordid and small as that of old Bru in Emile Zola's *L'Assommoir*. Finally, when things appear at their worst, help comes from an unexpected quarter. He is offered a small room by the owner of a café. Unable even to thank him, he does at least intuit that this means that he has been granted a reprieve until tomorrow. There are few more vivid representations of the emptiness experienced by many Frenchmen after the war. There is no plot. Very little happens. The narrator symbolizes the numbed condition produced by experiences so overwhelming that all action seems superfluous, all emotion redundant. *On vous parle* anticipates the world of Samuel Beckett's fiction of the 1950s.

The second volume of the trilogy is entitled *Les Premiers Jours* (The First Few Days, 1947). The narrator now has a name, Armand, and a job loading trucks. He has also discovered an appetite, but only for food and not yet for life. He lives with a couple, Albert and Lucette. Although vaguely aware that he loves Lucette, he dare not admit this even to himself. One day he defends her when Albert treats her badly in a restaurant. His gesture is a first clumsy step toward assuming responsibility for his own feelings. Lucette recognizes this and tries to seduce him. Unable to assimilate this new situation, he leaves the apartment and wanders into a store. The following events are the prototype for much of Cayrol's work. They consist of a vivid waking fantasy which culminates in his realizing that everything is happening inside him ("tout se passe en moi"). The novel climaxes in a fight between him and Albert, after which he sees not only Albert but also Lucette for the first time: he has learned to accept responsibility for his feelings. The novel, however, ends uncertainly with him admitting that he still does not know what tomorrow will bring.

Cayrol himself has provided the best commentary on his early work in two essays—"Les Rêves lazaréens" (Lazarean Dreams) and "Pour un romanesque lazaréen" (In Defense of Lazarean Fiction)—published together as *Lazare parmi nous* (Lazarus in our Midst, 1950). In the first of these he describes how men in the concentration camps used to have vivid dreams. A Lazarean dream is one which impresses itself on a dreamer in such a way as to leave him or her with no appetite for real life. Men afflicted by such dreams become increasingly isolated until finally they accept the conditions of a provisional existence. Instead of meeting the demands of a real relationship, they indulge in a yearning for an abstract love which they project onto others. Thus, the Lazarean hero "can discover only in others the profound meaning of love, its harmony, its joy, its plenitude." Fantasy, instead of being used to feed life, replaces it. Cayrol's entire work may be seen as an exploration of a Lazarean mentality. His novels trace a protagonist's efforts to escape from the limbo in which he exists as a result of his self-imposed isolation.

Armand is the Lazarean hero par excellence. He cannot recognize his own desires, let alone respond to them. His notions about others are correspondingly flawed. He sees them not as they are, but only insofar as they reflect his personality. For example, he says of one acquaintance: "Il est noyé continuellement par la vie quotidienne; il fait des efforts désespérés pour paraître vivant" (He is continually being swamped by everyday life; he makes desperate efforts to seem alive). The same applies to Armand. Lucette is always vaguely looking for someone, even when that person is by her side, and Albert is unintentionally callous, because indifferent. Armand is also vaguely looking for someone; he too is unintentionally callous. He sees in others only the reflection of his own face. He lives in a world of his own making. Consequently, he is, to all intents and purposes, dead—like Lazarus. His eventual recognition that his notions are composed entirely of his own projections is a first step toward freeing himself from his emotional isolation. The first two parts of *Je vivrai l'amour des autres* are a powerful representation of the plight of postwar man. They earned Cayrol the Prix Théophraste Renaudot for 1947.

The third part of the trilogy, announced as "Je ne veux pas savoir" (I Don't Want to Know), did not appear for another three years. In the meanwhile, Cayrol wrote another novel, *La Noire* (The Depths, 1949), whose relation to the trilogy is suggested by the name of the heroine, Armande. *La Noire*, which spans the war years, appears at first to be the story of Armande. In 1939 she is living with her mother and two sisters near a lake in the southwest of France. Her lover, Tristan, who has been called up, comes to bid her goodbye. Although she subsequently admits that she never enjoyed a moment of their intimacy (Tristan = *tristes temps* = sad times), she is shaken when he leaves her. She begins to daydream of him. The third chapter introduces an anonymous male narrator whose relation to Armande is not at first clear. Gradually it emerges that he is Tristan, describing the events objectively, and that Armande's narrative is a dream within *his* dream: the story of her increasing isolation reflects his inability to commit himself to her. The novel offers a symbolic representation of the consequences. Armande, now alone, lives an increasingly abject and dreamlike existence. She meets a young girl, Catherine, who leads her into the deepest part of the lake (*la noire*) and tries to drown her. Finally, exhausted both physically and mentally, Armande dies, and the narrator is forced to acknowledge his part in her tragedy. He marries Anne, Armande's sister, who functions as a voice of truth in the narrator's unconscious. As he says, "Armande can *also* be Anne." It is an ironic ending, but optimistic–for it signals that the narrator has at last learned the value of commitment. *La Noire* is a fascinating example of the double plot.

The change in title for the final volume of the trilogy–from "Je ne veux pas savoir" to *Le Feu qui prend* (The Fire Which Catches, 1950)–suggests that the lesson Cayrol learned in writing *La Noire* was essential for the completion of the three-part work. *Le Feu qui prend* takes up Armand's story. He has continued to live with Lucette and sunken to crime. To avoid the police, he returns to his mother's home. But instead of finding a "last refuge," he finds a disordered household. His mother has married a M. Flouche, who has two children: Tom, who belongs to the local underworld, and Francine. Although drawn to Francine, Armand–like the narrator of *La Noire*–is wary of relationships. The turning point occurs when he returns home one evening to find the house cold and deserted. He manages to light the fire, only to discover that his mother is dying in her bedroom. She asks him to bring a priest; he fetches a doctor. It is Francine who brings a priest, but Mme Flouche dies before he can do anything for her. The priest then challenges Armand to recognize his need of God, but Armand evades his questions. Mirroring his evasiveness, Francine attaches herself to a theosophical sect. But Armand has learned that he needs her, and it is not long before they meet again. The novel ends with Lucette's unexpected appearance. She has been mortally wounded in an accident but is proud to discover that Armand has at last committed himself to someone. Francine thanks her, Lucette dies, and Armand and Francine are now ready to face life together.

The narrative direction of *Je vivrai l'amour des autres* might suggest allegory. Cayrol, a committed Catholic, was undoubtedly aware of its Christian overtones and clearly intended these. But there is nothing to suggest that he had the outcome clearly in his mind when he sat down to write the trilogy. In fact, the evidence is very much to the contrary. The novel is not allegory. It is an expression of its author's spontaneous imagination. The ending represents an intima-

tion of the change of attitude needed if Armand is to free himself from his Lazarean limbo. The change involves not Christian love but commitment to another human being. The novel played a considerable part in the revolution in fictional technique which took place in France in the 1950s. Its mood reflected the disillusion felt by many writers with mere story telling. Cayrol's novel is not to be assessed at the level of its plot but at the level of its language, which progresses from the bleakness of the impersonal "on" (someone) in the first volume to the much more confident "il" (he) in the third. It is about the relation between Armand's gradual awakening and the language with which this is described.

Cayrol's subsequent works constitute an amplification of the trilogy's themes. Gérard, the hero of *Le Vent de la mémoire* (The Wind of Memory, 1952), is a middle-aged writer who is unconsciously fleeing from himself. He "discovers" a manuscript which he shows a friend. Discussing it with Roger triggers memories which he has long repressed: the mysterious manuscript is in fact an autobiographical novel revealing a side to his personality which he would rather not acknowledge. Gradually he is compelled to admit how selfish he has been, and to make a tentative resolution to accept himself as he is, in order to meet the obligations of relationship. Many of Cayrol's heroes recall episodes from their past. He has been called "le romancier de la mémoire" (the novelist of memory). But memory is not the same as having an intimation that one must recover something. Perhaps the best explanation of what it is that his heroes must recover is given by Cayrol in a quite different context. In *Lectures* (On Reading, 1973) he argues that the purpose of reading is to "recueillir ce que nous sommes, accueillir ce que nous devinons" (recover what we are, to assimilate what we intimate). Memory, as in Proust, is misleading, for it is never accurate; it can be invented. Strictly speaking, it is not memory which is at issue in Cayrol's fiction, but his characters' present intimations.

In his next two novels the action takes place between two moments in time. *L'Espace d'une nuit* (1954; translated as *All in a Night*, 1957) is one of Cayrol's most perfectly realized works. François, who is thirty, receives an ill-explained invitation to return home to see his father, a bully who dominated his childhood and still dominates his imagination. He gets off the train just before it reaches his father's village, and walks through the night. The novel consists of his extended reverie, which culminates with his arrival home, the death of his father, and François's acceptance of life and responsibilities. It was enthusiastically reviewed by Roland Barthes, who makes two points about Cayrol's novels. The first is that they record a *process* ("l'histoire d'une œuvre qui *est en train* de se faire"). It is as such that they are most profitably read. Barthes's second point is that criticism must resist the temptation to read Cayrol's novels at a symbolic level. *L'Espace d'une nuit* can be read literally. But it is so obviously a variation on the theme of "the dark night of the soul" that its symbolism also deserves consideration. In all Cayrol's works the action moves dexterously between the literal and waking fantasy. To approach the latter literally is to miss the play between the two very different kinds of reality on which they are based.

Le Déménagement (The Move, 1956) explores a similar situation from a woman's point of view. Cate (Catherine) has lived all her life in one apartment, first with her parents and then with her husband. Forced to move, the fabric of her life crumbles. The experience calls up all sorts of memories which cause her to understand how mean and empty her life has been. Unable to accept this insight, she attempts suicide. She fails, and regains consciousness to hear her husband's reassuring voice. Cate learns that she has used her home to shelter herself from life, and that one must immerse oneself in life if one is to realize one's personality: "Une vie doit se frotter aux autres vies, s'user pour briller" (One's life must rub against other lives, get worn in order to shine). This is also the theme of *La Gaffe* (The Blunder, 1957), whose protagonist, Jean, is a young medical student. He goes to a summer resort in Brittany, ostensibly for a short holiday but in fact to try to resolve the dilemmas natural to his age. He takes to wandering in the streets, in the course of which he makes friends with a group of carefree adolescents, the most important of whom is Christiane. After one of their pranks, he thinks he has killed Félicien and Sergine. Shocked by what he has done, he wants to assume responsibility for his action. He discovers that they are not dead, but he has learned a lesson. By taking charge of his life, he has gained a sense of his own personality.

The narrative technique of *Les Corps étrangers* (1959; translated as *Foreign Bodies*, 1960) is reminiscent of Cayrol's first novel. It too is a *récit* written in the first person. It is about a character called Gaspard who endlessly tells and retells the

story of his life. As he does so, he corrects himself, realizing that such and such an event never happened. His so-called memories are "foreign bodies" which he rids himself of only to replace them with others, which he subsequently also discredits. Gradually it becomes clear that Gaspard has no memory as such. He is seeking to create a past which corresponds to his desires; he is afflicted by a nostalgia for a past which he has not soiled for himself. It is the most unrelenting of Cayrol's early works and thus marks his increasing disillusionment with the world to which he had returned as if from the dead. Henceforth, his novels were to have less and less anchorage in an outer reality.

In the 1950s Cayrol also published two collections of poetry. The themes of *Les Mots sont aussi des demeures* (Words Are Also Dwelling Places, 1952) are the same as those found in his fiction: memory, nostalgia, and the struggle to discover one's own identity through language. *Pour tous les temps* (For All Time, 1955) continues the quest and once again illustrates his mastery of visual imagery.

The parallels between Cayrol's fictional technique and the cinema need no underlining. His work is essentially visual. The male narrator in *La Noire* says of himself: "Je vois ce que je pense" (I see what I think). He speaks not only for many of Cayrol's other heroes but also for Cayrol himself. It was not surprising, therefore, that he should become interested in filmmaking. In 1955 he was invited by Alain Resnais to contribute the dialogue for a film about the concentration camps, *Nuit et brouillard* (Night and Fog, 1956). The results were memorable and encouraged Cayrol to participate in other projects. In the early 1960s he collaborated with Claude Durand on a succession of short films: *Spécialité de la mer* (The Nature of the Sea, 1960) for television; *On vous parle* (Someone Is Speaking to You, 1960); *La Frontière* (The Border, 1961); *Madame se meurt* (Madame is Dying, 1961); and *De tout pour faire un monde* (Everything to Make a World, 1962). Cayrol and Durand also collaborated on a feature-length film, *Le Coup de grâce* (The Deathblow, 1965). But the most lasting of his contributions was again with Resnais, for whom he wrote the screenplay for *Muriel* (Muriel, 1963), one of the key films of the French New Wave cinema. He also wrote and directed *La Déesse* (The Goddess, 1966), a short film about a young soldier, Icare, who steals a Citroën DS (= déesse) in order to visit his girlfriend.

Cayrol could not resist putting his thoughts about the cinema on paper. In 1963, again with Claude Durand, he published *Le Droit de regard* (The Right to See), an essay on filmmaking written in four main sections. The first is a somewhat predictable attack on traditional techniques as "cinéma prêt à porter" (ready-to-wear cinema); the second looks at technique and expression; the third is a brilliant argument in favor of the short film (the *court métrage*); the last concerns the filming of objects. The major contention is that a film should concern itself not with a story but with the juxtaposition of sound and images in such a way as to stimulate the spectator into "imagining" a narrative for him- or herself. It should aim to surprise the viewer. The importance of Cayrol's films and film theory in his literary development can scarcely be exaggerated, for it was the challenge represented by the cinema which did much to help him put his war experiences behind him. The experience of collaborating helped him discover new directions in his own art form.

Cayrol was now working at Editions du Seuil. In 1956 he founded "Ecrire" (Writing), a series of anthologies devoted to first works. Many of the writers who owe their first publications to him subsequently found their way to *Tel Quel*, the progressive literary journal founded in 1960. Not surprisingly, Cayrol became a regular and respected contributor. When *Tel Quel* did a series of interviews called "La Littérature, aujourd'hui," it seemed appropriate to place him between Michel Butor and Alain Robbe-Grillet.

Les Pleins et les Déliés (1960) is one of Cayrol's key works. Its title is untranslatable. Literally, it means "the heavy downstrokes and lighter upstrokes" in handwriting, but in context it suggests that each given subject is treated with dexterity. The volume consists of a series of prose poems, some on man-made phenomena (a harbor, a town, houses), but most on natural phenomena such as trees, snow, sand, a flower, the sea. In each, the writer's imagination moves freely, creating a reality with confidence in its own narrative skill. By dispensing with a main character, Cayrol was able to experiment with his use of language to evoke a subject. The lesson gave his next work renewed vigor.

Bernard, the traveling-salesman hero of *Le Froid du soleil* (The Cold of the Sun, 1963), is killed in a car accident. The novel retraces his life as if projected on the "screen of his consciousness." His dreams of himself as a kind of knight-errant—his steed is his car—conflict with the banality and repetitiveness of his life. The narrative insists on this point: an ordinary life makes a bad novel. But it is also claiming that even the most ordinary life can make a good novel if its events are handled with artistry. It is not the peculiarity of Bernard's character which is at issue. The action of *Le Froid du soleil* is pure fantasy. Its subject is the skill with which Cayrol creates a world out of words.

Midi Minuit (Midday Midnight, 1966) is the story of Martine, who has left her husband and taken their son, Patrick, with her. On her way to her hometown, she stops by the sea. The novel consists of her thoughts and fantasies, including her seeing her husband everywhere she looks. The novel owes much to Cayrol's recent experience with filmmaking, especially in its way of controlling the tempo of events. Although the outcome is bleak, there are moments which vibrate in the reader's mind long after the book has been closed.

Je l'entends encore seems at first to be the story of Julien Reize, a writer whose life appears before him in reverse on his deathbed. But, as so often in Cayrol's work, another story soon emerges, quite different from that expected. The main protagonist turns out to be the writer's son, Jean-Pierre, a journalist now approaching thirty, still haunted by events which occurred in his childhood during the war. For twenty years he has lived a provisional life, at first with his grandmother, more recently with his girlfriend, Claudie. His obsession with his past has prevented him from ever fixing himself in time and space. The climax comes in a vividly described hallucination, in the course of which he is arrested by the police for unseemly behavior. At the police station he meets two young students who have been picked up during a demonstration against U.S. involvement in Vietnam. The novel ends with their release, because it is Saturday night, and them gamboling in the snow. There is a faint suggestion that Jean-Pierre has at last accepted his present reality, has learned to enjoy life.

De l'espace humain (A Man-made World, 1968) is a collection of short essays on various aspects of French city life. The ostensible subject—whether *les concierges* or *les restaurants*—is merely the starting point for a series of reflections on changing customs in France. There is considerable nostalgia expressed for traditional ways which seem threatened with extinction. Some of the essays are marred by this conservatism, but almost all reveal insights whose expression or governing idea deserves consideration. For example, Cayrol says that ready-to-wear shops provide the opportunity for young people to become the creations of their own fantasies. This reversal of what one would expect–that such shops express the fantasies of the young–is what makes Cayrol such a stimulating writer. His constant preoccupation is with the way people relate to their dreams.

His reputation was by now firmly established. In 1968 he was awarded the Prix Prince Pierre de Monaco for his work to date. He became deeply interested in the events of this crucial year. *Poésie-Journal* (Poetry-Diary, 1969) is a record of his impressions of 1968, notably of the student riots in Paris and the Soviet invasion of Czechoslovakia. It is an extraordinary work. Alain Bosquet has called it the only successful work about these events. It shows a new face of Cayrol: a man deeply troubled by the social tendencies of his time. But above all, it shows his despair at the way in which the media translate fact into fiction, thus causing the public to assimilate the news as if it were a best-seller. When the distinction between fact and fantasy is blurred, life is impoverished. It becomes provisional, that is, Lazarean.

Histoire d'une prairie (The Story of a Prairie, 1969) is the first of a series of novels which explore the properties of a location. Its hero is Joé, who lives sometimes alone and sometimes with Léna, his wife, and a woman with the extraordinary name of Irish Closet. At one moment, he is a survivor of the 1999 war; the next, he is watching the soldiers climb out of the wooden horse of Troy. Time gives way to space. Only the prairie is eternal; but, paradoxically, the prairie exists only insofar as it is observed by Joé. The novel unfolds like a dream; its action, if action it can be called, takes place entirely in the reader's mind. It constitutes the logical development of Cayrol's interest in waking fantasy. It is also the first real evidence of his sense of humor. This is serious novel writing as a game. Cayrol, already a master of language, has learned to play with it.

It was perhaps because he thought that he had become too abstract that he returned to a more conventional form in his next work. *N'oubliez pas que nous nous aimons* (Don't Forget That We Love One Another, 1971) is about a forty-eight-year-old businessman, Frank, whose second marriage has recently collapsed. His daughter by his first marriage, Christiane, who lives with her aunt, comes home unexpectedly to announce that she wants to be allowed to marry. Although he has never paid her much attention, Frank is irrationally and violently opposed to the idea. The novel is not just an analysis of the generation gap; it is an extremely tightly knit story told on two distinct levels of experience. Frank's attitude toward his daughter symbolizes what is wrong with his own conjugal relationship and thus tells the reader why he finds himself in the situation he is in. His inability to respect Christiane's emotional needs explains why his own marriage has broken down. Although it is undeniably well written, this is one of Cayrol's weakest works, published the year he married Jeanne Durand. Fortunately, for his next work he returned to the form he had employed with such success in *Histoire d'une prairie*.

Histoire d'un désert (The Story of a Desert, 1972) is about a middle-aged man who has been imprisoned during the war. The novel traces his search for his wife and two children, who may be just a figment of his imagination. It unfolds in a series of encounters with men, women, and even speaking animals. These confrontations increasingly reveal the degree of his emotional isolation. Like Lear, he has to learn to recognize his erroneous attitudes. The novel ends with him waking after a particularly vivid dream in which he thinks he has come full circle. In a sense, he has, but with the all-important difference that he is richer for the experience.

Histoire de la mer (The Story of the Sea, 1973) is a fantasy modeled on two classics of English literature: Charles Kingsley's *The Water Babies* (1863) and Lewis Carroll's *Alice's Adventures in Wonderland* (1865). A fairy tale for adults, it tells the story of Géraldine, a ten-year-old girl, and takes place in the time between a plane crash into the sea and her waking in a lifeboat. Like the other *histoires*, it consists of a series of encounters, this time mostly with various sea creatures. They give her advice, such as "Cherche l'aide qui te mène vers le but final de la vie" (Seek help which leads you to your ultimate goal in life), with the same mixture of humor and seriousness as in Lewis Carroll.

On finishing this work, Cayrol turned again to a novel he had started in 1957, planned to turn into a film in 1963, and then abandoned. *Kakemono Hôtel* (1974) is the story of an estate agent whose desire to appropriate a villa is so strong that he agrees to paying his aunt a life income in order to inherit it after her death. The sum becomes more than he can afford. His life collapses around him. Then his aunt's maid, Paquita, reveals that she is as greedy for the house as Maurice. The final scene has him burning the villa he so wanted to own, with Paquita inside it. It is a well-told and enormously cinematic story.

To many, Cayrol's election to the Académie Goncourt in 1974 was long overdue. It did not interrupt his work. His series of *histoires* continued with *Histoire de la forêt* (The Story of the Forest, 1975), which is about a teenage boy, Jérôme, who flees from his parents after they punish him for spying on his sister. It is an elaborate version of the myth of Narcissus and is also extremely witty. For example, at one moment Jérôme hears voices in a tree: Cayrol has always admitted his debt to the German romantics. They tell him that they are the same voices that spoke to Joan of Arc and that they are looking for someone who will listen more attentively than she did. When Jérôme shows little interest, one of them reflects: "Je prédis que Jeanne reviendra sous la forme d'une mère de famille qui lave son linge . . ." (I predict that Joan will return in the form of a mother who takes care of her family's laundry . . .). Cayrol does not dwell on this, or any, point, for one scene follows another with bewildering speed. At one stage, Jérôme meets a pregnant girl who tells him that she is carrying him in her belly. Is this his mother? The scenes which make up Cayrol's novels cannot be pinned down; they have all the ambivalence of dream.

The next novel in this series is *Histoire d'une maison*, which reverts to a more conventional type of narrative. It opens just before the war. Siméon, an accountant, wants to build a house. When war breaks out, the building still lacks a roof. He enlists and is eventually taken prisoner. He escapes, but his only thought is of his house. Meanwhile, his wife sets out to look for him. She does not find him where she expected, but they meet all the same, as if by accident. They return to Paris. It is with great difficulty that Odette, who has become pregnant, persuades him to return to work. Instead, he becomes involved in spying, for the sole purpose of keeping an eye on his house. He is arrested again and taken to Fresnes, where he spends his time planning to escape in order to build another house. He is removed to Mauthausen but is becoming increasingly ill. Still dreaming of a house, beside which he can no longer even see his family, he is found dead one morning. The novel is a vivid portrait of an obsession and how a Lazarean dream can

take possession of a man. Clearly, it is in part autobiographical, but this element should not be exaggerated. Cayrol's work unfolds like a spiral, returning to the same issues, but always from a fresh perspective and with renewed insights.

Like most novels about childhood, *Les Enfants pillards* (The Thieving Children, 1978) is based on its author's personal experiences. Indeed, Cayrol has claimed that it is entirely true. This, again, should not be taken literally. Whatever its basis in fact, the story is a novel. Its hero is Jean-Baptiste, and the narrative follows his relation with a group of children during a summer holiday of 1918. The adults have their thoughts elsewhere; the children are allowed to run about as they please. They witness violence and, when a pilot is washed up on the beach, death; they turn toward crime and then cruelty, but always with that innocence that Cayrol's heroes manifest even in their least likable moments. André, the leader of the group, teaches Jean-Baptiste about survival. *Les Enfants pillards* is a disturbing but provocative recollection of a childhood as it might have been.

The last of the *histoires* to date is *Histoire du ciel* (Story of the Sky, 1979). Its hero is Julien, a retired pilot whose relation with Edgard, a stargazer and guru, is the narrative axis. The novel consists of a series of improbable encounters which the reader follows avidly, for this work is as easy to read as Antoine de Saint-Exupéry's *Le Petit Prince* (The Little Prince, 1943), with which it has been compared. It delights because it reflects the skyscape of the reader's own imagination.

Exposés au soleil (Exposed to the Sun, 1980) is a collection of fifteen short stories, some of them first published in *Tel Quel* twenty years previously. They are remarkable not only for their concision but also for the variety of their moods. The collection ends with an essay in which Cayrol discusses the short-story form. He writes that his aim in writing a *récit court* is to capture "un instant qui fut intense mais rapide" (an instant which was at once intense and fleeting). One of the most vivid stories, first published in *Biblio* in November 1963, is about Perse, a young woman who is staring out of a window at a parked car trying to come to terms with the turmoil inside her. She half-fantasizes escaping in the car. The original story ends with the bare statement: "Mais on ne monte pas avec un inconnu" (One doesn't get into a car with a stranger). The revised version adds a new element. The narrator tells us that he wrote the story after visiting Haworth parsonage: the parallel between the Brontë home and Perse's thoughts is evident. The following day a local antiquarian offers him a print. To his astonishment, it shows the same young woman staring out of the same window. The addition illustrates the development of Cayrol's writing between the two versions. He has become a conjurer not only with words but also with the events he describes. His touch is as light and as sure as that of the early Jorge Luis Borges.

L'Homme dans le rétroviseur (The Man in the Rearview Mirror, 1981) is a tour de force. It is a variation of James Thurber's Walter Mitty story. Gaspard is a grocer's assistant who undergoes innumerable metamorphoses in the course of the novel, which emerges as an extremely witty exploration of the autonomy of a fictional character. The pace lets up only when Cayrol interrupts his story with tongue-in-cheek reflections on what he is doing. Enormously enjoyable, it is also a provocative commentary on the relation between a writer and his work.

It was perhaps inevitable that Cayrol should one day write an autobiography. It was equally predictable that it would tell the reader very little about his life. *Il était une fois Jean Cayrol* (Once Upon a Time There Was Jean Cayrol, 1982) is composed of short chapters on the most important events in his life: his childhood, the war, the concentration camps, his return to France, and his long struggle to come to terms with his experiences. He writes, he says, in order to give himself the impression he is alive ("J'écris, donc je suis"). He has never forgotten whence he returned; never forgotten that, in his words, people died in order that he could live ("On est mort pour que je vive"). On the one hand, this work is an attempt to share with his readers what has haunted him; on the other, it is an affirmation that he is none of his fictional personae, nor even their author: he is–always–"other." Cayrol is never more evasive than when he is writing about himself.

Cayrol's next work, *Un Mot d'auteur* (A Word by the Author, 1983), is a novel about a historical novelist called Golo: the name is derived from the Combray section of Marcel Proust's *A la recherche du temps perdu* (Remembrance of Things Past, 1913-1927). Golo's latest work, "Les Eaux dures" (The Hard Waters), has been lost in a flood, and he now sets out to reconstruct it. All he has to go on is the name of his heroine, Geneviève, and the rudiments of a plot. He advances obsessionally, even accusing Gustave Flau-

bert of having plagiarized a phrase he had used in his lost work. The work is brilliant, witty, and ultimately tragic, for Cayrol has little admiration for Golo. In a January 1983 interview with Gilles Pudlowski he dismissed his character in one sentence: "Un écrivain ne perd jamais rien parce qu'il n'a rien" (A writer never loses anything, because he hasn't anything to lose). The novel is a moving and ironic elaboration of this premise.

Qui suis-je? suivi de Une Mémoire toute fraîche (Who Am I? followed by An Ever-Present Memory, 1984) is composed of two short stories in which Cayrol continues his exploration of the themes which have interested him throughout his career. The first story is about Gratien Personne, a young locksmith obsessed with the notion that he must rediscover the womb from which he emerged. *Une Mémoire toute fraîche* is perhaps more successful. Gallia has lost her memory after an accident in which her sadistic husband was killed. She is haunted by a guilt arising from a false memory of events, by which she is finally overcome. Neither of these works ends optimistically, but one senses that this is not important. Cayrol uses his protagonists simply to explore notions which catch his imagination. In 1984 he was awarded the Grand Prix National des Lettres.

Léopold, the hero of Cayrol's most recent novel, *Les Châtaignes* (1986), is an adolescent who leaves home (Les Châtaignes = The Chestnut Trees) without any clear notion of where he is going. The novel consists of a series of encounters which come to nothing. The day after he meets Elisa, she arrives at their rendezvous on his brother's arm. He throws himself into the Garonne River in despair, but he is rescued by a passing ship. Inevitably, his brother appears again, this time knocking him into the ship's hold where he falls dead (*les châtaignes*, in this context, are beatings). Léopold, however, is not an alter-ego figure, nor does Cayrol identify with him. He is an image of a young man in an old man's fantasy. The novel is an exploration of a state of mind which must be brought to an end. It is only the temptation to indulge in a regressive fantasy which is killed with Léopold, leaving the author free to prepare another novel.

Since 1969 Cayrol has published two further volumes of his *Poésie-Journal*. Volume 2 (1977) covers the years 1975-1976 and shows Cayrol more removed from the events he observes than he was eight years before. The poems in *Poésie-Journal*, volume 3 (1980) no longer discuss political events, nor are they dated. Their tone, which verges on the pastoral, is that of a man who has fully come to terms with his own identity. They prepare the way for his 1985 verse collection, *Poèmes clefs* (Key Poems). Although more conservative in form, evoking sometimes Victor Hugo and sometimes the great poets of the French Renaissance, this volume contains some of his most striking images to date. In 1988 Cayrol's poems were collected in a single volume, *Œuvre poétique,* whose 830 pages confirm his place as one of the great poets of twentieth-century France. The work includes his most recent collection, "De Jour en jour" (From Day to Day), in which he explores the nature of words, memory, and time. It is fitting that the last poem is about Bordeaux as he remembers it, and that the final page should bear the motto "In my end is my beginning."

Cayrol's mastery of atmosphere is nowhere more evident than in his latest collection of short stories, *Des nuits plus blanches que nature* (Nights Whiter than Nature, 1987). Some as short as three pages, others of a more standard length, they combine fairy-tale elements with a vivid realism. For example, "Les Hirondelles" (The Swallows) is about some German soldiers who occupy a family house. The swallows, feeling their space has been invaded, leave. In 1945, when the owner returns from a concentration camp, the swallows arrive with him, effacing the past defeat. With such simple material, Cayrol conjures up extraordinarily haunting prose poems. His poetic imagination is the strength of his work. Although Cayrol has never enjoyed a wide readership, it is worth noting that he has received praise from many other writers. Each year his readers eagerly await his new work, for his odyssey has also been theirs. He always has something new to say, and the ability to say it with consummate ease. He almost certainly has more surprises up his sleeve. Jean Cayrol is one of the finest novelists of the twentieth century.

Interviews:
Albert Béguin, "Dialogue au balcon," *Revue de l'Alliance Française,* 34 (October 1947);
"La Littérature, aujourd'hui–V," *Tel Quel,* 13 (Spring 1963): 50-60;
Denise Bourdet, "Jean Cayrol," *Revue de Paris,* 70 (1963): 127-131;
Serge Groussard, "Je puis rompre ma chaîne et briser mon destin," *Biblio,* 31 (November 1963): 6-8;

Pierre Mertens, "Cayrol parmi nous," *Synthèses* (Brussels), 23 (April 1968): 23-33;
Jean-Louis Ezine, "Cayrol," in his *Les Ecrivains sur la sellette* (Paris: Seuil, 1981), pp. 189-193;
Gilles Pudlowski, "Jean Cayrol: le feu follet," *Nouvelles Littéraires,* no. 2870 (20-26 January 1983): 42;
Jean-Pierre Salgas, "Kafka, mon frère aîné," *Quinzaine Littéraire,* 413 (16 March 1984): 22-23.

Bibliography:
Catharine Savage Brosman, "Jean Cayrol," in *A Critical Bibliography of French Literature,* volume 6: *The Twentieth Century: Part Three,* edited by Douglas Alden and Richard Brooks (Syracuse: Syracuse University Press, 1979).

References:
Roland Barthes, "Jean Cayrol et ses romans," *Esprit,* 20 (March 1952): 482-499;
Barthes, "La Rature," in Cayrol's *Les Corps étrangers/Pour un romanesque lazaréen* (Paris: Union Générale d'Editions, 1964), pp. 231-247;
Albert Béguin, "Jean Cayrol," *Cahiers du Sud,* no. 287 (1948): 88-100;
Marc Bertrand, "Les Avatars de Lazare: Le Romanesque de Jean Cayrol," *French Review,* 51 (April 1978): 674-682;
Alain Bosquet, "Histoire du ciel," *Magazine Littéraire,* 147 (April 1979): 38;
Bernard Dort, "Jean Cayrol ou l'avènement du roman," *Cahiers du Sud,* no. 326 (1954): 132-140;
Claudine Guégnan Fischer, "Silence, mensonge et déception dans *Les Corps étrangers* de Jean Cayrol," *Selecta,* no. 3 (1984): 37-41;
Léon-Gabriel Gros, "Une Voix de l'ouest: Jean Cayrol," *Cahiers du Sud,* no. 265 (1944): 271-290;
Gennie Luccioni, "La Mort apprivoisée," *Esprit,* 36 (April 1968): 743-750;
Carlos Lynes, Jr., "Jean Cayrol," in *The Novelist as Philosopher: Studies in French Fiction, 1935-1960,* edited by John Cruickshank (London: Oxford University Press, 1962), pp. 183-205;
Gérard Mourgue, "Jean Cayrol," in his *Dieu dans la littérature d'aujourd'hui* (Paris: France-Empire, 1961), pp. 105-121;
Daniel Oster, *Jean Cayrol* (Paris: Seghers, 1973);
Oster, *Jean Cayrol et son œuvre* (Paris: Seuil, 1967);

Bernard Pingaud, "Jean Cayrol et le trésor," *Lettres Nouvelles*, no. 52 (1957): 619-628;

Catharine Savage, "The Trilogy of Jean Cayrol," *Thought*, 44 (Winter 1969): 513-530.

Hélène Cixous
(5 June 1937-)

Verena Andermatt Conley
Miami University

BOOKS: *Le Prénom de Dieu* (Paris: Grasset, 1967);

L'Exil de James Joyce ou l'art du remplacement (Paris: Grasset, 1968); translated by Sally A. J. Purcell as *The Exile of James Joyce* (New York: David Lewis, 1972; London: Calder, 1976);

Dedans (Paris: Grasset, 1969); translated by Carol Barko as *Inside* (New York: Schocken, 1986);

Le Troisième Corps (Paris: Grasset, 1970);

Les Commencements (Paris: Grasset, 1970);

Un Vrai Jardin (Paris: Editions de l'Herne, 1971);

Neutre (Paris: Grasset, 1972);

La Pupille (Paris: Gallimard, 1972);

Tombe (Paris: Seuil, 1973);

Portrait du soleil (Paris: Denoël, 1974);

Prénoms de personne (Paris: Seuil, 1974);

La Jeune Née, by Cixous and Catherine Clément (Paris: Union Générale d'Editions, 1975); translated by Betsy Wing as *The Newly Born Woman* (Minneapolis: University of Minnesota Press, 1986);

Un K. incompréhensible: Pierre Goldman (Paris: Christian Bourgois, 1975);

Révolutions pour plus d'un Faust (Paris: Seuil, 1975);

Souffles (Paris: Des Femmes, 1975);

LA (Paris: Gallimard, 1976);

Partie (Paris: Des Femmes, 1976);

Portrait de Dora (Paris: Des Femmes, 1976); translated by Anita Burrows as *Portrait of Dora, Gambit International Theatre Review* (1977); republished in *Benmussa Directs* (London: Calder/Dallas: Riverrun, 1979);

Angst (Paris: Des Femmes, 1977); translated by Jo Levy (London: Calder/New York: Riverrun, 1985);

La Venue à l'écriture, by Cixous, Annie Leclerc, and Madeleine Gagnon (Paris: Union Générale d'Editions, 1977);

Chant du corps interdit, le nom d'Œdipe (Paris: Des Femmes, 1978);

Préparatifs de noces au-delà de l'abîme (Paris: Des Femmes, 1978);

Ananké (Paris: Des Femmes, 1979);

Vivre l'orange/To Live the Orange, bilingual edition, with translation by Ann Liddle and Sarah Cornell (Paris: Des Femmes, 1979);

Illa (Paris: Des Femmes, 1980);

With ou l'art de l'innocence (Paris: Des Femmes, 1981);

Limonade tout était si infini (Paris: Des Femmes, 1982);

Le Livre de Promethea (Paris: Gallimard, 1983);

La Prise de l'école de Madhubaï (Paris: Avant-Scène, 1984);

L'Histoire terrible mais inachevée de Norodom Sihanouk roi du Cambodge (Paris: Théâtre du Soleil, 1985);

Entre l'écriture (Paris: Des Femmes, 1986);

Théâtre (Paris: Des Femmes, 1986);

La Bataille d'Arcachon (Laval, Quebec: Trois, 1987);

L'Indiade ou l'Inde de leurs rêves (Paris: Théâtre du Soleil, 1988);

Manne (Paris: Des Femmes, 1988).

PLAY PRODUCTIONS: *Portrait de Dora*, Paris, Théâtre d'Orsay, 1975;

La Prise de l'école de Madhubaï, Paris, Théâtre de l'Odéon, 1984;

L'Histoire terrible mais inachevée de Norodom Sihanouk roi du Cambodge, Paris, Théâtre du Soleil, 1984;

L'Indiade ou l'Inde de leurs rêves, Paris, Théâtre du Soleil, 1986.

Hélène Cixous

OTHER: "Extreme Fidelity" and "Tancredi Continues," in *Writing Differences*, edited by Susan Sellers (Milton Keynes: Open University Press, 1988), pp. 9-36, 37-53;

Clarice Lispector, *Agua Viva*, preface by Cixous (Minneapolis: University of Minnesota Press, 1989).

PERIODICAL PUBLICATIONS: "The Character of 'Character,'" translated by Keith Cohen, *New Literary History*, 5 (Winter 1974): 383-402;

"Le Rire de la Méduse," *Arc* (1975): 39-54; translated by Keith and Paula Cohen as "The Laugh of the Medusa," *Signs: Journal of Women and Culture in Society*, 1 (Summer 1976): 875-893;

"At Circe's, or The Self-Opener," translated by Carole Bové, *Boundary 2*, 3 (Winter 1975): 387-397;

"Fiction and Its Phantoms: A Reading of Freud's 'Das Unheimliche' ('The Uncanny')," translated by R. Denommé, *New Literary History*, 7 (Spring 1976): 525-548;

"La Missexualité, où jouis-je?," *Poétique*, no. 25-26 (1976): 240-249;

"Quant à la pomme de texte," *Etudes Littéraires*, 12 (December 1979): 411-423;

"L'Approche de Clarice Lispector," *Poétique*, 10 (November 1979): 408-419;

"Introduction to Lewis Carroll's *Through the Looking-glass* and *The Hunting of the Snark*," translated by M. Maclean, *New Literary History*, 13 (Winter 1982): 231-251;

"Cahier de métamorphoses," *Corps Ecrit*, 6 (1983): 65-75;

"12 Août 1980," bilingual version, with translation by Betsy Wing, *Boundary 2*, 12 (Winter 1984): 8-39;

"Reaching the Point of Wheat, or a Portrait of the Artist as a Maturing Woman," *New Literary History*, 19 (Autumn 1987): 1-21.

Over the past two decades, French literature has explored new ways of expressing the self and the relationship between the self and the world. With the advent of the human sciences—linguistics, anthropology, and psychoanalysis—literary texts have undergone radical transformation. The very boundaries between literature and other disciplines have been called into question. Writers and readers alike claim that the written text is not just an expression of a self or an imitation of a preexisting reality. Rather, they put emphasis on language itself and assert that the writing self structures himself, herself, in the text through the choice of rhetorical figures, insistences, and omissions—in a word, through styles. From the inception of her *œuvre* some twenty years ago to the present, Hélène Cixous writes at the crossroads of the human sciences and literature.

Passionately interested in limits, boundaries, and frontiers, she has continually read and written about them in an effort to test them, push them back, and, often, surge ahead. Accepting the general belief psychoanalysis took from science that life must be conceived in terms of an alternation of life *and* death drives, Cixous reexamines the ties between life and writing and sees the latter as a means to push back death. This sets her apart from most other contemporary writers who, in accord with philosophical presuppositions inherited from Hegel and others, put death at the center of their enterprise. This is not to say that Cixous denies the inevitable presence of death, but that while acknowledging it, she sets out to privilege life in all its forms. This concern has been central to her *œuvre*, which has also been marked by the many changes in the concept of knowledge in contemporary France.

Hélène Cixous was born on 5 June 1937 in Oran, Algeria. In the colonial environment where Cixous grew up, she was clearly in the minority. Her father, a doctor of French-colonial background, died when she was a girl. Her mother, Eve, was of Austro-German origin, and German, rather than French, is Cixous's native tongue. She makes this quite clear. German for her is a richer, more guttural language than the more abstract idiom of French. Members of her family were Sephardic Jews, and she lived through the persecutions of World War II. She never lost her strong desire to fight the encroachment of power in all of its forms upon the human body and the human mind. Her texts reveal that she has always felt imprisoned, enclosed on the inside, and that she felt the need to break out of the world in which she was born, to go beyond, to look for other worlds or realities less marked by the horrors of twentieth-century Europe. Already as a child, she found these worlds in fiction. Sensitive to the influence of power at every institutional level—familial, academic, political—she delighted in reading myths. In her later work she claims that myths are neutral until they are read and interpreted. They are usually read by a group in power who uses interpretation for justificatory and repressive purposes. Cixous strives to find out where, historically, such repression occurs and where exclusions are located and articulated. In addition to reading myths and the German romantics, such as Heinrich von Kleist, Cixous began to study English literature in her teens. In her late teens she went to France to study. Her great love was Shakespeare, whose passionate and diverse writings held special attraction. *Antony and Cleopatra* and *The Tempest*, with their scenes of transformation between man and woman, father and daughter, marked her.

A desire to privilege life and a growing insistence on the fictional, on the poetic are distinctive aspects of her work. The poetic, for her, is not limited to lines and verse. It deals with the imaginary, with deliverance from social stigmas through a freeing of language, through invention of new ways of speaking and writing, as well as other ways of seeing, hearing, touching, and tasting. It is always her relationship with the other, with otherness, that allows for an opening. A transformation of the dynamics of self and other constitutes the political dimension underlying all of her writing.

Cixous began her career as an academic. In 1959, at the age of twenty-two, she passed the prestigious *agrégation* in English. She married and had two children, a daughter and a son, born in 1959 and 1962. In 1962 she became *assistante* at the Université de Bordeaux. In 1965 she and her husband were divorced and Cixous moved from Bordeaux to Paris. She was *maître assistante* at the Sorbonne from 1965 to 1967 and was appointed *maître de conférences* at Nanterre in 1967. Also in 1967 she published her first text, *Le Prénom de Dieu* (God's First Name). In 1968 she became *docteur ès lettres*. She was appointed *chargé de mission* to found the experimental Université de Paris VIII-Vincennes, now at Saint Denis, in the aftermath of the student riots of May 1968. An alternative to the traditional and, in the view of many, repressive French academic environment, Paris VIII was to be a center of learning where time-honored power structures and hierarchies would be kept to a minimum. The new university, though never much appreciated by the French government, soon distinguished itself through its exceptionally high-quality faculty. Since 1968 Cixous has been professor of English literature at Paris VIII.

In 1969 Cixous, having become very active on the intellectual scene, founded with Tzvetan Todorov and Gérard Genette the experimental review *Poétique*. The review was to be a forum for new ways of reading literary texts, a departure from the still largely Lansonian or literary-historical approach prevalent in French academe under the influence of nineteenth-century positivism. The review became a prestigious mouthpiece on both sides of the Atlantic. As a university professor of English literature, Cixous continued her career with the publication of her thesis, *L'Exil de James Joyce ou l'art du remplacement* (1968; translated as *The Exile of James Joyce*, 1972). Cixous never hid her ambivalence toward Joyce. On the one hand, she was interested in his techniques, his belief that transformations of linguistic structures would alter mental structures, and his awareness of ideological and political manipulations through language. On the other, she always marked her distance from a writing caught up in guilt and the anguish of paradox. Though Joyce influenced her work through his insistence on the necessity to create new languages, on musicalizing literature and joining body and spirit, she criticized him for his creative paradox: for Joyce, one must lose in order to have. In other words, one must kill in order to live. The movement to life starts with a killing of the other, death, and guilt, a concept that differs significantly from Cixous's recognition that loss and death are inevitable and indeed necessary for life.

Several articles on English literature published in the avant-garde reviews *Tel Quel* and *Poétique* also marked the period of the late 1960s and early 1970s. Critics at the time classified her as a highly politicized vanguard writer and critic, someone interested in transforming language and writing. In the United States she was especially known for her work on Joyce and as an editor of *Poétique*. Her fictional writings, few of which have been translated into English, are less well known, although they have received attention in France. Cixous's production is abundant. Her texts can be divided into several groups, each loosely gravitating around a center of interest, along a path marked by Cixous's continued endeavor to push death back from the horizon of life.

The first texts are animated by a desire for autoanalysis in the wake of Cixous's discovery of Freud and such modern avatars as Jacques Lacan. Drawing her own portrait analytically, she works through her family structures, her childhood in Algeria, the death of her father, the influence of her German mother and grandmother, and her relationship with her brother. These familial structures are best rendered in *Dedans* (1969; translated as *Inside*, 1986), which earned her the Prix Médicis and confirmed her reputation in literary circles.

The trilogy, *Le Troisième Corps*, *Les Commencements*, and *Neutre* (The Third Body, Beginnings, and Neuter), published from 1970 to 1972, marks a period of great hope. In the aftermath of 1968, everything seemed possible. Students and professors had joined workers in the streets. Transformations in linguistic and ideological structures seemed unquestionable. Cixous's experimental texts of those years were written at the boundary of new theories and fictional invention. Cixous developed her own fictions influenced by Derrida's theories of writing as displacing oppositions into differences, by Lacan's pronouncements on language as a chain of signifiers, a combination of metaphors and metonymies, and by Gilles Deleuze's texts undermining the logic of meaning which would put writing on the side of appropriation and death. The trilogy, like all of Cixous's subsequent work, is marked by an effort to undo repression, question power structures, free writing and the self. Written at a time when the euphoria of new discoveries outweighed theoretical divergences, these texts combine many incompatible theories. The freeing of the subject and the undoing of repression go along with a re-evaluation of what has been repressed: body, woman, writing. Cixous works through Lacan's pronouncements about the insistence of the letter in the unconscious and Derrida's affirmation about origin as repetition. Like these theorists, she privileges the letter phonically and graphically.

Le Troisième Corps, as its title suggests, is a writing born of the crossing of two desires, Cixous's and that of her lover. The title insists on the bodily importance of writing, on the process of birth, on giving life. These preoccupations are constant in her work, though the emphasis changes. The text becomes a way of freeing the self. It is written at the limit of conscious and unconscious, at the limit of repression and the laws of prohibition. The freeing of the self comes from and through the other, through the desire of the other. The self, including the writing self, exists only in a differential relationship with other selves. It never exists independently, that is, autonomously, or identical to itself.

This analogy can be extended to literature and the writing process. The book, considered as a whole or self-sufficient unit, is replaced by the text. The text never simply is; it is always to come—*à venir*, as Maurice Blanchot would say. It is an intertextual web, a system of signifiers referring to other signifiers. This is not to say that meaning is merely a network of cross-references but that there is always an open-endedness and a plurality. The text can never be fully interpreted. Writing, then, also has to do with the freeing or deliverance of the book from commodity into endless text. Cixous replaces the book, with its emphasis on closure, on the spiritual and on repression of the body, with text, always linked to *deliverance* and to all its related signifiers; *lit* (both as reading and bed), *dé-lit* (as un-reading and misdemeanor, a crime transgressing established norms). The *lit* is a place of exchange, of love, where one lies down, where one reads, where body and mind are conjoined.

Dialogue among different voices, and, in the form of intertextual references, with other writings, replaces the monologue of authorial control to keep the text open. In *Le Troisième Corps* the voice of the lover echoes that of other fictional lovers, especially those of Kleist's Jeronimo and the count F. from "Das Erdbeben in Chili" ("The Earthquake in Chile") and "Die Marquise von O" ("The Marquise of O"), respectively. Freud's rewriting of Wilhelm Jensen's *Gradiva*, a love story dealing with fetishism, entombment, entrapment, life and death in the archaeological setting of Pompeii, examining passion in its relation to life and death, also haunts Cixous's text.

Similar preoccupations underlie *Les Commencements*, an oneiric, plotless text which explores the relationship between writing and painting through allusions to Titian, Tintoretto, Klee; between literature and psychoanalysis through quotations from Freud's case of Dora, one of his studies on hysteria. Dora, the young girl who rebelled against being a pawn in her father's adulterous relationship and who, despite Freud's interest in her, terminated her analysis with him of her own free will, was one of the first figures who interested Cixous in the course of her exploration of the "feminine question." *Les Commencements* also subverts the classical, linear story by developing another, more Freudian temporality, which, following the postulation of life and death

drives, places emphasis not on continuity but on beginnings. In *Neutre*, a "textual opera," the numbers, three, four, and twelve structure the text. This work broaches the theme of sexual difference and questions sexual identity by asserting that both genders contain masculine and feminine at the same time and thus are *ne-uter*, neither one nor the other. So-called social identities, always related to repression and ideological manipulations, are exploded. Again, the writer is in dialogue with other voices, with her lover, her family, as well as with a procession of revolutionary writers from other times and other countries: Marx, Freud, Shakespeare, Dante, Hölderlin, Milton, and Poe. Throughout her work Cixous insists on the necessity of plurality, on the braiding of voices into an operatic song, on the absence of closure.

Cixous's political and ideological commitments are clear. In the 1970s she took a stand on a trial that polarized the French, that of Pierre Goldman, a Jewish immigrant, accused, without sufficient evidence, of murder. Cixous, like Foucault and others, wrote in his defense. *Un K. incompréhensible: Pierre Goldman* (An Incomprehensible Kase: Pierre Goldman, 1975), the letter *K* playing on echoes from Kafka's *Der Prozess* (*The Trial*) and "Vor dem Gesetz" (Before the Law), is a violent outcry against prejudice in the French legal system.

Her stance against repression and social injustice, which she sees as one with the death drive, led Cixous to espouse the cause of women. Her theoretical *Prénoms de personne* (Nobody's Name, 1974), a collection of essays on Freud, Hoffmann, Kleist, Poe, and Joyce, deals with the association of the unified (phallic) subject, narcissism, and death. Cixous analyzes how, in pre-Freudian times, such writers as Hoffmann and Kleist used doubles and similar figures in their efforts to represent otherness and to undermine the repressive unity of the subject. Through Poe and Joyce, Cixous denounces the attempt to put woman on the side of death, and shows how these writers' dialectical structures enclose women in a "limited economy" and an exchange dominated by a desire for death. To this, she opposes a general economy, a term that Georges Bataille, the contemporary French writer and philosopher, popularized via his works on anthropology and psychoanalysis. Cixous proposes an economy of the gift, related to spending and loss. Because for Cixous and other contemporary theoreticians the subject exists only in a differential relationship with other subjects, the insistence is on the modes of exchange. Exchange, thought of in terms of giving and receiving, plays a crucial role in the women's question. How does one give, how does one receive? What, in such an exchange, is the relationship to alterity and the other? How does exchange affect language and writing? Like many contemporary French writers and thinkers, Cixous believes that there is no social change possible without linguistic change. Hence, she pays special attention to attitudes or "positions" toward language. How do other writers inscribe exchange, desire, passion and love in their works?

In 1974 Cixous established the Centre de Recherches en Etudes Féminines. The following year she published "Le Rire de la Méduse," translated in 1976 in the review *Signs* by Keith and Paula Cohen as "The Laugh of the Medusa." Cixous focuses on a small but crucial text by Freud that deals with castration, a founding concept of phallic society. Man, horrified by woman's genitals, turns to stone. The turning into stone, a defensive measure, becomes simultaneous with erection, or man's entrance into a symbolic system which excludes woman. The symbolic system is based on the primacy of the phallus, on the privilege of the concept and of the spirit, and on the exclusion of woman, body, and, as Derrida has shown, of writing. Laughter undermines meaning. Woman, claims Cixous, does not have to take man's constructs of truth; the law is nothing but a man-made word; and woman, contrary to Kafka's K. in "Before the Law," does not have to heed it. Yet, to go against it would be the same as to support it; oppositions cancel each other out. Laughter, however, as Bataille has shown repeatedly in his neo-Hegelian readings, explodes meaning and opens a gap. Cixous goes beyond a simple explosion of meaning. Laughter is decentered toward something more positive, toward joy and an affirmation of life.

Affirmation of life functions as the most important concern of *La Jeune Née* (1975; translated as *The Newly Born Woman*, 1986), a book by Cixous and Catherine Clément. The title *La Jeune Née* plays at the same time on "Là-je-nais," there I am being born, and La Genet, a female version of the author Jean Genet, whose poetic writings insist on the general equality of all human beings. In *La Jeune Née* Cixous insists on the necessity of displacing the desire for recognition, always based on sexual war, which ends, symboli-

cally, with the succumbing of one of the partners. To this, she opposes a desire for alterity, by which, through a journeying toward the other, through a process of identification without fusion, the self goes as far as possible toward the other, lets herself be altered by the other, yet does not become the other. This desire keeps the other alive. To bring about change, Cixous urges women to break their silence, to "write themselves." They must write their bodies, their desires which heretofore have only been talked about by men. Freud's Dora is a central concern in *La Jeune Née*. Dora's "no," which terminates prematurely and on her own volition her sessions with Freud, leaves the latter despondent and defensive. Like laughter, Dora's "no" momentarily stops the merry-go-round, in this case one of adultery and familial lies. It also undermines Freud's authority. Yet, and this is quite clear, Dora's "no" represents a strategic moment in a historical configuration, a moment which must be exceeded. Cixous does not hide her ambivalence about Dora. Her admiration for the girl's decision to stop participating in a sick familial structure is tainted by her disapproval of Dora's basal sexuality. Dora is one of Cixous's major preoccupations during the 1970s and appears in several texts. There had been allusions to Dora in the trilogy. *Portrait du soleil* (Portrait of the Sun, 1974) is a poetic rewriting of Freud's case study. A play, *Portrait de Dora*, performed at the Théâtre d'Orsay in 1975, published in 1976, and translated in 1977, put Freud onstage to show the analyst's own projections in his treatment of Dora and his writings on her.

Feminine pleasure, which has been denied to women and confiscated by men, is a preoccupation of such texts as "La Missexualité, où jouis-je?" (The Missexual, Where Am I Having Pleasure?), published in *Poétique* in 1976, and *La Venue à l'écriture* (The Coming to Writing, 1977), written in collaboration with Annie Leclerc and Madeleine Gagnon. In the latter, playing on *la venue*, she who has come, and *l'avenue*, the path, Cixous traces the origin of women's writing to the mother's voice and body. Although she is in accord with such theoreticians as Derrida, who insist on the necessity of decapitating paternal authority by removing a fixed point of origin, she nevertheless insists on the strong masculinity of such a gesture.

In *Souffles* (1975)—the title evokes breath, inspiration, rhythm—Cixous proposes to analyze the origin of writing in terms of the mother-daughter relationship. Men have made women into hysterics; they have vitiated the relationships between women, especially between mother and daughter. Cixous insists on the origin of writing as song, as something that comes from the body. *Souffles* insists on the necessity of rewriting mythology, the Bible, and literary history from a feminine point of view.

Cixous's personal difficulties contributed to the 1977 text *Angst,* which deals with the breakdown of a love relationship. The pain and anguish are not expressed in existential, representational terms, but in a metaphoric exchange of letters. The text, as always one of transformation, led Cixous to another phase in her consideration of women's issues. For the next few years Cixous espoused the cause of women in a more militant language and her work appeared almost exclusively under the imprint of the publishing house Des Femmes, where Cixous enjoyed a close association with Antoinette Fouque, cofounder of the Mouvement de Libération des Femmes. She explained this decision in an interview (published in Verena Andermatt Conley's *Hélène Cixous: Writing the Feminine,* 1984) as reflecting her having attained an intellectual limit which, she felt, had to be surpassed. Consequently, she developed a more marked interest in relationships among women, though men are never completely absent in her writing. If, as Cixous claims, women need to pay more attention to each other, it is because any real transformation in relationships has to come from women. Always having been opposed to the use of such concepts as *man* and *woman* because of their repressive qualities, she urged the temporary, strategic use of *masculine* and *feminine,* attributes of two respective "economies." Just as Freud in his description of stages of development had made clear that these stages exist in various degrees and combinations at all times in every individual, so it is, Cixous argues, with masculine and feminine. The attributes are found in both men and women, though for cultural reasons, Cixous claims, a feminine economy belongs more often to women and a masculine one to men. Masculine is said to qualify an economy that is reappropriating, short, cutting, and feminine, an economy that is continuous, abundant.

Cixous's work from this period intersects with both Derrida's essay on Kant, "Economimesis," in *Mimesis désarticulation* (1975), and Jean-François Lyotard's *Economie libidinale* (1974). The attributes masculine and feminine will eventually be replaced by other descriptive terms,

which, like adjectives of color, make no reference to sexual difference. In this time of transition Cixous clearly privileges woman, or certain women, who are, in her terms, capable of giving. She redefines the maternal. The daughter is always in tune with the mother. The woman gives because she nourishes the child. Because she is able to contain the child, the mother is both container and contained; her relationship to otherness is different from that of men to whom things happen from the outside.

In her works from the late 1970s and early 1980s, influenced by her reading of Heidegger on poetry and language, Cixous asks and works through questions of knowledge, innocence, the law, life, and death in *Préparatifs de noces au-delà de l'abîme* (Wedding Preparations Beyond the Abyss, 1978), *Ananké* (1979), *Illa* (1980), *With ou l'art de l'innocence* (With or the Art of Innocence, 1981), and *Limonade tout était si infini* (Lemonade All was So Infinite, 1982). She tries to develop a writing that would be as close to life as possible, a writing that keeps the other alive. Cixous is in dialogue with, among others, Kafka, whose concerns are similar to hers but who constantly, and, in her words, tragically, opts for death. Invoking her poetic freedom, she reintroduces a whole vocabulary that had been out of favor since the mid 1960s, although she gives it a different inflection. Her militancy has taken a different turn. Less into flight, flow, and abundance, she now meditates on the sublime and develops the notion of the infinitely small. The sublime is not related to the colossal, the infinitely large, but, on the contrary, to the small.

For Cixous, it is a question of finding a language adequate to the privileging of life in its smallest forms, a language that gives birth. It has been a commonplace that words kill. The word as sign is put in the place of the person or the thing. The sign erects a symbolic wall between people, preventing communication at the same time as it makes exchange possible. As Bataille had stated, ideal communication would be silence, but people, in order to express themselves, must have recourse to words. The choice of words is of extreme importance. Words can make symbolic wounds; they can be symptoms; they can be spent in abundance while nothing is said. Verbal contact, Cixous holds, should be analogous to a slight touch between two people. To speak, close to the psychoanalytic notion of the full word, is an act which occurs in conjunction with a moment of transformation, when the word is transparent, not hidden or cloaked. This full but transparent word, like an arrow, is direct and takes the shortest route possible to its mark. The insistence is on *le nu*, but not the much-fetishized naked female body always related to castration and to a voyeurism that stops on the threshold of a scene. The naked word and body, uncovered and transparent, are engaged in a process of giving and receiving in such a way that the "thank you" of the art of receiving or the obligation created by the acceptance of the gift is already tuned into the "birth music" of the gift.

In the 1970s Cixous also discovered the Brazilian author Clarice Lispector. Influenced to a degree by the French *nouveau roman*, but with a strong voice of her own, Lispector meditated on writing and on the relationship between life and writing. Lispector, in her interest in quotidian objects, preoccupation with passion, and insistence on the flowing quality of the word, on the coming into language and writing, had already put into practice what Cixous had been seeking. Cixous's article in *Poétique*, "L'Approche de Clarice Lispector," appeared in 1979, the same year as the bilingual text *Vivre l'orange/To Live the Orange*. These texts play on fruit, but very differently from the earlier *Portrait du soleil*. There Cixous had punned in her opening statement: "D'Oran-je" (from Oran I am), linking her native city Oran to the orange. She had insisted on the cut made in the orange, on the gap or wound, from which the text had been written. Now, sweet nourishing juices replace the wound. The insistence is on the metaphor of the world as fruit, as product, as something nourishing that one keeps alive: to live, not to consume; to keep alive, not to kill. From the sadism of a scene linked to eating, Cixous shifts toward another orality where the insistence is on the living experience of tasting.

This oral scene is not one of cannibalistic communion or of fascistic fusion; neither is the relationship postulated one ruled by the dialectic victor/vanquished. The orange is closely related to the child and birth, to life, as well as to that other paradisiacal fruit, the apple, read simultaneously in English and French as fruit and calling, as apple and *appel*, which had been mistreated by the Church Fathers. Orange, as noun and adjective, as fruit and color, functions as a locus of correspondences of sight, touch, smell, taste, affecting reading and writing. It establishes relationships of harmony and is crucial to Cixous's next texts.

A break with Antoinette Fouque in the early 1980s prompted Cixous to leave Des Femmes temporarily. Her relationship with the publishing house had been increasingly strained. Cixous claims that she resented the limits a certain militancy imposed on her freedom. Another text, *Le Livre de Promethea* (The Book of Promethea, or Promethea's Book, 1983), written after her encounter with Ariane Mnouchkine, the director of the experimental Théâtre du Soleil, marks a turn. The book is a celebration of their encounter and a feminine rewriting of the Promethean myth, which, along with the myths of Orpheus and Ulysses, has figured prominently in literature. *Le Livre de Promethea* marks the culmination of a search for a positive passion, for a positive love and a language that touches lightly, intermittently, without seizing, appropriating, but infusing with life. The Promethean myth, from its epic dimensions of freeing the world and mankind, is transposed to quotidian passion, to detail, to a market scene, to fruits and flowers.

Cixous's encounter with Ariane Mnouchkine proved decisive. Mnouchkine was known for her innovative productions of Shakespeare, linking the Elizabethan stage with Far Eastern techniques. Cixous had already herself produced *Portrait de Dora* and was preparing *La Prise de l'école de Madhubaï* (The Taking of the School of Madhubaï), staged in 1984. With Mnouchkine, Cixous traveled to Cambodia to study a group of people that had been disinherited by their neighbors. Cixous's play *L'Histoire terrible mais inachevée de Norodom Sihanouk roi du Cambodge* (The Terrible but Unfinished Story of Norodom Sihanouk, King of Cambodia), performed in 1984, is the story of a people that had lived happily, amid dancing, singing, and harmony. They paid for their innocence with their lives. Always haunted by the notion of paradise, of a garden in the *hic et nunc* and not in the distant promises of an afterlife, Cixous found in Cambodia the remnants of a people who had lived according to these ethics. They had paid a high price for their beliefs. The lengthy but successful play directed by Mnouchkine was performed in two three-hour sessions. Such an overtly political play is a continuation of Cixous's fight against all forms of bodily and spiritual repression. The play is infused with a contemporary reading of the concept of freedom which, for her, is linked to poetry and writing. *L'Indiade ou l'Inde de leurs rêves* (The Indiade or India of their Dreams), a play produced in

1986, deals with the problems of colonialism, the liberation of India, and pacifism.

In addition to her writing for the theater, Cixous has continued to publish fiction. *La Bataille d'Arcachon* (The Battle of Arcachon, 1987) extends her experiments with new ways of writing about love, of linking absence and presence, self and other. She has also produced *Entre l'écriture* (Between Writing, or Enter Writing, 1986), a collection of new and previously published meditations on writing and painting. Cixous has begun to focus increasingly on the relationship between history and writing. *Manne* (Manna, 1988) is a lyrical text about the irruption of history in the personal lives of poets. It is a tribute to Osip Mandelstam, a victim of the Stalin regime, and Nelson Mandela, the fighter of apartheid in South Africa, and also to women poets, from the Russian Marina Tsvetaeva to the concentration-camp victim Etty Heilsum. Her involvement in theater marks a new departure in Cixous's work which is likely to continue for some time. She is currently at work on another play. At the same time, she is still directing the Centre de Recherches en Etudes Féminines at the Université de Paris VIII and is affiliated with the Collège International de Philosophie.

Cixous will undoubtedly continue to write with the same passion, energy, and force. From fictional texts to theater and theory, Cixous's writings are always challenging and provocative. Situated in the mainstream of contemporary French thought, Cixous manages to have a distinctive, archaic, lyrical voice that is noteworthy for never being militantly strident.

References:

Carol Armbruster, "Hélène-Clarice: Nouvelle voix," *Contemporary Literature*, 25 (Summer 1983): 145-157;

Boundary 2, special issue on Cixous, edited by Verena Andermatt Conley, 12 (Winter 1984);

Colette Camelin, "La scène de la fille dans *Illa*," *Littérature*, 67 (October 1987): 84-101;

Beatrice Cameron, "Letter to Cixous," *Sub-Stance*, 6 (1977): 159-165;

Verena Andermatt Conley, *Hélène Cixous: Writing the Feminine* (Lincoln & London: University of Nebraska Press, 1984);

Diane Griffin Crowder, "Amazons and Mothers? Monique Wittig, Hélène Cixous and Theories of Women's Writing," *Contemporary Literature*, 24 (Summer 1983): 117-144;

Françoise Defromont, "Faire la femme, différence sexuelle et énonciation," *Fabula*, 5 (1985): 95-112;

Defromont, "Le Jardin des délices," *Fruits*, 1 (1983): 49-59;

Brian Duren, "Cixous' Exorbitant Texts," *Sub-Stance*, 10 (1981): 39-51;

Martha Noel Evans, "Portrait of Dora: Freud's Case History as Reviewed by Hélène Cixous," *Sub-Stance*, 11 (1982): 64-71;

Lucette Finas, "Le Pourpre du neutre," in her *Le Bruit d'Iris* (Paris: Flammarion, 1981);

Claudine Fisher, *La Cosmogonie d'Hélène Cixous* (Amsterdam: Rodopi, 1988);

Fisher, "Le Vivant de la mort chez Hélène Cixous," *Bérénice: Letteratura Francese Contemporanea*, 10 (March 1984): 345-351;

Anna Gibbs, "Cixous and Gertrude Stein," *Meanjin*, 38 (September 1979): 281-293;

Ann Rosalind Jones, "Inscribing Femininity: French Theories of the Feminine," in *Making a Difference: Feminist Literary Criticism*, edited by Gayle Greene and Coppélia Kahn (London: Methuen, 1985), pp. 80-112;

Jones, "Writing and Body: Toward an Understanding of *L'Ecriture féminine*," *French Studies*, 7 (Summer 1981): 247-263;

Vivian Kogan, "I Want Vulva! Cixous and the Poetics of the Body," *Esprit Créateur*, 25 (Summer 1985): 73-85;

Annette Kuhn, "Introduction to Hélène Cixous's 'Castration or Decapitation?,' " *Signs*, 7 (Autumn 1981): 36-40;

Marguerite Le Clézio, "Psychoanalyse-poésie. Le Rite de Cixous la Méduse," *Bonnes Feuilles*, 9 (Fall 1980): 92-103;

Christiane Makward, Interview with Cixous, *Sub-Stance*, 5 (Autumn 1976): 19-37;

Makward, "Structures du silence ou délire: Marguerite Duras, Hélène Cixous," *Poétique*, 9 (September 1978): 314-324;

Elaine Marks and Isabelle de Courtivron, eds., *New French Feminisms* (Amherst: University of Massachusetts Press, 1980);

René Micha, "La Tête de Dora sous Cixous," *Critique*, 33 (February 1977): 114-121;

Judith G. Miller, "Jean Cocteau and Hélène Cixous," in *Drama, Sex and Politics*, edited by James Redmond (Cambridge: Cambridge University Press, 1985), pp. 203-211;

Toril Moi, "Cixous: An Imaginary Utopia," in *Sexual/Textual Politics* (London & New York: Methuen, 1985);

Michèle Richman, "Sex and Signs: The Language of French Feminist Criticism," *Language and Style*, 13 (Autumn 1980): 62-80;

Pierre Salesne, "*Ou l'art de l'innocence*: The Path to You," in *Writing Differences*, edited by Susan Sellers (Milton Keynes: Open University Press, 1988), pp. 113-126;

Dina Sherzer, "Postmodernist Feminist Fiction," in her *Representation in Contemporary French Fiction* (Lincoln & London: University of Nebraska Press, 1986);

Domna C. Stanton, "Language and Revolution: The Franco-American Disconnection," in *The Future of Difference*, edited by Hester Eisenstein and Alice Jardine (Boston: G. K. Hall, 1980), pp. 73-87;

Sharon Willis, "Hélène Cixous's *Portrait de Dora:* The Unseen and the Un-Scene," *Theater Journal*, 37 (October 1985): 287-301;

Willis, "Mis-translation: *Vivre l'orange*," *Sub-Stance*, 16 (1987): 76-83.

Louis-René des Forêts
(28 January 1918-   )

John T. Naughton
Colgate University

BOOKS: *Les Mendiants* (Paris: Gallimard, 1943); translated by Helen Beauclerk as *The Beggars* (London: Dobson, 1948); revised French edition (Paris: Gallimard, 1986);

Le Bavard (Paris: Gallimard, 1946); revised edition, with an afterword by Maurice Blanchot (Paris: Union Générale d'Editions, 1963); translated in *The Children's Room* (1963);

La Chambre des enfants (Paris: Gallimard, 1960); translated in *The Children's Room* (1963); revised French edition, omitting one story (Paris: Gallimard, 1983);

The Children's Room, translated by Jean Stewart (London: Calder, 1963)—comprises *Le Bavard* and *La Chambre des enfants*;

Les Mégères de la mer (Paris: Mercure de France, 1967);

Un Malade en forêt (Montpellier: Fata Morgana, 1987);

Le Malheur du Lido (Montpellier: Fata Morgana, 1987).

OTHER: "Lettres de Gerard Manley Hopkins," translated by des Forêts, *Ephémère*, no. 3 (1967).

PERIODICAL PUBLICATIONS: "Notes éparses en mai," *Ephémère*, no. 6 (1968);

Ostinato (excerpts), *Nouvelle Revue Française*, no. 372 (January 1984): 1-64; *Ire des Vents*, no. 15-16 (April 1987): 203-239;

"Poèmes de Samuel Wood," *Ire des Vents*, no. 13-14 (March 1986): 11-27.

Author of a small but influential body of work, Louis-René des Forêts has played an important role in the postwar movement in France that has sought to question, to renovate, and to transform traditional modes of narration. In addition to writing in several genres, des Forêts has done translations, coedited a literary review, drawn and painted; he has dreamed of making motion pictures and played small parts in obscure films. His influence may be seen in the work of writers as diverse as Albert Camus and Marguerite Duras.

Born in Paris on 28 January 1918, Louis-René des Forêts comes from a long line of distinguished naval officers on his mother's side. As a young boy, he spent the winter months with his family in Paris and the summer months at a country house in the Berry region of France. The house, called Les Pluies, once served as a kind of rendezvous station for hunters. Des Forêts continues to divide his time between these two worlds.

Educated in boarding schools from the age of eight, des Forêts spent his most important formative years in a Catholic secondary school in Brittany. As a boy, he had dreamed of pursuing a naval career, and he was sent to the school in Brittany with this end in mind. He proved to be an undistinguished, rather undisciplined student, and his later literary work suggests that he was often severely punished. His deepest, most lasting impressions were formed in boarding school—in a special, isolated world of austerity, even cruelty, and above all loneliness. Almost all of des Forêts's work is haunted by memories of the years spent in this environment. It was here that he first began to experiment with writing.

Before the outbreak of World War II, des Forêts studied political science and law in Paris because his parents hoped that he might one day make a place for himself in the diplomatic service. He was not much interested in his work, however, and his studies were unsuccessful. It was also during this period that des Forêts published his first essays on music, his lifelong passion and the medium in which he would most have wished to work. These essays appeared in various obscure and ephemeral reviews of the time and have not been collected or republished. Des Forêts also did some traveling from 1936 to 1938, visiting Holland, England, Italy, and Austria, where he spent three months and was witness to the *Anschluss.*

In 1938 he began work at Les Pluies on his first novel, *Les Mendiants.* Called to active service in the war in 1939, he was soon mobilized. In 1941 he returned to the country to finish *Les Mendiants,* which was published in 1943 (and translated as *The Beggars* in 1948). Active in Resistance groups for the remainder of the war, des Forêts was forced to suspend work on a new novel entitled *Le Bavard.* (A long autobiographical story entitled "Un Malade en forêt" [A Sick Man in the Forest] documents his wartime experience as a member of a clandestine group given the task of rescuing, then lodging or evacuating Allied paratroopers.) After the Liberation, des Forêts returned to the country to finish *Le Bavard,* which, though it was eventually to become one of his most discussed works, met with considerable indifference when it was first published in 1946. It was not translated into English until 1963, when it appeared as "The Bavard" in *The Children's Room.*

After the war and the publication of *Le Bavard,* des Forêts worked for a year in Paris as literary adviser at the publishing house of Robert Laffont. He married in 1947 and retired to Les

Dust jacket for the 1963 volume that includes Jean Stewart's translations of Le Bavard *and* La Chambre des enfants

Pluies to work for five years on a novel he eventually abandoned. His friend Raymond Queneau's judgment of it as disappointing confirmed des Forêts's own doubts, and he rejected the work as too mechanical and contrived, despite having written over six hundred pages. He then left Les Pluies to work in Paris, convinced that the isolation of the country and the leisure to write were, in fact, detrimental to his work.

Des Forêts was employed by Gallimard in 1953, and he collaborated in the preparation of the multivolume *Encyclopédie de la Pléiade* before becoming a reviewer on the Comité de lecture (Evaluation Committee) in 1965. He served in this capacity for eighteen years, reading and evaluating manuscripts submitted to Gallimard for possible publication. It was after he was employed by Gallimard that des Forêts became friends with Georges Bataille and Maurice Blanchot, whose ideas and work were to have a decisive influence on his own development. Des Forêts's book *La Chambre des enfants*, a collection of narratives with interconnecting concerns, was published in 1960 and won the Prix des Critiques. It was translated into English in *The Children's Room*, 1963. The same year *Le Bavard* appeared in a revised edition that included an important afterword by Maurice Blanchot entitled "La Parole vaine" (Vain Speech). From 1966 through 1972 des Forêts collaborated on the review *Ephémère*, which he had founded with his friends Yves Bonnefoy, André du Bouchet, and Gaëton Picon. He published translations of several letters by Gerard Manley Hopkins in the third number of *Ephémère* in 1967. (He has said that Hopkins is, with Shakespeare, Pascal, and Rimbaud, one of the few writers of abiding influence and importance for him.) In 1967 des Forêts's poetic masterpiece, *Les Mégères de la mer* (The Shrews of the Sea), appeared, published by Mercure de France. The work is the poetic reconstruction of a fragment of an unfinished novel. Like many other French intellectuals, des Forêts took a lively interest in the Castro revolution in Cuba and made a trip to that country in 1967 to participate in the activities of an international cultural congress. When Paris was rocked by student and worker demonstrations in May and June 1968, des Forêts felt a sense of promise and new hope which he recorded in "Notes éparses en mai" (Scattered Notes in May), published in the sixth number of *Ephémère*.

During the long interval between the 1967 appearance of *Les Mégères de la mer* and the publication in 1984 of extracts from a new work entitled *Ostinato*, des Forêts turned for a time to drawing and painting, activities which, by his account, gave him more pleasure than he had ever received from writing. His efforts in the visual arts had begun at the suggestion of Denis Roche, who wanted to publish a book of drawings by writers and texts by painters. Des Forêts was encouraged by Pierre Bettencourt to pursue this new medium, and important exhibitions of his work were held at Ancy-le-Franc and at Beaubourg in 1978.

A new edition of *La Chambre des enfants* was published in 1983 by Gallimard in the series L'Imaginaire. In the new edition of the work what had been the first story of the earlier version has been dropped. This narrative, "Un Malade en forêt," was published separately by Fata Morgana in 1987. In 1985 Fata Morgana published an important interview with des Forêts enti-

tled *Voies et détours de la fiction* (Paths and Bypaths of Fiction). The interview, conducted by Philippe Sollers, was first published in 1962 in the review *Tel Quel*. A new, slightly revised edition of *Les Mendiants* was published by Gallimard in 1986. A film version of the novel was made by Benoît Jacquot in 1987.

Parts of *Ostinato*, des Forêts's ambitious project of an autobiographical nature, appeared in the *Nouvelle Revue Française* in January 1984, and new lyric poems that seem to translate a renewed faith in life were published in 1986 in *Ire des Vents* under the title "Poèmes de Samuel Wood."

Des Forêts has become an exemplary figure for many writers, and for theoreticians of writing as well, since his work is fundamentally a meditation on the activity of writing and a rigorous consideration of the inescapable insufficiencies that come into play the moment one projects one's thoughts in words. Thus, the preoccupation with a past eroded by time and approached by the inadequacies of a deficient memory, the questioning of the status of the self deployed in and by writing, and yet the hope that writing might be able to commemorate the value of existence and aid the reader in rediscovering his own moments of special intensity have made des Forêts's work particularly compelling to those engaged in similar pursuits. "Une Ecriture de notre temps"–a writing of our time–this is how poet Yves Bonnefoy has described des Forêts's scrupulous, doubt-ridden enterprise in an article for the *Nouvelle Revue Française*. In his work one senses a bitter, sometimes violent spiritual combat between a lyrical exhaltation seeking to express itself and the seemingly cruel lucidity that restrains it. It is not surprising that his *œuvre* is often viewed as rarefied, even sacrificial, and that it has been interrupted by long periods of silence. It has seemed to many that des Forêts's work seeks to modify the traditional relation of reader to writer and that it strives to formulate a new kind of "negative" rhetoric. Raymond Queneau has compared des Forêts to Herman Melville's Bartleby, the scrivener who "would prefer not to."

Des Forêts's first novel, *Les Mendiants*, is in many respects a remarkable work. Though possessing several flaws characteristic of first novels, *Les Mendiants* manages to develop a broad range of interesting characters through an intricate and compelling plot. A particularly striking feature of the novel is the fact that it presents two distinct yet intermingling spheres–the world of the adolescents and that of the adults. The skill with which des Forêts develops the similarities between these worlds, while respecting their obvious differences, is one of the book's most noteworthy achievements.

Distinguished contemporary readers were quick to point out the limitations of the work. Jean-Paul Sartre felt that the influence of William Faulkner was too dominant. And it is true that the narrative is structured in a manner strikingly reminiscent of Faulkner's *As I Lay Dying* (1930) in that the story unfolds from several points of view, as each of the many characters considers the events in turn and imbues them with his or her own special perspective. Des Forêts has himself maintained that the work reflects the influence not so much of Faulkner as of Stephen Hudson. He has also acknowledged the considerable influence that American writers such as John Dos Passos and Sherwood Anderson had on him at this stage of his development. Roger Martin du Gard, in fact, complained that all the characters in the novel tend to talk the same way and that the work is doused in too much American whiskey.

The edition of 1943 was badly printed and full of typographical errors. On rereading the work in preparation for the new edition of 1986, des Forêts was appalled by the plethora of adjectives. The 1986 edition contains a certain amount of revision in points of detail, and one of the monologues of the enigmatic character called simply The Stranger has been substantially rewritten. On the whole, however, des Forêts allows the work to remain itself: the first novel of a very young and gifted writer.

The action of the book is set in an unidentified port city and involves a gang of smugglers whose members include an aging shipbuilder and his grandson; a professional actor; an escaped convict; and a steely and disillusioned woman named Annabelle. The plot in part develops around the operations of the smugglers, tracing events that lead to their discovery and arrest. A group of adolescents has simultaneously organized its own gang, with its own hierarchy and structure. The boys "play" at smuggling, deferring to their uncontested leader, Sani.

Des Forêts uses aspects of conventional detective fiction to focus on elements in human experience and in human relations that are viewed as perennial, operative in the affairs of both children and adults. These elements include loneliness, the quest for power and dominance over others, and the need to fill the emptiness of existence

with meaning or sensation. Des Forêts is especially preoccupied in this novel with playacting and the taking on of roles in human behavior. Annabelle sums up some of these ideas when she maintains that the part of oneself one considers the most important always remains hidden to others and that what one shows to other people are faces and roles without real interest. And yet, she says, this is all as inescapable as original sin, for if every person is filled with the desire to share his secret side, no one wants to know anything about anyone else's.

The title of the book in fact highlights the idea that in human relations people are often required to "beg" for the attention and affection of others. This kind of unfulfilled yearning is especially manifest in the character Hélène, who is in love with a fellow actor, the philandering cad, Grégoire. Some of des Forêts's most masterful strokes are achieved in the depiction of this tormented relationship, since the role that each character plays onstage in Shakespeare's *Othello* is a reversal of the role each assumes in real life. Thus Hélène, who plays Desdemona onstage, is in fact tortured by Othello-like pangs of jealousy. Des Forêts here introduces a theme to which he will return in his mature fiction: the notion that the artist is only provisionally incarnate in his roles and in his representations, that there is never a perfect equivalence between an artist's life and his work.

Des Forêts's first novel is also marked by the doubt and suspicion that characterize his later work. Toward the end of the book, for instance, one of the characters, Guillaume, grown older and looking back on events described for him by his brother Fred, insists that the recollections are not exact but that his brother is obviously filled with the desire to talk about what he has in fact forgotten. It is difficult and exhausting, Guillaume maintains, to describe in precise words those images that were filtered at the time by drunken eyes and reconstructed as well as possible today by a memory blunted by the years. And in any case, he concludes, words cannot do much, which is why they are not very important.

The suspicion brought to bear on words is clearly projected into the many failed relationships depicted in the novel. The absence of authority, of a founding discourse, reduces all human activity to futility and cynicism. The illicit trafficking of goods externalizes the fraudulence and cruelty implicit in the abortive or inauthentic efforts at intimacy that frustrate all the characters' inner lives. The *idée fixe* professed by Fred–to fill up the emptiness of existence in any way possible–is what motivates all the characters, all the "beggars" in this novel of thwarted dreams and lust for power. Beneath the veneer of an action novel, des Forêts begins, in *Les Mendiants*, to raise some of the existential and epistemological questions that reemerge in the later work.

What is striking about *Les Mendiants*, though, is that it is, by comparison to subsequent works, so decidedly a novel of action, of exteriors, and that it deals with such a wide range of characters and social types. The works that follow it are, by comparison, interior, self-reflexive–concerned not so much with characters and plot as with the problems of narrative as such. It is true that "Un Malade en forêt," in the original edition of *La Chambre des enfants*, is a narrative of action. Set in wartime, and clearly autobiographical, it tells the story of the evacuation of a wounded African soldier from the battle zone to a place of safety, where he arrives already dead from appendicitis. It is significant, however, that des Forêts decided to exclude the story from the 1983 edition of *La Chambre des enfants*. Clearly, des Forêts saw that the story did not mesh with the more introspective pieces of the collection and that it would be more appropriate to republish the work separately.

First published in 1946, des Forêts's second novel, *Le Bavard*, has had wide influence and has been the object of considerable attention. Albert Camus seems to have taken the narrator of *Le Bavard* as the model for the narrative voice in his novel *La Chute* (*The Fall*, 1956). Maurice Blanchot, as well as many other contemporary readers, agreed with Georges Bataille, who felt that the work was one of the strangest and most upsetting ever written.

Readers have commented on the dizzying or "vertiginous" quality of the narration, on its subversion of the established rules and conventions of the "game" of writing. The title of the work designates a person who talks a great deal, often repetitiously and without seriousness or focus. And it is true that the narrator systematically undermines and discredits the veracity of the narrative he seemingly seeks to establish.

The narrative is rooted in the nameless narrator's avowed self-fascination. He loves, as he says in the first words of his story, to look at himself in the mirror. Indeed his narrative becomes a kind of reflecting surface in which he studies himself, assumes stances, tries poses. He asserts that he feels the need to express himself, though he is not sure of his theme or of his ability to maintain a line of coherence in his remarks. Similarly, when he recounts an incident in a bar, during which he tries to woo the female companion of another man, he underlines the fact that he is inebriated when he approaches the woman. The essential thing, he tells us, is the chatter. The nature, the content of his prattle or coquetry is without importance. Des Forêts seems to be identifying the impulse toward narration with euphoria and eroticism, with the need to parade, impress, seduce, or dominate.

After being rebuffed by the woman's cruel burst of laughter, the narrator leaves the bar and wanders through the snowy streets, though he is filled with the dread of being followed. He takes refuge on a park bench and is invaded by the music of memories which comes to possess him. Once again, however, absorption in feelings of euphoria is punished by the brutal imposition of limitation and disappointment. The lover of the woman in the bar suddenly appears and beats the narrator, knocking him down in the snow. In his utterly reduced state of exhaustion and pain, the narrator is all at once moved by the sounds of a children's choir which float through the icy air and into the park from a nearby church and seem to annul all sense of suffering and humiliation. Thinking that he has been chosen for a privileged moment of ethereal music, the narrator is once again awakened to a less self-flattering reality: the sounds come from the voices of otherwise disagreeable schoolchildren. Nevertheless, the music is able to invade and overwhelm his bruised sensibilities entirely. For a moment at least, he is transformed by the intense warmth of the music, with its hints of freedom and joyful innocence. It seems to speak of a distant realm, at once sexless and sensual, existing far from human worries and concerns, far from the familiar odor of sin. The music also conjures up more precise memories of the moments spent in the chapel of a boarding school in Brittany, during the narrator's youth. These memories evoke the image of a young man with a proud capacity for life and for truth with which the narrator's present sense of himself as doubt-filled and insufficient is painfully dissociated. They reconnect the narrator with deeply buried aspects of himself and grant him a feeling of joyful rebirth. After having heard such singing, he wonders, how will he ever be able to open his mouth again?

The final section of the book seems to dismantle all the elements it has set up. The narrator suggests that he has invented all the events in his previous narration. The story was a means, he says, to hold the reader captive. He has no real existence other than in the words he uses to constitute and project himself. The reader, too, has no absolute ontological status, since he is at the mercy of an unreliable and equivocating narrator who presents the world to him. The thrust of the narrative therefore seems to become a kind of process of disintoxication and demystification. The narrator asks the reader to imagine that he is like a magician who has grown weary of exploiting the credulity of the public he has been holding in deceit and illusion, and who has therefore set himself the task of replacing his joy at mystifying with the joy of demystifying. This task is just the opposite of what is usually praised, and it carries the risk of the loss of all the benefits that might be gained from a reputation as miracle worker. Since narrations–confessions, apologies, explanations of events–are mendacious instances of self-assertion and garrulity, they need to be deconstructed as fictions and ruses. The reader of *Le Bavard* is thus witness to a "crisis in prattling"–a crisis in which his own capacity for lying and hypocrisy is implicated.

When all is said and done, however, the narrative does in fact exist–which suggests that for des Forêts the need to express oneself, to try to connect with a listener, with the other, is a human and unalienable one, even if there is "nothing to say," even if there is little to reveal other than the dishonesties inherent in speaking. Exhausted then by what Blanchot has called "vain speech," the narrator at last falls silent, leaving the reader with the task of trying to sort out what, in the strange narrative, might be truth and what mere lying.

The importance given to the section on the children's singing seems to suggest that one may sometimes experience feelings of great power and depth, which suddenly and unpredictably reconnect one with the fullness of life and with the capacity for wonder and joyful participation in existence, although such miraculous moments cannot be consciously sought or easily expressed. And it is to this kind of experience that the work of des Forêts often points readers–through the scrupulous discrediting of the capacity of words in themselves to convey this experience. And in this resides the "negative" power of his achievement: by designating their own insufficiency, words hint at what is beyond them; they open onto what is beyond their grasp. The relation of des Forêts's work to negative philosophies and theologies, his contention that what human beings are trying to reach is always diverted and modified by the ultimately unsuccessful effort to communicate, does not, however, lead to an absolute silence. Although, in des Forêts's view, every writer lives the temptation of silence, few yield to it, he feels, as though some mysterious force withdrew the right and even the power of making so grave a decision. In his interview with Philippe Sollers, des Forêts cites the well-known observation of Maurice Blanchot which his own experience had taught him to approve: "Se taire est une manière de s'exprimer dont l'illégitimité nous relance dans la parole" (Silence is a means of expression, the illegitimacy of which thrusts us back into speech).

What one therefore finds in des Forêts's work are dialectical elements: precarious speech emerging from a silence seeking ascendancy; the search for the richness of past experience and the sense of its corrosion by time and dream; the meditation on the radical difference between real life in real time and artistic representation. These are the elements that are particularly evident in the collection of short narratives with interconnecting themes, *La Chambre des enfants*.

The first story, "Les Grands Moments d'un chanteur" (The Great Moments of a Singer), takes up certain ideas touched upon in *Les Mendiants*, particularly the evocation of the differences between roles assumed in art and those played in real life. Frédéric Molieri, an obscure oboist with unrevealed vocal talents, is called upon to play the part of Don Giovanni in Mozart's opera when the lead singer succumbs to an unexplained indisposition. Molieri becomes a star performer for a time, while steadfastly insisting that the grandeur of his representations has nothing to do with his own inherent simplicity and insignificance as a man. He is loved, he maintains, for what he is not.

Followed by an adoring woman admirer, Anna Fercovitz, who is unable to understand fully or deal with the discrepancy between the artist, whom she reveres, and the man, whom she despises, Molieri seems too weary of his powers and his capacity to manipulate the public. Feeling suddenly "dispossessed," he begins to sabotage his performances, and eventually, having lost all his glory and prestige, he resumes his modest position as oboist.

Narrated by a not wholly reliable observer who gradually becomes passionately involved in Molieri's destiny, "Les Grands Moments d'un chanteur" focuses on the artist's capacity to produce effects, on his ability to lose himself in his roles or in his representations. The narrative thus emphasizes the "elastic" dimension of the artistic personality: nothing in itself, everything in its metamorphoses and illusory incarnations.

The second story, entitled "La Chambre des enfants," is a highly complex, somewhat elusive discussion of such issues as the relation of speech to silence, of freedom to rules and regimentation, of past event to present awareness, of role-playing to authenticity. The narrative presents its themes in the form of abstract dialogues between children and in the context of a vaguely allegorical tableau. Assailed by youthful voices, an observer designated only by the pronoun "he" secretly stands watch by a children's room, listening to their efforts to force a silent companion, named Georges, to speak. The observer, it is learned at the end of the piece, is called Georges. It is only when the children fall silent that Georges feels impelled toward speech: it is for him alone to break the silence and to assure both his own salvation and that of the children. How can he convince himself of his identity and of his presence, he wonders, if not through the dubious affirmation of speech?

"Une Mémoire démentielle" (An Insane Memory) deals with the insufficiencies of memory, with the inevitably flawed reconstruction of the past, with all the difficulties involved in re-creating former events. Constituting a kind of *ars poetica,* "Une Mémoire démentielle"–which has had considerable influence on Marguerite Duras's aesthetic ideas–provides an important and relentless investigation of the way memory works, of the way fantasies and fictions are elaborated, while developing at the same time a series of vivid evocations of a boarding-school childhood.

The narrative traces the evolution of an artistic position–in part summed up by the awareness attributed to the "he" of the text–that although his experience eludes every rational reconstruction, the obsession with transmitting it and with imposing it has come to replace the obsession with simply reliving it minutely. Thus the artist devotes his waking hours to the effort to give expression to the ineffable and order to what is irremediably chaotic. One of the "obligations" he comes to impose on himself is to justify the search for

what is precious in his past: not to fix its perishable matter in words, but to invent reasons to establish why it is worthy of being saved from forgetfulness.

Although undertaking an endless and impossible task, the writer establishes "versions" that, though imperfect, perpetuate his obsession with the resurrection of the past. In the last lines of the narrative there is an abrupt shifting to the first-person voice which affirms both literary aspirations and the obstinate search for the truth about one's being: "Je suis ce littérateur. Je suis ce maniaque. Mais je fus peut-être cet enfant" (I am this literary man. I am this maniac. But I was also perhaps this child).

"Dans un miroir" (In a Mirror), the last and longest piece in the collection, is a tour de force that achieves a rare degree of self-reflexivity and autocriticism. The narrative discusses the ways in which writing becomes a mirror to reflect subjective conflicts in seemingly objective fashion. In the first part of the narrative the reader encounters four characters. Leonard comes each day to the apartment of a friend who maintains a position of reclusiveness and silence over which his sister Louise stands guard; completing the group is a cousin of the brother and sister, a schoolboy who listens to and records "word for word" the conversations taking place in the adjacent rooms of the apartment. The first part of the narrative is filled with the conversations between Louise and Leonard concerning the latter's struggle to engage his silent friend in an intimate dialogue. All the movements and exchanges between these characters are recorded by the young schoolboy cousin for their future edification. He arranges the discovery of the notebook in which all their activities have been faithfully transcribed, and, in the second part of the narrative, this "fiction of an allegorical nature" is analyzed and dismissed by the sister as fallacious misrepresentation. Isn't the purportedly faithful record of the conversations overheard and the actions silently witnessed a simple revision, a fraudulent reconstruction? In the mirror of this reconstruction, images are so distorted as to be unrecognizable, and memory, in any case, is unable to verify the truth or falseness of representation. The most irrefutable truth about the notebook, the sister maintains, is that it reflects not the objective truth about others, but the subjective reality, the "inner debate," of the author himself. Thus, the first part of the narrative, which ostensibly transcribes the conversations of those observed from behind a half-closed door, is interpreted, in the second part, as the schoolboy's own desire for intimacy, and the silent and reclusive friend constantly evoked in the "record" of the first phase of the narrative is seen as in fact the mirror-image of the hidden observer-author. This interpretation disarms the schoolboy cousin, who nonetheless hopes that another, misplaced version of the events will soon seem a more truthful reflection.

A scrupulous examination of the ways in which the self is constituted by language and imagination, and of the manner in which the past is transformed in the effort to preserve it, *La Chambre des enfants* is made up of narratives that are so rigorously concerned with the problems of the narrative as such that they seem something like discourses on method. Des Forêts's preoccupation with the insufficiencies of language and his unremitting scrutiny of the unreliable forces at work in the worlds created by writing are hallmarks of his moral and ethical determination. And the painful awareness of the inability of language to recapture the beauty and power inherent in certain moments of the past, particularly in childhood, also haunts des Forêts's long poem, *Les Mégères de la mer.*

The poem deals with the relation of subjectivity to inspiration, creating a vivid decor and rich symbolism to evoke its problematic theme. Several specific details establish the Brittany coast as the setting for the poem's drama. The language is noble and restrained, but with the vocabulary that attaches the poem to an epic and chivalric tradition, there is also a colloquial diction that conjures up the language of children and the hours spent in parochial boarding school.

The voice speaking remembers, across the frail bridge of memory and words, the special relationship he once had with equivocal feminine forces identified in the title of the poem as the "mégères de la mer," or shrews of the sea. His present position is thus seen as diminished with respect to the intensity of a proximity now lost. "Comprends-moi dont la svelte gloire est aujourd'hui éteinte, / Cette citadelle agreste fut le théâtre de ma passion / Et dans ma mémoire souffrante qui est mon seul avoir / Je cherche où l'enfant que je fus a laissé ses empreintes" (Understand me, though my own slim glory be now extinct, / This uncouth citadel was once the only theater of my passion / I suffer now in memory which is my last possession / As I look for any mark the child I was might have left).

The nature of the "shrews," however, is as ambiguous as that of the witches in Shakespeare's *Macbeth.* Maternal and sometimes protective, the weird sisters of the sea are also dangerously alluring, even imprisoning, and their "son" is repeatedly seen as caught in their power. Nevertheless, his first encounters with the hags are remembered as occurring at moments when, as a boy, he would escape from the mundane pleasures of his comrades during the periods of recreation at school to spy on the old women preparing strange dishes. Watching them, listening to an unknown and hermetic idiom, seals forever his entrance into the darkness.

The problem for the narrating "double" of this lost child is that he can never fully recapture his initial and all-determining experiences with these wild forces. He feels walled up in words, groping in the darkness of images, yet spurred on by a cruel child within him who demands that nothing be buried. The person speaking thus becomes, as he says, like one who has escaped from shipwreck. Wishing neither to attenuate nor exaggerate the importance and power of his affiliation, the narrator must struggle to commemorate through words an essentially ineffable experience.

A major part of the poem focuses on the equivocal status of the shrews. At times caressing and nurturing, the chief among them–a figure full of white splendor–while capable of loosening the knots of fear and taming the misgivings of a developing sensibility, is nonetheless also depicted as an "old daughter of hell" ("vieille fille de l'enfer"). Will the pursuit of her mean perdition or entrance into some unexpected sanctuary of desire? Speaking a strange language full of all the ways of death, she is also a dispenser of justice capable of restoring the narrator to an original land of nothingness from which he has been snatched to lead a life of dreams and untruths. It is to this nameless land that the poet would return, free of all false words and unreal history. Entrance into this land is seen as blocked, however, and the narrator imagines himself treading forever the sorrowful country called himself, endlessly dragging behind him his todays and tomorrows. And yet, he resigns himself to his fate as perpetual guest at these obscure rites and agrees to be faithful to the rendezvous, realizing that the weird sisters are of those messengers who last forever and knowing that he will always be haunted by their hypnotic force.

The poem ends with the hope that through the evocations of this lost realm, through fidelity to the powerful experiences of childhood, the narrator might gain access to a region beyond the worlds betrayed by fraudulence, a region where feelings of deficiency and doubt would disappear beneath "l'arche intemporelle où trône la toute pure nullité" (the timeless arch where all-pure nullity reigns). Still, the poet disavows the journey he has made and asks that there be no memorial for it, since he knows that his path has been an uncertain and an unclear one and that the witches of the sea–those outcast, wild, and enticing forces that inflame imagination and desire–lead the child away from the common life and into a deeper, more dangerous apprehension of reality.

After the publication of *Les Mégères de la mer* no major work by des Forêts appeared for quite some time. Then, in January 1984, the *Nouvelle Revue Française* presented extracts of a new work entitled *Ostinato*, the first important literary publication by des Forêts in almost twenty years. Projected as a kind of autobiography in six parts, *Ostinato* is composed of fragments of poetic prose of varying lengths. They constitute what Virginia Woolf called "moments of being"–those experiences of special intensity, the "vestiges" of the shipwreck wrought by time. Des Forêts evokes, with particular power, the cruelty and perversity of the boarding school authorities against whom a fiercely proud youngster must struggle–through cunning, through silence–for his liberty. The enclosed world of school days stands in vivid contrast to the tranquil joys provided by the natural world, with its bird songs and open fields. Many of the themes treated in the earlier works reemerge here, and several passages discuss, in a manner reminiscent of the Pascalian meditation, the methodology of the work itself.

The title, *Ostinato*, is a musical term signifying that a rhythmical formula is maintained throughout a part or the whole of a composition. And in des Forêts's work there is neither crescendo, nor diminuendo, but a steady production of fragments, each constituting a new vision, a new departure, and produced not so much by memory as by language itself–by a phrase, for instance, which will then seek to find its relation to memory and past experience.

Presented in an unvarying present tense and evoking the experiences of an unnamed "he," the work, which contains, as the author admits, the inescapable element of fiction and transformation, strives to record, among other things, the irreducible and untranslatable experience of suffering brought about by the death of a child. With the "Poèmes de Samuel Wood," which treat some of the same themes and which were published in *Ire des Vents* in 1986, *Ostinato* represents des Forêts's painful return to literary speech after years of self-imposed silence–broken at last by what the poet has called bright life's shattering force.

Interviews:

Philippe Sollers, "La Littérature aujourd'hui," *Tel Quel*, no. 19 (February 1962); republished as *Voies et détours de la fiction* (Montpellier: Fata Morgana, 1985);

Jean-Pierre Salgas, "Les Lectures de Louis-René des Forêts," *Quinzaine Littéraire*, no. 410 (January 1984): 11-13.

References:

Marianne Alphant, "Louis-René des Forêts: A silences rompus," *Libération* (22-23 September 1984): 30-31;

Jean-Louis Baudry, "Louis-René des Forêts et le thème du miroir," *Tel Quel*, no. 7 (Autumn 1961): 42-49;

Jacques Bens, "*La Chambre des enfants*," *Nouvelle Revue Française*, no. 90 (June 1960): 1161-1162;

Maurice Blanchot, "La Marche de l'écrevisse," *Nouvelle Revue Française*, no. 91 (July 1960): 90-99;

Blanchot, "La Parole vaine," afterword to des Forêts's *Le Bavard* (Paris: Union Générale d'Editions, 1963);

Yves Bonnefoy, "Une Ecriture de notre temps: Louis-René des Forêts," *Nouvelle Revue Française*, no. 402 (July 1986)-no. 408 (January 1987): 38-55;

D. Bourdet, "Louis-René des Forêts," *Revue de Paris*, 71 (5 May 1964): 126-131;

Serge Canadas, "L.-R. des Forêts: L'Inabordable Question," *Critique*, 40 (March 1984): 229-244;

Pierre Chappuis, "Vertige lucide," *Revue des Belles Lettres*, 103, no. 3-4 (1980): 123-129;

Marc Dambre, "Louis-René des Forêts: Entre Méduse et Persée," *Magazine Littéraire*, no. 146 (March 1979): 40-41;

Antoine de Gaudemar, "*Les Mendiants* revu par le cinéma, corrigé par des Forêts," *Libération* (25 April 1986): 36-37;

Patrice Delbourg, "Derrière la porte grise," *Nouvelles Littéraires* (17-23 November 1983): 32;

Florence De Mèredieu, "Louis-René des Forêts: *Ateliers d'aujourd'hui*," *Nouvelle Revue française*, no. 307 (August 1978): 170-171;

Jean Grosjean, "Lettres d'Avant," *Nouvelle Revue Française*, no. 92 (August 1960);

Edmond Jabès, "Louis-René des Forêts ou le malaise de la question," in *Le Livre des marges II: Dans la double dépendance du dit* (Montpellier: Fata Morgana, 1984), pp. 380-382;

Vincent Kaufman, "Contrats sans paroles," *Texte*, 2 (1983): 35-47;

Pierre Klossowski, "En marge des tableaux de Louis-René des Forêts," *Ateliers d'aujourd'hui* (Paris: Centre Georges Pompidou, 1978);

Carol J. Murphy, "Des Forêts's Dizzy Narrator: Ironic Transformations in *Le Bavard*," *Stanford French Review*, 5 (Winter 1981): 353-362;

John T. Naughton, *Louis-René des Forêts* (Amsterdam: Rodopi, forthcoming 1989);

Claude Perruchot, "La Littérature du silence," *Etudes Françaises*, no. 2 (February 1966): 109-116;

Bernard Pingaud, "Louis-René des Forêts," in *Ecrivains d'aujourd'hui*, edited by Pingaud (Paris: Grasset, 1960), pp. 227-233;

Pingaud, "Le Pouvoir de la voix," in his *L'Expérience romanesque* (Paris: Gallimard, 1983), pp. 265-281;

René Proslier, "Louis-René des Forêts," *Nouvelles Littéraires* (16 June 1960): 4;

Pascal Quignard, *Le Vœu de silence* (Montpellier: Fata Morgana, 1985);

Dominique Rabaté, "L'Impossible Mémoire de Louis-René des Forêts," *Poétique*, no. 61 (February 1985): 91-99;

Rabaté, "Parole d'excès, poésie de silence," *Pleine Marge*, no. 1 (May 1985);

Jean Roudaut, "Le Bavard ou le secret diffusé," *Nouvelle Revue Française*, no. 336 (January 1981): 63-76;

Roudaut, "Rendre justice à Louis-René des Forêts," *Magazine Littéraire*, no. 49 (February 1971): 51;

Jean-Luc Seylaz, "Le Bavard," in *Les Critiques de notre temps et le nouveau roman* (Paris: Editions Garnier, 1972), pp. 99-107;

Steven Ungar, "Rules of the Game: First-Person Singular in des Forets' *Le Bavard*," *Esprit Créateur*, 20 (Fall 1980): 66-77.

Marguerite Duras
(Marguerite Donnadieu)
(4 April 1914-)

Carol J. Murphy
University of Florida

BOOKS: *Les Impudents* (Paris: Plon, 1943);

La Vie tranquille (Paris: Gallimard, 1944);

Un Barrage contre le Pacifique (Paris: Gallimard, 1950); translated by Herma Briffault as *The Sea Wall* (New York: Pellegrini & Cudahy, 1953); translated by Antonia White as *A Sea of Troubles* (London: Methuen, 1953);

Le Marin de Gibraltar (Paris: Gallimard, 1952); translated by Barbara Bray as *The Sailor from Gibraltar* (London: Calder & Boyars, 1966; New York: Grove Press, 1967);

Les Petits Chevaux de Tarquinia (Paris: Gallimard, 1953); translated by Peter DuBerg as *The Little Horses of Tarquinia* (London: Calder, 1960; London: Calder/New York: Riverrun, 1985);

Des Journées entières dans les arbres (Paris: Gallimard, 1954); translated by Anita Barrows as *Whole Days in the Trees and Other Stories* (London: Calder/New York: Riverrun, 1984);

Le Square (Paris: Gallimard, 1955); translated by Sonia Pitt-Rivers and Irina Morduch as *The Square* (London: Calder, 1959; New York: Grove Press, 1959);

Moderato Cantabile (Paris: Editions de Minuit, 1958); translated by Richard Seaver (New York: Grove Press, 1960; London: Calder & Boyars, 1966);

Les Viaducs de la Seine-et-Oise (Paris: Gallimard, 1960); translated as *The Viaducts of Seine and Oise* in *Three Plays* (1967);

Dix Heures et demie du soir en été (Paris: Gallimard, 1960); translated by Anne Borchardt as *Ten-thirty on a Summer Night* (London: Calder, 1962; New York: Grove Press, 1963);

Hiroshima mon amour (Paris: Gallimard, 1960); translated by Seaver (New York: Grove Press, 1961; translation republished, 1966);

Une Aussi Longue Absence, by Duras and Gérard Jarlot (Paris: Gallimard, 1961); translated (1966);

L'Après-midi de Monsieur Andesmas (Paris: Gallimard, 1962); translated as *The Afternoon of Monsieur Andesmas* (1964);

Miracle en Alabama, adapted by Duras and Jarlot from *The Miracle Worker*, by William Gebson, published with *L'Homme qui se taisait* by Pierre Gaillot (Paris: Avant-Scène, 1962);

Le Ravissement de Lol V. Stein (Paris: Gallimard, 1964); translated by Seaver as *The Ravishing of Lol V. Stein* (New York: Grove Press, 1967); translated by Eileen Ellenbogen as *The Rapture of Lol V. Stein* (London: Hamilton, 1967);

The Afternoon of Monsieur Andesmas, translated by Borchardt; *The Rivers and the Forests*, translated by Bray (London: Calder, 1964);

Théâtre I: Les Eaux et forêts, Le Square, La Musica (Paris: Gallimard, 1965); *Les Eaux et forêts* translated as *The Rivers and the Forests* (1964); *Le Square* translated as *The Square* in *Three Plays* (1967); *La Musica* translated (1975);

Des Journées entières dans les arbres (Paris: Avant-Scène, 1966); translated as *Days in the Trees* in *Three Plays* (1967);

Le Vice-Consul (Paris: Gallimard, 1966); translated by Ellenbogen as *The Vice-Consul* (London: Hamilton, 1968; New York: Pantheon, 1987);

Hiroshima mon amour, translated by Seaver; *Une Aussi Longue Absence*, translated by Barbara Wright (London: Calder & Boyars, 1966);

L'Amante anglaise (Paris: Gallimard, 1967); translated by Bray (London: Hamilton, 1968; New York: Grove Press, 1968);

Three Plays, translated by Bray and Sonia Orwell (London: Calder & Boyars, 1967)—comprises *Le Square*, *Des Journées entières dans les arbres*, and *Les Viaducs de la Seine-et-Oise*;

L'Amante anglaise (Paris: Cahiers du Théâtre National Populaire, 1968); translated (1975);

Théâtre II: Suzanna Andler; Des Journées entières dans les arbres; "Yes," peut-être; Le Shaga; Un Homme est venu me voir (Paris: Gallimard, 1968); *Suzanna Andler* translated (1975); *Des Journées entières dans les arbres* translated as *Days in the Trees* in *Three Plays* (1967);

Détruire, dit-elle (Paris: Editions de Minuit, 1969); translated by Bray as *Destroy, She Said* (London: Hamilton, 1970; New York: Grove Press, 1970);

Abahn, Sabana, David (Paris: Gallimard, 1970);

Les Papiers d'Aspern, adapted by Duras and Robert Antelme from Michael Redgrave's stage adaptation of "The Aspern Papers," by Henry James (Paris: Paris-Théâtre, 1970);

L'Amour (Paris: Gallimard, 1971);

Ah Ernesto! (Paris: François Ruy-Vidal, 1971);

India Song: Texte-théâtre-film (Paris: Gallimard, 1973); translated by Bray as *India Song* (New York: Grove Press, 1976);

Nathalie Granger, suivie de La Femme du Gange (Paris: Gallimard, 1973);

Suzanna Andler; La Musica & L'Amante anglaise, translated by Bray (London: Calder, 1975);

Le Camion, suivi de Entretien avec Michelle Porte (Paris: Editions de Minuit, 1977);

L'Eden Cinéma (Paris: Mercure de France, 1977);

Le Navire Night; Césarée; Les Mains négatives; Aurélia Steiner, Aurélia Steiner, Aurélia Steiner (Paris: Mercure de France, 1979);

Véra Baxter ou Les Plages de l'Atlantique (Paris: Albatros, 1980);

L'Homme assis dans le couloir (Paris: Editions de Minuit, 1980); translated by Mary Lydon as *The Seated Man in the Passage, Contemporary Literature,* 24 (Summer 1983): 259-275;

Les Yeux Verts, Cahiers du Cinéma, no. 312-313 (June 1980);

L'Eté '80 (Paris: Editions de Minuit, 1981);

Agatha (Paris: Editions de Minuit, 1981);

Outside (Paris: Albin Michel, 1981); translated by Arthur Goldhammer (Boston: Beacon, 1986);

L'Homme atlantique (Paris: Editions de Minuit, 1982);

Savannah Bay (Paris: Editions de Minuit, 1982; revised edition, 1983);

La Maladie de la mort (Paris: Editions de Minuit, 1982); translated by Bray as *The Malady of Death* (New York: Grove Press, 1986);

Théâtre III: "La Bête dans la jungle," d'après Henry James, adaptation de James Lord et Marguerite Duras; "Les Papiers d'Aspern," d'après Henry James, adaptation de Marguerite Duras et Robert Antelme; "La Danse de mort," d'après August Strindberg, adaptation de Marguerite Duras* (Paris: Gallimard, 1984);

L'Amant (Paris: Editions de Minuit, 1984); translated by Bray as *The Lover* (New York: Pantheon, 1985; London: Flamingo, 1986);

La Douleur (Paris: P.O.L., 1985); translated by Bray as *The War: A Memoir* (New York: Pantheon, 1986; London: Collins, 1986);

La Musica deuxième (Paris: Gallimard, 1985);

La Mouette de Tchekhov (Paris: Gallimard, 1985);

Les Yeux bleus cheveux noirs (Paris: Editions de Minuit, 1986); translated by Bray as *Blue Eyes, Black Hair* (New York: Pantheon, 1988; London: Collins, 1988);

La Pute de la côte normande (Paris: Editions de Minuit, 1986);

La Vie matérielle (Paris: P.O.L., 1987);

Emily L. (Paris: Editions de Minuit, 1987).

PLAY PRODUCTIONS: *Le Square*, Paris, Studio des Champs-Elysées, 1957; abridged version, Paris, Théâtre des Mathurins, 1960;

Les Viaducs de la Seine-et-Oise, Paris, Théâtre de Poche, 1960;

Les Papiers d'Aspern, adapted by Duras and Robert Antelme from Michael Redgrave's stage adaptation of "The Aspern Papers," by Henry James, Paris, Théâtre des Mathurins-Marcel Herrand, 1961;

La Bête dans la jungle, Paris, Théâtre de l'Athénée, October 1962;

La Musica, Paris, Studio des Champs-Elysées, 8 October 1965;

Les Eaux et forêts, Paris, Théâtre Mouffetard, 14 May 1965;

Des Journées entières dans les arbres, Paris, Odéon-Théâtre de France, 1 December 1965; revised version, Paris, Théâtre d'Orsay, 15 October 1975;

"Yes," peut-être, Paris, Théâtre Gramont, 5 January 1968;

Le Shaga, Paris, Théâtre Gramont, 5 January 1968;

L'Amante anglaise, Paris, Théâtre National Populaire, Salle Gémier, 16 December 1968;

Suzanna Andler, Paris, Théâtre des Mathurins, December 1969;

La Danse de mort, Paris, Théâtre du Palais de Chaillot, 21 February 1970;

L'Eden Cinéma, Paris, Théâtre d'Orsay, 25 October 1977;

La Musica deuxième, Paris, Théâtre du Rond-Point Renaud-Barrault, 20 March 1985.

Marguerite Duras (photograph by Erica Lennard)

MOTION PICTURES: *Hiroshima mon amour*, screenplay by Duras, 1959;

Une Aussi Longue Absence, screenplay by Duras and Gérard Jarlot, 1961;

La Musica, screenplay by Duras, directed by Duras and Paul Seban, 1966;

Détruire, dit-elle, screenplay and direction by Duras, 1969;

Jaune le soleil, screenplay and direction by Duras, 1971;

Nathalie Granger, screenplay and direction by Duras, 1972;

La Femme du Gange, screenplay and direction by Duras, 1973;

India Song, screenplay and direction by Duras, 1975;

Baxter, Vera Baxter, screenplay and direction by Duras, 1976;

Son Nom de Venise dans Calcutta désert, screenplay and direction by Duras, 1976;

Des Journées entières dans les arbres, screenplay and direction by Duras, 1976;

Le Camion, screenplay and direction by Duras, 1977;

Le Navire Night, screenplay and direction by Duras, 1978;

Césarée, screenplay and direction by Duras, 1979;

Les Mains négatives, screenplay and direction by Duras, 1979;

Aurélia Steiner, dite Aurélia Melbourne, screenplay and direction by Duras, 1979;

Aurélia Steiner, dite Aurélia Vancouver, screenplay and direction by Duras, 1979;

Agatha et les lectures illimitées, screenplay and direction by Duras, 1981;

L'Homme atlantique, screenplay and direction by Duras, 1981;

Dialogue de Rome, screenplay and direction by Duras, 1982;

Les Enfants, screenplay and direction by Duras, with Jean Mascolo and Jean-Marc Turine, 1985.

OTHER: "Notes on *India Song*," in *Marguerite Duras*, by Duras, François Barat, and Joël Farges (Paris: Editions Albatros, 1975).

One of the most important literary figures in France, Marguerite Duras won international acclaim after she was awarded the 1984 Prix Goncourt for her autobiographical novel *L'Amant* (translated almost immediately into English as *The Lover*). Although Duras had been writing fiction and directing films for over forty years, she was always considered a rather inaccessible author by the general public. The publication of *L'Amant* sparked interest in all her work, which was speedily republished to meet the overwhelming demand. Featured in numerous interviews on television and in popular magazines in France, Duras became something of a national literary phenomenon. *The Lover*, elegantly translated by Barbara Bray, won the Ritz Paris Hemingway Award in 1986, and, in the United States, the cover article of the *New York Times Book Review* (23 June 1985) featured an elogious review of the novel, comparing it, in terms of popularity and interest for an American reader, to Thomas Mann's *Death in Venice* and D. M. Thomas's *White Hotel*. Articles in such nonliterary magazines as *Vogue, Vanity Fair,* and *People* also chronicled the event.

L'Amant is the tale of a passionate love affair lived by a young French *lycéenne* in Saigon with a wealthy young Chinese man during the 1930s. The story is recounted by a sixty-year-old woman ravaged by the pain of life, who, to those familiar with Duras's biography, is not unlike the author herself. *L'Amant* is indeed representative of most of Duras's fiction, informed as it is by memories of her youth spent in French colonial Indochina, now Vietnam. The experiences of those years marked her emotionally and physically; the first few paragraphs of *L'Amant* are a description of the narrator's aged face: "J'ai un visage lacéré de rides sèches et profondes, à la peau cassée . . . détruit" (My face is lacerated with deep, dry lines and broken skin . . . destroyed). These personal scars were to furnish the stuff of her fiction. Her first important novel, *Un Barrage contre le Pacifique* (translated as *The Sea Wall* in 1953), is set in the rice paddies of the Mekong River delta. The exotic landscape of Vietnam colors the decor of much of Duras's fiction with a sensual but oftentimes suffocating eroticism either implicit, in novels set in non-Oriental places, such as *Le Marin de Gibraltar* (1952; translated as *The Sailor from Gibraltar*, 1966) and *Dix Heures et demie du soir en été* (1960; translated as *Ten-thirty on a Summer Night*, 1962), or explicit, as in *Le Vice-Consul* (1966; translated as *The Vice-Consul*, 1968) and *India Song* (1973; translated, 1976). *Des Journées entières dans les arbres* (1954; translated as *Whole Days in the Trees*, 1984) also recalls the lush landscape of Duras's youth and was published first as a short story, then staged and published as a play (1966) and finally produced as a film (1976), directed by the author. In consistently rewriting this period of her life, often in several genres or blends of genres, Duras has evolved what might be called a core story of passionate love and desire undercut with death. Successive texts echo or decant the story in an increasingly fragmented, lyrical style which has come to characterize Duras's poetic prose.

Duras was born Marguerite Donnadieu on 4 April 1914, in Giandinh, near Saigon. Her parents, Henri and Marie Legrand Donnadieu, had left the north of France for teaching positions in the French colony. The death of her father when she and her brothers were young resulted in her mother's decision to farm a government land grant to support her family. Duras, whose pen name was inspired by a village in southwestern France where she spent part of her early childhood, has chronicled the feisty determination of her petite but domineering mother in many of her works. She paints an especially potent portrait in *Un Barrage contre le Pacifique*, in which the mother's force of character is rendered as justifiable anger against the corrupt colonial government which bilked her of her fortune by selling her a worthless piece of land. Duras's bitter attack against colonial injustice persists as a thematic thread in her works such as *Le Vice-Consul* and *India Song* and bespeaks a hatred of exclusion, exploitation, and misuse of power, whether it be political or sexual, public or private.

Duras's attempt to come to terms with her family, but especially with her mother, surfaces repeatedly in her interviews and in her fiction. The mother's continued support of Duras's philandering older brother is the subject of *Des Journées entières dans les arbres*. In both the stage and film versions, Madeleine Renaud created a memorable role. Renaud also played Duras's mother in *L'Eden Cinéma* (1977), a stage rendition of *Un Barrage contre le Pacifique* in which Duras recounts evenings spent in the movie house where her mother worked as a piano player to supplement her meager income. Descriptions of the mother testify to her presence as a strident "mother courage": "Mère de tous. Mère de tout. Criante. Hurlante. Dure. Terrible. Invivable" (Mother of all. Mother of everything. Screaming. Howling. Terrible. Impossible to live with). Acclaimed critically as a study in exquisite melancholy, the play's rhythm was compared to that of a silent film.

Duras's love of the cinema as well as her depiction of young female protagonists as passively engaged in erotic activity probably springs from her early acquaintance with the medium and its portrayal of the reigning female sexual fantasies of the time.

In *L'Amant*, the narrator says that she is finally free to talk about her mother and brothers now that they are dead. Duras's beloved younger brother was her constant companion during the carefree childhood days spent "under the trees" in Pnompenh, Sadek, and Vinh Long. He appears in the fiction, often as an older brother, such as Jacques in *Les Impudents* (The Shameless, 1943), Nicolas in *La Vie tranquille* (The Tranquil Life, 1944), and Joseph in *Un Barrage contre le Pacifique*. Of her real-life older brother, who left Indochina early for schooling in France, Duras has left the unflattering portrait of Jacques in *Des Journées entières dans les arbres*. The irresponsible young man gambled away the family heritage but always remained the preferred child of the mother, a circumstance which, as Duras has revealed in interviews, constituted a wound that would haunt her in both her life and fiction. In an excoriating passage in *L'Amant* she accuses her older brother of having been the "assassin" of the younger, who died of pneumonia at age twenty-two because of the unavailability of medication during World War II. The reappearing character of an adored but feared and hated sibling in the early novels is probably a composite portrait of both of her brothers. *Agatha*, an incestuous dialogue between an older brother and sister, published in 1981, is an example of this ambivalence.

Duras took her *baccalauréat* in Saigon in both Vietnamese and French and in 1931 left for Paris where she earned a *licence* in law and political science in 1935. While working as a secretary for the Ministère des Colonies from 1935 to 1941, she met and married Robert Antelme, an active member of the French Communist party and author of *L'Espèce humaine* (The Human Species, 1947). Duras, too, was a member of the Party and participated actively in political life, especially during the Resistance movement, when she became friends with François Mitterand. It was during the war that she began to write fiction. Although her first manuscript, "La Famille Taneran," was rejected for publication in 1941, she was encouraged by Raymond Queneau to continue writing. Duras later met Dionys Mascolo, a fellow Communist and a philosopher, with whom

she had a son, Jean. In "La Douleur," the autobiographical text which is the title work of a collection published in 1985 (translated as *The War: A Memoir*, 1986), she recounts the story of Antelme's return from a prisoner-of-war camp with the help of Mitterand. Duras's attentive care of the emaciated, corpselike figure whom she nursed back to life was all the more poignant in that the couple proceeded with an already agreed-upon divorce soon after, in 1946. In 1950 Duras was one of a number of intellectuals ousted from the French Communist party. As a result of this experience and the Parisian student-worker revolution of May 1968, she proclaimed her rejection of all ideology as well as of bourgeois values and social conventions. The spirit of May '68 in its quest for egalitarianism and liberation from authority is expressed in *Détruire, dit-elle* (1969; translated as *Destroy, She Said*, 1970) and in the Duras-directed film of the same title (1969), as well as in *Abahn, Sabana, David* (1970).

Duras has addressed social issues in her journalistic writing for newspapers and magazines as diverse as *France-Observateur*, *Vogue*, *Libération*, and *L'Autre Journal*. In 1963 she achieved notoriety for her exposé of the Ben Barka affair during the Algerian war. Most of her journalistic work has been collected and published in *Outside* (1981; translated, 1986) and *L'Eté '80* (Summer '80, 1981). In the latter, a collection of articles which she wrote at the request of *Libération* editor Serge July, passages of fiction and lyrical description alternate with startlingly vivid and moving accounts of the Polish labor strikes in Gdansk led by Lech Walesa of Solidarity. In an earlier article in *Libération*, "Sublime, forcément sublime" (Sublime, Necessarily Sublime, 17 July 1985), Duras took up the defense of accused criminal Christine Villemin by writing an unsettling fictionalized account of her case, thereby creating a stir over judicial procedure. A member of the editorial board of *L'Autre Journal*, she conducted for the liberal magazine a series of interviews with François Mitterand prior to the 1988 elections.

Duras's stance on feminism and feminist writing has been sporadically active and political, as seen in her writings for the French periodical *Sorcières* and in her interviews with Xavière Gauthier collected in *Les Parleuses* (1974; translated as *Woman to Woman*, 1987). For the most part, however, Duras has not espoused a consistent political position concerning the French feminist movement, which has been factious since the Mouvement de Libération des Femmes (Woman's

Liberation Movement) was founded in 1970. She influences French feminism through example rather than pronouncement. In *Marguerite Duras: Writing on the Body* (1987), Sharon Willis details Duras's essentialist view of femininity, especially as regards a particular "economy" of writing. In *Les Parleuses* and in an interview in the American feminist journal *Signs*, Duras spoke of a specifically feminine mode of writing. She affirmed in an interview with Michelle Porte, published in *Les Lieux de Marguerite Duras* (The Places of Marguerite Duras, 1977), that women write from desire, a posture which she maintained is fundamentally different from that of male writing. Elsewhere, Duras has spoken of her writing as a response to an inner music and, in the novel *Emily L.* (1987), as a response to fear.

Duras's cinematic work is at one with her novelistic vision of counterpoint, fragmentation, highly charged eroticism, and errant desire. Before the publication of *L'Amant*, she was probably best known in the United States for her deeply moving film script for Alain Resnais's film *Hiroshima mon amour*, which stunned the public at the Cannes Film Festival in 1959. The story of a public and private tragedy, intertwined and played out in remembering and forgetting, conferred an almost musical quality on the film which scandalized some moviegoers for what was perceived to be a diminishing of Hiroshima's tragedy. In her own filmmaking, Duras has favored low-budget movies, in part as a protest against the glibness of commercialized cinema. She created a controversy when she made *Le Camion* (The Truck) in four days and then entered it in the Cannes Film Festival in 1977. Although her films have had limited popular success, she is supported by a faithful coterie of stars, including Michaël Lonsdale, Delphine Seyrig, and Gérard Depardieu; technicians, such as the photographer Bruno Nuytten; and the composer Carlos d'Alessio, who wrote the haunting tango music of *India Song*. *India Song*, by its radical separation of the image and sound tracks, is a landmark of cinematography for which she won a special prize at the 1975 Cannes Film Festival.

Duras has long enjoyed the support of the Compagnie Renaud-Barrault and several of her plays, including *Des Journées entières dans les arbres* (produced, 1965; published, 1966; translated as *Days in the Trees*, 1967), *L'Amante anglaise* (produced and published, 1968; translated, 1975), and *L'Eden Cinéma* (produced and published, 1977) were part of the company's repertory at the Odéon, the former Théâtre d'Orsay, and the Théâtre du Rond-Point. Claude Régy's imaginative direction of Madeleine Renaud, Michaël Lonsdale, Bulle Ogier, and Catherine Sellers led to memorable performances. Other plays have been staged by the Lucernaire theater group and at the Théâtre Marie Stuart. Duras has also collaborated on stage adaptations of two of Henry James's stories, "The Aspern Papers" and "The Beast in the Jungle," and written as well an adaptation of Strindberg's *Dance of Death*. In 1983 she was awarded the Grand Prix du Théâtre de l'Académie Française.

Duras's life–and probably her fiction–have been marked by her near-fatal alcoholism. Indeed, the narrator of *L'Amant* refers to alcohol as having played a God-like role in her life: "L'alcool a rempli la fonction que Dieu n'a pas eue, il a eu aussi celle de me tuer, de tuer" (Alcohol filled the function that God did not in my life, and it also functioned to kill me, to kill). The ravaged face of the narrator in *L'Amant*, like Duras's own, bears testimony to her disease. In the fiction, heavy drinking is a characteristic of the earlier protagonists, a trait which certain critics attributed to the then prevalent influence on French writers of Hemingway and the so-called American-style novel. Maria in *Dix Heures et demie du soir en été* drinks to deny that her husband is unfaithful to her with her best friend. Both the French actress in *Hiroshima mon amour* and Anne and Chauvin in the 1958 novel *Moderato Cantabile* (translated, 1960) drink to forget so that, paradoxically, they can remember and re-create an impossible love situation. Drinking in *Le Marin de Gibraltar* and the 1953 novel *Les Petits Chevaux de Tarquinia* (translated as *The Little Horses of Tarquinia*, 1960) makes reality more hospitable to characters' illusions. Duras's own bout with alcoholism has been graphically related by Yann Andréa, her faithful companion since 1980, in *M.D.* (1983), a book that, by its perfect resonance with Duras's own prose, reveals stylistically the symbiotic bond between the two. *M.D.* recounts Duras's torments in 1982 while undergoing treatment for alcoholism at the American Hospital in Paris. Duras herself has written of this painful but miraculous turning point in her life in *La Vie matérielle* (Material Life, 1987). In that series of *textes dits* (spoken texts) to Jérôme Beaujour, in which Duras discusses her life and her fiction, she recalls meeting Andréa at the seaside resort of Trouville. Since that time, he has been at her side and is the subject of *L'Homme atlantique* (The

Atlantic Man), her 1981 film, published as a *récit* in 1982. He is also the probable referent for the male companion of the older female narrator in *Emily L.* In *La Vie matérielle* Duras discloses that she has forsaken her sixth-arrondissement Parisian dwelling for her apartment at Trouville where she spends most of her time. She also maintains a country home at Neauphle-le-Château which is featured in photographs in Michelle Porte's *Les Lieux de Marguerite Duras.*

It is clear that the intertwining of Duras's life experiences with those of her protagonists is a hallmark of her fiction. The zigzag narrative style of *L'Amant* is characteristic of the Durassian corpus as a whole. In *L'Amant* the narrator darts back and forth from the past to the present following the meanderings of memory and refers to herself both in the autobiographical first-person as well as in the more impersonal and fictional third-person narration. The refusal to occupy a fixed place or space and the anxious search for wholeness or identity as the motivating force of desire are equated with the task of writing the text in Duras's work. While certain themes persist—remembering, forgetting, desiring, and crossing boundaries—the stylistic and generic rendition of these themes varies. Fragments of past "texts," both fictional and actually experienced, reappear as if remembered, or relived, in more recent works. Duras seems to have found her particular voice in the late 1950s, in *Moderato Cantabile* and most especially in *Le Ravissement de Lol V. Stein* (1964; translated as *The Ravishing of Lol V. Stein,* 1967). Influenced perhaps by the New Novelists, with whom she was associated but from whom she distinguished herself by her lyrical style (Alain Robbe-Grillet is said to have called her the "Edith Piaf of the *nouveau roman*"), Duras progressively pared her texts down to all but the essential elements of her story of sustained desire, so as to emulate better her themes. *L'Amant* exemplifies this technique in that it is a "lightened" version of *Un Barrage contre le Pacifique* which, stripped of its epic sweep, reorchestrates poetically a past affective moment, the sensuousness and futility of a fifteen-year-old's desire. The music of memory and desire is sustained in these repetitions, and both writer and reader are left with the intangible reality of what Duras has called in her résumé of *India Song* "une histoire d'amour immobilisée dans la culminance de la passion" (a story of love immobilized in the culminating moment of passion). Far from a reduction of her story of desire, the Durassian rephrasings in

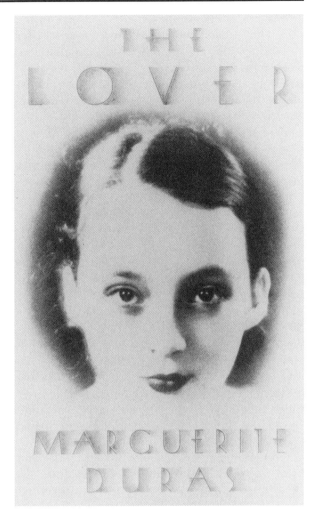

Dust jacket for Barbara Bray's 1985 translation of L'Amant. *The jacket photograph shows Duras in 1932, when she was eighteen.*

counterpoint accentuate the complexities and contradictions of a universal memory of an impossible love, or wholeness, which she delivers to the reader. Our task is to rewrite the story, transporting it to new narrative regions, as she indicated in the introduction to *India Song*: "de faire basculer le récit dans l'oubli pour le laisser à la disposition d'autres mémoires que celles de l'auteur" (to topple the story into oblivion so as to leave it at the disposition of other memories different from those of the author). In effect, Duras creates a gap of desire, memory, and meaning which is bridged through the medium of her writing and the reader's reading of her writing, which she sees in *La Vie matérielle* as "écriture flottante . . . ces aller-et-retour entre moi et moi, entre vous et moi dans ce temps qui nous est commun" (floating writing . . . these round trips between myself and myself, between you and me in this time which we share).

The swing between self and other, reader and writer, past and present is an intangible that Duras aims to conjure up for her reader, and it explains the questioning of borders that her work explores thematically, structurally, and compositionally. For example, characters are often confused, such as Alissa and Elisabeth in *Détruire, dit-elle*. The narrator of *Le Ravissement de Lol V. Stein*, Jacques Hold, abdicates narrative responsibility halfway through the text and admits to inventing the story of a woman whose very sense of self is built on a void. Interrogations of genre abound. Oftentimes, Duras's titles bear indications of how one is to read them. *India Song* is subtitled *texte-théâtre-film*. Duras referred to *Moderato Cantabile* as a poem and to *La Vie matérielle* as *textes dits*, or rewritten conversations. The 1976 film *Son Nom de Venise dans Calcutta désert* (Her Name of Venice in Deserted Calcutta) employs the same sound track as *India Song* with different images, those of a deserted chateau. In *Le Camion*, Duras and Depardieu are filmed reading the script of a movie called *Le Camion*, a work which "might have been," in alternation with footage of the film itself. The boundaries of fiction and reality are stretched in all of Duras's works but especially in *L'Amant*, *La Vie matérielle*, and *Emily L.*, which is the only one of the three she chose to designate as a novel. As Duras continually weaves and unravels her story for the reader, she spins an invisible thread of memory and desire at the borders and in the gaps of traditional narrative modes. Thus, the Durassian fictional thrust is progressively transgressive and the gradual breakdown in character psychology, narrative structures, and genre leads to the "free circulation of desires" which Xavière Gauthier posits as the point of convergence of the works.

A brief overview of the fiction confirms this trajectory. The early novels, *Les Impudents*, *La Vie tranquille*, and *Un Barrage contre le Pacifique*, portray young heroines in search of male companions to complete their boring, empty lives. Passive and lethargic, these women have not yet experienced the passionate love which will mark later protagonists who mourn melancholically the loss of such loves. Maud, Françou, and Suzanne are dominated by a brother and/or mother, and the plot revolves around their attempts to extricate themselves from family control. The suffocation and *ennui* of the settings of these novels recur, especially in *Les Petits Chevaux de Tarquinia*, where marital life is rendered in its quotidian mo-

notony, as well as in *L'Après-midi de Monsieur Andesmas* (1962; translated as *The Afternoon of Monsieur Andesmas*, 1964), where the loneliness of the aged male protagonist is juxtaposed with the gaiety of a village dance in the valley below, where his granddaughter is having an affair with a married man.

With *Le Marin de Gibraltar*, a slightly different fictional prototype develops. Anna's exotic travels on her yacht in search of a former lover, the sailor of the title, signal the futility of her task. In fact the very existence of the sailor is questioned by the strategies of the text. Her vagabondage and obsessive drinking in a torpid Mediterranean climate accentuate the void at the heart of her quest. This lack must be filled by the continual retelling of the tale of the sailor from Gibraltar. Echoes of Anna's travels and the self-conscious text reappear in Duras's script for Resnais's *Hiroshima mon amour* in which a French actress, in Japan to make a film about World War II, journeys mentally to her past in occupied France where she fell in love with a German soldier. The confusion of a past illicit love with a present one–her affair with a married Japanese architect–in a city that is a constant reminder of a tragic past situates the film's *élan* in the transgressive meanderings of memory and desire. In *Dix Heures et demie du soir en été*, infidelity and quest are rendered in a more fragmented, rhythmic style. The story of Maria, who is caught in a triangular situation with her unfaithful husband Pierre, is marked by free indirect discourse and scenic fragmentation so as to orchestrate allusively the perturbations of its protagonist. Maria's fugue with a criminal in a city besieged by violent storms is Duras's indirect affirmation of the destructive nature of love.

Infidelity, triangles, and musical motifs recur in *Moderato Cantabile*, which has been variously described as the "x-ray of a depression" (by Julia Kristeva in a 1987 *PMLA* article) and "Madame Bovary rewritten by Bela Bartok" (Claude Roy, in the afterword to the 1958 Minuit edition). This work portrays another illicit relationship, albeit a verbal one. Anne Desbaresdes, the wife of a local industrialist, and Chauvin, one of his workers, become enamored of one another after witnessing a crime of passion in which a deranged husband kills his unfaithful wife. They meet for a week in the café near the scene of the crime to try to understand the motivation for such an act. Their re-creation of the tale as mutual seduction in an increasingly alcohol-blurred vision takes place against the backdrop of a weekly piano lesson. During the lesson, Anne's child refuses to render the Diabelli sonatina *comme il faut*, that is, *moderato cantabile*. The musical motif which furnishes the book with its title also informs its structure. The *moderato* principle (marital fidelity, bourgeois social conventions, objective narration) is played off the *cantabile* (passionate love, criminal madness, subjective vision) in a stylized evocation of emotional transport. As in *Hiroshima mon amour*, death and love merge in a powerful but masterfully controlled narrative of Eros's dark underside. The contrapuntal technique which had already emerged in *Dix Heures et demie du soir en été* is perfected in *Moderato Cantabile,* where characters' motives, incidents of plot, and bits of dialogue and decor are repeated in carefully orchestrated fragments. The self-consciousness of the couple's rewriting of the crime is a comment on the writing and reading of the text.

With *Le Ravissement de Lol V. Stein* begins the "saga" of what has come to be known as the India Cycle, comprising, in addition to *Le Ravissement de Lol V. Stein, Le Vice-Consul, L'Amour* (1971), the text *La Femme du Gange* (Woman of the Ganges) and the film of the same title (both 1973), and the film *Son Nom de Venise dans Calcutta désert.* Duras's adolescent experiences anchor the story of desire in reverberation and repetition throughout these texts and films but with a thematic and stylistic minimalism which accentuates a central affective experience. The repetition of selected detail, the continued breakdown of discursive style, and a blurring in characterization and scenery create a hallucinatory erotic effect. Duras has said of *Le Ravissement de Lol V. Stein* that, unlike *Moderato Cantabile,* which she considered a finished product, the story of Lol is still in the process of being written, spilling out from generic borders to be evoked simultaneously in film and text. Although the theatrical version of *India Song* was never produced, the hybrid genre form is significant of a narrative break that comes to define Duras's project.

The title of *Le Ravissement de Lol V. Stein,* like that of *Moderato Cantabile,* highlights the conflictual elements at play in the novel both thematically and structurally. *Ravissement,* or ravishing, suggests simultaneously a physical and emotional state, ecstasy and rape. The heroine of this story totters on the edge of annihilation, for she is nothing but the memory of a past episode in which she was figuratively voided. At the Munici-

pal Casino of T. Beach in S. Thala, Lol V. Stein is forsaken by her fiancé for a seductive, older woman, Anne-Marie Stretter. Her identity is thus crystallized in "lack," a fact echoed by the mysterious sonority of the setting S. Thala (es-tu là? [are you there?]). Like other Durassian protagonists, Lol can (re)live passionate desires only by being the excluded element in a romantic triangle. The triangular mediation of desire which serves as catalyst for the plot is underscored by the novel's tripartite division. However, what appears to be an ordered text is upset by the narrator's intrusion halfway into the novel to proclaim that he is simply inventing Lol's story, thereby voiding any verisimilitude. Identity of protagonist and text is questioned in this work where typographical indications such as unfinished sentences and blank spaces riddle the novel with holes and constitute its grounding in lack. Lol vainly seeks "le mot-trou" (the word-hole) which would allow her to express the pain of her existence, and it is precisely this word that the narrator Jacques Hold cannot hold or make whole.

In the same way that *Le Ravissement de Lol V. Stein* echoes faintly the triangular affairs, characters, and settings of previous novels such as *Le Marin de Gibraltar, Dix Heures et demie du soir en été, Moderato Cantabile,* and so forth, *Le Ravissement de Lol V. Stein* is itself echoed or distilled temporally, psychologically, and linguistically in *L'Amour,* an allegorical rendition of the Durassian triangle of desire, published in 1971. The anonymous characters in this text mime a ballet of desire on a beach, in effect remembering, reliving, and rewriting Lol's ravishing at the ball which frames the 1964 novel. Metaphor is concretized in this ravaged version of the Durassian story where the reader confronts a devastated world: daylight becomes the intense light of fire accompanied by sirens, cries of alarm, and black smoke, all of which signify a thematic and textual paroxysm of memory's return to a past, personal destruction. Emotional breakdown is conveyed indirectly by the contestation or destruction of textual coherency. The title of *L'Amour* is ironic in that the absence of love is necessary to sustain the act of desiring that the book performs in its open-ended, elliptical style. As in *Le Ravissement de Lol V. Stein,* both text and female protagonist are anchored in a sustained negation.

The character of Anne-Marie Stretter, who served merely to reinforce Lol's alienation or exclusion in *Le Ravissement,* emerges as a central Durassian figure in an earlier novel of the India

Cycle, *Le Vice-Consul*. The wife of the French ambassador to Calcutta, she is sought after by colonial society for her charm and beauty but remains aloof, almost indifferent to those around her. Stretter is modeled on a woman who left a lasting impression on Duras during her childhood in Indochina. A quiet, unassuming wife and mother, Elizabeth Striedter was rumored to have caused the suicide of a young lover which occasioned her move to Vinh Long, where Duras was living at the time. In various interviews, Duras has spoken of her shock in learning that such an apparently ordinary woman could hold the sway of death over another. Emblematic of a feminine silence that is mortal, Striedter/Stretter became the focus of a Freudian primal scene for Duras which eventually propelled her to write. In *La Vie matérielle*, Duras defines this shocking new awareness—of the power of death shrouded in the silence of certain women—as a "connaissance interdite." Because this "forbidden knowledge" did not correspond to the young Duras's social and moral universe, it was blocked verbally and emotionally from understanding, whence Duras's need to find a "vocable qui dirait que, très clairement, on sait ne pas comprendre ce qu'il y a à comprendre" (a word which would very clearly say that one knows how not to understand what there is to be understood).

The inability to understand and the search for a word—Lol's *mot-trou*—to express an affective and verbal insufficiency is at the heart of the Stretter character, who embodies in her very vagueness the Durassian protagonist anchored in a melancholic search. Her encounter with the vice-consul of the title is one of complicity and desire. The latter shot at a pack of lepers in the Shalimar gardens and has been consequently condemned to social and professional exile, not for the heinous nature of his crime but rather for the lack of apparent motivation behind it. Both Stretter and the vice-consul are gripped by an inexplicable and ineffable need to rebel against lack, public and personal. In India, their individual and social distress finds its counterpart in the hunger and poverty of Calcutta's needy. Unable to express their awareness of pain, suffering, and exile, they communicate nonverbally in a "dance of desire" at the embassy reception which, given the vice-consul's condemnation, is viewed by the guests as a scandalous transgression of accepted social custom. An inarticulate protestation resounds also in the vice-consul's cry of despair when he is rebuffed by Stretter. His plaintive wail, which flays the soundtrack of *India Song*, is emblematic of the *cri de l'écriture* (the cry of writing) as protest against the unbearable.

Juxtaposed with the story of Anne-Marie Stretter and the vice-consul in this novel is another tale of famished desire, that of the *mendiante*, a young beggar woman, crazed and pregnant, who wanders through the forests in search of a metaphoric food which would satisfy her hunger. Like the vice-consul she cannot articulate her desire by communicating with others but can only repeat a nonsensical word, *Battambang*. The cry of the beggar woman and the vice-consul, together with the latter's dance with Stretter which is itself mirrored by the anxious march of the beggar woman, embody the desire to know, to be (w)hole, and to conclude that propels the writing of this text. The presence of a narrator, Peter Morgan, who avows the difficulty of his task, that is, to write something about which he knows nothing, or the beggar woman's story, further emphasizes the impossibility of writing the whole/hole story and showcases writing as desire.

Duras's dissection of the thematics of writing is further explored in the *texte-théâtre-film India Song* by her accentuation of the discontinuous. In separating the visual from the verbal in the film, she opens up the story to its universal implications. *India Song* is a reduplication of *Le Vice-Consul* but with the characters projected into new narrative regions. As Duras explained in an interview, the reader/viewer is invited to a new place, one which is not only described by new narrative strategies but is also the experience of a radically different narration. In the film, Stretter, played by Delphine Seyrig, moves silently and languorously through the rooms of the embassy surrounded by her faithful lovers, who glide after her in phantomlike fashion. Simultaneously, four narrative voices in voice-over comment on Stretter's story, on other stories of impossible love, and on directives for staging/filming the story. Mingled with these narrative blurbs are disembodied voices of guests and gossipers at the reception and snatches of tango and blues music, the *Diabelli Variations*, and so forth. Visual and auditory clues suggest that Stretter has already committed suicide and thus indicate that the story being told in the film/text is a flashback. The external voices amplify the memory of Stretter's life by recalling others who have succumbed to desire. Past and present are mingled in a modulation of memories and desires where the music *in* the text becomes a music *of* the text grounded in an absent, yet ever-present, death. The reader/viewer experiences this sustaining of fragmentation and recomposition in the immediacy of its expression, and this unusual film experience prompted one critic to exhort the French moviegoer to leave his/her "Cartesianism" in the cloak-room.

With *India Song*, Duras elaborated most successfully her themes of remembering and desiring conflated as writing, in a musical and visual reverberation of the India Cycle texts together with fragments of preceding novels. In the film *Son Nom de Venise dans Calcutta désert*, Duras used the exact sound track of *India Song* while the camera panned the abandoned, ruined set of the latter so as to distill further her story into a musical evocation or memory of a film that was itself a memory.

Other works develop thematic concerns touched upon in this cycle. In *L'Amante anglaise*, the novel and play, for example, the implications of a female character's madness in the enactment of a macabre crime are left up to readers and/or spectators who are delivered evidence in the form of fragments of taped interviews with the accused. Thus the reader/spectator assumes the role of a jury member who must reconstitute both the crime and the motives behind it. That the crime consisted of dismembering a corpse and shipping the body fragments in several freight cars throughout France only underlines ironically and in a somewhat grotesque manner the reader's task–to put together the story and to uncover the motives–as well as the impossibility of that task since, at the end of the tale, the corpse's head has still not been located. Further heightening the disconcerting nature of the plot is the fact that it is based on an actual crime. The drama was first staged at the Théâtre National Populaire in 1968 by Madeleine Renaud and was revived in 1970 when it became a stock play in the Compagnie Renaud-Barrault's repertory.

The loss or absence of the missing word/head that would piece together a body and a text, thereby restoring identity and making *sense* out of apparent madness, is a familiar Durassian motif. It acts to play off one term against another in oppositions such as madness-reason, absence-presence, forgetting-remembering, silence-speech and, in *Le Ravissement de Lol V. Stein*, hole/whole. In keeping with this ongoing sustaining of reversals, texts such as *La Maladie de la mort* (1982; translated as *The Malady of Death*, 1986) and *L'Homme assis dans le couloir* (1980; translated as *The Seated*

Man in the Passage, 1983) sound the sadistic violence of erotic passion and the undercurrent of death present in love. Together with some of the short stories collected in *La Douleur*, they investigate the relationship of sex, power, and need. Duras's use of the *vous* form in *La Maladie de la mort*, as well as in *L'Homme atlantique*, continues to implicate her reader, seeming to suggest that conflicting emotions are human and that every heroic or affirming action is capable of being reversed. By blurring boundaries between contradictories and within identities or categories, Duras trangresses thematically and textually black-and-white ways of thinking. *L'Homme atlantique* is a static moving picture about a film that "will be" made. *La Maladie de la mort* could equally well be entitled "La Maladie de l'amour," as Maurice Blanchot has indicated in his *La Communauté inavouable* (The Unavowable Community, 1983): "Ainsi revient la duplicité du mot *mort*, de cette maladie de la mort qui désignerait tantôt l'amour empêché, tantôt le pur mouvement d'aimer l'un et l'autre appelant l'abîme . . ." (Thus returns the duplicity of the dead word/of the word *dead*, of this malady of death which at times would designate thwarted love, at other times, the pure movement of loving, each of them summoning the abyss . . .).

The political implications of collapsing categories in the interplay of desire and violence, love and death, redemption and guilt, inflicting and receiving pain is brought home in *La Douleur*, a collection of six texts set in France at the end of World War II. Duras's pretense of having found the manuscript in a drawer where it sat for forty years is perhaps most interesting for the dimension of verisimilitude that it seeks to convey. Intending perhaps to plunge her reader into the actuality of the past, Duras's narrator tells of her anxious grief in awaiting the return of her husband, Robert L., from a prisoner-of-war camp. She loyally nurses him back to life with the support of D., the man whose child she would bear and for whom she wants to divorce Robert L. To anyone familiar with the author's life, Duras, her first husband Robert Antelme, and Dionys Mascolo are thinly disguised in this *récit*. As Francine du Plessix Gray commented (*New York Times Book Review*, 4 May 1986), "the sorrow of waiting becomes encrusted" in this spare prose which contains an outpouring of indignation at the sight of so many private and public tragedies. Outrage, loss, and the redemptive powers of love are so skillfully written here that, quite simply, the word *écrit* (writing/the written) does not apply, as Duras accurately indicates in the preface. The final cameo of the restored near-victim of Dachau smiling at his wife after having lost her to another man, his sister to the Nazis, and much of his physical strength is a compelling portrait of the regeneration after death that defined the times. Yet, in this very same collection there are three texts, also autobiographical, in which Duras questions heroic action and redemption. In "Monsieur X., dit ici Pierre Rabier" (Mr. X, here called Pierre Rabier) she relates her involvement in a compromising situation with a Gestapo agent whom, in a postwar trial, she testifies both for and against. "Albert des Capitales" (Albert of the Capitals) and "Ter le milicien" (Ter the Militiaman) concern the brutal torture of Nazi informers in which Duras and other members of the Resistance were involved. In the preface to "Monsieur X," which she claims is founded on fact, Duras offers us these stories in "doubt," hoping to describe the dual-edged nature of any sanction and the swiftness with which victim can become victimizer.

In 1986 Duras published *Les Yeux bleus cheveux noirs* (translated as *Blue Eyes, Black Hair*, 1988), which was an attempt to rewrite *La Maladie de la mort*, as she herself indicated in *La Vie matérielle*. A description, at times crude, of a prostitute and a homosexual caught in the impossibility of their love, *Les Yeux bleus cheveux noirs* is an investigation of sexual difference, not only between male and female but also and especially of the homosexual nature of the heterosexual male. The direct, clipped style is cut through with interventions of a character called the actor. He plays a choruslike role and imagines a dramatization of what the love affair of this anonymous couple "would be like" if enacted on stage. Impotency rendered potent or possible through the imagination of art is an important theme in this self-conscious text which, like *La Maladie de la mort*, engages the reader (through the interruptions of the actor) in a voyeuristic obsession reminiscent of scenes in *Le Ravissement de Lol V. Stein*.

More "joyous" a work, published in the same year, *La Vie matérielle* is a patchwork of digressive essays sprinkled with *sagesse* and humor in which Duras expresses her thoughts on a variety of topics, running the gamut from shopping lists to alcoholism. This range of subjects prompted Philippe Aubert (*Monde*, 7 October 1987) to qualify the work as "l'irruption surréaliste de l'Ajax et du Nescafé dans la cosmogonie de Marguerite Duras" (the surrealistic eruption of Ajax and Nescafé into the cosmogony of Marguerite Duras). At first glance an inconsequential work written to amuse and "pass the time," *La Vie matérielle* renders nonetheless a Durassian vision of the world where something is nothing, the material is intangible, and the impossible is seen as possible. Duras playfully engages the reader in this work which falls between the cracks of traditional genre classification in its blend of journalism, fiction, and autobiography.

Emily L. is the most recent of Duras's texts but one in which she picks up the threads of her preceding works and theme preoccupations in her ongoing story of paradox and (im)possibility. In part a rewriting of *Le Marin de Gibraltar*, in part a reinscription of the colonial experience of her youth, this novel is a meditation on the fear at the heart of writing and loving in their rapport with otherness, the other. Set in Normandy, *Emily L.* is a tale-within-a-tale, and each plays off or mirrors the other. The female narrator and her male companion, indubitably Duras and Yann Andréa, recount and "invent" the story of Emily L. and the Captain while simultaneously reflecting on their own impossible love affair. The fear which governs both stories is identified by the narrator as the silent underside of reason, what she calls the "congenial madness" of a reclusive self reaching out to the otherness of reason. Self-conscious statements about the fear of writing and about the fear of loving bathe this text in a generalized anxiety in which borders between writing and loving, concluding and dying, self and other, autobiography and fiction are suspended. Echoes of *L'Amant* and *Le Ravissement de Lol V. Stein* are manifest in the theme of an absence which generates the text. Just as *L'Amant* springs from an absent photo which, had it been taken, "would have captured" the past, likewise, in *Emily L.*, an absent poem—one written by Emily L. and destroyed by the Captain—"would have told" the story of the fear and exclusion at the heart of writing and loving. Like Lol and Anne-Marie Stretter, the *mendiante* and the vice-consul before them, Emily L. and the female narrator each experience the uneasiness of *not* seeing or *not* knowing, the *connaissance interdite* which Madame Striedter symbolized for Duras who incarnated her in Anne-Marie Stretter.

It is difficult to conclude a study of an author who has continually expressed the inability to conclude and is indeed still engaged in writing. From the earliest novels to the most recent, the trajectory of Duras's fictional enterprise remains firmly entrenched in desire–the desire to know how to understand and express that which continually slips away from human understanding, what Julia Kristeva has so accurately characterized as the "whiteness of meaning" at the heart of Duras's rhetoric. It is this impulse which informs the Durassian corpus and has established Marguerite Duras as a powerful and memorable voice in twentieth-century French fiction.

Interviews:

Xavière Gauthier, *Les Parleuses* (Paris: Editions de Minuit, 1974); translated by Katharine A. Jensen as *Woman to Woman* (Lincoln & London: University of Nebraska Press, 1987);

Susan Husserl-Kapit, "An Interview with Marguerite Duras," *Signs: Journal of Women and Culture in Society*, 1 (Winter 1975): 423-434;

Michelle Porte, *Les Lieux de Marguerite Duras* (Paris: Editions de Minuit, 1977).

References:

Sanford S. Ames, ed., *Remains to be Seen: Essays on Marguerite Duras* (New York: Peter Lang, 1988);

Yann Andréa, *M.D.* (Paris: Editions de Minuit, 1983);

Arc, special issue on Duras, 98 (1985);

Maurice Blanchot, *La Communauté inavouable* (Paris: Editions de Minuit, 1983), pp. 51-93;

Cahiers de la Compagnie Madeleine Renaud–Jean-Louis Barrault, special issues on Duras, no. 52 (December 1965); no. 89 (October 1979); no. 106 (September 1983);

Alfred Cismaru, *Marguerite Duras* (New York: Twayne, 1971);

Yvonne Guers-Villate, *Continuité/Discontinuité de l'œuvre durassienne* (Brussels: Editions de l'Université de Bruxelles, 1985);

Julia Kristeva, "The Pain of Sorrow in the Modern World: The Works of Marguerite Duras," *PMLA*, 102 (March 1987): 138-152;

Suzanne Lamy and André Roy, *Marguerite Duras à Montréal* (Montreal: Editions Spirale, 1981);

Marcelle Marini, *Territoires du féminin avec Marguerite Duras* (Paris: Editions de Minuit, 1977);

Michèle Montrelay, *L'Ombre et le nom sur la féminité* (Paris: Editions de Minuit, 1977);

Carol J. Murphy, *Alienation and Absence in the Novels of Marguerite Duras* (Lexington, Ky.: French Forum Monographs, 1982);

Jean Pierrot, *Marguerite Duras* (Paris: José Corti, 1986);

Rencontre des "Cahiers Renaud-Barrault" avec Marguerite Duras, Madeleine Renaud, Jean-Louis Barrault, Claude Régy, les spectateurs et les comédiens de la compagnie, Cahiers de la Compagnie Renaud–Barrault, no. 91 (September 1976);

Revue des Sciences Humaines, special issue on Duras, 202 (April-June 1986);

Trista Selous, *The Other Woman: Feminism and Femininity in the Work of Marguerite Duras* (New Haven: Yale University Press, 1988);

Jean-Luc Seylaz, *Les Romans de Marguerite Duras* (Paris: Minard, 1963);

Alain Vircondelet, *Marguerite Duras ou le temps de détruire* (Paris: Seghers, 1972);

Sharon Willis, *Marguerite Duras: Writing on the Body* (Urbana & Chicago: University of Illinois Press, 1987).

Romain Gary
(Romain Kacew)
(8 May 1914-2 December 1980)

Bette H. Lustig
Tufts University

BOOKS: *Forest of Anger*, translated by Viola Gerard Garvin (London: Cresset, 1944); French version published as *Education européenne* (Paris: Calmann-Lévy, 1945); translated as *A European Education* (New York: Simon & Schuster, 1960); revised as *Nothing Important Ever Dies* (London: Cresset, 1960); French edition revised and enlarged (Paris: Club de Libraires de France, 1961);

Tulipe (Paris: Calmann-Lévy, 1946; definitive edition, Paris: Gallimard, 1970);

Le Grand Vestiaire (Paris: Gallimard, 1948); translated by Joseph Barnes as *The Company of Men* (New York: Simon & Schuster, 1950);

Les Couleurs du jour (Paris: Gallimard, 1952); translated by Stephen Becker as *The Colours of the Day* (New York: Simon & Schuster, 1953; London: Joseph, 1953; revised, London: White Lion, 1976);

Les Racines du ciel (Paris: Gallimard, 1956); translated as *The Roots of Heaven* (New York: Simon & Schuster, 1958; London: Joseph, 1958); definitive French edition (Paris: Gallimard, 1980);

L'Homme à la colombe, as Fosco Sinibaldi (Paris: Gallimard, 1958); definitive edition, as Romain Gary (Paris: Gallimard, 1984);

Lady L, English version (New York: Simon & Schuster, 1959; London: Joseph, 1959); French version (Paris: Gallimard, 1963);

La Promesse de l'aube (Paris: Gallimard, 1960); translated by John Markham Beach as *Promise at Dawn* (New York: Harper, 1961; London: Joseph, 1962);

Johnnie Cœur (Paris: Gallimard, 1961);

The Talent Show, translated by Beach (New York: Harper, 1961; London: Joseph, 1961); French version published as *Les Mangeurs d'étoiles* (Paris: Gallimard, 1966);

Gloire à nos illustres pionniers (Paris: Gallimard, 1962); translated by Richard Howard as *His-*

Romain Gary

sing Tales (New York: Harper & Row, 1964; London: Joseph, 1964);

Pour Sganarelle: Recherche d'un personnage et d'un roman (Paris: Gallimard, 1965);

The Ski Bum (New York: Harper & Row, 1965); French version published as *Adieu Gary Cooper* (Paris: Gallimard, 1969);

La Danse de Gengis Cohn (Paris: Gallimard, 1967); translated by Gary and Camilla Sykes as *The Dance of Genghis Cohn* (New York: World, 1968; London: Cape, 1969);

La Tête coupable (Paris: Gallimard, 1968); translated as *The Guilty Head* (New York: World, 1969);

Chien blanc (Paris: Gallimard, 1970); translated as *White Dog* (New York: World, 1970; London: Cape, 1971);

Les Trésors de la Mer Rouge (Paris: Gallimard, 1971);

Europa (Paris: Gallimard, 1972); translated by Gary and Barbara Bray (Garden City, N.Y.: Doubleday, 1978);

Les Enchanteurs (Paris: Gallimard, 1973); translated by Helen Eustis as *The Enchanters* (New York: Putnam's, 1975);

The Gasp (New York: Putnam's, 1973; London: Weidenfeld & Nicolson, 1973); French version published as *Charge d'âme* (Paris: Gallimard, 1977);

Les Têtes de Stéphanie, as Shatan Bogat (Paris: Gallimard, 1974); translated by J. Maxwell Brownjohn as *Direct Flight to Allah*, by René Deville (London: Collins, 1975);

La Nuit sera calme (Paris: Gallimard, 1974);

Gros-Câlin, as Emile Ajar (Paris: Mercure de France, 1974);

Au-delà de cette limite votre ticket n'est plus valable (Paris: Gallimard, 1975); translated by Sophie Wilkins as *Your Ticket Is No Longer Valid* (New York: Braziller, 1977); republished as *The Way Out* (London: Joseph, 1977);

Les Oiseaux vont mourir au Pérou; Gloire à nos illustres pionniers (Paris: Gallimard, 1975);

La Vie devant soi, as Emile Ajar (Paris: Mercure de France, 1975); translated by Ralph Manheim as *Momo* (Garden City, N.Y.: Doubleday, 1978); republished as *The Life Before Us* (New York: New Directions, 1986);

Pseudo, as Emile Ajar (Paris: Mercure de France, 1976);

Clair de femme (Paris: Gallimard, 1977);

La Bonne Moitié (Paris: Gallimard, 1979);

Les Clowns lyriques (Paris: Gallimard, 1979);

L'Angoisse du roi Salomon, as Emile Ajar (Paris: Mercure de France, 1979); translated as the title work in *King Solomon* (1983);

Les Cerfs-volants (Paris: Gallimard, 1980);

Vie et mort d'Emile Ajar (Paris: Gallimard, 1981); translated as *The Life and Death of Emile Ajar* in *King Solomon* (1983);

King Solomon, translated by Barbara Wright (New York: Harper & Row, 1983; London: Harvill, 1983)—comprises *L'Angoisse du roi Salomon* and *Vie et mort d'Emile Ajar*.

MOTION PICTURES: *The Roots of Heaven*, adapted from Gary's novel *Les Racines du ciel*, screenplay by Gary and Patrick Leigh-Fermor, Twentieth Century-Fox, 1959;

Les Oiseaux vont mourir au Pérou/Birds in Peru, adapted from Gary's story, screenplay and direction by Gary, Regional Film Distributors, 1968;

Kill, screenplay and direction by Gary, Cocinor, 1971.

PERIODICAL PUBLICATIONS: "La Paz: The Man Who Ate the Landscape," *Holiday*, 24 (November 1958): 44, 46-47;

"Man Who Stayed Lonely to Save France," *Life*, 45 (8 December 1958): 144-146+ ;

"Colonials," *Holiday*, 25 (April 1959): 84-93;

"Party of One," *Holiday*, 27 (January 1960): 11+ ; 30 (July 1961): 8, 14-16, 18-19;

"Anger that Turned Generals into Desperados," *Life*, 50 (5 May 1961): 26-29;

"Here Is Might and Reassuring Promise," *Life*, 53 (21 December 1962): 4-5;

"Humanist," *Saturday Evening Post*, 236 (26 October 1963);

"Fake," *Ladies' Home Journal*, 80 (November 1963): 78-80;

"Oldest Story Ever Told," *Esquire*, 60 (December 1963): 144-147;

"I Know a Place in Paris," *Holiday*, 37 (January 1965): 54-57, 139-141;

"Twilight of the goddess?," *Ladies' Home Journal*, 82 (March 1965): 90-91;

"Flamboyant Guadeloupe," *Holiday*, 42 (August 1967): 54-59, 72-73;

"Dear Elephant, Sir," *Life*, 63 (22 December 1967): 126-139;

"Nympho in a Home Movie," *Time*, 92 (6 December 1968): 110-111;

"To Mon Général: Farewell, with Love and Anger," *Life*, 66 (9 May 1969): 26-29;

"Ode to the Man Who Was France," *Life*, 69 (20 November 1970): 42-44;

"La Vie dévalorisée," *Monde*, 15 November 1972, p. 13;

"Lettre ouverte de Romain Gary à l'Ambassadeur Jean Chauvel," *Figaro Littéraire*, 9 December 1972, pp. 1, 19;

"André Malraux ou l'honneur d'être un homme," *Monde*, 18 November 1977, p. 31.

Born Romain Kacew in Moscow 8 May 1914, Romain Gary spent the first fourteen years of his life in Russia and Poland. His mother, Nina Kacew, an actress and the daughter of a Russian-Jewish watchmaker, managed a millinery shop. Her husband, Lebja Kacew, was probably not Gary's father; he left his wife shortly after the child's birth. Although Gary never liked to discuss his father's identity, his recent biographer Dominique Bona theorizes convincingly that he was the son of the actor Ivan Mosjoukin. In Russia Nina Kacew's millinery business failed, and she and her son moved to furnished rooms in Warsaw. An ambitious, self-sacrificing woman, she prodded her son constantly and sought to direct his life. Despite her precarious financial situation, Kacew arranged for her son to have lessons in many areas in order to determine where his talents lay. His mother did not want him to become a painter, because she feared he would be indigent. He lacked the talent to be a violinist. She taught him French, and he began writing poetry in that language at the age of twelve.

In 1928 mother and son moved to Nice. For both of them France was the promised land. In France Nina Kacew presented him to others as a future ambassador. She expected him to defend her against others' insults, often provoked by her supercilious attitudes. In an effort to raise his status, she endeavored unsuccessfully to have him accepted by an exclusive tennis club. This humiliating experience, described in his memoir, *La Promesse de l'aube* (1960; translated as *Promise at Dawn*, 1961), was indelibly inscribed in his memory.

Prior to and during World War II Gary served as a pilot with the French Air Force (1937-1940) and with the Free French Air Force and the British Royal Air Force (1940-1945) in Africa, Russia, and Palestine. He began writing fiction when he was in the military. His first novel, *Education européenne*, published in English translation as *Forest of Anger* in 1944 and then in French in 1945, received the Prix des Critiques. For his military service Gary was awarded the Croix de Guerre and the Croix de la Libération; he was also made a Chevalier de la Légion d'Honneur. When Gary returned home from the war, he discovered that his mother had died of cancer in 1942. Gary was offered the presidency of the council on the administration of the brothels in France, but, with his *licence* in law from the University of Paris and a diploma in Slavic languages from the University of Warsaw, he began a diplomatic career. During his years as a diplomat he served in Sofia, Bulgaria; in Paris; in Berne; and as spokesman for the French delegation to the United Nations, first in New York, then in London. After his assignment in New York, apparently suffering from exhaustion, he was given a three-month leave, which he devoted to working on his Goncourt Prize-winning novel, *Les Racines du ciel* (1956; translated as *The Roots of Heaven*, 1958). After assuming for a short time in early 1956 the post of chargé d'affaires in La Paz, Bo-

livia, he became consul general at Los Angeles, a position he held until 1960. In 1967 and 1968 he served as *chargé de mission* for the government of Georges Pompidou.

During these years Gary married twice. His first wife was the English writer Lesley Blanch, whom he divorced in 1963 to marry actress Jean Seberg, whom he divorced seven years later. Much of his life with Seberg and their involvement in the Civil Rights movement are described in Gary's *Chien blanc* (1970; translated that year as *White Dog*). They had a son, Diego, who lived for a while in Spain with his governess; these two were the models for Momo and Mme Rosa in *La Vie devant soi* (1975; translated as *Momo*, 1978). Because of her association with political radicals in the 1960s, Seberg became the focus of a scandal created by the F.B.I. in 1970 and described in bureau documents of the period as an attempt to "cheapen her image with the general public." A rumor was circulated that Seberg was expecting the child of a Black Panther leader, although Gary always claimed that the baby was his. The child was born prematurely (a result of her shock at hearing the lie, Seberg claimed) and died a few days later. Seberg made several attempts to take her own life. She succeeded on 8 September 1979.

During his diplomatic career Gary wrote nearly a dozen novels. His writing began as an escape from reality, and he never used the name he was given at birth on his published works. In 1958 he published a novel entitled *L'Homme à la colombe* under the pseudonym Fosco Sinibaldi; in 1974, under the name Shatan Bogat, another, *Les Têtes de Stéphanie*, appeared (it was translated in 1975 as *Direct Flight to Allah* and published under the pseudonym René Deville). Gary created what biographer and critic Herbert Lottman called "the literary hoax of the century" when he began publishing under the name Emile Ajar in the 1970s while continuing to write as Romain Gary. *Gari* is the imperative mood of the Russian verb *to burn*; he chose the Americanized form, Gary, partly in recognition of his idol at the time, Gary Cooper. The name *Ajar* is semantically close to *gari* because it is the Russian word for *live coals*. The name Emile came from Paul Gauguin's illegitimate son.

His decision to write as Emile Ajar stemmed from his pleasure in disguises and from a need for freedom. Discouraged with the way the critics had catalogued him and filed his work away for thirty years, he hoped that the Ajar signature would earn his works more attention from critics and the public alike. In order to succeed in his plan, he had his cousin Paul Pavlowitch appear as Ajar at interviews. Gary carefully orchestrated these meetings and advised Pavlowitch to refuse to pose for photographs. When one newspaper insisted on publishing a photo, Pavlowitch's good rapport with the photographer assured that half his face was hidden.

Writing as Ajar, Gary won his second Prix Goncourt for *La Vie devant soi*, although the award was accepted by Pavlowitch, in keeping with the hoax. He wrote two more books, *Pseudo* (1976) and *L'Angoisse du roi Salomon* (1979; translated as *King Solomon*, 1983), under the Ajar name. That Ajar's popularity was increasing and Gary's sales were dwindling was proof, he thought, that the critics were still not reading his works attentively. In *Pseudo*, a "pseudo-confession," Gary attempts in part to falsify some of the biographical information which Pavlowitch had inadvertently revealed in an interview with *Monde* correspondent Yvonne Baby. *Pseudo* mirrors the strained relationship between Pavlowitch and Gary. Pavlowitch was outraged at Gary's betrayal of confidentiality in *Pseudo*. Gary insisted that the anguish he revealed was his own. Gary asked Pavlowitch to write an explanation for publication after Gary's death. Pavlowitch wrote *L'Homme que l'on croyait* (The Man Whom One Believed), published in 1981, and Gary wrote his own account, *Vie et mort d'Emile Ajar* (translated as *The Life and Death of Emile Ajar* in *King Solomon*, 1983), published the same year.

The year before these volumes appeared, on 2 December 1980, Gary died from a self-inflicted gunshot wound. Many believed that his death was related to that of Seberg, fifteen months earlier, but Gary left a suicide note in which he asserted: "No connection to Jean Seberg.... Obviously one could blame this on nervous depression. But then, one would have to admit that it had lasted since I reached manhood and had permitted me to carry on my literary work.... Perhaps one must seek the answer in the title of my autobiography, 'The Night Will Be Peaceful' [*La Nuit sera calme*, 1974]. And in the last words of my last novel.... 'I have finally explained myself fully.'"

Gary's first novel, *Education européenne*, depicts, amid the hardships of hunger, bitter cold, sickness, danger, and death experienced by partisans of the Polish Resistance, a mosaic of friendship, courage, imagination, and hope. The title sig-

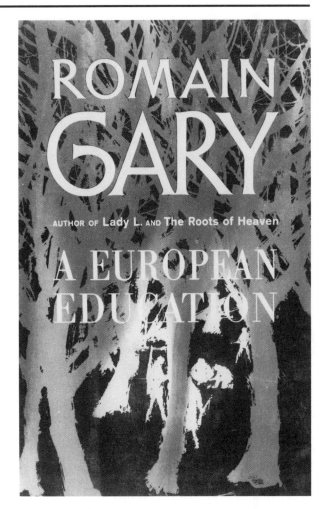

American edition dust jacket for the 1960 translation of Gary's award-winning first novel

nifies the juxtaposition of the great European universities, libraries, and cathedrals, and the ideals they were founded to promote, with the monstrous forms of destruction brought about by the war. Janek personifies this duality, because his love of music enables him to try to save from the partisans Augustus Schröder, a pianist and a maker of music boxes whose son is a Nazi. Yet this same compassionate mind conceives and cold-bloodedly perpetrates the murder of a German soldier. The myth, as Gary called the ennobling spirit which elevates human behavior above bestiality, is personified in the Messianic figure of Nadejda, a character in one of the stories within the novel, narrated by the partisan Adam Dobranski to distract his cohorts from their suffering. Nadejda is symbolized by the nightingale singing in the forest, as one sings alone at night to give oneself hope.

The metaphor of the nightingale, recurring in Gary's second novel, *Tulipe*, published in 1946, signifies the indestructibility of hope and courage. *Tulipe* is a short, dense work announcing several themes reappearing in later works: the hope for the evolution of more humane humans in the future, the coexistence of good and evil in man, the relationship between imposture and authenticity in the twentieth century, and the dichotomy between European historical culture or civilization and modern technology. Especially important is the stylistic similarity between *Tulipe* and the four later novels Gary wrote under the name Emile Ajar. "Tout Emile Ajar se trouvait déjà dans *Tulipe*" (All of Emile Ajar was already found in *Tulipe*), noted Gary in *Vie et mort d'Emile Ajar*, a statement with which Michel Tournier concurs in his *Le Vol du vampire* (The Vampire's Flight, 1981), adding that both use the same naive yet cruel humor.

Dedicated to his first wife, Lesley Blanch, Gary's third novel, *Le Grand Vestiaire* (1948; translated as *The Company of Men*, 1950), was hardly noticed in France, although the English translation became a best-seller in the United States. Ben Ray Redman wrote in *Saturday Review* (3 June 1950): "Romain Gary knows how to tell a story, how to hold his reader's interest on a tight rein; even better, he can people his tale with characters that exist uniquely yet convincingly. *The Company of Men* is singularly free of stock types and to say this of any novel is to say a great deal." In *Yale French Studies* (no. 8 [1951]), Jean Boorsch remarked that, on the basis of his first three novels, "Gary can be numbered among the greatest hopes of the new generation of novelists . . . [to] be counted on to throw more light on the human condition and the pitiful passion it entails."

Narrated in flashback in the first person by Luc Martin, who must come to grips with life following the death of his father, *Le Grand Vestiaire* describes the sordid lower echelons of Parisian society with Balzacian relish. Sleazy characters, shady financial dealings, and poor health form the backdrop of Luc's life as a Resistance orphan sent to Paris where he meets and lives with two other vagabonds, Léonce and Josette. In order to survive, this brother and sister exchange their illegal earnings for shelter with Gustave Vanderputte, a Nazi collaborator and thus a character whose beliefs are diametrically opposed to the ideals for which Luc's father died.

The pervasive psychological atmosphere of the novel is extreme loneliness. Luc accepts learning the survival skills of the Paris underworld, because he has no choice materially or emotionally. Vanderputte's loneliness, however, is that of an exile from humanity and, as such, is even worse. Observing the gestures and listening to the conversations of the sadomasochistic pair, Vanderputte, a criminal, and Kuhl, a police officer, Luc realizes they are drawn together to escape utter isolation. The pathologically impeccable Kuhl is a forerunner of the character of the baron appearing in Gary's next novel, *Les Couleurs du jour* (1952; translated as *The Colours of the Day*, 1953).

Vanderputte, in agony from a tooth abscess, tries to justify his Nazi collaboration to the dentist from whom he seeks treatment, explaining that his efforts affected mostly Jews. Dr. Lejbowitch, a Romanian Jew, refuses to treat him. The moral question raised here is similar to the one posed in Simon Wiesenthal's novel *Die Sonnenblume* (*The Sunflower*, 1970): can a Jew forgive a Nazi who, on his deathbed, asks for pardon? He cannot, wrote Wiesenthal, because he has no right to assume responsibility for the millions who were murdered. Gary's answer to the question is different: Vanderputte, he suggests, has lived too long and been rejected too often to be accountable to society, but his wretched state, rejected by Dr. Lejbowitch, reflects mankind's guilt in refusing to show compassion, to pardon.

At the monastery where Luc is refused shelter, he notes that the monk's frock, the sleeves billowing in the breeze, resembles a shell, a costume; it is a sham, not an indication of compassion within. Where are the men that his father said would take care of him? These are not human beings, but ridiculous masses of clothing walking around–a wardrobe only ("Le Grand Vestiaire")–with no hearts inside.

Written in a lyrical style, *Les Couleurs du jour* is a novel about the many facets of erotic love. In this work, made into the 1959 film *The Man Who Understood Women*, Gary creates tension between the happiness of some and the unhappiness of others, fantasy and reality, guilt and honor. The title, referring to the means by which RAF pilots distinguished friends from enemies, means, in the language of love, the use of the feminine "colors" of tolerance, sensitivity, and freedom over lies, hypocrisy, and deceit. This comic novel, set in Nice, was well received by the critics.

Influenced by fellow Slav Joseph Conrad, Gary wrote his first Goncourt Prize-winning novel, *Les Racines du ciel*. Although his book is considered by some to be the first novel on ecology,

Gary explained in an author's note that he wrote the work to focus upon the protection of the human environment in the global sense of respect for humanity, freedom, space, and generosity. Begun in New York in 1952 and completed upon his arrival as consul general in Los Angeles, in its English translation *Les Racines du ciel* sold over three hundred thousand copies in the United States.

Narrated by the missionary Saint-Denis in a series of flashbacks, in a time frame of less than twenty-four hours, *Les Racines du ciel* recounts the campaign led by Morel against the senseless slaughter of African elephants. Variously viewed as a hero, a saint, and a fanatic, his briefcase bulging with petitions, Morel pleads for a margin of beauty in life, an area of refuge outside the strictly utilitarian. For Morel, the margin is indispensable; civilization cannot endure without it, although the need to defend this haven can be learned only through considerable suffering; thus the protection of elephants in Africa is part of several larger issues. Morel's friend and supporter Peer Qvist explains that the Mexican Indians call this need for protection, justice, and love the "tree of life." The Moslem term is the "roots of heaven."

Gary believed, like the paleontologist and explorer Pierre Teilhard de Chardin, who was one of his friends, that man's brain had not yet completely evolved. Gary, in an interview with John Weightman on *Les Racines du ciel* (*Newsweek*, 20 January 1958), stated that no progress will be made until man's whole biological nature changes. He considered "present man. . . . a biological misfit, a premature phenomenon." He thought scientific progress would begin "not in outer space, but in inner space" and would transform man so that he would "take the protection of nature and himself into his own hands." He predicted, moreover, that "the next 20,000 years would be difficult." Morel, whose name is close to *moral*, incarnates the future moral human being envisioned by Gary.

Published in 1965, Gary's critical and theoretical treatise *Pour Sganarelle: Recherche d'un personnage et d'un roman* (For Sganarelle: The Quest for a Character and a Novel) is a preface to his *Frère Océan* series, which includes *La Danse de Gengis Cohn* (1967; translated as *The Dance of Genghis Cohn*, 1968), *La Tête coupable* (1968; translated as *The Guilty Head*, 1969), and *Charge d'âme* (1977; published originally in English as *The Gasp*, 1973). Continuing his treatment of World

War II in *La Danse de Gengis Cohn*, Gary focuses on the Holocaust. Murdered by a Nazi firing squad, Gengis Cohn, whose name suggests both Gary's Cossack/Jewish ancestry and the aggressor/victim duality, enters as a dybbuk the subconscious of Schatz, the SS officer who ordered the execution. Whereas in life, as Moishe Cohn, he was a Jewish comic actor at the Schwarze Schickse Cabaret, in the afterlife he dances relentlessly in the psyche of Schatz, who cannot exorcise him despite continual efforts, including psychiatric treatment and attempted suicide. Twenty-five years after Cohn enters Schatz's mind, Schatz is a police chief investigating the murders of some forty men found lying with their trousers dropped and expressions of beatitude on their faces. To Schatz the crime seems unmotivated, and he can recall no precedent for such violence. To remind him of a precedent, the Holocaust, Cohn dances in rage. He will not cease dancing in Schatz's psyche, symbolizing Nazi Germany, until a world of humane beings is created.

The murders turn out to be connected to a nymphomaniac named Lily, who represents humanity. Each of the victims had tried to satisfy her sexually, and when they failed one by one, Lily's constant companion Florian, a eunuch, killed them. Lily is portrayed as abnormal, constantly desiring, hoping the day will come when she will be satisfied, yet always condemned to failure. What she seeks but cannot find is an act offered out of love. Lily is unsatisfied by contemporary man, because all he offers her are techniques, systems, and ideologies; the metaphor of virility set forth by Lily's many partners signifies politically Hitler's aggression. Loving humanity means considering humankind as sacred, and since contemporary human beings do not or cannot offer love, Florian kills them.

La Danse de Gengis Cohn is thus a *roman engagé*, a novel committed to reiterating emphatically, like Cohn's dance, the worst human suffering of the twentieth century, equal to the worst in human history. It is also in many ways a comic novel, sparkling with puns, literary allusions, gallows humor (such as Schatz's refusal to wash his hands with soap, because he never knows who—which Jew—is in it), and outrageous, bitterly ironic statements (in a cultured society mothers holding babies are exempt from digging their own graves). *La Danse de Gengis Cohn* received good reviews in the United States but met with a cool reception in France. In a 1968 interview with Louis Monier and Arlette Merchez for

Nouvelles Littéraires, Gary attributed the French reaction partly to the prejudice of Parisian critics against him (Gary's bête noire) and partly to a lack of understanding in France of the Ashkenazic Yiddish context. It is also possible that Gary's mention of French anti-Semitism may have alienated some.

The thematic thread of changing one form of racism for another, set forth in *La Danse de Gengis Cohn* in Cohn's refusal to join a fraternity that would scapegoat blacks, becomes a major consideration in *Chien blanc*, Gary's first work written in French on an American subject. *Chien blanc* is a nonfiction account of the progress of Gary's adopted dog, Batka, trained first to attack blacks, then taught by a black to accept them, and, finally, in a symmetry of hatred, retrained to attack whites. Set against the background of black insurrections and the Civil Rights movement of the 1960s, it is at once an informative document and a glimpse into the domestic life of Gary and Jean Seberg. No longer Uncle Toms, blacks become strangers or, in existential terms, the others. Batka finally attacks his master and dies on Gary's doorstep in, as one commentator put it, a state of "schizophrenic disarray"; "the message seems to be that black hatred of whites is even more self-defeating than white hatred of blacks."

Inspired by the personal tragedy of his close friend Ilona Gesmay, a schizophrenic, Gary wrote *Europa* (1972; translated, 1978), which, using the metaphor of schizophrenia, reverts thematically to *Education européenne* in its focus on the schism in Europe between barbarism and civilization. Danthès, who was French ambassador to Rome twenty-five years before the action of the novel begins, has chosen his diplomatic career over marriage to Malwina von Leyden because her promiscuity was unacceptable in his social circle and because, as the result of an automobile accident in which both he and she were involved, she was permanently paralyzed from the waist down. The vileness of his rejection in his youth of Malwina juxtaposed to the "immense culture" and presumably high moral standards of his maturity proves Danthès to be a living example of the dichotomy which puts culture on one side and society on the other.

Through the character Dr. Jarde, Gary presents the damaging effect on the human brain of the absence of love. Love consists in imagining from the heart, inventing, idealizing a person; to be dreamed by another is to be finally created; imagining or inventing takes the *other* out of an-

other. The baron, first seen as an ally of love in *Les Couleurs du jour*, reappears in *Europa* as the companion and counterpart of Malwina, who has become intent on avenging herself by bringing about Danthès's mental collapse. In his "Note to the American Edition" Gary defines the baron as either a "self-mocking idealist forever seeking to reach that unattainable goal, a truly noble man," or one whose "quest for impeccable distinction of soul and mind ends up in a purely vestmental elegance." *Europa* contrasts stylistically with the linear narrative of *Education européenne*. Structurally more complex, *Europa* is kaleidoscopic in its treatment of time and space as it moves, sometimes humorously, from one century and location to another, with a repetition of texts suggestive of the writings of Alain Robbe-Grillet.

In 1974, the same year that Gary's autobiographical work *La Nuit sera calme* appeared, he produced his first book published under the pseudonym Emile Ajar. Shortened by fifty pages before its publication by Mercure de France, *Gros-Câlin* (Big Hug) recounts the tragicomedy of Michel Cousin and his pet python Gros-Câlin. The theme of loneliness, present in other works by Gary, is treated half-humorously here: Cousin has a neighbor, Professor Tsourès (*troubles* in Yiddish), so preoccupied with massacres and persecutions that he never notices him; Cousin takes ventriloquy lessons to simulate a dialogue with himself; he is even rejected by a blind person he tries to help across a street. In the absence of love he seeks, like Fosco Zaga in the 1973 novel *Les Enchanteurs* (translated as *The Enchanters*, 1975), sexual gratification with prostitutes, including Mlle Dreyfus, a Guyanese woman he loves.

Love continues to be an important concern in the Ajar novels, as it is in works published during the same period under the name Gary. *Au-delà de cette limite votre ticket n'est plus valable* (1975; translated as *Your Ticket Is No Longer Valid*, 1977) treats a sexagenarian's waning sexuality, variously interpreted as a metaphor for the decline of the West and its increasing dependence on third-world countries and as the author's fear of failure with his partner, the reader. *La Vie devant soi*, published the same year and made into the 1977 Oscar-winning film *Madame Rosa*, starring Simone Signoret, concerns every aspect of love except the erotic. *La Vie devant soi* is the story of the solitary boy Momo (for Mohammed) in search of love.

Momo is cared for by Madame Rosa, a retired Jewish prostitute who shelters prostitutes' children. After he sells his dog, Super, to give the animal a better home, Momo dresses up an umbrella as the object of his affections and calls it Arthur. He has no mother and fantasizes that in her place a lioness, renowned for her protection of her cubs, comes at night and licks his face. When Momo goes to a dubbing studio and watches the rewinding of a film, his mind reels in reverse to a scene where, seated on the floor, he remembers seeing his mother's boots, her leather miniskirt, but, unfortunately, not her face. Continuing in this self-psychoanalytic direction, he remembers two arms holding him closely and rocking him to comfort him when he had a stomachache. It is from his presumed father, Kadir Youssef, released from a mental institution where he was sent following the murder of Momo's mother, that Momo learns that his mother was Aïcha, a prostitute.

His quest for his mother becomes part of a larger search for love: he talks about love with M. Hamil, who teaches him the Koran, and he tries to arrange a marriage between Mme Rosa, his symbolic mother, and M. Hamil, his symbolic father. After Mme Rosa's death, Dr. Ramon, a psychiatrist who has taped the whole story narrated in the first person by Momo, retrieves Arthur, because, as Momo says, "il faut aimer" (one has to love).

In the late 1970s, between his third Ajar work, *Pseudo*, and his fourth and final one, *L'Angoisse du roi Salomon*, he published, under the name of Gary, *Clair de femme* (1977), a short novel about two couples, which was not well received. In 1978 he translated his 1973 novel *The Gasp* into French as *Charge d'âme*. He also did some reworkings of earlier books, producing *La Bonne Moitié* (1979), a two-act comedy based on *Le Grand Vestiaire*, and *Les Clowns lyriques*, drawn from *Les Couleurs du jour*.

L'Angoisse du roi Salomon continues the Ajar novels' examination of love. M. Salomon Rubinstein, a wealthy retired king of the garment industry now devoted to easing the pain of others, operates a charity help line for old, lonely, and sometimes desperate souls. It is thus that Jean, an autodidactic taxi driver who is M. Salomon's partner and the narrator of the novel, becomes acquainted with Cora Lamenaire, in her younger days a singer in the tradition of Edith Piaf but now a lonely elderly woman. Cora is one member of the "endangered species" that is humanity whom Jean tries to save, first with sexual favors, although he is barely able to tolerate her physical ap-

pearance, and then by encouraging her to perform on stage at the Slush nightclub, a fiasco which results in her suicide attempt. As he did in *Les Racines du ciel*, Gary uses nature and wildlife metaphors in *L'Angoisse du roi Salomon*–birds in a sanctuary in Brittany, their feet glued to the ground presumably because of an oil spill, baby seals looking up at clubs raised to kill them–to represent the frailty of the human species. The preservation of endangered humanity consists in keeping alive a sense of self-respect resulting from the knowledge that someone cares.

Many metaphors in the Ajar novels, based on vernacular expressions, are less poetic than those in Gary's other works. *Bricoler*, meaning literally to repair things, is often used to signify mending people. Momo is a "bricoleur" who tries unsuccessfully to persuade M. Hamil to marry Mme Rosa to help them both. Jean is also a "mender" of people's lives. Another Ajarism is the term *prêt-à-porter*, meaning ready-made garments and used to suggest that life, from an infant's first cry, is not cut to order or custom-made but must be accepted as it happens. *Gros-Câlin* exhibits experiments in sound play ("feotuscisme . . . fettucini . . . fétichisme . . . fascisme"), and *Vie et mort d'Emile Ajar* contains malapropisms ("l'amnistie" for "l'amnésie," for example).

Circular, illogical sentences sometimes appear in the Ajar works. Mme Rosa says, "Jamais il ne pleure cet enfant-là et pourtant Dieu sait que je souffre" (He never cries, that child, and yet God knows that I suffer). In *L'Angoisse du roi Salomon* Jean says, "On s'est tu tous les deux, sauf que moi je n'avais pas parlé du tout" (We had both stopped talking, except that I had not spoken at all). These circular, oversimplified sentences leave gaps which the reader must complete. The text, as Pavlowitch observed, functions suggestively, requiring greater reader involvement, like works of the New Novelists. The style of writing is more concise, and the Ajar works contain fewer descriptive passages.

Closing the circle begun with his first book, *Education européenne*, on the Polish Resistance, Gary's last novel, *Les Cerfs-volants* (The Kites, 1980), recounts in flashback the Allies' invasion of Normandy and chronicles the bravery and imagination of members of the French Resistance. Among the characters are Julie Espinoza, a Jewish madam in Paris who poses as Countess Esterhazy to spy on the Germans; Marcellin Duprat, owner and chef of the gourmet restaurant Clos Joli, who is determined to defend

France's honor with her cuisine; Ambroise Fleury, a retired postman who flies kites displaying yellow stars in defiance of the Germans; Ludo Fleury, the narrator, who works saving Polish pilots; and, finally, the brave Germans General von Teile and Hans von Schwede, who die heroically for having attempted to assassinate Hitler.

After miraculously returning from Auschwitz via Russia, Ambroise is seen flying a kite bearing the image of Gen. Charles de Gaulle, symbolizing freedom. The kites, a metaphor of one's ideals or values, must be held tightly and not allowed to escape "dans la poursuite du bleu" (in pursuit of the blue sky) where they will be destroyed. Moral values for Gary are the mythology that separates humanity from bestiality, and they must never be allowed to perish. *Les Cerfs-volants*, a unanimous success, reveals Gary's optimistic side. He was no longer settling old scores. Frédéric Vitoux wrote in the *Nouvel Observateur* (14-18 June 1980), "Les romans de cette qualité ne sont pas légion" (Novels of this quality are not numerous).

Certain themes, theories, and characters are distinctive of Gary's novels. For example, Gary never lets his readers forget the horrors of the Holocaust. Closely related to his continual reminders of the Holocaust is the theme of the dichotomy of Europe, of civilization and culture versus barbarism or, in his later works, versus modern technology and dependence on the raw materials of third-world countries. The metaphor of schizophrenia, used to express the dichotomy of Europe, is another theme, closely tied to Gary's (and others') theories of the evolution of the human brain and to his observation of the human need for love and other feminine, Christlike qualities, such as mercy, gentleness, warmth, tenderness, and compassion—attributes that help one human being imagine or invent another. To imagine with the heart is to re-mythify humanity, to reestablish the scale of values by which the human being is considered sacred. No ideology justifies human suffering and death. Such is the work of the great twentieth-century imposters, of Hitler, Stalin, and Mussolini, whose activity Gary denounces in his novels as charlatanism and swindling.

The noble prostitute is a recurrent figure in Gary's works that underscores his belief that sexual immorality is neither the most dangerous nor the only kind. He considered intellectual immorality—minds that design hydrogen bombs or run death camps—far worse. The prostitutes in Gary's books, who usually sell their bodies to ensure the survival of others or are generous in different ways, are treated with respect. Sexual metaphors in Gary's works are often used politically with virility signifying loveless power or brute force and frigidity indicating the need of humanity to love humanity. The world of Romain Gary evokes moral visions and social truths. He will perhaps be best remembered for *Les Racines du ciel*, *La Vie devant soi*, and for his first novel, *Education européenne*.

Interviews:

John Weightman, "Talk with the Author [of *The Roots of Heaven*]," *Newsweek*, 51 (20 January 1958): 92-93;

Louis Monier and Arlette Merchez, "Je suis un irregulier," *Nouvelles Littéraires*, 31 October 1968, pp. 1, 14;

J. J. Brochier, "Mes Beatniks par Roman Gary," *Magazine Littéraire* (July 1969): 46-47;

Jean Montalbelti, "L'Amerique contre les démons," *Nouvelles Littéraires*, 9 April 1970, pp. 1, 11;

Georges Klarsfeld, "Roman Gary: Les Trafiquants ne sont pas des humains," *Nouvelles Littéraires*, 24-30 January 1972, p. 24;

Pierre Sipriot, "Entre deux c'est pour moi la seule unité concevable," *Figaro Littéraire*, 12-13 February 1977, pp. I, III.

Biography:

Dominique Bona, *Romain Gary* (Paris: Mercure de France, 1987).

References:

Judith Kaufman, "La Danse de Romain Gary ou Gengis Cohn et la valse-horà des mythes de l'Occident," *Etudes Littéraires*, 17 (April 1984): 71-94;

Alexandre Lorian, "Les Raisonnements déraisonnables d'Emile Ajar," *Hebrew University Studies in Literature and the Arts* (Spring 1987): 120-145;

Bette H. Lustig, "Emile Ajar Demystified," *French Review*, 57 (December 1983): 203-212;

Jane McKee, "The Symbolic Imagination of Romain Gary," *Maynooth Review*, 2 (6 May 1982): 60-71;

Paul Pavlowitch, *L'Homme que l'on croyait* (Paris: Fayard, 1981);

Eli Pfeffercorn, "The Art of Survival: Romain Gary's *La Danse de Gengis Cohn*," *Modern Language Studies*, 10 (Fall 1980): 76-80;

Leonardo Sciascia, "Le Visage sur le masque," *Nouvelle Revue Française*, no. 356 (September 1982): 40-44;

N. Sjursen, "A Python as a Pampered Animal, or The Double Man Gary-Ajar," *Revue Historique*, 88, no. 2 (1988): 342-343;

Ted Spivey, "Man's Divine Rootedness in the Earth: Romain Gary's Fiction," in his *The Journey Beyond Tragedy* (Gainesville: University Presses of Florida, 1980), pp. 126-138;

Michel Tournier, "Emile Agar ou la vie derrière soi," in his *Le Vol du vampire* (Paris: Gallimard, 1981), pp. 340-355.

Julien Gracq
(Louis Poirier)
(27 July 1910-   )

Carol J. Murphy
University of Florida

BOOKS: *Au château d'Argol* (Paris: José Corti, 1938); translated by Louise Varèse as *The Castle of Argol* (London: Owen, 1951; Norfolk, Conn.: New Directions, 1951?);

Un Beau Ténébreux (Paris: José Corti, 1945); translated by W. J. Strachan as *A Dark Stranger* (London: Drummond, 1950; New York: New Directions, 1950?);

Liberté grande (Paris: José Corti, 1947);

André Breton, Quelques aspects de l'écrivain (Paris: José Corti, 1948);

Le Roi pêcheur (Paris: José Corti, 1948);

La Littérature à l'estomac (Paris: José Corti, 1950);

Le Rivage des Syrtes (Paris: José Corti, 1951); translated by Richard Howard as *The Opposing Shore* (New York: Columbia University Press, 1986);

Un Balcon en forêt (Paris: José Corti, 1958); translated by Howard as *Balcony in the Forest* (New York: Braziller, 1959; London: Hutchinson, 1960);

Liberté grande; La Terre habitable; Gomorrhe; La Sieste en Flandre hollandaise (Paris: José Corti, 1958);

Préférences (Paris: José Corti, 1961; enlarged edition, 1969);

Lettrines (Paris: José Corti, 1967);

La Presqu'île (Paris: José Corti, 1970);

Lettrines 2 (Paris: José Corti, 1974);

Les Eaux étroites (Paris: José Corti, 1976);

En lisant, en écrivant (Paris: José Corti, 1981);

La Forme d'une ville (Paris: José Corti, 1985).

PLAY PRODUCTIONS: *Le Roi pêcheur*, Paris, Théâtre Montparnasse, 25 April 1949;

Penthésilée, Paris, Théâtre Hébertot, 20 July 1955.

OTHER: Heinrich von Kleist, *Penthésilée*, translated by Gracq (Paris: José Corti, 1954).

PERIODICAL PUBLICATION: "Autour des sept collines," *Nouvelle Revue Française*, no. 381 (October 1984): 1-39.

When Julien Gracq refused the Goncourt Prize, which was awarded to him in 1951 for *Le Rivage des Syrtes* (translated as *The Opposing Shore*, 1986), it was with the conviction that literature and the writer must remain untainted by commercial interests and media exploitation. This same stance determined Gracq's association with the surrealists in the 1930s and 1940s. Refusing to become an orthodox member of the group, Gracq has consistently maintained his position as a loner in the literary world. Like Marcel Proust, he was forced to subsidize the publication of his first novel, *Au château d'Argol* (1938; translated as *The Castle of Argol*, 1951), after Gallimard refused to publish it. Ironically, Gallimard plans to publish a two-volume Pléiade edition of Gracq's works, some fifty years after its initial rejection.

Julien Gracq (photograph copyright © Jean
Gaumy: Magnum)

Born Louis Poirier in St. Florent-le-Vieil, near Nantes, in 1910, Gracq is a writer by avocation, a historian and geographer by training. After his boarding-school days at the Lycée Clemenceau in Nantes (recalled in imaginative detail in *La Forme d'une ville* [The Shape of a City, 1985]), he pursued his studies of literature at the Lycée Henri IV in Paris, where he was inspired by Alain, the eminent pedagogue who influenced others of Gracq's generation, including Jean-Paul Sartre and Raymond Aron. Further training in geography at the Ecole Normale Supérieure along with studies at the Ecole Libre des Sciences Politiques were followed by successful completion of the *agrégation* in history in 1934. A career as a lycée teacher of geography and history in Nantes, Amiens, and Angers led to his appointment at the Lycée Claude Bernard in Paris in 1947, where he taught until he retired in 1970. Since then Gracq has divided his time between his apart-

ment in Paris and a country house in Anjou.

Gracq's works defy labeling, but one can point to several formative influences–both personal and literary–that have inspired them. In *Préférences* (1961), his first collection of critical essays, he recalls his bewilderment at the launching of the liner *Ile-de-France* in St. Nazaire. This event made an indelible impression on the fifteen-year-old, who was transfixed by the *élan,* or momentum, of the ship leaving its moorings. For Gracq, the author, the image of this moment captures what he tries to convey in his fiction: the dynamic thrust of departures that will never be betrayed by an arrival (that "aucune arrivée ne pourra jamais démentir"). For the historian, this magnetic force is that of History-on-the-move, the march of time toward an apocalyptic end which contains the promise of rebirth. Reinforcing this adolescent discovery of unbounding energy was the encounter with Wagner's *Parsifal,* which Gracq saw at the Paris Opera in 1928. The quest theme as enunciated by the Grail legend and the Arthurian cycle would provide him with the mythic "touchstone" of his novels, reminiscent in part of Breton geography and medieval history. It is the fatalistic aspect of the quest for ultimate knowledge–a search that must logically end in death–which fascinates Gracq, whose works highlight the suspenseful waiting at the heart of the quest.

An inveterate reader, Gracq first favored Jules Verne, Edgar Allan Poe, Gérard de Nerval, and Arthur Rimbaud, and later, Stendhal and the German romantics, among others. Their influence on his work is explicitly acknowledged in the critical essays, as well as alluded to in the prose. His one collection of prose poems, *Liberté grande* (1947), augmented in 1958 to include several other poetic texts, is clearly indebted to Rimbaud. In *En lisant, en écrivant* (On Reading, On Writing, 1981), his most recent volume of critical essays, Gracq underlines the importance of interaction between author and reader, a communion made possible by the presence of a subtext which magnetically attracts the enchanted reader. Gracq expresses his view of this *texte-en-filigrane* through Allan, a character in *Un Beau Ténébreux* (1945; translated as *A Dark Stranger,* 1950): "Toute œuvre est un palimpseste–et si l'œuvre est réussie, le texte effacé est toujours un texte magique" (Every work is a palimpsest–and if the work is a success, the erased text is always a magic one).

The emphasis on a charmed literary encounter is what ties Gracq to the surrealists. His meeting with André Breton, first through the reading of Breton's *Nadja* (1928), then in person in Nantes in 1939, was influential in inspiring the biographical essay *André Breton, Quelques aspects de l'écrivain* (André Breton, Some Aspects of the Writer), published in 1948. Breton's insistence on the electrifying dynamism of life and literature complements Gracq's notion of the thrust of history, a view which Gracq also shares with Ernst Jünger. In "Symbolique d'Ernst Jünger" (*Préférences*), Gracq points to *Auf den Marmorklippen* (*On the Marble Cliffs*, 1939) as an emblematic portrayal of History alternating between periods of harmony and decline. Gracq's reading led to a meeting with Jünger and a continuing friendship.

As a whole Gracq's work is highly allusive, written in a poetic language characterized by metaphorical overload and syntactic sinuosity. The author's style reflects his subject—the dynamism of magical forces that subtend History—in its vertiginous deployment of multiple clauses which flow headlong in a seemingly desperate attempt to avoid closure. Analogies continually dazzle the reader who confronts the themes of quest and departure refracted into many simultaneously maintained subthemes. The march of History, or time, is also that of the "(hi)story" of the text which moves toward a conclusion. In Gracq's scriptural universe, the metaphor of theatricality serves not only to dramatize life as art, but also to point to the self-referentiality of all writing. This view links Gracq to modernity and the New Novelists, despite his vehement rejection of the latter's overemphasis on technique in his essay "Pourquoi la littérature respire mal" (Why Literature Breathes Badly, in *Préférences*). Another extended metaphor offers a view of the cosmos as organic, one which Gracq inherited from the romantics. In his novels man is a human "plant," seen in his rapport with nature.

Thus the line of reference in Gracq's work stretches from the Grail myth to surrealism through French and German romanticism. Gracq has explicitly established a link between Breton's circle and the Arthurian knights of legend in the preface to his play, *Le Roi pêcheur* (The Fisher King, published in 1948). For Gracq, the quest of Arthur's knights for the Grail, one which would unite the sacred and the profane, corresponds to the surrealists' desire to resolve contradictions between waking life and the dream world. In both instances what interests Gracq is the portrayal of the *search* for an ideal treasure which "si obstinément qu'il dérobe nous est toujours représenté comme *à portée de la main*" (no matter how often it defies discovery is always represented as within arm's reach). Gracq's version in the play, which premiered on 25 April 1949 at the Théâtre Montparnasse in Paris, concentrates on possession of the Grail as death (of desire and of hope) and petrification, an inevitable conclusion of the search which, in the legend, only Kundry is willing to undertake. In addition to his own play, Gracq was commissioned by Jean-Louis Barrault to do a translation of Heinrich von Kleist's *Penthesilea* (1808), produced in Paris in 1955.

When *Au château d'Argol* appeared in 1938, it received scant attention. Only 150 copies were sold, but one of them reached André Breton, who pronounced Gracq's novel the only true surrealist novel—a great compliment given Breton's condemnation of the genre in *Manifeste du surréalisme* (The Surrealist Manifesto, 1924). In his preface Gracq renders homage to Poe and other Gothic novelists but warns his reader against a facile reduction of events, places, and objects to static symbols. In fact, *Au château d'Argol* is much more than a pastiche of the *roman noir*. A diabolical version of *Parsifal*, it contains the seeds of all of Gracq's novels, in which a protagonist, a somewhat marginal figure, sets off in quest of an ideal which is viewed as a salvation. The search leads to the threshold of an answer, a death which is, at least implicitly, a redemption or rebirth.

The story, told by an omniscient narrator and devoid of dialogue, is divided into ten chapters whose titles, such as "Argol," "Le Cimetière" (The Cemetery), "La Forêt" (The Forest), and "La Mort" (Death), seem to herald a straightforward and conventional narration of a rite of passage, an impression which is belied by the text.

At the beginning of the novel Albert, the last scion of a noble family, sets out to visit the castle of Argol, a Breton manor that he has purchased sight unseen on the recommendations of a friend. In the spirit of surrealism, he is said to be savoring "l'angoisse du hasard" (the anguish of chance). Blond and delicate, Albert is scornful of women and indeed of earthly matters in general, preferring the more exalted activities of the mind. He has set himself the ambitious task of resolving the enigma of life. The essence of a nomadic and meditative savant, this Perceval figure is especially drawn to the philosopher Hegel and his attempt to articulate a science of totality. Albert's arrival at Argol coincides with a sudden terrifying storm which overcomes him with a sense of the ominous. It is then that he learns that his longtime friend and soul mate, Herminien, is to arrive at the castle with a woman unknown to Albert, Heide. In the first of many premonitory scenes in the novel, Albert carves Heide's name on an ancient tombstone in the cemetery.

Herminien is the dark underside of Albert's idealism. Possessed of a demonic lucidity, he treads the earth in pursuit of the material. Whereas Albert is struck with the grace of literature, Herminien seeks to understand its mechanics. He plays Mephistopheles to Albert's Dr. Faust, the nickname that he has conferred on his blond friend. Both men communicate instinctively in a love-hate relationship where each sees in the other "le fantôme à la fois de son double et de son contraire" (the phantom at one and the same time of his double and his opposite).

Heide's role, like that of most of Gracq's female characters, is that of a catalyst. She is a contradictory being, virginal and chaste, but also a "colonne de sang" (pillar of blood), the Grail figure sought by Albert-Perceval. Heide symbolizes the "seuil magique interdit aux hommes" (magical threshold forbidden to men), and her arrival transforms the setting into a stage of deadly desire.

Moments spent in idyllic harmony are interspersed with scenes of tension and separation in the interactions of the trio. In the chapter entitled "Le Bain" (The Bath) individual barriers yield to a physical and spiritual communion through the unifying qualities of water. Later the men affirm their "virile fraternity" in a mysterious subterranean chapel where objects emblematic of the Grail quest—lamp, helmet, lance, and tombstone—represent spatially for Albert the meaning of the metaphysical enigma that he has been trying to solve.

Separation occurs when Herminien brutally rapes Heide in the forest and flees Argol. By violating Heide, Herminien takes possession of the Grail and becomes a figure of the Fisher King. In the symbolic schema of the novel Albert also partakes of the Grail by nursing Heide back to life. Visions of the bloodstained, naked Heide haunt him in dreams of fountains spurting blood which pierce him like a lance. He thus experiences on the level of carnal desire the separation

implicit in the quest that he has been acting out intellectually.

The return of Herminien and the passage of the two men through a secret, womblike tunnel underneath the castle to the forbidden "magical threshold" of Heide's room is yet another stage in Albert's quest. Tempted again by his satanic double, Albert decides to remove the unbearable "open wound" that Heide represents by preparing to kill her. Aware of her impending doom, Heide kills herself, a sacrificial victim in the male rite of initiation. Her death prepares the way for the ultimate resolution of the story. Albert, reduced to the ephemeral sound of his footsteps ("ses pas"), stealthily follows Herminien into the courtyard of the castle. When the echoing footsteps (Albert's) join those of his "âme damnée" (damned soul; that is, Herminien), the sensation of an "icy bolt of lightning" piercing Herminien's shoulders like "a handful of snow" signifies the death of a double which is also a moment of reconciliation or union. Albert's act—never explicitly stated—symbolizes his own death and redemption. The Hegelian myth of the Fall of Man, as expressed by Albert at the beginning of the novel, is thus fulfilled: "La main qui inflige la blessure est aussi celle qui la guérit" (The hand which inflicts the wound is also the one which cures it).

The novel contains a *mise en abyme* (interior reproduction of itself) of its central focus in the engraving that Albert beholds, with fascination and horror, in Herminien's room. It is a picture of Perceval touching Amfortas's wound with his lance, causing the Fisher King's blood to fill the chalice. In Albert's eyes, the lance acts as a "hyphen," an agent of union containing the knight, the king, and the Grail in a circle. The cyclical nature of the Grail legend is inscribed on a golden ring in the corner of the engraving: "Rédemption au Rédempteur" (Redemption for the Redeemer). The engraving, together with the conceit of flowing blood which unifies the text, exemplifies meaning in its plenitude where the juxtaposition of opposites creates a new reality, the "sur-reality" formulated by Breton in *Second Manifeste du surréalisme* (*The Second Surrealist Manifesto*, 1930). Albert's uneasiness at the sight of the engraving stems from the realization that it is a work which is "entièrement significatif" (entirely significant), containing in dynamic, flowing form an "ingouvernable contradiction" (ungovernable contradiction) in a "sacrilège équivalence" (sacrilegious equivalence). He understands finally the enigma of life where good cannot exist without evil. Consequently, Albert, although horrified at Heide's "stigmata" and aware of Herminien's role as "l'ange noir de la chute" (the black angel of the fall), comes to accept evil (that is, Herminien) in a "fraternelle connivence" (fraternal conspiracy). This revelation–the acceptance of evil as necessary for redemption–constitutes the "pierre de scandale," or scandalous touchstone, of the novel.

Gracq's version of the Grail legend as surrealist principle is manifest in his style. His saturation of the text with analogies, descriptive passages, and syntactical complexity tends to "clot" or block static signification. The reader is indeed carried into a rhythmic world of sustained contradictions.

Oscillation and flow characterize the text as a search for meaning in the interplay of communion and separation. Moments of calm, fertility, and harmony are interrupted by storms, shadows, and images of death. Horizontal spaces intersect with the vertical, the feminine with the masculine, images of birth with those of death and separation. At times the castle is a Grail filled with blood; at other times it is portrayed as a giant vessel borne by the "waves" of the forest. Time, like space, is also distorted. Night fuses with day, and the overall effect is a *clair-obscur*, or chiaroscuro, theatrical lighting. Time is mechanical and inevitable and is represented in its fatalistic nature both by the relentless hourglass in the cemetery and the massive iron clock in the chapel. It yields no escape, signifying the suspense of an ongoing quest and a fatal rush to a predetermined end. At other moments, however, time is subsumed into the *rêverie* of Bergsonian *durée* (the duration of perceived time) where it merges with cosmic rhythms.

Thus, the style of the narration is one of deferral–consonant with Albert's quest–and the emphasis is on writing as prolongation of desire and suspension of meaning. The metaphor of drama occurs throughout in references to the *trois coups* (three knocks) which signal the beginning of a play or the momentary raising of the curtain which, if it were raised, would signal the end of the text and death. In *Au château d'Argol*, then, Gracq elaborates a metaphor not only for the redemption of life but also for the reading of the text. This latter motif is developed as an important theme in his second novel, *Un Beau Ténébreux*.

Un Beau Ténébreux has a more realistic setting than *Au château d'Argol*, but the same themes presented there in allegorical form are here repeated and amplified. The site is a seaside resort in Brittany during a summer and fall in what could be the 1930s. A major portion of the story is conveyed through the eyes of Gerald, a character whose journal ends abruptly before the conclusion of the novel. The story is continued by an unidentified narrator who attempts to piece together events and complete the tale, albeit "dans un obscur sentiment d'incertitude" (with a vague feeling of uncertainty). Contrary to the homogeneous narrative style of *Au château d'Argol*, the story of *Un Beau Ténébreux* is told through journal entries, letters, *récits*, or narrations (mainly of dreams), and dialogue–a polyphony of narrative forms which lends a rhythm of dialectical interplay to the text.

A group of friends, "la bande 'straight,'" has gathered to spend a summer together at the Hôtel des Vagues. As presented by Gerald, a would-be writer and literary critic, the characters are types. Irene, newly married to Henri Maurevert, is the epitome of vitality and sensuality; she is compared to bright daylight and is contrasted with the nocturnal and chaste Christel, whose influence on the group is of a dramatic nature. In fact, Christel's only desire is to lead a theatrical life, having been overwhelmed as an adolescent by the powerful conclusion of Puccini's *Tosca*. She is pursued by Jacques, the "poet" of the group, who is fascinated by her enigmatic manner. Not surprisingly, Gerald is most at ease with Gregory, whom he describes as a "biblical prophet," one who exists to make way for another, much as he, Gerald, mediates the story for the reader. The religious characterization of Gregory proves to be an apt one, because his primary role in the novel is to introduce Allan, who quickly becomes the "dieu de la bande" (the God of the Group).

Allan's arrival on the scene has a catalytic effect on the guests, as does Heide's in *Au château d'Argol*. In his "electric" presence, the group's elective affinities manifest themselves and propel the action of the story which is, in reality, a long prelude to a final scene which is itself a threshold. The notion of the text as prelude or waiting is suggested by Gerald's introductory description of the resort. A barren landscape bathed in a hazy light lends a theatrical effect to the setting, matching the ambiguities of the story whose themes are refracted into a blurred "aura" of possible meanings. The proliferation of such words as *vide* (empty), *vague*, and *désert* underlines the empty and provisional nature of vacation (*vacances*) seen as vacancy (*vacance*). Together with the comparison of the hotel to a ship being prepared to "traverser l'été" (cross summer), they evoke the air of expectation surrounding a departure or quest.

Allan, the "dark stranger" of the title, serves to awaken the group from the somnolence of its summer. Characters' dreams play an important role in this novel, but Allan is the only character who lives his dreams while awake. As such, he is an embodiment of the "rêve éveillé," or waking dream, a posture that the surrealists so eagerly sought to articulate and equated with artistic creation. Gerald refers to Allan as the "roi de théâtre" (king of theater), and his obsession with gambling and games of all types identifies him as a player in quest of an answer or clue. Like Albert in *Au château d'Argol*, Allan is fascinated with solving puzzles. He sees the world variously as a hieroglyph, chess game, or a text to be read, not for its surface structure, but for its hidden meaning whose traces are barely perceptible as on a palimpsest. Unlike Albert, however, Allan is cognizant of the implications of his search. The "magic text" he is seeking is one which will unite divine and earthly, sacred and profane in a vertiginous, noncontradictory moment, which he qualifies as Rimbaldian: the possession of truth in body and soul ("Je ne puis me contenter à moins que . . . je ne possède la vérité dans une âme et dans un corps" [I cannot be content unless . . . I possess truth in a soul and a body]). For Allan, this means acting in a God-like manner to control his own death. Consequently, he has made a Mephistophelian pact with his companion Dolores to commit suicide together. Their agreement, a "rewriting" of Alfred de Vigny's tale "Les Amants de Montmorency," is made explicit as such when the couple appears at the masked ball–a pivotal moment in the novel's plot–disguised as Vigny's lovers. The story of *Un Beau Ténébreux*, intertextual in its references to Vigny, Poe, Nerval, Rimbaud, Shakespeare, and many others, is also metatextual; Allan's dramatic conclusion to his search governs the action of the text and is equated with the rewriting of an already existent text either explicitly, as in the case of Vigny, or implicitly, by analogy with Faust, the myth of the Grail, *Tosca*, *The Divine Comedy*, and *Lohengrin*.

Allan's intentions are gradually made known to the group and the reader in a series of "revelations." One's first awareness of his obsession with death is transmitted by Gregory's letter to Gerald relating a boarding school incident in which Allan, a troubled adolescent, spent an entire night at the side of a dead classmate, transfixed by the horror of "le néant" (nothingness). Later, during an outing to the ruins of Roscaër castle, set atop a cliff surrounded by a luxurious forest, Allan is spellbinding in his eerie tale of a night spent alone in a church. For Allan, this experience was a mystical one, allowing him to fuse with the nocturnal side of life. A final moment of revelation occurs at the masked ball where, paradoxically, the characters' intentions are "unmasked" by disguises revealing their prototypes in literature. The ball scene is yet another signal to the reader that all writing is intertextual, cut through with magic meanings that exist in trace form. It emphasizes the fact that the characters are types and their roles–the action of the text–are predetermined and fatalistically tragic. As in *Au château d'Argol*, Gracq saturates the story with an overdetermination of meaning that acts to precipitate the action to the threshold of a conclusion, thus privileging desire and suspense.

Analogies are abundant and dizzying in their array. In an extended metaphor, Gregory compares Allan's life–and "act"–to Victor Hugo's downward spirals (*Les Feuilles d'automne*, 1831) leading to an infernal abyss. Hugo's reading of *The Divine Comedy* transforms Dante's progressively tighter circles into ever-widening ones, which explode in a vertiginous burst. Such is Allan's alarming rush to embrace death, according to Gregory. Allan, not only a Perceval figure but also an incarnation of Lohengrin and Faust, is portrayed as an anti-Christ who seeks out the nocturnal, "dark" side of life, a predilection he shares with Christel. His pact with Dolores is an attempt to gain ultimate knowledge, that is, an understanding of good *and* evil, life *and* death. For Allan, the Grail had to be an earthly, incarnate reality before it could be incorporated into myth and endowed with a sense of the marvelous. Allan's quest is Gracq's: the merging of the sacred and the profane in a rewriting of both the Grail legend and the incarnation of Christ in terms of a surreal quest.

Allan sparks a liberation of yearnings and dreams among the vacationers for whom he represents a "conduit" of desires. He exists as both redeemer and–by his potential act–redeemed, initiating the group by a "baptism of fire" into a new language of dreams, one which is continually associated with Rimbaldian vertigo. Most like Allan in his capacity to dream while awake, Henri is a marginal being, described as "désorbité" (out of orbit), and thus incapable of satisfying his wife's more earthly passions. His recurring dream constitutes some of the most lyrical and poetic passages of the text and is an allegorical version of the novel's dizzying quest for an ending. In his car at the edge of an abyss, he experiences a vertiginous moment where his life appears to embrace death, where the height of the cliff confronts the depth of the void beneath him, and where he seems constantly on the verge of waking from his dream, as in "un dernier acte de tragédie" (a last act of tragedy). Christel also dreams. She is, rather blatantly, a Christ figure, not only by her name but also by her attempt to "save" Allan from his fate while simultaneously being attracted to it. Both she and Gerald are haunted by nightmares of labyrinthine passages, unfinished plays, and cavernous theaters engulfed by waves. Gerald sees his dreams as the comic version of the role that he seems to be playing while awake. Like the emblematic objects and places in the setting, dreams and the theatrical motif are signs which direct the reader to focus on the text as ludic object whose rules or meaning are continually suspended. Allan's search for the magic text barely visible beneath the surface of the palimpsest is the reader's. In its evocation of art, opera, theater, literature, and games, *Un Beau Ténébreux* sets forth the task of "unmasking" it, one suggested by the Shakespearean epigraph: "They rightly do inherit Heaven's graces.... /They are the lords and owners of their faces...."

As in *Au château d'Argol*, however, the text ends at the threshold of a resolution. When Allan, alone in his room before the "poisoned glass," hears a knock at the door, one reads: "Il vit venir à lui sa dernière heure" (he saw his last hour coming toward him). Dolores? death? The reader is left to conclude.

Gracq's masterpiece, *Le Rivage des Syrtes*, is also the story of a journey toward death. It incorporates familiar Gracquian motifs: the quest theme, reconciliation of opposites, and the self-referential text, but is magnified to reflect History as representative of an imminent, inevitable Apocalypse. The *clair-obscur* tones of the preceding novels are transformed into the twilight world of a dying city, a lighting which is simultaneously suggestive of the dawn of a new civilization. Louis Poirier, the historian-geographer influenced by a Spenglerian view of history, emerges most clearly from Gracq's third novel.

In an imaginary setting, reminiscent of the Italian city-states of the Renaissance, Gracq evokes the decadence of a moribund, mercantile state, Orsenna. The time is equally vague but seems to be around 1900. Aldo, the young descendant of a wealthy political family, is tired of his unchallenging life and sets off to undertake a new position as Observer at the Admiralty, a lonely outpost on the Sea of Syrtes. For three hundred years Orsenna has been at war with the country of Farghestan. Although the war has stagnated into an uneasy peace, the separation between the two countries, symbolized by the yawning gulf of the Syrtan sea, is stressed from the outset of the novel. Equally, Aldo's departure from his family and bourgeois comforts is seen as a solemn break ("brèche") from the past and a thrust to an uncertain future. The plot centers on a gradual illumination—for the reader and for Aldo—of the protagonist's mission: to close the gap between Orsenna and Farghestan by journeying to the forbidden land. Aldo's transgressive act is the decisive factor which plunges the two countries headlong into a violent clash which awakens them from their sleep in order to face death and destruction. Aldo's quest for death in *Le Rivage des Syrtes* recalls Allan's in *Un Beau Ténébreux* but with connotations of universal destruction.

Aldo is torn between two poles or points of view concerning the status of Orsenna and Farghestan. His captain at the Syrtan front, Marino, represents the forces of order who want to preserve peace at all costs. Consequently, Marino is willing to look the other way when Aldo discovers a foreign patrol boat in Orsenna's waters. At the other extreme is Vanessa, fiery daughter of the renegade Aldobrandi family. A seductive temptress, she introduces Aldo to the pleasures of the illicit by enticing him on a journey beyond the forbidden threshold between the two countries to witness the fury of the Tängri, the "calm" underwater volcano of Farghestan's capital, Rhages. Aldo's first vision of the shimmering column of fiery water—lancelike in its verticality—is a signal of the beginning of the end. Described as the apparition of fire on water and compared to a midnight sun, the Tängri symbolizes inversion of the existing order on a cosmic level. When Aldo returns to the Tängri in the Admiralty's official boat, he sets off the long-stagnant but potential war.

As in the other novels, revelatory places and events signal the direction of the plot. Aldo repeatedly seeks refuge in the womblike Chamber of Charts containing the maps of the Syrtan sea. There he is magnetically drawn to the thin red line indicating the border–qualified as "magic"–between the two countries. Likewise, the sensual and decadent city of Maremma, dubbed Venice of the Syrtes, fascinates Aldo with its promise of death. Metaphors of the imminent war as fever and malady abound in Gracq's description of this city, where mysterious rumors of transgression circulate like infected blood through the veins of a dying body. For Aldo, Maremma's stench contains both an uncertain wager and a promise which gradually comes to mean the paradoxical return to life implicit in the preparation for war. The baroque ruins and cemetery of Sagra are the strange setting for Aldo's sighting of the enemy patrol boat that he had glimpsed earlier. With this discovery, he realizes that the threat to the status quo comes from an agent from within. The decision of the Admiralty's crew to refurbish the dilapidated fortress, together with Marino's apparent suicide, removes the last barriers to the war and prepares the way for a dénouement which is never explicitly described.

Signs proliferate in this novel in which the theme of interpreting signs is central. The fact that one learns, in a sudden flash-forward of the narrator, two-thirds of the way through the novel, that the destruction of Orsenna has already taken place serves to underline the focus on the *activity* of reading the signs in the novel that point to its inevitable conclusion, that is, death. Aldo, another Perceval in search of a Grail, is a figure for the reader as well as for the writer. His search for intelligibility (*sens*) is clearly identified with the fatal destruction occasioned by the war. In *Le Rivage des Syrtes* Gracq equates this ending in meaning as the fate of the text whose operation is to suspend the search for as long as possible. Three key passages serve as clues or constructs of the activity of reading/writing the novel.

The Council of Orsenna's response to Aldo's report on the rumors of war is an enigmatic document which forces Aldo to read between the lines and incarnate the "timbre" that has informed it. His *explication de texte* of the implicit instructions in the letter mirrors the readers' activity. Another *mise en abyme* of the reading of the novel occurs in the Christmas Eve sermon delivered in the church of St. Damase in Maremma. The pastor points to his message as a polysemous one, where, in essence, the story of Christ's birth is transformed into the story of his death. It is a "ténébreuse naissance" (dark birth); therein lies the meaning of his birth. When trans-

posed to the level of the book that one is reading, where the central subject is the reversal of death in life (stagnant peace) to life in death (preparations for war), the suggestion is that the resolution of the book (its conclusion) is also a moment of death. Gracq's enterprise is to prolong the moment of the book's conclusion by portraying the activity of reading as prelude to a crystallization in meaning.

A third passage–less a *mise en abyme* than an illuminating conversation–opens up the activity of reading a text ("histoire") to include that of reading History. It occurs at the end of the novel in Aldo's discussion with the sage Danielo. The latter, a disillusioned historian (a double for Gracq?) and author of a *Histoire des origines* (History of Origins) thirty years earlier, has abandoned traditional historical methodology in order to read between the lines of History ("dans les intervalles"). Danielo is a reader whose goal–to locate historical origins and causes–is doomed to failure; as such, it mirrors Aldo's quest in the novel. In effect, only *signs* point to the origins of the war, and, even though the war has already taken place, it is never described. Gracq's use of the metaphor of the "jeu du furet" (hunt-the-slipper), where an object runs along an invisible cord through the hands of the players, is emblematic of Aldo's (and the reader's) inability to locate the origin of the rumors about the war in which everyone is an accomplice but no one person is responsible. As such, it illustrates the absent thread along which Gracq deploys his plot.

In this novel Gracq's elaboration of the Grail myth as surrealist principle is rendered in a masterly prose in which the exaggerated style of the *roman noir* is replaced by the ornamentation and majesty of the baroque. Paradoxically, however, the surfeit of decor and plot serves less to dramatize and set the scene than to point to the emptiness of the stage (that is, the book), thus simultaneously maintaining and voiding the setting and action. The last lines of the novel, Aldo's observation of Orsenna, clearly indicate Gracq's metaphor of the book as empty theater and as absent conclusion: "je croyais marcher au milieu de l'agencement bizarre et des flaques de lumière égarantes d'un théâtre vide ... et je savais pourquoi désormais le décor était planté" (I seemed to walk in the strange setting and alienating floodlights of an empty theater ... and I knew at once why, for all time, the stage was set).

The absent center of both text and History is reiterated in Gracq's fourth novel, *Un Balcon en forêt* (1958; translated as *Balcony in the Forest*, 1959). However, the majesty and cosmic tonality that characterize *Le Rivage des Syrtes* are here replaced by a melancholic tale of an inward journey toward death.

Published in 1958, *Un Balcon en forêt* was heralded as a departure from the preceding novels in that its plot and protagonist, Lieutenant Grange, are, at first glance, firmly anchored in a historical moment and geographical place, the time span being that of the "drôle de guerre," September 1939 to May 1940, and the place being the Franco-Belgian border. Grange is stationed at a blockhouse in the Ardennes Forest, where his task is to await the German attack. During this suspenseful period he falls in love with a young woman named Mona who is finally forced to flee her home when the German advance becomes imminent. Wounded in the initial skirmish which kills most of his company, Grange retreats to Mona's abandoned cottage where, at the end of the novel, he falls asleep in her bed.

A simple *récit*, *Un Balcon en forêt* would seem to portray the poignant anxiety of the period of waiting that immediately followed the declaration of World War II in 1939, and to a certain degree, it does. Closer scrutiny, however, reveals a text whose surface is constantly flayed by other preoccupations central to Gracq's entire corpus. In this novel Gracq posits an actual historical moment in order to contest its existence. This opposition of contradictories recalls the dialectical dynamism of the other works but gains force in the questioning of a documented event. In this respect, *Un Balcon en forêt* emerges as the most "surreal" of Gracq's works. Ironically, in the uneasy period of waiting that was the "drôle de guerre," history provided an exact replication of a surrealist moment.

War is literally in the air in this novel and reverberates in the numerous references to the past and its wars: the "guerre de '14," the Commune, Napoleon's "Grande Armée," and conflicts of both the Merovingian dynasty and Romanic Gaul. Gracq conveys an impression of historical depth and texture by frequent allusions to figures associated with France's medieval past: Gilles de Rais (Bluebeard), Jeanne d'Orléans, the Prince d'Aquitaine, among many others. The constant return to the past with the emphasis on deciphering its signs in light of the present apocalyptic moment designates History–and, by association, the text–as a palimpsest which beckons to be read.

Grange, like Gracq's other protagonists, is a quester who, at the beginning of the novel, is en route to a frontier outpost. On a train which sinuously follows the course of the Meuse River, Grange imagines himself to be setting off for the "Domaine d'Arnheim," the utopian setting of Poe's short story of the same title. That the reader is embarking on a mythical quest as lived by the protagonist is suggested not only by the trip along the river, a metaphor of the journey of life, but also by the epigraph of the story, taken from Wagner's *Parsifal*. It entreats the guardians of the wood leading to Amfortas's legendary haunt to remain watchful until dawn. Together with the descriptions of the Ardennes forest, which evoke Brocéliande, Arthur's legendary haunt, the epigraph points to Grange's journey as a search for the Grail. Unlike Aldo, who seeks an answer in confronting an external Other (Marino, Vanessa, Farghestan, and so forth), Grange retreats into himself, gradually detaching from the world around him. He experiences the dizzying sensation of being perched on a crack, isolated both from his past and future as in "les failles profondes qui séparent les pages d'un livre" (the deep crevices which separate the pages of a book). The *clair-obscur* of dusk which pervades the setting of the other novels is here transferred to Grange's inner state; he is said to suffer from an "angoisse crépusculaire" (twilight anguish). Whereas, in the other works, privileged places evoke the *élan* of a boat about to be launched, in *Un Balcon en forêt* the boat is Grange. In talking with Mona, he feels a drifting sensation as if, lifted from below, a "coque géante, déjà soulevée par la respiration de la mer" (giant hull lifted by the sea's breath) were carrying him away from her into the recesses of his imagination.

Grange's favorite retreats–Mona's bed and the blockhouse–are clearly uterinelike and thus evocative of birth and renewal. Like Gracq's other female protagonists, Mona is a mediator who advances Grange along on his quest for self-knowledge. She is described as an ephemeral, fairylike child and is constantly associated with water. Gracq's pervasive use of water imagery, not only in the portrayal of Mona but also in his depiction of the forest, the climate of the "drôle de guerre," and so forth, saturates the text with what seems to be a feminine principle of life, cleansing and initiation. However, this imagery is double-edged with the menace of death. The waters are stagnant, heavy and murky, suggestive of the death instinct paradoxically present in life. Thus, even though Grange feels a sense of womblike peace when cramped inside the blockhouse, the space is an oppressive one, where "le corps remuait là-dedans comme l'amande sèche dans son noyau" (the body moved inside like a dried-out almond in its shell).

Like Aldo, Grange is confronted with the signs of History, much as the reader is confronted with the text. While reading the newspapers which arrive from the village, he is struck by the *absence* of commentary about the overwhelmingly present threat. He spends long nights in the blockhouse "reading" the stars. The suspended state of peace/war which characterized France in 1939 is equated with the process of deferral of meaning and closure which occurs in the act of reading. Grange, who feels trapped between the pages of a book, is a reflection of France's marginal position. An emphasis on borders in the novel points to the precarious position of both the protagonist and the reader perched on the bar of interpretive possibilities and invited to find meaning. That reading is a dizzying activity is underlined both in the ubiquitous water imagery and in the vertiginous series of reversals or opposites which govern the text: history/fiction, reality/fantasy, death/life, war/peace. Thus, a text which, on the surface, is a discourse on the Phony War is, in its deep structure, a self-conscious discourse on the quest implied in interpretation.

As in the other novels, an extended metaphor of theatricality limns the text, giving it an aura of artificiality and vague unreality. Literally and figuratively, Gracq conveys the sense of the "theater of war." Enemy planes darting across the sky light it up like a "stage." The forest is described as a "set for an opera," and the watch for the enemy is compared to waiting for a curtain to rise. The text in its entirety is again a prelude to a conclusion which is itself a threshold.

At the end of the novel, when the wounded protagonist returns to Mona's cottage (presumably to die), he looks at himself in a mirror but sees only an "ombre grise" (gray shadow). In Grange's journey inward toward death he gradually passes "to the other side" ("Je suis peut-être de l'autre côté" [I am perhaps on the other side]). In the imagery of the novel, this passage suggests the crossing of a threshold to a death which would be an emptying out of the self in a paradoxical *affirmation* of one's negation. In *Le Rivage des Syrtes*, Aldo's final revelation (of why the

stage had been set) takes place in an empty theater. In *Un Balcon en forêt* the revelation is of an "inner" emptiness and comes to Grange when he sees his "voided" self in the mirror. It is then that he realizes that "la vie ne se rejoignait pas à elle-même" (life no longer mirrors itself in the image), and, in the concluding words of the novel, he is said to pull the covers over his head and fall asleep. ("Puis il tira la couverture sur sa tête et s'endormit"). Likewise, left at the border of a conclusion, the reader is left to surmise that the only meaning which counts is the suspension of meaning, the quest seen as "une attente pure," that is, pure waiting and desire.

With *Un Balcon en forêt*, Gracq seems to have arrived at an end point in his novelistic writing. His fascination with the physicality of space, as evinced in the numerous descriptive passages in the novels, informs the posterior works of fiction which include three short stories ("La Route" [The Road], "La Presqu'île" [The Peninsula], "Le Roi Cophetua" [King Cophetua]) collected under the title *La Presqu'île* (1970) and two semi-autobiographical works, *Les Eaux étroites* (Narrow Waters, 1976) and *La Forme d'une ville* (1985). The titles alone are suggestive of Gracq the geographer, whose careful eye for topographical detail comes to take preference over the studied narration of plot. For the most part, these short works are lyrical evocations of landscape akin to the *rêveries* of Rousseau's *Rêveries du promeneur solitaire* (The Reveries of the Solitary Walker).

In the autobiographical works, Gracq's meanderings through the labyrinth of memory take the form of a mental and physical geography. *Les Eaux étroites* consists of lyrical descriptions of the countryside culled while floating down the Eure river in a canoelike bark, and this contemplation of nature stirs up the murky waters of the past. In *La Forme d'une ville*, Gracq's surrealistlike wanderings through the city of his adolescence, Nantes, recall André Breton's *Nadja* (1928) and Louis Aragon's *Le Paysan de Paris* (Nightwalker, 1926). He guides the reader through a personalized past time and place intimately linked to his boarding-school days. The themes found in the novels remain constant in these works, but they are rendered in a different light, as if distilled or decanted.

In the short story "La Route," a fragment of an unfinished novel, Gracq articulates once again the theme of the quest. Although the journey evoked by the unidentified first-person narrator appears to be a trip through Brittany, it is almost immediately transformed into an oneiric version of the apocalyptic *élan* elaborated in *Le Rivage des Syrtes*. A lyrical meditation on "l'étrange–l'inquiétante route!" (the strange, alarming road!), the text is an emblem of the journey of life as continuous departure without arrival. The other short stories in the collection convey the same sense of waiting and desire. "Le Roi Cophetua" is a more sustained narrative than "La Route." Set in France in 1917, it concerns an unidentified first-person narrator who has come from Paris to an isolated provincial village at the behest of an old army friend. While waiting for his friend–who never arrives, the reader is led to believe, because he has been killed in the war–the visitor wonders about the woman who has greeted him. Is she a servant or his friend's mistress? The woman's anxious longing for the return of her master merges gradually with the excruciating day-long wait of the friend, and their mutual expectancy culminates in a tortured portrait of amorous loss. When, inevitably, they spend the night together, in unspoken pain and desire, their story becomes a reflection of a painting that earlier captured the attention of the visitor. In the flickering candlelight of evening the painting was barely visible, but the visitor finally recognized it to be a rendition of the story of King Cophetua in love with a beggarmaid told in Shakespeare's *Love's Labour's Lost*. A *mise en abyme* for the story and for the enigma of the woman, the painting serves to generate the tale and governs its conclusion in the visitor's silent departure the next day. In an allusive style Gracq sketches a moving portrait of melancholic desire.

"La Presqu'île" is more stylized in plot than "Le Roi Cophetua" but the theme of anxious waiting is the same, albeit magnified by a minute examination of a lover's thoughts projected onto nature. The deceptively simple story is about a man named Simon who is en route to the train station at the edge of the Breton peninsula of Guérande to meet his mistress, Irmgard, due on the 7:53 P.M. train. When she does not arrive as expected, he is obliged to return later in the evening. In between the two trains, his reflections on the ocean and surrounding countryside betray the ambivalence and fear at the heart of his relationship

with the woman. The story's "conclusion," at the moment when Simon glimpses Irmgard's descent from the train, freezes its focus in the gap between hated separation and fearful reunion. The reader, like Simon, is caught up in undecidability and unrelieved expectancy.

Indeed, in the short works of fiction as well as in the novels and poetry, Gracq continues to dazzle his readers with verbal magnificence and, paradoxically, eloquent silence. He transports them to (into) a magic universe of dreams and desires which exist just beneath the surface of the quotidian. As André Breton pointed out, Julien Gracq is a surrealist writer in the finest sense of the term and merits the place of honor that he holds in contemporary French literature.

Bibliography:
Peter Hoy, *Julien Gracq: Essai de bibliographie, 1938-1972* (London: Grant & Cutler, 1973).

References:
Ruth Amossy, *Les Jeux de l'allusion littéraire dans "Un Beau Ténébreux" de Julien Gracq* (Neuchâtel: Baconnière, 1980);

Amossy, *Parcours symboliques chez Julien Gracq: "Le Rivage des Syrtes"* (Paris: SEDES, 1982);

Elisabeth Cardonne-Arlyck, *La Métaphore raconte: Pratique de Julien Gracq* (Paris: Klincksieck, 1984);

Georges Cesbron, ed., *Julien Gracq: Actes du Colloque International, Angers, 21-24 mai 1981* (Angers: Presses de l'Université d'Angers, 1981);

Annie-Claude Dobbs, *Dramaturgie et liturgie dans l'œuvre de Julien Gracq* (Paris: José Corti, 1972);

Marie Francis, *Forme et signification de l'attente dans l'œuvre romanesque de Julien Gracq* (Paris: Nizet, 1979);

Jean-Louis Leutrat, *Julien Gracq* (Paris: Editions Universitaires, 1967);

Leutrat, ed., *Julien Gracq* (Paris: Editions de l'Herne, 1972);

Marginales, special issue on Gracq, no. 134 (October 1970);

Jacqueline Michel, *Une Mise en récit du silence: Le Clézio, Bosco, Gracq* (Paris: José Corti, 1986).

J. M. G. Le Clézio

(13 April 1940-   )

Stephen Smith
Central Connecticut State University

BOOKS: *Le Procès-verbal* (Paris: Gallimard, 1963); translated by Daphne Woodward as *The Interrogation* (London: Hamilton, 1964; New York: Atheneum, 1964);

Le Jour où Beaumont fit connaissance avec sa douleur (Paris: Mercure de France, 1964);

La Fièvre (Paris: Gallimard, 1965); translated by Woodward as *Fever* (London: Hamilton, 1966; New York: Atheneum, 1966);

Le Déluge (Paris: Gallimard, 1966); translated by Peter Green as *The Flood* (London: Hamilton, 1967; New York: Atheneum, 1968);

L'Extase matérielle (Paris: Gallimard, 1967);

Terra Amata (Paris: Gallimard, 1967); translated by Barbara Bray (London: Hamilton, 1969; New York: Atheneum, 1969);

Le Livre des fuites (Paris: Gallimard, 1969); translated by Simon Watson Taylor as *The Book of Flights* (London: Cape, 1971; New York: Atheneum, 1972);

La Guerre (Paris: Gallimard, 1970); translated by Taylor as *War* (London: Cape, 1973; New York: Atheneum, 1973);

Haï (Geneva: Albert Skira, 1971);

Mydriase (Montpellier: Fata Morgana, 1973);

Les Géants (Paris: Gallimard, 1973); translated by Taylor as *The Giants* (London: Cape, 1975; New York: Atheneum, 1975);

Voyages de l'autre côté (Paris: Gallimard, 1975);

Mondo et autres histoires (Paris: Gallimard, 1978);

L'Inconnu sur la terre (Paris: Gallimard, 1978);

Vers les icebergs (Montpellier: Fata Morgana, 1978);

Voyage au pays des arbres (Paris: Gallimard, 1978);

Désert (Paris: Gallimard, 1980);

Lullaby (Paris: Gallimard, 1980);

Trois Villes saintes (Paris: Gallimard, 1980);

La Ronde et autres faits divers (Paris: Gallimard, 1982);

Celui qui n'avait jamais vu la mer, suivi de La Montagne du dieu vivant (Paris: Gallimard, 1984);

Le Chercheur d'or (Paris: Gallimard, 1985);

Villa Aurore, suivi de Orlamonde (Paris: Gallimard, 1985);

Balaabilou (Paris: Gallimard, 1986);

Voyage à Rodrigues (Paris: Gallimard, 1986);

Les Années Cannes: 40 Ans de festival (Paris: Hatier, 1987);

Le Rêve mexicain ou la pensée interrompue (Paris: Gallimard, 1989).

OTHER: Flannery O'Connor, *Et ce sont les violents qui l'emportent*, translated by Maurice Edgar Coindreau, preface by Le Clézio (Paris: Gallimard, 1965);

Isidore Ducasse, Comte de Lautréamont, *Œuvres complètes: Les Chants de Maldoror, Lettres, Poésies I et II*, edited by Hubert Juin, preface by Le Clézio (Paris: Gallimard, 1973);

Les Prophéties du Chilam Balam, translated, with a preface, by Le Clézio (Paris: Gallimard, 1976);

Max Jacob, *Derniers Poèmes en vers et en prose*, preface by Le Clézio (Paris: Gallimard, 1982);

Relation de Michoacan, translated, with a preface, by Le Clézio (Paris: Gallimard, 1984).

Jean Marie Gustave Le Clézio achieved instant celebrity when his first novel, *Le Procès-verbal* (1963; translated as *The Interrogation*, 1964), published when he was twenty-three, received the Prix Théophraste Renaudot. From that time he has been consistently treated as one of France's major contemporary literary figures. His second novel, *Le Déluge* (1966; translated as *The Flood*, 1967), was one of only four French novels recommended in the *Quinzaine Littéraire* as among "the best books" of 1966, and his essay *L'Extase matérielle* (Material Ecstasy, 1967) was similarly listed the following year. His novel *Désert* was chosen by the staff of *Lire* as the best French book (nonfiction as well as fiction) of the year in 1980, second only to Norman Mailer's *The Executioner's Song* among books from all countries published in France at that time. Many of his works have been best-sellers, no mean tribute to the taste of the French book-buying public, for Le Clézio remains remarkably constant in his artistic

J. M. G. Le Clézio (photograph copyright © Jerry Bauer)

integrity, never making a compromise for the sake of popular favor.

His publications include not only novels but also some of the most interesting short stories currently being produced, along with penetrating, intensely personal essays which reflect most of the major currents of contemporary French thought. At the same time, Le Clézio continues his activity as a literary critic and scholar, as a student of several American Indian cultures, both past and present, and as a professor of French literature. Significantly, he prefers to see himself more as an artisan than as an artist, and he identifies more closely with the public scribe than with the man of letters.

Le Clézio, born 13 April 1940, in Nice, to Raoul Le Clézio, a medical doctor, and his wife, Simone, née Le Clézio, emphasizes the duality of his family's background. He was descended from a Breton settler who immigrated to l'Ile de France (now Mauritius) just after the French Revo-

lution; his grandfathers were brothers, and his parents, therefore, cousins. Yet, because of the curious quirks of history, his mother was a French citizen, his father, British, and all Le Clézio's early works dutifully report that he was born of an English father and a French mother. He identifies so strongly with the Mauritian phase of his family's past that he speaks of having grown up feeling separated from his roots, alienated and foreign. Although his education was predominantly French, he spent a part of his childhood in Nigeria, studied for awhile in Bristol (at the same time he was teaching at Bath Grammar School), then in London, and feels so much at ease in English that he pondered using that language rather than French as his primary mode of expression. As for his degrees, he holds the *licence-ès-lettres* (1963) from what is now the University of Nice, the *maîtrise* from the University of Aix-en-Provence (1964), and is a *docteur-ès-lettres* (1983) from the University of Perpignan.

His writings reflect his love of travel, his interest in knowing numerous peoples and cultures. He performed his military service as a teacher at the Buddhist University of Bangkok and at the University of Mexico. For some four years he spent most of his time living with Indian tribes in Panama, and he has traveled extensively throughout Mexico, the United States, Canada, and in the islands of the Indian Ocean. In recent years he has given courses at several U.S. institutions, including Boston University, the University of Texas at Austin, and the University of New Mexico at Albuquerque.

Admittedly reserved, excessively shy when he was younger, he prefers that his personal life remain private, letting his works speak for themselves. Occasionally he chooses to give the merest glimpse of the domestic side of his existence, as, for example, when, for the tenth anniversary issue of the magazine *Lire*, he provided his own drawing of his daughter Amy. Sketching is, in fact, one of his favorite pastimes; some of his earliest creations were cartoons, and several of his books include samples of his pen-and-ink drawings.

His novels, ultimately, all center around the great questions of the philosophers: the meaning of life, of death; the individual's relation to the physical world, as well as to the social order, and, in particular, the ways in which these relations are mediated through language. Nature is both the great enigma and the great answer, but ever the great fascination, and natural forces–the sun and the sea perhaps above all–play a prominent role throughout his canon. As cognizant as Nietzsche and Jacques Derrida that every event, every idea, every mode of relating is "always already" derived from a long history of similar phenomena, that every mask one removes in the search for truth reveals only another in the infinite series of masks, he persists at the same time in manifesting a Rousseauistic nostalgia for origins. If there is a single dominant characteristic of Le Clézio's style, it is his enthusiastic espousal of an aesthetics of opposites, contradictions, paradoxes, decidedly not in an effort to reconcile them into a synthesis, but rather, it seems, for the sheer love of the beauty of their dialectical tension, or perhaps from a vision of reality so broad that all exclusions must count as falsehoods.

The same problematics lies at the basis of his interest in an oft iterated questioning of language per se. Neither believing in its ability to communicate (a stance made fashionable by the decon-

structionists), nor yet willing to renounce the will to express, Le Clézio, like Albert Camus, Samuel Beckett, Marguerite Duras, and to a certain degree those writers loosely referred to as the New Philosophers, grounds his texts in an epistemology of impotence, continuing the heroic attempt to realize tasks known to be impossible.

Le Clézio's grappling with universal themes correlates naturally with the omnipresence in his works of archetypal figures and situations: cosmogony, the Magna Mater, the fall from innocence, death and rebirth, the flood, the double, the magic flight, the hero's journey, the scapegoat, the shape-shifter, the trickster, the belly of the whale, the toothed vagina, the world navel (and the world tree), the eternal return, the wise fool–these and others of the world's preeminent mythopoetic motifs influence, coincide with, or underlie aspects of his fiction, ranging from details of imagery to some of the most fundamental components of characterization and structure.

Though these writings are profoundly unified thematically, they exhibit wide diversity in technique and a marked progression in tone. In the first works, the quintessential Le Clézian hero passively observes the world around him, submits to its aggressions, attempts to flee from it or to become one with it, but never to act upon it, to change it. Sporadic outbursts of gratuitous violence are his most revealing interactions with his surroundings. A sense of social outrage, a desire even for revolutionary upheaval is present but manifested essentially on the peripheries of the hero's world, in that part which he merely notes rather than in that wherein he actually participates. *Les Géants* (1973; translated as *The Giants*, 1975) marks a turning point, for, even though Bogo and Tranquilité remain primarily victim-figures, Machines, the third major character, actively revolts against sources of repression. Lalla's journey in *Désert* is not a flight but an archetypal quest leading to knowledge and comprehension, terminating, unlike J. H. Hogan's endless wanderings in the 1969 novel *Le Livre des fuites* (translated as *The Book of Flights*, 1971), in a return to her origins. Moreover, the vital secondary story line is the historical tale of a desert tribe's valiant resistance against French aggression. In *Le Chercheur d'or* (The Gold Seeker, 1985), Alexis, impractical idealist though he be, pursues his dream rather than submitting to fate; he, too, unlike the early protagonists, attains a mature sense of satisfaction and understanding.

Le Clézio's experimentations with writing techniques were so varied in his beginning works that some critics chose to group him with the New Novelists, but such a categorization hardly seems applicable. His style embraces everything from the most prosaic and matter-of-fact descriptions, timetables, and lists, to passages of soaring lyricism. He mingles genres, and his novels, stories, and essays include poetry, graphics, multiple distancing mechanisms, and a fair amount of autocriticism. Characters in the first books tend to be allegorical, frankly mythical, self-consciously fictitious, or possessed of a realism which waxes and wanes at the author's whim; the later books are more likely to focus on individualized personages convincing in their verisimilitude.

Adam Pollo, Le Clézio's first fictional hero, the protagonist of Le Procès-verbal, is also the first of several of the author's avatars of Everyman, but the human experience that he represents is one of anomie, frustration, alienation. Unsure whether he has escaped from an insane asylum or deserted from the military, he lives as a squatter in an abandoned house at some remove from town, but near the sea. He spends his days indolently, writing letters, not meant to be sent, to Michèle (a girl he once tried to rape), or just sitting in the sun. He walks to the beach or through the city; watches animals in a zoo; follows a dog; meets Michèle a few times and has sex with her; kills a rat in the house; has a fight with a man he sees with Michèle. After the police come to the house, Adam escapes to the city, where his harangue of a crowd on the street ends in gibberish; when he exposes himself, the police are again called, and they finally capture him in a nursery school. Interned in a mental institution, he is interviewed by students in psychiatry. As the book closes, Adam has withdrawn into total aphasia and regressed into a state of fetuslike dependency.

The interest of Le Procès-verbal lies in its powerful evocation of Adam's estrangement from the social order; the accurate, though slanted, descriptions of the world about him resulting from his attentive obsessions; the imaginative force of his efforts to become one with the physical universe; the psychological acuity of the presentation of his anxieties concerning death, life, sexuality. To these qualities must be added the novel's complex mythological resonances, and the young author's command of narrative techniques, the felicitous lyricism of his prose.

As a result of this novel, and the ensuing Prix Théophraste Renaudot with which it was honored, the timid, unknown twenty-three-year-old who had sent his manuscript through the mail, without agent, without fanfare, to the prestigious Gallimard publishing house, became an instant celebrity. Adulated by the press, which delighted in printing pictures of his "Nordic" good looks, he was much interviewed, quoted, praised. Though such notoriety was excellent for the sales of his book, it accorded ill with Le Clézio's love of privacy.

La Fièvre (1965; translated as Fever, 1966) is a collection of "neuf histoires de petite folie" (nine stories of slight madness), abnormal states provoked by an overdose of sun, a mild fever, a toothache, a passing fit of anger—those few minutes during which "c'est le règne du chaos, de l'aventure" (it is the reign of chaos, of adventure). The title story tells of Roch Estéve's feverish experience on a summer afternoon, when he causes a fight; breaks a window at work; hallucinates that he is becoming his wife, Elisabeth, who, meanwhile, meets an artist who sketches her in a café. The story closes, as it had opened, with Roch's taking a revivifying swim in the sea. "Le Jour où Beaumont fit connaissance avec sa douleur" ("The Day Beaumont Became Acquainted with His Pain"), separately published (1964) before its inclusion in La Fièvre, relates the title character's bout with a severe toothache. His perceptions, already distorted by the suffering he endures, are further affected by the bottle of brandy he drinks as a palliative. A telephone call to Paule pleading for her presence brings only her promise to come the next day and Beaumont's sense of abandonment and anger. He retreats into the aching tooth, sheltered by his very pain. As the story ends, he is sitting on a rooftop in the sunshine, surrounded by bird droppings.

The remaining stories in the collection have scarcely more plot than these two, and sometimes even less: "Il me semble que le bateau se dirige vers l'île" ("It Seems to me the Boat is Heading for the Island") and "Arrière" ("Backwards") close with a quasi-mystical disappearance of the narrator. J. F. Paoli in "L'Homme qui marche" ("The Walking Man"), the very quintessence of the Le Clézian personage of this period, walks, sees, feels, fears, and flees, but finally finds joy and happiness in the sentiment of being in rhythm with universal reality. "Martin," the book's most complex story, can be read as Le Clézio's self-parody, mocking himself both as creator and as the media's fair-haired boy. As a genius, Martin invents a language, defines the state of ecstasy (and thus explicates the condition which marks each of the stories of *La Fièvre*), and condemns the falseness of a social ensemble which treats him "comme un prince et parfois même comme un petit prophète" (like a prince and sometimes like a little prophet). As a hydrocephalic, a helpless victim, he must submit to human brutality as he learns bitter lessons about life in society.

"Le Monde est vivant" ("The World is Alive"), one of Le Clézio's most lyrical passages, describes a mountain valley in minutest detail, "le portrait de quelques kilomètres de lumière, de bruits et de senteurs" (the portrait of a few kilometers of light, sounds, and odors). "Alors je pourrai trouver la paix et le sommeil" ("Then Shall I be Able to Find Peace and Slumber") recounts the narrator's tumultuous physical and psychic sensations after he lies down to sleep. "Un Jour de vieillesse" ("A Day of Old Age") is the boy Joseph Charon's attempt to fathom death as he witnesses the agony of old Maria Vanoni. This volume devoted to the minor madnesses of which life is full, revealing the volcanic nature of each being, underscores death and the extinction of inner fires as Maria writes her final words: "J'ai froid" (I am cold).

These stories, some of which have subsequently appeared in English-language anthologies, all show the heightened sensory experiences of characters in hypersensitive states of consciousness. As consciousness of the body increases, the boundaries between it and the surrounding world seem to fade, and receptivity to the material universe intensifies also. The characters, recognized by their author as "excessive," are shocked into realizing that they truly belong to life.

Le Déluge, Le Clézio's second novel, tells the story of another alienated Everyman, François Besson (the name can be interpreted as "the Frenchman's twin"). Living in the vividly delineated nightmarish hell of the modern city, he cracks under its pressures when, just as he hears a siren, a girl passes by on a motorbike and disappears among concrete buildings, seemingly sucked up by annihilation, just as the siren stops. From that moment on, François sees death everywhere. In the twelve following days he ritualistically divests himself of all links with society (breaking with his mother, with his girlfriend Josette, then forming and breaking a liaison with

Marthe), with various comforts (food, drink, warmth), and with the temptation of a religious solution to his anxieties. Finally, he burns out his eyes by staring at the sun, and survives in apocalyptic delirium. Framing François's story is his friend Anna's: on the first day of his ordeal, he listens to the beginning of a tape she had made for him on which she recounts her own solitude, confusions, and fears. After he has become blind, he listens to the rest of the tape: Anna had recorded her suicide.

Le Clézio's universe had assumed distinctive patterns by this time. Characterized by the dichotomy between a magnificent but inexorably forceful and indifferent nature, and the stridulous aggressivity, the irritations of light, sound, and odors, the crowding, the domination found in civilization, this double decor wracks the nerves and destroys every possibility of peace the protagonist might fashion through the contemplation of both natural and artificial beauty.

Le Déluge received high praise for its power, its poignancy, its inventiveness. Yet Le Clézio was mildly reproved by some critics for what they saw as an exaggerated reliance on certain techniques which they took as mere mannerisms: plays on words, letters, sounds; enumerations; the indiscriminate addition of materials only distantly related to the whole of the text. One critic, however, confessed his unwillingness to quibble over such trifles when dealing with what he viewed as a great book.

L'Extase matérielle, a lengthy essay, is described in a blurb on the cover as a series of meditations written in the manner of a gloss on Le Clézio's own fiction, a discussion of his conviction that the beauty and energy of life derive not from the spirit but from matter. The tripartite structure of the work (before the author's birth, during his life, after his death) will be repeated, with virtually identical meanings, in the novels *Terra Amata* (1967; translated, 1969) and *Voyages de l'autre côté* (Travels to the Other Side, 1975). The ideas developed here will infuse the author's subsequent fictions as prominently as they had his prior ones.

Of primordial importance is the notion that writing provides a uniquely efficacious access for giving meaning to existence. Systems, especially linguistic systems, raise barriers between the self and the world; the goal of plenitude in reunion can be achieved perhaps only in death and in silence, and Le Clézio shows no desire to reconcile these apparently contradictory positions. Much of the vigor of this challenging but essential statement of many of his deepest preoccupations grows out of his refusal to lock his ideas into restrictive systematizations. The very quest for meaning is reflected in the essay's styles. Critics have spoken of the verbosity, the sprawling proliferative disorder, the predilection for oxymora, and other traits which distinguish the book's opening sections–the perfect transcription, indeed, of the doubts, confusions, and anxieties Le Clézio discusses. The final section, "Le Silence," though considered by some to be repetitious, has been lauded by others as "le superbe finale" (the superb finale) for its coherence and for the wisdom it communicates, earning Le Clézio the epithet conferred by Jacques Bersani in the *Nouvelle Revue Française* (July 1967), "notre grand tragique" (our great tragedian).

Terra Amata (the title of the English translation bears the same Latin words, meaning "beloved earth") casts its protagonist once again in the role of Everyman. Here his name is Chancelade, and between the author's "Prologue" and "Epilogue" Chancelade's life from pre-birth to post-death and burial unfolds. He plays, grows up, loves Mina (Jennifer R. Waelti-Walters suggests in *J. M. G. Le Clézio* [1977] that the name is possibly related to Le Clézio's wife, Marina, though an allegorical connection with the medieval German word for love seems highly probable), fathers a son, knows happiness: one of the obscure billions who have peopled the earth and about whom it is wondered whether anything at all of his life will remain after the passage of time.

The sense of angst comes through as strongly here as before, the horror of individual annihilation, too, but this novel depicts a more fully realized zest for living than its predecessors. Furthermore, from the beginning, *Terra Amata* is a self-conscious fiction: the prologue questions the reader's motives in reading this particular book. Le Clézio eventually points out that Chancelade has never existed except as an authorial projection behind the words. His techniques, moreover, call extensive attention to themselves and away from the story: passages in Morse code, in sign language, in incomprehensible words, in "indiscreet" questions, lists, enumerations combine indiscriminately with more conventional prose. One reviewer drew an analogy between these techniques and some of Jean-Luc Godard's cinematic practices. The novel was perceived as a re-creation of Le Clézio's typical novel-

istic universe, which nevertheless corresponds with a quotidian reality barely filtered through the author's personal optics, recalling contemporary American literature and especially J. D. Salinger.

Le Livre des fuites reflects Le Clézio's period spent in the Orient and in Central America to fulfill his military obligations beginning about the time *Le Déluge* was published. It traces Jeune Homme Hogan's (Young Man Hogan, obviously another Everyman, as well as an overt double of the author) voyages through space, time, and various incarnations as he seeks to penetrate the veil which separates him from reality and, simultaneously, to escape from certain socially imposed but personally revolting roles; he wishes also to elude constraints of definition, both in the necessary conventions of language-based communication and in the physical limits inflicted upon human individuality, including those ineluctable frontiers of time beyond which the person no longer exists. Unity or multiplicity? This crucial philosophical content of the work translates into its technical aspects. Le Clézio yields constantly to the temptation of multiplicity: the author is also the personage, the "I" is "he" and vice versa; the "he" is Jeune Homme Hogan, but he is also a host of other names and identities; the novel is, additionally, a commentary on itself and on fiction in general. There is, thus, the recognition that all these escapes from unity can happen only in fiction, this "malhonnêteté désespérante de celui qui n'ose pas dire 'je'" (despairing dishonesty of whoever dares not say "I"). There is, equally, rejection of the concept that language can communicate reality, or unity, that the human spirit can be analyzed, reduced to a few gestures and words. In spite of a consistent calling into question of fiction, Le Clézio proceeds to create, imagine, invent, and the work closes with statements indicating an equivalence between true lives and true books (neither has an end), followed by the phrase "(A suivre)" ([To be continued]), which recalls the ending of *Le Procès-verbal* when the author claims that the reader will probably hear more about Adam Pollo or about some other one "d'entre lui" (from among him).

In his flight, Hogan remains as passive as Le Clézio's other central figures, his travels serving largely to permit an ever-changing field of vision. Social injustices, outrageous tragedies figure conspicuously in what he observes, none worse than in the village of Bilisario Dominguez, where Hogan feels a perfect peace. The village lies amid coffee plantations; the plantation owners have private jets and Rolls Royces–but the workers are all blind, their sight lost because of a malady that could have been averted by insecticides for which the owners refused to pay. Le Clézio's writing achieves peaks of power in the quietly understated ironies of such descriptions.

The previously used techniques of collage, enumerations, the mélange of literary genres recur here in large measure, along with the stylistic resource of refusal or specificity. The signal difference is that in *Le Livre des fuites* these techniques, which might appear gratuitous elsewhere, integrate precisely with the ideas and themes of the novel as a whole. Introduced with a degree of discretion that almost causes them to pass unnoticed, and as well suited to the text as are the numerous less-conventional devices, are the first of Le Clézio's graphics. Because of its skillful matching of form with content, and its intense integration of the author's philosophical, artistic, and social concerns, *Le Livre des fuites* constitutes one of Le Clézio's most satisfying accomplishments and was hailed as such by critics.

It was around this period that Le Clézio began his long sojourns among Panamanian Indians, though *La Guerre* (1970; translated as *War*, 1973), published the year after *Le Livre des fuites*, does not yet echo those experiences. For the first time, Le Clézio places a woman, Bea B., at the center of one of his novels. In truth, she is no more substantial than J. H. Hogan, and, like him, she changes name, identity, and even sex. Similarly, she functions as a fictionalized authorial double who shifts at will between third and first persons. The introduction of Monsieur X, a further double of Bea B., but, too, an independent personage whom she greatly admires, likewise stresses the complexities of Le Clézio's distancing artifices and the difficulties of his search for identifiable truth and reality.

Just as *Terra Amata* was, in a sense, a history of the entire human race, *La Guerre* is, from one perspective, the story of all civilization, including the conflicts among nations. But the very notion of war stands throughout the Le Clézian canon not merely as literal, ugly fact but also as potent image of aggression, symbol of everything that threatens the individual's precarious selfhood. War is all the forces of voluntarism within humanity and no less such external aggressors as technology or the modern city. Thought is war, as is birth itself, which projects us into troubled and troubling life. The novel closes with fourteen pages of photographs, most of which on the surface show rather banal aspects of ordinary modern existence, but all of which can be seen, in the light of Le Clézio's text, as examples of isolation, hostility, regimentation, domination. *La Guerre* amplifies the account of Le Clézio's and his personages' quest for understanding, a search which does not exclude certain elements of mysticism, a kind of belief, sometimes in spite of the evidence to the contrary, that somewhere there lies, there must lie, a magical word, a sign, a design which will stop "war" and somehow explain the whole universe.

Le Clézio's years with the Embera Indians in Panama provided the material for his next three works, all nonfiction, one of which has not been published. *Haï* (1971), a book about Indian art, is Le Clézio's contemplative essay on subjects which lie at the core of all his writings. Approximately a third of the work reproduces photographs of Indian art (including skin-painting) and Western advertisements. In the contrast between the living, magical, utilitarian art of the Indians and the malevolent instruments of tyranny that he sees in Western publicity, he finds matter for reflection on the interrelations between language and thought, between art and nature, between humanity and the universe. The quest to break down the obstacles separating the individual from the material world recurs, as does the desire to transcend the restraints of language and the linguistically imposed necessity of categorization. Language, the tool of domination, is also a mode of access to the cosmos.

A fundamental part of the discussion revolves around the implications of the difference between Western notions of individual artists, the uniqueness of the creative genius and the value accorded to their constructs, and the Indian's anonymous art, eminently disposable, for the Indians prize thought, not objects. Not feeling alienated from the world, they have no need to re-create it, no necessity for affirming the self. Art for them is a collective form of medicine, and Le Clézio holds their attitude in the highest esteem. *Haï* was extolled by critics as important both for what it reveals about the development of Le Clézio's thought and for its cogency as a document concerning the meaning and functions of art.

Mydriase (mydriasis, a protracted or excessive dilation of the pupil), published in 1973 in a limited edition with engravings by Vladimir Velickovic, is a short text that evokes and discourses upon a drug-induced trance. The Le Clézian thematic syndrome of looking/seeing/ blindness/light/darkness predominates, and other motifs reappear: the relations between language and the physical world, anxiety and solitude, creativity, oppression, the wish for direct experience of the universe, the retreat to the security of the womb. Drugs give an aura of mystical insight into the sense of one's entire existence, that kind of awareness which many of Le Clézio's characters seek. Intimately linked though it be with Le Clézio's major works, *Mydriase* has received but the scantiest of critical attention.

Le Clézio's next major work would have had for its title, if possible, only a graphic symbol: the lightning bolt used throughout Europe to warn of mortal danger. It does, indeed, bear this symbol, but for practical reasons it has the secondary title *Les Géants* (enclosed within parentheses on the book's cover, although not on the title page). Symbolical languages and graphics, multiple typefaces, stock-market quotations, advertising copy, all play major roles in this work, which is as much a warning and an exhortation to vigilance and revolt as it is a novel.

The tone is set in the dedication to "Ch'in Shih Huang Ti," the first Chinese emperor, "très respectueusement, admirativement" (very respectfully, admiringly), and, one might add, very ironically. Ching's major achievements include ordering the burning of books, the killing of scholars assembled to read or discuss the classics, the branding of anyone found still possessing books, and the forced labor of such persons (when they were not buried alive) on his pet project, the Great Wall.

Today's equivalents of such tyrants are the Masters of thought and language, the giants of capitalism, technology, marketing, of government. Interspersed with a running intertext concerning the methods of marketing based on motivational research (most of this information is easily accessible in, say, Vance Packard's 1957 book on the psychology of advertising, *The Hidden Persuaders*), Le Clézio's novel discloses the effects of giant corporate greed and violent desire for total control over the lives of his three principal characters, a young woman named Tranquilité, her friend Machines, and a solitary child, Bogo the Mute, who spends his days as a passive onlooker, seeing life from the parking lot surrounding the immense supermarket Hyperpolis (the super-city, but also, far more menacingly, the super-police-state) where Machines works.

The characters are slightly developed, cardboard figures set up to represent the giants' legion of innocent victims.

Les Géants ends with deliberately enigmatic ambivalence, suggesting that one's fears can be transcended, that one might successfully revolt, but that the wolves have already completed their bloody slaughter of the sheep; and the ultimate act of burning Hyperpolis is still in the hortatory, not the declarative mode. Although reviewers noted the persistence of the author's primary concerns and methods in *Les Géants* and admired the powerful passions inspiring the work, along with the skill of much of the writing, there was a decided amount of critical disaffection with regard to the end result.

Voyages de l'autre côté, Le Clézian in every essential facet, nevertheless offers fuller ramifications of the author's thought which had existed earlier only in more rudimentary form. Happiness appears in this novel as a given, and it is guaranteed by the benevolence of Naja Naja, a mythical incarnation of the Great Mother. Structured like *L'Extase matérielle* and *Terra Amata*, with the central panel of a triptych representing life, preceded by pre-birth, followed by after-death, this novel depicts Naja Naja as she leads a band of barely differentiated followers in a quest for totality, penetrating to the other side of language, of the senses, of solitude and anguish, to find the immemorial truths of immutable eternity. Poetic, visionary, filled with masterfully elaborated descriptions and highly charged imagery, and with a notable degree of childlike simplicity (all the other characters *are* like children in their relationship with Naja Naja), *Voyages de l'autre côté* was acclaimed for its extraordinary, beautiful writing as well as for its profundity.

Le Clézio's interest in Central American Indian societies inspired his next major publication, a translation of ancient Mayan texts titled *Les Prophéties du Chilam Balam* (1976). His preface emphasizes several Le Clézian themes: the view of language and books as magic, the importance of the sun, the desire for harmony with the universe, undertaking escape from death, an awareness of solitude.

The next two books, *Mondo et autres histoires* (Mondo and Other Stories, 1978) and *L'Inconnu sur la terre* (The Unknown One on the Earth, 1978), were written during the same period and published a week apart. They display numerous analogous thematic preoccupations: a dominance of the sun and the sea, light and shadow; the primordial roles given to language and the senses, especially "le regard" (gaze); the need for liberty and authenticity; the desire for beauty.

Each of the eight stories of *Mondo et autres histoires* narrates the tale of a visionary child, literally or figuratively orphaned, mystically connected with an ideal which may or may not actually exist alongside the everyday world of adults, but which is always purer, more beautiful, more intense. Their relationships are with other children or with persons who live on the margins of normal society, a privileged case being that of the friendship between an old person and a child. There are occasional glimpses of Le Clézio's indignation at the manipulation and mistreatment of society's weaker members ("Mondo," and especially "Hazaran"); but these often powerful and moving stories are essentially lyrical evocations of childhood's wonder-filled vision of the universe, where aspects of ugliness and terror only highlight the overriding presence of happiness and delight. Every story emphasizes the child's heightened sensitivity and passionate awareness of the natural world and its enigmas. Gallimard subsequently published various stories from *Mondo et autres histoires* in its children's series Folio Junior. *Lullaby* appeared in 1980; *Celui qui n'avait jamais vu la mer, suivi de La Montagne du dieu vivant* (He Who Has Never Seen the Sea; The Mountain of the Living God) is from 1984.

Le Clézio himself does not see *L'Inconnu sur la terre* as an exploration of mysteries or an attempt to invent myths; it is, he has suggested, perhaps just the story of an unknown little boy wandering near the sea, reveling in the extreme light of day. The work has been referred to as an intimate journal, detailing what Le Clézio believes, what he loves, outlining his *ars poetica*, and composed largely of prose poems tending toward religious exercises. In *L'Inconnu sur la terre* the author is still hoping to discover ways of overcoming all the obstacles separating humanity from the "real world." His descriptions, aimed to make the reader *see* familiar objects, rather than merely ascertain them, focus on such subjects as flowers, vegetables, insects, seashells, storms, clouds, bread, rocks, trees, smiles, sleep, or on such common activities as flying kites and eating oranges.

The "unknown one" of the title is an inscrutable child, close cousin of Antoine de Saint-Exupéry's little prince, even more closely related to children in the stories of *Mondo*, in particular the "god" of "La Montagne du dieu vivant." Le Clézio's fictions only rarely display interest in the creation of "characters"; this child receives even less such attention than do most. Sometimes serving as the protagonist in anecdotes involving a specific child, the figure is rather a reminder of the child in each of us, the potential for a purer contact with the world, less inhibited by customs and codes, more open to magic and marvel.

Critics, reviewing the two books together, judged the stories as charmingly strange and extolled the limpidity and simplicity of the style. *L'Inconnu sur la terre*, though deemed somewhat repetitious and naive, was nonetheless perceived as stylistically pleasing when read in small portions at a time and as an essential commentary on the deeper meanings of the stories. One critic proclaimed Le Clézio the visionary writer "le meilleur de sa génération" (the best of his generation).

Vers les icebergs (Towards the Icebergs, 1978) mirrors Le Clézio's fascination with Henri Michaux's poetry. The essay's treatment of certain of the poet's themes, and in particular its discussion of his language, help elucidate the affinities between the two authors.

Voyage au pays des arbres (A Journey to the Land of Trees, 1978), a children's bedtime story lavishly illustrated by Henri Galeron, revolves around a child figure, like Le Clézio's two major works of this same year. In an interview published at the time, Le Clézio avowed his own profound identification with this child, who remains basically similar from story to story despite changes of name and circumstances.

The 1980 novel *Désert* intersperses two narratives recounted in alternating sequences. The hallucinatory account of the "blue men" of the desert in their holy war against the infidel French invaders provides a historical backdrop and contrast to the story of Lalla, the novel's principal character. In the winter of 1909-1910 the great sheik Ma el Aïnine led his army of believers across the desert, while their number diminished daily because of the hardships of the journey. Even Ma el Aïnine dies, but he passes his spiritual power on to Nour, the youth around whom this section of the novel is articulated. The army's encounter with the French ends in a general massacre, and the few survivors return to the desert, disappearing as though in a dream.

In counterpoint with this sympathetically related episode of suffering and defeat is Lalla's tale. A descendant of the blue men, she embodies happiness itself for Le Clézio. Growing up in a shantytown, fully in harmony with the beauties of nature–light and dark, sea and desert, stones and clouds–she has visions of Es Ser (The Secret), whom she identifies with the Blue Man, and in whose words and gaze she finds guidance. Loving and becoming pregnant by the Hartani, she can follow him only so far into the desert before she turns back. Naman, an old fisherman whose stories enthralled Lalla, predicts she will go to France. After his death she does, and experiences life "chez les esclaves" (among the slaves) in Marseilles. She toils as a scrubwoman before achieving celebrity as a cover girl, but when the moment of her delivery approaches, she goes back to the desert to give birth to her daughter. In 1986 one of the stories told by Naman was extracted for publication under the title *Balaabilou*, with illustrations by Georges Lemoine.

Trois Villes saintes (Three Holy Cities, 1980), published simultaneously with *Désert*, adds to Le Clézio's writings on Central American Indian societies. A short text concerning present-day Mayans, it depicts the inhabitants of the only three villages which have not forgotten the religious promise of prophecies predicting liberation from the Spanish. The book's structure follows a mystic progression from the dust and dryness of the beginnings, when old soldiers watch and wait for the water that represents both vengeance and liberty, through the nightlong prayer of an old man whose powers will produce the cycle of water, to the ending when the clouds (or perhaps the gods) begin to gather and the first drops of rain fall.

Désert was termed one of the biggest literary events of the year, a magnificent meditation, one of Le Clézio's most beautiful books. *Trois Villes saintes*, though found somewhat inaccessible by certain reviewers (the obscurities can be cleared up by recourse to Le Clézio's introduction to *Les Prophéties du Chilam Balam*), was discussed mainly as further expounding those themes of the enduring strength of vanquished peoples and their cultures. In the year these two books appeared, Le Clézio was selected as the first recipient of the Paul Morand literary prize awarded by the Académie Française.

La Ronde et autres faits divers (The Round and Other News-in-Brief Items, 1982) plunges the reader back into the darker side of Le Clézio's imaginings. These eleven stories, some (perhaps all?) inspired by news items of preceding years, concern human suffering and victims of the social order. Solitude, anguish, injustice,

repression, lack of understanding once more thwart characters' instinctual strivings for love, beauty, security, and liberty. Subjects include rape, theft, manhunts, imprisonment, demolitions of cherished buildings, betrayal, violent accidents resulting in death or mutilation.

The characters, many in close sensory union with nature, envision a possible happiness, at times in a lost childhood paradise, at others in an improbable future, but in every case this chance for fulfillment, when it is not completely negated, lies under a terrible menace. *La Ronde et autres faits divers*, another critical success, was referred to by *Nouvel Observateur* reviewer Claude Roy as Le Clézio's "merveilleux dernier livre" (marvelous latest book). In a notice headlined "Le Clézio de meilleur en meilleur" (Le Clézio, Better and Better), Roy described the work as a new summit in Le Clézio's ascensional movement of creation and declared the author himself one of "les grands écrivains" (the greatest writers). Two of the stories from *La Ronde et autres faits divers* were extracted and published in the Folio Junior series in 1985 under the title *Villa Aurore, suivi de Orlamonde*.

Relation de Michoacan (1984), another Indian text translated and prefaced by Le Clézio, demonstrates his abiding insistence upon preserving the memory of past cultures, the spirit and grandeur of their people. The volume recounts the history of the Porhépechas' faith and beliefs, the names and qualities of their gods and heroes. Le Clézio's introduction, not surprisingly, makes clear his own special identification with this ancient book filled with mystery and magic.

The 1985 novel *Le Chercheur d'or* begins with facts from the file of the author's paternal grandfather, allies them with certain mythological themes, in particular the story of Jason and the Argonauts and the biblical account of the Garden of Eden, and thereupon filters them through Le Clézio's unique creative vision. One meets with expected themes: solitude and dread; the threat of death, loss, abandonment; the call to evasion; the quest for meaning; revolt against oppression and social exploitation; sympathy for marginal characters; identification with childhood and with childlike attitudes and perceptions; the superiority of nature and the natural state.

The novel comprises Alexis L'Etang's search for a corsair's treasure believed to be hidden on the island of Rodrigues. After his father's death and the loss of the family estate, Alexis sets out to find the fortune he hopes will reestablish his mother and sister in their former life of peace and happiness. His journey, lasting years, turns out to be both successful (he believes he has broken the codes, found the pirate's retreat) and futile (the hiding place is empty). The sojourn on Rodrigues is interrupted by a period of service in the British army during World War I. Over these many years, he meets, loves, and twice loses the beautiful Ouma, from whom he learns that all true values are permanent interior ones, not related to gold, a symbol of false and evanescent exterior values.

Le Chercheur d'or, so similar stylistically and thematically to the rest of the Le Clézian corpus, was accorded a curiously mixed press. The book was criticized for juvenile metaphors, for lacking verisimilitude in the evocation of Alexis's world, for its disappointing anticlimactic conclusion. The review *Lire*, normally one of Le Clézio's champions, published a notice that was not only totally negative but downright vicious as well, deriding the work as boring, the style as laborious exoticism, the images as derived from postcard aesthetics, and the ideas as those of a metaphysical Boy Scout. On the positive side, the work was hailed in other quarters for its "force prodigieuse" (prodigious strength), for the beauty of its descriptions, the emotional impact of such scenes as the helmsman's death and burial, the exactness and sensorial quality of its style.

The journal *Voyage à Rodrigues* (1986), meant to be read in conjunction with *Le Chercheur d'or*, is the author's account of the real-life drama that had inspired the novel, as well as of his own visit to the island where his grandfather's adventures had transpired. His sense of identification with this grandfather, whom he had never known, leads him into further reflections on the significance of time and eternity, the powers of dreams and of their preservation. The work has been declared a classic of the genre of book which describes travels and the transformations they effect on those who undertake them, to be considered in a class with Michel Leiris's *L'Afrique fantôme* and Claude Lévi-Strauss's *Tristes Tropiques*.

Les Années Cannes: 40 Ans de festival (The Cannes Years: Forty Years of Festivals, 1987) is somewhat of a curiosity in the Le Clézian canon. Essentially a picture book, presenting a year-by-year account of the Cannes film festival, it opens with an essay by Le Clézio entitled "La Magie du cinéma" (The Magic of the Cinema). In this trib-

ute to directors, stars, and films he has admired, Le Clézio touches on many of the ideas and themes that dominate the rest of his production: the transforming powers of the imagination, the beauty of the world, childhood, the cosmogony, the infinite and that which exceeds all limits, metamorphoses, anxiety and death and rebirth. Recurring images in the essay include such familiar and major ones as those of penetration, the gaze, the center, the abyss, light, and heat.

Le Rêve mexicain ou la pensée interrompue (The Mexican Dream, or Thought Interrupted, 1989) continues Le Clézio's reflections on native cultures of the Americas, already evoked in *Haï*, *Trois Villes saintes*, and in the translations and presentations in *Les Prophéties du Chilam Balam* and *Relation de Michoacan*. This collection of essays is important for many reasons. The first of Le Clézio's "Indian" works to achieve popular success, it includes a great amount of information on Mexico before the conquest, its history, peoples, religion, and customs. Le Clézio considers the destruction of this ancient civilization to have been "le plus grand désastre de l'humanité" (the greatest disaster in human history). He assumes here the role of an eloquent, impassioned apostle proclaiming the necessity of conserving and propagating the memory of this vanished culture.

Although the provenance of the book is nowhere clearly indicated, it is a collection of essays, at least some of which had already been published, including one that Le Clézio wrote in Spanish. A natural consequence of the book's diverse origins is an unfortunate propensity toward repetition of ideas, illustrations, and even quotations from other texts.

In several instances Le Clézio's efforts to simplify, to make these materials accessible to the general public, cause the work to become simplistic. Anecdotes removed from their context are used to prove ideas that differ slightly from what they actually demonstrate. Le Clézio resorts to a rhetoric of antitheses in order to contrast the sixteenth-century Europeans—entirely rational and materialistic—with the Indians, portrayed as living in a mythical, intuitive relation with the cosmos—nonrational, nonmaterialistic. The resulting exaggerations necessarily weaken some of his arguments. At times, Le Clézio attributes great originality to certain Indian concepts that are actually widely attested in other cultures.

Le Rêve mexicain stands, nevertheless, as an essential work, as much for the lessons of history and culture to be found therein as for the urgency of its message, and especially for all that it reveals about the development of Le Clézian thought. The work received a curiously dispassionate (reverential perhaps?) reception in the French press. One critic speculated on the possibility that the work may be "une introspection déguisée en recherche historique" (an introspection disguised as historical research); another pointed out that the work depicts the confrontation between two grand dreams, that of the Indians and that of the conquerors, and that both dreams are "superbement décrits" (superbly described). But mostly the reviews are coupled with brief interviews with the author and either a short excerpt from the book or an objective recounting of its contents.

J. M. G. Le Clézio is one of France's most highly regarded literary figures. Though individual works are sometimes severely criticized, the consensus is that even his lesser works deserve the attention that only the most important writers receive. The recent rapid rise of *Le Rêve mexicain ou la pensée interrompue* on the best-seller lists, in spite of its defects and difficulties, says much about the general perception of the writings of this prolific author.

Three more of his books have been announced as forthcoming: a novel describing the childhood and adolescence of a young Palestinian girl, a collection of short stories entitled "Printemps" (Spring), and an autobiographical narrative about Le Clézio's trip when, as a child, he traveled to rejoin his father in Africa. It appears that Le Clézio is becoming more comfortable with the idea that the public wants to know the person behind the books. The frankly autobiographical aspects of *Voyage à Rodrigues*, the proposed volume about his boyhood trip, and his appearance on the television program *Apostrophes* during the fall of 1988 seem to bespeak a newfound ease about revealing himself to his public. (In 1978 he would permit photographs only at thirty meters' remove; close-up shots of him have recently become common in the French press.) Perhaps someday it will be possible to write a biography of Le Clézio with the author's full consent and cooperation.

Interviews:

Madeleine Chapsal, "Etre jeune, c'est un peu répugnant," *Express*, 21 November 1963, pp. 31-32;

Alain Jouffroy and François Bott, "Godard, Le Clézio face à face," *Express*, 9-15 May 1966, pp. 128-130, 135-138;

Pierre Lhoste, *Conversations avec J. M. G. Le Clézio* (Paris: Mercure de France, 1971);

Pierre Boncenne, "J. M. G. Le Clézio s'explique," *Lire*, 32 (April 1978): 20-49;

Jean-Louis Ezine, "J. M. G. Le Clézio," in his *Les Ecrivains sur la sellette* (Paris: Editions du Seuil, 1981), pp. 47-51.

References:

Jacques Bersani, "Le Clézio sismographe," *Critique*, no. 238 (March 1967): 311-321;

Bersani, "Sagesse de Le Clézio," *Nouvelle Revue Française*, no. 175 (July 1967): 110-115;

Pierre de Boisdeffre, "Le Clézio, Beckett . . . vers un 'au-delà de la littérature,' " in his *Où va le roman? Essai*, revised and enlarged edition (Paris: Del Duca, 1972), pp. 263-277;

Maurice Cagnon, "J. M. G. Le Clézio: The Genesis of Writing," *Language and Style*, 5 (Summer 1972): 221-227;

Cagnon, "J. M. G. Le Clézio, l'impossible vérité de la fiction," *Critique*, no. 297 (February 1972): 158-164;

Cagnon and Stephen Smith, "J. M. G. Le Clézio: Fiction's Double Bind," in *Surfiction: Fiction Today and Tomorrow*, edited by Raymond Federman (Chicago: Swallow Press, 1975), pp. 215-226;

Cagnon and Smith, "Le Clézio's Taoist Vision," *French Review*, 47, special issue no. 6 (Spring 1974): 245-252;

Cagnon and Smith, "*Martin:* A Portrait of the Artist as a Young Hydrocephalic," *International Fiction Review*, 2 (1975): 64-67;

Cagnon and Smith, "*Mors et anima:* La Dialectique du paradoxe plausible," *Revue du Pacifique*, 1 (Spring 1975): 33-42;

Teresa Di Scanno, *La Vision du monde de Le Clézio: cinq études sur l'œuvre* (Naples: Liguori, 1983);

Ruth Holzberg, *L'Œil du serpent: Dialectique du silence dans l'oeuvre de J. M. G. Le Clézio* (Sherbrooke, Quebec: Editions Naaman, 1981);

Salij H. Jathar, "J. M. G. Le Clézio's *Le Déluge* and American Criticism," *Œuvres et Critiques*, 2 (Winter 1977-1978): 117-124;

Patricia J. Johnson, "Adam Pollo and the Greek Connection: The Mythological Dimensions of Le Clézio's *Le Procès-verbal*," *Classical and Modern Literature*, 4 (Fall 1983): 5-14;

Marguerite Le Clézio, "L'Etre sujet/objet: La Vision active et passive chez Le Clézio," in *Ethique et esthétique dans la littérature française du XXᵉ siècle*, edited by Maurice Cagnon, Stanford French and Italian Studies, volume 10 (Saratoga, Cal.: Anma Libri, 1978);

Le Clézio, "Langage ou réalité: La Phénoménologie platonicienne de J. M. G. Le Clézio," *French Review*, 54 (March 1981): 530-537;

Roger Mathé, *L'Exotisme d'Homère à Le Clézio* (Paris: Bordas, 1972);

Jacqueline Michel, *Une Mise en récit du silence: Le Clézio, Bosco, Gracq* (Paris: José Corti, 1986);

Neal Oxenhandler, "Nihilism in Le Clézio's *La Fièvre*," in *Symbolism and Modern Literature: Studies in Honor of Wallace Fowlie*, edited by Marcel Tétel (Durham: Duke University Press, 1978), pp. 264-273;

Wanda Rupolo, "La narrazione metafisica di Le Clézio," *Nuova Antologia*, no. 520 (February 1974): 190-200; reprinted as "Le Clézio e il linguaggio matematico," in her *Il Linguaggio dell'Immagine* (Rome: Bonacci, 1979), pp. 217-232;

Pierre-Henri Simon, "J. M. G. Le Clézio," in his *Parier pour l'homme* (Paris: Seuil, 1973), pp. 303-313;

Stephen Smith, "Le Clézio's Search for Self in a World of Words," *Modern Language Studies*, 10 (Spring 1980): 49-58;

Jennifer R. Waelti-Walters, *Icare ou l'évasion impossible: Etude psycho-mythique de l'œuvre de J. M. G. Le Clézio* (Sherbrooke, Quebec: Editions Naaman, 1981);

Waelti-Walters, *J. M. G. Le Clézio* (Boston: Twayne, 1977);

Waelti-Walters, "Narrative movement in J. M. G. Le Clézio's *Fever*," *Studies in Short Fiction*, 14 (Summer 1977): 247-254;

Gerda Zeltner, "Le Clézio: Le Roman antiformaliste," in *Positions et oppositions sur le roman contemporain*, edited by Michel Mansuy (Strasbourg: Klincksieck, 1971), pp. 215-228.

Françoise Mallet-Joris
(Françoise Lilar)
(6 July 1930-)

Marie Naudin
University of Connecticut

BOOKS: *Poèmes du dimanche*, as Françoise Lilar (Brussels: Editions des Artistes, 1947);

Le Rempart des béguines, as Françoise Mallet (Paris: Julliard, 1951); translated by Herma Briffault as *The Illusionist* (New York: Farrar, Straus & Young, 1952); republished as *Into the Labyrinth* (London: Secker, 1953);

La Chambre rouge (Paris: Julliard, 1955); translated by Briffault as *The Red Room* (New York: Farrar, Straus & Cudahy, 1956; London: Allen, 1956);

Les Mensonges (Paris: Julliard, 1956); translated by Briffault as *House of Lies* (New York: Farrar, Straus, 1957; London: Allen, 1958);

Cordélia (Paris: Julliard, 1956); translated by Peter Green as *Cordelia and Other Stories* (New York: Farrar, Straus & Giroux, 1965; London: Allen, 1965);

L'Empire céleste (Paris: Julliard, 1958); translated by Briffault as *Café Céleste* (New York: Farrar, Straus & Cudahy, 1959; London: Allen, 1959);

Les Personnages (Paris: Julliard, 1961); translated by Briffault as *The Favourite* (New York: Farrar, Straus & Cudahy, 1962; London: Allen, 1962);

Lettre à moi-même (Paris: Julliard, 1963); translated by Patrick O'Brian as *A Letter to Myself* (New York: Farrar, Straus, 1964; London: Allen, 1964);

Marie Mancini, le premier amour de Louis XIV (Paris: Hachette, 1964); translated by O'Brian as *The Uncompromising Heart: A Life of Marie Mancini, Louis XIV's First Love* (New York: Farrar, Straus & Giroux, 1966; London: Allen, 1966);

Enfance ton regard (Paris: Hachette, 1966);

Les Signes et les prodiges (Paris: Grasset, 1966); translated by Briffault as *Signs and Wonders* (New York: Farrar, Straus & Giroux, 1966; London: Allen, 1967);

Françoise Mallet-Joris (photograph copyright © Jerry Bauer)

Trois Ages de la nuit: Histoires de la sorcellerie (Paris: Grasset, 1968); translated by Briffault as *The Witches: Three Tales of Sorcery* (New York: Farrar, Straus & Giroux, 1969; London: Allen, 1970);

La Maison de papier (Paris: Grasset, 1970); translated by Derek Coltman as *The Paper House* (New York: Farrar, Straus & Giroux, 1971; London: Allen, 1971);

A propos de Madame de Sévigné (Liège: Dynamo, 1971);

Le Roi qui aimait trop les fleurs (Tournai: Casterman, 1971);

Les Feuilles mortes d'un bel été (Paris: Grasset, 1973);

Le Jeu du souterrain (Paris: Grasset, 1973); translated by Briffault as *The Underground Game* (London: Allen, 1974; New York: Dutton, 1975);

Le Cirque (Paris: Robert Mouret, 1974);

J'aurais voulu jouer de l'accordéon (Paris: Julliard, 1975);

Juliette Gréco, by Mallet-Joris and Michel Grisolia (Paris: Seghers, 1975);

Allégra (Paris: Grasset, 1976);

Jeanne Guyon (Paris: Flammarion, 1978);

Dickie-Roi (Paris: Grasset, 1979);

Un Chagrin d'amour et d'ailleurs (Paris: Grasset, 1981);

Le Clin d'œil de l'ange (Paris: Gallimard, 1983);

Le Rire de Laura (Paris: Gallimard, 1985);

Marie-Paule Belle (Paris: Seghers, 1987);

Tristesse du cerf-volant (Paris: Flammarion, 1988).

OTHER: *Nouvelles*, edited by Mallet-Joris (Paris: Julliard, 1957);

"Les Personnages féminins dans l'œuvre de François Mauriac," in Mauriac's *Le Désert de l'amour* (Paris: Amis du Club du Livre du Mois, 1959), pp. 35-37;

"Un Roman de solitaire: Un Ouragan de passions," in Emily Brontë's *Haute-Plainte*, translated by Jacques and Yolande de Lacretelle (Paris: Club des Amis du Livre, 1961), pp. 19-24;

Yaël Dayan, *Sables*, translated by Mallet-Joris (Paris: Julliard, 1963);

Rendez-vous donné par Françoise Mallet-Joris à quelques jeunes écrivains, edited by Mallet-Joris (Paris: Julliard, 1963);

John Cheever, *Les Wapshot*, translated by Geneviève Naudin, preface by Mallet-Joris (Paris: Julliard, 1965);

Honoré de Balzac, *Les Célibataires (Pierrette, Le Curé de Tours)*, edited by H. A. Ducourneau, preface by Mallet-Joris (Paris: Livre de Poche, 1967);

Gertrude von Le Fort, *La Femme éternelle; La Femme dans le temps; La Femme hors du temps*, translated by André Boccon-Gibod, preface by Mallet-Joris (Paris: Editions du Cerf, 1968);

"Madame de Sévigné vue par Françoise Mallet-Joris," in *Lettres de Madame de Sévigné* (Paris: Club des Classiques, 1969), pp. 5-31;

Marc Attali, *Attali*, preface by Mallet-Joris (Paris: Balland, 1971).

PERIODICAL PUBLICATION: *Un Goût de miel*, translated and adapted by Mallet-Joris and Gabriel Arout from Shelagh Delaney's play *A Taste of Honey*, *Avant-Scène*, 217 (1 April 1960): 9-29.

"Membre de l'Académie Goncourt, championne du best-seller qui devient feuilleton de télévision, professionnelle jusqu'au bout des ongles, Françoise Mallet-Joris, avec sa coiffure stricte de grande bourgeoise, ses sourires télévisuels quand il faut et son ton conciliant un peu chantant de petite fille bien élevée, semble installée dans sa carrière de femme de lettres comme on peut l'être dans ses meubles" (Member of the Goncourt Academy, champion of the televised best-seller, professional down to the tip of her toes, Françoise Mallet-Joris, with her classy hairdos, her on-cue TV smiles, and the conciliatory manner of a refined lady, seems to be settled into her career of woman of letters as one might settle into an armchair). This portrait from the 1980s by Jacques Bofford, a Swiss radio commentator, accurately depicts the image that Mallet-Joris evokes in French-speaking European countries. As an individual and as a spokesperson, she is representative of the generation that was in its teens at the end of World War II. Her novels acknowledge a period of change and explore the problem of human values.

Françoise-Eugénie-Julienne Lilar was born in Antwerp, Belgium, on 6 July 1930. Her father, Albert Lilar, was a lawyer, a professor of maritime law, and four times minister of justice. Her mother, Suzanne Verbist Lilar, a writer and member of the Belgian Academy, was the first woman to practice law in Antwerp. Her sister, Marie Lilar, was born in 1934. Until the age of four, Françoise Lilar spoke mainly Flemish with her maid, Maria. She continued to study this language and became bilingual. In 1936 she entered a private school in Antwerp. She discovered literature through Hans Christian Andersen's tales. The wartime exodus took her to Brive-la-Gaillarde, in France, for several months. At sixteen she ran away in the company of a playwright, Louis Ducreux. In 1947 she left for America, where she studied at Bryn Mawr College and married Robert Amadou, a professor of French. Her son Daniel was born 25 December 1947. Mallet-Joris's marriage ended in divorce. She returned to Europe, settling in Paris, and at nineteen she took courses in literature at the Sorbonne.

At twenty she wrote *Le Rempart des béguines* (1951; translated as *The Illusionist*, 1952), which was published by Julliard under the pseudonym Françoise Mallet, chosen (at random) so as not to disrupt her father's political career. After a summer traveling by motorcycle in Greece she began to work for Julliard as a reader in 1952. In order to avoid confusion with the writer Robert Mallet, she added the Flemish first name Joris to her pseudonym. That same year she married the historian Alain Joxe, whom she divorced soon thereafter. The following years were punctuated by her conversion to Catholicism, proven to be a durable one, a trip to Tunisia, and her marriage to the painter Jacques Delfau, with whom she had a son, Vincent, in 1955, and two daughters, Alberte, in 1958, and Pauline, in 1960. Although married to a Frenchman, she remains very attached to Belgium, where she regularly spends time.

Mallet-Joris claims that she always had a penchant for writing. Her mother encouraged her, corrected her, and gave her advice. Her first novel (unpublished), "La Maison sous la mer" (The House under the Sea), dates from her ninth year, and her first verse, *Poèmes du dimanche* (Sunday Poems), which the Belgian playwright Fernand Crommelynck admired, appeared in 1947, her seventeenth year, under her maiden name. Having been brought up by relatively liberal parents, she did not hesitate, as did most of the younger generation after World War II, to venture forth at an early age in worldly pursuits. The hopes and disappointments she experienced are reflected in her first two published novels, even though she claims that the plot of *Le Rempart des béguines* was derived from a story told to her at the age of twelve by a school friend.

Both *Le Rempart des béguines* and *La Chambre rouge* (1955; translated as *The Red Room*, 1956) are written in the form of a confessional novel in the first person, and their subject is the romantic awakening of the same heroine, Hélène Noris. In the first novel, as a motherless child Hélène falls in love with her father's mistress. Homosexual relations develop between Hélène and Tamara, a prototype of the liberated woman. However, once Tamara marries her father and blends into the very society which she had mocked, Hélène discovers that her friend is incapable of true love. In the sequel Hélène learns that she, too, has limitations. Stealing a potential lover from Tamara, who is now her stepmother, Hélène receives permission from this lover to carry on other relationships as well. This she does and thus destroys what could have been a lasting relationship between them. With some bitterness, Hélène realizes that true love comprises a transhuman dimension that requires much patience and self-denial.

These two novels constitute the point of departure for all of Mallet-Joris's subsequent work, in view of their acknowledgment of a tenacious desire for the absolute and their simultaneous recognition that absolutes are incompatible with an existence made up of compromises and lies. Novels of apprenticeship, they reveal disappointment in the confidences shared by human beings. In a style which foreshadows the works of Mallet-Joris's contemporary Françoise Sagan, these two works are also reminiscent of the libertine trend of the eighteenth century as well as of the perverse heights of Colette. They have had more than an ephemeral success occasioned by their shock value. The first novel has had numerous printings (more than five hundred thousand copies to date). In addition, both works have been made into films: *Le Rempart des béguines* in 1972, directed by Guy Casaril, and *La Chambre rouge* in 1973, directed by Jean-Pierre Berckmans.

A former brothel, hotel rooms, carnivals–all of the sensuality of northern Europe is found under a good-natured, virtuous veneer in *Les Mensonges*, published in 1956 (and translated as *House of Lies*, 1957). The setting is Antwerp with alternating foci on the van Baarsheim residence and a hovel known as the Triangle d'Or. A first-person narrative gives way to an objective fresco depicting the last days of a wealthy bourgeois fallen prey to his legitimate and illegitimate heirs. No sooner has Klaes van Baarsheim's illegitimate daughter Alberte left the Triangle d'Or for shelter in the van Baarsheim home than she willingly returns, finding more authenticity there than in the hypocrisy of the upper-middle class. This book, which one might describe as Balzacian, was followed by a collection of short stories, *Cordélia* (1956; translated as *Cordelia and Other Stories*, 1965). The young vagabond of the title story is from the same milieu as Alberte; the eleven stories accompanying this one relinquish a Belgian setting for others in the United States, Austria, Italy, and France. One of them, "Les Poubelles" ("The Garbage Cans"), broaches the typically French theme of workers on strike. It was made into a film in 1959, directed by Louis Grospierre and entitled *Le Travail c'est la liberté* (Work Is Freedom).

The years 1957 and 1958 were decisive ones in Mallet-Joris's career. In 1957 she received the Prix des Libraires de France for *Les Mensonges*, and King Baudoin of Belgium awarded her a medal of honor. In addition, Julliard asked her to edit some anthologies of short works by young writers; *Nouvelles* (Short Stories) was published that year, and *Rendez-vous donné par Françoise Mallet-Joris à quelques jeunes écrivains* (Françoise Mallet-Joris's Rendezvous with Some Young Writers) appeared in 1963. Her 1958 novel, *L'Empire céleste* (translated as *Café Céleste*, 1959), received the coveted Prix Fémina. Money from the literary prizes allowed Mallet-Joris to buy a second home, a farmhouse known as Gué-de-la-Chaîne, in the Orne region of lower Normandy.

L'Empire céleste concludes a series of works dominated by themes involving lust and money. This study of residents of a Parisian apartment building is reminiscent of Emile Zola's *Pot-Bouille*; however, it is as much a psychological novel as it is a behavioral study. The main character, Stéphane, ironically falls victim to the facade that he himself has constructed. Contrary to Alberte's situation in Mallet-Joris's preceding novel, Stéphane must forsake his lodgings and his comfortable surroundings against his will. Stéphane's wife, Louise, and the concierge's daughter are vibrant female characters.

Although critics have described the interlaced plots as a "nest of vipers" worthy of François Mauriac, Mallet-Joris differs from this author in her treatment of women. In a short preface to a 1959 edition of Mauriac's *Le Désert de l'amour* (*The Desert of Love*) she reproaches Mauriac for not having included realistic portraits of women in his works and for excessively emphasizing the demise of carnal desire.

In 1960 Mallet-Joris collaborated with Gabriel Arout on a translation and adaptation of *A Taste of Honey*, the play by Shelagh Delaney in which two women boldly explore their own outer limits. In 1961, in a preface to a translation of *Wuthering Heights*, Mallet-Joris praises Emily Brontë for her enigmatic work, a "deforming mirror," in Mallet-Joris's words, that reflects the world through fevers and anguish.

Les Personnages (1961; translated as *The Favourite*, 1962) initiated a series of historical novels which include *Marie Mancini, le premier amour de Louis XIV* (1964; translated as *The Uncompromising Heart: A Life of Marie Mancini, Louis XIV's First Love*, 1966); *Trois Ages de la nuit: Histoires de la sorcellerie* (1968; translated as *The Witches: Three Tales of Sorcery*, 1969); and *Jeanne Guyon* (1978). These novels depict heroines who live their beliefs whatever the cost may be. The first work of this group is a masterpiece that has enjoyed numerous printings. Here the author strays from themes and styles of Colette, Honoré de Balzac, and Zola and approaches Pierre Corneille and Mme de La Fayette, whose sister-in-law, Louise de La Fayette, maid of honor to Louis XIII's queen, Anne of Austria, may well have been a source of inspiration. The period of Louis XIII is described as a time of anticlericalism and voluptuous atmosphere, yet the novel's structure reflects the rigors of a classical tragedy with its unities of time, place, and action and with the great dignity exhibited in the character of Louise. One could draw a parallel between Mallet-Joris's own conversion to Catholicism, narrated in a rambling style in her 1963 autobiography, *Lettre à moi-même* (translated as *A Letter to Myself*, 1964), a sort of self-assessment as a woman and a writer, and Louise de La Fayette's conversion in *Les Personnages*. In each case the novelist shows how God works with and against human mediocrity.

Marie Mancini well depicts the atmosphere of the Fronde, with its abundant energy and violence. Although the heroine seems quite different from that of the preceding novel, one may distinguish a relationship between the two which must have attracted Mallet-Joris. Both are in love with kings and are worthy of the highest love because of the quality of their souls. Infatuated with the absolute, they both rapidly climb to the top, yet through lack of cunning, they find themselves incapable of securing this position. What determines their triumph also ensures their defeat. To the house of God—the cloister—Mancini prefers the infinity of despair. Certainly Mallet-Joris places Mme de Sévigné among those idealistic heroines of the seventeenth century who were dissatisfied by reality. She wrote two studies on this "femme de lettres." One appeared in 1969 as the preface to an edition of Mme de Sévigné's letters, and the other, entitled *A propos de Madame de Sévigné*, appeared in 1971. These works focus upon the compensatory role that writing plays for one who is a victim of existential malaise.

In 1963 Mallet-Joris translated into French the mythic and symbolic novel *Dust*, by Yaël Dayan, daughter of Israeli statesman Moshe Dayan. In 1964 Prince Rainier awarded her the Prix de Monaco in recognition of her works. In 1965 she was active in François Mitterand's unsuccessful presidential campaign. The same year she became a member of the editorial board at Grasset, which served as her principal publisher until 1983. She also wrote a preface to a translation of John Cheever's 1957 novel *The Wapshot Chronicle*. In 1967 she provided a preface for an edition of Balzac's *Les Célibataires* (The Celibates), praising the author for having preserved the presentiment of mystery behind his realistic portrayals.

Mallet-Joris's 1966 novel, *Les Signes et les prodiges* (translated the same year as *Signs and Wonders*), is the first of several works treating both contemporary French issues and the depths of her characters' souls. Set in 1962 under Charles de Gaulle's regime, the novel is suffused with the lingering effects of World War II and the Algerian conflict. It reveals the bitterness of the *pieds-noirs* (French Algerians) repatriated to the south of France and the schemes involved in launching a magazine. In this atmosphere two brothers, Nicolas and Simon Léclusier, confront the problem of evil. While writing cannot relieve the atheist Nicolas's struggle with existence itself, the ministry of Simon, a priest in the ghettos of Lyons, does not relieve him either. Nicolas's attempts to begin afresh in new surroundings culminate in two failures: his refusal to assume responsibility for a child he has fathered and his suicide.

Although the pessimism of this work is perhaps too severe, the pessimism of *Trois Ages de la nuit* comes across as more realistic because it is sustained by Mallet-Joris's psychological analyses of her characters. The problem of evil also haunts these three historical novellas set in the sixteenth and the seventeenth centuries. The three women concerned, all supposedly witches demonically possessed, are at first presented as victims of their education, as well as of negative examples they received as children. They are subsequently depicted as victims of the malevolence of their peers. With sarcasm Mallet-Joris flays the judges who condemn the accused in advance and who contribute to the proliferation of evil by their insatiable hunger for fables, extravagances, horrors, and obscenities.

Mallet-Joris complained of this work's lack of success and attributed it to the Parisian student revolts that were taking place at the time the book was published. Indeed, as the French reviews attest, readers seemed most interested in the theme of protest. The third novella, "Jeanne ou la révolte," was adapted for television in 1974 and directed by Christian Mesnil. The English

translation of *Trois Ages de la nuit* was widely reviewed and read in the United States.

In 1968 Mallet-Joris also wrote the preface to a new edition of Gertrude von Le Fort's *La Femme éternelle; La Femme dans le temps; La Femme hors du temps* (*The Eternal Woman; The Woman in Time; The Timeless Woman*), translated from the German by André Boccon-Gibod. In this piece she counseled moderation for contemporary women in transition, who stand to profit more from conjugal harmony than from domestic strife. Moving from women to children, during the years 1966-1974 Mallet-Joris devoted a series of works to themes of childhood. During this time she was living in an old building on the rue Jacob and playing the roles of writer and mother.

In 1966 *Enfance ton regard* (Childhood Look) appeared. In this work Mallet-Joris comments on a series of photographs and traces the historical importance of children in world literature since the development of psychoanalysis and the advent of surrealism. In 1970 she witnessed the monumental success of her familial chronicle *La Maison de papier* (translated as *The Paper House*, 1971), which has sold more than one million copies. In this autobiographical best-seller conversations with children, immigrant servants, and friends and acquaintances predominate, revealing a great deal of humor and wisdom. Mallet-Joris takes up such questions as whether it is possible to reconcile motherhood or political involvement with a writer's career and how, in the words of one commentator, "to be available to all and still be able to retreat into solitude at will." The information she discloses ranges from her favorite time of the day–7 A.M.–to the operation preventing her from having more children, to her first guitar lessons, to her work as host of the television series *Lectures pour tous*.

In 1971 and 1973 Mallet-Joris produced two children's books: *Le Roi qui aimait trop les fleurs* (The King who Loved Flowers Too Much) and *Les Feuilles mortes d'un bel été* (Dead Leaves from a Beautiful Summer). In 1974 a volume entitled *Le Cirque* (The Circus) appeared, with lithographs by Hilaire. In this book Mallet-Joris imparts her love of mime and the circus in a well-documented text inspired by her cherished poster depicting Myra Baracito, the dancer, tightrope walker, and juggler from the 1920s.

In 1969 Mallet-Joris was elected to the jury for the Prix Fémina; in 1970 she was elected to the Académie Goncourt. She is the only woman on the prestigious jury, and she carries the title of vice-president of the academy. These duties did not hamper Mallet-Joris's creative activities. In 1971, in collaboration with the composer Michel Grisolia, she began to write lyrics for the popular singer Marie-Paule Belle. In 1975, with Grisolia, she produced a biography of Juliette Gréco, the well-known singer in Saint-Germain-des-Prés after World War II. For Mallet-Joris, song is "un défoulement formidable" (a wonderful release) which allows her to leave the prison of her own image, an image of a writer cut off from group creativity.

The writer-artist became the subject of three of her works in the 1970s, all dealing primarily with reflections on creativity: an essay that serves as preface to *Attali* (1971), a volume of photographs by Marc Attali; the novel *Le Jeu du souterrain* (1973; translated as *The Underground Game*, 1974); and the autobiographical *J'aurais voulu jouer de l'accordéon* (I Would Have Liked to Play the Accordion, 1975). *Le Jeu du souterrain*, which was inspired by André Gide's *Les Faux-Monnayeurs* (*The Counterfeiters*), relates how the ups and downs of an author, Robert Guibal, supercede those of his main character Pierre Sorel in the novel which Guibal will never finish. Mallet-Joris seems to reiterate in this work the message of *La Maison de papier*, according to which a writer cannot separate himself from all that surrounds him, conditions him, and nourishes him. In other words, as Guibal emphasizes, there are treasures everywhere.

In the preface to *Attali* and in *J'aurais voulu jouer de l'accordéon*, she justifies the splicing of most of her novels into apparently unordered sequences. She borrows from Attali methods—collage, restructuring of photographs—that allow a particular treatment of reality by exploiting the fissures. In *J'aurais voulu jouer l'accordéon* she explains that she was also inspired by her painter-husband's use of cardboard cut-outs to explore further color possibilities in already completed paintings. In an interview in the 1970s with Jean-Louis de Rambures, Mallet-Joris noted that she writes or records stories she has heard and that after having read the newspaper, she works regularly from 7:30 A.M. to 12:30 P.M., except on Sundays. She discussed also her tendency to digress, adding that she usually accepts the cuts and revisions suggested by friends who have read her manuscripts. Although toying with various ways of structuring her works amuses her, playing with words and taking great pains with her style bores her. The owner of a studio in Nice, a frequent traveler (to Sweden in 1972, to Finland in 1974, to Canada in 1975 with members of the Académie Goncourt, to Mexico in 1978), the reader, on the average, of one book a day, Mallet-Joris has continued to produce a book every two years. Among them, although quite distinct from the rest, is the work she considers the most important, *Jeanne Guyon* (1978).

This historical novel commissioned by Flammarion is the fruit of ten years of research. It relates the story of the founder and apostle of quietism, a seventeenth-century sect. Although Mallet-Joris does not emphasize Guyon's mysticism, she works well with the subjects of Guyon's youth, her years of marriage, and the beginning of her widowhood. It seems, however, that Mallet-Joris tires of her heroine in the course of Guyon's confrontations with other historical characters: Mme de Maintenon, Jacques Bossuet, and François Fénelon. The book includes a good bibliography, a chronology, and some insights into the education of girls in the seventeenth century.

The novels published by Mallet-Joris since 1976 tackle certain contemporary social problems and problems of daily life. In an interview granted to Katy Barasc in 1983, she deplored the fact that since 1974 French literature has been devoted more to research than to lived experience and human relationships, and she claimed that there was not a single book which offered cheer or companionship of any kind. Her recent books constitute, in part, a response to this situation. In *Allégra* (1976) she treats the joys and worries caused by handicapped children and the issue of female roles; in *Dickie-Roi* (Dickie-King, 1979), the world of show business, religious sects, and drug crimes; in *Un Chagrin d'amour et d'ailleurs* (More than a Broken Heart, 1981), working immigrants, the building of a cultural center and other municipal accomplishments; in *Le Rire de Laura* (Laura's Laugh, 1985), the world of medicine and surgery, abortion, the record industry, and the exploitation of youth. *Allégra* and *Dickie-Roi* were adapted for television in 1978 and 1981 respectively. In all of these novels Mallet-Joris analyzes the anguish which besets individuals of goodwill and the likelihood that they will either opt for suicide or integrate themselves into life through a certain degree of compromise.

Allégra incarnates the type of woman Mallet-Joris prefers throughout her novels: a seemingly aloof and ordinary woman plagued by worries and passions. What develops in the character of Allégra and in her sister Jo is a maternal love capable of moral crimes. While Jo drags her handicapped son to a charlatan with the foolish hope of finding a miraculous cure, Allégra fears the cure which will restore speech to the four-year-old mute Arab boy she has come to love as her son. When she becomes pregnant by her husband, she goes so far as to have an abortion performed by the quack Jo had consulted, so as not to harm the uniqueness of her frenzied love for the Arab child. The operation precipitates her death. For Mallet-Joris the moralist there are no miracles, only propriety and good sense. This is the lesson Laura, the mother in *Le Rire de Laura*, learns at the bedside of her son Martin following an overdose he has taken in a moment of despair in the face of his own unscrupulousness.

Dickie-Roi (whose real name is Frédéric Roy) is a music idol, inspired by Claude François, a popular singer who died an accidental death. This character seems to borrow traits from Daniel of *La Maison de papier* as well, in his love of the absolute. Whereas Dickie, a victim of those who cultivate him, falls into an abyss, his fan Pauline, probably modeled in part after the author's own daughter Pauline, matures and preserves her equilibrium. The novel depicts the milieu of star exploiters and young admirers, and of the less young who seek in an idol or in the advice of a guru human warmth, a dream, a hope, an escape from mediocrity.

Song, which meets profoundly human needs, contrasts with the impersonality of the cultural center in *Un Chagrin d'amour et d'ailleurs*. Gilbert Lefèvre, mayor of the town of A., considers himself a bulwark against sentimentality, religion, and violence, and the cultural center which he has had built in A. is a symbol of his political ideals. His private life, however, is in ruins. His wife Jeanette, once an advocate of political action as a solution to mankind's problems, has become, over the years of longing and existential angst, an alcoholic and a victim of despair. In a manner reminiscent of Racinian tragedy, the final breakup of Gilbert and Jeanette is played out in one place, in one day. During the dedication of Gilbert's cultural center Jeanette retreats on tiptoe, in the direction of the railroad station.

While 1983 marked the beginning of Mallet-Joris's work at Gallimard as a reader as well as her debut as a writer published by this prestigious house with her novel *Le Clin d'œil de l'ange* (The Angel's Wink), the source of this "suite romanesque" dates from 1981. In that year she underwent a serious operation, and in the clinic where she was convalescing she had the impression that her life was suspended: reality became parenthetical; in a flash all options were opened to her. She thinks that all people have some of these momentary intuitions, or "winks," of fortune, but it is rare that they are answered. On this theme she wrote the seven stories of *Le Clin d'œil de l'ange*, all concerning more or less well-adjusted couples and upsetting encounters. Two sequences have the United States as their setting, "Nantucket" and "Disneyland," while another, the first, takes place in Antwerp, that "réservoir d'images et d'émotions fortes et pures" (profound and genuine emotional reservoir).

The novel *Le Rire de Laura*, with at least one hundred thousand copies in print, deals in part with adolescence. Martin, Laura's son, is a young man of the 1980s, more realistic and disillusioned than the youth of the 1970s. He knows how to manipulate others and to crush those weaker than he. At the peak of his enterprise Martin becomes acutely aware of his faults and attempts suicide. Saved at the last minute, and nursed back to health by his mother, he will in turn help her by forcing her to leave her ivory tower, to deal with him as an equal, to question herself, and to discover that she had erred by investing everything in her husband. Laura's laugh has a tearing quality: life without compromise is unlivable. *Le Rire de Laura*, like *Un Chagrin d'amour et d'ailleurs*, also exemplifies the problems of communication between a husband and wife who love each other.

In May 1985 Mallet-Joris finished her first libretto, written in Dutch and intended for production in Antwerp. The libretto was set to music by Jean Bergmans, and the theme is that of the life, trial, and execution of Caryl Chessman. In February 1986 the French government honored her by conferring upon her the Ordre National du Mérite. The years 1987 and 1988 saw the publication of two books dedicated to two women close to Mallet-Joris. The first is a biography, *Marie-Paule Belle*. The second is a novel, *Tristesse du cerf-volant* (Kite's Sadness), dedicated to Mallet-Joris's mother.

Interviews:

Jean-Louis de Rambures, "Françoise Mallet-Joris: 'Je me sers des histoires qu'on me raconte,'" in his *Comment travaillent les écrivains* (Paris: Flammarion, 1978), pp. 111-115;

Katy Barasc, "Rencontre(s) avec Françoise Mallet-Joris, Il y a des sirènes qui tricotent," *Masques*, 19 (Autumn 1983): 5-12;

Michel Lambert, "Françoise Mallet-Joris: 'Je reste une Lilar,' " *Télé-Moustique*, no. 3113 (26 September 1985): 26-27, 29.

Bibliography:

Auguste Grisay, "Bibliographie des éditions originales de Françoise Mallet-Joris," *Le Livre et l'Estampe*, no. 45-46 (1966): 107-108; "Supplément à la bibliographie des éditions originales de Françoise Mallet-Joris," *Le Livre et l'Estampe*, no. 89-92 (1977): 105-106.

References:

Lucille Frackman Becker, *Françoise Mallet-Joris* (Boston: Twayne, 1985);

Alexis Curvers, "Un Roman théologique: *Les Personnages* de Françoise Mallet-Joris," *Revue Générale Belge*, 97th year (November 1961): 85-95;

Geneviève Delattre, "Mirrors and Masks in the World of Françoise Mallet-Joris," *Yale French Studies*, no. 27 (1961): 121-126;

Monique Detry, *Françoise Mallet-Joris: Dossier critique et inédits; suivi de Le Miroir, le voyage et la fête* (Paris: Grasset, 1976);

Michel Georis, *Françoise Mallet-Joris, essai; suivi de Une Inconnue: Françoise Lilar, poétesse de 15 ans*, by Frédéric Kiesel (Brussels: P. de Méyère, 1964);

Marcel Lobet, "Françoise Mallet-Joris et la confession féminine," *Marginales* (September 1964): 17-21;

Rima Drell Reck, "Françoise Mallet-Joris and the Anatomy of the Will," *Yale French Studies*, no. 24 (1959): 74-79;

Madeleine Rumeau-Smith, "Rôles, images et authenticité dans *Allégra* de Françoise Mallet-Joris," *Bulletin de la Société des Professeurs Français en Amérique* (1980-1981): 91-101;

Emese Soots, "The Only Motion is Returning: The Metaphor of Alchemy in Mallet-Joris and Yourcenar," *French Forum*, 14 (January 1979): 3-16.

André Pieyre de Mandiargues

(14 March 1909-   )

David J. Bond
University of Saskatchewan

BOOKS: *Dans les années sordides* (Monaco: A.P.M., 1943);

Hedera, ou la persistance de l'amour pendant une rêverie (Monaco: Hommage, 1945);

L'Etudiante (Paris: Fontaine, 1946);

Le Musée noir (Paris: Laffont, 1946);

Les Incongruités monumentales (Paris: Laffont, 1948);

Les Sept Périls spectraux (Paris: Pas Perdus, 1950);

Soleil des loups (Paris: Laffont, 1951);

L'Anglais décrit dans le château fermé, as Pierre Morion (Oxford & Cambridge, 1953); republished under Mandiargues's name (Paris: Gallimard, 1979);

Marbre (Paris: Laffont, 1953);

Astyanax (Paris: Terrain Vague, 1956);

Le Lis de mer (Paris: Laffont, 1956); translated by Richard Howard as *The Girl Beneath the Lion* (New York: Grove, 1958; London: Calder, 1959);

Les Monstres de Bomarzo (Paris: Grasset, 1957);

Le Belvédère (Paris: Grasset, 1958);

Le Cadran lunaire (Paris: Laffont, 1958);

Feu de braise (Paris: Grasset, 1959); translated by April Fitzlyon as *Blaze of Embers* (London: Calder & Boyars, 1971);

Cartolines et dédicaces (Paris: Terrain Vague, 1960);

Sugaï (Paris: Georges Fall, 1960);

L'Age de craie, suivi de Hedera (Paris: Gallimard, 1961);

La Nuit l'amour (Paris: Pierre Loeb, 1961);

Deuxième Belvédère (Paris: Grasset, 1962);

La Motocyclette (Paris: Gallimard, 1963); translated by Howard as *The Motorcycle* (New York: Grove, 1965); translated by Alexander Trocchi as *The Girl on the Motorcycle* (London: Calder & Boyars, 1966);

Le Point où j'en suis, suivi de Dalila exaltée et de La Nuit l'amour (Paris: Gallimard, 1964);

Beylamour (Paris: Jean-Jacques Pauvert, 1965);

Porte dévergondée (Paris: Gallimard, 1965);

Critiquettes (Montpellier: Fata Morgana, 1967);

Jacinthes (Paris: O. Lazar-Vernet, 1967); trans-

André Pieyre de Mandiargues, 1981 (photograph by Kiyomi Yaruaji)

lated by Edward Lucie Smith as *Hyacinths* (Paris: O. Lazar-Vernet, 1967);

La Marge (Paris: Gallimard, 1967); translated by Howard as *The Margin* (New York: Grove, 1969; London: Calder & Boyars, 1969);

Le Marronnier (Paris: Mercure de France, 1968);

Ruisseau des solitudes, suivi de Jacinthes et de Chapeaugaga (Paris: Gallimard, 1968);

Le Lièvre de la lune (Milan: M'Arte, 1970);

Eros solaire (Paris: Tchou, 1970);

Bona l'amour et la peinture (Geneva: Skira, 1971);

La Nuit de mil neuf cent quatorze, ou Le Style liberty (Paris: L'Herne, 1971);

Troisième Belvédère (Paris: Gallimard, 1971);

Mascarets (Paris: Gallimard, 1971);

Croiseur noir (Paris: O. Lazar-Vernet, 1972);

Isabella Morra (Paris: Gallimard, 1973);

Terre érotique (Paris: Tchou, 1974);

Chagall (Paris: Maeght, 1975);

Sous la lame (Paris: Gallimard, 1976);

Arcimboldo le merveilleux (Paris: Laffont, 1977); translated by Mark Paris as *Arcimboldo the Marvelous* (New York: Abrams, 1978);

L'Ivre Œil, suivi de Croiseur noir et de Passage de l'Egyptienne (Paris: Gallimard, 1979);

La Nuit séculaire (Paris: Gallimard, 1979);

Le Trésor cruel de Hans Bellmer (Paris: Sphinx, 1979);

Arsène et Cléopâtre (Paris: Gallimard, 1981);

Le Deuil des roses (Paris: Gallimard, 1983);

Sept Jardins fantastiques (Tokyo: Muleta, 1983);

Aimer Michaux (Montpellier: Fata Morgana, 1983);

Cuevas Blues (Montpellier: Fata Morgana, 1986);

Tout disparaîtra (Paris: Gallimard, 1987).

PLAY PRODUCTIONS: *Isabella Morra*, Paris, Théâtre d'Orsay, May 1973;

Arsène et Cléopâtre, Paris, Centre National d'Art et d'Essai, January 1986.

TRANSLATIONS: Tommasso Landolfi, *La Femme de Gogol* (Paris: Gallimard, 1969);

Octavio Paz, *La Fille de Rappuccini* (Paris: Mercure de France, 1972);

W. B. Yeats, *Le Vent parmi les roseaux* (Paris: O. Lazar-Vernet, 1972);

F. de Pisis, *La Petite Bassaride* (Paris: L'Herne, 1972);

Yukio Mishima, *Madame de Sade* (Paris: Gallimard, 1976);

F. de Pisis, *Onze plus un poèmes* (Montpellier: Fata Morgana, 1983).

OTHER: *Masques de Léonor Fini*, preface by Mandiargues (Paris: Parade, 1951);

Marcel Béalu, *L'Araignée d'eau et autres écrits fantastiques*, preface by Mandiargues (Paris: Nouvel Office d'Edition, 1964);

Les Corps illuminés, photographs by Frédéric Barzilay, text by Mandiargues (Paris: Mercure de France, 1965);

Yves Bayser, *Le Jardin*, preface by Mandiargues (Paris: Tchou, 1970);

Saint-Pol Roux, *Le Trésor de l'homme*, preface by Mandiargues (Limoges: Rougerie, 1970);

Hans Bellmer, *L'Œuvre gravé*, preface by Mandiargues (Paris: Denoël, 1971);

Unica Zürn, *L'Homme jasmin*, preface by Mandiargues (Paris: Gallimard, 1971);

Honoré de Balzac, *La Peau de chagrin*, preface by Mandiargues (Paris: Gallimard, 1974);

Leonora Carrington, *Le Cornet acoustique*, translated by Henri Parisot, preface by Mandiargues (Paris: Flammarion, 1974);

Irina Ionesco, *Liliacées langoureuses aux parfums d'Arabie*, preface by Mandiargues (Paris: Editions de Chêne, 1974);

Macé, *Le Jardin des langues*, preface by Mandiargues (Paris: Gallimard, 1974);

Jean Paulhan, *Douze Lettres à Fautrier*, preface by Mandiargues (Paris: O. Lazar-Vernet, 1975);

Guido Ballo, *Alphabet du soleil*, preface by Mandiargues (Paris: Seghers, 1976);

Pauline Réage, *Retour à Roissy*, preface by Mandiargues (Paris: Jean-Jacques Pauvert, 1976);

Marie-Thérèse Souverbie, *Le Grand Livre de la rose*, preface by Mandiargues (Paris, Vilo & Lausanne: Clairefontaine, 1976);

Isaure de Saint-Pierre, *L'Ombre claire*, preface by Mandiargues (Paris: Belfond, 1977);

Sandro Zanotto, *Le Delta de Vénus*, preface by Mandiargues (Paris: Jean-Jacques Pauvert, 1977);

Ninette Lyon, *Le Guide culinaire des poissons et mollusques*, preface by Mandiargues (Verviers: Marabout, 1979);

Georges Lambrichs, *Chaystre, ou Les Plaisirs incommodes*, preface by Mandiargues (Paris: Editions de la Difference, 1983);

Henri Cartier-Bresson, *Photoportraits*, preface by Mandiargues (Paris: Gallimard, 1986).

PERIODICAL PUBLICATIONS: "Le Prisonnier," *Biblio*, 34 (November 1966): 15-16;

"Texte inédit: Leonora Carrington," *Combat*, 13 (April 1974): 2;

"Inédit: Hommage à la rose," *Figaro*, 6 November 1976, p. 17.

André Pieyre de Mandiargues is a writer of fiction, poetry, literary and art criticism, and drama. Although not one of the best-known contemporary writers (especially outside of France), he has always received praise from critics for his work. His fictional writing in particular has been singled out as constituting a special world unlike any other in French literature today. With its mixture of fantasy and detailed description, its baroque décor, its often dreamlike atmosphere, its cruel eroticism, and its appeal to the reader's senses, it is a very unusual realm of strange characters and unexpected events. The language used in this fiction (and, indeed, in all his work) has been praised for its elegance and its classical purity. Peter Brooks calls Mandiargues "a superbly evocative writer" (*Partisan Review*, Winter 1966); Jean d'Ormesson says that he is "un des rares stylistes de notre littérature contemporaine" (one of the few stylists in our contemporary literature; *Nouvelles Littéraires*, 14 May 1971), and Mark J. Temmer speaks of "prose cadences worthy of Bossuet or Bourdaloue, rhythmic forms into which are poured, like gold and silver, the counterparts of his sensations" (*Yale French Studies*, no. 31 [1964]). According to Robert Kanters, Mandiargues belongs to "le très petit nombre d'écrivains qui font honneur à la littérature présente" (the very small number of writers who do honor to current literature; *Revue de Paris*, January 1968).

One possible reason why Mandiargues's reputation has been slow to spread beyond the circle of professional critics is that he has always preferred to avoid the public gaze. He has said that he finds it difficult to speak about himself, although he has given interviews, including two long ones in book form: *Le Désordre de la mémoire* (The Disorder of Memory, 1975) and *Un Saturne gai* (A Happy Saturn, 1982). He probably consented to such interviews because he believes, as he commented in *Un Saturne gai*, that "l'on ne peut pas avoir vraiment confiance en un livre d'entretiens pour faire connaître quelqu'un" (one cannot rely on a book of interviews to reveal a person). Despite these reservations, however, the main events in Mandiargues's life, and his ideas on art and literature, are fairly clear from what he has said and written.

Mandiargues, the son of David and Lucie Bernard Pieyre de Mandiargues, was born in Paris in 1909. After the death of his father, killed in 1916 in World War I, he and his younger brother were brought up by his mother and a governess. He was a timid child, afflicted by a stutter, who did not do particularly well at school. He was sent to a variety of private institutions, passed the first part of his *baccalauréat* examination at the fourth attempt, and the second part at the age of eighteen. At his mother's insistence, he prepared (and failed) the entrance examination for the Ecole des Hautes Etudes Commerciales, but he was later accepted by "cette sinistre école" (that sinister school, as he calls it in *Le Désordre de la mémoire*). Having failed to pass from the first year to the second, he abandoned commercial studies and registered for a literature degree at the Sorbonne. These studies were not pursued beyond the first examination.

At the age of twenty-one Mandiargues received a modest inheritance that enabled him to travel widely in Germany, Poland, Austria, Hungary, the Balkans, and, above all, Italy, a country that he has always particularly loved. He was accompanied on many of these journeys by his friend Henri Cartier-Bresson, who was later to become famous as a photographer. Yet, despite Cartier-Bresson's friendship, and despite the opportunity to travel, the sense of solitude and melancholy that had always haunted him became stronger. His stuttering grew worse, as did his misanthropy and his intolerance toward a bourgeois milieu that he found stifling. When in Paris, he spent much of his time in nightclubs, bars, and brothels. He was particularly attracted to those nightclubs where he could listen to jazz until the early hours of the morning.

Meanwhile, from the age of twenty-three Mandiargues had been writing regularly, but he kept secret all that he wrote. He had always read widely, but, as he says in *Le Désordre de la mémoire*: "Mon amour des livres me faisait considérer les écrivains comme des êtres tellement supérieurs au reste des humains qu'il eût été ridicule, imbécile ou criminel de prétendre à m'élever un jour jusqu'au rang de ceux-là" (My love of books made me consider writers as beings so superior to the rest of humanity that it would have been ridiculous, idiotic or criminal to aspire to raise myself one day to their rank). When he began writing, it was in an attempt to perfect his style and to recapture the emotion that he had felt when reading those authors whom he particularly admired. He rejected the idea that the writer is inspired by the need to communicate with others, believing that his own early writings were born more of a need to communicate with himself. He has no patience with those young writers whose only concern is to see their works in print, for he argues that the writer must first undergo a process of apprenticeship and perfecting of his art.

Mandiargues spent the period of World War II in Monte Carlo, where he lived a solitary life. He devoted much of his time to provoking dreams by the use of coca leaves. He would then, on awakening, note down what he had dreamed. He seems slowly to have undergone a personality change, for he began to lose his timidity and his

Portrait of Mandiargues, painted in 1950 by his wife, Bona (by permission of the author)

stutter. Even more important was his decision to publish some of his writing, although in limited editions for his own satisfaction and that of a few friends. *Dans les années sordides* (In the Sordid Years), which appeared in Monaco in 1943, is a collection of prose poems evoking the atmosphere of the "sordid" war years and is based largely on images drawn from his dreams. In *Un Saturne gai* he says that this work was "à l'âge de trente-quatre ans la justification d'une existence qui jusque-là n'avait eu aucune valeur, aucun sens" (at the age of thirty-four the justification of an existence that, until then, had had no value, no meaning).

One of the few significant events in Mandiargues's life until this point had been his love for Méret Oppenheim, a surrealist painter of German origin. His second published work, *Hedera, ou la persistance de l'amour pendant une rêverie* (Hedera, or The Persistence of Love During a Dream), which appeared in 1945, is a long love poem in irregular verse dedicated to Oppenheim. Mandiargues has called it "le plus surréaliste de mes poèmes" (the most surrealist of my poems) and says that: "Il sort directement du rêve et de la rêverie" (It comes directly from dream and reverie).

After the war Mandiargues returned to Paris. The period of apprenticeship was now over, and he began publishing regularly in editions available to the general public. The short story "L'Etudiante" (The Girl Student) was followed in the same year (1946) by a volume of short stories called *Le Musée noir* (The Black Museum). These tales of the fantastic already show a mixture of elements that will reappear in his later fiction: unusual events, a cruel eroticism, and the mysterious links between individuals and nature. The most interesting of these stories is "Le Sang de l'agneau" (The Blood of the Lamb), the tale of a girl's loss of childhood innocence and her bloody initiation into womanhood. The heroine, Marceline Caïn, loses her childhood when she is raped by a black shepherd. She is, as it were, a sacrificial lamb, but, when the shepherd, overcome by remorse, hangs himself, she refuses to save him. She later takes his knife and, becoming the sacrificer that her name suggests she will be, kills her parents, who are her last link to childhood.

Le Musée noir met with little success at a time when existentialist philosophy dominated French intellectual life and literature had to be "committed." In *Le Désordre de la mémoire* Mandiargues dismisses this philosophy as "une pseudo-philosophie aussi médiocre qu'arrogante" (a pseudo-philosophy, as mediocre as it was arrogant), and he condemns its scorn for stylish writing. He much preferred the surrealists, whose work he had admired since he had first discovered it in 1926 or 1927. Although surrealism never regained the prestige and influence it had had before the war, it did experience a renewal once the war ended. Mandiargues found this "seconde époque du surréalisme" (second age of surrealism) more to his taste than the reigning existentialism, and he drew close to André Breton and his group. Although he never "joined" the surrealists, he was associated with them for several years until a coolness developed between him and Breton. The cause of this rift was principally Mandiargues's admiration for certain writers whom Breton considered unimportant (Mallarmé, Ronsard, Rabelais, and Ernst Hoffmann) and a disagreement over the importance of "literature." Breton despised "literature" as a vulgar, commercialized product, inferior in every way to poetry, while Mandiargues describes much surrealist work as literature and sees no harm in writing work that is accessible to a wider public. Consequently, although one cannot say that

Mandiargues broke with the surrealists, they drifted apart. Yet Mandiargues has always continued to express his admiration for Breton and the surrealists.

Another important event of these years was his meeting with Bona Tibertelli in October 1947. Bona, who was a painter in her own right, had accompanied to Paris her uncle, the Italian painter Filippo de Pisis. Mandiargues was already an old friend of de Pisis and had arranged accommodation for him during this visit. He remembers little of his first meeting with Bona, except being struck by the beauty of her eyes. The two were married in Modena on 2 February 1950. Although they were divorced at Bona's insistence in 1960, they later came together again and were remarried. Mandiargues says that: "Bona est pour moi surtout la femme que j'aime" (Bona is above all for me the woman I love). She is the inspiration for many of his poems, for several of the short stories, and for the heroine of *Le Lis de mer*. They have one daughter, Sybille, born on 24 July 1967.

In 1951 Mandiargues published *Soleil des loups*, the title of which means Wolf's Sun and is thieves' slang for the moon. In fact, the moon is a cold and eerie presence brooding over the six stories in the volume. The longest and most important is "L'Archéologue" (The Archaeologist), the story of Conrad Mur, who dislikes women because they remind him of death and corruption. He becomes engaged to a cold, statuesque beauty called Bettina, whom he meets, under the moonlight, on a frozen lake. On a trip to Italy, Conrad and Bettina are shown the wax figure of a girl from whose belly spills a profusion of strawberries—an obvious representation of the fertility, femininity, and forces of nature that Conrad fears. Bettina now falls ill, and, in her suffering body, Conrad discovers a woman like any other, so he abandons her. In a dreamlike trance, he seems to be transported to the seabed, where he encounters a huge statue of a goddess. He removes a ring from her finger, places it on his own, then symbolically rejects this marriage by putting it back on the statue. The goddess later appears before him and destroys him. This strange tale, with its dreamlike sequences, introduces a figure that reappears in other fiction by Mandiargues: a goddess who incarnates the forces of nature, the powers of life and death, and who avenges insults to these forces. *Soleil des loups* was awarded the Prix des Critiques for 1951.

Mandiargues's first novel, *Marbre* (Marble), was published in 1953. It follows the fortunes of Ferréol Buq, who travels in Italy and encounters strange adventures. It is divided into five almost distinct parts, preceded by an introduction explaining the circumstances of the novel's composition and the reasons for the choice of location and characters' names. These self-conscious references to the novel's construction continue in the body of the work, where the author addresses the reader directly and talks of the death of the traditional writer and reader. The work finishes with a suggested ending and an invitation to the reader to invent an alternative one if he or she prefers. One may see in *Marbre*, written at a time when the *nouveau roman* was beginning to be dominant in France, a reflection of that genre's exploration of the techniques of novel-writing. One of its scenes, in which Ferréol discovers a hollow statue of a hermaphrodite surrounded by regularly shaped monuments, offers a fine example of Mandiargues's love of geometric shapes and mandalas. In another scene Ferréol observes a ceremony in an isolated village during which a dying woman is exposed in an erotically charged atmosphere to the gaze of the male population, gathered in an arena. This is an excellent example of Mandiargues's taste for ritual and ceremonial settings, and it also conveys a theme that recurs in his work: the identity of the forces of life and death, which are inherent in nature, and which manifest themselves in certain privileged moments.

In 1956 Mandiargues published *Le Lis de mer* (translated as *The Girl Beneath the Lion*, 1958), a short novel set in a Mediterranean world of sun, sea, and sensual pleasure. It describes how a young girl, Vanina, on holiday in Sardinia, suddenly decides to give herself to a man encountered by chance on a beach. She instructs the man carefully on the site that he is to choose and the manner that he is to adopt, turning the process into a kind of ritual rape in which she is a willing victim. The presence of the god Pan, incarnation of the forces of nature, is felt in the sun, the sea, and the vegetation throughout the novel. When Vanina finally joins in sexual union with the man, these "panic" forces enter her in such a way that she feels in total communion with nature. One may see this story as depicting a voyage of initiation, a kind of mythical quest for the divine forces in nature.

Le Lis de mer was followed in 1959 by *Feu de braise* (translated as *Blaze of Embers*, 1971), another collection of stories based on dreams, reverie, and strange happenings. It contains one of Mandiargues's most complex tales, "Le Diamant" (The Diamond), which tells how a young girl, the daughter of a Jewish diamond dealer, falls inside a diamond while examining it. When the sun's rays strike the diamond, a tiny figure, half-man and half-lion, appears and couples with her. She awakes outside the diamond, which now has a small flaw. This flaw grows as does the child inside her, who will be "la gloire de la race longtemps persécutée" (the glory of the long-persecuted race). This story too tells of a girl's union with the forces of nature, and it contains allusions to myth and alchemy. It also has an element of fantasy found in several other stories: a sudden change of shape or size by a character. *Feu de braise* was a critical success and was awarded the Prix de la Nouvelle for 1959.

La Motocyclette (1963; translated as *The Motorcycle*, 1965) was the first work that brought Mandiargues to the notice of a wider public, possibly because of its manifestly erotic component. The heroine of the work, Rébecca Nul, leaves her sleeping husband one morning and rides off to Heidelberg on her motorcycle to meet her lover, Daniel. As in a *nouveau roman*, the reader is placed inside the heroine's consciousness, which moves between observation of the actual journey, memories of the recent past (the house that Rébecca has just left), the distant past (her meetings with Daniel before her marriage), the more distant past (her life in Switzerland before she married), and the future (anticipation of her arrival at her lover's home). Many of her memories are erotic in nature, evoking scenes in which she experienced "panic" communion while coupling with Daniel. It is also the story of a mythic quest in which the heroine crosses frontiers and bridges, follows signs, goes past thresholds and guardians, and finally meets, not the godlike lover whom she expects to meet, but death. The novel ends as her motorcycle crashes into the back of a truck on which is painted a face of Bacchus–the trademark of the beer that the vehicle is carrying. As the face seems to swallow her, Rébecca realizes that "l'univers est dionysiaque" (the universe is Dionysiac). Her death is described in deliberately erotic terms: "Des milliers de lames sont acharnées sur elle et ... il lui semble qu'elles ne lui font qu'une seule plaie, par où son amant se répand en elle" (thousands of blades plunge into her and ... it is as though they made one single wound through which her

lover spreads inside her). Like Ferréol in *Marbre*, Rébecca here discovers that the forces of life (manifested in the sexual urge) are the same as the forces of death, and that they are inherent in the world around her. Dionysus (who is also known as Bacchus or Pan) is, of course, the symbolic representation of these forces.

La Motocyclette, despite its mythic overtones, is a realistic novel in that it describes precisely the functioning of motorcycles, the towns and highways on Rébecca's route, and the sights that she sees. In fact, Mandiargues carefully traveled on several occasions the route taken by his heroine in order to note all the details he needed for the novel. The book was mentioned as a possible winner of one of the annual literary prizes in France, but was not successful. It was, however, made into the 1968 film by Jack Cardiff: *Naked Under Leather*.

Porte dévergondée (published in 1965; the title means roughly Shameless Door) is a collection of short stories of which Mandiargues writes in the preface: "Le propre de ces aventures ou de ces histoires est de choquer le spectateur ou l'auditeur" (The essence of these adventures or stories is to shock the spectator or listener). This typically surrealist desire to shock, which is evident in much of what he has written, is conveyed in this case by the explicitly erotic content of the volume. The same overt eroticism appears in *La Marge* (1967; translated as *The Margin*, 1969), which is Mandiargues's most important novel and one which received high critical acclaim. It was awarded France's most important literary prize, the Prix Goncourt, and this, in its turn, made it, of all his works, the one that is best known and that has reached the widest public.

La Marge is the story of Sigismond Pons, who replaces his cousin, a traveling salesman, on a business trip to Barcelona. While in that city, he receives a letter that he opens and begins to read. His eyes fall on a sentence that seems to indicate that his wife has died. He puts the letter away, without reading any more, and spends several days wandering around the prostitutes' quarter of Barcelona, where he observes the teeming streets, the bars, cinemas, nightclubs, and passersby. He uses the services of a childlike prostitute who catches his eye and enters several of the bars and nightclubs. Finally, he opens the letter and reads that his son has drowned and his wife has committed suicide. He then drives off to a deserted spot outside the city and kills himself.

This novel has many levels of meaning. It can be seen as another mythic quest in which the hero discovers himself and death. Like all such quests, it is full of signs (words spoken by a lottery-ticket seller, names of hotels, small incidents) that point the hero toward his goal. *La Marge* is also based on close observation and detailed description, for Mandiargues portrays the streets of Barcelona and the city's inhabitants with great precision. The description reminds the reader of the *nouveau roman*, especially as the reader is again placed within a consciousness that observes, registers every detail, and often repeats observations. The description of the "real" world is mingled with dream and memories as Sigismond remembers his honeymoon in Rome, his wife, and his father. Through evocation of memories, several layers of time are manipulated as Sigismond moves freely in his mind between past and present. By setting aside his normal concerns, by turning his back on news of death, by immersing himself in this district of the city, and by traveling in time, Sigismond creates another world set *en marge*. He seems, for a while, to escape the normal flow of time.

Another object of Sigismond's activity is to hold death at bay. He blots out knowledge of his wife's death and holds back his own demise by his wanderings, but also by erotic activity. His expression of the sexual urge, seen in his commerce with the prostitute, is also an expression of the life force in the face of death. Sex as a response to death is likewise suggested when Sigismond buys a bottle of liqueur shaped like the Columbus Monument in Barcelona. When he returns to his hotel, he places this phallic bottle on the letter announcing death like "une queue virile plantée sur la lettre fatale pour la sceller momentanément" (a virile member placed on the fatal letter to seal it momentarily). But Sigismond eventually opens the letter, accepts death, and, as he dies, reconciles all the opposing forces in his life.

An unusual feature of this novel is its attacks on Francisco Franco's regime in Spain. The Spanish dictator is described as *le furhoncle* (an untranslatable pun that combines *Führer* with *furoncle*, the French for a boil). He is seen as the oppressor of the Catalan people, a tyrant responsible for the physical and moral decay observed by Sigismond. Such openly political stances are not common in Mandiargues's work, for he is not a very political person. He did go to Cuba in 1968 to attend a congress of writers friendly to

Castro's regime, and he does express in *Le Désordre de la mémoire* his opposition to American involvement in other countries and his support for the regimes in China, Algeria, and Cuba. These statements should, however, be balanced against the fact that, before World War II, he felt sympathy for Italian fascism, and that, in recent years, he has changed his attitude toward China and Cuba. The fact is that Mandiargues's political statements are moral ones and represent reactions to events of the day. He disapproved of American actions in 1975 because he opposed American involvement in Vietnam. He supported, at that time, regimes which he thought were unjustly attacked, but he has changed his opinion of them now that they, in their turn, are oppressive. Likewise, when he signed the "Manifeste des 121" in 1960 (a protest by writers and intellectuals against the war in Algeria), it was because he found France's involvement in Algeria morally repugnant.

Mandiargues's main preoccupations have always been literary and artistic. In 1971 he published *Mascarets*, a collection of stories whose tone is conveyed by the title, which means Tidal Bore, and which is slang for orgasm. "La Marée" (The Tide) is the most interesting of these tales. Written originally at the request of André Breton for inclusion in a catalogue of an exhibition on eroticism, it was also incorporated in a film by Walerian Borowczyk (*Immoral Tales*, 1974). It tells how a young man takes a girl to a lonely part of a beach, where they are cut off by the tide, and makes her fellate him. (She is not entirely an unwilling participant, it should be pointed out.) At the exact moment of high tide, he experiences an orgasm that seems to link him to the tide, nature, and the forces that control the very functioning of the universe.

Sous la lame (Under the Blade, 1976) is another collection of stories that, as the title suggests, are full of sadism, blood, and violent death. The longest of them is "Mil neuf cent trente-trois" (Nineteen Thirty-three), a story dedicated to the "Shades of Mishima," a writer who fascinated Mandiargues. Mandiargues had met Yukio Mishima on a trip to Japan, and in 1976 he translated Mishima's *Madame de Sade* (from English) into French. "Mil neuf cent trente-trois" is the story of a man who, almost overcome by a sudden urge to kill his wife, flees from her to the city of Ferrara. There, in the midst of a wild fascist celebration, he comes to terms with the darker side of himself, which he symbolically accepts by accepting the services of a prostitute. The latter, who wears a large artificial phallus, represents, by her hermaphrodite disguise, the double nature of the human psyche, its mixture of opposites, among which are both good and evil.

In 1979 Mandiargues published under his own name a work that had appeared under the assumed name of Pierre Morion on 2 June 1953 (the date, he maliciously points out, of Queen Elizabeth II's coronation). *L'Anglais décrit dans le château fermé* (The Englishman Described in the Closed Castle) is an openly pornographic work set in an isolated castle owned by an English lord. Here the characters engage in sadoerotic activities, culminating in the murder of a child before the eyes of its mother, who is then raped. The narrator, finally overcome by what he has seen, flees the castle, which is destroyed in an explosion some days later. This book, described by Mandiargues in the preface as "un récit érotique aussi sadique et scandaleux qu'il se pourrait" (as erotic, sadistic, and scandalous a story as possible), is best seen as another attempt to shock and go beyond the limits of decorum.

Le Deuil des roses (Roses in Mourning, 1983) is a collection of stories that again mingle eroticism, cruelty, and dreams. The main story, after which the volume is titled, relates the abduction of a man one night in Paris by three beautiful Japanese girls. They take him to a house where he is made to watch the death of their mistress, a Japanese actress. Mandiargues mingles erotic sensation, an atmosphere of unreality, and death in a way familiar from much of his previous fiction.

Tout disparaîtra, the most recent of Mandiargues's fiction, was published in 1987. It is the story of Hugo Arnold, who meets a beautiful young woman in the Paris metro and decides that he must know more about her. After a lengthy conversation between the two of them, conducted partly from platforms on opposite sides of the metro station and interrupted frequently by the arrival of trains, she takes him by a tortuous route to an old house in a district that he does not recognize. There she submits passively to him. Shortly after, she receives a telephone call and is suddenly transformed into a dangerous, far from passive woman. She puts on razor-sharp fingernails and performs a dance over Hugo's naked body that covers it with cuts and almost emasculates him. He is no longer the dominant, assertive male, but a terrified and bleeding victim who runs half-dressed into the street when the woman dismisses him. He now wanders beside the Seine River until he sees another woman swimming toward him. He helps her out of the river and discovers that she is the reincarnation of a woman from the ancient Middle East. The story ends when she stabs herself before his eyes, and he is arrested for her murder. *Tout disparaîtra* shows Mandiargues's usual obsessions with the cruel and the erotic, but this time the man is clearly the victim of the cruelty.

The fiction published by Mandiargues between 1946 and 1987 is the best known and most easily accessible of his work. But he has also written and published a great deal of poetry, and he considers himself as much a poet as a writer of fiction. In fact, the two domains constantly merge in his work. One may find in his poems many of the themes encountered in his fiction: eroticism, dreams, love of the natural world, and communion with that world. Woman, depicted as a figure of adoration, a goddess, an incarnation of nature or a cause of wonder, dominates much of his poetic work. Many animals also appear: hares, wolves, stags, frogs, otters—all of them depicted as representatives of a natural world that also manifests itself in forests, snow-covered plains, the moon, and the sea.

One collection of poetry, *L'Age de craie* (The Age of Chalk, 1961), contains some early poems composed before his first published works. Many of the pieces in the volume evoke the seashore and chalk cliffs of Normandy, which Mandiargues visited frequently as a child, and for which he has always had a special affection. When women are depicted, they are seen as incarnations of forces inherent in the world of nature, forces that carry with them decomposition and death. Hence the description of the three girls in "Les Filles des Gobes" (The Daughters of the Gobes): "Trois filles nues battues du vent du nord/ Le sel brillait au bout de leurs menus seins gris/ Leurs pieds dans l'eau faisaient un clapotis/ Monotone. Et la mort habitait leurs yeux clairs" (Three naked girls battered by the North wind, the salt shone on the tips of their tiny naked grey breasts, their feet splashed monotonously in the water, and death lived in their clear eyes).

Among his several other volumes of poetry, one should mention *L'Ivre Œil, suivi de Croiseur noir et de Passage de l'Egyptienne* (The Drunken Eye, followed by Black Cruiser and Passage of the Egyptian Woman, 1979). This is one of Mandiargues's finest collections of poems, which won the French Academy's Grand Prix de la Poésie and was instrumental in earning him the

Aigle d'or du Festival de Nice for the ensemble of his poetic work. The first part of the volume contains a series of poems dedicated to such artists and writers as Max Ernst, André Masson, Joan Miró, Jean Follain, Louis Aragon, and, of course, Bona. "Croiseur Noir" (originally published separately in 1972) is a rather frightening poem that depicts evil in the form of a huge black vessel that carries what appear to be nuclear weapons, but this ugly vision pales when the poet invokes "la chevelure ardente/De la grande comète rouge/Dont le moteur est l'amour" (the burning hair of the great red comet whose motive force is love). "Passage de l'Egyptienne" recounts the legend of Saint Mary the Egyptian, who, in order to obtain her passage across a river, paid the boatman with her body. It is a sensuous evocation of sexual union consummated amid the papyrus and plovers of the river bank, while "La flore et la faune palustres/S'accordent pour célébrer/L'heureux cérémonial des sens" (The paludal flora and fauna unite to celebrate the joyful ceremonial of the senses).

Mandiargues has also shown an interest in the theater and has published three plays. *Isabella Morra* was published in 1973 and performed in Paris, with Jean-Louis Barrault and Anny Duperey in the main roles. Written in a highly poetic language, it is set in sixteenth-century Italy and has poetry and love of dreams as its main themes. It revolves around Isabella Morra, who is based on a historical character. Isabella's father has been exiled and her brothers rule the home. She carries on a correspondence in poems with Don Diego Sandoval, a Spanish grandee living in Italy, but her brothers discover this and accuse her of illicit sexual relations with the Spaniard. Rather than bow to her brothers, who represent a sordid and brutal reality that she refuses, Isabella lies to them and claims that she is indeed Don Diego's mistress. She thus affirms her right to her own poetic world and tells her brothers: "J'existe dans un monde qui vous est interdit" (I exist in a world that is forbidden to you). Enraged by this defiance, in a scene with clearly incestuous overtones, her brothers torture and kill her. Perhaps because of its deliberate anachronisms (the three brothers ride motorcycles), perhaps because it bases its effects on poetic language rather than dramatic events, the play was not a success and had only a short run.

La Nuit séculaire, which means approximately The Age-Old Night, was published in 1979 but as yet has not been performed. It deals with time and escape from it and is set on the night of 31 December 1899, a moment poised between two days, two years, and two centuries. During this night, in the Norwegian city of Bodo, the aged Baroness Bjorn (one hundred and twenty years old) and her daughter Lovisa Axelius (a mere ninety-nine years old) receive some sailors from the visiting Russian vessel *Aurora*. This ship anticipates the future, for it later played a role in the Russian Revolution, while the baroness's memories link the play to the past. Because of their great age, the women seem to defy time. In fact, Lovisa is practically immortal, for she dies but is reborn as herself when she was thirteen years old.

Arsène et Cléopâtre (published in 1981) has been performed only in a small experimental theater that is part of the Centre National d'Art et d'Essai in Paris, with Marie Trintignant and Lou Castel in the main roles. While fairly lighthearted in tone, it deals with the serious theme of the relations between art and life, theater and the "real" world.

In addition to the work mentioned so far, Mandiargues has written many articles of literary and artistic criticism, most of them gathered in *Le Belvédère* (The Belvedere, 1958), *Deuxième Belvédère* (Second Belvedere, 1962), *Troisième Belvédère* (Third Belvedere, 1971), and *Le Cadran lunaire* (The Moondial, 1958). Throughout his life, Mandiargues has been the friend of painters and artists, especially ones connected with surrealism. His many articles cover artists and artistic movements ranging from El Greco to Max Ernst, from the baroque to cubism, and from Bernini to Bellmer, but with an obvious predilection for the avant-garde and revolutionary. His literary criticism covers an even wider field, for he has written about Balzac, Baudelaire, Mallarmé, Péret, Novalis, Hoffmann, Kleist, Gambini, Ponge, Réage, Aragon, and many others. He reserves special admiration for the English Elizabethans, the German romantics, the surrealists, André Breton, Jean Paulhan, Marcel Jouhandeau, Yukio Mishima, and, of course, Sade. He has also written articles on places, curious events, objects, and people that have caught his eye. In "L'Espion des Pouilles" (The Spy of Apulia; collected in *Le Cadran lunaire*), for example, he describes Castel del Monto, Frederic II's curious castle in Italy; in "Un Monument d'horlogerie" (A Clockwork Monument; collected in *Le Cadran lunaire*), a strangely ornamented clock seen in a shop window; in "Les Monstres de Bomarzo" (The Monsters at

Bomarzo; collected in *Le Belvédère*), the hideous but disturbingly fascinating statues of monsters at Bomarzo, in Italy. Such articles as these show Mandiargues's avid curiosity, his delight in the strange and unusual, his ability to see the marvelous all around him.

Throughout a very productive career, Mandiargues has shown an exemplary dedication to his art. This has been recognized by critics and rewarded by a series of prizes, the most recent of which was the Grand Prix National des Lettres, awarded in 1985 for his work as a whole. It is difficult to summarize a body of work that is so rich, covers so many fields, and is written in such a brilliant but elusive style. Perhaps the best way of describing him is to quote Octavio Paz, who, in *Corriente alterna* (*Alternating Current*, 1964), says that he is "uno de los escritores en verdad originales que han aparecido en Francia después de la guerra" (one of the truly original writers to have appeared in France since the war).

Interviews:

"Une Rencontre avec André Pieyre de Mandiargues. Interview de René Lacôte," *Lettres Françaises*, no. 1256 (6 December 1967): 3-4;

"Goncourt, moto et cinéma. Une interview de Pieyre de Mandiargues," *Nouvelles Littéraires*, no. 2103 (21 December 1967): 14;

Le Désordre de la mémoire: Entretiens avec Francine Mallet (Paris: Gallimard, 1975);

"André Pieyre de Mandiargues: Je suis un érotomane puritain. Interview avec Gille Costaz," *Galerie des Arts* (June 1978): 76-80;

"Les Mandiargues. Interview d'Isaure de Saint-Pierre," *Elle* (6 August 1978): 50-53;

"Claude Bonnefoy: L'un et l'autre Mandiargues. Interview," *Nouvelles Littéraires*, no. 2690 (21-28 June 1979): 5;

Un Saturne gai: Entretiens avec Yvonne Caroutch (Paris: Gallimard, 1982);

"Arlette Arnel. Entretien: Les Multiples Visages d'André Pieyre de Mandiargues," *Magazine Littéraire*, no. 257 (September 1988): 98-104.

References:

David J. Bond, "André Pieyre de Mandiargues and the Discovery of the Self," *International Fiction Review*, 6 (Summer 1979): 133-136;

Bond, "André Pieyre de Mandiargues: Some Ideas on Art," *Romanic Review*, 70 (January 1979): 69-79;

Bond, *The Fiction of André Pieyre de Mandiargues* (Syracuse: Syracuse University Press, 1982);

Bond, "Jung and Pieyre de Mandiargues," *Esprit Créateur*, 22 (Summer 1982): 53-62;

Bond, "Mystic and Erotic Experience in the Fiction of André Pieyre de Mandiargues," *Kentucky Romance Quarterly*, 27 (May 1980): 205-213;

Susan Campanini, "Alchemy in Pieyre de Mandiargues's 'Le Diamant,'" *French Review*, 50 (March 1977): 602-609;

Campanini, "Blood Rites: Pieyre de Mandiargues's 'Le Sang de L'Agneau,'" *Romanic Review*, 73 (May 1982): 364-372;

Hanna Charney, "The Tide as Structure in 'La Marée,'" *Dada/Surrealism*, 5 (1976): 5-10;

André Gascht, "André Pieyre de Mandiargues ou le goût de l'insolite," *Marginales*, 74 (October 1960): 18-33;

Angela Habel, "'L'Archéologue' de Pieyre de Mandiargues: Entre le fantastique et la psychanalyse," *Symposium*, 36 (Summer 1982): 129-148;

Stirling Haig, "André Pieyre de Mandiargues and 'Les Pierreuses,'" *French Review*, 39 (November 1965): 275-280;

Bettina Knapp, "André Pieyre de Mandiargues," in her *French Novelists Speak Out* (Troy, N.Y.: Whitston, 1976), pp. 48-56;

Octavio Paz, "La metamórfosis de la piedra," in his *Corriente alterna* (Mexico City: Siglo XX, 1964), pp. 94-104; translated as "The Metamorphoses of Stone," in *Alternating Current*, translated by Helen R. Lane (New York: Viking, 1973), pp. 91-95;

André Robin, "André Pieyre de Mandiargues ou l'initiation panique. I," *Cahiers du Sud*, no. 383-384 (1965): 138-156;

Robin, "André Pieyre de Mandiargues ou l'initiation panique. II," *Cahiers du Sud*, no. 385 (1965): 195-213;

Salah Stetié, *André Pieyre de Mandiargues* (Paris: Seghers, 1978);

Mark J. Temmer, "André Pieyre de Mandiargues," *Yale French Studies*, no. 31 (1964): 99-104.

Claude Mauriac
(25 April 1914-   )

Gretchen Rous Besser

BOOKS: *Introduction à une mystique de l'enfer* (Paris: Grasset, 1938);

Jean Cocteau; ou, La Vérité du mensonge (Paris: Odette Lieutier, 1945);

Aimer Balzac (Paris: Table Ronde, 1945);

La Trahison d'un clerc (Paris: Table Ronde, 1945);

Malraux; ou, Le Mal du héros (Paris: Grasset, 1946);

André Breton (Paris: Editions de Flore, 1949);

Conversations avec André Gide (Paris: Albin Michel, 1951); translated by Michael Lebeck as *Conversations with André Gide* (New York: Braziller, 1965);

Hommes et idées d'aujourd'hui (Paris: Albin Michel, 1953);

L'Amour du cinéma (Paris: Albin Michel, 1954);

Petite Littérature du cinéma (Paris: Editions du Cerf, 1957);

Toutes les femmes sont fatales (Paris: Albin Michel, 1957); translated by Richard Howard as *All Women Are Fatal* (New York: Braziller, 1964); translated by Henry Wolff as *Femmes Fatales* (London: Calder & Boyars, 1966);

L'Alittérature contemporaine: Artaud, Bataille, Beckett, Kafka, Leiris, Michaux, Miller, Robbe-Grillet, Nathalie Sarraute, etc. (Paris: Albin Michel, 1958); translated by Samuel I. Stone as *The New Literature* (New York: Braziller, 1959); revised and enlarged French edition (Paris: Albin Michel, 1969);

Le Dîner en ville (Paris: Albin Michel, 1959); translated by Merloyd Lawrence as *The Dinner Party* (New York: Braziller, 1960); republished as *Dinner in Town* (London: Calder, 1963);

La Marquise sortit à cinq heures (Paris: Albin Michel, 1961); translated by Howard as *The Marquise Went Out at Five* (New York: Braziller, 1962; London: Calder & Boyars, 1967);

L'Agrandissement (Paris: Albin Michel, 1963);

La Conversation (Paris: Grasset, 1964);

L'Oubli (Paris: Grasset, 1966);

Théâtre (Paris: Grasset, 1968)—comprises *La Conversation*; *Ici, maintenant*; *Le Cirque*; *Les Parisiens du dimanche*; and *Le Hun*;

De la littérature à l'alittérature (Paris: Grasset, 1969);

Une Amitié contrariée (Paris: Grasset, 1970);

Un Autre de Gaulle: Journal 1944-1954 (Paris: Hachette, 1971); translated by Moura Budberg and Gordon Latta as *The Other de Gaulle: Diaries 1944-1954* (New York: John Day, 1973; London: Angus & Robertson, 1973);

Le Temps immobile, volume 1 (Paris: Grasset, 1974);

Les Espaces imaginaires, volume 2 of *Le Temps immobile* (Paris: Grasset, 1975);

Et comme l'espérance est violente, volume 3 of *Le Temps immobile* (Paris: Grasset, 1976);

La Terrasse de Malagar, volume 4 of *Le Temps immobile* (Paris: Grasset, 1977);

Une Certaine Rage (Paris: Robert Laffont, 1977);

L'Eternité parfois (Paris: Pierre Belfond, 1977);

Aimer de Gaulle, volume 5 of *Le Temps immobile* (Paris: Grasset, 1978);

Le Bouddha s'est mis à trembler (Paris: Grasset, 1979);

Un Cœur tout neuf (Paris: Grasset, 1980);

Laurent Terzieff (Paris: Stock, 1980);

Le Rire des pères dans les yeux des enfants, volume 6 of *Le Temps immobile* (Paris: Grasset, 1981);

Radio Nuit (Paris: Grasset, 1982);

Signes, rencontres et rendez-vous, volume 7 of *Le Temps immobile* (Paris: Grasset, 1983);

Zabé (Paris: Gallimard, 1984);

Qui peut le dire? (Lausanne: L'Age d'Homme, 1985);

Bergère ô tour Eiffel, volume 8 of *Le Temps immobile* (Paris: Grasset, 1985);

François Mauriac, sa vie, son œuvre (Paris: Frédéric Birr, 1985);

Mauriac et fils, volume 9 of *Le Temps immobile* (Paris: Grasset, 1986);

L'Oncle Marcel, volume 10 of *Le Temps immobile* (Paris: Grasset, 1988).

PLAY PRODUCTIONS: *La Conversation*, Paris, Théâtre de Lutèce, 6 January 1966;

Les Parisiens du dimanche, Montreal, Expo '67, French Pavilion, 1 June 1967;

Ici, maintenant, Paris, Théâtre du Lucernaire, 22
    June 1971;
Le Cirque, Paris, Théâtre de la Huchette, 18 Octo-
    ber 1982.

OTHER: *Marcel Proust par lui-même*, edited by
    Mauriac (Paris: Seuil, 1953);
"Les Paliers de décompression (1922-1972)," in
    New Views of the European Novel, edited by
    R. G. Collins and Kenneth McRobbie (Winni-
    peg: University of Manitoba Press, 1972);
Jeanne Mauriac, *Mauriac intime: Photographies de
    Jeanne François Mauriac*, preface by Claude
    Mauriac (Paris: Stock, 1985).

PERIODICAL PUBLICATION: "Ma Rencontre à
    Venise avec Pasolini," *Figaro Littéraire*, 24 Au-
    gust 1974, pp. 7, 10.

During his youth and for much of his adult
life, Claude Mauriac enjoyed the privileges and
suffered the handicap of his father's fame. As
the son of François Mauriac, celebrated Catholic
novelist and member of the Académie Française,
Claude Mauriac rubbed shoulders at an early age
with such luminaries as André Gide, Jean Cocteau, Paul Claudel, Georges Duhamel, Louis Aragon, Marcel Jouhandeau, Jules Romains, Francis
Ponge, and Paul Valéry, among others. These acquaintances provided the subject matter for early
books of criticism and personal reminiscence. At
the same time his father's renown hampered the
young Mauriac in his desire to write. Unwilling
to tread on his father's turf, he tried his hand at
everything but fiction–literary criticism, journalism, film reviews, and a private journal which he
kept from age fourteen on. When he composed
his first novel, in 1957, Claude Mauriac ventured
far afield from the conventional structure, plot,
and characterization which the elder Mauriac
had brought to the pinnacle of classical purity.
Where his father was traditional, he was experimental; where his father was religious, he was ag-
nostic; where his father was a political conservative, he became a left-wing activist (although
tinged with Gaullist tendencies). In fact, Claude
Mauriac's career can be read as a constant struggle to emerge from his father's shadow into the
light of his own literary achievement.

Born 25 April 1914 to François and Jeanne
Lafon Mauriac, Claude Mauriac led a comfortable, sheltered childhood with his two younger sisters in their parents' book-filled apartment at 83,
rue de la Pompe in Paris. The family paid fre-

*Claude Mauriac, February 1977, at Malagar, the family
château in the Gironde (photograph by Paul Paviot)*

quent visits to the Mauriac ancestral château of
Malagar in the Gironde, a region celebrated in
Mauriac *père*'s Nobel-prize-winning fiction. As a
youngster, Claude Mauriac's twin passions were
aviation and the French Revolution, which he
knew as intimately as if he had personally
stormed the Bastille. He and his beloved cousin,
Bertrand Gay-Lussac, put out a boys' newspaper
about biplanes and dreamed of flying. Gay-
Lussac's sudden death from mastoiditis in 1928,
at age fourteen, marked the adolescent Mauriac
for life. Again and again in his journal, over the
years, he relives his grief for his cousin and his horror at the "scandal" of death. He attributes to
this loss, from which he never recovered, his serious, even tragic, nature: "Il me semble que s'il
avait vécu, j'aurais été tout autre" (It seems to me

that, if he had lived, I would have been altogether different).

Mauriac studied law in the late 1930s at the Université de Paris, writing a dissertation entitled *La Corporation dans l'état* (The Corporation in the State), a work he judged mediocre, although it was published in 1941. He received his doctorate in 1943, but he never practiced law, nor do any of his subsequent writings–novels, plays, critical studies, or journal–reveal an interest or his training in jurisprudence.

When World War II broke out, Mauriac was mobilized briefly before spending most of the Occupation in Paris, with occasional visits to Malagar, where a German SS officer and his troops were billeted during the winter of 1940. Writing about that period, Mauriac has described the physical inconveniences (glacial cold, lack of water, scarcity of food) and moral suffering occasioned by this propinquity with the enemy, by their mutual embarrassment and masked antagonism. He has also expressed discomfiture with his unheroic civilian role, perhaps in contrast with the exploits of his brother-in-law, Alain Le Ray, who was a Resistance leader, and with the patriotic efforts of his father, who, despite the German occupation, managed to publish subversive articles under a pseudonym.

In 1944 Claude Mauriac was appointed personal secretary to Charles de Gaulle, a position he held until 1949. De Gaulle was a second father to young Mauriac. Captivated by the general's magnetism and conscious of this opportunity to witness history in the making, Mauriac kept an exhaustive journal recording his encounters and conversations with de Gaulle, which were to form the basis for two later books.

Mauriac's duties did not prevent him from writing several works of literary criticism during his years with de Gaulle. *Aimer Balzac* (To Love Balzac, 1945) communicates his admiration for the master with almost proselytizing fervor. *Jean Cocteau; ou, La Vérité du mensonge* (Jean Cocteau or The Truth of the Lie, 1945), on the other hand, is so blunt in exposing Cocteau's showman traits that it wounded its subject deeply. *Une Amitié contrariée* (A Thwarted Friendship) of 1970 is an attempt to repair the damage and rehabilitate Cocteau's memory. The early studies were followed in quick succession by *Malraux; ou, Le Mal du héros* (Malraux or The Hero's Evil, 1946) and *André Breton* (1949), which received the Prix Sainte-Beuve.

Mauriac has said that his works of criticism came about almost by accident. He would read a writer he admired, take notes, then realize he had assembled material for a book. Mauriac maintains that he is not a true critic or theoretician. Asked what external criteria he applies to a work of art, he replied, "Absolument aucun, que les résonances qu'elle a pour moi, que le plaisir intellectuel qu'elle me donne, que l'enrichissement qu'elle m'apporte, que ce qu'elle m'apprend" (Absolutely none, except the resonances that a book creates within me, the intellectual pleasure it affords, the enrichment or enlightenment it provides). These principles guided him during his years as a columnist for the *Figaro* (1946-1977) and as film critic for the *Figaro Littéraire* (1947-1972).

While working for de Gaulle, Mauriac met Georges Pompidou, whose office was down the hall. In 1949 Pompidou helped Mauriac found a review called *Liberté de l'Esprit*, of which he was director until 1953. Revenue was so minimal that by 1952 Mauriac could no longer afford to pay himself a salary. In 1951 his *Conversations avec André Gide* (translated as *Conversations with André Gide*, 1965) had appeared, with its youthful portrait of Gide at age seventy. Here Mauriac traces the steps from his early intellectual adulation for the great writer through their burgeoning friendship and increasing intimacy to his eventual reservations about Gide's spontaneity and honesty. That same year, he married Marie-Claude Mante, grandniece of Marcel Proust and of Edmond Rostand. Mauriac had always felt a strong affinity for Proust as a writer, and in 1953 he edited *Marcel Proust par lui-même* (Marcel Proust by Himself). He also published *Hommes et idées d'aujourd'hui* (Men and Ideas of Today), which went virtually unnoticed. Two books of film criticism followed: *L'Amour du cinéma* (1954) and *Petite Littérature du cinéma* (1957).

Mauriac made his international mark as a critic with *L'Alittérature contemporaine* (published in 1958 and revised in 1969), in which he coins the term *aliterature* (analogous to the word *amoral*) to denote "la littérature délivrée des facilités qui ont donné à ce mot un sens péjoratif " (literature freed from the facilities that have given this word a pejorative meaning). *The New Literature*, as it was called in the American translation of 1959, helped publicize the innovative efforts of such New Wave novelists as Nathalie Sarraute, Alain Robbe-Grillet, Michel Butor, Robert Pinget, Claude Simon, and Philippe Sollers. Among these disparate writers Mauriac detects common concerns: metaphysical anguish, a distrust of language, and an all-consuming search for truth, for an absolute that lies always out of reach.

Mauriac had heretofore felt that fiction was a field in which he could do nothing but repeat, less well, what his father had accomplished. However, a trip to the United States in 1956 helped him overcome this inhibition. During the summer of his return, he composed his first novel, *Toutes les femmes sont fatales*. It was refused many times. Finally, through the efforts of André Sabatier, Albin Michel agreed to publish the book in 1957 in an edition of twenty-five thousand copies, an exceptional number for a first novel. The first English translation, *All Women Are Fatal*, appeared in 1964. Mauriac was disappointed that the book elicited no important criticism and that his attempts to undermine the conventions of fictional technique were ignored or misunderstood. *Toutes les femmes sont fatales* was the first of a tetralogy which Mauriac called "Le Dialogue intérieur"–a variation on the concept of interior monologue, where the unspoken thoughts of two or more characters converge and converse. The same protagonist, Bertrand Carnéjoux, appears in different places and at different ages of his life, thinking about the various women he has desired, all of whom become anonymous, interchangeable, in his mind.

This initial novel was followed in 1959 by *Le Dîner en ville*, published in translation as *The Dinner Party* (1960) and *Dinner in Town* (1963), which earned for its author the Prix Médicis and resulted in his being classified as an exponent of the French New Novel. (Mauriac is now a member of the Médicis jury.) Mingling the spoken conversation and unspoken thoughts of eight dinner guests whom the reader must identify through their habits of speech or unvoiced preoccupations (assisted by a diagram of their respective places at the table), *Le Dîner en ville* is more than a conundrum or a literary tour de force. The protagonist–again, Bertrand Carnéjoux–is a writer obsessed by his craft and by questions that will return as leitmotivs in Mauriac's future work–a preoccupation with the passage of time and its corollary, death; the interaction between literature and cinema; the interchangeability of personalities; and the problem for the writer of transposing reality into words. If Proust's aim was to recapture time, Mauriac's is to immobilize time, to arrest its headlong course–in this instance, by a dinner party, which provides a momentary re-

spite from life's movement toward death. In this early novel Mauriac introduces a phrase (supposedly quoted from Bertrand Carnéjoux's book) which will crop up repeatedly in his writings: "Le temps nous tue mais il n'existe pas" (Time kills us, but it does not exist).

La Marquise sortit à cinq heures (1961; translated as *The Marquise Went Out at Five*, 1962) is more complex in construction and more ambitious in scope than its predecessors; in the space of one hour–from five to six o'clock of a summer evening–it registers the words and thoughts of people who pass through a specific crossroads in Paris–the Carrefour de Buci, of which a detailed map is included–in the present and over the course of eight centuries. The title is taken from Paul Valéry's remark to André Breton that he would never write a novel that began: "La Marquise sortit à cinq heures." Taking up the gauntlet, Mauriac begins his novel with these words–supposedly the opening sentence of a novel that the fictional Bertrand Carnéjoux is writing. Bertrand stands on the balcony of his flat and looks down on the Carrefour de Buci–as does his neighbor, Claude Desprez (both alter egos for Mauriac). The reader finds himself turn by turn inside the minds of the people that these two see, eavesdropping on snatches of conversation, privy to secret thoughts and impressions. Desprez introduces a historical dimension by viewing the intersection as "couches superposées de présents qui n'ont point tout à fait disparu en cessant d'être, coexistant ici virtuellement à jamais" (superimposed layers of present moments which have not completely disappeared upon ceasing to be, which coexist here virtually forever). The anonymity of characters is not a gratuitous procedure but stems from Mauriac's conviction that human beings are interchangeable in time, that the living of today will be the dead of tomorrow, in a continuum of history that remains constant while its individual components are replaced.

Bertrand Carnéjoux, like Mauriac, is immersed in the problems of writing fiction (his novel, *Le Déjeuner au bistro* [Lunch at the Café], is a mirror-image of his creator's novel, *Le Dîner en ville*). The writer, Mauriac feels, must be part of his creation, must descend among his characters and infuse life into his book from within. Just as Bertrand Carnéjoux contemplates sending his marquise, his alter ego, out onto the fictional scene, Mauriac enters his own novel at the end, appearing as the author and creator of Carnéjoux: "Romancier animé par un romancier que romancier moi-même j'ai mis dans un roman où rien pourtant ne fut inventé" (Novelist brought to life by a novelist that, as novelist, I have myself placed in a novel where, nevertheless, nothing has been invented). The novel disintegrates as Mauriac steps into the text and "purifies" his book of its "last traces of fiction" in favor of what he calls truth. "The seriousness and the ultimate realism of the novel that mirrors itself could have no more vivid demonstration," concluded Robert Alter, in a 1975 assessment in *TriQuarterly*. Gilbert Highet, who approached *La Marquise sortit à cinq heures* with ambivalence, was won over after a painstaking, persistent reading. "As I finished *The Marquise Went Out at Five*," he wrote in a review for *Horizon* (May 1962), "I forgot that I was reading a book and felt as though I were standing on a balcony above the Carrefour de Buci, sharing for an hour the life of those gay, harassed, volatile, intelligent, sensual, xenophobic people of Paris, who are the real hero of Mauriac's eloquent and penetrating novel."

Each of the novels in Mauriac's tetralogy is contained in germ in its predecessor. *L'Agrandissement* (Enlargement, 1963) expands four pages taken from *La Marquise sortit à cinq heures* into two hundred pages of text. Whereas the time span of *Le Dîner en ville* was the length of a meal and that of *La Marquise sortit à cinq heures* an hour, *L'Agrandissement* covers a mere two minutes, the amount of time it takes the traffic light on the corner of the Carrefour de Buci to turn from amber to red, then green, and back to amber. Mauriac's intention is to blow up a moment in time, a tiny corner of space, sufficiently so that he does not lose its essential detail. "La plus infime fraction de temps concevable dure encore trop pour que je puisse espérer l'épuiser" (The most infinitesimal fraction of time conceivable lasts too long for me to hope to exhaust it). *L'Agrandissement* consists of a single long paragraph containing a potpourri of thoughts, scenes, imaginings, memories, and reflections by the narrator, Bertrand Carnéjoux, about the novel he is writing (and the reader is reading). Recalling the past, meditating on the present, he experiments with the notion of simultaneity and the immobilization of time. At the end, Mauriac calls the book "l'histoire d'un monsieur qui se demande comment il va écrire un roman que j'ai déjà écrit" (the story of a man who wonders how he is going to write a novel which I have already written).

Aside from *Le Dîner en ville* Mauriac's novels received scant recognition when they appeared.

Claude Mauriac and his father, François, pictured on the cover for volume 9 of Le Temps immobile

In fact, the fictional Carnéjoux voices his creator's complaints when he says in *L'Agrandissement*: "Mais je n'écris pas si mal. J'écris même plutôt bien. Pourquoi, dès lors, ce silence autour de mes ouvrages, non point en ce qui concerne mes travaux universitaires, là je n'ai relativement pas à me plaindre, mais à l'égard de mes recherches personnelles, comme si je ne méritais pas, moi aussi, qu'on me commente?" (I don't write so badly. In fact, I write rather well. Why, then, this silence surrounding my works, not my scholarly writings, there I have relatively no complaints, but with respect to my personal strivings, as if I weren't worth a comment?). Almost in reply, Vivian Mercier, in *The New Novel from Queneau to Pinget* (1971), called *L'Agrandissement* "Claude Mauriac's most original work by far, and at least the equal in originality of any other work by the New Novelists." Leon Roudiez's praise was fainter, in his *French Fiction Today* (1972): "If it does not provide an exciting esthetic experience, it certainly is not uninteresting. I might even say that it generates considerable intellectual enjoyment."

Mauriac transferred some of his themes to drama with the 1964 publication of his first play, *La Conversation*. The dramatic format is a conversation between a man and a woman from the time they are engaged until after he dies. Time is telescoped, years pass, wars come and go, children are born, grow up, and have children of their own, while the conversation is repeated in successive generations. The second part, "Conversation II," consists of an exchange between the woman and another man (an old friend and one-time lover) which is lifted directly out of the first part of "Conversation I"–like the blowup of a segment of dialogue–and is accompanied by an "interior dialogue" in which they express their true thoughts. *La Conversation* was staged in 1966 by Nicolas Bataille at the Théâtre de Lutèce in Paris where, despite a laudatory article by Eugène Ionesco in *Combat*, it played to a near-empty house. It was simultaneously produced by Michel Mitrani for Télévision Française.

Originally conceived as a filmscript, *L'Oubli* (Forgetfulness, 1966) is a detective-style novel which centers on the protagonist's attempts to identify a beautiful woman who claims to know him but whom he fails to recognize. As he searches his memory, he discovers that forgetfulness is the capital experience of life. Once again, the fictional hero is the author's spokesman. Having just completed a play titled *Ici, maintenant* (Here, Now) (a work which Mauriac himself had written), Nicolas has begun a novel, the novel we are in fact reading. "Il n'y a qu'un sujet: le temps" (There is only one subject: time). Forgetfulness is a function of time, which not only alters and destroys one's physical being but also erases the memory of all one has felt, thought, and been. *L'Oubli* was poorly received. Roudiez said of the book: "In my opinion [*L'Oubli*] had best be forgotten. The mock detective-story plot that holds things together . . . is more grotesque than burlesque and somewhat embarrassing in its inanity."

Ici, maintenant was published in 1968 in *Théâtre*, a volume of plays which includes *La Conversation*, *Le Cirque* (The Circus, produced by Nicolas Bataille in 1982), an "impromptu" entitled *Les Parisiens du dimanche* (The Sunday Parisians) which Bataille staged in Montreal at the French Pavilion of Expo '67, and *Le Hun* (The Hun). These plays are all concerned, in one way or another, with the interchangeability of individuals and the ineluctable passage of time.

By 1972 Mauriac had been experimenting with various forms of writing, seeking his way, for more than thirty-five years. He wrote in 1941, "Il reste que je puis et dois faire mieux qu'une œuvre critique. Je sens en moi le grondement de cette œuvre encore informe" (I can and must do better than a critical work. I sense within me the rumbling of this still-unformed work). Although his major themes and ideas were present in his mind, he felt he had not discovered a suitable way to express them, a form capable of sustaining the major opus he dreamed of writing. On the afternoon of 26 June 1957, as he was driving past the Tour Saint-Jacques on his way to the dentist at precisely 13:45 (he has pinpointed the place and moment), he experienced a revelation. This was nothing less than the method of composing what was to become *Le Temps immobile* (Time Immobilized, 1974-1988); the concept dazzled him as being unique. However, so great was his diffidence that it was more than fifteen years before Mauriac succeeded in "mounting" the first text of an opus which by 1988 ran to ten volumes.

It is incorrect and a violation of the author's intention to view his *Temps immobile* as memoir or autobiography. Mauriac refers to this work as "le roman de ma vie," "un roman où tout est vrai" (the novel of my life, a novel in which everything is true). Like much of his fiction, it is constructed from authentic texts–letters, historical documents, excerpts from other writers' diaries, passages from other writers' works–which are interpolated among his own writings (in this case, dated entries from a journal covering nearly sixty years). These entries are arranged in thematic but nonchronological order. The structure resembles a montage of clippings–not unlike those inserted in *La Marquise sortit à cinq heures*, which Mauriac has called the germ of *Le Temps immobile*, except that the documents he draws on are his own. These are not invented or historical texts, "mais de petits fragments de temps pur empruntés à ma vie" (but tiny fragments of pure time borrowed from my life). Mauriac cuts, rearranges, and pastes, juggling and juxtaposing journal notations that span scores of years. In this assemblage, intertextuality is carried to its extreme. For Mauriac, the texts themselves are less important than the effect achieved by their contiguity:

"C'est entre les textes, de leur contact, que naît l'essentiel" (It is between the texts, through their contact, that the essential arises). *Le Temps immobile* acquires its density through such temporal associations, which emphasize "le vertige du temps et son inexistence" (the vertigo of time and its nonexistence). Authenticity is guaranteed by the uncorrected, unretouched texts. Mauriac's journal furnishes a means of recapturing time, à la Proust, but with more accurate documentation than mere memory affords. What makes this account more reliable and immediate than any writer's journal is that it is composed not of reminiscences, a retelling of the past, but is made up entirely of present moments, the innumerable present moments of Mauriac's life. Although the author insists he has not written a *journal intime* and serves merely as a mirror to reflect events and people, his personality endows the book with a warm human quality. Mauriac is scrupulously honest, determined at all costs to be fair, unpretentious, reserving his severest criticism for himself.

Although the ten volumes of *Le Temps immobile* cover similar terrain and echo basic themes, each stands as an entity with its own power and perspective. The opening volume, entitled simply *Le Temps immobile* (1974), is, in the author's words, "pure réflexion sur le temps pur" (pure reflection on pure time). The passage of time is rendered even more acute when it is experienced as a function of space–when the same scene recurs among the same participants on the same site (the family home at Vémars or the château of Malagar) but after an interval of years. When innumerable scenes of this kind are repeated, the effect is a dizzying plunge into the fourth dimension–time. Excerpts from his father's *Bloc-Notes*, entries from his grandfather's journal dated 1873, texts by de Gaulle, André Malraux, Paul Claudel, Michel Foucault, and others contribute the historical density that Mauriac achieved in *La Marquise sortit à cinq heures*. Much of this first volume centers on the process of creation–his consciousness of attempting an experimental writing form allied to cinematographic technique, the unsettling experience of reviving the past, the Proustian hope that his writing will help to vitiate the effects of time, and the fear that he will never bring his life's work to fruition.

While pursuing many of the themes from volume 1–time and death, his father's presence, the importance of his journal, the construction of his present work–*Les Espaces imaginaires* (Imaginary Spaces, 1975), or *Le Temps immobile*, volume 2, includes material of a more personal nature which Mauriac treats with uncommon candor. The picture of his father is less roseate, more realistic than it was in the previous volume. Mauriac is sensitive to his father's disapproval, dismayed by his unenthusiastic reaction to the proofs of *Le Dîner en ville*, conscious of the barrier of "la non-communication, absolue, totale, irrémédiable" (absolute, total, irremediable noncommunication) between them. Included in *Les Espaces imaginaires* are accounts of political events, demonstrations against the Stavisky ministry (1934), reactions against the Vichy government, sidelights on the Spanish civil war, pages on the German occupation, on his admiration for de Gaulle, and on his present political activities. Mauriac is no longer so self-consciously aware of his technique; the transitions flow more smoothly, and he seems more firmly in control of his method and material. The critic Pierre de Boisdeffre, who found the procedure artificial in volume 1, judged this book to be extremely successful. The author, he says, has furnished "un témoignage irremplaçable sur son temps et sur son propre cheminement spirituel–un témoignage qui est aussi une œuvre d'art" (an irreplaceable testimonial to his time and his own spiritual progress–a testimonial that is also a work of art [*Revue des Deux Mondes*, July 1975]).

Volumes 3 and 5 of *Le Temps immobile* are more political and historical in emphasis. *Et comme l'espérance est violente* (And How Violent Hope Is, 1976)–the title refers to a verse by Apollinaire–is divided into two parts, which correspond roughly to Mauriac's contradictory political leanings. The first section focuses on the two giants of postwar France, de Gaulle and Malraux. The former remains a gigantic shadow on the wall–the object of a feudal-type allegiance by a clan of devotees, among them Malraux. Mauriac provides a rare series of "film clips" showing Malraux dominating a dinner-party conversation with his dazzling erudition, reminiscing about de Gaulle, discoursing about mysticism, and fascinating the younger Mauriac with his virtuosity and encyclopedic knowledge. The second half of the book marks a passage from "sentimental" Gaullism to active *gauchisme* as Mauriac joins forces with Foucault, Jean Genet, and Jean-Paul Sartre to investigate police brutality, champion the causes of disaffected Algerians, press for prison reform, and combat the death penalty. Attracted by the camaraderie of this closed world of outcasts into which he is grudgingly admitted, Mauriac finds it difficult to accept their militant doctrines. A spokesman for moderation and reason, Mauriac is invariably gentle, fair-minded, and a voluble opponent of violence. Because the passages (as always) are excerpted from his journal without explanatory background, the reader may have difficulty in following the minutiae of outdated events. The impression is that of reading last year's newspaper. To Foucault's suggestion that he furnish footnotes, Mauriac countered that he had neither the time nor patience to include them.

La Terrasse de Malagar (*Le Temps immobile*, 4) of 1977 marks a return to the familial atmosphere of the first two volumes, with Malagar and the terrace of the family house providing a fulcrum of stability around which the years spin. Malagar represents for Mauriac, as it did for his father (in François Mauriac's words), "une halte dans la fuite des jours" (a halt in the flight of days). Here, father and son feel themselves outside time's orbit. There are pages of intimate revelation about François Mauriac: his anguish at growing old, his delight in his grandchildren, recollections of his own youth at Malagar. After François Mauriac's death, Claude sounds the entire register of grief and relives his despair at losing Bertrand Gay-Lussac. Again, the gestation of his book forms its subject. He recounts the revelation of his life's work, the "crystallization" of an idea he had ruminated for years. The book he is now writing, which he compares to a mania, folly, asceticism, and a drug, is his only profound justification for living. He recognizes (in 1976) that he has attempted, if not succeeded in, writing his major work–and the serenity with which he reads the writings of others guarantees the worth of his own.

Like his open-ended *Temps immobile*, *Une Certaine Rage* (1977) consists of journal extracts, many of which testify to Mauriac's political ambivalence. Although he sides with Michel Foucault, Jean-Paul Sartre, Maurice Nadeau, and others in activist support of liberal causes, championing prisoners–Iranian student protesters, a teacher, an accused murderer–whose innocence he proclaims, denouncing the death penalty, and inveighing against injustice, Mauriac cannot shrug off his conservative background nor forget that he was brought up the child of privilege. He basks in his acceptance by leftist friends, stressing the anomaly he represents as "un gaulliste de gauche" (a left-wing Gaullist).

Although *L'Eternité parfois* (Eternity Sometimes, 1977) was to have been the core of *Le Temps immobile* 6, it did not appear under the Grasset imprint. At the request of his friend Bruno Lagrange, Mauriac published the novel with Pierre Belfond, and hence it exists apart from the series. Mauriac continues to ponder the effects of time, the discrepancy (and identity) between the young man he was and the older man he has become. Waves of nostalgia for the past, of love for his children, of yearning for his dead father and persistent grief for his cousin Bertrand permeate this book with an autumnal melancholy. Letters and conversations dating back to 1953 and 1955 reveal the father's hopes for his son's conversion, the latter's groping for faith, his ambivalent spirituality. His father writes him (1953): "Tes professions répétées d'agnosticisme rendent un son qui est très près d'être celui de la prière" (Your repeated professions of agnosticism render a sound which is very close to that of prayer).

Aimer de Gaulle (To Love de Gaulle, 1978) reorchestrates the earlier book *Un Autre de Gaulle* (1971; translated as *The Other de Gaulle*, 1973) in order to fit it into the framework of *Le Temps immobile* as volume 5. Aside from glimpses into Mauriac's engagement, marriage, and the birth of his first child, the book revolves around de Gaulle. During his years as de Gaulle's private secretary, in charge of his voluminous correspondence and heading an office that at one point numbered twenty under secretaries, Mauriac met with de Gaulle almost daily. These privileged encounters provide an intimate view of the French leader: his courage and imperviousness to danger (he risked his life twenty times in two days following his arrival in Paris), his patriotism (including an undeviating wariness of his English and American allies), his dignity, aloofness, and political acumen (the threat to step down was a favorite ploy because he knew–or thought–he was irreplaceable). His proximity to de Gaulle continues to awe young Mauriac. Together with pride in his post goes the occasional humiliating consciousness of collaborating in political expediencies with which he does not concur. His ambivalences, as recorded in these pages, are not the revised evaluations of a later date but feelings that are presented at the time they arise; their immediacy and freshness are startling.

With *Le Bouddha s'est mis à trembler* (Buddha Began to Tremble, 1979), Mauriac published his first novel in thirteen years that was not written as part of "le roman de ma vie," *Le Temps immobile*. Brief, enigmatic, filled with symbolic imagery—tulips, cats, bird song—and visual scenes presented like film sequences, the book serves to illuminate *Le Temps immobile* and vice versa. Bertrand, now a gifted actor/director, meets a stranger, Camille, with whom he strikes up an immediate, passionate friendship. They plan a film about friendship in which they will play themselves—no, they will play the parts of Montaigne and La Boétie. Bertrand later tells Camille the "great secret" he has learned about time—that it is possible to discover that motionless lake where time does not flow and to float there in a perpetual present. Even death can be transcended, he says. Death is just another voyage, which can be effaced in our thoughts as we visit—not in space, but in time—with the person we love. He explains that after suffering from his father's death, he no longer feels grief: "non parce que le temps a fait son œuvre, comme on dit. Mais parce que j'ai fait, dans le silence de moi-même, une œuvre sur le temps" (Not because time has completed its work, as they say. But because, in the silence of myself, I have completed a work about time). This is as close to a confessional as Mauriac comes.

In April 1968 Mauriac had served on a film jury for Les Rencontres Internationales du Jeune Cinéma with the actor/director Laurent Terzieff. The ensuing friendship prompted him to write *Laurent Terzieff* (1980), in which Terzieff appears as a romantic hero. By means of journal entries and a taped interview, Mauriac presents Terzieff's background, stage debut, meteoric success, and anecdotes about the directors with whom he worked—Roberto Rossellini, Pier Paolo Pasolini, Luis Buñuel, Arthur Adamov. Much of the book reflects Mauriac's awed fascination with his younger friend. Not only did Terzieff produce *Ici, maintenant* on the Paris stage (1971) but he also suggested that Mauriac write a play about the friendship between Montaigne and La Boétie; this idea became the germ of the novel *Le Bouddha s'est mis à trembler*.

Un Cœur tout neuf (A Brand New Heart, 1980) is a novel concerned with time, aging, futile love, and the interchangeability of identity. In the first section Rachel, an older woman who has received a heart implant, finds that her lover has fallen for the surgeon's assistant; in despair and unable to work, she takes up with a young black man. In the second part the roles are reversed (due to a computer error, the author explains): the narrator is a man with a heart im-

plant who takes up with a young black woman (it is her lover, killed in a car crash, who furnished his new heart) because Rachel, the woman he loves, has gone off with his surgeon.

Excursions into fiction did not prevent Mauriac from continuing to work on his *Temps immobile*. Volume 6 (1981) has a gentle, pleasing title taken from a poem by Pasolini—*Le Rire des pères dans les yeux des enfants* (Fathers' Laughter in Their Children's Eyes)—which is consonant with its emphasis on family relationships, especially the bridge between Mauriac's love and admiration for his father and his devotion to his children. He includes reminiscences about Gide, Duhamel, Roger Martin du Gard, and "Papa"—the old guard—together with more recent literary acquaintances—Alain Robbe-Grillet, Nathalie Sarraute. The second half of the book plumbs his deepest emotions as his children—Gérard, Natalie, Gilles—are born, learn to speak, grow independent, and his father becomes ill, declines, and, in 1970, dies. Mauriac's grief was so great that for years he was unable to reread the diary entries following his father's death. Now he can face this loss with equanimity and acceptance. He realizes that his father's death has freed him to be himself: "Surtout: mon père n'étant plus là, je n'ai plus besoin de m'affirmer autrement qu'en étant moi-même, dans le plein soleil de la vie, de la mort, sans cette ombre immense qu'il mettait sur moi" (Especially: with my father no longer here, I no longer feel the need to assert myself otherwise than by being myself, in the full sunlight of life and death, without that immense shadow he cast over me).

In the third section Mauriac refers to his previous novels as first drafts of this volume of *Le Temps immobile* in which he is immersed and which he variously calls an impossible book, "un livre effrayant" (a frightening book), and a work "sans véritable intérêt" (without veritable interest). These inconsistencies, moments of pride followed by bouts of discouragement, ups and downs of hope and despair, exposed with utmost sincerity, give the book its universal appeal and poignancy. There are, Mauriac holds, several ways to read *Le Temps immobile:* as anecdote (the history of an era), as literature (a new form of writing based on journal entries), but above all as "une expérience existentielle qui seule a un véritable prix à mes yeux" (an existential experience, which alone has true value for me). His son Gérard's wedding (1979) in the same church where his father had worshipped, his uncle had served mass, and he, Claude, had once been a choirboy, reunites all the Mauriac generations in one setting–continuity in time is served by sameness of place. In *Le Rire des pères dans les yeux des enfants* there is a sense of peace, of acceptance, missing from the previous volumes. Mauriac has come to terms with his father's death, even the possible loss of Malagar. His serenity derives most of all from a sense of accomplishment: he has finally found his path, is convinced of the value and authenticity of his work. He is his own person, no longer François Mauriac's son.

In spite of repeated protestations that he will not write fiction again, that composing *Le Temps immobile* fulfills his needs and exhausts his resources, Mauriac has continued to produce new novels. The most recent, *Radio Nuit* (Radio Night, 1982) and *Zabé* (1984), are incursions into the realm of the supernatural and soundings of spiritual concerns. The process of creation is implicit in the product of creation; the genesis of a novel is recorded in its pages. The opening paragraph of *Radio Nuit* is a dated journal entry describing the idea for this particular book–a work of capital importance for Mauriac, who says: "Ce roman, si roman il y a, j'y ai mis l'essentiel de ma vie, ce qui reste au fond du tamis, ce très peu d'or qui est sans prix pour moi" (In this novel, if novel it be, I have put the essence of my life, what remains at the bottom of the sieve, this bit of gold that is priceless to me). The initial section is composed of an ongoing conversation between the first-person narrator, Raphael, and an old professor (both spokesmen for the author), supplemented by quotations from Proust, Jean-Jacques Rousseau, Søren Kierkegaard, Charles Péguy, Denis Diderot, Alexandr Solzhenitsyn, Graham Greene, Gustave Flaubert, and W. H. Auden, dealing with questions of time and eternity, death and consciousness, nonbelief and morality, the existence or nonexistence of God, and the possibility of communicating with the dead. Interpolated are Mauriac's dated notes describing the composition of the present book, which is both novel and journal; it is precisely in the back-and-forth momentum between the two forms, "dans ces hésitations entre l'autobiographie et le romanesque" (in these hesitations between autobiography and fiction), that the book's essence may be perceived.

The second section skirts the supernatural and surrealistic. The new narrator, Rodolphe, Raphael's friend, has been listening to a strange radio program in the middle of the night, which he is convinced emanates from the realm of the dead. Upon seeing a grave with his name in the Père-Lachaise cemetery, he believes he has died. In the radio studio where he is to be interviewed, he sees the father and young brother (Bertrand) he lost many years before. In succeeding scenes Rodolphe becomes his younger self (selves), traversing back and forth in time, exchanging identities with his brother and with his black twin, escaping from time and from selfhood, in dreamlike travels and hallucinatory metamorphoses. In the closing section Raphael, the first narrator, reviews the incidents of section 2 and concludes that Rodolphe is really his old professor, a messenger from the world of the dead. There is no difference among men through time and history. All men are the same man, with the same thoughts, hopes, loves, and sufferings.

Signes, rencontres et rendez-vous (Signs, Encounters, and Meetings) of 1983 (*Le Temps immobile*, 7) again considers the passage of time: time passes, and he, Mauriac, remains unchanged. He is present in 1927 when his cousin Bertrand is still alive; in 1930, when he is in love with a girl named Camille; in 1932, when his father has an operation. He achieves a day-by-day correspondence between the same dates in 1932 and in 1982, with a bewildering suppression of the intervening years. Historical events evoke personal experiences and vice versa: his father's illness, Hindenburg's election as German president, his father's election to the presidency of the Société des Gens de Lettres, the assassination of French president Paul Doumer, his father's election (1933) to the Académie Française, the German menace, fear of war, unemployment, the dissolution of the League of Nations. Mauriac's political activities are cataloged here, from his conservative upbringing and early association with La Roque's Croix-de-Feu group to the left-wing swing that brought him in contact with Foucault, interested him in the Meinhof-Baader affair (1977), sent him to Thailand and Malaysia to interview Vietnam refugees and to participate with other French intellectuals on the Boat for Vietnam committee (1978), and sent him back to Bangkok in 1980 to take part in a symbolic March for Survival to the Cambodian border.

In *Bergère ô tour Eiffel* (Shepherdess, O Eiffel Tower, *Le Temps immobile*, 8) of 1985, whose title refers to a verse from Apollinaire quoted in *Radio Nuit*, Mauriac again plays tricks with time, again contrasts diary entries fifty years apart (1931 and 1981). Although he claims that his work is unique, that no one except Henri-Frédéric Amiel (1821-1881) had written so long a journal and no one ever had used a journal as the springboard for another work which would not have existed without it, Mauriac experiences fatigue, exhaustion, in thus delving into and reliving the past. Paradoxically, the only time he considers worth living is the time consecrated to the composition of his *Le Temps immobile*. He ventures into a deeper stratum of confession than ever before, revealing an inferiority complex dating to earliest childhood, his adolescent dissatisfaction with his looks, and a youthful consciousness of physical weakness and intellectual incapacity. Now his resource texts include *Le Temps immobile* itself. He is prey to mixed emotions upon rereading volume 1: satisfaction at having achieved a project long contemplated and deferred, vertigo in discovering portions he had forgotten, pride mingled with doubt and disquiet.

Primarily, he is concerned with the gestation of this work, especially because he now feels, at his present age, that time has ceased being immobile; he envisages for this volume the title "Le Temps s'écroule" (Time Crumbles). Pages taken from the Occupation years emphasize his dismay (guilt?) at living a life of peace and happiness during a period of wartime suffering; claiming he was unaware of the concentration camps and Jewish extermination, he comes upon journal entries proving the contrary—and he is not proud of this part of his past. In fact, this becomes the most oppressive of the *Temps immobile* volumes because for the first time Mauriac confronts the Occupation and a self he finds antipathetic. Mauriac's obsession, reiterated in *Le Bouddha s'est mis à trembler*, *Radio Nuit*, and *Zabé*, is to "vaincre la vieillesse . . . et connaître l'éternité" (vanquish old age . . . and know eternity). The sale of the family home and of his parents' apartment, with the distribution of their belongings, saddens him—but he keeps the past alive and fresh in his journals; it is in *Le Temps immobile*, and only there, he realizes, that his childhood home remains intact, inviolate, unchanged. Although *Bergère ô tour Eiffel* tends to be wordy, repetitious, even tedious at times, it provides, uncorrected by the lens of memory or hindsight, an authentic image of a man and his times.

According to the author, *Mauriac et fils* (Mauriac and Son, 1986) is the penultimate volume of *Le Temps immobile*. The title of the book is the name of the wine-cask company operated by François Mauriac's father and grandfather at a time when it was common for a trade to be handed down from father to son (the allusion to François and Claude is obvious). Thematic material from previous volumes is repeated: the fifty-year interval between dates is again emphasized, the writer's activist friendship with Michel Foucault is expounded upon, his legacy from his father is plumbed. Prewar events in Prague (1938) are contrasted with a quieter visit in 1985. The book ends with the account of a trip through Central America with the Médecins sans Frontières (a refugee aid group) in the summer of 1985 and Mauriac's invitation to his readers to make a similar, internal voyage "hors du temps, dans l'éternité de leur temps immobile à eux" (outside of time, in the eternity of their own *temps immobile*).

Since August 1986 Mauriac has written a weekly column on politics for the *Matin*. In 1988 he published volume 10 of *Le Temps immobile*, entitled *L'Oncle Marcel* (Uncle Marcel). In this latest brick in the edifice of his masterwork, Mauriac continues to question relationships of time, place, politics, and family filiation, especially with his omnipresent father and his distant relative Marcel Proust. Again he is overwhelmed by the deliberate diffraction of time—in this case, 1936 and 1986.

Mauriac's recent work has received cursory attention from French critics. Dominique Autrand was impressed by *La Terrasse de Malagar* (*Quinzaine Littéraire*, 1-15 May 1977); Jean-Didier Wolfram called *Le Rire des pères* an important work (*Magazine Littéraire*, April 1981), and Henri-François Rey found *Zabé* to be a successfully executed novel, "un beau livre, d'abord parce que l'auteur a su avec une apparente simplicité marier le rêve et la réalité dans des noces qui sont toujours heureuses" (a fine book, primarily because the author has been able with apparent simplicity to wed dream and reality in a marriage that is always happy [*Magazine Littéraire*, March 1984]). In spite of this sporadic praise, the majority of critics tend to side with Douglas Johnson's appraisal of *Le Temps immobile* in the *Times Literary Supplement* (17 September 1976): "it was because of François that Claude Mauriac has constantly been surrounded by the distinguished and famous, and it is this which has enabled him to write a journal which other people will want to read. There are always those who like to hear anecdotes, and all that M. Mauriac has had to do is to record the stories which he heard in the course of the day. . . . To this extent M. Mauriac has published a book which is bound to be successful."

Perhaps Mauriac's work—especially his *Temps immobile*—will best be appreciated by Stendhal's "happy few." True, his book affords uncommon close-ups of the great and famous, which may account for the disproportionate sales of *Temps immobile* volumes—ten to twelve thousand for *Aimer de Gaulle* and *La Terrasse de Malagar*, five thousand or so for the rest. But for some readers, what is chiefly endearing is the personality of the writer—humble, modest, self-effacing, passionate in his devotions, ironbound in his principles, and utterly sincere. Mauriac does not pose for posterity or disguise his insecurities, failures, anxieties, and self-criticism. He is eminently, almost embarrassingly, truthful. One is not accustomed to candor of so non-self-serving a nature. Although he claims he has tried to obliterate his presence as much as possible, to step aside and allow others to speak, it is Claude Mauriac who appears as the central character, the true hero of his story, suffusing his book(s) with his sensitivity and quiet strength.

Interviews:

"Le Temps pris au piège," *Magazine Littéraire*, 46 (November 1970): 33-34;

Alain Clerval, "Entretien. Claude Mauriac: 'J'ai eu de la chance. Je ne m'en suis pas senti tout à fait indigne,'" *Quinzaine Littéraire*, no. 231 (16-30 April 1976): 14-15;

Gretchen R. Besser, "Entretien avec Claude Mauriac," *French Review*, 52 (March 1979): 611-617.

References:

Gretchen R. Besser, "Claude Mauriac and *Le Temps Immobile*," *World Literature Today*, 35 (Spring 1979): 242-244;

Pierre de Boisdeffre, "La Revue littéraire: Du côté du journal intime," *Revue des Deux Mondes*, no. 7 (July 1975): 163-172;

Stuart Johnson, "Structure in the Novels of Claude Mauriac," *French Review*, 38 (February 1965): 451-458;

Vivian Mercier, "Claude Mauriac: The Immobilization of Time," in his *The New Novel from Queneau to Pinget* (New York: Farrar, Straus & Giroux, 1971), pp. 315-362;

Leon Roudiez, "Claude Mauriac," in his *French Fiction Today* (New Brunswick: Rutgers University Press, 1972), pp. 132-151.

Patrick Modiano
(30 July 1945-)

Gerald Prince
University of Pennsylvania

BOOKS: *La Place de l'Etoile* (Paris: Gallimard, 1968);

La Ronde de nuit (Paris: Gallimard, 1969); translated by Patricia Wolf as *Night Rounds* (New York: Knopf, 1971; London: Gollancz, 1972);

Les Boulevards de ceinture (Paris: Gallimard, 1972); translated by Caroline Hillier as *Ring Roads* (London: Gollancz, 1974);

Lacombe Lucien, by Modiano and Louis Malle (Paris: Gallimard, 1974); translated by Sabine Destrée (New York: Viking, 1975);

Villa Triste (Paris: Gallimard, 1975); translated by Hillier (London: Gollancz, 1975);

Interrogatoire par Patrick Modiano suivi de Il fait beau, allons au cimetière, by Emmanuel Berl (Paris: Gallimard, 1976);

Livret de famille (Paris: Gallimard, 1977);

Rue des Boutiques Obscures (Paris: Gallimard, 1978); translated by Daniel Weissbort as *Missing Person* (London: Cape, 1980);

Une Jeunesse (Paris: Gallimard, 1981);

Memory Lane (Paris: Hachette/P.O.L., 1981);

De si braves garçons (Paris: Gallimard, 1982);

Poupée blonde (Paris: P.O.L., 1983);

Quartier perdu (Paris: Gallimard, 1984);

Dimanches d'août (Paris: Gallimard, 1986);

Une Aventure de Choura (Paris: Gallimard, 1986);

Une Fiancée pour Choura (Paris: Gallimard, 1987);

Remise de peine (Paris: Seuil, 1988).

PLAY PRODUCTION: *La Polka*, Paris, Théâtre du Gymnase, 16 May 1974.

MOTION PICTURE: *Lacombe Lucien*, screenplay by Modiano and Louis Malle, 1974.

PERIODICAL PUBLICATION: "Courrier du cœur," *Cahiers du Chemin*, no. 20 (15 January 1974): 35-40.

Among the French novelists born toward the end of World War II or after it, Patrick Modiano has created one of the most distinctive fictional universes. His works, written in a pure and graceful style, present a decomposing world marked by shadowy events and inhabited by protagonists who know above all fear, alienation, and regret. They struggle with the labyrinths of memory and time in a fumbling search for their murky origins; they find themselves at the mercy of the monstrous hazards of life, and they explore absence, death, and the disappearance of beings and things.

Though Modiano has granted several interviews and has appeared on television and though he has confirmed the autobiographical basis of much of his writing, few details about his personal life have become public knowledge. Modiano was born in Boulogne-Billancourt, a suburb of Paris. His mother, a Flemish actress named Louisa Colpeyn, and his father, Albert Modiano, a Sephardic Jew of Middle Eastern background who often seemed hostile to him, met during World War II in German-occupied France. Modiano is, as it were, French by accident. Although he was born after the liberation of France and the defeat of Germany, like many of his protagonists, Modiano feels inextricably tied to the nightmarish and shameful period of the Occupation. Like many of his protagonists, too, he went to a boarding school, the Collège Saint-Joseph in Thônes, a small village of Haute-Savoie near Annecy frequented by the idle rich, the fake or fallen aristocrats, the movie starlets who people café society, and the demimonde. Finally, like many of his protagonists, Modiano is very tall and remarkably inarticulate in conversation; he has no university training; and he became a writer because he did not know what else to do and because writing represents for him the possibility of discovering who he is.

The epigraph to Modiano's first novel is a Jewish joke which reflects the tone and tenor of the work: "Au mois de juin 1942, un officier allemand s'avance vers un jeune homme et lui dit: 'Pardon, Monsieur, où se trouve la Place de l'Etoile?' Le jeune homme désigne le côté gauche de sa poitrine" (In the month of June 1942, a German officer walks up to a young man and says to him: "Pardon me, sir, where is the Place de l'Etoile [the place of the star or Star Square]?" The young man points to the left side of his chest). The title *La Place de l'Etoile* (1968) designates not so much a famous Parisian site and not only the star that Jews had to wear under Nazi rule; it also designates the space of the heart, the space of an incurable wound, estrangement, and loss.

The protagonist, Raphaël Schlemilovitch–whose very name constitutes a sign of his foreignness in France and who has a love-hate relationship with things French–is a hero within whom countless possible figures of Jewishness mingle in a delirious phantasmagoria. Through hallucination, daydreaming, and fantasy Schlemilovitch evokes and plays the role of the Jew as martyr and the Jew as king, the Jew as clown and as avenger, Einstein and Jesus, Shylock, Judas, and the Marx Brothers, the industrialist, the snob, the wheeler-dealer, the Nazi, the neurotic, and many more. But whatever the role, Schlemilovitch remains a foreigner and is condemned to radical otherness and pain.

La Place de l'Etoile contains many of the elements that characterize Modiano's later work, from the creation of a fraudulent, dangerous, and dizzying world, the artful mixing of historical and fictive characters, and the protagonist's ambition to be a writer, to the hero's fundamental alienation and stubborn concern with origins and identity and his obsession with events from a past (in Schlemilovitch's case World War II and the Holocaust) that is paradoxically both dead and alive. Yet the novel's amalgamation of savage buffoonery and poignant tragedy as well as its exploitation and explosion of the resources of fiction are pursued to a degree that is perhaps unique in Modiano's work. It is a stunning achievement and was greeted as such by the critics. Josane Duranteau entitled her review of it in the *Monde* (11 May 1968) "Un Début exceptionnel" (An Exceptional Beginning), and *La Place de l'Etoile* won two literary prizes: the Prix Roger Nimier in 1968 and the Prix Félix Fénéon in 1969. The year after winning the Fénéon prize, Modiano married Dominique Zehrfuss, on 12 September 1970. They have two daughters, Zénaïde and Maria.

With his second novel, *La Ronde de nuit* (1969; translated as *Night Rounds*, 1971), Modiano continued the exploration of German-

occupied Paris. The capital city is an infernal amusement park, inhabited by ghosts and potential ghosts of whom nothing will remain but a few yellowed photographs, a bunch of old letters, a key ring, a handkerchief, a tie. Out of passivity, laziness, and alienation, the protagonist, Swing Troubadour, who wants nothing more than to be left alone, works for both the French Gestapo and the French Resistance. He does not have the qualities required for being a full-time traitor or a full-time hero, and, at the end, he opts for martyrdom, deciding to let himself be killed by the French Gestapo. The rounds of wanderings, police raids, fears, and underhanded collusions between executioners and victims multiply; accident takes on the look of fate; betrayal of self and others proves unavoidable; and the novel functions as a kind of exorcism against a past which Modiano did not experience but by which he feels irremediably affected. Something happened, and remembering it, imagining it, is both a duty and a need.

In *Les Boulevards de ceinture* (1972; translated as *Ring Roads*, 1974) the protagonist-narrator goes on a horrified and tender quest for his father, who, like many fathers in Modiano's work, has had to disappear. This quest for a man who is a hounded Jew as well as a black marketeer in Nazi-occupied France proceeds along the twin roads of remembrance and imagination and leads the protagonist to plunge into an ugly, turbid, and threatening universe. It is a quest for uncertain origins, one that underlines the fleeting nature of memories and the difficulty of recovering or explaining the past.

Les Boulevards de ceinture received the Grand Prix du Roman de l'Académie Française (awarded to a young prose writer for a "lofty work of fiction"). It can be said to constitute the last volume of a trilogy on the Occupation begun with *La Place de l'Etoile*. With it, what was already perceptible in the earlier novels becomes clearer: it is not so much a particular period that interests Modiano but, more generally, the hardship of being and living in time. The author said, during an interview with Jean-Louis de Rambures (*Monde*, 24 May 1974): "Ce n'est pas l'occupation pour elle-même qui me fascine, mais tout autre chose. Mon but est d'essayer de traduire une sorte de monde crépusculaire. Si je recours à l'occupation, c'est parce qu'elle me fournit ce climat idéal, un peu trouble, cette lumière, un peu bizarre. Mais il s'agit en réalité de l'image démesurément grossie de ce qui se passe

Advertisement that appeared in the Nouvel Observateur *for 8-14 January 1988.* Remise de peine, *about a ten-year-old boy's life in a small village near Paris, is Modiano's most openly autobiographical novel.*

aujourd'hui" (It is not the Occupation for itself that fascinates me, but something totally different. My goal is to try to express a kind of crepuscular world. If I resort to the Occupation, it is because it supplies me with this ideal–somewhat turbid–climate, this somewhat bizarre light. But, in reality, it is a matter of the inordinately magnified image of what is happening today).

"Courrier du cœur" (which means Mail from the Heart but can also be translated as Miss Lonelyhearts Column) is a short story by Modiano published in a 1974 issue of *Cahiers du Chemin* which exhibits many of the traits and concerns found in his first novels, though it does not use the Occupation as a background. Sometime in the late 1960s or early 1970s, somewhere on the desolate coast of Normandy, a man who has fled from Paris–"On me voulait du mal" (They wanted to do me harm)–feels hounded by a group of natives whose past is dubious at best. He writes a letter to his favorite movie star while waiting to be killed. The town casino looks like a Chinese pagoda and seems strangely out of place; the past is full of menace; fear and evil have not vanished; the hunt is still on.

In two other works dating from 1974 Modiano does resort to the Occupation. The seventeen-year-old protagonist of *Lacombe Lucien*, a screenplay Modiano coauthored with Louis Malle, the producer and director of the movie, would like to join the French underground. He meets a group of French collaborationists, unwittingly reveals to them the identity of a resistant, and starts working for the German police. After falling in love with a young Jewish woman and saving her and her grandmother from the Germans, he is executed by the French Resistance. Like many of Modiano's characters, Lucien is an abandoned child–his father was imprisoned–who lacks direction in a supremely ambiguous world and falls prey to the banality of evil.

In *La Polka* (The Polka, 1974), Modiano's only play to have been staged, a physician who has been barred from practice because he gave cocaine to his patients lives in a dark apartment littered with empty champagne cases. He is visited by phantoms from his past, friends who, like him, prospered during the Occupation. They exchange memories of that strangely happy era. Peopled with phantasms and bathed in a deathly atmosphere, the play insists on a theme that becomes increasingly prominent in Modiano's later works: nostalgia for the past (Modiano contributed to what the French call "la mode rétro"). However equivocal or appalling a former life may have been, Modiano's characters experience yearning for the space and time of youth, for circumstances obtaining before something ineluctable happened. Because it relies essentially on mood, tone, and style, *La Polka*–which premiered at the Théâtre du Gymnase 16 May 1974 but has never been published–can be said to lack dynamism and dramatic force. It was not well received by the critics. Indeed, Michel Cournot wrote in the

Monde (24 May 1974): "Cette pièce est exception-nellement faible" (This play is exceptionally weak).

The narrator of *Villa Triste* (1975; this title–meaning Sad Villa–was retained for the English translation, published the same year) tries to remember a summer he spent, twelve or thirteen years before, in a small French resort of Haute-Savoie. Stateless, rootless, fatherless, and ready to leave for nearby Switzerland at a moment's notice, he had taken refuge from the Algerian war and a deep sense of foreboding. In this provincial town, which paradoxically resembles a Caribbean island, Victor Chmara frequents cosmopolitan and dissolute groups, falls in love with a young movie starlet, and–unable to feel at ease in France–decides to go with her to America: she will become a star; he will develop into a great Jewish writer. But she does not share his dreams and leaves him for another man. He should have asked her to marry him, perhaps; everything would have been different. He should have acted but he felt paralyzed. Chmara was eighteen then. He finds it difficult to recapture that youthful period after which it is always too late. He knows now that the security of Switzerland does not exist and that human beings, particularly in the modern era, are survivors of dead worlds. But even though time buries the past in an untearable veil, he is determined not to forget.

Villa Triste may not be as immediately affecting as Modiano's first three novels. Nevertheless, its masterful choreography of shadows, its delicate weaving of tenuous links between what happened and what is, and the suggestive music of its style are admirable. It was awarded the 1975 Prix des Libraires, given annually by an association of booksellers to a writer whose work has not yet received the recognition it deserves.

Interrogatoire (Examination, 1976) results from a series of questions Modiano asked Emmanuel Berl, an independent-thinking essayist and novelist who wrote speeches for Marshal Philippe Pétain, leader of Vichy France, before quitting his job in disgust. Berl, whose work most probably influenced the younger man, lost his mother and father when he was a child, was particularly active between the two world wars, and, as a Jew, led a difficult life during the Occupation. The examination yields a highly engaging portrait of him as a lucid twentieth-century man who often had to change sides, out of loyalty to his ideals. The volume also includes Berl's *Il fait beau, allons au cimetière* (The Weather is Nice, Let's Go to the Cemetery).

Modiano returned to prose fiction in 1977 with *Livret de famille* (Family Album or Family Booklet). In France a *livret de famille* is an official document containing a series of names and dates: parents, weddings, divorces, children, baptisms, deaths. The narrator and protagonist of *Livret de famille*, Patrick Modiano, is fascinated by his past and dissatisfied with the administrative record of a life. He composes a different kind of family booklet: in fifteen chapters–fifteen stories–that artfully blend autobiographical data and imaginary memories, he evokes the German occupation of France, the beginning of his mother's career as an actress in Antwerp, his Jewish father hiding from the Gestapo in Paris, as well as scenes from his own adolescence and young adulthood.

With his usual elegance and economy of means, Modiano draws a penumbral world peopled with rootless phantoms and develops his privileged themes: the difficult necessity of remembering, time as a curse, chance as destiny. He restores an image of a period and a life on the basis of a few scattered elements just as an archaeologist might reconstruct a statue on the basis of some fragments. Ultimately, *Livret de famille* shows the power of imagination in substituting a partial kind of truth for an ungraspable reality. It is a moving and funny autobiographical fiction.

In *Rue des Boutiques Obscures* (1978; translated as *Missing Person*, 1980) an amnesiac detective using a borrowed name attempts to slip into the past and to recover his lost identity. Guy Roland's quest may well be doomed: the evidence that human beings have existed evaporates as quickly as a child's tears, and little, if anything, remains of their lives. Roland's inquiries take him back to the period of the Occupation and to one Pedro McEvoy (probably an assumed name), a.k.a. Jimmy Pedro Stern (another assumed name?), who was caught in the uncertainties and turpitudes of the period and, one day, disappeared. But perhaps Guy Roland was not Pedro McEvoy. He will have to go to Rome and check at least one more address, on the "rue des Boutiques Obscures" (Street of Somber Shops). Who am I? Who was I? What links are there between the two?

Along with the transient and cut-up nature of human existence, the novel explores the intricate character of remembrance and that of narrative as a builder of possible memories. Modiano's skill at creating an ambiguous world from bits and scraps, his ability to stage one ballet of wandering phantoms after another, his masterful blending of collective history and individual fate, and the artistry of his narration–lucid and dreamy, hesitant and precise–combine to yield what is perhaps his masterpiece. In 1978 *Rue des Boutiques Obscures* won that most prestigious of French literary awards, the Prix Goncourt.

Louis and Odile Memling, the protagonists of *Une Jeunesse* (A Youth, 1981), lead a peaceful life in an Alpine cottage with their two children. They are thirty-five and their youth is over. At twenty, they lived in the Paris of the 1960s, a Paris as treacherous and frightening as that of the Occupation. She wanted to be a singer. He worked for a trafficker and swindler who had been a hero in the French Resistance. Their loneliness, poverty, and innocence brought them together, and, together, they cheated Louis's employer by keeping for themselves a large sum of money they were supposed to smuggle into Switzerland. They seemed destined to lose, and they inexplicably won. They have survived, and they are lucky. But nothing can happen at thirty-five.

Though not one of Modiano's best productions, the novel is notable for the fluid simplicity of its style and for its characterization of a disquieting past lying beyond the present, the accidents making up a life, and the quiet resignation that sometimes comes with the years. It is, moreover, the only novel in which Modiano adopts the third-person as opposed to the first-person mode of narration.

In 1980, in the *Nouvelle Revue Française*, Modiano published "Memory Lane," a short story which appeared the following year as a book illustrated by Pierre Le-Tan. The narrator, whose youth is coming to an end, evokes a small group of people he frequented when he was making his beginning in life. He remembers the houses they lived in, the bars where they met, the games they played, the songs they sang ("Memory Lane" functioned as their anthem, and its lyrics are eloquent: "Memory Lane/Only once do horses go down Memory Lane/But the traces of their hooves still remain . . . "). There was Paul Contour, a once brilliant lawyer who, for the narrator, acted as a father figure (again, the biological father is absent); Maddy Contour, his wife, whom the young man loved in silence; an aging antique dealer; an aspiring actor; the first male fashion model in France; and a few others.

Modiano's story communicates how strangely groups coalesce and disintegrate; how quickly time passes; how mysteriously people become what they are. This magnificent text exemplifies not only Modiano's matter but his manner: with a few insignificant happenings, half a dozen ghostly figures, the misty landscape of a faded past, the melancholy music of a weary narrative voice, "Memory Lane" constitutes a magic web that catches the faint glimmers of a bygone world.

Like "Memory Lane," *Une Jeunesse,* and many other works by Modiano, *De si braves garçons* (Such Good Boys, 1982) could have been entitled "Twenty Years After." Through a dozen narratives having in common characters who were all students at the Collège Valvert, a boarding school for the lonely sons of rich and/or uncaring parents, *De si braves garçons* sketches the hopeful Eden of childhood and adolescence as well as the aborted projects, shattered promises, and missed appointments that can make up adulthood. The musketeers grow old. The children who were such good boys become caricatures of themselves (there is an unsuccessful actor, a drug addict, a potential murderer, a once brilliant and now broken dandy). The world is hard and incomprehensible, time is unforgiving, and something happened. Delicately and patiently Modiano excavates the crumbling vestiges of a youth that was, erects fragile presents and futures doomed to defeat, and sings in a muted and haunting fashion the rigor of surviving.

Poupée blonde (Blonde Doll, 1983), by Modiano with illustrations by Le-Tan, assumes the form of a kind of theater program for a play (also entitled *Poupée blonde*) by the fictitious playwright Pierre-Michel Wals and includes the text of this play. Notes introducing the playwright, actors, and producer, drawings of the costumes and design for an imaginary performance, and several specious ads (for gloves, for perfume, for nightclubs) accompany a text which presents situations and develops themes familiar to Modiano's readers. The protagonists–Louise Bermondsey, a beautiful blonde singer; her fiancé, the drummer Aldo Eykerling; Félix Decaulaert, who played solo guitar; Guy Marca-Rosa, who was on bass; and his friend Geneviève Werner–were twenty once and, in reference to the boy who did not grow old, called themselves the Peter Pans. Their first song–"Poupée blonde"–was enormously successful. Twenty years later only three of them are alive. Aldo never married, and he became a doctor, but he can no longer practice because of his indiscretions; Geneviève, his onetime mistress, is now the unhappy Mrs. Guy Marca-Rosa; and her husband is a wreck of a man. At least Louise, who committed suicide, and Félix, who died under mysterious circumstances, never had to experience aging. By way of imagination, dream, and memory, the five are brought together again, and the confrontation between them is a confrontation between ghosts from among the dead and ghosts from life, what might have been and what turned out to be, the sweet smell of nostalgia and the stench of despair. The meaning of passing time is explored once again, and, once again, Modiano's personal signature captures and transfigures the flavor of a lost world.

In 1984 Modiano received the Prix de Monaco, awarded to a writer of French for the totality of his work. Modiano's novel *Quartier perdu* (Lost Quarter) dates from the same year and constitutes still another version of his distinctive fictional world and another proof of his talent at evoking the spells of the past and the whims of fate. Ambrose Guise (the last name is revealing), a successful writer of English detective novels, comes to Paris for the first time in twenty years to meet with his Japanese publisher. It is summer. The city is deserted and seems as strange to him as a once familiar world would to a returning ghost.

When last in Paris, Ambrose Guise was Jean Dekker (this last name also is suggestive: it has a Flemish resonance and furthermore connotes by sound the Middle East and Cairo which, in French, is *Le Caire*). He frequented a group of profligates who liked nothing more than nocturnal ramblings. One day a young woman shot a member of the group; Dekker helped her to escape; he had to disappear. Overcome by uneasiness in the now alien capital, Guise decides to elucidate the circumstances of the crime and to understand his own relation to the past. The young marginalized French bachelor he was and the mature English paterfamilias he has become have little, if anything, in common. Yet, through memory, research, and writing, a fragile bridge is established between them, and a fragmentary autobiography is fashioned.

In 1986 and 1987 Modiano published two children's books, *Une Aventure de Choura* (An Adventure of Choura) and *Une Fiancée pour Choura* (A Fiancée for Choura), both illustrated by Dominique Zehrfuss. His novel *Dimanches d'août* appeared in 1986. The title, literally August Sundays, evokes in French "Dimanches doux," or Sweet Sundays, a phrase whose pronunciation is identical. The protagonist, Jean, lives a somnambulist's life in Nice and works in a garage that is soon to be closed. Seven years earlier Jean was in La Varenne, on the banks of the river Marne, preparing a photographic album he planned to call *Plages fluviales* (River Beaches). There he met Sylvia Villecourt; they had an affair; and–after a violent argument between her and her husband Frédéric (but was he really her husband?)–they left La Varenne and ended up in Nice. She took along an invaluable diamond–the Croix du Sud (the Southern Cross)–that had come into Frédéric's possession. In Nice, Jean and Sylvia met a strange American couple, Barbara and Virgil Neal, who befriended them, expressed interest in buying the stone, and, one night, disappeared with it and Sylvia. Was Sylvia kidnapped and killed? Was Virgil an American or the French gangster Paul Alessandri who, at one point, had dealings with Frédéric? Where exactly did the Croix du Sud come from? And what was the relationship between Frédéric's mother and the actor Aimos, who was killed during the Liberation of Paris? From one unsolvable enigma to another, Modiano weaves a haunting story of love and loss. Jean is now not much more than a ghost in a city seemingly inhabited by ghosts: it takes life little time to renege on its promises. Nevertheless, for a brief period after leaving La Varenne, Jean did manage to live a few sweet August Sundays.

In 1988 Modiano published *Remise de peine* (Deferral of Pain), his first openly autobiographical text. Patrick, the forty-year-old narrator, recalls his life in a small village near Paris when he was ten and people called him Patoche. Three women took care of him and his little brother; the youngsters' mother, an actress, was away on tour, and their father only saw them briefly, between business trips. The narrator recalls the caretakers–Annie, her mother Mathilde, and their companion Hélène Toch–and their friends–Roger Vincent with his big American convertible, Jean D., who eventually spent seven years in jail, Andrée K., Frédé, and others still. Their activities are tinged with mystery, and the entire group projects an aura of unconventional or dubious morality. One day, when Patoche comes home from school, he finds that the women have disappeared. The police are there; something "very serious" has happened. What is left of that time? A few objects; memories (the school Patoche attended and the Robin Hood Inn, his attachment to Annie, the books he liked, the first movie he saw, the games he played, the beginnings of his vocation as a writer); but also the feeling that life is full of accidents and the anguish provoked by that feeling; and an unanswerable question: what exactly happened? *Remise de peine* is quintessential Modiano. Though avowedly autobiographical, it recapitulates and summarizes the writer's fiction. Its universe is hazy and murky; its characters are phantomlike; its themes underline the passage of time and things, the powerful hold exerted by the past, the fragmentariness and poignancy of memory, the mysterious ominousness of life; and Modiano's style infuses all elements of the narrative with poetry.

Patrick Modiano in many ways belongs to a well-established tradition of French writing. His novels have the look and dimensions of the classic French *récit:* they seldom go over two hundred pages and, like his other works, they show a remarkable sense of scale. His themes, too, are classic: the search for self, the traps and tricks of life, the passing of time, the labyrinth of memory. His fictional universe is both elegantly lean and powerfully suggestive. His style seems effortless and achieves a melodious transparency. At the same time, Modiano subverts this tradition and is a kind of postmodernist traitor. Like his characters, who slip into lives that are perhaps not their own and live in places where they do not belong, Modiano adopts familiar structures and uses them as if they were not really made for him. The narrators' melancholy voices come to resemble voices heard on worn-out tapes; the plot repeatedly dissolves: narrative lines are not wholly adequate to the discontinuity of the past, memory, life; and the narration–elliptical, wandering, somnambulistic–tells quite a story without quite telling one. The self is not thoroughly illuminated. The past is not entirely recaptured. The quest does not exactly reach an end. But something happened. This is the moving refrain of the human condition.

References:

Jacques Bersani, "Modiano, agent double," *Nouvelle Revue Française*, no. 298 (November 1977): 78-84;

Janine Chasseguet-Smirgel, "*La Place de l'Etoile* de Patrick Modiano (Pour une définition psychanalytique de l'authenticité)," in her *Pour une psychanalyse de l'art et de la créativité* (Paris: Payot, 1971), pp. 217-255;

Jean-Marie Magnan, "Un Apatride nommé Modiano," *Sud*, 19 (Third Trimester 1976): 120-131;

Pierre-Jean Morel, "Une Dissertation de Modiano," *Nouvelles Littéraires*, no. 2862 (18 November 1982): 37-38;

C. W. Nettelbeck and P. A. Hueston, "Anthology as Art. Modiano's *Livret de famille*," *Australian Journal of French Studies*, 21 (May-August 1984): 213-223;

Nettelbeck and Hueston, *Patrick Modiano pièces d'identité: Ecrire l'entretemps* (Paris: Lettres Modernes, 1986);

Gerald Prince, "Re-Membering Modiano, or Something Happened," *Sub-Stance*, no. 49 (1986): 35-43;

Jean-Louis de Rambures, "Comment travaillent les écrivains. Patrick Modiano: 'Apprendre à mentir,' " *Monde*, 24 May 1974, p. 24.

Claude Ollier
(17 December 1922-   )

Cecile Lindsay
University of Nevada at Reno

BOOKS: *La Mise en scène*, volume 1 of *Le Jeu d'enfant* (Paris: Editions de Minuit, 1958); translated by Dominic Di Bernardi (Elmwood Park, Ill.: Dalkey Archive Press, 1988);

Le Maintien de l'ordre, volume 2 of *Le Jeu d'enfant* (Paris: Gallimard, 1961); translated by Ursule Molinaro as *Law and Order* (New York: Red Dust, 1971);

Eté indien, volume 3 of *Le Jeu d'enfant* (Paris: Editions de Minuit, 1963);

L'Echec de Nolan, volume 4 of *Le Jeu d'enfant* (Paris: Gallimard, 1967);

Navettes (Paris: Gallimard, 1967);

La Vie sur Epsilon, volume 5 of *Le Jeu d'enfant* (Paris: Gallimard, 1972);

Enigma, volume 6 of *Le Jeu d'enfant* (Paris: Gallimard, 1973);

Our ou Vingt Ans après, volume 7 of *Le Jeu d'enfant* (Paris: Gallimard, 1974);

Fuzzy Sets, volume 8 of *Le Jeu d'enfant* (Paris: Union Générale d'Editions, 1975);

Marrakch Medine (Paris: Flammarion, 1979);

Nébules (Paris: Flammarion, 1981);

Souvenirs écran (Paris: Cahiers du Cinéma/Gallimard, 1981);

Mon Double à Malacca (Paris: Flammarion, 1982);

Cahiers d'écolier (1950-1960) (Paris: Flammarion, 1984);

Fables sous rêve (1960-1970) (Paris: Flammarion, 1985);

Une Histoire illisible (Paris: Flammarion, 1986);

Déconnection (Paris: Flammarion, 1988).

MOTION PICTURES: *L'Accompagnement*, screenplay by Ollier and Jean-André Fieschi, Sociéte Gaumont-France, 1966;

Ecoute voir, screenplay by Ollier and Hugo Santiago, Sociéte Gaumont-France, 1978.

RADIO: *La Mort du personnage*, France-Culture, 1964;

Régression, France-Culture, 1965;

Cinématographe, by Ollier and Jean-André Fieschi, France-Culture, 1965;

Claude Ollier (photograph by Jacques Sassier, Document Gallimard)

Le Dit de ceux qui parlent, France-Culture, 1969;

Pèlerinage, France-Culture, 1969;

La Fugue, by Ollier and Fieschi, France-Culture, 1969;

Les Dires des années trente, France-Culture, 1970;

L'Oreille au mur, France-Culture, 1971;

Les Ailes, France-Culture, 1971;

Une Bosse dans la neige, France-Culture, 1971;

La Recyclade, France-Culture, 1971;

Our-Musique, music by Christian Rosset, France-Culture, 1975;

Réseau-Ollier-Navettes, France-Culture, 1975;

Opérettes entre guillemets, music by Rosset, France-Culture, 1977;

Loi d'écoute, France-Culture, 1979;

Computation, France-Culture, 1979;

Détour, France-Culture, 1980.

OTHER: "Vingt Ans après," in *Nouveau Roman: Hier, aujourd'hui*, proceedings of the colloquium at the Centre Culturel International de Cerisy-la-Salle, 20-30 July 1971, 2 volumes, edited by Jean Ricardou and Françoise van Rossum-Guyon (Paris: Union Générale d'Editions, 1972), II: 199-214.

PERIODICAL PUBLICATIONS: "Lecture-écriture-lecture," *Nouvelle Revue Française*, no. 214 (October 1970): 202-204;
"Les Pulsions motrices dans l'acte d'écriture," *Marche Romane*, 21, nos. 1-2 (1971): 33-35;
"Comment j'ai écrit *Our*," *Quinzaine Littéraire*, no. 200 (16-31 December 1974): 7;
"French Version," translated by Cecile Lindsay, *Review of Contemporary Fiction*, special issue on Ollier and Carlos Fuentes, 8 (Summer 1988): 30-37.

With the publication in 1958 of his first novel, Claude Ollier was immediately associated with the group of writers who came to be known in the 1950s and 1960s as the New Novelists. Although these writers (Alain Robbe-Grillet, Michel Butor, Claude Simon, and others) differed significantly from each other, they shared some important common denominators: a questioning of narrative form, of point of view, of temporality, of representation in fiction. Like his contemporaries, Ollier was interested in fiction's capacity for problematizing its own conventions, while at the same time proposing formal innovations that would challenge the ways in which fiction is usually read, evaluated, and categorized. However, Ollier's work soon took on a configuration that made it both unique and exemplary with respect to the New Novel movement: after completing his second novel in 1961, Ollier decided to link all his novels in an ongoing fictional "cycle" which would form, with subsequent books, a serial investigation into the nature and functioning of fiction itself. Eventually comprising eight works, with the last published in 1975, the cycle was entitled *Le Jeu d'enfant* (translatable as Child's Play or Child's Game). The eight books are divided into two cycles of four novels each and are linked to each other in a complex pattern of recurring characters, structures, situations, and passages. The principal thread binding all the works is eventually revealed to be a single protagonist who undertakes, in various guises, a voyage of investigation in a foreign setting. Analogously, the author and reader can be seen as exploring the nature of texts which become more and more alien with respect to traditional narrative forms and conventions.

The cycle's impetus is thus a dual one: it seeks both to reflect upon its own nature as fiction and to challenge the foundations of narrative convention by proposing alternatives to traditional forms and procedures. Thus Ollier's cycle addresses many of the important theoretical questions raised by the New Novel movement and, indeed, by much of the intellectual inquiry of recent years: what happens to the traditional protagonist in experimental fictions? to what extent is the author in control of the writing process? what is the role of the reader with respect to these demanding, ambiguous works? what, finally, is the nature and origin of a fictional text? These interrogations take place in works of high artistic quality where meticulous construction combines with lyric skill to create memorable fables of reading and writing.

Since the appearance in 1975 of the last volume of *Le Jeu d'enfant*, Ollier has published eight books, and a ninth is in progress at the time of this writing. These works vary in format and subject. While echoing some of the subjects and concerns of *Le Jeu d'enfant*, these more recent texts deal in new ways with the questions of perception and memory in relation to writing. Although its quality and interest are undisputed, Ollier's work has to date received considerably less critical attention than that of his contemporaries among the New Novelists. The reason for this comparative lack of analysis lies, perhaps, in the difficult and rigorous unity of Ollier's major cycle, whose scope, size, and intricacy make special demands upon the critic.

Claude Ollier was born 17 December 1922 in Paris. After studies in law and commerce at the Ecole des Hautes Etudes Commerciales, Ollier held various posts in industry, agriculture, banking, insurance, and in colonial administration in Morocco. In 1955 he began devoting himself solely to writing. He lived for eight years in Morocco and has traveled in North and Central America, the Middle East, and the Far East. In 1969 he taught at the Université Laval in Quebec. Married in 1969, he has resided since 1975 in Maule, a small village near Paris, with his daughter, Ariane, born in 1972.

Ollier is most reluctant to talk with interviewers about his life and provides only the sketchiest of biographical information. His attitude toward the question of any author's private life is best summed up by his answer to an interviewer who asked him to say something about himself. Ollier replied: "Il y a l'homme, et il y a l'auteur. L'homme est sans grande importance en l'affaire. L'auteur est probablement né d'une rencontre avec un film, vers 1930, ou une musique, un peu plus tard" (There is the man, and there is the author. The man is without much importance in the matter. The author was probably born from an encounter with a film, around 1930, or with a type of music, somewhat later).

Ollier's first book, *La Mise en scène* (1958; translated, 1988), received the Prix Médicis. He has written numerous radio pieces and coauthored two screenplays. In 1984 he finished work on a third screenplay, of *La Mise en scène*, but it has never been produced. Ollier has collaborated with such artists as Claude Garanjoud, Roberto Matta Echaurren, Bernard Dufour, and René Bonargent; typically, Ollier supplies a text to accompany etchings, drawings, or engravings. He received the 1980 Prix France Culture for his 1979 work, *Marrakch Medine*.

La Mise en scène, which became the first novel of the fictional cycle that Ollier eventually baptized *Le Jeu d'enfant*, contains elements of several different fictional genres: the mystery, the colonial adventure, and the traditional *Bildungsroman*, among others. Its protagonist is Lassalle, a French engineer whose job it is to establish a potential mining road in a remote region of the North African mountains. Lassalle is a typical Westerner, ill at ease and disoriented by the alien climate, language, and customs. He is aided by the enigmatic Ba Iken, an Arab who has served in the colonial army and who offers his services as translator and guide. Lassalle's initial task is soon doubled and complicated by another investigation: he becomes obsessed by what appears to be a local intrigue involving adultery and a double murder. The victims were a young village girl and a geologist named Lessing who had quite recently followed much the same itinerary as Lassalle. Although Ba Iken creates a plausible *mise en scène* in which the deaths are seen as unrelated or accidental, Lassalle persists in exploring the contradictions he uncovers. As he reconstructs what appears to be covered up by Ba Iken's version of events, Lassalle feels himself to be increasingly identified with the murdered predecessor, and increasingly threatened with the same fate.

The hostility he senses in the village and an ambiguous encounter with the dead girl's twin sister lead Lassalle to replace Lessing in an imagined or dreamed scenario; the protagonist of the scene is denoted only as *l'étranger* (the stranger, the foreigner), and his adventure is that of Lassalle transposed to the site of Lessing's encampment. The rampant "doubling" of protagonists, scenes, and situations threatens to destroy Lassalle. His singular identity is called into question in the same way that the various versions of the mysterious events call into question the possibility of ever establishing a single meaning. Lassalle prepares to leave without ever confronting Ba Iken with the evidence of an alternate scenario; his uneasy feeling that he had somehow been in the same danger as Lessing is increasingly dispelled as his own identity reasserts itself. Lassalle's name, which did not appear for five chapters during which links with Lessing's fate multiplied, finally reappears as he prepares to return to the innocuous colonial sphere (where he reports nothing of what he suspects).

Although Lassalle has managed to rescue a precarious identity and deduce a plausible solution to the mystery he uncovered, the final totality of meaning achieved from the outcome seems fragile, disjointed, and unvoiced in proportion to the three hundred pages it has filled. Lassalle's character is never plumbed in any psychological sense; the array of conflicting scenarios and evidence complicates any conclusions one might draw about the novel's meaning. *La Mise en scène* provides an apparently traditional setting–a colonial adventure–for a subversive "set-up" of certain novelistic conventions (a singular hero and a solvable mystery) and of the expectations associated with those conventions. The challenge posed to traditional ways of writing and reading novels initiated by his first work is extended and amplified in Ollier's subsequent fictions.

Le Maintien de l'ordre (1961; translated as *Law and Order*, 1971) presents a crime in which the protagonist has been followed and is being watched by two men. The title chosen for the English translation points to the continued interrogation of a coercive Western sense of order faced with a non-Western ordering of perception and events. The setting is a North African city during the Algerian war. What is given to be read in this narrative seems to be the unspoken observations and mental processes of an unnamed subject. Vague clues are gradually pieced together: the "hero" appears to be a French colonial official who has witnessed some events which seem to point to criminal activities–notably the torture of Arab youths–on the part of the police. The protagonist is not sure if the surveillance to which he is subjected aims at actual harm or simple intimidation.

The events, observations, and hypotheses are presented in a narrative sequence in which progression is disrupted and nonlinear. The protagonist himself is incapable of providing a coherent account of events, in the form of a letter he tries to write to a friend or colleague. Each time he sits to compose the letter, he is distracted by a map of the city fixed to the wall. Much of the narrative is given over to a contemplation of the map's complexities. The profusion of the city and the multiplicity of its possible readings provide a figure of the protagonist's inability to put into words a single coherent reading of recent events.

Much of the narrative details what the official sees from his seventh-floor window. Despite his panoramic elevation, his perception is never clear or stable: everything is seen through a vibrating screen of dust, smoke, mist, or heat; any scene viewed is framed and masked by grills, windows, doors ajar, or curtains. The partiality of his vision, along with his inability to solve the mystery of this crime story, makes the protagonist a singularly ineffectual fictional "hero." Indeed, by conventional standards, this character is most unsatisfying. His efforts to assert himself as a presence and take control of his experience never achieve the verisimilitude of the conventional hero; the interior monologue which constitutes the major part of the narration is never interior in any psychological sense. Lacking a definable personality, the fictional subject is seen here as a device for focusing and processing description; the hero has become one of many windows in a text whose frames and hinges have suddenly imposed themselves on the reader's field of vision.

There is no resolution to this crime drama. The protagonist never leaves his room, never writes his letter, and is never attacked. The plot that can be reconstructed from the narration is even more partial and less conclusive than the colonial adventure of the first novel, based on a protagonist who is correspondingly less credible or tangible. While an ironic order is being maintained in the corrupt colonial city, an order of textual instability, fragmentation, and theatricality which began to appear in *La Mise en scène* has increasingly asserted itself.

Eté indien (Indian Summer, 1963) returns to a named protagonist; Morel's adventure is nominally that of a love story. The initial and final sections of the novel present a narration in which any overt reference to the protagonist is suppressed; both sections describe, in almost identical terms, an aerial view of a wild, marshy peninsula which might be located in Mexico. Morel's vision directs the central portion of the narration. He has just landed in what appears to be New York City, in late summer. He has been commissioned to investigate the possibility of producing a film in the primitive terrain glimpsed, remembered, or imagined in the initial segment. He will spend a weekend in the metropolis in order to interview an archaeologist, J. J. The narration of Morel's encounters and excursions switches frequently from New York to Mexico, incorporating scenes imagined by Morel and passages borrowed from the first two novels of *Le Jeu d'enfant*.

While sightseeing, Morel meets Cynthia. Their romantic interlude causes him to miss his flight and extend his stay through Monday. Morel is doubtful of his qualifications for the assignment he has been given. And indeed, he does not conduct his investigation or even his tourism with much enthusiasm or competence: he gets lost, is nearly run over, is consistently late, and even forgets the archaeologist's name. His decreasing efficacy is accompanied by a growing passivity in comparison to the earlier protagonists: the engineer's curiosity and the official's meticulous observations have degenerated, with Morel, to a vague inattention, a uniform inability to concentrate. Even a sexual episode with Cynthia is punctuated by descriptions of the view outside the hotel window. A certain difficulty with light, elevation, and means of transportation provokes a perpetual nausea, headache, and somnolence that recall certain reactions on the part of the earlier protagonists. Morel finds perception painful and sustained attention impossible; he is particularly ill-suited for his function as an investigator or as a vehicle for focusing meaning in a fictional text. The stability, coherence, and unity of the narration are called into question by the strange vertigo of the subject whose vision directs it.

Ultimately the stability and singularity of this very subject are called into question in *Eté indien*. The increasing intertextuality of the third novel gives the reader a sense of familiarity which is confirmed by two photos of himself that Morel offers to Cynthia: the first one is unmistak-

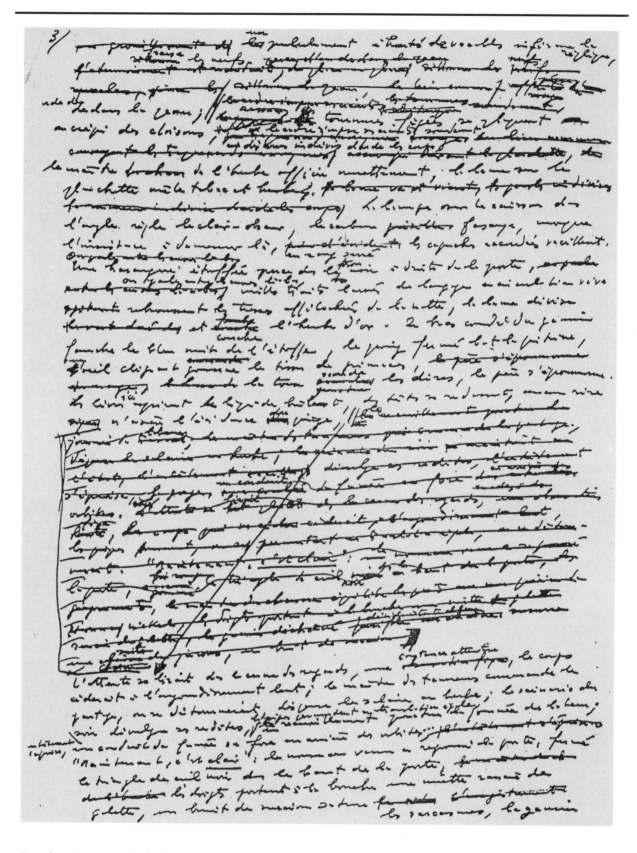

Page from the manuscript for Our ou Vingt Ans après, *volume 7 of Ollier's* Le Jeu d'enfant *(by permission of the author)*

ably of Lassalle, while the second one is of the protagonist of *Le Maintien de l'ordre*. There is apparently nothing original or singular about Morel or any other element of *Été indien*, and the contagion of repetition and reabsorption extends back to the earlier protagonist(s). This dissolution of the hero as the unique perceptual center and anchor of the novel is accompanied by an ironic recognition, on Morel's part, of his own obsolescence.

Thus the third novel of *Le Jeu d'enfant* has presented the Indian summer of the traditional hero and the kind of stories in which he has traditionally starred: during the final days of a prolonged summer in New York, a fragmentary, derisory love story takes place. As Cynthia and Morel end their last day together at an outdoor film (a story of global catastrophe), snow begins to fall. The final section of the book appears to present Morel's real flight to Mexico, in which his typical somnolence is broken by the plane's brutal descent into the aquatic terrain described in the book's first scene. The submersion of the fictional subject has been presaged since the beginning by a play on names: the itineraries of Lassal(Le)ssing both led to Assameur (*à sa mort*, to his death), but Lassalle manages to recover enough identity to escape the textual pitfall. Subsequent developments weaken his hold, and in the incarnation of Morel (*le mort*, the dead man), the protagonist acknowledges his own trajectory toward destruction.

The failure of the traditional narrative hero is explored in *L'Echec de Nolan* (Nolan's Failure, 1967). The fourth book of *Le Jeu d'enfant* is divided into four "reports," in which an unnamed investigator from a mysterious intelligence agency attempts to explain the recent disappearance of another agent, Nolan. The first report presents the investigator's visit to Scandinavia to interview the sole survivor of a plane crash in which Nolan disappeared; since no body was recovered, Nolan might yet be alive. No real information is discovered, however, and the investigator is told to delve further into Nolan's past for clues to his fate. Thus the subsequent reports take the investigator to the other cardinal points circling Western Europe. In each interview various clues link Nolan with one of the protagonists of the first three novels of the cycle. The reader concludes that Nolan was the real name of the single hero featured in various guises and settings in those fictions. Their adventures were only covers masking the real mission of a legendarily successful agent.

Nolan's exemplary methods involved writing clear and perceptive accounts of his discoveries. But despite his legendary talent, it is revealed, Nolan gradually developed some difficulty in composing his reports; his efforts began to be contaminated by references to his cover, by extraneous descriptions and unrelated details. The inquest into Nolan's disappearance thus becomes a critique of his written reports.

The investigator himself is preparing a report, at least in the first two interviews. Soon, however, he begins to experience the same writing problems as Nolan, and he exhibits symptoms of discomfort and malaise that recall all the other protagonists. The investigator is increasingly linked with the Nolan composite; digressions in his report repeat adventures experienced by his alphabetical predecessors, Lassalle and Morel. In the last interview the agent learns that he has been doubled by yet another investigator also asking about Nolan. Assuming that the agency has doubts about his efforts, he decides to pursue the question of Nolan's failure on his own; the text ends with him climbing to the top of a mountain. Instead of solving the mystery of Nolan's failure, the latest protagonist merges with him, commits the same errors, and effects a similar disappearance. With Nolan, the protagonist is ultimately *non-là*, not there.

In the fourth novel, then, the fictional protagonist has unwittingly operated an inquest into his own demise, his own failure to function as a conventional hero should. But the death of the hero cannot yet be registered: Morel metamorphoses into Nolan, whose body was never found; the final investigator disappears equivocally, leaving behind a double. Morel's dramatic death has in no way inaugurated a fiction devoid of characters; in fact, phantoms of the same protagonist continue to haunt *Le Jeu d'enfant*. Just as Nolan had both a cover and a real mission, so the fictional protagonist has pursued a dual track in the first relay of the cycle. The real mission of the protagonist was to uncover and indict the assumptions and conventions behind the traditional novelistic hero. An ongoing project of demystification has aimed at the reeducation of readers and writers through the progressive subversion of the *Bildungsroman* genre. But the figurative death of the protagonist is followed by a swift resurrection which complicates any facile dismissal of the old regime's hero. *L'Echec de Nolan* concludes with a protagonist of fiction who is multiple and ambiguous, but still in search of himself in the space of the fiction.

It soon becomes clear that the peregrinations of the protagonist(s) of the first cycle of *Le Jeu d'enfant* are to be continued in the realm of outer space, with the fifth book, *La Vie sur Epsilon* (Life on Epsilon, 1972), taking place on the fifth planet of the distant "système du prisme." Epsilon is a planet of sand and snow. The four astronauts sent to explore it are inexplicably stranded by mechanical failure. The reader is not surprised to find hints that the leader, O., is the newest avatar of the composite protagonist of the first relay of *Le Jeu d'enfant*. The spaceship has landed on a frontier which seems to divide the planet into equally virgin hemispheres. The astronauts follow this line of demarcation in hope of discovering some information that will help them escape. In their exploration of the planet's topography, they seem to be walking in a *book* magnified to delirious dimensions: pursuing the median line between sand and snow, they cross perpendicular furrows like lines on a page. Soon after their arrival the explorers become aware of clouds of dancing blades or strips of cloth or paper which resemble the turning pages of a book. When penetrated, the blades produce a peculiar hallucination: inside the cloud each astronaut relives as if it were his own an experience previously undergone by a companion on one of the other four planets of the system, and subsequently recounted to the future "hero" of the episode.

On Epsilon, then, space, time, and identity have become floating and heterogeneous; the unoriginality of the borrowed experiences points as well to the fundamental intertextuality of fiction, where any text can reevoke and recirculate previous texts. On Epsilon the fictional subject finds himself within the very space and matter of textuality; he wanders among the words, lines, and pages of the book that contains him. This situation provokes in O. a specific and significant anxiety. Immensely and stubbornly blank, the surface of Epsilon elicits from O. the same reaction Freud posited as that of the male child viewing the female organ: fear of castration, of indifference, of loss of identity. Epsilon cannot be "read," and its surface slowly erases any ordering traces left by the explorers. It is precisely by its traits which are perennially linked to the "feminine"–blankness, absence, castration–that the planet/book of Epsilon refuses domination or

appropriation, presenting a new vision of textuality.

O.'s anxiety escalates into terror with the final episode; previously the only climatic variations on the planet were subtle changes in the color of the light. But just as everything seems about to return to order, with all astronauts safe and communications restored, O. notices a bright circle of red on the snow. Soon communications are disrupted as a wave of red covers the planet like a tide of blood. And indeed, the fearful tide conveys the image of menstrual blood: if Epsilon is allegorically a text, then that text is profoundly "feminine," representing all that is fearful to the "masculine" subject seeking identity, meaning, order, and closure. The "maternal" capacity for metamorphosis and reproduction presents a delirious regression into the textual past for the subject, who would try to discover the source and explanation of his own condition. It is the feminine, maternal principle on Epsilon which terrifies the fictional subject, threatening the foundations of his subjectivity and eventually driving him mad; when rescued, O. is found sitting at his desk, writing in the air.

On the stellar landscape of Epsilon, O. conducts a quest which figures fiction's own search for its origins. In *La Vie sur Epsilon* this quest shakes the very foundation not only of fiction but of Western thought in general, for what is put into question is the unified nature of subjectivity and perception.

The derangement brought about in O. by the events on Epsilon is manifested in *Enigma* (1973), the sixth book of *Le Jeu d'enfant*, through two symptoms. First, he has forgotten his past. He remembers nothing of the events of Epsilon or of his earlier missions. Second, in his capacity as the leader of a survey team on the planet Iota, he exhibits a familiar tendency toward deviation and digression. The symptoms of O.'s madness are also those of fiction: O. must find his own past, just as a self-reflexive fiction continually seeks its own origin. And like O.'s deranged itinerary, fiction is composed of unpredictable digressions. If the source and elaboration of fiction are thus figured by O.'s crisis, then the allegorical enigma to be resolved is that of O.'s insanity.

On Iota, therefore, O. undergoes an experimental form of treatment. This treatment resembles psychoanalysis in that it constitutes a reliving of the past. It is O.'s daily task to lead a team of four men on a close inspection and mapping of a given sector of the planet. O.'s treatment also involves two females corresponding to the two sections of *Enigma*. In the first part, Naïma is an extremely advanced, apparently female computer whose task is to analyze and explain O.'s behavior. This analysis provides the narrative voice for a considerable part of the first section of the book. A recurrent vocabulary of textuality links O.'s aberrations to reading and writing, so that Naïma's analysis takes on the character of both literary criticism and dream interpretation. In recreating on Iota his earlier situation on Epsilon, O. gradually reenacts and remembers his past.

Although O. has remembered Epsilon as his most recent adventure, that maternal planet does not seem to constitute for him his absolute and earlier origins, for he continues his obsessional wandering when sent to Earth to convalesce in the second part of *Enigma*. In contrast to the computer-style language of the first part, the prose here becomes highly poetic as it evokes O.'s pastoral convalescence. In the Sudanese city of Ezzala, O. continues to reestablish contact with his own incarnations of the previous fictions. Here, Nejma is instructed to seduce O., to entertain him, and to aid in his recovery. She is a familiar figure, linked to a series of other women glimpsed or encountered (sometimes sexually) in the preceding fictions. In Nejma's presence O. continues to remember his earlier life. What he has forgotten about Epsilon was the feminine quality of that planet, which threatened his very identity and subjectivity. In Ezzala, O.'s dreams chart the progress of his recognition of that feminine principle and his attempted repression of it. The resolution of O.'s illness comes with his acceptance of a nonprivileged place within a feminine textuality characterized by continual permutation and flux. At the end of *Enigma*, O. abandons his wanderings in favor of a domestic life as a laborer.

O.'s cure in *Enigma* is also, allegorically, a corrective for traditional ways of viewing fiction as a finite, original work with a single decipherable meaning and a hero who is the privileged vehicle for conveying that meaning. In its place, a new view of fictional origin and elaboration is enunciated. In this view, an individual fiction is seen as a fragment of a larger text: its heroes recall other heroes, and its origin is lost in the infinite regress of other stories.

In *Our ou Vingt Ans après* (Ur or Twenty Years After, 1974) the reader deduces that the protagonist is O.'s unnamed son (although it eventually becomes impossible to distinguish between fa-

ther and son). He has been sent from Ezzala to accomplish a mission at the modern-day site of ancient Ur, where writing is said to have originated. As in the Alexandre Dumas novel echoed in the title, O.'s "cause" is taken up again in twenty years' time—that is, by the next generation. Like O., the son conducts an investigation on the question of writing, on the "corpus" of the feminine. But this time the inquest centers on the role of the father of a fiction: the author. In the seventh novel of *Le Jeu d'enfant*, the search centers on the archaeological foundations of writing and the paternity of fiction.

The radical intertextual model of fictional origin and elaboration that was proposed at the end of *Enigma* would seem to minimize the role of the writing subject. And indeed, much that has been written about the New Novel stresses its challenge to the traditional view of the author as the single autonomous "father" of a purely original textual offspring. Even more in *Our ou Vingt Ans après* than in his previous works, Ollier makes use of personages and passages borrowed, usually in slightly altered form, from past literature and mythology. These intertextual inserts come from sources as diverse as Lautréamont's *Les Chants de Maldoror*, the *Iliad*, and the myths of ancient Sumeria. The metaphor of writing as the weaving of intertextual threads into the fabric of a fiction characterizes this radicalized view of the author's task. And yet a recurring motif of biological filiation, in the form of many sets of fathers and sons, serves to complicate this new vision.

The narration of *Our* is composed of fragments from various sources: dreams, telepathy, hieroglyphic tablets, an omniscient narrator, and accounts by individuals who inhabit the archaeological site at Ur. The narration does not tell the story of the young man's visit, but rather recounts how that visit was recorded on clay tablets, and what becomes of those tablets. These secret tablets are the responsibility of the scribe Nabou (in Babylonian legend Nabû is the patron of scribes and the inventor of writing). At the end of the novel Nabou betrays his companions by permitting a young girl, Tiamât, to steal the secret tablets.

In Babylonian legend Tiamât is a feminine presence, a primeval watery chaos. It is from her body that the world was created. The allegory of fictional genesis in (and of) *Our ou Vingt Ans après* reposes on Tiamât's connection with textuality. Just as the body of the goddess was sacrificed so that the material world could be shaped, so the young Tiamât is presented as a ritual victim. Tiamât is twice raped by the visitor; each time, the text of *Our* is a pastiche or an outright borrowing from past literature, for example Flaubert's *Salammbô*. The primeval, originary "feminine" is the body of all textuality, which is figuratively pillaged to form a new fiction. Tiamât's rebellious flight at the end of the novel inaugurates a new chapter in the ongoing investigation into the source and nature of fiction. *Our ou Vingt Ans après* concludes with the young visitor in pursuit of Tiamât.

Although traditional notions of the author have been challenged and changed in *Our ou Vingt Ans après*, the person of the author is not ousted from the scene of fiction. Like the protagonist, the writing subject remains central to the cycle's interrogation, and it must be remembered that O. is also, in some sense, Ollier himself.

"Suis-je dans le livre?" (Am I in the book?): with this password, O. seeks to board the *Octopus*, the spaceship where he thinks Tiamât has taken refuge in her flight from Ur. O.'s question inaugurates an allegory of reading in *Fuzzy Sets* (1975), the last and most unconventional fiction of *Le Jeu d'enfant*. For after having incarnated the protagonist and the author, O. now comes to represent the reader of fiction. In the branching structure of the eight-armed vessel, O. seeks the secret space where the woman and her secret tablets are hidden. The *Octopus* becomes a figure not only of the eight-volume cycle, but of the structure of fiction itself. O.'s initial question points to an interrogation of the reader's relationship to the text read. While the reader is typically considered a passive spectator, in an unconventional fiction like *Fuzzy Sets* the reader is called on to become actively involved in making sense of a demanding, hermetic textuality. The format of this book is a sort of computer printout with many graphic gaps in the form of ellipses, parentheses, and pages on which the text is arranged into or around certain geometric shapes without respect to semantic continuity. Certain passages lack the beginning, middle, or end of every line; the text is traversed visually, semantically, and syntactically by the elliptical. If the space-age configuration of *Fuzzy Sets* presents a vision of the future's fiction, then that fiction is a text in flux whose fuzzy borders and exaggerated lacunae point to the impossibility of a linear, integral reading.

In *Fuzzy Sets*, Tiamât comes to figure the elusive meaning contained in textual ellipses. O.'s success in deducing her location culminates in his raping her. This episode should logically conclude a parable of reading in which the active reader steps in and fills in the text's semantic and typographical gaps. Yet a strange reversal complicates the analogy, for Tiamât reveals that O. has been set up to play just such a role in the scenario. Instead of actively conquering his place within the book, O. becomes a sort of foil in some larger scheme. His ordeal reflects in many respects that of the readers of avant-garde texts, who are led to form certain hypotheses as to the meaning of a work, only to see those notions turned against them in a perpetual subversion of their habitual ways of reading.

At the end of *Fuzzy Sets*, Tiamât's hypnotic, masturbatory ritual culminates in her triumphant escape from the spaceship. Allegorically, her flight precludes assigning any definitive, singular meaning to the fiction, which remains a "fuzzy set" of elliptical, shifting elements. *Fuzzy Sets*–and *Le Jeu d'enfant*–concludes with a reporter's account of O.'s return to his birthplace, to what appears to be Europe, specifically Paris. The cycle has spiraled back to its place of origin: Western Europe, the birthplace of the traditional novel, and Paris, the birthplace of Claude Ollier. But the "vieux continent de prose" (old continent of prose) to which O. returns is now a futuristic landscape. The report and the cycle end with an apostrophe to the reader: " 'Lecteur, vois-tu? Ce reportage est une introduction; à sa manière. Didactique: je l'ai écrit dans le style ancien' (Chroniques d'Ile de France)." ("Reader, do you see? This report is an introduction; in his/its way. Didactic: I have written it in the old style" [Chronicles of the Ile de France]). The cycle's conclusion suggests that while a cyclic return to the point of departure has been made, the nature of fiction has been radically altered by the eight-volume interrogation. The system returns to its point of departure, but the intervening developments have brought about the reeducation of all involved: the writer, the reader, and the form itself.

Published in 1967 along with the last book in the first cycle of *Le Jeu d'enfant*, *Navettes* is composed of fifteen short texts spanning fifteen years. Ranging chronologically from before *La Mise en scène* to the relay moment between the two cycles, these texts recall many situations, scenes, and passages from the first cycle while also anticipating certain aspects of the second. The title of this collection of texts evokes the image of weaving and texture as a metaphor for textuality: a *navette* is a shuttle, and these short works weave new connections between the longer works and larger movements of the major cycles. In so doing, they weave as well a net of further reflection on the questions raised by *Le Jeu d'enfant*.

The texts in *Navettes* participate in a variety of genres: descriptive vignettes, dream records, critical essays, and meditative travel narratives from Ollier's lengthy visit to North America (Times Square, the Baha'i temple near Chicago, the Golden Gate Bridge). Even the earliest of these pieces reflect the same careful construction and meticulous attention to language that characterize *Le Jeu d'enfant*. A subtle humor circulates in the measured, poetic prose of *Navettes*.

Participating in the major system while also illuminating it from outside, *Navettes* reiterates Ollier's insistence that fiction be its own analyst, its own critic. For example, the first text of the collection is entitled "Nocturne" and the last, "Nocturne entre guillemets," or Nocturne in Quotes. Although the narrative situations of the two texts are on the surface quite different, the second provides an ironic commentary on the kind of fiction allegorized by the first. Read in this way, the texts of *Navettes* constitute a microcosm of the cycle and a commentary of sorts on the entire cycle's movement toward greater self-consciousness. Thus *Navettes* counteracts any effect of tidy closure that might be attributed to the eight volumes of *Le Jeu d'enfant*.

Marrakch Medine is a work which defies generic classification. Published in 1979, four years after the last volume of *Le Jeu d'enfant*, this work represents a departure from the earlier cycle, while at the same time extending some of its issues and concerns, some of its terms and tones. The book is composed of passages (separated by blank space) varying in length from several lines to several pages. Stories and dialogues accompany the observations and investigations of the Moroccan city of Marrakesh and the area known as the *medine* by an unnamed narrator who is apparently part of a small group of Westerners visiting the Islamic city.

This reflective travel narrative is often doubled, as is customary in Ollier's texts, by cryptic meditations on perception, memory, and writing. Intertextual ties to Ollier's earlier works give the reader a sense of both familiarity and disorientation not unlike that of the tourist viewing the city through the filter of his own culture and assumptions. For *Marrakch Medine* also forms an extended meditation on the position of the Occidental spectator of an alien culture, language, religion, and landscape. Here Ollier ponders the lure of Orientalism, the possibility of achieving a noncolonizing perspective in a site of former colonialism, and the impossibility of penetrating the secrets withheld by the alterity that is Islam. But *Marrakch Medine* does not fall into the trap of a facile exoticism or self-castigation, for it also shows how the mythologizing of the other culture works in both directions, and it provides a figure of the encounter between the West and its Other, between Islam and its Other:

Le mythe, tu le liras dans les yeux des gosses, si tu vas dans le sud; ils copieront sur un carnet le numéro de ton automobile et tendront le crayon pour que tu inscrives ton nom, ton adresse; et ils voudront monter, et s'en aller, quitter le pays sec, c'est si bien chez toi Monsieur, on a tout ce qu'on veut, le cinéma, les femmes, la grosse paye, c'est l'Amérique! Le garçon te regarde, tu l'entrevois en bleu de travail, dans le grand ensemble, très loin de l'oasis; lui, voit passer les étrangers en djellaba et babouches. Chassé-croisé des regards, où se livrent les sentiments tels des émois, des élans recouverts, sitôt croisés que chassés—et où se lit aussi comme un raccourci de l'affaire.

(The myth, you will also read it in the kids' eyes, if you go to the south; they will copy in a notebook your car's number and hand you the pencil to write down your name, your address; and they'll want to get in, and go away, and leave the dry country, it's so nice where you live, Mister, you have everything you want, movies, women, good pay, it's paradise! The boy looks at you, you glimpse him in his blue work clothes, in the large view, very far from the oasis; *he* sees the foreigners pass by in djellabas and babouches. Exchange of glances, where feelings like agitations, like buried movements, give themselves up, no sooner exchanged than turned away—and in which can also be read something like a synopsis of the affair.)

The title of *Nébules* (1981) lends itself to multiple interpretations. First, *nébules* are architectural ornaments in the form of scallops; and in one sense, the twenty texts published in various journals from 1961 to 1978 and collected here can be considered as appendices or appendages of the major architecture of *Le Jeu d'enfant*. But in another sense the term evokes the cloudiness of the adjective *nébuleux* which, when applied to a writer or a theory, connotes obscurity. Thus any easy interpretation or clear classification of these nebulous texts is made hazy, and the collection stands freely on its own literary merits.

Nébules is divided into three parts. The title of the first section is "Fabules," or Little Fables. These texts are fictional fragments and descriptions of the Islamic world. The reader of *Le Jeu d'enfant* will recognize many elements from the fictional cycle. In French, *notules* are notes or annotations of another text, and the second section of this book, which bears that title, is composed of critical pieces on some modern paintings, a photograph, and the filmmaker Josef von Sternberg. The final section, "Modules," consists of four primarily theoretical essays on reading and writing. These texts are a valuable guide to the evolution of Ollier's views on writing and on his techniques of composition. The final text, "Pulsion," is a complex, poetic tribute to and pastiche of the writing of the influential philosopher Jacques Derrida.

Souvenirs écran (literally, Memories Screen, 1981) is a collection of texts written on a variety of films and filmmakers in the crucial cinematic decade from 1958 to 1968 (roughly the period of the French New Wave). These articles were originally published in journals devoted to film, literature, or both: *Cahiers du Cinéma, Mercure de France,* and *Nouvelle Revue Française*. The directors treated include Jean-Luc Godard, Fritz Lang, Sternberg, Alfred Hitchcock, Luis Buñuel, Michelangelo Antonioni, Satyajit Ray, Ernst Lubitsch, and Robert Bresson. Some of these pieces are simply notes and observations, while others are substantial analyses. Ollier assigns to cinema a significant influence on his own childhood, hence the title's allusion to Freud's notion of screen memories. These articles also make explicit the link between Ollier's concerns as a writer and his interests as a film critic. Ollier's involvement with cinema has not been limited to the role of spectator, however, for he has written several film scripts, and he played a cameo role as a doctor in Bresson's 1969 film, *Une Femme douce*.

Mon Double à Malacca (My Double in Malacca, 1982) is the account of a summer vacation in Malaysia. Its protagonists are Chloé, five years old, and Paul, her fifty-five-year-old father. Along with *Marrakch Medine*, this work continues an evolution toward the more openly biographical in its depiction and transmutation of Ollier's own travels. And like its predecessor, it defies generic categories; it is somewhat fictional, somewhat autobiographical, and very lyrical in its pro-

gression through the series of short passages that compose it.

Chloé, a confirmed reader of comic strips, imagines that she and her father are being followed and watched by several mysterious figures. Paul goes along with this fantasy, which eventually turns into reality as the two move against the exotic background of jungles, rivers, and beaches, from a colonial house on the island of Pinang to the sweltering eastern coastline.

But *Mon Double à Malacca* is much more than a poetic travel narrative or a mystery story; it is also another stage in Ollier's ongoing meditation on the disorientation (both bodily and cultural) produced by distant travel, and on how writing deals with experience. One thread spun throughout the text is the theme of a double of Paul back in a room in Europe, infested with exotic imaginings of the Far East. Similarly, the narrative switches back and forth from *je* to *tu* to *il*, grammatically reflecting Paul's psychic schisms. It is the contact with the Other, Islam, that triggers the doubling: "le survol d'Islam a partagé ton corps" (the flight over Islam divided your body). The effect of the trip and of the narrative is to double or multiply many aspects of existence, to blur the boundaries that people assume keep things separate around and within one; for example, the hot, humid climate of Malaysia destroys the distinction between inside and outside with respect to both houses and bodies. The effect of this disorientation of presumed categories is not the acquisition of some spiritual wholeness or oneness (as a mystification or Orientalist vision might conclude) but rather the confirmation of duality, division, and nonintegrality with respect to an individual subject and his or her perception and memories.

With *Une Histoire illisible* (An Unreadable Story, 1986) Ollier again explores the relation between writing and the remembered past. The unreadable to which the title refers is the personal past, which can never successfully be rendered as a chronology, an ordered continuity. The traditional way of writing biography is revealed to be an impossible enterprise, one which is permeated by naturalistic ideology. Such a way of writing the past is in reality a repression of the remembered givens of lived experience. The narrative of *Une Histoire illisible* thus eschews chronology, moving through various narrative genres which differ significantly from each other.

In *Déconnection* (Disconnection, 1988) Ollier explicitly treats what had been, in *Le Jeu d'enfant*, only an unspoken given: the experience of World War II, which shook all accepted values and left the European psyche permanently altered. In this fascinating and disturbing work two narratives unfold simultaneously, in alternating passages of two or three pages in length. One narrative is the story of Martin, an adolescent (probably French) conscripted to work in a German munitions factory in the final years of the war. The other story takes place toward the end of the present millennium. Certain unspecified "events" have caused a progressive decline in civilization; a mature man, a writer, lives alone in a small house on the outskirts of a village which could well be in France. His narrative is told in the first person. The population has dwindled, electricity and television broadcasts are sporadic, there is no mail; the few remaining people exchange tobacco and alcohol for food. The historical catastrophe of the mid century and the "events" of its conclusion are both seen through the eyes of single individuals. At the conclusion of this enigmatic text, civilization as it has been is ending and the stage is set for something radically different to begin.

Cahiers d'écolier (Student Notebooks, 1984) and *Fables sous rêve* (literally, Fables under Dream, 1985) are the first two volumes of the diary that Ollier has kept more or less regularly since 1950. *Cahiers d'écolier* covers 1950 to 1960, and *Fables sous rêve* continues on to 1970. A third volume, "Les Liens d'espace" (literally, Bonds of Space), is in progress and will bring the journal up to 1980. Ollier began publishing the journal at the prompting of two of his friends, Bernard Noël and Denis Roche, who felt that this work would be of interest to those familiar with Ollier's books and curious as to how they were written. And indeed, the journal offers fascinating glimpses into the complex genesis and elaboration of Ollier's texts. The entries include fragments of narrative, records of dreams, notes and ideas for future books, comments on work in progress, travel notes, and daily observations. The language of these entries is as meticulously crafted as that of Ollier's works written expressly for publication.

But this journal is not a personal diary containing the intimate biographical details and sentiments typically associated with the genre in question. Again, generic expectations are frustrated by Ollier's unconventional approach to writing. Those readers hoping to learn something more about Ollier the citizen will have scant clues to follow apart from the psychoanalytic conclusions they are free to draw from the dream narratives recorded there. However, those readers interested in the process and nature of writing will find a wealth of material there.

Interviews:

"Claude Ollier: Une Patience maniaque . . . ," *Magazine Littéraire*, no. 12 (November 1967): 36-37;

Bettina Knapp, "Claude Ollier," in her *French Novelists Speak Out* (New York: Whitson, 1976), pp. 148-164;

Bernard Noël, "Les Jeux de Claude Ollier," *Magazine Littéraire*, no. 213 (December 1984): 96-101.

References:

Phillipe Boyer, "Topographies pour jeux de piste," preface to Ollier's *La Mise en scène* (Paris: Flammarion, 1982), pp. 9-38;

Cecile Lindsay, "Le Degré zéro de la fiction: La Science du Nouveau Roman," *Romanic Review*, 74 (March 1983): 231-232;

Lindsay, "Textual Intercourse: Reader Theory and the New Novel," *Structuralist Review*, 2 (Spring 1984): 99-115;

Lindsay, "The Topography of (Science) Fiction: Claude Ollier's *Life on Epsilon*," *Science-Fiction Studies*, 11 (March 1984): 39-44;

Review of Contemporary Fiction, special issue on Ollier and Carlos Fuentes, 8 (Summer 1988);

Jean Ricardou, "L'Enigme dérivée," in his *Pour une théorie du Nouveau Roman* (Paris: Seuil, 1971), pp. 159-199;

Léon Roudiez, "Le Jeu du texte et du récit chez Claude Ollier," in *Nouveau Roman: hier, aujourd'hui*, volume 2 (Paris: Union Générale d'Editions, 1972), pp. 177-198;

Sub-Stance, special issue on Ollier, 13 (1976).

Georges Perec

(7 March 1936-3 March 1982)

Warren F. Motte, Jr.
University of Colorado

BOOKS: *Les Choses: Une Histoire des années soixante* (Paris: Julliard, 1965); translated by Helen R. Lane as *Les Choses: A Story of the Sixties* (New York: Grove, 1968);

Quel petit vélo à guidon chromé au fond de la cour? (Paris: Denoël, 1966);

Une Homme qui dort (Paris: Denoël, 1967);

La Disparition (Paris: Denoël, 1969);

Die Maschine, translated by Eugen Helmlé (Stuttgart: Reclam, 1972);

Les Revenentes (Paris: Julliard, 1972);

La Boutique obscure: 124 rêves (Paris: Denoël/Gonthier, 1973);

Espèces d'espaces: Journal d'un usager de l'espace (Paris: Galilée, 1974);

Ulcérations (Paris: Bibliothèque Oulipienne, 1974);

W ou le souvenir d'enfance (Paris: Denoël, 1975); translated by David Bellos as *W or The Memory of Childhood* (Boston: Godine, 1988; London: Collins, Harvill, 1988);

Alphabets (Paris: Galilée, 1976);

Je me souviens (Paris: Hachette, 1978);

La Vie mode d'emploi (Paris: Hachette, 1978); translated by Bellos as *Life, A User's Manual* (Boston: Godine, 1987; London: Collins, Harvill, 1987);

Un Cabinet d'amateur (Paris: Balland, 1979);

Les Mots croisés (Paris: Mazarine, 1979);

La Clôture et autres poèmes (Paris: Hachette, 1980);

Récits d'Ellis Island: Histoires d'errance et d'espoir, by Perec and Robert Bober (Paris: Sorbier, 1980);

Théâtre (Paris: Hachette, 1981)—comprises *L'Augmentation . . . , La Poche Parmentier*;

Epithalames (Paris: Bibliothèque Oulipienne, 1982);

Tentative d'épuisement d'un lieu parisien (Paris: Bourgois, 1982);

Penser / Classer (Paris: Hachette, 1985);

Les Mots croisés II (Paris: POL/Mazarine, 1986).

PLAY PRODUCTIONS: *L'Augmentation, ou Comment, quelles que soient les conditions sanitaires,*

Georges Perec (photograph by Anne de Brunhoff)

psychologiques, climatiques, économiques ou autres, mettre le maximum de chances de son côté en demandant à votre chef de service un réadjustement de votre salaire, Paris, Théâtre de la Gaîté-Montparnasse, 26 February 1970;

La Poche Parmentier, Théâtre de Nice, 12 February 1974.

OTHER: Perec, Pierre Lusson, and Jacques Roubaud, *Petit Traité invitant à la découverte de l'art subtil du GO* (Paris: Bourgois, 1969);

Oulipo, *La Littérature potentielle: Créations, re-créations, récréations*, includes contributions by Perec (Paris: Gallimard, 1973);

Harry Mathews, *Les Verts Champs de moutarde de l'Afghanistan*, translated by Perec (Paris: Denoël, 1974);

Oulipo, *Atlas de littérature potentielle*, includes contributions by Perec (Paris: Gallimard, 1981);

Oulipo, *La Bibliothèque oulipienne*, includes contributions by Perec (Geneva: Slatkine, 1981);

Mathews, *Le Naufrage du Stade Odradek*, translated by Perec (Paris: Hachette, 1981);

Oulipo, *La Bibliothèque oulipienne*, 2 volumes, includes contributions by Perec (Paris: Ramsay, 1987).

From the middle 1960s until his death in 1982, Georges Perec produced a score of major texts which, in their richness and their diversity, stand as one of the most impressive bodies of work in contemporary French literature. The salient constant in this corpus is change itself, particularly formal change: Perec wrote novellas, novels, poetry, plays, radio plays, essays, filmscripts, libretti, as well as other texts which resist traditional generic taxonomy. "Mon ambition d'écrivain," said Perec in 1978, "serait de parcourir toute la littérature de mon temps sans jamais avoir le sentiment de revenir sur mes pas ou de remarcher dans mes propres traces, et d'écrire tout ce qu'il est possible à un homme d'aujourd'hui d'écrire" (My ambition as a writer would be to traverse all of contemporary literature, without ever feeling that I am retracing my own steps or returning to beaten ground, and to write everything that a man today can possibly write). If many of Perec's works may be situated firmly within the tradition of the French avantgarde, several attained a far broader audience. The literary prizes he won, the Prix Théophraste Renaudot in 1965 and the Prix Médicis in 1978, testify amply to his popular appeal. In the years immediately preceding his death, his reputation among critics both in France and abroad had begun to burgeon considerably; since then, this process has accelerated. As various homages, special issues of journals, and colloquia devoted to his work succeed each other, Perec's place in the canon seems assured. One is left to reflect upon the ambivalence with which Perec himself would have regarded this phenomenon.

On both sides of his family Perec's antecedents were Polish Jews. His mother, Cyrla Szulewicz, emigrated from Poland to France after World War I; his father, Icek Judko Peretz, arrived in France in 1926, in the process changing his name to André Perec. They were married in Paris in 1934. Georges Perec, their only child, was born on 7 March 1936; in the first years of his life, the language he heard around him was Yiddish, rather than French. At the outbreak of World War II Perec's father enlisted in the French army; he was killed on the day of the armistice, 16 June 1940. In 1942 Perec's mother sent him to the Unoccupied Zone with the Red Cross. She herself, along with her sister, was arrested and imprisoned in the Drancy internment camp in January 1943; on 11 February she was deported to Germany, where she was murdered along with millions of others in the camps. Perec spent the duration of the war with family members in the Unoccupied Zone and in a Catholic boarding school in Villard-de-Lans. After the war he returned to Paris with his paternal aunt and her family. He attended the Collège des Estampes, a secondary school where one of his teachers was Jean Duvignaud (who would go on to become a major scholar and critic). After his graduation in 1954 he attended the Sorbonne, where he studied sociology. During this time he contributed short pieces to literary journals such as the *Nouvelle Nouvelle Revue Française*, as it was then called, and *Lettres Nouvelles*. Perec performed his compulsory military service in 1958-1959 and then returned to Paris, earning his living as a public-opinion pollster. He spent over a year in Tunisia in 1961-1962, then returned once again to Paris. He worked as a research librarian in neurophysiology at the Centre National de la Recherche Scientifique until 1979, when financial circumstances finally permitted him to devote himself full-time to writing. Perec died of lung cancer on 3 March 1982.

Although Perec's work is characterized by its heterogeneity, there are certain themes, tendencies, and concerns that recur with regularity in his writing. Perec himself suggested on more than one occasion that four of these are particularly insistent. First, what he called a "sociologie du quotidien," or sociology of everyday life, which focuses upon the minimal, the seemingly banal aspects of human existence: the gestures that a person makes in parking a car, or the ways in which people shelve the books in their libraries. The close observation demanded in this aspect of Perec's work leads to experimentation with a variety of descriptive techniques in the writing process. A second tendency is autobiographical. His work incorporates progressively more autobiographical detail; indeed, one of the projects interrupted by his death was a history of his family, a sort of grand fresco of personal and familial memory. As might be expected, in view of the events of his early life, the autobiographical current in his work is dominated by the themes of death, loss, and absence. Third, a ludic impulse is apparent throughout Perec's writings, a high delight in games and puzzles of all sorts. He privileged verbal games and played them constantly, exploiting them in order to heighten the aesthetic efficacy of his work and inviting his reader to play along. He argued that formal constraint, inherent in all word games, was crucially important to the literary text, illustrating this argument by example. Finally, there is a marked concern for narrative in his work, for the story well told. Thus, several of his texts, although their structural principles are as arcane as those of the most outlandish avant-garde experiments, may be read (and have been) as traditionalist works. This oscillation between the experimental and the traditional or, rather, the painstaking conflation of the two, accounts for a good measure of Perec's force and serves as the foundation upon which his literary reputation will come to rest.

His first novel, *Les Choses: Une Histoire des années soixante* (1965; translated as *Les Choses: A Story of the Sixties*, 1968), is the story of a young couple living in Paris, a chronicle of their peregrinations in an exceedingly material world. Their fascination with *things (les choses)*–Church shoes, English hunting prints, Oriental carpets–and their efforts to acquire them lead inexorably toward vacuity. As they progressively define themselves through things, those things gradually subsume them, finally erasing the couple's all-too-human emotions, reflections, and hopes. The structure of *Les Choses* is that of a traditional novel of apprenticeship, but with a crucial, ironic twist, for Jérôme and Sylvie never accede to insight: their failure to understand (far less transcend) their dilemma is as complete at the end of the novel as at the beginning.

The high degree of coincidence between Jérôme and Sylvie's life and that of Perec may lead one to read *Les Choses* as an autobiographical novel. Although some of the more obvious parallels are striking–Perec, like the couple, earned his living polling public opinion in Paris; like them, he spent a year in Sfax, Tunisia–such a reading is too reductive, in that it trivializes other important aspects of the text. Perec himself said that part of his intent in *Les Choses* was to rewrite Gustave Flaubert, and indeed his novel can be read as a contemporary response to *L'Education sentimentale*. Actually, *Les Choses* was received as a text announcing a new genre, the sociological novel, in which the techniques of sociological analysis are deployed in the service of the fictional narrative. Its success was resounding and immediate: *Les Choses* won the Prix Théophraste Renaudot (one of France's five principal literary prizes), confirming and guaranteeing its popular appeal. It was subsequently translated into sixteen languages, including English; indeed, for the moment, only three of Perec's works are available in English translation. As late as 1980, fifteen years after its first publication, *Les Choses* continued to sell at the rate of twenty thousand copies per year in France alone.

Perec's second novel, *Quel petit vélo à guidon chromé au fond de la cour?* (Which Little Bike With Chrome Handlebars at the Far End of the Courtyard?, 1966), is far different both in tone and in form. Perec himself called it a "récit épique en prose" (epic tale in prose), a generic tag whose ironic intent becomes apparent in the first pages of the text. Written in mock-heroic style, *Quel petit vélo* tells of the efforts of a group of friends on behalf of a young French soldier faced with the prospect of military service in Algeria during that country's war of independence. The political dimension of the novel is important: the narrator's anticolonialist, antimilitarist position and other sorts of implicit and explicit commentary are obvious and unavoidable. But, after all, the text is a novel rather than a political tract, and its principal motor is satire. The distance between the young intellectuals and the benighted conscript whom they try to help is the source of considerable irony, as are the means, progressively more ridiculous and uniformly ineffectual, which they choose.

Perec indulged his taste for the ludic far more in *Quel petit vélo* than in *Les Choses*: the situations he erects are clearly absurd. The narrator, for instance, is never quite certain of the soldier's family name; consequently, the latter is subjected to continual transformation in the course of the novel. The narration itself, in the best tradition of the eighteenth-century satirical text, is highly intrusive, and much of the narrator's commentary is metaliterary in nature. In the middle of the novel the narrator remarks, "Le lecteur, qui voudrait ici marquer une pause, le peut. Nous sommes arrivés, ma foi, à ce que d'excellents auteurs (Jules Sandeau, Victor Margueritte, Henri Lavedan, Alain Robbe-Grillet même, dans son tout dernier *Carême de Noël*) appellent une articulation naturelle" (Any reader who wishes to pause here may. We have come, upon my word, to what excellent authors [Jules Sandeau, Victor Margueritte, Henri Lavedan, even Alain Robbe-Grillet in his recent *Christmas Lent*] call a natural articulation). At the end of the volume Perec obligingly supplies a list of rhetorical figures used in the text. One hundred and sixty-four of these are inventoried and arranged in alphabetical order, but the index (and the consequent illumination it sheds upon the text) stops with the letter *P*: clearly, Perec offered this index as a pig in a poke.

The humor in *Quel petit vélo* is refreshing and self-deprecating. Some aspects of the story may reflect Perec's experience with the Ligne Générale (General Line), an activist group which he joined in the late 1950s; indeed, the novel is dedicated to "L. G. en mémoire de son plus beau fait d'armes" (L. G. in memory of its noblest feat of arms). Many aspects of the text recall Raymond Queneau's novels: that writer, more than any other, served as Perec's literary touchstone, and his admiration of Queneau was boundless.

Un Homme qui dort (A Sleeping Man), Perec's third novel, was published in 1967. Again Perec demonstrated his refusal to redeploy previous literary modes. The text is particularly anomalous insofar as it is narrated in the second person singular (the only other extended example of this sort of narrative structure in contemporary French litterature that springs readily to mind is Michel Butor's *La Modification* [*A Change of Heart*], published in 1957). *Un Homme qui dort* is the account of a young man's spiritual crisis: its narrator-protagonist (indeed he is the only character in the novel) traverses a period of profound depression. The principal symptom of his malady is an overwhelming somnolence. It becomes apparent that this condition is more metaphysical than physical, constituting an existential dilemma of sorts. Granted this, Perec's protagonist takes his place in a long line of literary sleepers, from Ivan Goncharov's Oblomov to John Barth's Jacob Horner, including such other figures as Kafka's K., Thomas Mann's Hans Castorp, and Sartre's Lucien Fleurier.

It is tempting to read *Un Homme qui dort* as a late existentialist novel. There is an insistent pattern of allusion to some of the more formidable beasts in the existentialist menagerie, particularly to Sartre's *La Nausée* (*Nausea*). But the tone of the allusions is often ironic and sometimes explicitly parodic. Moreover, much of the protagonist's crisis results precisely from his ingenuous reflection upon, and imitation of, models of behavior proposed by canonical twentieth-century novels. It is only when he lucidly rejects these models that he can begin to come to terms with his own dilemma: "Combien d'histoires modèles exaltent ta grandeur, ta souffrance! Combien de Robinson, de Roquentin, de Meursault, de Leverkühn! Les bons points, les belles images, les mensonges: ce

n'est pas vrai. Tu n'as rien appris, tu ne saurais témoigner. Ce n'est pas vrai, ne les crois pas, ne crois pas les martyrs, les héros, les aventuriers!" (How many exemplary stories exalt your grandeur, your suffering! How many Robinsons, Roquentins, Meursaults, Leverkühns! Good points, pretty images, lies: it's not true. You have learned nothing, you could never testify. It's not true, don't believe them, don't believe the martyrs, the heroes, the adventurers!).

Un Homme qui dort, like *Les Choses*, is a novel of apprenticeship, a *Bildungsroman*, but it is far more faithful to the traditional norms of that genre. The protagonist experiences a modest epiphany at the end of the story, and his consequent self-knowledge will, it is clear, allow him to resolve his crisis. Although its commercial success fell short of that of *Les Choses, Un Homme qui dort* was warmly received by the critics and the public. In 1974 Bernard Queysanne directed a film based on the novel.

Georges Perec joined the Ouvroir de Littérature Potentielle (Workshop of Potential Literature) in 1967. It was a choice which would be determinative both in his career and in that of the group as a whole. The Ouvroir de Littérature Potentielle (Oulipo, for short) was founded in 1960 by Raymond Queneau and François Le Lionnais. Composed of people from various walks of life (poets, mathematicians, historians, computer scientists), the Oulipo today includes twenty-five members. The group draws no distinction between living members and those who have died; thus, Marcel Duchamp and Italo Calvino are still inscribed on its rolls along with living members such as Harry Mathews and Jacques Roubaud. The Oulipo is dedicated to the pursuit of form in literature, and it has traditionally divided its activity into two distinct yet mutually complementary spheres. First, analysis, or the location and recuperation of formal experiments in the history of literature: ancient forms such as the palindrome, the tautogram, and rhopalic verse are particularly prized by the group. Second, synthesis, or the invention of new structures for the literary text.

For many years the Oulipo worked in voluntary obscurity, meeting once a month and shunning publicity of any sort. Such inhabitual reticence on the part of a literary group afforded the Oulipo, paradoxically, a certain degree of notoriety, as rumors of its activity filtered out into the French literary world. The whisperings about savant literary alchemists bending the more taboo literary arcana to their will certainly did no harm to the group's reputation in its early years. Gradually, the Oulipo began to open itself to public scrutiny, through participation in cultural events, colloquia, and workshops of various sorts. It also began to publish the results of its research: ironically, this did little to dispel the fog of mystery and misrepresentation with which mainstream opinion continues to envelop the group.

Quite simply, at the center of the group's aesthetic lies the belief that rigorous formal constraint is beneficial to the literary text, that the text must be erected (to adopt Raymond Queneau's metaphor) using a scaffolding of rigid structure, a preelaborated formal grid. Perec quickly took this axiom to heart, as well as the diverse corollaries resulting from it; each of his subsequent texts in some manner bears its stamp.

La Disparition (The Disappearance), published in 1969, illustrates this point nicely. It is a novel of three hundred pages in which the letter *E* never occurs. Perec was prompted to embark on the project by the Oulipo's research on the lipogram, a literary form in which one or more letters of the alphabet is omitted from a text; examples of the lipogram have been traced as far back in literary history as the sixth century B.C. This deliberate formal constraint goes far beyond mere whim, however: *La Disparition* is a sort of detective story whose mystery devolves upon the fact that the *E* has absconded from the alphabet. The disappearance of the *E* is reflected in every aspect of the text, which may consequently be read as a meditation upon its own process of production.

The chapters are numbered from one to twenty-six, but there is no fifth chapter, reflecting the absence of the fifth letter of the alphabet; the parts are numbered from one to six (reflecting six vowels if one counts the semivowel *Y*), but the second, like the second vowel, is absent. The French word *disparition* also means death, and indeed death haunts the pages of the novel, lurking in wait for any character who approaches the solution of the mystery. Moreover, the letter *E* is phonetically identical to the disjunctive pronoun *eux* (them): it may be conjectured that the principal death inscribed in the text is that of Perec's parents. Writing a novel without the most frequently used letter in the alphabet (it occurs four times, for instance, in Georges Perec's name) is a severe handicap, comparable, on another level, to facing life after the death of one's

parents. Successful completion of the project is thus, in a sense, an affirmation of survival.

It testifies to Perec's linguistic virtuosity that in breaking the record of the longest lipogram he also wrote an eminently readable novel. But the verbal pyrotechnics again mask more sober intent. Perec's purpose, as he expressed it in the final pages of *La Disparition*, was to adumbrate new possibilities for the novelistic genre itself: "L'ambition du 'Scriptor,' son propos, disons son souci, son souci constant, fut d'abord d'aboutir à un produit aussi original qu'instructif, à un produit qui aurait, qui pourrait avoir un pouvoir stimulant sur la construction, la narration, l'affabulation, l'action, disons, d'un mot, sur la façon du roman d'aujourd'hui" (literally, if not lipogrammatically, translated: "The author's purpose, his wish, his constant wish, was above all to produce something as original as it is instructive, something which would have, which might have, a power to stimulate the construction, the narration, the plot, the action, and, in a word, the making of the contemporary novel).

Perec collaborated with Pierre Lusson and Jacques Roubaud on *Petit Traité invitant à la découverte de l'art subtil du GO* (A Short Treatise Inviting the Discovery of the Subtle Art of GO, 1969), a primer of the Japanese game of Go. The authors review the rules, the strategy, the history, and the philosophy of that game, as well as proposing workshops to be held at the Moulin d'Andé, near Chartres. All of this discourse on the game drifts toward a meditation upon larger ludic systems; perhaps inevitably, granted the coauthors' status as poets, the direction of this drift is toward literature itself. At the end of their introduction, they explicitly declare their own game: "Il n'existe qu'une seule activité à laquelle se puisse raisonnablement comparer le GO. On aura compris que c'est l'écriture" (There is only one activity to which GO can reasonably be compared. This activity, it goes without saying, is literature).

Die Maschine (The Machine, 1972) is a radio play. It was commissioned by Saar Radio in 1968 and translated into German by Eugen Helmlé (Perec's original French version has not been published). The text attempts to simulate a computer analysis of Goethe's "Wanderers Nachtlied." For the computer, Perec postulated a group of six data banks containing, respectively, the poem, information about Goethe, a German vocabulary, alphabets arranged according to a phonological key, a syntactical key (a grammar), and a selection of other poems from world literature. The logical unit of the computer, the control, issues commands to the data banks. There are four voices in the radio play (three speakers and the voice of the control) which communicate the output of the computer. The analysis of the "Wanderers Nachtlied" that constitutes the text of *Die Maschine* proceeds according to categories (or registers) which the computer applies to the poem successively: an analysis of the individual word material, a modification of the semantic element, an examination of the relations between the poem and its author, and, finally, a comparison of the poem to other poems in order to extract that which Perec called "the essence of poetry." *Die Maschine* is a minor text within Perec's work, but it prefigures in striking manner the more ample experiments in literary combinatorics which follow upon it.

Les Revenentes (literally, The Ghosts; more appropriately perhaps, The Resurrected, 1972), like *La Disparition*, is a lipogrammatic novel. Unlike the latter, which excludes the *E*, *Les Revenentes* excludes all the other vowels: in 126 pages of text, the only vowel employed is the *E*. Consequently, the language of *Les Revenentes* is singularly anormative, although, once again, the text remains surprisingly readable: "J'erre près des berges de l'Elster. Elles sentent le genêt et les evergreens. Des gens blêmes, sevrés de mer, pêchent des brêmes et des espèces de flets" (literally: "I wander near the banks of the Elster. They smell of gorse and evergreens. Pale folks, cut off from the sea, are fishing for bream and species of halibut").

Curiously, a comparison of *La Disparition* and *Les Revenentes* reveals both symmetry and dissymmetry. Although both are lipogrammatic novels, because of the nature of the formal constraints which respectively rule them, they share not one word in common. Perec himself suggested that there remained a third logical possibility: a text composed of the words excluded from both *La Disparition* and *Les Revenentes*, that is, words in which both the letter *E* and another vowel figure. He excused himself from this task on the same occasion, remarking that it was time for him to devote himself to some other *idée fixe*.

In *La Boutique obscure: 124 rêves* (The Dark Boutique: 124 Dreams, 1973), Perec recounted the dreams he had from May 1969 to August 1972. Themes of death and arbitrary persecution abound, as does the theme of writing. Indeed, Perec stated that during this period he felt that

he was dreaming more and more *in order to write*, that his dreams were beginning to resemble texts, springing fully armed out of his dreamer's head, a circumstance that led him finally to call a halt to the experiment. It should be noted that Perec underwent psychoanalysis from May 1971 to June 1975; according to him, he published *La Boutique obscure* in the middle of this process to annoy his analyst (the relations between Perec and the latter were apparently not of the most cordial).

Perec's contributions to the first anthology of the Oulipo's work, *La Littérature potentielle: Créations, re-créations, récréations* (Potential Literature: Creations, Re-Creations, Recreations, 1973), are significant. They include an essay on the history of the lipogram, tracing that form from Lasus of Hermione in the sixth century B.C. to the present, as well as the world's longest palindrome, a text comprising more than five thousand letters (for this last feat, and for his record-breaking lipogram, Perec is enshrined in the *Guinness Book of Records*). Also included is an "alphabetical drama," a short play whose spoken lines homophonically recapitulate the alphabet. Perec elaborated a form called "L.S.D.," or "Littérature Sémo-Définitionnelle" (Semo-Definitional Literature) with his longtime friend and fellow Oulipian, Marcel Bénabou. Choosing two different utterances, the authors playfully show that they can be made to converge, through the substitution of a dictionary definition for each word in those utterances. "Petit Abécédaire illustré" (Little Illustrated Abecedary), Perec's other major contribution to the anthology, is a series of riddles, the answers to which parody the exercises in a child's reading primer.

Espèces d'espaces: Journal d'un usager de l'espace (Species of Space: Journal of a User of Space), published in 1974, resists ready generic classification: it is a meditation upon space and its uses. Its formal organization reflects an expanding spatial order, as chapters are devoted successively to the page, the bed, the bedroom, the apartment, the apartment building, the street, the neighborhood, the city, the countryside, France, Europe, the World, and (finally and inevitably) Space. But the principal concerns in *Espèces d'espaces* devolve upon writing and its various modes; Perec speaks revealingly of his past, present, and future literary projects. More particularly, *Espèces d'espaces* may be read as a handbook in the techniques of literary description.

Ulcérations (Ulcerations, 1974) was published as the first volume in the Bibliothèque Oulipienne (Oulipian Library), a series of works by members of the Oulipo, published privately in editions limited to 150 copies. The text is an example of heterogrammatic poetry, a form in which each "line" is a perfect anagram of every other "line" in the poem. Thus, *Ulcérations* is composed of 399 anagrams of its title, which itself is composed of the eleven most frequently used letters in the French alphabet. An example may serve to clarify this point; the poem begins:

Cœur à l'instinct saoûl
reclus à trône inutile,
Corsaire coulant secourant l'isolé,
crains-tu la course intruse?

(Heart of drunken instinct
recluse on a useless throne,
Foundering pirate saving the isolated,
do you fear the trespassing race?)

This passage in free verse reveals its own principle of composition when set in a heterogrammatic grid:

COEURALINST
INCTSAOULRE
CLUSATRONEI
NUTILECORSA
IRECOULANTS
ECOURANTLIS
OLECRAINSTU
LACOURSEINT
RUSE

Each eleven-letter "line" in the poem is thus a perfect anagram of the word *ulcérations*. Without dwelling upon Perec's innovation and obvious virtuosity, it must be remarked that *Ulcérations* is a very fine poem indeed; it exemplifies, moreover, in its very exaggeration, the essential combinatory nature of all poetry.

W ou le souvenir d'enfance (1975; translated as *W or The Memory of Childhood*, 1988) is a hybrid text in which a fictive narrative alternates, chapter by chapter, with an autobiographical narrative. The text is thus bipartite, in fact, doubly so, a caesura being defined by the moment in the autobiographical narrative when Perec takes final leave of his mother. The heavy masking of autobiographical elements which characterizes Perec's earlier writings is largely attenuated in *W*. The fictive narrative seems to serve this function at the outset of the text and yet, progressively, fiction

Dust jacket for the 1988 translation of the work in which autobiographical narrative alternates with an allegorical tale about the mythical island W

and autobiography converge, as images of persecution, cruelty, death, and absence are multiplied in both. It becomes clear that *W ou le souvenir d'enfance* is a book about holocaust, in both the particular and the universal sense, and about the ways in which personal and collective history reflect each other and mutually cohere.

W is also a speculation upon the ways in which literature may deal with events, either personal or historical, that, in their enormity, seem to refuse representation of any sort. The book is dedicated to "E," figuring, as the reader has seen, Perec's parents, whom he insistently inscribes in the text: "J'écris: j'écris parce que nous avons vécu ensemble, parce que j'ai été un parmi eux, ombre au milieu de leurs ombres, corps près de leurs corps; j'écris parce qu'ils ont laissé en moi leur marque indélibile et que la trace en est l'écriture: leur souvenir est mort à l'écriture; l'écriture est le souvenir de leur mort et l'affirmation de ma vie" (I write: I write because we lived together, because I was one among them, shadow among their shadows, body close to their bodies; I write because they left their indelible mark in me, and its trace is writing: their memory died in writing; writing is the remembrance of their death and the affirmation of my life).

W ou le souvenir d'enfance resulted, according to Perec, from a long, cathartic process of introspection and autoanalysis; he suggested that the writing of this work during his period of psychoanalysis was so therapeutic that any further formal therapy became unnecessary. *W* thus represents a pivotal point in Perec's career as a writer: it is a formidable, elegant, lucid book that must be considered, along with *La Vie mode d'emploi* (1978; translated as *Life, A User's Manual*, 1987), as his masterwork.

Alphabets (1976) is a collection of heterogrammatic poems. Each of these employs the ten most frequently used letters in the French alphabet, *A, E, I, L, N, O, R, S, T,* and *U*. The remaining sixteen letters are used in eleven poems each. The collection, logically enough, is organized alphabetically: the eleven poems with *B* as the variant letter are followed by eleven poems with *C*, and so forth until one reaches *Z*. Each poem has eleven heterogrammatic verses, and there are eleven poems for each of the sixteen variant letters. Consequently, and by no means coincidentally, there are 1,936 lines of poetry in *Alphabets* (11 X 11 X 16 = 1,936), a number which corresponds to the year of Perec's birth. Obviously, there is much method in this madness, as well as a firm belief (unanimously shared within the Oulipo) in the mutual complementarity of mathematics and literature.

Je me souviens (I Remember, 1978) is composed of 480 very short passages, each prefaced by the phrase "je me souviens." The passages allude to recent history, political, cultural, and popular. Perec's intent is to recuperate minuscule chunks of the past, to assemble a collection of "micro-memories" common to all Parisians of his generation; the text thus reflects his interest in the sociology of the quotidian. In an interview he stated that none of these short evocations of the past was really important, and yet one of the most interesting aspects of *Je me souviens* is how memory makes the past cohere, organizing events of radically different import into a progressively more isotopical pattern. Thus, the banal and the catastrophic rub elbows in the text, as Perec evokes Ray Ventura's big band, famine in Biafra, advertisements for cocktails, and Adolf Eichmann's trial.

Resulting from ten years of work, *La Vie mode d'emploi* is a chronicle of the life of a Parisian apartment building; it is, at seven hundred pages, the longest of Perec's writings. It won the 1978 Prix Médicis and has thus far elicited more critical scrutiny than any of his other books. It is perhaps in *La Vie mode d'emploi* that Perec achieved the most felicitous integration of the four concerns that animate his literary enterprise as a whole, the sociology of the quotidian, autobiography, Oulipian experimentation, and what Roland Barthes called "readerly" narrative.

Perec inscribed the generic tag *romans* (novels) on *La Vie mode d'emploi* to announce the plurality of narrative therein. As the various stories in the text intersect, complement, and gloss each other, one is accorded particular privilege. It is the story of Percival Bartlebooth, a dilettante millionaire, who as a young man elaborates a project to occupy the rest of his life. During ten years he would take lessons in watercolor painting. Then during twenty years he would travel the world, painting a watercolor of a different port every two weeks; as each painting was finished, he would send it back to Paris, where an artisan, Gaspard Winckler, would glue it on a sheet of wood and cut it up into a jigsaw puzzle. Upon his return, Bartlebooth would find, then, five hundred jigsaw puzzles waiting to be solved: to the solution of the puzzles he would devote twenty years (one puzzle every two weeks). As each puzzle was solved, it would be taken to the port where it had been painted twenty years prior, and dipped into the water until nothing remained except the original blank paper. "Aucune trace, ainsi, ne resterait de cette opération qui aurait, pendant cinquante ans, entièrement mobilisé son auteur" (No trace, thus, would remain of this project which, for fifty years, would have wholly occupied its author).

La Vie mode d'emploi is a highly specular text; the struggle between Winckler and Bartlebooth, puzzle maker and puzzle solver, is figural of the relations between author and reader. The insistent discussion of puzzles suggests that Perec proposes his text to the reader as precisely that, a puzzle to be solved. And indeed, the formal organization of the text confirms this. The apartment building described in *La Vie mode d'emploi* is ten stories high by ten units wide, suggesting an expanded chessboard. To each living space in the building, Perec devoted a chapter: one hundred squares in the grid, each corresponding to a chapter in the book. To organize the sequence of the chapters, Perec used a modified version of a celebrated chess problem called the Knight's Tour, in which a knight must visit all the squares on the board, never landing twice on the same square. He also established a series of themes, allusions, and objects to be integrated into *La Vie mode d'emploi*, choosing a mathematical figure to order them. This figure, known as the *Orthogonal Latin Bi-Square Order Ten*, assures the symmetrical distribution of pairs of numbers in a grid of ten by ten. As Perec deployed the figure, each number corresponded to a list of twenty-one items: in each chapter of *La Vie mode d'emploi*, then, there are forty-two predetermined constitutive elements.

Here again, the crucial paradox that accounts for so much of the aesthetic efficacy in Perec's work becomes apparent: *La Vie mode d'emploi* is a spectacularly innovative avant-garde experiment; it is also a "readerly" novel. To return to Queneau's term, the "scaffolding" that allowed the edifice to be constructed is not apparent in the finished product. The book, read as traditionalist narrative, will furnish considerable reward; but to any reader who is prepared to play Perec's game, *La Vie mode d'emploi* will offer the delights of the most intricate and *savant* of puzzles.

Un Cabinet d'amateur (A Collector's Study, 1979) is a novella about an art auction and its consequences. Perec indulged his taste for description as he cataloged the paintings in the collection. Moreover, after publication of the book, he suggested that all of the paintings described in *Un Cabinet d'amateur* allude in some manner to various chapters in *La Vie mode d'emploi*. Particular attention is accorded in the text to one painting, itself entitled *Un Cabinet d'amateur*: it is a portrait of an art patron among the works he has acquired. One of these reproduces the portrait that contains it, and so forth, in a structure of infinite regression. Clearly and explicitly, the *mise-en-abyme* technique of the portrait is proposed as that of the novella; like *La Vie mode d'empoi*, *Un Cabinet d'amateur* is a specular text whose principal concerns devolve upon the norms, the modalities, and the possibilities of literature itself.

Perec contributed crossword puzzles to the weekly magazine the *Point* from 1976 until his death; *Les Mots croisés*, published in 1979, collects 130 of these; a second volume of puzzles, *Les Mots croisés II*, appeared in 1986 with 102 puzzles. As a cruciverbist, Perec was known for the technical virtuosity of his puzzles, which included relatively few black spaces. More important, perhaps, are the striking parallels between this and his other activities. Formally, a crossword puzzle is not so very different from, say, a heterogrammatic poem, insofar as both involve the distribution of letters in a grid according to certain rigorous, predetermined rules. And here is where Perec's cruciverbal work serves to illuminate his literary work: like the crossword puzzle, in Perec's aesthetic the literary text is a ludic system, a game to be played by author and reader in strict interaction.

La Clôture et autres poèmes (Closure and Other Poems) was published in 1980. The title piece is a long heterogrammatic poem with what Perec called "jokers." These are variable letters in each line of heterogrammatic verse; each line uses the letters *A, C, E, I, L, N, O, R, S, T*, and *U* (those used in *Ulcérations*), plus one other letter which may vary from line to line. This, of course, renders the constraint considerably more supple, providing for more leeway in composition. The result on the level of the text is that the language of "La Clôture" seems to be more normative than that of *Ulcérations* or *Alphabets*. Thematically, the poem is strongly autobiographical, dealing with the rue Vilin, where Perec lived with his parents.

"Trompe l'œil," also included in the collection, is a group of six bilingual poems, works which may be read in both French and English (although the French readings are somewhat more convincing). "Métaux" (Metals) includes four heterogrammatic poems with jokers. Three other pieces deserve special mention. In "Deux 'Morales élémentaires' " (Two "Elementary Morals"), Perec adopts a poetic fixed form invented by Raymond Queneau; using it, he paints the portraits of two friends and fellow Oulipians, Jacques Roubaud and Harry Mathews. "La Belle Absente" (The Beautiful Absent One) is a sort of reverse acrostic. Each line of the poem uses twenty letters of the alphabet; *K, W, X, Y*, and *Z* never appear; the remaining absent letter varies from line to line. In the first line, no *C* is used, in the second, no *A*, and so forth, until, by omission, the name Catherine is inscribed in the text. "Dos, caddy d'aisselles" (Back, Caddy of Armpits) is a "syllabic palindrome." In the traditional palindrome, the operative integers are letters; here, they are syllables. Perec's text, read backwards syllable by syllable, homophonically imitates Gérard de Nerval's "El Desdichado" (The Disinherited), one of the most celebrated sonnets in French literature.

Récits d'Ellis Island: Histoires d'errance et d'espoir (Tales of Ellis Island: Stories of Wandering and Hope, 1980) resulted from a project Perec undertook in collaboration with the cinematographer Robert Bober, as did a film of the same title, shown on French television in November 1980. Perec was largely responsible for the verbal text of the project, Bober for the visual. The book is composed of four parts: a history of Ellis Island, a personal essay by Perec, a description of the way the authors proceeded, and a collection of accounts which they gathered from people who had passed through Ellis Island as immigrants. *Récits d'Ellis Island* was another step in Perec's examination of his personal history, an oblique inquiry into his own Judaity, a direct inquiry into historical exempla of loss and exile.

Atlas de littérature potentielle (Atlas of Potential Literature, 1981) is the Oulipo's second anthology: it offers examples of their research produced after 1973. Again, it demonstrates that Perec's contribution to the collective effort of the Oulipo was significant indeed. Included in the *Atlas* is a short piece entitled "Quatre Figures pour *La Vie mode d'emploi*" (Four Figures for *La Vie mode d'emploi*; also published in the special issue of *Arc* devoted to Perec), in which he glosses his novel, suggesting some of the formal devices operative therein and locating them firmly within the Oulipian aesthetic.

La Bibliothèque oulipienne (The Oulipian Library), published in 1981, makes available in a single trade anthology the first sixteen volumes of the Oulipo's "library," previously published in private, limited editions. The texts are intermediate forms, longer and more developed than the illustrative exercises in *La Littérature potentielle* and *Atlas de littérature potentielle*, shorter than more ambitious Oulipian texts such as Perec's *La Disparition*, Italo Calvino's *Se una notte d'inverno un viaggiatore* (If on a Winter's Night a Traveler, 1979), and Harry Mathews's *The Sinking of the Odradek Stadium* (1975). *Ulcérations* is the first piece in the anthology; Perec contributed "Dos, caddy d'aisselles" to the homage to Queneau originally published as volume 4 in the library. The final entry in this anthology, originally Oulipo's volume 16, is also a collective effort. Entitled *La Cantatrice sauve* (a phonetic pun on the title of Eugène Ionesco's play *La Cantatrice chauve*–a pun which could be rendered in a rough equivalent as The Bold Soprano), it is a series of one hundred homophonic exercises on the name Montserrat Caballé, the celebrated, anthroponymically

bizarre diva. In 1987 the Editions Ramsay published a two-volume anthology, comprising volumes 1-37 of the *Bibliothèque oulipienne*.

Théâtre (1981) includes two plays. *L'Augmentation, ou Comment, quelles que soient les conditions sanitaires, psychologiques, climatiques, économiques ou autres, mettre le maximum de chances de son côté en demandant à votre chef de service un réadjustement de votre salaire* (The Raise, or How, Whatever the Sanitary, Psychological, Climatic, Economic, or Other Conditions, To Maximize Your Chances When Asking Your Boss for an Adjustment of Your Salary) was first performed at the Théâtre de la Gaîté-Montparnasse on 26 February 1970. It chronicles the foredoomed efforts of an office worker as he struggles up his company's organigram asking for a raise. *La Poche Parmentier* (The Parmentier Pocket), first performed at the Théâtre de Nice on 12 February 1974, is a play about potatoes and theater. Pastiche and parody, it sounds a convincing death knell for the theater of the absurd.

Théâtre was the last of Georges Perec's major books published during his lifetime. In the period preceding his death, he was at work on a novel entitled "53 Jours" (53 Days); he gave the final draft of the first half of this bipartite text to his publisher shortly before he died. Since then, three books have been published. The first, *Epithalames* (Epithalamia, 1982), appeared thirteen days after Perec's death as volume 19 in the Bibliothèque Oulipienne. As its title suggests, it is a collection of marriage poems composed for friends. The structural technique used in all of them is what Perec called the "Beau Présent" (The Handsome Present One, in contrast to La Belle Absente); here, only those letters occurring in the names of the bride and groom are used in the poems, literal fusion in the verbal text auguring spiritual fusion in married life.

Tentative d'épuisement d'un lieu parisien (Toward the Exhaustion of a Place in Paris, 1982) republishes in book form a text that initially appeared in the journal *Cause Commune* in 1975. It reflects an abandoned project called "Les Lieux" (Places) that Perec began in 1969. Choosing twelve places in Paris where he had lived or which held some strong association for him, he undertook to describe two of them each month, one from memory, and one directly, by actually going to the place and describing what he saw there. The entire project was to have taken twelve years; each place would be described twenty-four times. Perec relied on an algorithm similar to the one used in *La Vie mode d'emploi*, the *Orthogonal Latin Bi-Square Order Twelve*, in order to organize the experiment such that each place would be described in each month of the year (once from memory and once "live"), and that no pair of places would ever be described in the same month. The project would thus unite three of Perec's major concerns: the sociology of the quotidian, autobiography, and experimentalist writing. For a variety of reasons, Perec renounced the project in 1975. *Tentative d'épuisement d'un lieu parisien* assembles nine exercises in "live" description of the Place Saint-Sulpice.

Penser/Classer (To Think/To Classify, 1985) recuperates and arranges thirteen short pieces published in more ephemeral form (newspapers, journals) between 1976 and 1982. Perec's fascination with the minute runs throughout "Notes concernant les objets qui sont sur ma table de travail" (Notes on the Objects Sitting on My Desk); "Considérations sur les lunettes" (Considerations on Eyeglasses) is an exhaustive, comic foray into the banal; "Lire: Esquisse socio-physiologique" (Reading: A Socio-Physiological Sketch) is a parodic compendium of some of the most egregiously trivial commonplaces of sociological analysis. More sober intent is apparent in "Les Lieux d'une ruse" (Places of a Ruse), which deals with his four-year period of psychoanalysis. In "Notes sur ce que je cherche" (Notes on What I Seek), Perec reflects upon his literary enterprise, invoking a recurrent image in his writings as a totalizing metaphor, a figure of his own work as well as of the literary tradition that nourished him; Perec's words may serve any discussion of his work as a fitting point of closure: "Je sens confusément que les livres que j'ai écrits s'inscrivent, prennent leur sens dans une image globale que je me fais de la littérature, mais il me semble que je ne pourrai jamais saisir précisément cette image, qu'elle est pour moi un au-delà de l'écriture, un 'pourquoi j'écris' auquel je ne peux répondre qu'en écrivant, différant sans cesse l'instant même où, cessant d'écrire, cette image deviendrait visible, comme un puzzle inexorablement achevé" (I feel vaguely that the books I have written inscribe themselves and take on meaning in a global image of literature that I conceive, but it seems to me that I will never be able to seize this image precisely, that it is, for me, something beyond writing, a "why I write" to which I can respond only by writing, constantly deferring the very instant when, ceasing to write, this image would become visible, like an inexorably finished puzzle).

References:

Arc, special issue on Perec, 76 (Summer 1979);

Claude Burgelin, *Georges Perec* (Paris: Seuil, 1988);

Cahiers Georges Perec, 1 number to date (1985-);

Littératures, special issue on Perec, 7 (Spring 1983);

Magazine Littéraire, special issue on Perec, no. 193 (March 1983);

Warren F. Motte, Jr., *The Poetics of Experiment: A Study of the Work of Georges Perec* (Lexington, Ky: French Forum Monographs, 1984);

Oulipo, *A Georges Perec* (Paris: Bibliothèque Oulipienne, 1984);

John Pedersen, *Perec ou les textes croisés* (Copenhagen: Revue Romane, 1985);

Jean-Michel Raynaud, *Pour un Perec lettré, chiffré* (Lille: Presses Universitaires de Lille, 1987);

Paul Schwartz, *Georges Perec: Traces of His Passage* (Birmingham, Ala.: Summa Publications, 1988).

Robert Pinget

(19 July 1919-)

Robert M. Henkels, Jr.
Auburn University

BOOKS: *Entre Fantoine et Agapa* (Jarnac: Tour de Feu, 1951); translated by Barbara Wright as *Between Fantoine and Agapa* (New York: Red Dust, 1982);

Mahu ou le matériau (Paris: Robert Laffont, 1952); translated by Alan Sheridan-Smith as *Mahu or The Material* (London: Calder & Boyars, 1967);

Le Renard et la boussole (Paris: Gallimard, 1953);

Graal Flibuste (Paris: Editions de Minuit, 1956; enlarged edition, 1966);

Baga (Paris: Editions de Minuit, 1958); translated by John Stevenson (London: Calder & Boyars, 1967);

Le Fiston (Paris: Editions de Minuit, 1959); translated by Richard Howard as *Monsieur Levert* (New York: Grove, 1961); translated by Richard N. Coe as *No Answer* (London: Calder, 1961);

Lettre morte (Paris: Editions de Minuit, 1959); translated by Barbara Bray as *Dead Letter* in *Plays*, volume 1 (1963);

La Manivelle, bilingual edition, with English translation as *The Old Tune* by Samuel Beckett (Paris: Editions de Minuit, 1960);

Clope au dossier (Paris: Editions de Minuit, 1961); translated by Bray as *Clope* in *Plays*, volume 1 (1963);

Ici ou ailleurs, suivi de Architruc et de L'Hypothèse (Paris: Editions de Minuit, 1961); *Architruc* and *L'Hypothèse (The Hypothesis)* translated by Bray in *Plays*, volume 2 (1967);

L'Inquisitoire (Paris: Editions de Minuit, 1962); translated by Donald Watson as *The Inquisitory* (London: Calder & Boyars, 1966; New York: Grove Press, 1967);

Plays, 2 volumes, translated by Bray and Beckett (London: Calder, 1963, 1967); republished as *Three Plays* (New York: Hill & Wang, 1966, 1967)–volume 1 comprises *La Manivelle, Clope au dossier*, and *Lettre morte*; volume 2, *Architruc, Autour de Mortin*, and *L'Hypothèse*;

Autour de Mortin (Paris: Editions de Minuit, 1965); translated by Bray as *About Mortin* in *Plays*, volume 2 (1967);

Quelqu'un (Paris: Editions de Minuit, 1965); translated by Wright as *Someone* (New York: Red Dust, 1984);

Le Libera (Paris: Editions de Minuit, 1968); translated by Wright as *The Libera me domine* (London: Calder & Boyars, 1972; New York: Red Dust, 1978);

Passacaille (Paris: Editions de Minuit, 1969); translated by Wright as *Recurrent Melody* (London: Calder & Boyars, 1975); republished as *Passcaglia* (New York: Red Dust, 1978);

Identité, suivi de Abel et Bela (Paris: Editions de Minuit, 1971);

Fable (Paris: Editions de Minuit, 1971); translated by Wright (London: Calder, 1980; New York: Red Dust, 1980);

Paralchimie. Suivie de Architruc. L'Hypothèse. Nuit. (Paris: Editions de Minuit, 1973);

Cette voix (Paris: Editions de Minuit, 1975); translated by Wright as *That Voice* (New York: Red Dust, 1982);

L'Apocryphe (Paris: Editions de Minuit, 1980);

Monsieur Songe (Paris: Editions de Minuit, 1982);

Le Harnais (Paris: Editions de Minuit, 1984);

Charrue (Paris: Editions de Minuit, 1985);

Un Testament bizarre, suivi de Mortin pas mort; Dictée; Sophisme et sadisme; Le Chrysanthème, Lusie (Paris: Editions de Minuit, 1986);

L'Ennemi (Paris: Editions de Minuit, 1987).

PLAY PRODUCTIONS: *Lettre morte*, Paris, TNP-Théâtre Récamier, 22 March 1960;

Ici ou ailleurs, in German, translated by Gerda Scheffel, Zurich, Grand Theatre, 1961;

Architruc, Paris, Comédie de Paris, 5 August 1962;

La Manivelle, Paris, Comédie de Paris, 5 August 1962;

L'Hypothèse, Paris, Odéon-Théâtre de France, 7 March 1966;

Abel et Bella, Paris, Café-Théâtre de l'Absidiole, January 1971;

Identité, Paris, Petit Odéon, November 1972.

In literature and the arts, as in history, the vital process of rebellion and regeneration needs to be activated by cataclysmic events. Just as World War I released the creative energies channeled into dada and surrealism, post-World War II Europe saw a vigorous rejection of narrative conventions dealing with character, time, and space that coalesced in the French New Novel beginning in the 1950s and 1960s. Like the other novelists published by Editions de Minuit with whom he is frequently compared, Robert Pinget found the techniques of the nineteenth-century narrative inadequate to a vision of man informed by the discoveries of Einstein, Jung, and Joyce. He set out in his own way to reconsider and reexpress man's relationship to himself, to the world, and to language.

Praised by his colleagues Alain Robbe-Grillet, Claude Simon, and Nathalie Sarraute as a writer's writer; author of a novel described by Samuel Beckett as "one of the most important books of the last twenty years"; hailed by John Updike as "one of the noblest figures in world literature," Pinget has long been recognized by critics as one of the towering figures of the New Novel. For although the sales of the works of these eight or ten demanding writers have been small, the interest in their work has been extraordinary, resulting in the award of two Nobel prizes (to Samuel Beckett and Claude Simon) over a period of the last twenty years. Pinget's mastery has grown and developed during a productive career spanning thirty-five years. Whereas other experimental novelists have fallen silent, Pinget's voice rings ever clearer, particularly in *L'Apocryphe* (Apocrypha, 1980), his twentieth book, which many consider his best. In addition to this record of sustained creative energy and ingenuity Pinget stands out as one of the most rewarding of the New Novelists for three reasons. His skill as a parodist and his keen sense of humor cause his writing to oscillate between the nineteenth-century conventions he questions and the forms of self-expression he is striving to create, thus giving the reader the impression that he is in a very real sense "present at the creation" as Pinget's texts are written. Pinget has also given his work the format of an expanding, cyclical novel, thus giving the reader the opportunity to observe his characteristic themes and techniques as they apply to and develop

around a core of recurring material. Finally, because Pinget's central theme has been the act of writing (which in his case serves as a metaphor for the quest to find order and transcendent meaning), many of his concerns anticipate and are best understood in relation to the so-called *nouvelle critique* that has emerged in France over the last twenty years.

Some time ago Pinget began systematically destroying his papers, tearing up notes, and tossing yellowed correspondence into the huge fireplace of his sixteenth-century farmhouse. This relentless annihilation of personal memorabilia and professional papers has caused great consternation to his prospective biographers and literary heirs. But in this case life is simply imitating art, for one of the situations to which Pinget returns with glee and horror in his fiction is the failed attempt of a dead author's surviving friends and family to reconstruct the departed's life or to piece together one of his lost or incomplete manuscripts for posthumous publication. From the plumes of smoke issuing from Pinget's chimney near Amboise, one judges that such a fate will never befall him. To Pinget, for whom the act of putting words on paper is at once a vital necessity and a metaphor for the human predicament, writing is everything and everything is writing. There is nothing else–save the ultimately terrifying blank page of death. Guarded in his autocritical comments, reluctant to part with his manuscripts (although he did sell one to buy a cello), Pinget has long considered his fiction as the sole expression of his life. He has thus suppressed biographical documents as superfluous and irrelevant.

Yet, strange as it may seem, Pinget's obsession with the writer's quest makes it possible, even revealing, to consider the corpus of his work as a sort of stylized spiritual autobiography. This approach to Pinget's fiction must be used with some caution, however, because the "facts" known about him are of interest to Pinget (and, because of his obliteration of the biographical record, to us) only as they affect the written record of his work.

Pinget was born 19 July 1919 into a comfortable Catholic middle-class family in Geneva. He studied at the Collège de Genève and at the school of law, where he took a *licence*. According to Bettina L. Knapp (*French Review*, March 1969), after his law studies he moved to Paris, where in the late 1940s he studied painting as a pupil of Souverbie and acquired a certain renown as an artist. Pinget, who enjoys a long-standing friendship with Samuel Beckett, has written radio plays for the BBC and for Radio Stuttgart; his work for the theater has been performed by the Comédie-Française. He has traveled extensively and spent time working on a kibbutz in Israel. He has never married.

In considering Pinget's writing as a sort of oblique autobiography of the artist, one might note, for example, that his stubborn search for the precise word seems to reflect his early training in the law. The fact that he has never married may explain the importance in his writing of the themes of the lost letter and the adopted child. His fascination with painting appears in his work in detailed descriptive passages, and his delight with baroque music is perhaps recalled by the fuguelike structures of the later works. Finally, Pinget's keen interest in Jung, Henri Michaux, Max Jacob, and Raymond Roussel has led him to a vision of the author as alchemist of words, or re-sayer of what can never completely be said. For the sake of clarity, Pinget's work can be divided into three periods: the early novels, 1951-1958; those of the "middle period," 1959-1967; and those since 1968.

When Pinget's first books began to appear in the early 1950s, existentialism and existentialist writers dominated the Parisian literary scene. Thanks largely to the influence of Sartre it was widely accepted that writers had a moral obligation to involve themselves in the political issues of the day and to express their political convictions in their work. Sartre and Camus dealt frequently with the themes of alienation and the absurd. Stated very simply, the existentialists wrote of a world without transcendent order or purpose. In their view, because man is endowed with reason and because his quest for some kind of logic or pattern in the chance occurrences of daily life must end in failure, he is condemned to live in and accept the absurd as a permanent condition over which he has no control but against which, as a logical being, he must rebel. Curiously enough, however, Sartre and Camus express this absurdist viewpoint through rational literary forms and structures shaped by nineteenth-century science which had been based on the very opposite premise that the natural order is comprehensible and predictable; the literary corollary of this posture is that a text must "make sense" to the reader.

Pinget's first books set out in directions diametrically opposed in content and form to these political and aesthetic trends. His writing was (and has remained) resolutely apolitical. As for the form of his work, although Pinget describes an irrational world with no discernible purpose or pattern, the way in which his stories are told emphasizes irrationality. The irrational and unpredictable are not absurdist themes grafted onto logically comprehensible forms. They have become an organic part of the writing itself. Such stock-in-trade devices of the so-called well-made novel as chronological time, linear narration, cause and effect, a sure sense of place, and predictable psychology (all common in the work of Sartre and Camus) are gently spoofed and abandoned.

Pinget's first volume, *Entre Fantoine et Agapa* (1951; translated as *Between Fantoine and Agapa*, 1982), emerges as a zesty, fanciful parody of the conventional short story. Freedom of association and the generative force of the unfettered imagination serve as reigning principles in Pinget's world. Figures of speech take on flesh and blood. Words become characters. People turn into things. Objects become human. In short order Pinget places the reader in a zone where the conscious and the unconscious do cartwheels. The dictionary becomes not a restrictive, normative definer of terms but a cornucopia of nonrational linkages. In his first venture into print Pinget produces a prose that has much of the muscular verve and vitality of Rabelais, and his flights of fancy recall the writings of Lewis Carroll, Jacob, and Michaux at their most whimsical.

Mahu ou le matériau (1952; translated as *Mahu or The Material*, 1967) expands the author's narrative focus from the short story to the novel. Written in two parts, this work in its first section exposes the limits of the genre as it existed in the "well-made" tradition through the transparent device of a series of would-be novelists who use the conventions of the traditional novel so heavy-handedly that their artificiality becomes amusingly apparent. The second half centers on a series of questions posed helter-skelter by Mahu, the narrator, who describes his prose experiments as "warm-up scales" for the efforts to come. In his third novel, *Le Renard et la boussole* (The Fox and the Compass, 1953), Pinget combines a parody of the voyage narrative with his more free-flowing experiments in verbal association. The book contains a novel within a novel (rather like André Gide's *Paludes* [*Marshlands*, 1895]). It is a device which Pinget will use in practically every narrative after this one. On the one hand, the novel recounts the journey to the Middle East of two characters, David and Renard. On the other, it describes the would-be narrator's failure to squeeze that story into adequate expression in words. The limits of language and of literary conventions become again the novel's subject and object.

Graal Flibuste (the title of this 1956 novel is virtually untranslatable) begins with a cautionary chapter that transcribes the blurry impressions of a drunkard. The man's vision comes in and out of focus. This chapter should serve as fair warning to the unwary that the journal to follow will recount a voyage to a world in which the norms and distinctions of everyday life do not apply. Indeed, *Graal Flibuste* unfolds as the travel journal of an explorer to an imagined world like that described in *Alice in Wonderland* or Savinien Cyrano de Bergerac's *L'Autre Monde; ou, Les Etats et empires de la lune et du soleil* (*Voyages to the Moon and the Sun*). The title "character" Graal Flibuste reigns as deus ex machina of this bizarre land. Momentarily putting aside the unpredictable quality of the introductory chapter, the narrator sets out to write his impressions of this new land in the bland, objective tone and with the keen attention to detail of a nineteenth-century naturalist reminiscent of Charles Darwin. It is this tension between the earnest attempt to write things down fully and completely and the intrusion of such irrational or suprarational elements as sound association, wordplay, and chance that gives the book its vitality and freshness. As the title indicates with its overtones of the Grail Quest ("graal") and piratical adventures ("flibuste/flibustier" [buccaneer]), the novel moves back and forth between the known and the unknown, trundling on to the next mystery once the last one has been more or less elucidated. When the narrator launches into an enumeration of the members of Graal Flibuste's family tree, the pseudoscientific tone of his journal is quickly undermined by the sounds and the combinations of sounds of the names that burp and belch across the page:

> Affaful enfanta [begat] Boute-Boute.
> Boute-Boute enfanta Lapa.
> Lapa enfanta Miamsk.
> Miamsk enfanta Loin.
> Loin enfanta Peute.
> Peute enfanta Peute-Peute.

As in Rabelais's genealogies the wheezes, sneezes, puns, and translingual puns produced by the list of names casts doubt on the accuracy of the very process of naming, and if read aloud, the geneal-

ogy sounds like a vintage motor car being started after a long rest in the garage.

Similarly Pinget's flora and fauna spring to life as baffling but arresting hybrids. The recognizable first parts of their names represent the familiar realm of everyday reality and, by extension, the novel's straightforward narrative impulse. But the second element calls upon the poetic imagination and acts out the text's baroque digressions and elaborations. The traveler does not encounter "écureuils" (squirrels) but "écureuils-bougies" (squirrel-candles); not "oublieuses" (forget-me-nots), but "oublieuses d'amertume" (forget-me-ills); not "merles" (blackbirds) but "merles-blancs" (white-blackbirds). Like the hyphens in the samples of inventive nomenclature, Pinget's prose serves a mediating function between a world of prosaic fact and a no less real domain of poetic fancy. The use of hyphens expresses, simultaneously the desire to name, to order and to classify, and the equally valid realization that the process of naming is ephemeral and arbitrary. On a more general level of discourse the narrative episodes of the voyager's account are interspersed with shaggy-dog stories, run-on non-sequitur sequences, and exhaustingly complete descriptions in which writing the description becomes an end in itself unrelated to the advancement of the plot or any other aspect of the narrator. Such passages are clearly intended to block linear development of the story line and to send it off in a series of bifurcations and arabesques. It is fitting, therefore, that the last chapter of the 1966 enlarged edition of the novel ends with a long description of the sculptural details that embellish a huge, mysterious triumphal arch. As the narrator expands his detailed account of the figures and designs that cram each cranny of the structure with suggestive, enigmatic symbols, it becomes evident that his description (and the entire account of the kingdom of Graal Flibuste as well) could go on forever. There can be no end to the narrator's journal since words can never capture completely the wonders of this or any other world. At this point in the narrative, that is, the elaboration of a seemingly infinitely expandable account of a monument opening onto an uncharted horizon, the text simply comes to a halt. Thus the end of the narrative praises and calls into question the spontaneous nature of the creative act and the validity of *Graal Flibuste* itself.

Pinget applies his tongue-in-cheek parody technique to the genre of the "mémoire" in *Baga* (1958; translated into English, 1967), his fifth novel. As in many of his books, the title here works by indirection. The novel's protagonist is not in fact Baga but rather Architruc, the king of a run-down mythical kingdom whom Baga serves as prime minister and confidant. In *Baga* the voyage of discovery is directed inward to the search for the self. Le Roi Architruc (King Thingamajig) seeks his identity through a series of daydreams and flights of fancy. But after projecting himself into a succession of avatars (warrior-king, adoptive parent, hermit, postulant nun) he ends his tale no surer of who he is than when he took up his pen.

The compressed prose of Pinget's first period crackles with the free-wheeling associations more usually found in poetry. The lack of conventional punctuation, the brevity of the chapters, and the catch-as-catch-can transitions heighten this feeling. Pinget himself was aware of this poetic effect. He has stated that what he was looking for when he began writing was to convey a poetic view of things firmly grounded in the prosaic. To keep his imaginative sentences and paragraphs earthbound, Pinget has harnessed his flights of fancy by giving his work the structure of prose narration. Unconventional though they may be, Pinget's early tales and novels all have a beginning, a middle, and a not-quite-end, trailing off so abruptly that their final pages call into question the very notion that anything is ever completed or fully expressed. Nothing in Pinget's fictional province is ever truly finished because everything and anything is subject to recurrence from one book to the next. Nothing can be stated, represented, or described once and for all since everything can be said again (and again . . .). Many characters and place names recur throughout Pinget's work. In cyclical novels of the nineteenth century (particularly Balzac's *Comédie humaine*) repeated elements are more clearly defined each time they appear. In Pinget's cycle each recurrent item appears in slightly altered form, thus satisfying the demands of poetry and prose.

The two-part structure of *Mahu ou le matériau* reflects Pinget's fascination with the ebb and flow of recurrence and alteration. Just as Mahu's musings rework and undermine the assertions advanced by his conventional fellow novelists in the first part of *Mahu ou le matériau*, the adventurous "warm-up scales" of Pinget's vigorous, zestful first period will be taken up and altered in the works to come. Like Pinget's "characters" who, as Robbe-Grillet remarked, are not characters in the accepted sense of the word but rather

"des *créations pures* qui ne relèvent que de l'esprit de création" (*pure creatures* who take shape purely from the spirit of creativity), the contents, themes, and techniques of Pinget's early works recur later but in increasingly sober tones.

To characterize the texts of Pinget's early period as "exercises" is not to relegate them to a position of minor importance. These texts which lay the groundwork for the books to come were well received by the critics. Robbe-Grillet wrote an extremely favorable review of *Mahu ou le matériau*, which he included in his collection of theoretical essays *Pour un nouveau roman* (*For a New Novel*, 1953), the unofficial manifesto of the New Novel group. Indeed, Robbe-Grillet's enthusiasm for Pinget's early work brought Pinget to Editions de Minuit, which became his publisher in 1956, with *Graal Flibuste*. His supralogical romps dramatize a curious paradox: that language is at the same time open to multiple associations and inadequate to express anything completely. When a word is bound by narrow dictionary definitions, it becomes a dead cipher. And yet when a word or phrase can trigger so many associations that it seems without limit, it means nothing. From the publication of *Mahu ou le matériau* on, Pinget was unequivocally associated with the New Novel group.

Pinget believes that every affirmation implies its own contradiction–whence the lack of closure in his novels and the reappearance of material from one book to the next. As his writing gained in confidence and scope, Pinget applied the same paradoxical principle to a variety of broader narrative structures and genres, specifically the epistolary novel and the detective story. The novel of letters, so popular in the eighteenth century, is based on the assumptions (dubious at best to Pinget) that a carefully reasoned written exchange is an adequate, even an elegant, means of communication and that the correspondents will understand each other through words. Pinget's second target for parody, the detective story, may be considered as the transposition in fictional terms of a rationalistic, Cartesian worldview in which everything in the text is there for a reason. Both genres affirm implicit faith in the efficacy of the written word. Both led Pinget to craft his most amusing and troubling parodies of linear narration.

Le Fiston (1959; translated as *Monsieur Levert* in the United States and as *No Answer* in Great Britain, 1961) is told through what appear at first to be successive drafts of a letter. The narrator, M.

Levert, seems to be writing to his runaway son to convince him to return home. Each draft of this letter that will neither be completed nor sent begins with a description of the burial of the local shoemaker's daughter, Marie Chinze. What does it have to do with the purpose of his letter? Familiar with the mystery-story genre in which all narrative threads will eventually "make sense," the reader begins almost unconsciously to weave together the disparate elements. To explain Levert's preoccupation, one might consider the possibility–hinted at by Sophie Narre, a character whose name evokes the verb *narrer* (to narrate)– that Levert had a clandestine affair with Mme Chinze and that Marie was their illegitimate daughter. Suppose also that Levert's son and Marie fell in love. Suppose finally that when they learned they were half brother and sister the boy left town never to return and the girl died of a broken heart. But wait. Each hypothesis is undone or qualified by Pinget's use of repetition, contradiction, ambiguous pronouns, the conditional tense, and other such rhetorical devices. No explanation will do because Levert begins writing his account again, and again–and again.

Assume then that his tortuous drafts are not to be taken literally but that they represent the writer's compulsion to state what can never be completely and finally said. The first edition of *Le Fiston* was printed without page numbers, and this elimination of conventional and convenient points of reference obliged the reader to thrash about in a sea of words like M. Levert writing his drafts and Pinget writing *Le Fiston*. Perhaps too Levert's attempt reflects Pinget's struggle to cast a net of words over such eternal mysteries as life, death, creativity, and aging. Like a Chinese box, the narrative opens into stories within stories. No definitive answers are provided, but neither Pinget nor Levert may abandon his attempt since, as the novel's last words proclaim, "En dehors de ce qui est écrit c'est la mort" (Outside of what is written there lies only death).

Clope au dossier (1961), in many ways Pinget's most hermetic book, purports to recount, in conversations among the patrons at a café, the unsuccessful attempt to unearth a legal brief or to reconstruct the events of a day in order to free the hermit, Clope, from suspicion of murder. Transitionless shifts cause the "facts" in the narrative to run together in a blur until writing itself becomes the narrative's subject and object. *Clope au dossier* contains the earliest and one

of the most fully developed variations on the theme of the search for the lost manuscript. In this case it is the dossier which may or may not have been tossed into a well, making a dull, "clope" sound as it sank from view. Although *Clope au dossier* is subtitled *roman*, it was translated for English-speaking audiences, as *Clope*, in volume one of Pinget's *Plays* (1963).

Quelqu'un (1965; translated as *Someone*, 1984) centers around another kind of manuscript. The absentminded narrator has mislaid notes he needs to finish a botanical treatise. He runs over the various events of the day trying to jog his memory, but his search will be to no avail. The act of remembering brings forth a touching narrative during which the narrator evokes among other things his relationships with the tenants of his boardinghouse and his friendship with the idiot orphan boy Fonfon. The theme of failed communication reappears. This time, however, the narrator tries to give himself a feeling of identity by telling a coherent story. As in *Le Fiston*, that attempt ends in failure. The notes are never found, and Fonfon is taken away. The narrator remains abjectly unsure of himself and completely alone.

L'Inquisitoire (1962; translated as *The Inquisitory*, 1966), Pinget's magnum opus of the period 1959-1967, grew out of a bizarre wager between the author and his publisher, Jérôme Lindon. Pinget's publisher had expressed concern that his books seemed to be suffering from a sort of "literary anorexia"–they were getting thinner and thinner. So Pinget bet him that he could bring in a five-hundred-page manuscript in six months. He then sat down, wrote day and night for six months, and did precisely that. "Yes or no answer," the novel begins. A voice that seems to belong to an investigator of some kind badgers an old, half-deaf retired servant for information about goings-on at his employer's home. The entire book is structured in question and answer form. As the questioner and the old man exchange queries and replies, a seemingly endless set of names, places, and events (some from previous Pinget books; others new) pours forth. The narrative, half inquisition, half repository, hones in on a series of scandals, orgies, tax frauds, and drug deals. Any one of them would explain the questioner's aggressive tone and the old man's evasiveness. But it gradually dawns on the reader that the book's investigative structure is a Chinese puzzle, another metaphor for the author's solitary task of creation. The opening admonitory

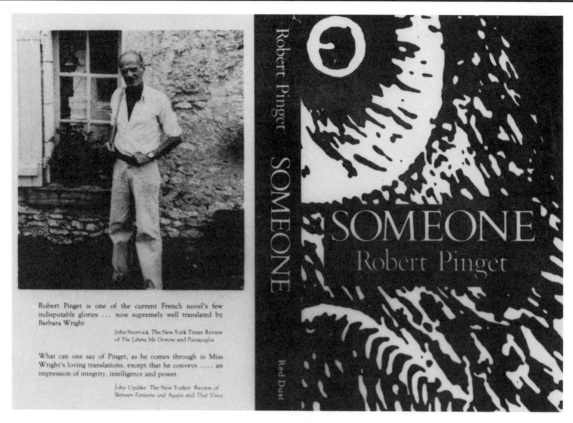

Dust jacket for Barbara Wright's translation of Quelqu'un, *Pinget's 1965 novel detailing the absentminded narrator's attempt to reconstruct the immediate past and find his lost notes for a botanical treatise*

phrase "yes or no answer" is spoken not only by the inquisitor but also by Robert Pinget to Robert Pinget as he sits at the typewriter and pecks out the manuscript that will become *L'Inquisitoire*.

The longest and most extensively developed of Pinget's novels, *L'Inquisitoire* marks a turning point of sorts in his career. Recognized by critics as his most ambitious and most successful work, the novel barely missed winning the Prix Fémina, one of France's most prestigious literary awards. Instead it received the Prix des Critiques as a sort of consolation prize. Three years later, as if in recognition of the near miss in 1963, the selection committee for the Fémina gave the prize to *Quelqu'un*.

This award proved to be a curse and a blessing for Pinget. The awarding of the Prix Fémina is watched with attention by the French reading public. It is almost a ritual for middle-class readers to pick up a copy of the year's prizewinner to read on vacation. French readers in droves stuffed copies of *Quelqu'un* into their suitcases, assuming it would provide light vacation reading. Needless to say most were disappointed. Although it is one of Pinget's most accessible works,

funny, touching, and beautifully written, many were not willing to perform the close reading required to appreciate the novel, and they expressed their disappointment most volubly in a spate of angry postcards and letters to Editions de Minuit.

Pinget is far from being the only major figure in contemporary French letters praised by respected critics who has failed to attract large numbers of readers. Beckett's novels, for example, are read mainly by academics, and in 1985, when Claude Simon, another of the New Novel group, won the Nobel Prize for Literature, the French media were hard-pressed to find prominent intellectuals well enough acquainted with his work to comment for French television.

The divergence between critical interest and public indifference has been influential in shaping Pinget's writing. The publication of *Quelqu'un* showed him that his work would never appeal to a large audience, and that fact hurt and disappointed him, deepening the theme of the misunderstood author. Stung by the low sales figures of *Quelqu'un*, Pinget briefly turned his attention to writing for the theater in the late 1960s, but he never completely abandoned prose narrative and gradually worked his way back to it. The experience with *Quelqu'un* helped sharpen Pinget's concentration on refining his themes and techniques without worrying about reader appeal. Someone once wrote that easy writing makes poor reading. Pinget's work is not easy to read, but it rewards the reader in direct proportion to his effort. It is difficult to imagine that he would have achieved as much had he been concerned with popular acclaim.

Pinget has described the creative process through which his narratives come to being as the identification of one of the many tones making up his own voice and the fullest possible expression of that inner voice through a written text. By 1968 Pinget had gone through his sometimes exuberant warm-up scales. In the early 1970s he found his own voice and expressed himself with growing clarity and urgency in books whose formal mastery and unsparing demands validate the quest begun with *Entre Fantoine et Agapa*. Over the years Pinget has become even more concerned with how his books are written than with what they have to say, reflecting the circumstance that, without realizing it, one listens at least as much to how voices sound as to what they say. In some respects the structures of his narratives have come to resemble the forms of baroque music.

In retrospect *Le Libera* (1968; translated as *The Libera me domine*, 1972) may be seen to herald this shift of direction. The text wheels from one scandal to another: a child killed in a traffic accident, a child molested and murdered, Mlle Lorpailleur's mad ravings, Mortin's futile attempts to write about it all. In a 1968 issue of *Critique* Tony Duvert wrote of this book that the conflict of the demands of the novel within the novel condemns the narrative to "un conflit perpétuel (et du reste passionnant) entre les exigences de conventions non avenues et les procédés perturbateurs qui prennent appui sur elles" (a perpetual [and also engrossing] conflict between the requirements of cancelled-out conventions and the disturbing forms growing out of them). The book ends with a series of suggested alternative developments to the narrative lines already suggested, a seemingly endlessly expandable series of "ors" and "buts." In the final pages, a litany of entreaty, the "Libera me Domine," from the Prayer for the Dead, hovers over the fiasco of interchangeable alternatives. A faint hope arises that something may one day break the circle of idle chatter and transcend it. But that transformation could come only at the dreadful moment of silence feared as death. Until then the chatter of gossip and story telling continues, and the narrative records it in its waves of contradictory verbiage.

Pinget's 1969 novel, *Passacaille* (translated in Great Britain as *Recurrent Melody*, 1975, and in the United States as *Passcaglia*, 1978), speaks about many things: the loneliness of an author at his desk in the country in winter, a mutilated body discovered on a manure pile, a broken clock, a mysterious stranger's comings and goings around the village. *Fable* (1971; translated, 1980) deals with passion in the physical, romantic, and religious sense. Its prose weaves together themes and images that touch upon the despair of lost love.

Cette voix (1975; translated as *That Voice*, 1982) moves back and forth among such considerations as a solitary writer living like a hermit in the village cemetery, the layout of headstones in the graveyard, women gossiping at the outdoor market, the training of the writer's young disciple, the murder of the old recluse at his home, the grape harvests in October, painful efforts to make sense of the writer's unfinished manuscript, efforts to have it published posthumously, the slate on which the author feverishly writes and erases his observations, All Saints' Day, a yellowed letter saved from the past, the struggle over the old writer's will. Pinget originally chose "L'Amnase" (The Amnesis) as the book's title. The term *amnesis* comes from psychoanalysis and describes the detailed recollection required as part of the healing process in therapy. The anecdotal fragments of *Cette voix* serve as analogues to the bits and pieces from the past recalled in analysis. Writing is another sort of amnesis because recall is deeply involved in the recurrence of themes, words, and events that bring Pinget's chronicle into being. They are Pinget's raw material, and he reworks them in new variations. Recurrence becomes the generative energy of the text.

That recurrence takes several patterns in Pinget's novels published since 1968. He moves farther from the nonsystematic repetition of leitmotivs and themes of earlier books. Recurrence may be partial and random, a sort of sporadic recapitulation as in *Le Libera*. It may also take the form of total recall in reverse order by which the return begins toward the middle of the book and works back to the beginning, as in *L'Apocryphe* where Pinget goes back over material initially presented in the first part of the book serially and completely. Parts 1 and 2 of *L'Apocryphe* begin with a description of a painting of a shepherd on an antique shard of Greek pottery. Then they work back and forth among several Pinget commonplaces: the daily routine of the aging writer, town gossip, conjecture over the cause of the old recluse's death, the comings and goings of a mysterious prowler, quarrels over the old writer's will, attempts to piece together the scraps of his unfinished manuscript. The repetition is not word for word or incident for incident. Like the melodies in baroque music, Pinget's subtle alternations make the overall pattern of return seem as inevitable as the succession of the seasons.

As each spring is fresh and new yet part of past springs, so it is with the pattern of returns in the Pingetian narrative. Elements lose none of their individuality for taking place in a recurrent cycle. As Pinget has noted, the repetition of themes with modifications, distortions, and variations undermines the reader's expectations and creates the impression that the book is being composed, and decomposed, before his very eyes. The reader then has become the writer, or at least the distance between them has been reduced to a minimum.

The impression of a common quest underlying all of Pinget's work is heightened for the reader acquainted with his writing for the theater and the diarylike texts he published from 1982 to 1985. The latter, *Monsieur Songe* (Mister Dream), *Le Harnais* (The Harness), and *Charrue* (Plow), may be best understood as pieces incidental to the composition of *Cette voix* and *L'Apocryphe*, much like self-deprecating and stylized variants of the *Journal* Gide published concurrently with *Les Faux-Monnayeurs* (*The Counterfeiters*, 1925). Pinget's plays are worth reading in their own right, although here, as in his fiction, the central theme is the act of writing and the primary structural and stylistic device is recurrence. Like his fiction, too, Pinget's dramatic work went against a marked literary trend. French theater of the 1950s and 1960s had become increasingly kinetic, oriented toward action. Peter Wiess's *Marat/Sade* (1966), a great financial and critical success from this period, relied heavily on crowd scenes, movement, and gesture. In the final scene the criminally insane charge the audience, separated from them only by a barrier of intertwined ropes, thus illustrating in kinetic terms that the barrier between the sane and the insane comes down to the exclusion imposed by the state. Working against

this current, Pinget's plays, like those of the French classical period, are essentially verbal.

Architruc (1961; translated in *Plays*, 1967), his most frequently performed play, is a one-acter. Loosely adapted from *Baga*, the main action shows how Prime Minister Baga plays at charades to amuse his bored master until Death comes on stage to strike Baga dead. *L'Hypothèse* (1961; translated as *The Hypothesis* in *Plays*, 1967), another one-act play, makes effective use of rear projection of slides and silent film to dramatize the struggle of Mortin, a writer, to complete his manuscript or to piece together its fragments. *La Manivelle* (published in 1960 in a bilingual edition that includes Beckett's skillful translation, *The Old Tune*) blends a darkly comic dialogue between duffers with defective memories from *Clope au dossier*. As in the genealogy in *Graal Flibuste*, their remembrances stumble over mutual misunderstandings in a hilarious exercise in language slowly silencing itself. In *Paralchimie* (1973), of which the title is a neologism formed from the Greek *para*, which can mean "closely resembling," and the French word for alchemy, Mortin, again the principal character, searches for a science of words that will make them reveal their magic possibilities. In *Autour de Mortin* (1965; translated as *About Mortin* in *Plays*, 1967) and *Un Testament bizarre* (1986) Pinget has adapted the radio play to his fascination with recurrence by presenting a series of interviews with friends, neighbors, and acquaintances of the recently deceased Mortin. As in *L'Inquisitoire*, the more the listener hears about the dead man, the less he knows about him, because although certain details recur from one speaker to the next, each sees them, and therefore Mortin, in a different light.

Pinget's most recent work, *L'Ennemi* (The Enemy, 1987), is marked by many of the features of his earlier fiction. Composed of 144 numbered paragraphs, it deals with provincial life and the shady, even criminal events that may have occurred (the evidence is incomplete or contradictory) in a small town. The narration is fragmented, with different threads of the sketchy plot scattered throughout the text, and distributed among different narrators, not identified as such but discernible through their points of view and speech patterns. The language is conversational, reflecting a wide range of tones. Below the fragile plot lines lie thematic concerns that make the work something other than a fictional game—notably the concern with aging (which is the true enemy) and the attempt to use words to deal with it. The two blank pages at the end, unlike the blank page in Gide's *Paludes*, are not intended for the reader to fill in but instead to mark the difficulty (not necessarily the failure) of the writer's undertaking–of any writer's undertaking.

Pinget's work is of importance to those interested in French fiction since World War II for several reasons. The New Novelists' break with narrative convention sent French fiction of the 1950s and 1960s in an entirely new direction, one which Pinget's fiction articulates with inventiveness and panache. Moreover, because his work uses parody to reject the conventions he finds outmoded, his chronicle provides a bridge between the old and the new. That is to say, his novels contain both the narrative structures whose validity they undermine and the new structures that are put in their place. Finally, many of the most provocative questions about literature posed in theoretical terms over the last ten years by such New Critics as Roland Barthes, Jacques Derrida, and Julia Kristeva lie at the heart of Pinget's concerns. For example, Pinget has stated unequivocally that his systematic use of recurrence and alternation obliges the reader to "deconstruct" the text. His use of quotation and self-quotation acts out the dynamic reciprocal textual relationships described in Kristeva's theoretical work on intertextuality. Pinget's innovative use of word as sound association is of great interest in semiotics. In short, in Pinget's work the New Novel and the New Criticism coexist in a mutually enlightening symbiosis. To learn from one is to learn about the other.

More important, Pinget is a writer who plays with language at all levels and who, while displaying a delight in whimsy rare for a Francophone writer, conveys in the most compelling fashion his conviction that writing is play for mortal stakes. The major themes of Pinget's work make it clear that this least maudlin and narcissistic of authors has been writing, as all writers ultimately must, of himself. The distance between the fictional Mortin at his desk and Pinget recounting Mortin's struggles at *his* desk is small but significant. Pinget, after all, is writing of Mortin writing. It is his will that serves as organizer in the triad of the writer, the writer-character, and the writer-character's characters. Nevertheless, Pinget realizes that, strive though he may, all writing is apocryphal, that everything can, and must be said again–and again. His discreet but excruciatingly honest invitation to the reader to participate in the impossible quest for the text that will speak the final word makes Pinget one of the most compellingly autobiographical of major contemporary French writers.

Interviews:

Bettina L. Knapp, "An Interview with Robert Pinget," *French Review*, 42 (March 1969): 548-554;

Jean Roudaut, "Monsieur Pinget," *Magazine Littéraire*, no. 232 (July-August 1986): 90-97.

References:

Cahiers de la Compagnie Madeleine Renaud–Jean-Louis Barrault, issue on Ionesco, Beckett, and Pinget, no. 53 (February 1966);

Victor Carrabino, "Pinget's *Passacaille*: The Endless Sonata of the Dead," *Neophilologus*, 69 (January 1985): 59-66;

Tony Duvert, "La Parole et la fiction," *Critique*, no. 252 (May 1968): 443-461;

Etudes Littéraires (Montreal), special issue on Pinget, 19 (Summer 1987);

Robert Henkels, *Robert Pinget: The Novel as Quest* (Tuscaloosa: University of Alabama Press, 1979);

Jean-Claude Liéber, "Réalisme et fiction dans l'œuvre de Robert Pinget," doctoral dissertation, Université de Paris, 1985;

Liéber, "Robert Pinget et le théâtre," *Théâtre/Public*, no. 76-77 (July-October 1987): 16-19;

Michèle Praeger, *Les Romans de Robert Pinget* (Lexington, Ky.: French Forum Monographs, 1987);

Review of Contemporary Fiction, special issue on Pinget, 3 (Summer 1983);

Revue de Belles Lettres (Geneva), special issue on Pinget, no. 1 (1982).

Jean Ricardou

(17 June 1932-   )

Tobin H. Jones
Colorado State University

BOOKS: *L'Observatoire de Cannes* (Paris: Editions de Minuit, 1961);
La Prise de Constantinople (Paris: Editions de Minuit, 1965);
Problèmes du nouveau roman (Paris: Seuil, 1967);
Les Lieux-dits: Petit Guide d'un voyage dans le livre (Paris: Gallimard, 1969);
Pour une théorie du nouveau roman (Paris: Seuil, 1971);
Révolutions minuscules (Paris: Gallimard, 1971); revised as *Révélations minuscules, en guise de préface à la gloire de Jean Paulhan, suivi de Révolutions minuscules* (Paris: Impressions Nouvelles, 1988);
Le Nouveau Roman (Paris: Seuil, 1973);
Nouveaux Problèmes du roman (Paris: Seuil, 1978);
Le Théâtre des métamorphoses (Paris: Seuil, 1982);
La Cathédrale de Sens (Paris: Impressions Nouvelles, 1988).

OTHER: *Que peut la littérature?* (Paris: Union Générale d'Editions, 1965)—comprises contributions by Ricardou, Simone de Beauvoir, Jean-Paul Sartre, Jean-Pierre Faye, and others;
"Fonction critique," in *Théorie d'ensemble,* edited by Philippe Sollers (Paris: Seuil, 1968), pp. 234-265;
"Esquisse d'une théorie des générateurs," in *Positions et oppositions sur le roman contemporain,* edited by Michel Mansuy (Paris: Klincksieck, 1971), pp. 143-150;
Nouveau Roman: Hier, aujourd'hui, proceedings of the colloquium at the Centre Culturel International de Cerisy-la-Salle, 20-30 July 1971, 2 volumes, edited by Ricardou and Françoise van Rossum-Guyon (Paris: Union Générale d'Editions, 1972)—volume 2 includes "Naissance d'une fiction," by Ricardou, pp. 379-392;
Claude Simon: Analyse, théorie, proceedings of the colloquium at the Centre Culturel International de Cerisy-la-Salle, 1-8 July 1974, edited by Ricardou (Paris: Union Générale d'Editions, 1975);

Jean Ricardou

Robbe-Grillet: Analyse, théorie, 2 volumes, proceedings of the colloquium at the Centre Culturel International de Cerisy-la-Salle, 29 June-8 July 1975, edited by Ricardou (Paris: Union Générale d'Editions, 1976);
Problèmes actuels de la lecture, proceedings of the colloquium at the Centre Culturel International de Cerisy-la-Salle, 21-31 July 1981, edited by Ricardou and Lucien Dällenbach (Paris: Clancier-Guénaud, 1982).

PERIODICAL PUBLICATIONS: "Le Roman: Michel Butor, ou Le Roman et ses degrés," *Nouvelle Revue Française,* no. 90 (June 1960): 1157-1161;
"Description et infraconscience chez Alain Robbe-Grillet," *Nouvelle Revue Française,* no. 95 (November 1960): 890-900;

"Par-delà le réel et l'irréel (simple note sur un fragment d'*Un Régicide*)," *Médiations*, no. 5 (Fall 1962): 17-25;

"Rudiments d'une analyse élaborationelle: La Révolution textuelle," *Esprit*, 42 (December 1974): 927-945;

"Pour une lecture rétrospective," *Revue des Sciences Humaines*, no. 177 (1980): 57-66;

"Pour une théorie matérialiste du texte," *Homme et la Société*, no. 59-62 (1981): 197-215;

"L'Escalade de l'autoreprésentation," *Texte*, no. 1 (1982): 15-25;

"Le Texte survit à l'excité (réponse à Michel Holland)," *L'Intertextualité. Intertexte, autotexte, intratexte*, special issue of *Texte*, no. 2 (1983): 193-215;

"Pluriel de l'écriture," *Texte en Main*, no. 1 (1984): 19-29;

"Les Raisons de l'ensemble," *Conséquences*, no. 5 (1985): 62-77;

"Degrés de l'illusoire," *Texte en Main*, no. 3/4 (1985): 151-153;

"Dédoubler la recouverte," *Texte en Main*, no. 5 (1986): 91-94.

Jean Ricardou's literary work is generally associated with the *nouveau roman* (the French New Novel). His three novels, his two collections of short fiction, one of which has undergone radical revision, and his theory and criticism incorporate many of the same technical and thematic concerns found in the works of Alain Robbe-Grillet, Claude Simon, and Claude Ollier. However, Ricardou's novels are even more extreme examples of literary self-consciousness and more difficult, involuted, and arcane structures than most works characteristic of the *nouveau roman*. Ricardou's novels also have major significance as aesthetic and artistic statements about the means and ends of the literary experience. As important as is his fiction, however, Ricardou's innovative and insightful literary criticism and theory are generally better known. He has authored highly original treatises on the techniques and theoretical and aesthetic functions of the narrative in the fiction of both earlier writers such as Poe, Flaubert, Proust, and Raymond Roussel and the writers of the *nouveau roman*. Indeed, Ricardou's theoretical and critical work has earned him such an important role in the dialogue that has taken place between writer and critical reader of the *nouveau roman* that it has overshadowed his considerable importance as a novelist.

Jean Ricardou, born 17 June 1932 in Cannes, has made public almost no details of his personal life. His career as a theorist and practitioner of the novel and as a perceptive and original critic of literature has grown more from pursuit of his creative interests than from his early academic preparation for teaching at the primary and secondary levels in the French educational system. After the award of a first baccalauréat, Section Moderne (1950), and a second baccalauréat, Section Sciences Expérimentales (1951), at the University of Aix-Marseilles, Ricardou studied for three years in Paris at the Ecole Normale d'Instituteurs, receiving his Certificat d'Aptitude à l'Enseignement Primaire in 1953. He then taught at the primary level from 1953 to 1961.

Beginning with his first literary and critical successes in 1960, when he published a short fiction, three brief literary reviews, and three critical studies, Ricardou's involvement in both the theoretical revolution and the technical experimentations of the *nouveau roman* gained momentum rapidly. By the end of 1961, he had published two more short fictions, his first novel, *L'Observatoire de Cannes* (The Cannes Observatory), three reviews, and two more articles representing the theoretical stances of the French New Novelists, who were, by then, already moving into a second stage of development as they explored the creative implications of self-generative and auto-representational fictional forms.

During the decade and a half following the publication of his first novel, Ricardou became one of the most visible and most militant of the French New Novelists. While teaching at the secondary level from 1961 to 1977, he formed close associations with the writers at Seuil and Editions de Minuit as well as the reviews *Tel Quel* and *Médiations*. During these years, he published two more novels, numerous short fictions, nearly sixty articles, and four collections of theoretical essays while also participating in dozens of debates and colloquia devoted to theoretical developments and practical concerns in the contemporary novel. It is perhaps Ricardou's visibility and militancy during these tumultuous years which have most contributed to his notoriety as a writer and theorist at odds with the critics representing the academies.

In the public forums on the *nouveau roman* during these years, Ricardou was both a very public and a very private person. He readily accepted critical challenges and responded with a spirited defense of his views, often provoking the critical establishment with theoretical positions extreme even to those familiar with the initiatives of the New Novelists. At the same time, he seemed to cultivate a certain mystery. Virtually never seen without his dark glasses, which he wore at all hours, indoors and out, he was remarkably reticent about his personal activities and preferences. His identity as an authorial persona seemed bound up in and, occasionally, even a creation of his fictions, as evidenced in his later works, such as those published in *La Cathédrale de Sens* (The Cathedral of Sens/Meaning, 1988) and the fictionlike preface to his revised *Révolutions minuscules* (1988).

Despite a de facto practice of non-self-disclosure, the interrelationships among his works of criticism, theory, and fiction provide a record of Ricardou's development as a writer. Because the early years of his career provide evidence to suggest that his theory and criticism influenced his vision as a novelist, critics have usually studied his novels as extensions and illustrations of that theory. This preferential focus has been exaggerated because the novels have known only limited popularity even among devotees of the *nouveau roman*. Moreover, because their radically experimental forms are extremely self-conscious literary exercises, reading Ricardou's fiction is much like reading his theory. Frequently offering a laboriously intellectual process whose aesthetic rewards are often hidden in extremely complex and convoluted forms, his novels refuse to play to traditional moral and social concerns. However, they do command one's attention for reasons of a formalist nature and, because of their innovative meld of theory and fiction, deserve study on their own merits. Equally important, for the reader sensitive to pattern and attentive to structure, they are exceptionally rich in intricate thematic and formal relationships, having considerable potential for eliciting and sustaining aesthetic interest.

To understand Ricardou as both writer and theorist of the novel, one must therefore recognize that, in his novels, fiction and theory interact and merge to form an aesthetic whole. One should note, too, that Ricardou's practices in the novel's composition–its creation at the hands of the writer tuned to the dynamics of the interaction between the novelist as *scriptor*, the linguistic make-up of the written text, and the *scriptor* as reader–often set the stage for his later development of theoretical approaches. Indeed, until *Le Théâtre des métamorphoses* (The Theater of Meta-

morphoses, 1982) and *La Cathédrale de Sens*, Ricardou's fiction proves a fertile ground from which the figure of theory springs with its thematically coherent structure to illustrate how an idea in fictional form has, as a process, preceded the theoretical conceptualization of that form. Thus it should not surprise one to find that the first novel, *L'Observatoire de Cannes*, incorporates elements that anticipate theoretical developments in subsequent fictions, such as *La Prise de Constantinople* (The Taking of Constantinople, 1965); *Les Lieux-dits* (The So-Called Places, 1969); "Communications," the four-part fiction incorporated into *Le Théâtre des métamorphoses;* and the short fictions of *Révolutions minuscules* and *La Cathédrale de Sens*.

Ricardou's first novel, *L'Observatoire de Cannes*, and his first short fiction, "Sur la pierre" (On the Stone, *Tel Quel*, Summer 1960; collected in *Révolutions minuscules*), reflect the early stages of his interest in the creative potential of narrative description and descriptive techniques evident in his articles, "Description et infraconscience chez Alain Robbe-Grillet" (Description and Infraconscience in Alain Robbe-Grillet, *Nouvelle Revue Française*, November 1960), "Réalités variables, variantes réelles" (Variable Realities, Real Variants, *Tel Quel*, Winter 1963; collected in *Problèmes du nouveau roman*, 1967), and "Aspects de la description créatrice" (Aspects of Creative Description, *Médiations*, no. 3 [Fall 1961], collected in *Problèmes du nouveau roman*). However, the major concern in *L'Observatoire de Cannes* was not simply to realize Robbe-Grillet's goal of exploiting the creative potential of the descriptive modes in a narrative in order to imply the existence of a creating narrative consciousness. It was also to anticipate an aesthetic structure and from that anticipation generate the patterns of a story.

The "story" of *L'Observatoire de Cannes*, ungoverned by traditional notions of plot, is perhaps best characterized as a quest. The novel opens with a deceptively conventional description of four people in the compartment of a train departing Cannes and heading west along the French Riviera: a blond girl, a young couple, and a bald, camera-carrying tourist. Through a series of scenes described as photographs, drawings, and observations, the narrative develops an implicit center of consciousness obsessed by the pursuit and conquest of the girl. In this process, Ricardou's subversion of the distinction between what is imaginary and what is "real" results in the elimination of conventional narrative chronology and an intertwining of three distinct orders of description whose hierarchical relationships supplant the causal order usually associated with more conventional visions of the fictional universe. One of these orders organizes the fictional reality as "perceived" from within the train's compartment, a moving, enclosed space that metaphorically frames the novel's visionary narrative consciousness. The second order of description is reflected in the reality portrayed in the photographs, sketches, or other forms of graphic representation describing locales which have potential for the development of the novel's themes. The third occurs as a synthesis derived from the linguistic confusion of the first two levels, whose representational functions are dialectically opposed throughout the novel.

Throughout *L'Observatoire de Cannes*, the narrative draws on the associative potential of the persons and objects it describes to motivate inference of the obsessive intent behind the thematic implications of "observation." From a montage of descriptions of persons, places, objects, and their relationships, the narrative generates themes of pursuit and domination. For instance, when imagined doubles of the blond girl appear in a striptease act in a cabaret called L'Observatoire de Cannes and in a photo essay, each is stripped bare in a ritualistic description that emphasizes the thematic importance of three modes of spatial movement. The first two forms of movement represent distance as an obstacle to be overcome through subjective and physical approach. The third, which eliminates distance through violence, corresponds to the realization of a goal and thus to closure.

The description of the photo essay depicting the onslaught of a storm-tossed sea on the unsuspecting blond girl is a classic example of the transformation of a static scene into a dynamically obsessive fantasy. Observed from the visual perspective of the sea, the sunbathing girl is first described in terms of the scant protection she would have were a storm suddenly to rise. The intentionality implicit to this perspective surfaces initially as speculation and is then realized in a violent scene depicting the sea overpowering all obstacles between it and the girl.

In such passages, Ricardou develops the connotative values of key words to imply the emotional changes in the narrative consciousness. The waves' violent onslaught corresponds to the overwhelming force of erotic motivation and the eventual consummation of desire in the image of foam-fissured rocks. The word *aigrette* is an example; initially connoting the feathering of the wave's crest, it foreshadows later use to denote a plume adorning the blond stripper's costume in the cabaret. *Culbuté*, which describes the overturning of the stone slabs protecting the girl from the sea, is charged with sexual connotations even as it represents denotatively the elimination of established structures. Paronymic wordplay creates further correspondences of both thematic and emotive kinds. *Dalles* and *sandales* join to destroy the established order, since *dalles* leads to *san[s] dal[l]es*. Meanwhile the two letters, *s* and *l*, which are excluded from the homophonic anagram, become key elements linking the transformations of word and meaning in this first novel to Ricardou's two subsequent novels, in which *S* and *L* will play major roles in the generation of thematic content. Such wordplay, which already has an important role in *L'Observatoire de Cannes*, later becomes critical to the structuring principles of *La Prise de Constantinople* and eventually finds its theoretical explanation in Ricardou's critical studies "La Bataille de la phrase" (The Battle of the Sentence, *Critique*, March 1970; collected in *Pour une théorie du nouveau roman*, 1971), "L'Initiative aux mots" (The Initiative for Words, a chapter in *Nouveaux Problèmes du Roman*, 1978), and "Esquisse d'une théorie des générateurs" (Sketch of a Theory of Generators, in *Positions et oppositions sur le roman contemporain*, 1971), as well as its allegorical illustration in his third novel, *Les Lieux-dits*.

Ricardou's most innovative achievement in such passages was to develop systematically two functional understandings of the word as image. One was conventionally associative and stressed possibilities of semantic combination to evoke new thematic associations. The other was more creative, since the word could be manipulated as a "logoform" to provoke the narrative imagination and generate new realities. The associative function of language implies understanding the narrative imagination as an activity of a consciousness which, though perhaps still unrevealed, already exists. Accordingly, as Ricardou later explained in "Expression et fonctionnement" (Expression and Functioning, *Tel Quel*, Winter 1966; collected in *Problèmes du nouveau roman*), language would thus be no more than an instrument of expression and representation. Ricardou's second interpretation of verbal motifs highlights a more aesthetically independent role and suggests that the narrative consciousness functions only in the present as it responds to the cues of the narrative language. This view implies a very different kind of creative intent, one in which the narration invites the reader to induce those motivating principles which generate the fiction's elements—its characters, places, and events—and which guide its composition.

Also among those techniques in *L'Observatoire de Cannes* whose theoretical and practical implications Ricardou would develop further in later works was the *mise en abyme,* or internal mirroring of the thematic, psychological, and aesthetic principles governing the creative process. An example is the description of graffiti etched on a water tower. These include a cylinder, which might represent the girl's rolled beach towel, her beach bag, or even the water tower rising above the clearing where the novel's erotic development reaches or is imagined to reach its climax. Seven other objects are also represented: a rectangular form recalling the checkered pattern of the girl's bikini; an inverted *V* resembling the recumbent girl's flexed legs; two forms resembling the soles of beach sandals; a tangle of lines suggesting paths in a forest, wrinkles of a ruffled neckline, or eddies of foam; two triangles joined at one of their angles, suggesting the bra of the bikini; and a third, inverted triangle, suggesting the bikini's bottom. The eighth form, a kind of signature, represents a knife, probably, it is suggested, the very instrument used to etch the graffiti. Stressing the importance of spatial contiguity in his description of the eight graffiti, Ricardou suggests cause as a function of the sequence and association of narrative relationships. Despite their apparently coincidental spatial relationships, the forms thus draw from their context the power to define meaning and generate a coherence that is aesthetically satisfying.

To achieve aesthetic satisfaction, however, the reader must be open to experiencing the novel as an elaboration of the thematic principles motivating its own composition. Because *L'Observatoire de Cannes* never draws its reader into a world of social relationships, it lacks much of the human interest expected of the conventional novel. Moreover, questions of how to distinguish the "real" from the virtual and how to interpret actions as a reflection of character prove inconsequential in the experience of the novel. Instead, in exploring the creative functions and effects of narrative description, *L'Observatoire de Cannes* raises questions to which Ricardou would return in a half dozen articles published from 1961 to 1965. Several of these treat in depth the theoreti-

cal implications of structural metaphor and the *mise en abyme,* the virtuality he believed implicit to all narrative description, and the differences between narrative function and narrative expression.

Ricardou explored further the practical side of all these concerns in his second novel, *La Prise de Constantinople,* in which he developed techniques whereby a fiction might generate its own content and reveal the principles of its organization. As the narrative assumes its form, the novel evolves as an emerging conceptualization of its composition. This process is represented thematically in terms of the fictional text's quest for its identity as a literary form.

Ricardou gave this second novel a striking format which, as he later claimed in "Naissance d'une fiction" (Birth of a Fiction, in *Nouveau Roman: Hier, aujourd'hui,* 1972), had a generative function in the process of the novel's writing. The novel has two titles, *La Prise de Constantinople,* which appears on the front cover, and *La Prose de Constantinople* on the back. These titles, which translate as the "taking" and the "telling" of Constantinople, reveal both the mutual dependence of the two acts and the transformational function of the narrative in passing from either one to the other. Within the front and the back covers two dedications to the Egyptian goddess Isis and two epigraphs stress convergence as an organizing principle. The text of the fiction is divided into three parts, each having eight chapters. The chapters are unnumbered and are further divided into blocks of narration, with noticeable blank spaces separating them on the page. The absence of any chapter titles and all pagination reinforces the initial impression that the novel's composition arises in a symmetrically dialectical opposition of various textual and spatial elements.

The plot of the novel proves to be equally unconventional. The novel's first word, "rien" (nothing), which is set off from the following text, generates a series of intertwined adventures that occur in several different temporal and spatial contexts. The physical presence of the word *rien* as something denoting nothing enables a connotative postulation of a content. Both a conceptualization and a description thus evolve in response to the existence of the word and to the opposition between the black of its type, suggestive of a void, and the white of the page, which, by contrast, makes possible a visualization of "nothing." The concept is next given analogous visual form, first as a zero and then as a circle. The circle, in turn, becomes a sphere and then takes the form of a full moon lighting the black, night-darkened fictional landscape, where "nothing" else is as yet perceived. The fictional universe thus expands as a narrative response to the void represented by the first word. And as the fictional universe evolves in a process of opposition and postulation, it forms a complex system of objects, scenes, and characters which, in turn, generate apparently different "plots," each taking place at different times and in different places.

The proliferation and fragmentation of content in the early chapters, where the reader witnesses the number of elements grow without clear relationship to actions or systems of causality, are in obvious conflict with the epigraphs' stress on the importance of convergence as a ruling principle. Indeed, divergence and diversity, not convergence and unity, govern the generation of the novel's multiple plots and thematic and formal elements. There are three initially distinct plots which describe the play of eight young children, the social games of eight young adults, and the adventures of eight space travelers who visit Venus to find La Cité Interdite (The Forbidden City). Gradually, however, textual repetitions of descriptive passages recur in different contexts, and the distinctiveness of these plots gives way to confusion. In the third part of the novel, a fourth group of characters emerges from the textual interplay of the three initial groups. This last set has only three characters, a doctor, Baseille, a nurse, Isa, and a mental patient, Edouard, who seeks his identity in the form of his experiences.

The accumulation of scenes and characters reveals a potential for both expansion and restriction stemming from the thematic and linguistic similarities of their presentation. On the one hand, verbatim repetitions of descriptive passages, sentences, and motifs associated with different plots or levels of reality undermine established relationships. Consequently, they strip from the descriptive passage any individuality it might have had as part of a distinct order of events in the fictional universe. On the other hand, textual repetitions also prove instrumental in defining structural patterns, since they mark new intersections among the variant scenes in the multiple plots. Ricardou's use of textual repetitions thus gives rise to a constant vacillation between the narrative as a presentation of a fictional universe and as a responsiveness to the linguistic character of that universe's composition.

As the narration establishes and destroys relationships among the various fictions, introducing new patterns and evoking new hypothetical orders of plot, causal motifs evolve thematic means to control the conceptual and textual generation of content. Eventually the theme of the quest for identity subsumes all causal relationships in a hierarchical structure, and the narrative consciousness synthesizes the identity of the mental patient Edouard in a fusion of the child Edouard, the young adult Edmond, and the space explorer Ed. Word.

The thematic motifs, the quest-oriented plots, and the textual reiterations of Ricardou's novel ultimately achieve a unity of development in a thematic convergence of the quests on all levels of the fiction. And when Edouard's "psychological" identity emerges from the continuum of the assumed and then abandoned identities of other characters in the various fictions, a comparable synthesis occurs on the level of writing in the narrative form. These two threads of the double quest for psychological (social and emotional) and formal (textual and fictional) self-definition finally merge in the novel's last sentence. "Certaine lecture consciencieuse suffit maintenant pour que l'irradiation de toute la figure élabore qui **JE SUIS**, et par un phénomène réflexif point trop imprévu, en un éclair, me **LE LIVRE**" (A certain conscientious reading now suffices for the irradiation of all the figure to elaborate who **I AM** and through a not-too-unforeseen, reflexive phenomenon to disclose in a flash **MY** con**TEXT**). With this pun on "livre," the narration draws to a close, and, having united the parallel quests and created from them the allegory of its own genesis from nothing, a dynamic form of writing as a process of self-generation, self-election or -determination, and self-elucidation reveals itself as the novel *La Prose de Constantinople*.

Unlike most other New Novelists, Ricardou has relied extensively on both external and internal "texts" to reflect the principles of formal composition. A suggestion that access to the meaning of *La Prise de Constantinople* lies at the juncture of opposites invites the reader to look to the novel's physical center, where passages prescribe two opposed methods of critical reading that might elucidate meaning. The first supposes that every literary work belongs to a vast library whose traditions form its intertextual infrastructure. The second suggests that an understanding of the fiction depends on both intuitive and deductive responses to its text alone. Ricardou explores the implications of these two approaches to reading in his experimentation with techniques of linguistic generation and control of the narrative.

Ricardou's experimentation with the generative potential of wordplay is much more radical in *La Prise de Constantinople* than in *L'Observatoire de Cannes*. In his second novel, he exploits phonic and semantic variations in the verbal forms of puns, homonyms, paronyms, anagrams, and cryptograms to derive conceptual and structural associations among words and their immediate contexts and create correspondences among the larger elements of the text. Homophonic puns (for example, the name of the Venusian city Silab Lee and the phrase, "syllabe-les," meaning syllabize them) or paronymic confusions ("prose" in the semantic context of "pose") draw attention to the ambiguous nature of language in the reading experience. Homonyms and paronyms, like those based on the pronunciation of *S* and *L* (*est-ce elle, aisselle, Hessel*) relate otherwise independent fictional developments. But such kinds of verbal plays do not integrate the associated elements in a meaningful way by subordinating them to the demands or priorities of a system. It is through exploitation of the generative and convergent characteristics of the anagram that Ricardou chooses to create thematic centers for the constellation of those elements. In this process of concentration and convergence, it is Isabelle who becomes the focus. An acronym formed from the first initials of the eight persons in each of the three groups of characters described in the novel, "ISABELLE" is also a source of anagrams capable of linking the various quests: the quest for the lost Venusian city Silab Lee, the castle Bel Asile, the doctor Baseille (who treats Edouard), and the Lac des Abeilles. Ricardou also uses partial anagrams to allow for even more suggestive associations. From Bel and Isa, for instance, he formed Blaise and Basile–names whose historical importance bears on the thematic organization of Ricardou's novel.

The reorganization of letters to form and interrelate new names has its analogous fictional correlation among elements in a system of mythological (fictional) and cultural (historical) references that allude to the narrative's quest for literary self-definition. Reigning over this system is the figure of Isis, who reunited the scattered parts of Osiris's dismembered body and who thus represents the themes of structural generation and inte-

gration. Another name, Basile, interrelates three complementary thematic perspectives. The Byzantine rulers Basile le Macédonien and Basile II belong to a set which evokes the historical "reality" of a documentable past. Basile le Vénusien in the space adventure, *La Cité Interdite*, and Basile l'Epouvantable from the medieval adventure "La Princesse interdite" belong to the realm of the fictional, stand for the figurative nature of the literary text, and thus represent the imagined. Finally, the alchemist Basile Valentin stands for the hermetic symbolism of the literary form as a quest structure. Allusions to structural metaphor in the gnostic and symbolic traditions of the Middle Ages thus intersect thematically with references to ancient Egyptian history and mythology to emphasize the metaphorical role of the novel's fictional events and characters in the physical elaboration and theoretical explanation of its form.

Ricardou merges the concerns of the theory, criticism, and practice of writing already clearly evident in *La Prise de Constantinople* even more overtly in his third novel, *Les Lieux-dits*, whose plot takes form in the play of tensions between the travel guide and the novel. Ricardou's subtitle to the novel, *Petit Guide d'un voyage dans le livre* (Short Guide to a Voyage in the Book), suggests the nature of the analogy at work in the novel's formal makeup. It also provides a clue to interpretation of the text as an allegory of the dialectical resolution of the differences among the narrative forms, semantic conceptions, and aesthetic intents of guidebook and novel.

As the reader progresses through the description of each of eight cities on the novel's itinerary, it becomes clear that novel and guidebook cannot be separated. The reader learns of a historical conflict between two doctrinaire sects. One maintains that the character of a place always lies at the origin of its name. The opposing sect defends the creative functions of language and argues that because words lie at the origin of our conception of reality, we must intuit the character of a reality on the basis of the meanings words evoke in the process of their own interactions. Although introduced as a parenthetical note to the guidebook's description of the city, this conflict soon becomes the central theme of the fiction.

Ricardou allegorizes the opposing theoretical stances in the creation of his characters. For instance, the principal character, Olivier Lasius, comes into being only as a narrative convention, a hypothetical visitor to Bannière whose creation permits the introduction of a fictional point of view. When he learns that a girl dressed in red following an identical itinerary has been asking the same questions as he about certain allegorical paintings by Albert Crucis, he sets out to meet her. The two characters eventually meet and follow a common itinerary of discovery which comes to embody metaphorically the themes of quest and conflict—the former in the process of search, pursuit, and capture and the latter in the antagonisms of sexual oppositions, conceptual reversals, and thematic and formal paradoxes.

Only near the novel's conclusion does it become clear how completely the composition of *Les Lieux-dits* reflects its own development. Invited to form an acrostic of the chapter titles, the reader discovers Belcroix to be the middle ground where the two modes of narration intersect (cross) in fundamental opposition. Returning to Belcroix, Olivier, who has come to represent the forces of the poetic, seeks first to seduce the girl Atta, who embodies the representational, and then imagines her destruction. The final lines of the novel, however, shift the emphasis again from the conflict between the two allegorical characters to the interpretation of the plot as a dialectical form of structural metaphor.

After the publication of *Les Lieux-dits*, Ricardou's writing turned increasingly to the thematics of the confrontation and mutual transgression of theory and fiction. In this development, his short fictions collected in *Révolutions minuscules* (1971) and its subsequent revision (1988) are a creative reordering of short experimental texts which he had begun to compose even before the publication of his first novel in 1961. In the order of presentation in the first edition of the collection, these short fictions mark the stages of Ricardou's experimentation with descriptive modes of narrative fiction and give form to the creative potential of the word freed of the constraints of its representative functions. The short fictions of the first version of *Révolutions minuscules* thus map the evolution of Ricardou's thought on relationships between theory and fiction in the written text. The fictions, as cast in the order of the revised edition of 1988, also achieve these ends, but they add a provocative new theme, that of the identity of the narrative text as inseparable from the evolving identity of the narrative consciousness of the text's creation.

Both thematic similarities and like technical characteristics link these short fictions to Ricardou's earlier novels. The order of the fictions

reflects Ricardou's development of narrative description as a means to generate a literary self-consciousness and to derive new texts from the ambiguous nature of language itself. These literary concerns appear in semantic fields such as that of water (sea, waves, currents, foam, cataracts, and the like) already evident in *L'Observatoire de Cannes* and *La Prise de Constantinople*. However, in the short fictions, "Jeu" (Game), "Sur la pierre," "Lancement d'un voilier" (The Launching of a Sailing Ship), and "Plage blanche" (White Beach), the imagery acquires a more clearly marked ambiguity of function. In "Plage blanche," for instance, the *plage* (beach) becomes the *page* which, in turn, is the arena (derived from *arénuleux* or sand-covered) for the verbal play of the text's dreamlike creation. The imagery of water also appears in other fictions, where it combines with the familiar themes of sexual quest and conquest as well as themes of opposition, transgression, and transformation. These thematic forces are, in turn, linked to the development of the fiction itself. For example, sexual conflict and domination through pursuit and conquest, inversion of values and functions, repetitions and aberrant variations of words and whole passages to motivate self-generation and composition are all present in "Diptyque," where the quest leads to the theme of death as closure in the textual opposition of beginning and ending.

"Autobiographie," the final fiction of *Révolutions minuscules*, merges the textual self-generation of the narrative "I" with the thematic concerns of the literary autobiography. Here, fiction evolves from the illusion of an autobiographical form which seems initially an account of events in the author's life which might have inspired his writing of the eight preceding fictions. The end of "Autobiographie" reaffirms once again, however, the creative power of the word. In the final two paragraphs, the reader finds that the images and themes which have recurred in the apparent context of an autobiographical explanation are reduced, fictionally distilled as it were, to "huit jets minimes, en voie de parfaite extinction" (eight little streams on the way to perfect extinction) and to insignificant curves traced in the sand which will only be complicated by future writings.

In many respects, Ricardou's blending of fiction and theory in *Le Théâtre des métamorphoses*, which he described as a mixed genre, achieves just that complication. Transformation or metamorphosis of fiction into theory, as seen in the allegorization of theoretical concerns in his earlier work, gives way in *Le Théâtre des métamorphoses* to the exploration of the fictional character of both criticism and theory. Thus, the meaning of "mixte" to describe the merging of the concerns and forms of a given fiction with the critical and theoretical representations of fiction in general should be interpreted as a meld or synthesis rather than an aggregation or simple combination. Just as the theater is a means for the representation of an illusory reality, the book becomes the means for the mutual transgressions and metamorphoses of the two languages.

The composition of *Le Théâtre des métamorphoses* reveals how problematical this potential dialectic can become. The work is composed of four major parts. Two of these, "Mixte" and "Principes pour quelques transformations" (Principles for a Few Transformations), which are predominantly theoretical and autocritical in nature, embrace the two central, primarily fictional works, "Communications" and "Improbables Strip-teases." Both of the fictions had already seen print in forms virtually the same as those they have in *Le Théâtre des métamorphoses* and have many thematic and textual elements in common with Ricardou's earlier fictions. Although the apparent opposition of the two languages is maintained by the clear separation of texts, linguistic and thematic transgressions occur throughout. Transgression, or what Ricardou later would discuss as "l'art du X" (the art of the X, of the crossing, or of the intersection), is marked in *Le Théâtre des métamorphoses* by various signs of the cross—the *X*, the crossing, the crusade, and the syllable *ptyx* (the *petit* x or little *x*) found in a number of titles and proper names. The many transgressions in this work take form in the familiar thematic developments of erotic pursuit and conquest (the quest), sexual conflict and domination (belligerence), and generation and unification. Both "Communications" and "Improbables Strip-teases" incorporate many elements from his earlier fictions. Among these are characters and thematic elements derived from *La Prise de Constantinople* in "Communications" and textual repetitions such as the strip-tease from *L'Observatoire de Cannes* which, already reproduced virtually unchanged in *La Prise de Constantinople*, appears again in "Improbables Strip-teases." Ricardou also developed the literary connotations of such themes as those of the quest for formal and conceptual self-definition; of conflict, realized in the dialectical resolution of opposing forces and val-

ues; and of doubling, seen in the *mise en abyme* and the mirroring of form and its underlying principles. The presence of these themes in *Le Théâtre des métamorphoses* reveals a wholeness of conception spanning two decades and highlights threads of continuity through Ricardou's work that provide keys to some of the most puzzling aspects of his novels.

The most characteristic and overt example of this continuity is Ricardou's emphasis on the number eight in all his fiction. In *L'Observatoire de Cannes*, there are eight graffiti whose images are basic to the obsessive generation of the plot. In *La Prise de Constantinople*, there are eight chapters in each of the novel's three parts, eight persons in each group of characters, and eight letters, forming the name Isabelle and its many anagrams. In *Les Lieux-dits*, the number occurs in the descriptions of Albert Crucis's allegorical painting, of a postcard depicting a factory, and of a package of Pall Mall cigarettes. In *Révolutions minuscules*, eight narratives precede the final, short fiction, "Autobiographie," which alludes to associations of a "personal" nature which one might construe as constituting an identity in a way similar to that which occurs in *La Prise de Constantinople*.

It seems reasonable to assume the number to be a figure associated with the organizing principles of the fictions in which it is found, even though it does not reveal the semantic functions of the formal aspects it emphasizes. The number also can be understood as a kind of signature, such as that to which Ricardou alluded in his first novel. This interpretation, though speculative, has some support of a nontextual kind. In 1972 Ricardou visited several universities in the United States and discussed the generation of *La Prise de Constantinople* from elements—such as the publisher's name and logo—which would be visible on the cover of a novel published with Editions de Minuit. His own name, he claimed, was a partial anagrammatic generator of the name of Villehardouin, a chronicler of the Fourth Crusade and, hence, one of several sources of the novel's thematic and formal composition. Until the publication of *Le Théâtre des métamorphoses* and his most recent collection of short fictions, *La Cathédrale de Sens*, and the revised edition of *Révolutions minuscules*, with its literarily self-conscious preface, critics considered this explanation a bit specious. But all three of these most recent works stress again these same associations and the generative function of Ricardou's name.

It thus seems even more reasonable to assume that in the consistent use of the figure and homological counterparts of eight, there is indeed a kind of signature of a personally thematic kind which reflects the meld of theory, criticism, and fiction that has become the benchmark of Ricardou's writings.

With the publication of his last major works of fiction in the 1988 edition of *Révolutions minuscules*, Ricardou has shown renewed activity in the realms of theory and criticism, with promises of another novel, "Le Centre de gravité" (The Center of Gravity), announced in March 1988 by Impressions Nouvelles as ready for publication. The reader must hope that unlike "Un Enchantement se dépare," a novel alluded to in 1978 as still in preparation, and which still has not yet appeared, "Le Centre de gravité" will soon see publication.

References:

Mireille Calle-Gruber, "Effets d'un texte non-saturé: *La Prise de Constantinople*," *Poétique*, no. 35 (September 1978): 325-335;

Pierre Caminade, "Analogie et métaphore structurelles de Jean Ricardou," in his *Images et métaphore, un problème de poétique contemporaine* (Paris: Bordas, 1970), pp. 90-96;

Ursula Fried, "Lecture créatrice à base structuraliste de 'Plage blanche' par Jean Ricardou," *Bonnes Feuilles*, no. 6 (Fall 1976): 3-17;

Lynn A. Higgins, "Literature 'à la lettre': Ricardou and the Poetics of Anagram," *Romanic Review*, 73 (November 1982): 473-488;

Higgins, *Parables of Theory: Jean Ricardou's Metafiction* (Birmingham, Ala.: Summa Publications, 1984);

Higgins, "Typographical Eros: Reading Ricardou in the Third Dimension," *Yale French Studies*, no. 57 (1979): 80-94;

Tobin H. Jones, "In Quest of a Newer New Novel: Ricardou's *La Prise de Constantinople*," *Contemporary Literature*, 14 (Summer 1973): 296-309;

Bruce A. Morrissette, "Generative Techniques in Robbe-Grillet and Ricardou," in *Generative Literature and Generative Art: New Essays*, by Alain Robbe-Grillet and others (Fredericton, N.B.: York Press, 1983), pp. 25-34;

Hélène Prigogine, "L'Aventure ricardolienne du nombre," *Nouveau Roman: Hier, aujourd'hui*, volume 2 (Paris: Union Générale d'Editions, 1972), pp. 353-378;

Jean-Claude Raillon, "Une Étude périlleusement excessive du texte cité," *Sud*, no. 8 (1972): 47-58;

Donald B. Rice, "The Ex-centricities of Jean Ricardou's *La Prise/Prose de Constantinople*," *International Fiction Review*, 2 (July 1975): 106-112;

Pierre-Henri Simon, "De Jean Ricardou: *L'Observatoire de Cannes*," in his *Diagnostic des Lettres Françaises Contemporaines* (Brussels: Renaissance du Livre, 1966), pp. 321-326.

Alain Robbe-Grillet
(18 August 1922-   )

John Fletcher
University of East Anglia

BOOKS: *Les Gommes* (Paris: Editions de Minuit, 1953); translated by Richard Howard as *The Erasers* (New York: Grove Press, 1964; London: Calder & Boyars, 1966);

Le Voyeur (Paris: Editions de Minuit, 1955); translated by Howard as *The Voyeur* (New York: Grove Press, 1958; London: Calder, 1959);

La Jalousie (Paris: Editions de Minuit, 1957); translated by Howard as *Jealousy* (New York: Grove Press, 1959; London: Calder, 1960);

Dans le labyrinthe (Paris: Editions de Minuit, 1959); translated by Howard as *In the Labyrinth* (New York: Grove Press, 1960); translated by Christine Brooke-Rose (London: Calder & Boyars, 1967 [i.e. 1968]);

L'Année dernière à Marienbad (Paris: Editions de Minuit, 1961); translated by Howard as *Last Year at Marienbad* (New York: Grove Press, 1962; London: Calder, 1962);

Instantanés (Paris: Editions de Minuit, 1962); translated as *Snapshots,* in *Snapshots, and Towards a New Novel* (1966); translated by Bruce Morrissette (New York: Grove Press, 1966);

L'Immortelle (Paris: Editions de Minuit, 1963); translated by A. M. Sheridan Smith as *The Immortal One* (London: Calder & Boyars, 1971);

Pour un nouveau roman (Paris: Editions de Minuit, 1963); translated by Howard as *For a New Novel* (New York: Grove Press, 1966); translated as *Towards a New Novel,* in *Snapshots, and Towards a New Novel* (1966);

La Maison de rendez-vous (Paris: Editions de Minuit, 1965); translated by Howard (New York: Grove Press, 1966); translated by Sheridan Smith as *The House of Assignation* (London: Calder & Boyars, 1970);

Snapshots, and Towards a New Novel, translated by Barbara Wright (London: Calder & Boyars, 1965 [i.e. 1966]);

Projet pour une révolution à New York (Paris: Editions de Minuit, 1970); translated by Howard as *Project for a Revolution in New York*

Alain Robbe-Grillet (photograph copyright © Jerry Bauer)

(New York: Grove Press, 1972; London: Calder & Boyars, 1973);

Rêves de jeunes filles, text by Robbe-Grillet, photographs by David Hamilton (Paris: Robert Laffont, 1971); translated by Elizabeth Walter as *Dreams of a Young Girl* (New York: Morrow, 1971); translation also published as *Dreams of Young Girls* (London: Collins, 1971);

Les Demoiselles d'Hamilton, text by Robbe-Grillet, photographs by Hamilton (Paris: Robert Laffont, 1972); translated by Martha Egan as *Sisters* (New York: Morrow, 1973; London: Collins, 1976);

Glissements progressifs du plaisir (Paris: Editions de Minuit, 1973);

La Belle Captive, text by Robbe-Grillet, illustrations by René Magritte (Lausanne: Bibliothèque des Arts, 1975);

Construction d'un temple en ruines à la déesse Vanadé, text by Robbe-Grillet, etchings by Paul Delvaux (Paris: Le Bateau-Lavoir, 1975);

Topologie d'une cité fantôme (Paris: Editions de Minuit, 1976); translated by J. A. Underwood as *Topology of a Phantom City* (New York: Grove Press, 1977; London: Calder, 1978);

Temple aux miroirs, text by Robbe-Grillet, photographs by Irina Ionesco (Paris: Seghers, 1977);

Un Régicide (Paris: Editions de Minuit, 1978);

Souvenirs du triangle d'or (Paris: Editions de Minuit, 1978); translated by Underwood as *Recollections of the Golden Triangle* (London: Calder, 1984; New York: Grove, 1986);

Le Rendez-vous, school edition, with exercises and vocabulary by Yvone Lenard (New York: Holt, Rinehart & Winston, 1981); trade edition, *Djinn: Un Trou rouge entre les pavés disjoints* (Paris: Editions de Minuit, 1981); translated by Lenard and Walter Wells as *Djinn* (New York: Grove Press, 1982; London: Calder, 1983);

Le Miroir qui revient (Paris: Editions de Minuit, 1984); translated by Jo Levy as *Ghosts in the Mirror* (London: Calder, 1988; New York: Grove, 1989);

Angélique ou L'Enchantement (Paris: Editions de Minuit, 1988).

MOTION PICTURES: *L'Année dernière à Marienbad*, screenplay and dialogue by Robbe-Grillet, 1961;

L'Immortelle, screenplay and direction by Robbe-Grillet, 1963;

Trans-Europ-Express, screenplay and direction by Robbe-Grillet, 1967;

L'Homme qui ment, screenplay and direction by Robbe-Grillet, 1968;

L'Eden et après, screenplay and direction by Robbe-Grillet, 1970;

Glissements progressifs du plaisir, screenplay and direction by Robbe-Grillet, 1973;

Le Jeu avec le feu, screenplay and direction by Robbe-Grillet, 1975;

La Belle Captive, screenplay and direction by Robbe-Grillet, 1983.

Born in Brest, in Brittany, on 18 August 1922, Alain Robbe-Grillet, the most influential French writer of his generation, is the son of Gaston Robbe-Grillet, owner of a small manufacturing business (himself the son of a schoolteacher) and of Yvonne Canu Robbe-Grillet (the daughter of a navy petty-officer). He attended a Paris primary school and then *lycées* in Paris and Brest. In 1942 he passed the competitive entrance examination for the prestigious Institut National d'Agronomie. In common with many young men of his generation too young to fight in the campaign that preceded the fall of France in 1940, he found himself forcibly recruited to work for the Germans under the STO, or compulsory labor scheme. This obligation interrupted his studies and took him to Nuremberg in Germany, where he worked as a lathe operator in a factory producing Panther tanks from July 1943 to August 1944. On graduation in 1945 he joined the staff of the Institut National de la Statistique et des Etudes Economiques. In 1948 he visited Bulgaria as part of a voluntary youth aid scheme, the International Reconstruction Brigades, and was employed on the building of a railway between Pernik and Voluiek. From 1948 to 1951 he worked in Morocco, Guinea, Guadeloupe and Martinique for the Institut des Fruits et Agrumes Coloniaux, or Colonial Fruit Institute, but fell ill and had to be repatriated on health grounds. He never returned to his career as an agricultural scientist, but during his period of convalescence became a full-time writer instead. In 1957 he married Catherine Rstakian; there are no children from the marriage.

Robbe-Grillet has received several awards, none of them, it must be admitted, major ones. In 1955 he won the Prix des Critiques for *Le Voyeur* (*The Voyeur*), and in 1961 *L'Année dernière à Marienbad* (*Last Year at Marienbad*), the film he wrote for Alain Resnais, won the Golden Lion at the Venice Film Festival. In 1963 his own film *L'Immortelle* (*The Immortal One*) won the Prix Louis Delluc, and in 1969 *L'Homme qui ment* (*The Liar*) won the prize for best screenplay at the Berlin Festival. But so far both the Goncourt and the Nobel prizes have eluded him.

What is it, then, that makes this relatively under-honored author so well known, an inescapable presence on the cultural scene, a writer with whom many violently disagree but whom no one can ignore? The answer lies in the recent history of France. The humiliating wartime occupation of the country deeply marked people of Robbe-Grillet's generation and led them to question the grounds of the commitment to radical politics preached by intellectuals of the preceding generation, particularly by Jean-Paul Sartre, Simone de Beauvoir, and their associates. Robbe-Grillet spoke for many when he began, in the mid 1950s, to cast doubt on philosophical concepts such as meaning and identity which the elders still took for granted, however searching their political and moral inquiry. Robbe-Grillet and others saw only instability and relativity where Sartre and friends assumed firm ground, and they conveyed their perceptions of indeterminacy in works of the imagination to which the term *nouveau roman*, or New Novel, soon came to be applied. Writers such as Nathalie Sarraute, Claude Simon, Robert Pinget, Marguerite Duras, and Michel Butor all broadly subscribe to this tendency, which takes as its basic tenet that objectivity in literature–a notion derived from a now largely discredited metaphysics of transcendence– is an illusion which must be discarded together with what Robbe-Grillet calls old myths of profundity: myths on which, he alleges, the novel used to be based. Readers in the past were reassured by the notion that nature had depths which mankind alone could plumb, drawing comfort from their powers over the physical world and from their ability to gain access to the hidden soul of things. This assurance, Robbe-Grillet argued, was bogus, the product of a cozy but now-bankrupt humanism. In its place, he urged a new realism, a new attitude to time, a new conception of plot, and a new approach to character in literature, all of which had to be tougher, harder, and more transparent than in the writings of those he saw as the bankrupt humanists par excellence, Sartre and his associates. Robbe-Grillet himself is in favor of a literature that is all "on the surface," postulating nothing about what may or may not lie behind phenomena; of a novel that presents characters with little or no previous history, and without conventional names to identify them; of a treatment of time which renders faithfully the achronological leaps of the imagination and the temporal distortions of memory and emotion; and of narrative which is not afraid of being inconsistent and reflecting a reality that has its own recurring bafflements.

Robbe-Grillet gave literary form to these ideas in a novel, *Les Gommes* (1953; translated as *The Erasers,* 1964), which caused a considerable controversy in France when it was published. It soon made him famous, but it was not in fact his first novel. That was *Un Régicide* (A Regicide) which was written while he was still employed as a research scientist in 1949, although it was not

published until 1978, because Robbe-Grillet was unable to find a publisher for it. It is, ostensibly at least–such precautions are necessary in dealing with a writer who claims to have abolished story in the traditional sense–about the murder of a king (hence the title) which does not come off, indeed seems a figment of the hero's imagination. Like most first novels, it betrays its influences, owing a lot to surrealism and to the novelists Robbe-Grillet read at the time, a somewhat unlikely combination including Graham Greene, James Cain, Franz Kafka, and Raymond Roussel.

Les Gommes too is an act of homage, but this time to the art of the thriller as practiced by such masters as Raymond Chandler. Its subject is "vingt-quatre heures en trop," or the superfluous twenty-four hours during which the action takes place. Robbe-Grillet claims that *Les Gommes* is faithful to the mystery genre, having a murderer, a sleuth, and a body; indeed, the traditional functions are respected insofar as a killer fires a fatal shot, a victim dies, and a detective solves the crime to everyone's satisfaction. But the relationship among these functions is far from straightforward. The nature of this relationship is revealed in another of Robbe-Grillet's claims: that *Les Gommes* is the account of the twenty-four-hour period which starts at the moment the shot is fired and ends with that of the victim's death: the time it takes the bullet to travel a dozen feet, "twenty-four superfluous hours."

The novel opens in a provincial café in which the proprietor is preparing mechanically for the day and ruminating on the murder the previous evening of a neighbor, Daniel Dupont. He goes to wake a client in the only bedroom he has available to let, but the man has already left the house. Downstairs someone called Garinati asks after the customer, whose name is Wallas. Acting on orders from his boss, Bona, Garinati assassinated Dupont the previous evening, after hiding in Dupont's study while the latter was out of the room eating his evening meal. Or so he thought. In fact he fired one shot at Dupont as the latter entered his study after dinner, but missed, wounding his victim only slightly. But he does not know that Dupont has survived: the morning papers carry the news that Dupont died from several shots. This, however, is merely a story put about officially in order to mislead the would-be assassins; in reality Dupont is hiding at the clinic of a doctor friend and will be driven secretly to Paris later that day. Since the gang who tried to murder him is expected to strike again at another target, the authorities are anxious that Dupont's lucky escape should be concealed lest the gang take fright and go underground.

Wallas the special agent has been sent from the capital to investigate the murder (which, when he arrives, as the astute reader is not slow to notice, has only just been committed). His watch has stopped; indeed, by coincidence, it did so at 7:30 the previous evening, at precisely the moment when Dupont "died." Wallas arrived late that evening in this dreary town, which he hardly knows, having visited it previously only once, as a child. One of his first actions the following day (the day on which Dupont is due to be spirited away to Paris) is to buy an eraser. He also calls on the local police chief, with whom he is to work on the investigation, only to find that the matter has been taken out of the inspector's hands (naturally enough, since, as the reader knows, the authorities in Paris do not wish the fact that no crime has been committed to be revealed by zealous criminal investigators). In the conversation between Wallas and his colleague it transpires that one cartridge is missing from the magazine of Wallas's revolver, a weapon which happens to be the same caliber as the one fired at Dupont.

Starting his investigation, Wallas learns that a man he resembles interfered with the mechanism of Dupont's doorbell prior to the attempted murder, and when he goes to the local post office he is mistaken for someone else and given mail addressed to a Mr. André VS (Wallas is pronounced *Vallass* in French). Then Wallas remembers that when he visited the town as a child he was accompanied by his mother and that the purpose of the trip was to see his father, from whom his mother was separated. The development of the investigation leads him to hide in Dupont's study later that evening, but the man who enters the room is not, as he expects, a member of Bona's gang come to make a second attempt at assassination, but Dupont himself returning to collect some important papers prior to his departure for Paris. Seeing Wallas, whom he does not recognize, and aiming a revolver at him, he tries to fire first, but Wallas, who does not recognize Dupont either, is faster on the trigger and Dupont is shot dead. It is exactly 7:30 P.M.; the failed act has gone back to its starting point for a second go, and has succeeded. Wallas's watch begins ticking again, precisely twenty-four hours after it stopped.

Robbe-Grillet has deliberately built into this thriller the myth of Oedipus. Wallas is killing his father, whom he does not know, and thus fulfilling a destiny he could not avoid. The woman from whom he bought the erasers earlier in the day was (again unbeknown to him) his stepmother, and he had experienced sexual desire for her. The novel is even shaped like an ancient tragedy, with a prologue, five chapters like acts in a play, and an epilogue. And as in the Oedipus story, although Wallas never consciously intends to kill his father or to lust after a mother figure, an alter ego has been planning the crime, as the incident in the post office and the business of the doorbell show; so, like Oedipus, he is somehow obscurely guilty of a crime his unconscious mind, at least, had worked out carefully in advance. At the same time Robbe-Grillet skillfully creates a pastiche of the mystery genre: red herrings are dragged across the path, and the narrative builds a strong feeling of suspense, making the novel exciting to read. To a lesser extent, the espionage genre, which John le Carré has made his own, is also parodied, especially its enigmatic stories in which the systematic assemblage of the plot is more important than the subject matter. Incomplete disclosures and delayed resolutions characterize *Les Gommes* also: the reader is never precisely told for whom the assassins are working, but they certainly seem to pose a serious threat to the state.

Robbe-Grillet's ingenuity in this impressively plotted story has been rewarded by the book's sales—the highest in France of any of his works. It is the nearest this esoteric writer has come to producing a book likely to appeal to a wide audience. By the same token, however, *Les Gommes* is less centrally and urgently an expression of Robbe-Grillet's vision than either *Un Régicide* or his third novel (but second published), *Le Voyeur* (1955; translated as *The Voyeur*, 1958).

Around the time *Le Voyeur* was published Robbe-Grillet was writing several short prose texts later collected under the title *Instantanés* (1962; translated as *Snapshots*, 1966). These portray a state of unease, even of ill-contained hysteria, masked by meticulous, apparently dispassionate and objective description. Two of them feature the menacing power of the sea and the danger of being cut off by a rising tide, and in his autobiographical essay *Le Miroir qui revient* (1984; translated as *Ghosts in the Mirror*, 1988) Robbe-Grillet has revealed that as a child he was terrified of the ocean near which he was born. It is significant, then, that *Le Voyeur* is set in the same Breton coastal region where the author was born and later spent his holidays as a child.

Robbe-Grillet considered calling *Le Voyeur* "Le Voyageur" (The Traveler) because the hero is a traveling watch salesman visiting the island of his birth on a day trip from the mainland. He needs several good sales that day in order to restore his shaky finances, and he thinks the place where he once lived offers attractive prospects. He has not been long on the island when he hears of a girl of thirteen who, despite her youth, has already acquired a questionable moral reputation. Her name is Jacqueline Leduc. While trying to sell a watch to the girl's mother, the traveler—called Mathias—sees a photograph of Jacqueline which reminds him of another girl with whom he was evidently once emotionally involved. Her name was Violette. Thereafter in thinking of Jacqueline he will tend to apply to her the name of Violette. The confusion is significant, since the word *viol* means rape in French.

During the day Jacqueline disappears. Mathias is delayed on his return to the ferry and just misses it, and so has to spend a few more days on the island. The next day Jacqueline's body is washed ashore, and it is commonly assumed that she slipped and fell accidentally into the sea while playing on the cliffs. Certain marks on her body are not thought to be significant; she could have been nibbled by sea predators or dragged by currents over rough surfaces. Mathias eventually leaves the island when the boat calls again.

The reader quickly notices that something in the story has been left out. Mathias's schedule has a gap in it, a period of time during his first day on the island which is not accounted for in the otherwise detailed exposition of his activities. It must have been something carrying a high emotional charge because it has, as it were, burned a hole in the text. It is strongly hinted that Mathias sought Jacqueline out, found her playing on the clifftop, and then did something which disturbs him greatly whenever he thinks back to it afterward. After missing the return ferry—an act perhaps unconsciously intended—he returns anxiously to the place where she was last seen alive and removes certain objects which he seems to have left there. He is particularly careful to pick up some cigarette butts lying about in the grass. To his horror, he discovers that his actions have not gone unseen. There must have been a witness to whatever occurred before Jacqueline's

body fell—or was pushed—into the sea. This witness—perhaps the voyeur of the title—is a young man called Julien Marek. He makes no attempt to incriminate Mathias, however; perhaps, it is hinted, because he has his own reasons for wishing the girl dead. No suspicion falls on the traveler, therefore, who to his surprise and relief is allowed to leave the island unhindered.

It would be easy to reconstruct, from the various indications in the text, how Jacqueline was methodically and sadistically tortured, raped, and killed by Mathias, watched all the while by Julien and his terrifyingly accusatory eyes. But to do so would be to miss the point. Not only does the story center for Robbe-Grillet on this blank spot, but it is this void itself which presides over the writing of the entire book: this absence is the true generator of the text. If a criminal act were to be described or shown retrospectively, the book would be a quite different one, a much more conventional thriller. *Les Gommes* was a clever literary puzzle of that kind; *Le Voyeur* is an altogether more original work of art, a deeply unsettling book about genuine anxiety and about an obsessive, guilty fascination with evil. Indeed, despite Robbe-Grillet's declared aim of avoiding what passed for psychological analysis in the literature of earlier times, his insight into the workings of the criminal disposition is impressive. For example, Mathias betrays his disturbed state of mind by what can only be called obsessive mental arithmetic as he calculates such things as how many watches he can sell by the hour. It is true that his mental predicament has a physical basis in the migraine which afflicts him and which grows steadily more distracting, but the headache serves merely to reinforce a sense of alienation and estrangement which seems inseparable from his condition. He is a man haunted by sadoerotic obsessions—the text conceals several occurrences of triangles and other structures with sexual connotations—and is preoccupied with mazes and labyrinths, a common Robbe-Grillet trope.

This atmosphere of anxiety gives *Le Voyeur* much of its tight grip on the reader's attention, but it is also thrilling in a more conventional sense: there is straightforward suspense when Mathias is hurrying to catch the boat which will carry him away from the scene of the crime or accident, and there is stark terror when he realizes that young Marek has watched everything. In the black holes at the center of each of Julien's eyes Mathias's secret has been engulfed, just as at the level of the text it has been swallowed up by the yawning gap in the narrative. The resulting sense of guilt and fear reminds one of Alfred Hitchcock at his most remorseless, and yet, like Hitchcock's movies, *Le Voyeur* also has a kind of playfulness, as the narrator shares with the reader a wry amusement at Mathias's unsuccessful attempts to fast-talk his way to quick sales with the canny fisher-folk, or at the appropriateness of the title of the picture show at the island cinema: *Mr. X on the Double Circuit.* Indeed, this is itself particularly appropriate, because Mathias covers the same itinerary twice and because of the ubiquitousness in the novel of the figure-eight motif, represented, for example, by the two juxtaposed circles of the voyeur's eyes.

The text is dense with resonances of this kind. Just as *Les Gommes* is based on a "superfluous" twenty-four hours, Mathias "loses" about sixty minutes: sixty minutes during which something was done to harm Jacqueline. Or was it? The salesman indulges in manic attempts to account for his use of time on the island because he is torn between two conflicting impulses: that of his professional obligations as a salesman, on the one hand, and that of his sexual fantasies, on the other. All the reader can be sure of is that there was a death, but it could have been an accident: that indeed is what the local people assume, and they must be familiar with corpses washed up by the sea, sufficiently at least to tell the difference between cigarette burns and natural abrasions. If Mathias did not in fact kill this "Violette," he would have had no difficulty in fantasizing the whole business. He would then, quite naturally, have felt acute guilt over this fantasy. A man who can see—as Mathias does—an ambiguous mixture of surrender and constraint in a simple snapshot of Jacqueline would certainly experience little difficulty in embroidering richly upon the image. Without the hypothesis of murder, however, it is difficult to account for the role in the story of Julien who—if Mathias is a rapist—becomes the true voyeur, because he has derived pleasure from watching Mathias act out his own fantasies for him.

Le Voyeur is widely regarded as Robbe-Grillet's finest work, an impressive and moving piece of fiction in which the technique of narration is exactly appropriate to the subject, a novel which owes something of its form, manner, and tone to the traditional detective story but which transcends its model. It handles a serious and emotive topic—rape followed by murder—without sensationalizing or trivializing it. This is all the more

commendable because in later works Robbe-Grillet sometimes indulges in facile, frivolous attitudes to sadism. In *Le Voyeur* he handles Jacqueline's death with black humor, perhaps, but in such a way that the basic seriousness of Mathias's sick mentality is not ignored.

If *Le Voyeur* is probably Robbe-Grillet's masterpiece, his next novel, *La Jalousie* (1957; translated as *Jealousy*, 1959), is the one by which he is perhaps best known. The title itself provides a key to the double meaning which lies at the heart of the book: in French, *la jalousie* not only means jealousy but also is the ordinary word for slatted shutters or blinds. In this novel a jealous husband spies on his wife from the wide balcony of their house as she sits behind the blinds in her bedroom; the blinds give him an uneasy sense of security and yet also a voyeuristic thrill. Thus *La Jalousie* takes up where *Le Voyeur* left off: the narrator and the voyeur are now one.

Closely scrutinized by the voyeur for signs that they are beginning an affair are the voyeur's wife, designated simply as A, and Franck, the owner of a nearby plantation. For unlike *Le Voyeur*, this novel is set in the tropics where Robbe-Grillet worked for a time; indeed, he has acknowledged the autobiographical nature of the story: in real life, he was the neighboring planter. Since the jealous husband is telling the story in a deceptively objective manner, he does not refer to himself as "je" (I) but instead uses impersonal constructions, such as "le moment est venu de s'intéresser à la santé de Christiane" (the moment has come to inquire after Christiane's health), to indicate his own role in conversations over drinks on the veranda. Similarly he uses the present tense a great deal, since he is living in the continuous present of strong emotion. The almost geometric precision of the husband's tedious descriptions of the banana plantation is an attempt to conceal his unease about the relations between his attractive wife and their neighbor. Jealousy is never actually described—still less dissected, as it would be in a classic French novel—but is shown in the obsessive gazing, in the husband's morbid scrutiny of the presumed lovers' slightest utterance or gesture. The emotion is brilliantly symbolized by the adjustable blinds, through which the hero stares at the woman whose glance he cannot sustain when she happens to look in his direction.

Robbe-Grillet maintains that no chronological sequence of events can be established in *La Jalousie*, but there is a plot of sorts. It is clear that the two planters and their wives see each other often, which they are bound to do as isolated compatriots in a foreign land. When the story opens, Franck's wife is unwell and so no longer accompanies him on visits to the house. This suspiciously convenient illness starts the husband thinking his morbid thoughts, and after that everything which passes between A and Franck is grist to his mill. A detached observer would probably find little to get concerned about, but the husband is not a detached observer. At dinner the conversation turns on a book set in Africa which A is reading and which Franck has lent her. Since the husband does not know the novel which they are discussing he is excluded from their conversation.

He therefore watches all the more closely for any signs which might betray a growing intimacy between the two, and he thinks he catches a glimpse of a note being passed between them. Then, rather unusually, the wife appears to have failed to make herself understood by the native servant, and the husband is obliged to go in search of ice for their drinks. He suspects A and Franck of having taken advantage of his brief absence from the veranda to plot their next move. This motive appears to be confirmed when Franck announces that he is going to have to drive down to the port to arrange for the delivery of a new truck and A promptly suggests that she go with him to do some shopping. They agree on an early start so as to be able to be back the same night. In fact, they do not return until the following day.

All the time he is left on his own the husband prowls around the house. He searches his wife's room for incriminating evidence, and when in the evening A and Franck fail to return he gives in to his jealous fantasies, going so far as to imagine the car in which they are traveling hitting a tree and bursting into flames. When the presumed guilty pair turn up the next day they claim that they had to stop the night in a hotel because Franck's car had–again perhaps conveniently–broken down. Although closely watched, A behaves no differently from her normal immaculate self. Franck seems embarrassed, however; he makes an ambiguous apology about being an indifferent mechanic (which the husband takes of course to refer to his ineptness as a lover), and soon takes his leave. Apparently reassured that A shows no sign of wishing to leave him, the husband begins to relax and his fit of jealousy gradually subsides. Since the jealous fit *is* the novel–and the novel is a jealous fit–the one

ends with the other: they fade out together into a relatively calm silence. The novel closes on the neutral note with which it began, in objective description of the house and its surroundings.

Although it is not difficult to arrive at this simple outline of a story, Robbe-Grillet is right in saying that a precise chronology of events is impossible to establish, if only because narration and fantasy are inextricably linked, as are different kinds of memory. Indeed the odd contradiction in the narrative reflects the husband's own uncertainties: he will never know for sure whether in deciding to make the trip to the coast his wife was contemplating adultery. Nothing in her manner, at least, betrays any such intention. Shortly before the end the narrator thinks about the novel Franck and A have discussed so frequently, but he has only half-understood the story and gets into a frenzied muddle over it. Similarly he is himself part of, and deeply engaged in, a fiction the givens of which are as arbitrary as those of the book Franck and A have been reading. He keeps returning to events which he considers significant, such as the letter A appears to write and pass to Franck. In his mental rehearsal of occurrences like these he recalls (or thinks he recalls) different details, but he–or rather the text which expresses him–is prone to confuse different events, blur temporal distinctions, and even distort reality altogether. He is particularly anxious about events which he has not been able to observe directly, such as whether, when she leans inside Franck's car before his final departure, A kisses him goodbye in token of a shared night together, or whether she merely reaches in for something she has left in there.

For like all jealous men, he has a well-developed erotic imagination. The description of Franck destroying a centipede in the dining room while he is watched intently by A, herself scrutinized for her reactions by the jealous narrator, is paralleled later in a passage in which the solitary husband imagines Franck killing another insect in a hotel room he has rented with A. The analogy between the episodes–the one described and the other imagined–is assisted by another double meaning in French: the word *serviette* can mean both table napkin and hand towel. In the first occurrence Franck wads his napkin into a ball and crushes the insect with it, leaving a stain on the wall which later becomes inextricably associated in the narrator's mind with the possibility of a sexual relationship between his wife and his neighbor.

In the second passage–the imaginary one– Franck wads his *serviette* (now a hand towel) into a ball and squashes the centipede against the bedroom wall. The smooth transition from *serviette* as napkin to *serviette* as towel momentarily disguises from the reader that the narrative has slipped into the imaginary, indeed into erotic fantasy, in which the wife, excited by Franck's manly action against the insect, closes her elegant fingers in a tight grip on the sheet of the bed. In the dining room, she had been seen (or imagined) to clench the handle of her table knife, a natural enough reaction in the circumstances; this gesture is recalled, and developed erotically, in a quite exaggerated manner by the narrator when he imagines his wife watching her lover admiringly from the bed. Immediately after this orgy of fantasy the husband imagines the mosquito netting falling all round the lovers' bed, interposing an opaque veil as if to exclude the indiscreet gaze of the guilty voyeur.

Here and at other points in the narrative the hero betrays an awareness that his obsessive scrutiny of his wife is unhealthy, that it is as much the mark of a pervert spying on sexual activity as the action of a person with genuine cause to doubt the fidelity of a companion. So to calm himself he has recourse once more to describing banana trees. All of this makes *La Jalousie* a tour de force as a psychological novel. And yet Robbe-Grillet maintains that he has driven psychology out of narrative fiction and left behind a void of nonexplanation. But what he has done is, rather, to take psychological analysis a stage further than great predecessors such as Stendhal and Proust: he makes the jealous character an observer recounting the whole business in the third person as if it were of no direct personal concern to himself. But it is, of course: from this inherent contradiction between the hero's emotional involvement and his pseudo-objective stance Robbe-Grillet derives fine effects of irony–ones which Stendhal and Proust would have appreciated. The contradiction also accounts for the tone of suppressed hysteria, of violent feelings only just contained by a superficially dispassionate manner, which is the hallmark of Robbe-Grillet's best and most characteristic writing.

For, like the films *L'Année dernière à Marienbad* and *L'Immortelle*, *La Jalousie* is a love story only thinly disguised. The husband admires the symmetry of his wife's body and cannot take his eyes off her lustrous black curls moving in supple waves and brushing her shoulders lightly as she turns her head. Even when tortured by jealousy, he cannot resist quoting her witty rejoinders to Franck's sometimes crass remarks, just as he enjoys the spectacle of Franck's discomfiture when she suggests, à propos of the novel they are reading, that she can see nothing wrong in a white woman having a black lover, something which shocks the conventional neighbor. Even in its more somber moments, *La Jalousie* remains a humorous account of a love which is doubtful, tormented, and unhappy, certainly, but which survives acute suffering nonetheless.

After the disturbing eroticism of *Le Voyeur* and *La Jalousie*, Robbe-Grillet turned to something more epistemologically unsettling in his next novel, *Dans le labyrinthe* (1959; translated as *In the Labyrinth*, 1960). Like much else in Robbe-Grillet's writing, its method derives partly from Kafka: although every detail is drawn with painstaking clarity, the overall impression is one of confusion, as in a dream or imperfect recollection. In *Dans le labyrinthe* a soldier is wandering around a town in the depths of winter after a major military defeat; he searches for a man to whom he has, it appears, undertaken to give a parcel containing the personal effects of a dead comrade. When the advance guard of the enemy troops arrives to occupy the abandoned town the soldier is wounded in trying to escape, and eventually he dies in the flat of a young woman whose own husband is at the front and whose small son has befriended the lost soldier. Once again there is an autobiographical basis to the story: Robbe-Grillet has said that it arises out of the memory of seeing the victorious German army entering Brest in 1940.

In literary terms the novel grows out of what Robbe-Grillet was later to call "signes générateurs," or generative signs, in this case objects such as an infantry bayonet or *The Defeat at Reichenfels,* a picture of a military disaster which the narrator–who is perhaps a doctor, possibly the one called in to treat the wounded soldier– dwells upon in descriptions similar to those in *Instantanés.* Whether the entire text should be seen as developing out of a contemplation of this picture (depicting a café scene after a defeat) or whether the picture provides an objective correlative of the disaster in which the doctor indirectly takes part cannot and need not ultimately be determined.

As in Kafka, this uncertainty does not mean however that nothing can be known. The technique used in previous novels by Robbe-Grillet–

Dust jacket for Jo Levy's translation of Le Miroir qui revient *(Grove Press, 1989)*

that of returning to scenes previously described and modifying them in respect to this or that detail–is here perfected, but this internal ambiguity is continually being corrected by the care that is taken to pick things up where they were left off, so that a kind of narrative stability develops after all. The soldier's purpose in coming to the town is eventually, if belatedly, explained, and in spite of what are referred to as "small inconsistencies," something reasonably solid is established in the end. This is, after all, not so very different from the way one often has to learn things in real life, or attempt to recover them from memory; people find themselves frequently unable to reconstruct events to their entire satisfaction. That is no doubt why Robbe-Grillet insists in his preface to *Dans le labyrinthe* that the reality in question in this novel is strictly physical and totally without allegorical significance. He requests the reader therefore to see in it only the objects, the gestures, the words, and the events that are recounted, without seeking to give them either

more or less meaning than they would have in his or her own life. In other words, the soldier's story is his own and does not imply anything wider–as Sartre or Camus would–about the human condition in general.

Nevertheless this is a very "anxious" text, haunted by what is termed in the narrative exaggeration, strangeness, and death, and by the soldier's nightmares, panic, and dread of labyrinths, something encountered previously in *Le Voyeur*. The anxiety reaches its paroxysm as the soldier dies, after which the text gradually calms down, returning in the closing pages–like *La Jalousie*–to the same elements set forth in the opening pages.

Because Robbe-Grillet is experimenting in this novel with a self-generating work developed by "triggers" of various kinds, and even refusing on occasion textual excursions and plot developments which are not considered appropriate, it makes sense to speak of a form of vertigo in the text itself, a sort of controlled hysteria, which gives his writing its particular flavor and draws one into a world in which anxiety and enigma are not merely thematic concepts but, as in Kafka, are organizing structural elements in their own right. Thus Robbe-Grillet does not merely imitate the external features of Kafka's world–the aspects one thinks of as particularly Kafkaesque, such as claustrophobic mazes and contradictory utterances–he gets right inside it and re-creates it in his own terms.

Soon after the publication of *Dans le labyrinthe* Robbe-Grillet became involved in the cinema, first as scriptwriter for Alain Resnais, then as director himself. He has continued since then to make films that broadly reflect the preoccupations of the fiction which he has continued to write in parallel. The first two films, *L'Année dernière à Marienbad* (1961) and *L'Immortelle* (1963), explore the plangent theme of love and loss which is heard in *La Jalousie; Trans-Europ-Express* (1967) harks back in some respects to *Les Gommes*, especially to its pastiche of the thriller; and *L'Homme qui ment* (1968) carries over aspects of the political theme of *Dans le labyrinthe*. The films of the 1970s and 1980s, *L'Eden et après* (Eden and After, 1970), *Glissements progressifs du plaisir* (Progressive Slippings of Pleasure, 1973), *Le Jeu avec le feu* (The Game with Fire, 1975), *La Belle Captive* (The Beautiful Captive, 1983), explore (and exploit) pornographic stereotypes which the novels of these decades concentrate upon as well. Robbe-Grillet has always professed a fascination for the images and stereotypes of popular culture such as comic strips or James Bond movies. So it is not surprising that his later fiction offers sophisticated commentary on the clichés of the mass media.

His next novel, *La Maison de rendez-vous* (1965; translated in the U.S. in 1966 and, as *The House of Assignation,* in Great Britain in 1970) is set in the Hong Kong of the popular imagination, not the thriving business center which the British administer while the Chinese inhabitants make their pile. Robbe-Grillet's island is not the impressive but ultimately uninteresting economic miracle, but a city where illicit traffic in opium and young girls finances the most outlandish sexual indulgence and leads to the most ferocious gang warfare.

The particular stereotype in this novel–apart from a fantasy Hong Kong itself–is the Villa Bleue, a high-class brothel which is the "house of assignation" of the title. Various sinister characters inhabit the Villa, particularly Lady Ava, its madam, Lauren, its most expensive girl, and a phony Englishman, called Sir Ralph, who could have come straight out of the pages of a Victorian pornographic novel. The story is a deliberately contradictory one. Sir Ralph, alias Johnson, has murdered a man called Manneret, an associate of his in shady business dealings, and so has to leave Hong Kong in a hurry. But wishing to take Lauren with him, he needs to raise a large sum quickly to pay Lady Ava for the privilege. He applies to his associate Manneret for the money, and kills him when this is refused. He therefore has to leave Hong Kong in a hurry. But Johnson makes the mistake of returning to the Villa Bleue to carry off Lauren. He finds the British police waiting for him. In classic gangster style, the crook's moll has served as decoy and he has walked into the trap. The end is quite spine-chillingly effective:

> A l'étage au-dessus, la porte de Lauren est ouverte également. Johnson s'élance, pris d'une soudaine appréhension: quelque malheur serait arrivé en son absence . . . C'est au milieu de la pièce seulement qu'il aperçoit le lieutenant de police en short kaki et chaussettes blanches. Il se retourne d'un seul coup et voit que la porte s'est refermée et qu'un soldat, mitraillette au poing, se tient par devant, lui barrant la route. Plus lentement, son regard balaye toute la chambre. Le second soldat, devant les rideaux fermés du bow-window, le surveille aussi avec attention, tenant à deux mains sa mitraillette braquée sur lui. Le lieu-

tenant ne bronche pas, lui non plus, et ne le quitte pas de l'œil. Lauren est allongée sur le couvre-lit de fourrure, entre les quatre colonnes soutenant le ciel qui forme au-dessus d'elle comme un dais. Elle est vêtue d'un pyjama de soie dorée, moulant le corps, à petit col montant et manches longues, suivant la mode chinoise. Couchée sur le côté, un genou replié, l'autre jambe étendue, la tête relevée sur un coude, elle le regarde sans faire un geste, sans que bouge un seul trait de son visage lisse. Et il n'y a rien dans ses yeux.

(On the floor above, Lauren's door is also open. Johnson dashes in, seized with a sudden apprehension: something might have happened to her while he was away . . . It is only when he is in the middle of the room that he sees the police lieutenant in khaki shorts and white socks. He whirls round and sees that the door has shut behind him and that a soldier holding a machine-gun is standing in front of it, barring the way. More slowly now, his eye sweeps the whole room. The second soldier, who is by the closed curtains of the bay-window, is also watching him attentively, holding his machine-gun with both hands, trained on him. The lieutenant does not move either and does not take his eyes off him. Lauren is lying on the fur bedspread, between the four pillars that support the tester over her like a canopy. She is wearing pyjamas of golden silk that hug the lines of her body, with a small stand-up collar and long sleeves, in the Chinese style. She is lying on her side with one knee flexed and the other leg stretched out, her head raised on one elbow, looking at him without a single gesture, without moving a single feature of her smooth face. And there is nothing in her eyes.)

Although inconsistency is built into the narrative as an organizing principle, *La Maison de rendez-vous* is a good read for those who like exotic thrillers. It is certainly Robbe-Grillet's most attractive and amusing work. Like some of the books it parodies, it has a refreshing tendency not to take itself too seriously; the whole book, from the first paragraph (in which the narrator tells us that he is obsessed with sadoerotic imagery) onward, is firmly tongue-in-cheek.

After *La Maison de rendez-vous* Robbe-Grillet abandoned the novel for some years in order to concentrate on the cinema. He returned to prose fiction with *Projet pour une révolution à New York* (1970; translated as *Project for a Revolution in New York,* 1972), influenced by his increasingly frequent sojourns in the city. (In 1989 he served as visiting professor of French at New York University). This time the stereotypes are the American gangster story and the myth of urban violence in the United States. There is a deliberate spoof in evoking the idea of revolution in the distinctly unrevolutionary world of contemporary America; in any case Robbe-Grillet's revolution is more sadoerotic than political in character. The book–like the films he was making during the same period–exploits pornographic motifs, so that Robbe-Grillet's city of subways, skyscrapers, narrow straight streets, and ubiquitous fire escapes is no more (or less) like the real New York than the Hong Kong of *La Maison de rendez-vous* is like the British colony in southern China.

Not surprisingly, this novel was not well received by the critics. Robbe-Grillet's early books had been greeted for the most part with hostile incomprehension; then, when the reasons for his not writing novels with straightforward plots and identifiable characters had become clear, his works met with respectful acclaim. Now, however, the critics expressed unease about what they saw as shoddy sadism and a racist discourse which might almost be an act of blatant provocation toward those who might be genuinely preparing for a revolution in New York. Even if one does not find the book insulting, though, it is disappointing, even rather silly, and another instance of the way some Europeans, obsessed by the myth of America, have failed to understand it, preferring instead to turn stock images and tropes into transfigurations of the fantastic.

Beginning with *Projet pour une révolution à New York*, Robbe-Grillet's work, both in novel and in film, explores a world of bonds, fire, knives, and bites which draws so freely on the clichés of hard pornography as to leave the reader or spectator wondering if there is any difference. His next prose work, *Topologie d'une cité fantôme* (1976; translated as *Topology of a Phantom City*, 1977), is really a collection of discrete prose texts, some of which appeared in two books of photographs for which Robbe-Grillet provided the text and David Hamilton the plates. *Rêves de jeunes filles* came out in 1971 (and was translated as *Dreams of a Young Girl*, 1971) and *Les Demoiselles d'Hamilton* in 1972 (translated as *Sisters*, 1973), and both feature the soft-focus, mildly pornographic pictures which have made Hamilton famous through their poster and postcard sales throughout the world. But *Topologie d'une cité fantôme* also includes pieces written for *Construction d'un temple en ruines à la déesse Vanadé* (Construction of a Temple in Ruins

to the Goddess Vanadé, 1975), illustrated by Paul Delvaux, and *La Belle Captive* (The Beautiful Captive, 1975), illustrated by René Magritte; these clearly derive from the surrealistic images of both painters. The book written with Magritte also contains a fragment from Robbe-Grillet's most recent novel to date, *Souvenirs du triangle d'or* (1978; translated as *Recollections of the Golden Triangle*, 1984), which includes material from a pornographic photograph album, *Temple aux miroirs* (Temple of Mirrors, 1977), which features naked prepubescent girls, showing how the works of the late 1970s not only interrelate but also seem to feed off one another, as if, to paraphrase Robbe-Grillet's description of *Souvenirs du triangle d'or*, they were indulging in sadoerotic practices with the body of their own narrative, an incestuousness which is not accidental, or the result of shortgage of material, but an organizing principle in itself.

The principal stereotype in *Topologie d'une cité fantôme* and *Souvenirs du triangle d'or*–apart from the now ubiquitous triangle of the female pudenda–is apocalyptic writing made popular by science-fiction authors on both sides of the Atlantic. In the preface to *Topologie d'une cité fantôme*, the narrator describes how he imagines the "phantom city," and the terms he uses are decidedly apocalyptic:

Avant de m'endormir, tenace encore cependant, la ville morte . . .

Voici. Je suis seul. Il est tard. Je veille. Dernière sentinelle après la pluie, après le feu, après la guerre, j'écoute encore à travers des épaisseurs sans fin de glace blanche les imperceptibles bruits absents: derniers craquements des murailles brûlées, cendre ou poussière s'écoulant en menu filet d'une fissure, de l'eau qui goutte au fond d'une cave à la voûte fêlée, une pierre qui se détache à la façade éventrée d'un immeuble monumental, dégringole en rebondissant d'anfractuosités en corniches, et roule sur le sol parmi les autres pierres.

(Before I fall asleep, still stubbornly persistent, the dead city. . . .

Right. I am alone. It is late. I am keeping watch. The last watchman after the rain, after the fire, after the war, I listen still through endless thicknesses of white ice for the imperceptible, absent sounds: the last crackings of burnt walls, a thin stream of ash or dust pouring from a split, water dripping in a cellar with a fractured vault, a stone coming loose from the gutted façade of a large and important-looking building, tumbling down, bouncing from projection to cornice to roll on the ground among the other stones.)

However, Robbe-Grillet's rituals of violence and representation constitute a deliberately jokey apocalypse. Although he deals with some fairly extreme states of nightmare he is concerned with developing a form of fiction which is increasingly metatextual. For example, he is acutely conscious of the fact that a novel, however unconventional in form, has to stop somewhere. The writing of the end of a book is different in kind from the writing of the beginning, he maintains, because the text itself becomes conscious, as it were, that time is running out, that the material is exhausted, and that possibilities of prolongation have to be resisted. In the closing pages of *Projet pour une révolution à New York,* for instance, the word *chat* (cat) presents itself but is turned aside as an obtrusive irrelevance at this late stage in the proceedings as the narrator, haunted by what Frank Kermode has called "the sense of an ending," hastens to close the fictional shop and go home. In his last three novels, indeed, Robbe-Grillet has written the ultimate apocalyptic work: fictions about the end which bring themselves to an end in wry commentary on the popular genre of doom fiction, which owes as much to the fantasies of the Marquis de Sade as it does to any biblical vision of the end of things.

Since publication of these science-fiction-style books, Robbe-Grillet has written three relatively minor works. The first, *Le Rendez-vous,* was written and published in 1981 at the suggestion of Yvone Lenard, an American college professor who wanted a story for her students written in idiomatic French according to an order of grammatical progression supplied by Lenard with the needs of intermediate to advanced users in mind. "As a true writer would," writes Lenard, "Robbe-Grillet found in this progression the very elements, not only of his expression, but of the deep, underlying structure of his story." This reworks the now familiar stock-in-trade of puzzles, tailor's dummies, and the myth of Oedipus, but adds little (except in terms of humor, this is not a text, fortunately, which takes itself too seriously) to the Robbe-Grillet canon. A trade edition entitled *Djinn* (*Djinn* is the French pronunciation of the English name Jean) appeared the same year and was published in English translation in 1982.

The second work is the charming autobiographical essay *Le Miroir qui revient* (1984), which was hailed by most critics, weary no doubt of seeing Robbe-Grillet endlessly rehash his own clichés, as a fresh departure. The mirror of the title refers to a tall story about a looking-glass which floats in on the tide bearing the image of Henri de Corinthe's betrothed. She was drowned, the reader is told, off Montevideo, and her body was never found, but she is there, in the mirror, smiling up enigmatically at Henri with her pale blue eyes. Corinthe–the Oedipal associations are obvious–is (Robbe-Grillet claims tongue-in-cheek) a close friend of the Robbe-Grillet family, about which Robbe-Grillet himself has much to say in this work of self-revelation.

Critics were delighted to see shamelessly flaunted a backsliding into the discredited longing to recount one's past which Robbe-Grillet had seemed–especially in the collection of position statements entitled, with deliberate polemical intent, *Pour un nouveau roman* (1963; translated as *For a New Novel,* 1966)–to have put firmly behind him. That this same Robbe-Grillet, self-appointed high priest of objective writing, principal of an *école du regard,* should start talking about himself, his parents and sister, his protective love of his wife, and his dislike of children other than little girls, took most watchers of the French literary scene by surprise. Soon, though, the critics were rubbing their hands at the thought of all those American Ph.D. students who would be tearing up their chapters on creative methodologization and intertextuality in the works of the one contemporary "scriptor" who had been expected by academe to stick to his impersonalist guns.

But it was not as simple as that. "Je n'ai jamais parlé d'autre chose que de moi" (I have never spoken about anything but myself) were the opening words of an autobiographical fragment which had appeared some years previously and which should have put everyone on his guard. This fragment is the opening section in *Le Miroir qui revient,* and sets the tone for a remarkably frank memoir. It is also in places a moving one. For example, in one episode he tells how his father, age about six, went to bake a cake with his friends, taking with him a precious slab of butter which his mother had given him for the purpose. But the children squabbled, and the cake was never made, so the little chap came back alone in the hot sun, his heart suddenly overflowing with the misery of the world while the butter, clumsily rewrapped, slowly melted in his hands.

It is also very witty. Robbe-Grillet recalls, for instance, his instructor in the Nuremberg armaments factory, a Turk whose grasp of French was less than perfect, who, when he tried to introduce his pupils to technical terms, unwittingly made obscene puns in French, much to the ribald delight of his unwillingly recruited class. Humor has always been a feature of Robbe-Grillet's writing, but never before as explicitly and uninhibitedly as this.

He describes the family he comes from as a closely knit clan presided over by a father who was utterly devoted to his own people and totally mistrustful of everybody else. This "kind papa" was–Robbe-Grillet makes no bones about it–an extreme right-wing anarchist so perverse in his political attitudes as to be rather likable. Although an anti-Semite, he would never have dreamed of handing over individual Jews to the Germans. And although he hated the British as the traditional enemies of his country, he introduced his children to masterpieces of juvenile literature translated from English. Endearingly, and with a sense of humor which his son inherited, he was candid about his eccentricities and admitted that he was perhaps not "quite normal."

In *Le Miroir qui revient* Robbe-Grillet shows himself to be extremely percipient about the curious addiction of the French Right to irrational and even inconsistent policies. They aimed to restore to the French throne a pretender who had no time for them; supported vociferously a church which excommunicated them; and collaborated with an invader who had every intention, once final victory was secured, of making France a country of slaves in the service of the purer Aryan peoples. What cured him of such nonsense, Robbe-Grillet believes, was witnessing in wartime Germany where those political attitudes led. For the same reason he is astute in his assessment of Céline, one of the great novelists of twentieth-century France and yet a rabid anti-Semite.

More interesting, though, than his occasional stabs at literary criticism in this book are the insights he offers into the ways of creation themselves, particularly the manner in which the pseudo-objectivity of reality is subverted by human subjectivity. Relativity is, he believes, the only absolute. This is a lesson which his scientific training taught him, and he has held fast to it ever since. The novelist can write of the world only from a personal standpoint, limitedly, subjectively. This entails a radical approach to charac-

ter and an equally thoroughgoing reappraisal of plot, which, unlike those of Balzac, designed in a linear and consistent fashion, must proceed in fits and starts, with contradictions not teased out but actually built into the structure, as in *La Maison de rendez-vous*. Similarly, *Le Miroir qui revient* loops back on itself, so that it is not only the mirror which returns; topics, raised earlier, also return again.

Perhaps the most interesting avowal in this autobiographical essay is that Robbe-Grillet is a fanatically tidy person. This obsession of his for order underlies all his fictional writing, he confesses. It explains why his heroes behave so neurotically, checking and rechecking their schedules as in *Le Voyeur*, or counting and recounting the rows of banana trees as in *La Jalousie*. "Les choses ne sont jamais définitivement en ordre" (things are never definitively in order) are almost the last words of the dying Lady Ava in *La Maison de rendez-vous*. Robbe-Grillet clearly intends to suggest, through this witty essay in autobiography, that they shall be his epitaph too.

Le Miroir qui revient, which was followed by a wordier, less witty, more aggressively argumentative sequel, *Angélique ou L'Enchantement* (Angélique or Enchantment) in 1988, caused quite a stir in France when it was published, and it even sold quite well. In general, however, in spite of considerable notoriety, and with as many as forty percent of his French titles being marketed outside France, Robbe-Grillet is hardly a popular writer. His response to this circumstance is to claim that no one has ever really understood him. There is some truth in this assertion. As recently as 1971, one critic wrote that Robbe-Grillet "despises humanism" and prides himself on "rising above the weakness of human nature," whereas the fact is that he goes to great lengths in *Pour un nouveau roman* and elsewhere to make it clear that, far from setting himself above other people, he shares all the normal emotions and weaknesses, and that the only humanism for which he feels contempt is the facile anthropocentric illusion of nineteenth-century positivism and its twentieth-century offshoot, the "tragic" pessimism of such writers as Albert Camus. Since he is without religious belief himself, Robbe-Grillet would even claim, somewhat indignantly, that in his world mankind is on the contrary supreme, because it stands alone, subordinated to no being and nothing in the universe.

In spite of making what he thought were unambiguous statements of this kind, Robbe-Grillet has found, to his wry amusement, that there are almost as many Robbe-Grillets as there are critics of his work. Early reactions in France were predictably hostile and uncomprehending–the equivalent, on the level of literary criticism, of the pot of paint flung in the public's face–but these soon gave way, in serious organs of opinion, to more considered responses. In 1954 the then relatively little-known theorist Roland Barthes published an influential essay on *Les Gommes* and on one or two of the *Instantanés* texts. This commentary (collected in Barthes's *Essais critiques*, 1964) advanced a philosophical interpretation which stressed the epistemological questioning at the heart of Robbe-Grillet's enterprise, and projected him as a writer concerned above all with the surface phenomena of the world. For some years Barthes's *chosiste* (thingist) Robbe-Grillet remained the standard version. Then the American critic and friend of the novelist, Bruce Morrissette, in a major reinterpretation, *Les Romans de Robbe-Grillet* (1963; translated as *The Novels of Robbe-Grillet*, 1975), moved from Barthes's phenomenological stance almost to the other extreme, and adopted a psychological approach which stressed the subjectivity, accurately recorded, of the total vision of Robbe-Grillet's fictional world, and the obsessive quality of his narrators.

Younger critics such as Stephen Heath (*The Nouveau Roman*, 1972) and Ann Jefferson (*The Nouveau Roman and the Poetics of Fiction*, 1980) later drew attention to the possibility of a linguistics-based interpretation which stressed the novelist as user of language in a world in which human speech *is* reality, and not just its vehicle or what encodes it. Jefferson, for instance, argues that language creates ambiguity and paranoia in Robbe-Grillet's teleological structures; our view of history, she maintains, is "colored by our view of the language through which it is constructed, and our view of that language is equally determined by the kind of history which it elaborates."

In so energetically precipitating definitions in this way, Robbe-Grillet's novels reveal their strangeness (as well, paradoxically, as their richness, at first sight an unlikely word to apply to writing of this kind); but they also raise the suspicion that sophisticated approaches like these not only feed off, but also in their own way provoke, the kind of text Robbe-Grillet has been writing in recent years. In his later works, indeed, the influence of other critics and theorists can be discerned in ways often detrimental to the interest

and originality of the creative writing. He runs the risk of ending up in an impasse as a writer's writer of the most rarefied kind, an experimental, "laboratory" novelist whose appeal to a wider circle of readers is in serious jeopardy.

There are, in fact, signs that this has already happened. It is probable that posterity's verdict on Robbe-Grillet will be that he took literary postmodernism as far as it would go in terms of elaboration and stylistic experimentation, and in doing so forced his own work into a dead end. If the particular strand of postmodernism which Robbe-Grillet so typically and centrally represents is now exhausted–and there are strong indications that this is so–then his laudable efforts in the 1950s to find what he called in one of his essays "a way for the future novel" will be seen to have failed. Fortunately for him, one or two of the early novels, conceived before the theory was fully elaborated, transcend the dogma deployed to justify them after the event, and stand as impressive fictions in their own right, eruptions of the unconscious which subvert the sophisticated constructions of rational thought.

About 1960 Robbe-Grillet himself seems to have sensed that he could not repeat the achievement of *Le Voyeur* and *La Jalousie*. As a result, the novels published since *La Maison de rendez-vous* are mechanical and disappointing affairs, peddling an increasingly suspect form of near-pornography. It is one thing to probe the mentality of a character who derives satisfaction from imagining the torture of a young girl, as is the case in *Le Voyeur*, and quite another to present such notions as if they were universally shared fantasies, which is a claim implicit in Robbe-Grillet's later fiction.

Nevertheless, if his overall achievement is uneven, and if his recent statements to the effect that pornography is quite innocuous are merely silly, Robbe-Grillet remains a person of remarkable intellectual power who may well turn out to have had an importance in French literary and intellectual history in the twentieth century comparable only to that of Jean-Paul Sartre. He remains by far the best known of the so-called New Novelists in the United States, the highly articulate proponent of a certain kind of postmodernism which may now be moribund but which has been central to the literary history of France since World War II. He holds this position in spite of the fact that he has become in recent years something of a globe-trotting guru, a frequent presence at conferences and colloquia where his work and that of other New Novelists is discussed. In his early career, he had virtually the whole of the French literary establishment against him; now, as the forthright exponent of one form of French intellectualism, he has become a prominent member of that establishment. He is thus no longer the revitalizing force in contemporary French writing that he was in the 1950s. The time is perhaps ripe for a new Robbe-Grillet to appear on the French literary scene: one who will oppose his hegemony with all the zestful vigor which Robbe-Grillet himself deployed against the cultural leaders of his own generation.

Interviews:

Jean-Jacques Brochier, *Alain Robbe-Grillet, Qui suis-je?* (Lyons: La Manufacture, 1985).

Bibliography:

Dale Watson Fraizer, *Alain Robbe-Grillet: An Annotated Bibliography of Critical Studies 1953-1972* (Metuchen, N.J.: Scarecrow Press, 1973).

References:

Roland Barthes, "Littérature objective," in his *Essais critiques* (Paris: Seuil, 1964), pp. 29-40;

John Fletcher, *Alain Robbe-Grillet* (London & New York: Methuen, 1983);

Stephen Heath, *The Nouveau Roman: A Study in the Practice of Writing* (London: Elek, 1972);

Ann Jefferson, *The Nouveau Roman and the Poetics of Fiction* (Cambridge: Cambridge University Press, 1980);

Bruce Morrissette, *Intertextual Assemblage in Robbe-Grillet from Topology to the Golden Triangle* (Fredericton, N.B.: York Press, 1979);

Morrissette, *Les Romans de Robbe-Grillet* (Paris: Editions de Minuit, 1963), translated as *The Novels of Robbe-Grillet* (Ithaca: Cornell University Press, 1975);

Obliques, special issue on Robbe-Grillet, 16-17 (1978);

Leon S. Roudiez, *French Fiction Today: A New Direction* (New Brunswick: Rutgers University Press, 1972), pp. 206-232;

Ben Stoltzfus, *Alain Robbe-Grillet: The Body of the Text* (Rutherford, N.J.: Fairleigh Dickinson University Press, 1985);

John Sturrock, *The French New Novel* (London: Oxford University Press, 1969), pp. 170-235.

Emmanuel Roblès
(4 May 1914-   )

James A. Kilker
Southern Illinois University at Carbondale

BOOKS: *L'Action* (Algiers: Soubiron, 1938; Paris: Charlot, 1946);

La Vallée du paradis (Algiers: Charlot, 1941; Paris: Charlot, 1946);

La Marie des quatre vents (Algiers: Charlot, 1942);

Travail d'homme (Algiers: Charlot, 1943); translated by Dorothy Bolton as *The Angry Mountain* (London: Hutchinson, 1948);

Nuits sur le monde (Algiers: Charlot, 1944; Paris: Charlot, 1945);

Les Hauteurs de la ville (Paris: Charlot, 1948);

Montserrat (Paris: Charlot, 1949);

Garcia Lorca (Algiers: Editions du Cactus, 1949);

La Mort en face (Paris: Seuil, 1951);

Cela s'appelle l'aurore (Paris: Seuil, 1952); translated by Therese Pol as *Dawn on our Darkness* (New York: J. Messner, 1954; London: Collins, 1954);

La Vérité est morte (Paris: Seuil, 1952);

Porfirio (Algiers: Rivages, 1953); translated as *Porfirio* in *Three Plays* (1977);

Federica (Paris: Seuil, 1954); translated by Joyce Emerson as *Flowers for Manuela* (London: Redman, 1956);

Le Grain de sable (Paris: Editions de l'Empire, 1955);

Les Couteaux (Paris: Seuil, 1956); translated by Geoffrey Sainsbury as *Knives* (London: Collins, 1958);

L'Horloge, suivi de Porfirio (Paris: Seuil, 1958); *L'Horloge* translated as *The Clock* in *Three Plays* (1977);

L'Homme d'avril (Paris: Seuil, 1959);

Le Vésuve (Paris: Seuil, 1961); translated by Milton Stansbury as *Vesuvius* (Englewood Cliffs, N.J.: Prentice-Hall, 1970);

Jeunes Saisons (Algiers & Paris: Baconnier, 1961);

Un Raisin au soleil, adapted from Lorraine Hansberry's play (Paris: Seghers, 1963);

La Remontée du fleuve (Paris: Seuil, 1964);

Plaidoyer pour un rebelle, suivi de Mer libre (Paris: Seuil, 1965); *Plaidoyer pour un rebelle* translated as *Case for a Rebel* in *Three Plays* (1977);

Emmanuel Roblès

La Croisière (Paris: Seuil, 1968);

Un Printemps d'Italie (Paris: Seuil, 1970);

L'Ombre et la rive (Paris: Seuil, 1972);

Saison violente (Paris: Seuil, 1974);

Un Amour sans fin (Paris: Périples, 1974);

Capuche (Paris: Laffont, 1975);

Un Amour sans fin, suivi de Les Horloges de Prague (Paris: Seuil, 1976);

Les Sirènes (Paris: Seuil, 1977);

Three Plays, translated by James A. Kilker (Carbondale: Southern Illinois University Press, 1977)—comprises *Porfirio*, *L'Horloge*, and *Plaidoyer pour un rebelle;*

Clairières du temps (Paris: Atelier des Grames, 1978);

L'Arbre invisible (Paris: Balland, 1979);

Venise en hiver (Paris: Seuil, 1981);

Un Château en novembre, suivi de La Fenêtre (Paris: Seuil, 1984);

Emmanuel Roblès, Théâtre complet, 2 volumes
  (Paris: Grasset & Fasquelle, 1985, 1987);
La Chasse à la licorne (Paris: Seuil, 1985);
Routes tibétaines (Paris: Grasset & Fasquelle, 1986);
Thomas et Chat-gris (Paris: Grasset, 1986);
Norma ou l'exil infini (Paris: Seuil, 1988).

PLAY PRODUCTIONS: *Montserrat,* Paris, Théâtre Montparnasse, and Algiers, Théâtre du
  Colisée, 23 April 1948;
Porfirio, Algiers, Théâtre de la Rue at Salle Valen-
  tin, 25 March 1953;
La Vérité est morte, Paris, Comédie-Française, 26 No-
  vember 1953;
L'Espagnol courageux, translated and adapted
  from Miguel de Cervantes's play, Festival of
  Mers-el-Kébir, 1958;
Un Raisin au soleil, adapted from Lorraine Hans-
  berry's play, Paris, Comédie Caumartin,
  1960;
Carlota, adapted from Miguel Mihura's play, Pa-
  ris, Théâtre Edouard VII, 1960;
L'Horloge, Paris, Théâtre des Buttes-Chaumont,
  10 April 1965;
Plaidoyer pour un rebelle, Brussels, Théâtre Royal
  du Parc, 13 April 1966;
Desert Isle, translated by Anne-Marie de Moret,
  Saint Louis University, Busch Center, 30 No-
  vember 1973; French version produced as
  Ile déserte, Saint Louis, Studio Theater, 23
  March 1975.

OTHER: Arturo Serrano Plaja, *Les Mains fertiles,*
  translated by Roblès (Paris: Charlot, 1947);
Serrano Plaja, *Galop de la destinée,* translated by Roblès (Paris: Seghers, 1954);
Ramón Sender, *Le Roi et la reine,* translated by Roblès (Paris: Seuil, 1955).

PERIODICAL PUBLICATIONS: *Ile déserte, Revue
  Périples* (1948);
Carlota, translated and adapted from Miguel Mihura's play, *Paris-Théâtre,* no. 161 (1960);
L'Espagnol courageux, translated and adapted
  from Miguel de Cervantes's play, *Œuvres Libres,* new series, no. 217 (June 1964):
  209-280.

Emmanuel François Roblès was born 4 May
1914 into a family of preponderantly Spanish ancestry in the most Spanish of Algerian cities,
Oran, where his father Manuel (the Spanish equivalent of Emmanuel), a mason, had also been
born in March 1887. His mother, Antoinette

Hélène Roblès, née Ruvira, born in Sidi-Bel-
Abbès, in the department of Oran, in August
1890, was one-quarter French, her grandmother
having married a Frenchman named Pon, from
Lyons. Roblès's parents were married on 9 August 1911, at the Eglise du Saint-Esprit in Oran
and in a civil ceremony three days later. A first
son, René-Joseph, born to them a year later, died
at the age of seven.

A month after Roblès's father left Oran in
August 1913 to work on a new military hospital
in Morocco, his wife, pregnant with Emmanuel,
went to Casablanca to visit him. Stricken with typhus, Manuel Roblès died during her stay there,
on 26 September. The father's death and the
birth of Emmanuel several months later forced
Antoinette Roblès to work as a laundress, and
the young Roblès's maternal grandmother, who
lived with them, assumed the dominant role in
managing the family. Since Antoinette Roblès
also worked weekends as a maid, even scheduling
the child's christening was a problem; he was not
baptized until September 1915, in a service at
Oran's Cathedral.

The Hispanic influence noteworthy in many
of Roblès's works was nourished early by life at
home. Although his mother conversed with him
in French, his grandmother spoke only Spanish
to the child. The older woman would whet her
grandson's interest in Spain with tales of her
youth in Andalusia. At age four, Roblès began to
learn to read and write in French at a nursery
school run by the Trinitarian sisters. Just prior to
his second year there, death struck his family
again when his elder brother died from cardiac arrest after an attack of rheumatic fever.

In the autumn of 1920, six-year-old Roblès
began primary school at a public institution, the
Ecole Jules Renard, where his academic record
provided him the means to a secondary education. In view of his agnosticism as an adult, it is
noteworthy that, while at Jules Renard, Roblès
took religious instruction; he received first communion at the Oran Cathedral in May 1923.
Roblès next attended the Collège Ardaillon, in
the heart of Oran, on a scholarship that provided
for all his supplies as well as for his tuition.
Roblès had already become an avid reader, seeking out any book he could borrow or buy with
small sums he received for chores, such as securing coal or water for neighborhood women. At
the Collège Ardaillon his reading was directed
for the first time. A thirst for adventure and exotic places was satisfied by the works of Jules

Verne and Pierre Loti, then two of his favorite authors.

But Roblès's activities were not limited to studies, reading, and odd jobs. He joined a gang of boys his age whose conduct after school and on holidays was patently unrestrained. In common with Roblès, they were fatherless; their mothers worked, and they were left free to follow their whims and inclinations. Their fathers, mostly members of the poor Hispanic working class who had been drafted into the French infantry during World War I, had been killed or wounded on the western front. To make matters more difficult, Roblès lost his grandmother not long after entering Ardaillon, and with her death all parental restraint disappeared.

Though the boys expended much of their energy in sports, they also engaged in such high jinks as breaking street lamps with slingshots or smearing tar on bedsheets hung out to dry. Roblès evoked the era and events in his essay *Jeunes Saisons* (Young Seasons, 1961). Though he matter-of-factly describes the unbridled, sometimes reprehensible antics of his cohorts, there was a redeeming side to such camaraderie. The Oran of Roblès's youth was rife with racism and social prejudice. One leading city newspaper, the *Petit Oranais*, was anti-Semitic. Yet the Jews and mainly Hispanic Christians of Roblès's group were bound by feelings of loyalty and fraternity and harbored no prejudice or ill will toward the Muslims.

Other adolescent experiences, slightly fictionalized, were to find expression in a novel, much later: *Saison violente* (Violent Season, 1974), whose title is probably an echo of a poem by Guillaume Apollinaire. Madame Quinson, in fiction and reality, was a wealthy colonial woman (*pied noir*), the widow of a career army officer killed in World War I. Roblès met her through his mother who had done domestic work for her. When Antoinette Roblès was no longer able to support her son, Madame Quinson agreed to lodge him in her home. In the short time Roblès lived there he was able, probably for the first time, to measure the distance that separated rich from poor and colonized from colonizer.

Besides becoming more acutely aware of his own status in colonial Oran's socioeconomic structure, Roblès benefited from Madame Quinson's lending him books from her late husband's library. Because Monsieur Quinson had been stationed in many French colonies, his collection was especially well furnished in travel books on exotic areas, including Tonkin and Madagascar. At the same time, the husband of another of Madame Roblès's employers, Monsieur Epry, a professor and probably a socialist, opened to Roblès his own library of books on politics as well as travel. Monsieur Epry also encouraged and paid for Roblès's use of the municipal library.

During Roblès's stay with Madame Quinson, he met the man who would most influence his lifestyle, if not his literary career. Roblès began to attend physical training at a gymnasium established by a former foreign legionnaire, Emil Mosel, an Austrian who had become a French citizen. Roblès, who worked with weights and did Greco-Roman wrestling, came to admire Mosel and to regard him as the father he never had. Roblès followed his precepts to remain in good physical condition, but owing more to Mosel's example than his admonitions, Roblès has never taken alcohol nor smoked. His fixation on Mosel was probably increased by the fact that his mother was thinking of remarriage, which Roblès abhorred as a betrayal of his deceased father.

Although by the time of the wedding Roblès had almost come to accept his new stepfather, a widower named Pedroti, he left to live with his paternal grandmother. Two months later, he moved in with his mother's sister and her husband for a year. His acceptance of his new stepfather finally came when he was able to look upon his mother's remarriage as a *mariage de raison*, a sacrifice made for him, her only son, and, as he finished his studies at the Collège Ardaillon, he was living independently in a vacant laundry room offered him by his mother and stepfather on the top floor of the building in which they lived. Here Roblès studied for the competitive examinations that gave him a full scholarship to the Ecole Normale Supérieure in Algiers. The year was 1931.

The prospect of teaching offered comfortable security, even relative wealth, to a young man of Roblès's background. He went to Algiers to the Ecole Normale to prepare for that career. While he was studying there, a similar school opened in Oran, so Roblès returned there for his third and last year. In June 1934 he received his *brevet supérieur*, the equivalent of the *baccalauréat*.

During Roblès's normal-school years he earned extra money by writing for two Oran newspapers, *Oran-Républicain* and *Oran-Spectacle*. Savings he had from his part-time journalistic activities, along with free round-trip transportation offered him by Thomas Ibañez, a friend who was secretary of the Association des Amis de l'Union Soviétique, made it possible for him to participate in an organized tour to Russia, with return via Poland and Germany, in the summer of 1934. After seeing Leningrad, Moscow, Kiev, and Kharkov, on the way back to Paris, he left the group at Krakow and went to visit Berlin. This mid-August stay coincided with the German plebecite held to confirm Hitler as *Führer*. The violently polarized crowds, the sight of SA and *Wehrmacht* troops, hearing a speech by Goebbels in front of the Reichstag, and a glimpse of Hitler on a distant balcony marked Roblès's memory indelibly. He evoked those portentous events in an article for *Combat*, published 18 August 1945 and included by Jean-Louis Depierris in his 1967 book *Entretiens avec Emmanuel Roblès* (Conversations with Emmanuel Roblès).

During the 1934-1935 academic year Roblès taught in a small school named after Ernest Renan in the vicinity of Oran. He also wrote articles, without pay, for the *Semeur*, a socialist newspaper in that city. With no one to care for but himself, he had enough money from his teaching and journalism to allow him to take the kind of trips of which he had always dreamed. Under the spell of André Malraux's *Les Conquérants* (The Conquerors, 1928), *La Voie royale* (The Royal Way, 1930), and especially *La Condition humaine* (Man's Fate, 1933), which had won the Prix Goncourt, Roblès decided to travel to the Far East. At twenty-one he longed to write a full-length work, but he felt he needed more experience, more seasoning. First traveling to Paris in June 1935 to attend the first Congrès pour la Défense de la Culture, Roblès then went to Marseilles and set sail aboard the *Leconte de Lisle*. After stopovers at such ports as Port Said, Djibuti, Colombo, Madras, and Singapore, he reached Saigon, where the ship remained a week. Still inspired by Malraux, along with some shipboard companions, he made a side trip to Cambodia to see the ruins of Angkor Thom and Angkor Wat. The dances he witnessed there and an incident he observed while crossing the Mekong River on a ferry during a storm furnished material for a short story– almost a *reportage*–called "La Danse du dragon" (Dragon's Dance), later published by Charlot in a collection of his short fiction titled *Nuits sur le monde* (Darkness upon the World, 1944).

When he arrived in Haiphong, Roblès immediately implemented his plan of going to China via French Indochina. The itinerary would have taken him into the heart of China and on to Shang-

hai, but not many days into the trip Roblès fell ill with food poisoning and was rushed back to a Haiphong hospital.

Roblès, though weak, was able to return to Oran by 1 October, in time for the 1935-1936 school year. He was assigned to teach in nearby Mers-el-Kébir, but his health remained poor and he had suddenly become bald. A series of doctors proved unable to diagnose his illness, but one, toward the end of the school year, advised him to spend a few months at Pont d'Espagne, a station near Cauterets, in the Pyrenees. Roblès finally recovered to spend the rest of the summer at the home of his aunt and her husband, traveling once to Brussels to attend a peace rally.

While ill and teaching at Mers-el-Kébir, Roblès had written a romance which he later disposed of. With his health restored and a new teaching assignment in the Marine section of Oran, he began work on *L'Action*, his first novel, published in 1938. It revolves around a bus drivers' strike, inspired by the workers' struggles in Algeria, where the right to strike was not respected. Roblès was motivated by his working-class background and encouraged by the success of the Popular Front in France in 1936. The strike that he describes in *L'Action* actually took place in Oran, but Roblès, nostalgic for Algiers and the stimulating literary and artistic life he had enjoyed there, set the novel in that city. The hero of *L'Action*, Astone, was named after Aston, an English soccer player of the period whom Roblès admired. Another protagonist, Hadj, who under Astone's direction organizes fellow Muslim bus-company employees to strike, is the first Arab revolutionary hero in a French novel. Hadj, an intelligent, self-educated Arab denied not only the possibility of self-realization but also the opportunity to earn a decent wage in a closed colonial society, was a fictional harbinger in the 1930s of the widespread resentment and anger that would lead to the Algerian war of liberation starting in 1954. The character is a precursor of Smaïl, an Arab protagonist in Roblès's prophetic *Les Hauteurs de la ville* (The City Heights, 1948), published ten years later, which clearly indicates the inevitability of revolution in a society unresponsive to the basic needs of the majority of its people.

L'Action is a gripping story narrated with flair, but, like many novels, it has, as Roblès has admitted, certain weaknesses. Psychological insight, especially with regard to women characters, is slight, and verisimilitude is lacking in places. The lingering influence on certain passages of Malraux, as well as of American writers such as Steinbeck and Hemingway, whom he had rather recently discovered, became apparent to Roblès in retrospect. Yet many of the thoughts and attitudes, most notably the cult of fraternity and solidarity, found in Roblès's later works are already evident in his first novel.

Drafted into military service at Blida, near Algiers, 15 September 1937 for two years, Roblès was sent to l'Agha, a harbor seaplane base in Algiers, to be trained in meteorology. Roblès had spent the previous summer as a civilian in Paris, staying again with his aunt and uncle and attending the 1937 exposition. He had taken his manuscript of *L'Action* with him. A newspaper, *Œuvre*, offered to print it in serial form, but because Roblès felt the editor was trying to take advantage of him as an unknown writer, he refused.

In Algiers Roblès's military duties did not occupy all his time. Familiar with the city from his student days, he took full advantage of it. When he met Albert Camus at the Maison de la Culture, they immediately became friends, and he gave Camus *L'Action* to read. Favorably impressed, he suggested to Roblès that Edmond Charlot, who had just published Camus's *L'Envers et l'endroit* (1937), might also handle *L'Action*. Charlot, who ran his business on a shoestring, told Roblès that he presently lacked the capital to publish his work. Thus Roblès turned to the Soubiron brothers, Paul and Georges, also publishers in Algiers. They agreed to publish the novel and paid Roblès immediately. *L'Action* appeared in January 1938.

Although Roblès wanted to take courses in Spanish literature at the University of Algiers while he was stationed at l'Agha, his classes in meteorology did not leave him sufficient time. In addition, the international situation created by the Anschluss, Hitler's takeover of Austria, in March, and by the Sudeten crisis in September resulted in his unit often being restricted to quarters. He was, however, able to contribute articles to *Oran-Républicain* and *Alger-Républicain*. Because French soldiers at the time were not allowed to publish, Roblès used the pseudonyms Petrone and E. F. Chênes, the latter a French translation of his Spanish surname (in English, Oaks). The remuneration he received represented a welcome supplement to his meager military pay. Camus, who with Pascal Pia ran *Alger-Républicain*, virtually assured placement of Roblès's articles.

Camus also urged Roblès to write his second novel, in serial form, for the paper. Titled *La Vallée du paradis* (Paradise Valley, 1941) in book form, the longer serialized version was called *Place Mahon*, after a small square in the heart of Algiers, near the Place du Gouvernement and lower Casbah, where the action takes place. By the time the book version appeared, Place Mahon no longer existed, having been demolished to make way for a thoroughfare. But when Roblès was writing, in 1938, it was a picturesque district, reflecting the mixture of different nationals and underworld types it harbored. The serialized version of the novel was signed Emmanuel François Chênes. A lack of capital delayed Charlot's publication of a revised, tightened version of it "in boards" until September 1941.

La Vallée du paradis presents a recurring theme in Roblès's work: the desire to travel to faraway places, to escape the past and flee a milieu that will bring down upon the protagonist an unhappy destiny. Stegger, the protagonist of *La Vallée du paradis*, a World War I veteran who lives in an unidentified Mediterranean seaport, wants to start anew in the valley of the upper Paraná in Argentina, where he hopes to achieve independence and find happiness. Because of a woman, he had seriously injured a man in a fight and, as a result, was imprisoned. He escapes from prison, and, to acquire money for a passage to a better world, he robs the house of the man who had given him food and shelter when he was fleeing. Surprised by his benefactor in the act of stealing, Stegger, in a panic, strangles him. When he is pursued by the police, Stegger jumps to his death rather than be captured.

Symbolically Roblès names the company that promotes and recruits immigrants to the Paraná valley El Dorado, and the ship that is supposed to take them there bears the Spanish name *Valparaiso*, Valley of Paradise. Although the image of a beautiful ship called the *Valparaiso* and, especially, the distant colony to which it will take him represent paradise to Stegger, it is a goal he will never attain. Nonetheless, he has achieved a measure of happiness living out his revolt against an unjust society. It is this final struggle against evil and the genuine but temporary love of a woman in this port city that affirm his values and give him an identity in an absurd world. This may have been the only true happiness within Stegger's reach. After all, the tangible symbol of his happiness, the *Valparaiso*, is old, dirty, and ugly, and the attraction of the distant colony may well be illusory. The stoicism, if not satisfaction, with which Stegger accepts death in this early Roblesian novel points up an idea that recurs in some later works: the quest for the absolute may fall short and yet allow the protagonists to identify and appreciate retrospectively reasons for happiness that were at hand. Thus he may die at peace with himself.

In October 1938, with international tension eased for a time by the Western powers' capitulation to Hitler's demands for the Sudetenland, French military units were no longer on alert. Back in Algiers Roblès found time to begin work at the University of Algiers on a *licence* in Spanish literature, and he met and courted a second-year law student named Paulette Puyade. They married the following spring, on 22 April 1939. Paulette Roblès abandoned her studies to accept a position as teacher in Kouba, a suburb. In August, with his military duty coming to an end, Roblès was granted a *congé libérable*, a two-week furlough prior to discharge, during which he and his wife traveled to the Basque country and to Pau, in southwestern France, to visit her family. There Roblès received a telegram recalling him to Algiers and his unit. World War II was about to begin; he would not be discharged.

During the period of the Phoney War (September 1939-May 1940) Roblès served as a Spanish interpreter, but he soon became bored with his duties. Believing that the front in the West would remain stable because of the Maginot and Siegfried lines, and that an Allied offensive would eventually be launched against Germany from the Middle East through the Balkans, Roblès requested, and was eventually granted, a transfer to Rayak, a large French air base in Syria. He was to go as a meteorologist and thus went first to refurbish his meteorology skills at l'Agha. Simultaneously, Roblès studied Rumanian with a Rumanian doctor who was a refugee in Algiers.

Roblès was waiting to be assigned to a unit bound for Syria when the Germans launched their spring offensive, Belgium fell, and his unit received new orders. He was sent to Oued-Hamimine, the air base near Constantine in eastern Algeria, where, neglected by the French high command, with little to eat or to do, Roblès spent the month following the armistice with Germany. Finally, he was discharged on 29 July 1940.

Roblès immediately returned to his wife in Algiers. As a couple they applied for teaching posts and were named to a small school in the village of Turenne (now Sabra) west of Tlemcen,

not far from the Moroccan border and only an hour or so by train from Oran. The couple broke the monotony of their assignment by visiting Roblès's mother frequently as well as Camus, who had returned to Oran from France to marry Francine Faure.

The isolation Roblès felt in Turenne characterizes a short play he wrote there, titled *Ile déserte* (Desert Island). Of its six characters, only a married couple, Jérôme and Marie, have names; the others are interchangeable bureaucrats. Desiring to flee their island to seek happiness elsewhere, the couple is frustrated when they are obliged to see one bureaucrat after another for permission to emigrate, but to no avail. In this satire of a bureaucratic, faceless state, Roblès upholds, as he had in *L'Action* and would do in future works, the worth and dignity of the individual in a rigid, circuitous, indifferent society. The play was published in *Revue Périples*, a tiny Tunisian literary review, in 1948. It remained unproduced until the 1970s when it was produced, in French (1975) and in English translation (1973) in Saint Louis.

A more significant work Roblès began in this period was *Travail d'homme* (1943; translated as *The Angry Mountain*, 1948), a novel that brought him his first literary prizes, the Grand Prix Littéraire de l'Algérie, in 1943, and, in 1945, the Prix Populiste. Partially to dispel his feeling of isolation, also to satisfy his curiosity, Roblès occasionally visited the site of a dam under construction near Beni-Badel, a village a few kilometers south of Turenne, and his observations there became the inspiration for the novel.

Taking up again the workers' struggles and the poor working-class milieu of his early novels, Roblès describes the efforts of an army of workers in southern Spain against "an angry mountain." Raphaël, the hero, abandons a sales job in his uncle's furniture store for more virile work, a "travail d'homme," as a construction worker building a dam in a hostile environment. He runs a constant risk of death in his struggle against nature and the elements, and he is always in danger from the physical violence of some of his fellow workers. On the positive side of the struggle is the fraternity, the virile camaraderie he comes to feel for others among them. The conclusion pays tribute to the workers who risk their lives to keep the dam they are building for humanity from being swept away. However important the role of the individual, it is surpassed by the scope of the work in which he is engaged.

In the spring of 1941 Camus had organized an underground network to aid escapees from occupied Europe in reaching Gibraltar via Oran and Morocco. While at Turenne, Roblès was part of that network. On two occasions, at Camus's bidding, he guided individuals from Tlemcen to the Moroccan border. One of these occasions furnished material Roblès later used in his novel *Les Hauteurs de la ville,* in which the hero guides a member of the Resistance to the Moroccan border near Oujda. While they were living at Turenne, Paulette Roblès contracted typhus during an epidemic. Roblès incorporated details of the effects of the epidemic into *Les Hauteurs de la ville* and reported his observations to Camus, who was then writing *La Peste* (*The Plague,* 1947).

To recuperate Paulette Roblès returned to her mother's home in Algiers in spring 1941, and Roblès followed in the summer. Not wishing to return to Turenne, he obtained a teaching assignment at Grasel-Bizar, a village in the Kabylia region. Although Roblès liked the area, he was harrassed by police interrogations on several occasions. Because his novel *L'Action* showed leftist tendencies, and because he had translated poetry by Federico García Lorca into French, he was falsely accused of being a Communist. While he was in Algiers during the summer of 1942, he managed with the help of friends to be appointed instructor at the normal school in Bouzaréa, a suburb. Before the couple relocated, Paulette Roblès gave birth to a son, Paul, on 8 August 1942.

In this same period Roblès joined the local Resistance movement then preparing the way for the Anglo-American invasion of North Africa. Two days after the invasion, just as Roblès had resumed teaching, he was approached by two American officers familiar with his training in meteorology and his proficiency in Spanish. They offered him a job with the Psychological Warfare Branch (PWB), monitoring Spanish weather broadcasts and translating them into French. He accepted and immediately resigned from the Ecole Normale.

Besides allowing him a small but useful role in the prosecution of the war, the Americans' arrival benefited Roblès in ways he could not have foreseen. *Travail d'homme* had been completed, but a paper shortage was an obstacle to publication. The author succeeded in obtaining newsprint from the American military, and it was on this poor quality paper that the work was first published. When it won the Grand Prix Littéraire de l'Algérie, the recognition given Roblès was instru-

mental in securing him a position more attuned to his principal talent and interests. With the French armed forces rapidly rebuilding in Algeria, it was a question of time before he would be recalled for active duty. He left Listening Services, went back to the French air force as an *aspirant* (loosely, an officer candidate), and soon became a war correspondent.

Roblès worked for the newly created *Ailes de France,* a French air-force organ that disseminated both news and propaganda, with headquarters on rue Michelet in Algiers. While civilians carried out the technical work of publication, military personnel were correspondents who went on missions, most often with French units, and also reported on Allied air-force squadrons and activities. Correspondents were unarmed and their articles were subject to military censorship.

In the first months of his new assignment Roblès covered mainly French air-force flight-training schools in Morocco and Algeria which were being equipped with American aircraft and armaments. Shortly, however, he came closer to military action in Corsica, Sicily, Sardinia, and on the Italian peninsula. One article he wrote in Corsica concerned Antoine de Saint-Exupéry's last flight at the end of July 1944. Roblès had met the writer-pilot Saint-Exupéry the previous autumn in Algiers. Roblès's journalistic experiences gave him ideas and details for his short stories and novels. His "De l'autre côté de la vie" (On the Other Side of Life), included in *Nuits sur le monde,* is about a friend, Charles Andreï, sent to Corsica to work with the Resistance prior to French recapture of the island. Andreï was caught by the OVRA, the Italian fascist police, tortured, and shot. Experiences in Naples and a story he heard there about a young soldier who deserted because of love for a woman furnished Roblès the nucleus and setting for his 1961 novel *Le Vésuve* (translated as *Vesuvius,* 1970). In Rome conversations with Count Carlo Sforza, Italian minister of foreign affairs, about the German massacre of Italian hostages in the Ardeatine Caves, as well as a visit to the studio of an artist who had illustrated an article of his, led him to write *Un Printemps d'Italie* (A Springtime in Italy, 1970). Similarly, a charitable doctor he met in Sardinia became the model for the hero of *Cela s'appelle l'aurore* (1952; translated as *Dawn on our Darkness,* 1954). In short, the impact of World War II on Roblès was strong and durable, and incidents from the conflict came to replace the workers' struggles of his first two novels.

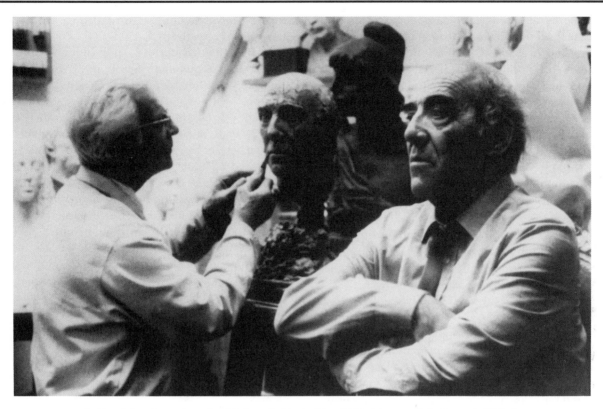

Roblès sitting for sculptor Paul Belmondo, Paris, May 1981 (photograph by James A. Kilker)

Following liberation in August 1944, Paris again became the center of French political and military power, and *Ailes de France* moved its headquarters there, changing its title to *Aviation Française*. Roblès served as its codirector, while remaining a war correspondent. On 16 December 1944 he was promoted to lieutenant. In the winter of 1944-1945 Roblès covered French fighter-squadron activities in Alsace, French heavy-bomber operations from an airfield near York, England, and fighting connected with the Remagen bridgehead in Germany. At the war's end he was with the French first fighter squadron near Kleinsachsenheim, a small village in Wurtenberg.

With the war over and the offices of *Aviation Française* now located in the rue Pierre-Charron, Paris, Roblès brought his wife and son from Algiers. His publisher, Charlot, had already established himself in Paris. On 22 February 1946, in Paris, Roblès was discharged for the second time from military service. As a civilian he was initially able to live on royalties from his books; from sales of articles to such journals as *Gavroche*, a literary weekly, *Le Populaire*, and Camus's *Combat;* and from continuing to write weekly articles for *Aviation Française*. In addition,

he started work on a play, *Montserrat*, destined to be his theatrical masterpiece, and on the novel *Les Hauteurs de la ville*. In the spring of 1946 Roblès had just completed the first act of *Montserrat*, and in May he read it to Camus, who expressed approval. Yet at this point Roblès put aside the play to concentrate on the novel.

Postwar economic conditions in France grew increasingly difficult, and the winter of 1946-1947 was especially trying. There were shortages of food and coal, and electrical failures were frequent. Given these hardships and having a young son to care for, Roblès decided his family would not spend the next winter in Paris but in Algiers, where life would be better and they could live with less expense. In April 1947 they left for North Africa, stopping for three weeks en route at Pau. In Pau Roblès completed *Les Hauteurs de la ville*.

Back in Algiers Roblès became literary critic at *Radio-Alger* and resumed work on *Montserrat*, which he finished that autumn. When Camus came back to Algiers in January 1948 on one of his regular visits, he saw Roblès and asked to read the finished play. Camus took the manuscript back to Paris. In March Roblès received a wire from Camus stating that *Montserrat* would be premiered at the Théâtre Montparnasse in Paris the next month. In fact *Montserrat* opened on the same day, 23 April 1948, both in Paris and at the Théâtre du Colisée in Algiers. Roblès attended the French opening; his wife, the Algerian one.

Except for some jibes from a few rightist critics, the play won critical acclaim and international popularity in theaters on both sides of the iron curtain. It was first published in *Monde Illustré* (5 June 1948) and in book form the following year. Unfortunately, the only version of *Montserrat*, either literary or theatrical, which was not a notable success was an English-language one. In 1949 Lillian Hellman, who acquired rights to the play, did an unfaithful adaptation that left playgoers with the false impression of a melodrama rather than the tragedy Roblès wrote.

Following on the heels of *Montserrat*, *Les Hauteurs de la ville* also appeared in 1948, under Charlot's imprint, and was a critical and commercial success. Whereas the principal and historical setting of *Montserrat* are owed to Roblès's reading of Latin American history while he was on his last military assignment, the plot of *Les Hauteurs de la ville* was suggested by Muslim uprisings around Constantine, Algeria, in May 1945. Yet the theme of the two works is the same: opposition to oppression. The action in *Montserrat* takes place against the backdrop of Simon Bolívar's struggle with Spain for South American independence. The Spanish mercilessly suppress freedom in Venezuela while struggling to rid themselves of the yoke of Bonapartist tyranny in nineteenth-century Spain. In *Les Hauteurs de la ville* the Muslims in Algeria, many of them ex-combatants who had fought for the freedom of France against the Germans, find that, paradoxically, they are in the same position vis-à-vis the French as the French were with respect to the Nazis. *Les Hauteurs de la ville* won the Prix Fémina in 1948.

While commuting between Algiers and Paris according to professional needs, Roblès took on new obligations in Algeria during 1948-1949. In addition to working for *Radio-Alger*, he accepted a position with the Service de la Jeunesse et des Sports and made literary lecture tours throughout Algeria. He and his wife had another child, a daughter, Jacqueline. His major writing project was a new play, one to express again his Hispanicism, *La Vérité est morte* (Truth is Dead, 1952). Centering on the siege of Saragossa during the Napoleonic campaign in Spain, the play was originally planned as the middle panel of a triptych fea-

turing *Montserrat* and a third drama which has never been completed.

In 1950 Charlot's publishing company failed. In September Seuil in Paris became Roblès's publisher, acquiring the rights to his publications with Charlot. The next year Seuil brought out *La Mort en face* (Facing Death, 1951), a book of three short stories with Spanish themes written earlier in Roblès's career. In 1952 Seuil published *La Vérité est morte*, which opened at the Salle Luxembourg of the Comédie-Française on 26 November 1953 and held the boards briefly. Although the play met with much success in later 1967 productions in Belgium and France, as well as in television and radio versions broadcast in several countries, including France, Belgium, and Czechoslovakia, Roblès felt its lukewarm initial reception could be traced in great part to a cabal organized to bring down Paul Descaves, a Freemason who was the newly named director of the Comédie-Française. It is true too that certain critics, among them Robert Kemp, writing in the *Monde*, felt that Roblès was unpatriotic to depict as aggressors French soldiers fighting in Spain during the Napoleonic invasion of that country.

In 1952 Roblès had one of his biggest commercial successes with the novel *Cela s'appelle l'aurore*. The hero, Valério, a selfless, charitable doctor, in his quest for happiness must choose between his wife, returning to Sardinia to join him, and his mistress, the woman he has come to love in her absence. Valério must also choose between turning in or protecting Sandro, a poor, downtrodden individual, a former soldier who had served under Valério in Libya and who has murdered a man. The murdered man had been the employer of Sandro's wife and had brought on her death by ill-treatment. The conflict is between social conventions or apparent justice and reality. True happiness for Valério, though, is not selfish, but rather bound up in his communion with humanity in general.

Among Roblès's activities in Algiers he had collaborated, in 1949, in founding a dramatic company called the Théâtre de la Rue. In 1953 he wrote for his company a comedy titled *Porfirio*. This farce, which pokes fun at the politics of a nameless banana republic dominated by the Star Company (United Fruit), was first produced in Algiers on 25 March 1953 and published that year in a limited edition. In 1958 it appeared in a volume with a play that has a Mediterranean setting, *L'Horloge* (The Clock). Its heroine, Vanina, incarnates the revolt against the rapacious Alfieri, a wealthy property owner who reigns over the town by terror, corruption, and exploitation of the weak.

Roblès's proclivity for Hispanic personages and settings came to the fore again in 1954 with the publication of his novel, *Federica* (translated as *Flowers for Manuela*, 1956), set in Spain and Algeria. Ricardo, the hero, much like Valério in *Cela s'appelle l'aurore*, feels a sense of honor and responsibility for a fellow creature, in this case, a young woman he has saved from rape. The same year Roblès went to Mexico to consult with Luis Buñuel, who made a film from the novel in 1956. Roblès's visit to Villahermosa during this trip sparked another novel, *Les Couteaux* (1956; translated as *Knives*, 1958). Roblès's hero, Pierre Mayen, a French veteran of World War I and an atheist, kills Salgado, a leader in the local struggle against what he believes to be religious fanaticism. For his scenes of pillaging and desecration of a church, Roblès was able to draw on events he had documented on a 1931 trip to Málaga, Spain, where republican anarchists carried out similar sacrileges.

Roblès had been to Japan in 1957 and, based on his experiences, he wrote a long story, "L'Homme d'avril" (The Man of April), which became the title work in a four-story collection published by Seuil in 1959. Two of the stories, "Un Matin de soleil" (A Sunny Morning) and "Le Rossignol de Kabylie" (The Nightingale of Kabylia), have been made into films. While Roblès was on the set in Algiers during the 1958 filming of "Un Matin de soleil," his son accidentally shot himself in the head with Roblès's revolver. Deeply grieved by Paul's death, the family moved to Paris.

From this base, where he had been made editor of Seuil's Mediterranean series consisting of works by writers from countries that bordered that sea, Roblès was constantly on the move. Europe, North and South America, Africa and Asia were on his itinerary. He lectured widely at universities, made lecture tours for the French government, and traveled throughout France on promotional trips for Seuil.

Despite his heavy schedule, Roblès continued to write prolifically. *Le Vésuve* and *Un Printemps d'Italie* both reflect his hatred of war—the horror it visits on combatants; the slaughter of innocents it entails (the German air force raids on Naples in *Le Vésuve*, the Allied raids on Rome in *Un Printemps d'Italie*); and the savagery it provokes in man, whatever the aims of the belliger-

ent powers (the rapes of Neopolitan women by American Rangers in *Le Vésuve* the massacre of civilians by the Germans in *Un Printemps d'Italie*). Yet if Longereau in *Le Vésuve* and Sainte-Rose in *Un Printemps d'Italie* both hate war and, for a time, seek personal happiness, both know ultimately that they must fight to eradicate fascism.

In both the factual *Jeunes Saisons* and in the autobiographical novel *Saison violente*, Roblès narrates versions of two periods of his boyhood in Oran. Despite the local color and the warmth of certain relationships that permeate the works, they constitute a condemnation of racism and colonialism. The boy of Spanish background will never be considered the equal of the French colonials, but merely "un cinquante pour cent," a fifty percenter.

A metaphysical concern not found in Roblès's other works appears in the protagonist André Gersaint of *La Remontée du fleuve* (Going Up the River, 1964). This work was well received by critics of the Right and less favorably by those of the Left. Obsessed by the absurd death of a young student in a motorcycle accident, Gersaint sees God as indifferent to human destiny and as a negation of his own values. God's apparently gratuitous act is answered by a gratuitous act on Gersaint's part: he fires at random on an unknown passerby. Behind the hero's despair lies the suffering of Roblès during the six years after the absurd death of his son. Gersaint is hired as secretary for Holberg, the man he has wounded, and thereby meets the woman who becomes his mistress. His love for her is his salvation—the means by which he is able to go "up the river."

Although not premiered until 1966, the drama *Plaidoyer pour un rebelle* (published in 1965 and translated as *Case for a Rebel* in 1977), written during the Algerian war, was prompted by the act of a prorebel Frenchman who had planted a bomb to sabotage the power plant where he worked. Roblès transposes the action to the Dutch East Indies, and the protagonist, Keller, is Dutch, but this matters not, for the theme is universal. Keller is caught disarming his bomb to prevent it from killing innocent workers. Keller has gone against his own cause in the interest of humanity and must pay the price. Before the judge, however, he indicts colonialism.

Mer libre (Open Sea), a play published in 1965 with *Plaidoyer pour un rebelle*, is set in the restricted space of a boat, giving it a unity of place seen also in *La Croisière* (The Cruise), a novel published in 1968. Magellan in *Mer libre* must confirm his theory that there is a passage around South America, refusing to turn back, despite the cowardice and mutiny of some officers and crew. In fact, he must lie to succeed in his quest. *La Croisière* dramatizes a class struggle between wealthy bourgeois, a French and a German couple, on the one hand, who have chartered a luxury yacht, and a proletarian crew, on the other. Georges Maurer, the protagonist, of working-class origin, has been hired as a guide and interpreter. Still obsessed by his experiences as a combatant in the Italian campaign in World War II, Maurer had hoped that final victory over the forces of oppression in that conflict would bring a better world. But nothing has changed. Victory over the Nazis has left intact the bonds of money and social class that transcend the communality of language and nationality and oppress the working classes. Although Maurer is at first perceived by the crew as being little more than a flunky to the rich, a conflict of interests brought about by the chance discovery of an abandoned, heavily damaged Greek cargo ship eventually reveals his depth of attachment to the working crew who represent the class of his origins.

In 1972 Roblès published a book of short stories, *L'Ombre et la rive* (The Shadow and the Shore). The following year he was elected to the Académie Goncourt and worked on *Saison violente* between lecture tours in Yugoslavia and in South America. In 1974, the year *Saison violente* was published, Paulette Roblès died in the course of surgery. He dedicated to her the short but touching book of poems bearing the title *Un Amour sans fin* (A Love without End, 1974). The poems were republished in 1976 in a volume that also included *Les Horloges de Prague* (The Clocks of Prague). Both *Un Amour sans fin* and *Les Horloges de Prague* reflect nostalgic reminiscences of the poet in various sites and cities of the world. One senses in most of the poems the loss of a companion who formerly accompanied him and whom he sometimes addresses.

Roblès's novel *Les Sirènes* (The Foghorns) was published in 1977. The action takes place in the English port of Liverpool, to which André Donat, an engineer in the merchant marine, comes to repair one of his company's ships. Donat is deeply distressed and depressed because of his wife's recent death, but he transcends his grief by striving increasingly for the happiness of others. The antagonism shown between the wealthy businessmen and the unemployed–and

even sailors–is reminiscent of the class conflict aboard the yacht in *La Croisière*.

Class distinction is apparent too in *L'Arbre invisible* (The Invisible Tree), a long story published in book form in 1979, but the focus of the story is on the suffering of the main character, Marc Andria, who unintentionally killed a young man in a barroom fight. A prison term has only made his suffering more acute and distorted his view of life. Granted probation after one year, on the condition that he will work as a repairman on the estate of a wealthy woman, Marc finds rebirth in his love of Lucienne, a beautiful, young laundress employed there.

Venise en hiver (Venice in Winter, 1981) and *La Chasse à la licorne* (In Pursuit of the Unicorn, 1985) are set in contemporary Venice and Paris respectively. The power of love to transform and regenerate the lives of a man and woman is central to each work. In the former, the heroine, Hélène Morel, breaks with an overbearing lover in Paris and goes to Venice as a guest of her aunt and uncle. There she meets Lassner, a reporter and photographer, with whom she falls in love, and in a climate of terrorism the two find meaning in life.

La Chasse à la licorne is the title of a play within Roblès's 1985 novel and, as it happens, the two protagonists of the novel, Pierre Martinange and Serge Moro, have roles in the play. A representation of a unicorn, a symbol of virtue in the Middle Ages, serves as a backdrop to the stage set; it is pursued by the protagonists in the play and, symbolically also, by Serge, a virtuous but somewhat unstable man who is sometimes provoked to acts of violence in reaction to the injustices of a corrupt society. On such occasions only his friend Pierre has the power to assuage him.

Pierre, however, who has fallen in love with Madeleine, the unhappy wife of a wealthy antique dealer, is not always immediately available on such occasions. As Pierre and Madeleine free themselves from bourgeois hypocrisy to live out their love, Serge is the victim of an injustice and reacts brutally. With the aid of Pierre he escapes a police net and flees into the night, pursued like a tracked animal. Although death is the final outcome for Serge, he has lived his last day intensely, assuming his identity through his acts. He derives a measure of satisfaction, if not happiness, from the fraternal solidarity shown him by Pierre. It is no doubt this same sense of solidarity, along with the authenticity of their love, that has given meaning to the lives of Pierre and Madeleine.

Love also occupies a predominant place in Roblès's two most recent plays, *Un Château en novembre* (A Castle in November) and *La Fenêtre* (The Window), published together in a single volume in 1984. The first was adapted for performance in Bucharest in 1988; the second was presented as a reading at the Loft Theater in Tampa, Florida, 24 January 1989. Jeanne de Castille in *Un Château en novembre,* drawn from sixteenth-century Spanish history, places love above politics and reasons of state. So does Clara in *La Fenêtre* when she is courted by Sergio, a resistance fighter in an unidentified Latin American or Mediterranean country. Although Sergio woos Clara initially because she has an apartment overlooking a prison that constitutes a useful observation post, Clara's love is real. Because of her love rather than for any identifiable belief in Sergio's political principles, Clara holds an arresting officer at bay with a gun to allow her suitor to escape. Sergio's escape assured, Clara surrenders to the officer, thus accepting the sacrifice of a long prison sentence for love, the one thing that gives meaning to her life.

In Roblès's most recent novel, *Norma ou l'exil infini* (Norma or The Infinite Exile, 1988), the theme of the sacrifice of a woman for love recurs in a more drastic form. Against the background of the Falkland Islands War, Charles, a young professor, helps Rodolfo Reyes, a recent refugee from the dictatorial regime in Argentina, who is working in Paris on research projects dealing with Amerindians. Although now old and in declining health, Reyes remains the philanderer he has always been. It is through another refugee from Argentina, Carmen, that Charles learns that Reyes's wife, Norma, died at the hands of her torturers rather than give information that would have resulted in the arrest and probable death of her husband. Thus Charles learns the extent to which a woman will sacrifice herself when her love has no limits.

The Roblès canon can be said to represent, in contrast to many modern works, a positive orientation to the human condition. Although Roblès has developed no formal personal philosophy like the one Camus expressed in *Le Mythe de Sisyphe* (The Myth of Sisyphus, 1942) or *L'Homme révolté* (The Rebel, 1951), his works reveal a view of man and the world similar to that of his compatriot. A partial explanation may lie in the striking similarity of their backgrounds. Born in the same country within six months of one another, of similar ethnic mixtures, fatherless, poor, educated on scholarships, influenced by many of the same authors, they began to write at the same time. The two men developed an approach to life characteristically atheistic and humanistic, seeking means by which man can give meaning to life and live with dignity in an absurd world.

Renouncing religion and belief in God, Roblès turned to humanity, despite its shortcomings, as the source of all values. While still too controlled by selfish forces of darkness traceable to the dawn of mankind, man represents to Roblès (as he does to Camus) much more to admire than to despise. Roblès's stand in favor of man recalls Pascal's wager with respect to God, except that all advantages accrue to this life.

Corollary with Roblès's emphasis on human values is his stress on the worth of each individual. The right of each to self-realization and thus to freedom from oppression must be attained through human solidarity and love. Given the real world and the forces of good and evil within a single person, any aspiration toward change may bring on conflict.

Many of Roblès's protagonists sense they are different; sometimes they feel humiliated in their social or political roles, or they may lack love. Seeking happiness, they break the status quo, often at the personal level. In time, however, the protagonist, witnessing surrounding poverty, oppression, or war, comes to recognize that personal, isolated happiness or interest is selfish. The immediate conflict, then, is between personal fulfillment and human solidarity. In the end, Roblès's heroes opt for the latter. Longereau's desertion in *Le Vésuve* of his mistress is illustrative: he leaves her to fight the Nazis. By acting on behalf of others, refusing to consent to the debasement of mankind or any individual, Roblès's heroes reveal their sense of honor. Thus Montserrat accepts torture and execution rather than put the cause of Venezuelan independence at risk. Dr. Valério of *Cela s'appelle l'aurore* stands ready to compromise himself professionally and socially to help the downtrodden; Ricardo defends Federica, the title character of Roblès's 1954 novel; the hero in *Plaidoyer pour un rebelle* sacrifices himself to prevent the possible death of innocents.

Because the world in which Roblès's characters evolve is often brutal and violent, their desire to love may take on the aspect of an absolute and, as such, the appearance of an escape from a corrupt society. Love is an escape, but it represents, at the same time, much more. Like the cause of human solidarity, it is capable of giving significance to a life otherwise without meaning. Several of Roblès's female characters–Sylvia in *Le Vésuve*, Clara in *La Fenêtre*, Norma in *Norma ou l'exil infini*–make this point. Another manifestation of the desire to escape appears in Roblès's works as a yearning to travel to distant lands, as in *La Vallée du paradis* and *Ile déserte*. Death is an ever-present phenomenon in Roblès's works, and his heroes have what some might term the Spaniard's obsession with it. They may abhor it but realize it to be the one inevitable reality. Yet apprehension of death enhances the value of life, which may be lost at any moment, with nothing existing beyond.

Judging from reviews of his recent novels, *La Chasse à la licorne* and *Norma ou l'exil infini* in the French, Belgian, and Swiss press, Roblès continues to remain in favor with the critics. The inventiveness of his narrative, the well-delineated psychology of his characters and his clear, poignant style assure him a wide reading public. At present Roblès is at work on a book of memoirs, provisionally titled "Mémoires éclatés" (Exploded Memoirs), which deals with many personal experiences, including his stay in Guatemala City during Colonel Castillo Armas's coup d'état against the Arbenz regime. Emmanuel Roblès continues to direct the Méditerranée series for Seuil and to make lecture tours. He has lived most of the past thirty years in the Parisian suburb of Boulogne-sur-Seine and often visits his daughter Jacqueline and her family in Limoges.

References:

Francis Ambrière, "Montserrat," in his *La Galerie dramatique* (Paris: Corrêa, 1949);

Georges-Albert Astre and Serge Groussard, *Emmanuel Roblès* (Paris: Livres de France, 1965);

Astre, *Emmanuel Roblès ou L'Homme et son espoir* (Paris: Périples, 1972);

Astre, *Emmanuel Roblès ou Le Risque de vivre* (Paris: Grasset, 1987);

Jean-Louis Depierris, *Entretiens avec Emmanuel Roblès* (Paris: Editions du Seuil, 1967);

Mouloud Feraoun, "Images algériennes d'Emmanuel Roblès," in *L'Anniversaire*, by Feraoun (Paris: Seuil, 1972);

Folio, special issue: *Emmanuel Roblès*, no. 15 (November 1983);

Josette Frigiotti, *Roblès dramaturge: Essai de théâtre comparé* (Paris: Scènes de France, 1972);

Georges Joyaux, "Emmanuel Roblès et le thème de l'honneur," *Kentucky Foreign Language Quarterly*, 11, no. 3 (1964): 134-141;

James A. Kilker, Preface to *Three Plays*, by Roblès translated by Kilker (Carbondale: Southern Illinois University Press, 1978);

Marie J. Kilker, "The Theatre of Emmanuel Roblès: An American Introduction with a Checklist on Criticism and Production," Ph.D. dissertation, Southern Illinois University, 1972;

Fanny Landi-Benos, *Emmanuel Roblès ou Les Raisons de vivre* (Paris: Oswald, 1969);

Henri Peyre, Afterward to *Vesuvius*, by Roblès (Englewood Cliffs, N.J.: Prentice-Hall, 1970);

Jean Rousselot and Marie-Jeanne Royer, *Dossier Roblès* (Paris: Editions J.T.F., 1965);

Micheline Rozier, *Emmanuel Roblès ou La Rupture du cercle* (Sherbrooke, Quebec: Naaman, 1973);

Pierre-Henri Simon, "Roblès et *Le Vésuve*," in his *Diagnostic des lettres françaises contemporaines* (Brussels: Renaissance du Livre, 1966);

Simoun, special issue: *Pour saluer Roblès*, no. 30 (December 1959);

Marcel Thiébault, "Sur *Les Hauteurs de la ville*," *Revue de Paris*, 56 (February 1949);

Jacques Vier, "Emmanuel Roblès et *La Remontée du fleuve*," *Table Ronde*, no. 200 (September 1964).

Jules Roy

(22 October 1907-   )

Catharine Savage Brosman
Tulane University

BOOKS: *Trois Prières pour des pilotes* (Algiers: Charlot, 1942; revised, 1944); bilingual edition, with translation by George Ellidge, published as *Three Prayers for Pilots* (Algiers: Charlot, 1944);

Chants et prières pour des pilotes (Algiers: Charlot, 1943; Paris: Charlot, 1945; revised edition, Paris: Gallimard, 1952);

Ciel et terre (Algiers: Charlot, 1943);

L'Œil de loup du roi de Pharan (Sétif, 1945);

La Vallée heureuse (Paris: Charlot, 1946); translated by Edward Owen Marsh as *The Happy Valley* (London: Gollancz, 1952);

Comme un mauvais ange (Paris: Charlot, 1947);

Le Métier des armes (Paris: Gallimard, 1948);

Passion de Saint-Exupéry (Paris: Gallimard, 1951); revised as *Passion et mort de Saint-Exupéry* (Paris: Julliard, 1964);

Retour de l'enfer (Paris: Gallimard, 1951); translated by Mervyn Savill as *Return from Hell* (London: Kimber, 1954);

Beau Sang (Paris: Gallimard, 1952);

La Bataille dans la rizière (Paris: Gallimard, 1953);

Les Cyclones (Paris: Gallimard, 1954);

Le Navigateur (Paris: Gallimard, 1954); translated by Savill as *The Navigator* (London: Turnstile Press, 1955; New York: Knopf, 1955);

La Femme infidèle (Paris: Gallimard, 1955); translated by J. Robert Loy as *The Unfaithful Wife* (London: Weidenfeld & Nicolson, 1956; New York: Knopf, 1956);

Nico à la découverte du ciel (Paris: Calmann-Lévy, 1956);

Les Flammes de l'été (Paris: Gallimard, 1956);

Le Fleuve rouge (Paris: Gallimard, 1957);

L'Homme à l'épée (Paris: Gallimard, 1957; enlarged edition, Paris: Julliard, 1970);

Sept Poèmes de ténèbres (N.p.: Privately printed, 1957);

Les Belles Croisades (Paris: Gallimard, 1959);

La Guerre d'Algérie (Paris: Julliard, 1960); translated by Richard Howard as *War in Algeria* (New York: Grove Press, 1961);

Autour du drame (Paris: Julliard, 1961);

La Bataille de Diên Biên Phu (Paris: Julliard, 1963); translated by Robert Baldick as *The Battle of Dienbienphu* (London: Faber & Faber, 1965; New York: Harper & Row, 1965);

Le Voyage en Chine (Paris: Julliard, 1965); translated by Francis Price as *Journey Through China* (London: Faber, 1967; New York: Harper & Row, 1967);

Le Grand Naufrage (Paris: Julliard, 1966); translated by Baldick as *The Trial of Marshal Pétain* (New York: Harper & Row, 1967; London: Faber, 1968);

Les Chevaux du soleil (Paris: Grasset, 1968; revised edition, Paris: Club Français du Livre, 1969); republished as *Chronique d'Alger* (Paris: Livre de Poche, 1975);

Une Femme au nom d'étoile, volume 2 of *Les Chevaux du soleil* (Paris: Grasset, 1968; enlarged edition, Paris: Tallandier, 1971);

Les Cerises d'Icherridène, volume 3 of *Les Chevaux du soleil* (Paris: Grasset, 1969);

La Mort de Mao (Paris: Christian Bourgois, 1969);

Le Maître de la Mitidja, volume 4 of *Les Chevaux du soleil* (Paris: Grasset, 1970);

La Rue des Zouaves, précédé de S. M. Monsieur Constantin (Paris: Julliard, 1970);

L'Amour fauve (Paris: Grasset, 1971);

Les Ames interdites, volume 5 of *Les Chevaux du soleil* (Paris: Grasset, 1972);

J'accuse le général Massu (Paris: Seuil, 1972);

Le Tonnerre et les anges, volume 6 of *Les Chevaux du soleil* (Paris: Grasset, 1975);

Danse du ventre au-dessus des canons (Paris: Flammarion, 1976);

Turnau (Sienne: Privately printed, 1976);

Pour le lieutenant Karl (Paris: Christian Bourgois, 1977);

Le Désert de Retz (Paris: Grasset, 1978);

Concerto pour un chien (Paris: Grasset, 1979);

Les Chevaux du soleil, revised and abridged edition, 1 volume (Paris: Grasset, 1980);

Eloge de Max-Pol Fouchet (Le Paradou: Actes-Sud, 1980);

Jules Roy, Vézelay, 1986 (photograph by S. Bassouls/Sygma)

Etranger pour mes frères (Paris: Stock, 1982);

A propos d'Alger, de Camus et du hasard (Pézenas: Haut Quartier, 1982);

La Saison des za (Paris: Grasset, 1982);

Une Affaire d'honneur (Paris: Plon, 1983);

Beyrouth viva la muerte (Paris: Grasset, 1984);

Prière à Mademoiselle Sainte Madeleine (Pézenas: Haut Quartier, 1984);

Guynemer, l'ange de la mort (Paris: Albin Michel, 1986);

Chant d'amour pour Marseille (Marseilles: Editions Jeanne Laffitte, 1988);

Mémoires barbares (Paris: Albin Michel, 1989).

PLAY PRODUCTIONS: *Beau Sang*, Paris, Théâtre de l'Humour, 1952;

Les Cyclones, Paris, Théâtre de la Michodière, 1954;

Le Fleuve rouge, Paris, Théâtre en Rond, 1960-1961 season.

OTHER: Peter Henn, *La Dernière Rafale*, translated by Henry Daussy, preface by Roy (Paris: Julliard, 1952);

Michel Mohrt, *Marin La Meslée*, preface by Roy (Paris: Editions de Flore, 1952);

"La Clé du mystère de sa mort," in *Saint-Exupéry*, edited by R.-M. Albérès (Paris: Albin Michel, 1961);

Claude Dufresnoy, *Des Officiers parlent*, preface by Roy (Paris: Julliard, 1961);

"L'Instruction du procès Djamila Boupacha," in *Djamila Boupacha*, edited by Simone de Beauvoir and Gisèle Halimi (Paris: Gallimard, 1962); translated by Peter Green (London: Deutsch, 1962; New York: Macmillan, 1962);

"La Tragédie algérienne," in *Camus*, edited by Albérès (Paris: Hachette, 1964);

Martine Lyon, *Les Chinois*, preface by Roy (Paris: Julliard, 1965);

Gabriel Audisio, *L'Opéra fabuleux*, preface by Roy (Paris: Julliard, 1970);

"Dodeigne," in *Chant de pierre: Dodeigne* (Auxerre: Centre Culturel de l'Yonne, 1983).

PERIODICAL PUBLICATIONS: "Retour au combat," *Confluences*, special issue on Antoine de Saint-Exupéry, 7, no. 12-14 (1947): 121-132;

"Camus, prix Nobel," *Nouvelles Littéraires*, no. 1573 (24 October 1957): 1;

"Un Africain," *Monde*, 6 January 1960, p. 2;

"L'Etoile qu'il portait sur son front," *Etudes Méditerranéennes*, special issue on Jean Amrouche, no. 11 (June 1963);

"Vézelay: Le Chant de la résurrection," *Figaro*, 31 March 1980, p. 32;

"Adieu ma mie, adieu mon espérance," *Nouvel Observateur*, no. 833 (27 October 1980): 86-88.

Jules Roy is the foremost French military writer of the twentieth century, and, after Antoine de Saint-Exupéry, the chief practitioner, along with Joseph Kessel, of a peculiarly modern genre, the literature of aviation. He is an outstanding example of the *moraliste*, that is, a writer who studies human behavior and mores, either in the personal or the impersonal mode, and proposes values and standards. Principally a novelist, he also composes plays, two of which were successful on the Paris stage; dozens of articles, some of the most important of which are collected in *L'Homme à l'épée* (The Man with the Sword, 1957; enlarged edition, 1970) and *Autour du drame* (Concerning the Drama, 1961); poems (especially at the outset of his career); and several biographical, historical, and polemical volumes and personal essays. During his military career, which spanned a quarter-century, he saw profound changes in warfare and in the military as well as the public attitude toward them–changes which he continued to observe after he left active duty in 1953 and which are a recurring theme in his work. He also witnessed the fall of the French colonial empire in the Far East and North Africa, and, as one born in that empire and long a member of the military which supported it, wrote of these developments with keen but critical insight; indeed, he can be considered one of the major anticolonialist authors in contemporary France. Yet, despite his great gifts as a stylist, creator of characters, and observer of men, and the value of his insights into the army as an institution and his reflections on the military ethic, his work has not been sufficiently appreciated. Important literary prizes he has won and the large sales figures for some of his books only partially offset the relative neglect of his work by critics, due in part doubtless to his subject matter and to his ideological independence.

The complexity of Roy's biography and the importance of his nonfictional writings make it necessary to examine these before discussing his novels. He was born 22 October 1907 in the Alge-

rian village of Rovigo, some forty kilometers from Algiers, to Henri Dematons, a schoolteacher who had arrived from France at the turn of the century after domestic difficulties in two previous marriages, and Mathilde Paris Roy, whose grandparents had settled in Algeria in the 1850s. At the time of Jules Roy's birth, his mother was married to Louis-Alfred Roy, a retired gendarme, with whom she had a son some seventeen years older than Jules. The liaison between Dematons and Mathilde Roy, which is recounted more than once in Jules Roy's later books, was the scandal of the village, where the Roy couple ran a small hotel. In December after Jules's birth, on the occasion of his baptism, Louis-Alfred Roy expulsed his wife and her illegitimate son from the hotel; she then went to live with her parents on their farm near the village of Sidi-Moussa. Thus, over Jules Roy's birth and childhood there lay the shadow of scandal and personal shame–of which he was not aware until his teens, and did not grasp wholly until years later, when he recognized and accepted what it meant to be the son of two rebels. This is the central fact of his life, playing a crucial role in what he has done and written.

In 1910 Louis-Alfred Roy's death left Mathilde free to marry Dematons, who had been removed from his school at Rovigo and named to another post. But Jules did not understand that this man was his father and long felt fatherless. The boy's progress at school was uneven, and at age twelve he was sent to the seminary at Saint-Eugène, to the west of Algiers, to continue his education and, presumably, prepare for the priesthood. He remained there for seven years, during which he acquired a solid foundation in French literature, Latin, and Church doctrine, and also developed his gifts as a singer. The habits of asceticism and moral and intellectual rigor which the priests instilled in him never left him. But, instead of finishing his training for the priesthood, he chose a military career, after having had, like his fellow seminarians, six months of officer's training. In 1927 he was assigned to his first post, and, at age twenty-one, he married Mirande Grimal. Leaving the seminary for the army was not, he noted, so radical a change as it appeared; he had exchanged one discipline, one code of behavior, for another, equally rigorous. It is not surprising that throughout Roy's work runs the motif of the soldier-monk, that medieval figure who wielded the sword for the sake of the cross, and that he refers frequently to the Crusades, the quest for the Grail, and the need for commitment and sacrifice.

By the mid 1930s Roy, who was stationed in France (a post which enabled him to become acquainted with some writers in Paris), decided that, in a Europe still at peace, though precariously so, he would find more challenges in aviation than in the infantry, and by 1937 he had been transferred to that branch. He participated in aerial operations in the war months of 1939-1940 and, after the fall of France in June 1940, left the country, with his equipment and fellow aviators, for Algeria, where what was left of most air-force squadrons gathered but were generally immobilized, according to the terms of the armistice with the Germans. Until November 1942, he remained a loyalist, that is, loyal to Marshal Philippe Pétain, head of the French state, instead of favoring the Free French of Charles de Gaulle. The drama of his change of allegiance to the Free French after the Anglo-American invasion of North Africa is told at length in his essay *Le Métier des armes* (The Profession of Arms, 1948), which explains how he realized that to continue serving Pétain was to serve not France but the enemy and occupant of France. The decision was reached with difficulty, however, for in strict terms, Roy had sworn obedience to his commanders and was in fact breaking a military oath by refusing to serve the Vichy government. He sought a place with the French contingent of the Royal Air Force and from 1944 through 1945 flew with Bomber Command, as bombardier, copilot, and crew captain, thirty-seven missions over Germany or occupied territories, for which he received the Distinguished Flying Cross.

At the close of the war in 1945 Roy, by then a major, returned to France to assume a desk job with the air force and pursue a writing career that had begun during the early 1940s, in Algeria, where his first poems and an initial *récit*, or narrative, *Ciel et terre* (Heaven and Earth, 1943), had been published by Edmond Charlot. His first postwar book, *La Vallée heureuse* (1946; translated as *The Happy Valley*, 1952), won the Prix Théophraste Renaudot and brought him fame. During the immediate postwar years, his marriage to his first wife, by whom he had two children, was dissolved, and he became acquainted with several other Algerian-born writers, of whom the most important, Albert Camus, was to become his closest friend.

Until 1953 Roy's career was double, that of military officer and writer. In 1953, with the war-

fare between the French and Indochinese insurgents expanding, Roy, who had been promoted to colonel, asked to be sent to Indochina to see the conflict for himself and assuage his vague feeling of guilt at holding a desk job while his fellow officers were in combat. The *état-major*, leery of him since his publication of *La Vallée heureuse*, chose to send him only as an observer. What he observed brought about a profound change in his thinking on the conflict. Knowing already that the war was unpopular and ill-supported at home, being fought chiefly by career officers, colonials, and mercenaries, he also discovered that it had little support from the Indochinese people in whose name it was being waged, and—the crowning evidence of its injustice—that French officers were not only using napalm but also applying to captive soldiers and suspect civilians the methods of "interrogation" which had been one of the abominations practiced by the Nazis.

Roy resigned from active duty and returned home; henceforth he would support himself by his *demi-solde* (half pay) and his books, plays, and articles. He began examining the war in print, at first discreetly, in articles and in the essay *La Bataille dans la rizière* (The Battle in the Rice Paddy, 1953), which avoided direct accusation, then with more forceful denunciations in the fictional *Les Belles Croisades* (Fine Crusades, 1959) and in his play *Le Fleuve rouge* (Red River), which was composed in 1953, but published in 1957, and not produced on stage until the winter of 1960-1961, when it was generally well received and won the Prix Pelman. He achieved further success with his *récit Le Navigateur* (1954; translated as *The Navigator*, 1955), which won the Prix de Monaco. Although his thoughtful and well-crafted early play *Beau Sang* (Fine Blood, with a wordplay on "Baussant," the flag of the Knights Templar, who are the topic of the play), produced and published in 1952, had only a *succès d'estime*, *Les Cyclones* (produced and published in 1954), a drama about military testing of high-speed planes, which, like so many of Roy's works, explores the moral problems involved in giving orders that can affect men's lives, was highly acclaimed. Its success on the stage, with Pierre Fresnay in a star role, was accompanied by the awarding of the Grand Prix d'Art Dramatique.

If the war in Indochina and the ultimate defeat of the French at Dien Bien Phu in May 1954—a defeat he had predicted and which distressed him greatly—marked for Roy the first half of the 1950s, over the second half fell the shadow of the Algerian colonial conflict, generally said to have begun in November 1954. Here he observed many of the same military, political, and moral problems which had characterized the Indochinese war, and was even more distressed by them, since Algeria remained his homeland, his mother, he used to say, along with the army. An early article (1955), entitled "Dans une juste guerre" (In a Just War–the title is an echo of a poem by Charles Péguy), while showing his understanding and support of a true military ethic, incorporating the notions both of just cause and just conduct in war, also stated his principle, adopted after the trip to Indochina, that when the people are against the war, it is no longer just; he even wrote that, if he had been born a "native" (Arab or Berber), he would be in the *maquis*, or underground.

This early, and courageous, statement did not go unnoticed, especially by the military, among whom it provoked ire, but it had no sequel for some years, because Roy decided that it would be inappropriate for him to take further initiatives in criticizing the conduct and grounds for the war. He retained some of the reluctance of one officer to criticize others publicly. In addition he was persuaded that Camus, his guru (as he calls him), so much more famous, should take the lead in speaking on Algeria. After the failure of Camus's civil truce proposal in 1956, both writers remained nearly silent on the matter, Roy reluctantly so sometimes, believing that ultimately he would have to speak out. Camus's death early in 1960 changed Roy's attitude toward taking a stand on Algeria. When several associates told him in the spring that he should travel there to assess the military situation for himself, he obtained a pass and toured the war-torn territory for several weeks, interviewing officers, soldiers, and civilians, visiting villages, and inspecting the barricade between Algeria and Tunisia. Upon returning, he composed *La Guerre d'Algérie* (1960; translated as *War in Algeria*, 1961), for which he found a publisher only with difficulty, because of fear of government seizure.

When the volume appeared at the end of the summer, it became an immediate best-seller, with over one hundred thousand copies sold shortly, and was soon translated into several languages. Its highly controversial argument, although set forth soberly and seeming modest at this remove, was that, despite the valor displayed often by the army in Algeria, despite the concern it demonstrated for reorganizing the territory on the basis of social justice, there were grave violations of military ethics committed by this same army, and that fundamentally the war was an unjust one, since it was an attempt to perpetuate a system which denied full citizenship and opportunities to most of the inhabitants. His position was bolder than any Camus ever took, and it can be argued that Roy had a more comprehensive view of the Algerian situation. Roy was attacked by the conservatives and received death threats; but the popularity of the book–one of the first written by a political moderate and former officer to state so plainly the case for a French military withdrawal and negotiations with the rebels–may well have been a factor in changing the political climate in France to the point where President de Gaulle's government could open negotiations some months later. Roy's essay was accompanied by a series of articles in the *Express*, the *Monde*, and other periodicals, in which he called on his military colleagues, de Gaulle, and the rebels to listen to what he considered his reasonable proposals; these articles and others, including an open letter to and interview with Ferhat Abbas, a rebel leader, are collected in *Autour du drame*.

With the attainment of Algerian independence in July 1962, the colonial empire about which he had already written a considerable amount, and was to write more, came to an end. He was both pleased and distressed, since the change had been brought about by great violence and since nearly all the Algerians of European ancestry, such as his half-brother, had been forced to leave, according to the rebel formula "The suitcase or the coffin." The agony of his motherland remained before his eyes and eventually helped inspire his masterful series of historical novels, *Les Chevaux du soleil* (The Horses of the Sun, 1968-1975).

In 1962 Roy turned his attention away from the Algerian situation to other matters. After revisiting Indochina and interviewing participants, including Gen. Vo Nguyen Giap, he published in 1963 one of his best documentary volumes, *La Bataille de Diên Biên Phu* (translated as *The Battle of Dienbienphu*, 1965), on the last French stand in Indochina. This was followed by a trip to China, during which he hoped to gather materials for a history of the Long March; his frustrations and disappointments and his unveiled criticisms of the People's Republic make his subsequent book, *Le Voyage en Chine* (1965; translated as *Journey Through China*, 1967), a highly idiosyncratic document. After his second marriage, in 1965, he and his wife Tatiana Soukhoroukoff, a journalist of Russian origin, went to live in the Morvan region of western Burgundy, in a series of houses they restored, finally settling in Vézelay. He published in 1966 his thoughtful legal and historical volume, *Le Grand Naufrage* (translated as *The Trial of Marshal Pétain*, 1967). In the mid 1960s he began his Algerian novels, for which, with his wife's and friends' encouragement, he carried out a long investigation in the archives of Algeria, preparing a solid foundation for the series, which required nearly a decade of labor. Meanwhile, two major awards attested to his literary stature: the Grand Prix de l'Académie Française for the whole of his work (1958) and the Grand Prix National de Lettres (1969). He was also awarded in 1975 the Grand Prix de la Ville de Paris. When Gen. Jacques Massu published in 1971 his self-serving memoirs on his Algerian campaigns, *La Vraie Bataille d'Alger*, Roy returned to the Algerian question. His *J'accuse le général Massu* (1972), its title echoing Emile Zola's celebrated requisitory on the Dreyfus Affair, which began "I accuse," is a stirring defense of the military ethic that refuses to use torture, no matter what is at stake, and is also a defense of the Algerian rebels.

During the late 1970s and 1980s Roy pursued his literary activity and continued to travel, although less widely than before. One of his trips, to Lebanon, led to the composition of his *Beyrouth viva la muerte* (Beirut, Long Live Death, 1984), an essay on the perennial political crisis there. Other volumes of the period include an important autobiographical narrative, entitled *Etranger pour mes frères* (Stranger to My Brothers, 1982), the title of which underlines the crucial themes of alienation and fraternity; two autobiographical novels, *Le Désert de Retz* (1978) and *La Saison des za* (The Season of Za, 1982); a history of the sinking of the French fleet by the British at Mers el-Kébir in 1940 called *Une Affaire d'honneur* (A Matter of Honor, 1983); and *Guynemer, l'ange de la mort* (Guynemer, the Angel of Death, 1986), a biography of the World War I aviator Georges Guynemer. Roy and his wife continue to reside at Vézelay. His most recent book, *Mémoires barbares* (Barbarian Memoirs, 1989), is a lengthy and detailed examination of his life and career. Beginning with a conversation he had with General de Gaulle in 1955, it retraces then his childhood, military career, and life in the Parisian literary milieux of the 1930s, late 1940s, and 1950s, affording glimpses of figures such as

Camus, André Malraux, Paul Léautaud, Ernst Jünger, and many others. The purpose, however, is not just to illuminate a literary career through anecdotes and portraits, but rather to reveal the relationships between his own development and the dramas of his century. As he writes on the book cover, "Après ce que je vis en Algérie, je devins un subversif. Je le suis toujours" (After what I saw in Algeria, I became subversive. I still am).

Roy's fiction, like his essays and plays, reveals an author who is both very much in a literary tradition and highly individualistic. A master psychologist, probing human conscience and treating with a sure, delicate touch such traditional subjects as love and infidelity, he recalls the great love analysts of French literature, from Mme de Lafayette and Racine through Stendhal, Constant, and Proust. Concerned as he is also with the army, he cites as his predecessors such early military authors as Montluc (1502-1577) and Vauvenargues (1715-1747) and especially the nineteenth-century poet Alfred de Vigny, whose *Servitude et grandeur militaires* evokes well the contradictions of military service, and the early twentieth-century officer Ernest Psichari, all of whom explored what it means to be a member of the military body, to follow military discipline to the point of giving one's life, to have authority over other men's lives, and to serve one's nation. Readers of these earlier military writers will find much that is familiar in Roy's work. Yet, under the changed circumstances of the mid twentieth century, he has developed highly personal viewpoints on the army and many other topics and cast them in a style and form very much his own.

Roy's early *récits* concern chiefly aviation and war, together; unlike Saint-Exupéry, he rarely deals with civilian aviation. *Ciel et terre* recounts the tribulations and successes of a pilot, Patrice, just before and during World War II. It is not a strong work aesthetically, but contains very interesting observations on flying, some of which are developed at greater length in Roy's pithy and poetic volume *Comme un mauvais ange* (Like an Evil Angel, 1947). *La Vallée heureuse* (the title refers antiphrastically to the Ruhr Valley) is an aesthetically more mature work, composed of several episodes concerning the RAF experiences of the autobiographical hero, Chevrier. Despite the episodic structure, the book, which was prefaced by the poet Pierre Jean Jouve, has some fictional unity, thanks to recurrent characters and themes and to a developed, if simple, plot line. It opens with the account of a collision in the air, which really did happen to Roy, over England, in which he just barely saved his plane though the other craft crashed, and ends after Chevrier has lost his closest friend in a raid and had an unsatisfactory love affair. Throughout, there are excellent accounts of night raids and battles with Bomber Command, which has not been the subject of much fiction. This text can profitably be read alongside Roy's sober and frank diary of his months in England, *Retour de l'enfer* (1951; translated as *Return from Hell*, 1954). His portrait in both texts of the flyers' dominant, obsessive emotion–fear–led to criticism from those who would have preferred more heroic, if less persuasive, characters.

These same themes are found, somewhat more subtly, in *Le Navigateur*, an excellent example of the classic French narrative, in which the stress is on struggle within a man's heart rather than battle in the sky. The eponymous hero is involved in a collision similar to Roy's; he meets an English woman who is interested in him but whose love he cannot effectively return; disobeying orders, he refuses to fly with a pilot who then is killed with all his crew. Because he feels guilty at surviving, and detached from his activity, which seems to have no meaning, the hero then consents to fly with another pilot who is having visual difficulties–really a failure of nerve–and whom the commanding officer will cashier if he does not prove himself; and both men are killed. With few characters and a unified, carefully spun-out plot, the story contrasts with much other war literature characterized by diffuseness and puts the reader at the heart of a military and psychological dilemma, while addressing some of the major themes of military aviation: strategy, obedience, sacrifice, friendship, loneliness, fear, endurance, the stupidity of senior officers. While in some of his later fiction Roy returns to the topic of air raids, it is not surprisingly with a somewhat more critical perspective on the war and his participation, but the sense of the immediacy of the action is reduced.

The same classic sense of composition demonstrated in *Le Navigateur* characterizes three other novels in the 1950s. In *Les Belles Croisades*, the author uses a more elaborate structure, with part of the story narrated in the third person, the rest in the first person. Autobiographical to a considerable degree, it concerns Major Fontane, who is sent to Saigon and Hanoi as an observer, his friendship with a colonel in the information office (the narrator), his unsuccessful romantic at-

Roy with his friend the poet Armand Guibert, 1936, at Le Larzac military base

tachment to the secretary of a crass bureaucrat, and his discovery that in the field, torture is used during interrogations. Fontane's views on the conflict are counterbalanced by those of the narrator, who argues that his chivalric expectations are out of place in modern warfare, particularly against colonial insurgents; he points out the very real political and military disadvantages of considering the war as a crusade which must be carried out morally. The arguments between the two friends and among others convey the range of views on the war both in Indochina and in France. Although the two characters seem to express different sides of Roy's own position, as if he had divided himself between them, Fontane's arguments clearly have the author's greater sympathy. The hero's death in an ambush, after he has unsuccessfully defended his views and realized that, in a sense, there is no place for him in the contemporary military structure, has moral and literary appropriateness alike. It was concerning this work that Roy received from de Gaulle the message, "Sachez que votre pensée vaut pour beaucoup, qu'elle va loin, qu'elle est en service" (Please know that your thinking is of value for many, that it goes far, that it is serving).

La Femme infidèle (1955; translated as *The Unfaithful Wife*, 1956) and *Les Flammes de l'été* (Summer Flames, 1956) both concern love. In the first, a pilot is lost during a mission off the Algerian coast. Two officers, who are friends, are charged with informing his widow. Their gradual discovery of her many infidelities, and of their own desire for her–which makes them rivals–also leads to strong guilt feelings with respect to the dead pilot. By means of this simple plot, the novelist explores the themes of flying, friendship and duty, love and desire, and the conflicts between men and women, making good use of the context of military aviation, where all matters can become matters of life and death. The second novel of this pair is even simpler and more soberly written; as unified as Racine's tragedies, it shows how the difficulties inherent in human love doom it to failure. The plot is elementary: a man and a woman meet, become lovers, share their lives briefly, and part, unable to prolong their affair, not because of exterior obstacles, but because of unspoken needs and mental reservations–women and men being fundamentally very different–and the basic inability of human beings to make desire and happiness endure.

Despite their qualities, little in these *récits* and in Roy's plays, diary, and essays written in the first years of his career would have led a reader to believe that by the end of the 1960s he would prove himself also an author of impressive historical novels of a vast scope, treating multiple themes. It is not that his talent went unnoticed. Many critics praised *La Vallée heureuse;* his other fiction and, to some degree, his dramas earned favorable notices in France and elsewhere. But his work was often pronounced thin, and his character portraits, while always striking a note of truth, were done with discreet touches rather than the strong brush strokes that create powerful personae. Nor had he made full literary use of his own complex personality and range of experience. The task of bringing before the reader's eyes Algerian history from 1830 to 1962, and giving voices to nearly mute generations of colonists and colonized, as well as to his family and himself, magnetized and developed his literary tal-

ent, revealing an impressive and visionary novelist.

Les Chevaux du soleil consists of six volumes, the first of which bears the same title as the whole. A revised and abridged version was published, in a single volume, in 1980, after a successful television series had been made from the novels, and, like the separate volumes, sold well. The idea of composing a great fictional fresco on Algeria was in some ways not a surprising one, but, after deciding in 1966 to launch the series, the writer found the project difficult: early Algerian colonial history posed problems because of its remove and its complexity; more recent decades, because of the terrible social turmoil and the atrocities of the war. Roy, moreover, wanted to tell, along with Algeria's story, his own. While he had no aspirations of competing with the New Novelists in their innovations in form, he effectively renewed the formula of the historical novel by the techniques of narration which he adapted to his complex subject, particularly his use of narrative voices. None of the six volumes is just a pure chronicle of the period, although the first, with its extensive military campaigns, may appear to be so. Each is built around individual as well as collective dramas, and the series is marked by strong character portraits, from Marshal Bourmont to General de Gaulle, from Bouychou, an illiterate but strong-willed, crafty soldier of the conquest, through dozens of other figures, real and imaginary. Roy combines historical material, based on his research, with scenes of his own fabrication, which have that higher poetic truth Aristotle praised. Through recurrent themes such as love, friendship, marriage and the family, women, natives' rights, education, patriotism, and the colonial enterprise–including what one might call the *idea* of Algeria as a historical and moral, almost spiritual, creation–and by following a few families for several generations, as well as through obvious topological and historical unity, the author gives to his series the coherence necessary to make a whole of six volumes. Recurring metaphors and narrative techniques provide added unity; yet there is also a significant variety of tone, voice, and compositional devices.

Volume 1, where the military theme prevails, includes vivid and elaborate battle scenes. It recounts the departure of the French fleet from Toulon in May 1830, the arrival near Algiers, encounters with the Turks, who resist fiercely after initial inactivity, and eventual military success and the occupation of the city. In the background is the political drama being enacted in Paris, leading to the July Revolution and the fall of the Bourbon monarchy. The cast of characters ranges from the prudent naval commander Duperré and Marshal Bourmont–rivals and a study in contrasts–through other historical figures, down to the lowliest foot soldier. The novelist directs his attention particularly toward Bouychou and his younger companion Passebois, who serve as the voices of those common soldiers who always pay the highest price in the battle. Their observations on the war and the mores of the Algerians show that they are not entirely duped by official rhetoric, which seeks variously to justify the expedition, in part by calling the natives barbarians. Another character of importance is Lieutenant de Roailles, whose noble mind and strict sense of military honor contrast with the crude opportunism and moral indifference that characterize so many officers and men. Throughout are visible Roy's ever-present concern for exploring military ethics and his desire to convey accurately a sense of both the reasons for the invasion and the manner of its execution. Artfully switching from large to small scene, from officers to infantrymen, he points to the roles played by individuals in the collective drama. Such themes as love, sexuality, friendship, and politics are woven into the military narrative, and descriptions of the landscape serve not only to interest the reader but also to suggest the powerful effect which, from the earliest days of the conquest, Algeria exerted on French imaginations.

In *Une Femme au nom d'étoile* (A Woman with a Star's Name, 1968), military action recedes into the background, and attention is concentrated on the early settlers of the Mitidja–the coastal plain of Algeria–who in the late 1850s laid the social foundations for later colonial development. The action concerns two families and several officers. A major character is Bouychou, who has married Marie Aldabram, the mountain woman with the star's name, who had driven him mad with love before the expedition; he has returned to Algeria with her and their children, to take up farming near Boufarik. Hot, passionate, bull-like–a temperament suited to Algeria–he is one of those who will help create the Algerian people. Roailles, now a general, and, as one critic wrote, Roy's "officer after his own heart," reappears when he comes to pay a visit to Bouychou–a gesture of goodwill toward an old soldier. In this volume he becomes even more the voice of conscience than before. His orderly, a lieutenant

named Hector Griès, forms a striking contrast with him. A womanizer, ambitious and violent, he discovers his own star, or pearl, in Bouychou's stunning daughter Marguerite. They hastily make love in the stable, a location not without significance, given the novel's system of symbols. The ensuing pregnancy leads to a marriage between Marguerite and Griès–that is, between the world of the settlers and the military. Jean-Pierre Paris, the son of farmers from Sidi-Moussa, marries Marguerite's sister Marie; they will be the grandparents of Hector Koenig, hero of the later volumes. The strange friendship that grows between Marguerite and Sabine de Roailles, the general's beautiful, childless, somewhat aloof wife, reveals the novelist's remarkable gifts as a psychologist. Similarly, his views on what is acceptable military conduct are apparent in the episode in which Roailles is asked to lead a punitive raid against restless natives in the south, a raid which, he knows, is supposed to be bloody and ruthless. He refuses the assignment, since he realizes that he is being chosen in order that his integrity may serve as a cover for the extermination of whole villages; instead, he decides to retire from the army. The farewell party given by Sabine is a splendid episode, rich in local color, perceptive observations on people and manners, and undercurrents of desire which fit well into the Algerian setting.

Volume 3, *Les Cerises d'Icherridène* (The Cherries of Icherridène, 1969), is perhaps the strangest, psychologically speaking, of the six because it depicts an unusual spiritual evolution. Superbly dramatic, it joins matters affecting the individual, such as love, loyalty, and marriage, to the wider concerns of war, rebellion by natives, justice, and military ethics. The dominant figure of the volume is Captain Griès, who plays a crucial role as a spokesman for the author and precedent for the autobiographical Hector Koenig. He is a woman's man in much more than the ordinary sense, for the three female figures who fascinate him also direct his conscience and his acts; for Roy, women inspire and empower men. In an early episode at Bach, the French country house to which Roailles and Sabine retreated, Griès learns that the general has just died, and in a strange moonlit room, with the corpse of his mentor a few feet away, and in a France violated by the Franco-Prussian War, he and Sabine engage in passionate lovemaking. This is not gratuitous, but rather a response to the deep call of the flesh threatened with loss and death, and a strange way of communicating with the deceased. Back in Algeria, Griès returns to his favorite occupation: fighting and exterminating natives. No imitator of Roailles, despite his affection for him, he has been violent and cruel. But Sabine, who returns to him in dream like a mystery woman, is changing him, although he is still fascinated by his wife Marguerite. When the cherry trees of Icherridène, beautiful, fruit-laden–one of the few riches afforded by a harsh land–are destroyed by the army, he begins to deplore the waste, and he takes no pleasure in seeing native women chased away, naked and humiliated.

In the final part of the volume, after Griès has shared a ritual meal with two women and an old man in a mountain village which his own troops have besieged and occupied, he undergoes another effect of the eternal feminine: the next day, he refuses to obey orders to evacuate the village so that it may be destroyed from below by artillery. His decision, though mysterious, as are all spiritual acts, is made plausible by the novelist's keen psychological insights and understanding of military pragmatism. The volume closes thus with an act of conscience, and Griès stands out as the spiritual heir of Roailles.

In volume 4, *Le Maître de la Mitidja* (The Mitidja Schoolmaster, 1970), Roy tells through a wholly imaginary diary the story of his father's arrival in Africa and courtship of Mathilde. What is perhaps most striking about this volume is the technique of creating fiction out of biography by giving to his father a voice which is like the novelist's own and yet which springs from, and illuminates, Dematons's drama. To the story of his passion for Mathilde are added other plots which reveal the political and social situation in Algeria around 1900. Relationships between colonizers and colonized, Algeria and France, liberals (few in number) and the rest of the colony are well portrayed. The most burning social question is the Jewish one, and, despite himself, Dematons is drawn into a web of events involving a Jew that end ultimately in tragedy. The relationship between this plot and his love for Mathilde is a close and significant one: Dematons tries to protect the Jew against village persecution because he does not accept the local prejudices, nor play by the rules; Mathilde, who stands by him when the tragedy is precipitated, likewise puts conscience above law, the voice of the individual above that of the group, no matter how sacrosanct the latter may be. What is visible here is not only Roy's fundamental romanticism but the con-

viction that the collectivity itself *needs* the individual who stands apart, to see and speak as he sees fit; otherwise, society degenerates into group tyranny. The volume also points to the most significant source of his liberalism on social issues (despite his conservative temperament): his mother's "fault," written in his very flesh, and connected thematically, by the motif of illegitimacy, to France's sin in Algeria, which created a caste of social bastards. The rhetoric of the novel thus joins that of *La Guerre d'Algérie*, where the author wrote, in what is perhaps his most-quoted phrase, that if the French soldiers in Algeria saw one day in their gunsights a tall, white-haired bastard, beside the rebels, they should shoot: it would be he.

The "forbidden souls" to which the title of volume 5, *Les Ames interdites* (1972), refers are primarily the native Algerians, to whom social advancement, respect, and citizenship are denied; they are also those who cannot find happiness, whether for social or personal reasons. The volume concerns Roy's family and his autobiographical hero in 1910, 1914, and 1930. Its scope widens to include several important native characters and deal with crucial issues of the early twentieth century in the territory. The first parts are told mostly by Marie Carnetto, Mathilde's sister, who recounts Mathilde's liaison and marriage and introduces the reader to other family members and their many tensions and conflicts. The boy Hector–son of Mathilde and Dematons–is the narrator briefly in the pages that concern 1914, as the way *he* sees events begins to become more important. To relate the events of 1930, Roy uses an omniscient narrator, but within this narration imbeds several long monologues, by Hassane, an Arab; Dematons; Hector Koenig, now an officer; and others. The whole volume is governed by violence–the war of 1914 in Europe, native uprisings and crimes, the violence of character and behavior which seems to be a fundamental trait of the settlers. The centennial celebrations of 1930 only exacerbate resentment among natives, and underline the profound flaws in colonial society, flaws which correspond to Hector's deep malaise, as one who is at once an officer (that is, a preserver of the status quo) and sympathetic to the natives; a member of an established family and the ruling caste, and yet illegitimate. Roy's technical achievement in the volume is to handle well a great deal of material, including historical and autobiographical elements. By means of multiple voices, he conveys different perspectives on the colonial problem, and, without heavy-handedness, foreshadows and illuminates the conflicts that would tear Algeria apart after 1954.

For the last volume, *Le Tonnerre et les anges* (1975), Roy chose a title with apocalyptic overtones: the thunder is that of the great storm of war; the angels, those who preside over such a cataclysm, which, although tragic, must ultimately be seen also as a part of that great historical development that, according to Roy's Christian understanding, will bring about the Kingdom of God. The action of the volume takes place under the Fifth Republic, from the events of the Forum in Algiers in 1958, which brought down the previous regime, to independence. The main characters include Hector, now a journalist; a young army captain in Algeria, Roailles, honorable and worthy of his ancestor, but smarting under the defeat of Dien Bien Phu; Raïssa, a half-breed rebel—daughter of Hassane and Hector's cousin Marguerite—with whom Roailles falls in love; Dr. Paris and other members of Hector's family; and several major historical figures such as generals Massu, Salan, and de Gaulle. Roy's portrait of the opium-smoking Salan, ambitious, determined to use the events of the Forum for his own purposes, is keen and enlightening. His portrait of "The Brontosaurus," de Gaulle—the first ever in a work of French fiction, and thus very bold—is even more telling. The general's calculated reactions, his attempts to foresee the future and use events, his secretiveness, and his hidden weaknesses are conveyed remarkably. Through multiple narrators and plots, Roy recounts episodes from the war and political intrigues in Paris, while he depicts the life of civilians in Algeria—both European and Arab—as tension and violence increase. The near-assassination of Dr. Paris, the suicide of Raïssa's father, who has joined the rebellion and been captured, and other acts of violence foreshadow the death of Hector, who, still feeling his private fraternity with the social bastards, has tried to understand the situation and has written articles in support of the revolt; he is shot in the cemetery where he has gone to visit his mother's grave. Yet Roy is at pains to show that, from this terrible travail of a people, where there have been wrongs on both sides, a new nation is to be born—a nation which he does not judge but merely loves, because it is created on his native soil—and to which the rhetoric of the series pointed from the first volume.

Roy's most recent narratives belong together both chronologically and thematically.

Throughout, one sees concerns and themes from his previous writing, such as World War II—especially the bombing raids—Indochina, Algeria, and human relationships, and new themes, such as animals. Those of the narratives which he calls *récits* are in the personal mode, with a first-person narrator who is clearly the author himself, and episodes from his own life, past and present. In others, which he calls novels, he uses a third-person narrator. But in all of them, his personality and experiences shine through. The effect is to shed a searching and yet mellow, mature light on his earlier work and reveal more of the man than previously. One could easily say about Roy what Montaigne wrote of his *Essais:* that he was himself the matter of his book. It is a paradox, but one which will surprise few, to observe that, as Roy's work acquired a much wider scope in his historical novels, dealing with a wide range of characters and topics removed from his experience, it also became more personal; the identification between his irregular birth and Algeria's suffering was both a profoundly felt experience and a masterly artistic device. Having made manifest in fiction Algeria's situation and his own, his parents' rebellion and that of the political rebels of the following generations, he was, as it were, freed to portray himself directly, and to reassess his earlier experiences.

The novels *Le Désert de Retz* and *La Saison des za* (the title is a quotation from Raymond Queneau, its untranslatable word *za* echoing the first syllable of the word *amours*, loves, as it would be pronounced in this phrase) focus on different periods of the author's life. In the former, under the guise of Colonel Krieg—a retired officer living in a country house near Retz's Desert, a ruined estate from the eighteenth century—Roy portrays himself during the difficult period following his resignation from the air force, but adds to this portrait a great deal of invented material. As though his sense of emptiness at having left the military were not enough, he feels guilt at having abandoned his fellow officers fighting in Indochina and listens with great distress to the news of the battle raging at Dien Bien Phu. Added to the self-doubts provoked by his resignation are the gnawing desires and doubts of love. Three women preside over his mind. Isolde Schutz, whom he met in Tokyo en route to Korea, is the wife of a banker from Hamburg, now residing in Paris. Her violet eyes and Valkyrie-like beauty remind him of another Isolde, encountered during the war when, as a bombardier, he was shot down over Germany and taken in by Herr Dancker and his daughter Isolde, who appear in retrospective, sometimes oneiric, passages. The third woman is an actress, Irene, who loves him, whom he perhaps loves, but cannot bring himself to acknowledge as one who should share his life. In this novel, as the name Krieg indicates, Roy is clearly as concerned with his own German heritage (Henri Dematons, born in eastern France, was descended from a Prussian) as with what it means to be a military man. The fact that Germans shelter Krieg and protect him against the SS awakens his conscience, smarting at having bombed so many cities, and also underlines the arbitrariness of fate and war: he could easily have been born farther east and become a Luftwaffe pilot. Irene's death and Isolde Schutz's departure resolve nothing; like the desolate estate around him, Krieg's heart is a ruin, though not without beauty.

In *La Saison des za*, Roy goes back to his literary debuts in Paris in the 1930s. Portraying himself under the name Paul Berg, he focuses first on the eccentric *littérateur* René-Louis Doyon, who was one of his principal mentors and whose personality and career, always on the edge of the main literary currents, are conveyed brilliantly. He also recounts his double military and literary career, throughout which his marriages and many love affairs both interfere with and inspire his work. Figures such as Camus and André Malraux pass in and out, and on the backdrop are major political and social events of his lifetime. Although much of the material appears for the first time in Roy's work, there are frequent echoes of scenes and periods described earlier, for instance, in *Le Tonnerre et les anges* and *Le Désert de Retz*, and it becomes clear that all of Roy's writing is a series of literary tapestries, with repeated motifs and constant cross-references. Such an intertextuality, both personal and historical, mirrors well the complexity of his own situation and the period during which he wrote.

Complementary to these two novels are the shorter and more personal narratives. *Danse du ventre au-dessus des canons* (Belly-dance Over the Cannons, 1976) and *Pour le lieutenant Karl* (For Lieutenant Karl, 1977) are both concerned with Roy's RAF experiences. In the former, a highway accident in which he and his wife and dog narrowly escaped death is the occasion to remember bombing raids, especially one in which a navigational error jeopardized the crew, which nevertheless dropped its bombs over Gelsenkircken. The questions of what is right and wrong, how to live one's life, and to what one should give value rush into his mind as he meditates on the fate of men and beasts. In the latter work, he recounts a visit to the RAF base at Elvington, thirty-one years after he was assigned there. The Karl of the title is an imaginary character who incarnates the thinking military man, one who asks questions and finally refuses to obey an order. In both of these works, echoes of *La Vallée heureuse* crisscross with the mature reflections of the officer who was spared but wonders why and meditates on the horrors of industrial warfare. These short narratives can be juxtaposed to three others, concerned with animals, a topic used in previous centuries by such French authors as La Fontaine and Fabre and in the twentieth century by Colette. *La Mort de Mao* (Mao's Death, 1969), *L'Amour fauve* (Wild Love, 1971), which deal with desert foxes and Roy's dog Mao, and *Concerto pour un chien* (Concerto for a Dog, 1979) reveal a highly developed, individual sensitivity to the problems posed by, and the rewards of, the coexistence of man and beast. Reflections of the author's daily life and his past join the moral and metaphysical considerations that are the currency of his work.

Seen as a whole, Roy's literary production, spanning nearly a half-century, is an impressive achievement. He has dealt with some of the most important social and military issues of the century, in a prose praised by many, including Paul Morand, who compared it to that of Chateaubriand. He is, as Rémi Laureillard put it in the *Quinzaine Littéraire* (15-31 July 1969), an author for our time, respected in many circles, although, decades after his essays on the Algerian war, he still received insulting letters and remained persona non grata to some former military colleagues. Thanks in part to a German translation of *Les Chevaux du soleil*, his work has been appreciated especially in Germany, where he was invited to give a series of lectures. His lasting concern for honor and ethics in the army and for justice, which characterizes almost all his writing, makes him one of the voices of conscience in modern France.

Letters:

D'une amitié: Correspondance Jean Amrouche-Jules Roy (Aix-en-Provence: Edisud, 1985).

Interviews:

Paul Guth, "Jules Roy ou de la soutane à l'hélice," in his *Quarante contre un* (Paris: Denoël, 1952), pp. 357-368;

André Gillois, "Jules Roy," in his *Qui êtes-vous?* (Paris: Gallimard, 1953), pp. 213-220;

Gabriel d'Aubarède, "Rencontre avec Jules Roy," *Nouvelles Littéraires*, no. 1352 (30 July 1953): 1,6;

André Bourin, "Je suis un 'demi-solde,' nous dit Jules Roy," *Nouvelles Littéraires*, no. 1607 (19 June 1958): 1,4;

Xavier Grall, "Passion de Jules Roy," *Signes du Temps*, no. 2 (November 1963): 37-38;

Jean-Francis Held, "Paroles recueillies de Jules Roy," *Nouvel Observateur*, 18 May 1966;

Francis Bueb, "Rencontre avec Jules Roy," *Combat*, no. 7769 (10 July 1969): 9;

Pierre Lhoste, "Jules Roy: Mes Mots de passe," *Nouvelles Littéraires*, no. 2201 (17 November 1969): 1,7;

Jacques Roque, "Jules Roy ou la rigueur," in Roy's *Une Femme au nom d'étoile* (Paris: Tallandier, 1971);

Philippe Bernet, "L'Etonnant Retour en Algérie du pied-noir Jules Roy," *Aurore*, 1 April 1975, p. 2;

Serge Bromberger, "Le Coup de soleil de Jules Roy," *Figaro Littéraire*, no. 1508 (12 April 1975): 13;

Jean-Marc Roberts, "Un Colonel Fracasse," *Nouvel Observateur*, no. 694 (27 February 1978): 84.

References:

Catharine Savage Brosman, *Art as Testimony: The Work of Jules Roy* (Gainesville: University of Florida Press, 1989);

Brosman, "Les Frères ennemis: Jules Roy et l'Algérie," *French Review*, 56 (March 1983): 579-587;

Brosman, *Jules Roy* (Philadelphia: Celfan Monographs, 1988);

Brosman, "Language, Family, Self: Jules Roy's Political Rhetoric," *Degré Second*, no. 11 (September 1987): 29-34;

Albert Camus, "On Jules Roy's *La Vallée heureuse*," in his *Lyrical and Critical Essays*, translated by Ellen Conroy Kennedy, edited by Philip Thody (New York: Knopf, 1968), pp. 242-247;

Pierre Daix, "L'Honneur des écrivains," in his *Réflexions sur la méthode de Martin du Gard* (Paris: Editeurs Français Réunis, 1957), pp. 112-118;

Jean-Louis Ezine, "La Littérature en piqué," in his *Les Ecrivains sur la sellette* (Paris: Seuil, 1981), pp. 195-199;

Claude Girault, "Compagnons d'âme," *Cahiers Henri Bosco*, 25 (1985): 91-113;

Lucien Guissard, "Jules Roy: *Le Métier des armes*," in his *Ecrits en notre temps* (Paris: Fayard, 1961), pp. 181-210;

Robert Kanters, "Jules Roy," in his *L'Air des lettres* (Paris: Grasset, 1973), pp. 225-237;

Kanters, "Jules Roy, croisé sans croix," in his *Des écrivains et des hommes* (Paris: Julliard, 1952), pp. 199-221;

Chester W. Obuchowski, *Mars on Trial* (Madrid: José Porrúa Turanzas, 1978);

J.-L. Prévost, "Jules Roy ou les exigences de l'honneur," *Livres et Lectures*, 5 (1960): 455-459;

Revue Celfan Review, special issue on Roy, 6, no. 1-2 (1987);

Jacques Romane, "Jules Roy," *Revue Nouvelle*, 11 (15 January 1955): 90-95;

A. Van Lennep, "Jules Roy, le témoin déchiré," *Levende Talen*, 32 (1958): 484-492.

Papers:

Jules Roy's papers are held at the Municipal Library of Marseilles.

Françoise Sagan
(Françoise Quoirez)
(21 June 1935-)

Marian Brown St. Onge
Boston College

BOOKS: *Bonjour tristesse* (Paris: Julliard, 1954); translated by Irene Ash (New York: Dutton, 1955; London: Murray, 1955);

Un Certain Sourire (Paris: Julliard, 1956); translated by Anne Green as *A Certain Smile* (New York: Dutton, 1956); translated by Ash (London: Murray, 1956);

Dans un mois, dans un an (Paris: Julliard, 1957); translated by Frances Frenaye as *Those Without Shadows* (New York: Dutton, 1957); translated by Ash (London: Murray, 1957);

Aimez-vous Brahms? (Paris: Julliard, 1959); translated by Peter Wiles (New York: Dutton, 1960; London: Murray, 1960);

Château en Suède (Paris: Julliard, 1960);

Les Merveilleux Nuages (Paris: Julliard, 1961); translated by Green as *Wonderful Clouds* (London: Murray, 1961; New York: Dutton, 1962);

Les Violons parfois (Paris: Julliard, 1962);

Landru, by Sagan and Claude Chabrol (Paris: Julliard, 1963);

La Robe mauve de Valentine (Paris: Julliard, 1963);

Bonheur, impair et passe (Paris: Julliard, 1964);

Toxique (Paris: Julliard, 1964); translated by Frenaye (New York: Dutton, 1964; London: Souvenir Press, 1965);

La Chamade (Paris: Julliard, 1965); translated by Robert Westhoff (New York: Dutton, 1966; London: Murray, 1966);

Le Cheval évanoui, suivi de L'Echarde (Paris: Julliard, 1966);

Le Garde du cœur (Paris: Julliard, 1968); translated by Westhoff as *The Heart-keeper* (New York: Dutton, 1968; London: Murray, 1968);

Un Peu de soleil dans l'eau froide (Paris: Flammarion, 1969); translated by Terence Kilmartin as *A Few Hours of Sunlight* (New York: Harper & Row, 1971); translated by Joanna Kilmartin as *Sunlight on Cold Water* (London: Weidenfeld & Nicolson, 1971);

Un Piano dans l'herbe (Paris: Flammarion, 1970);

Françoise Sagan (photograph copyright © Jerry Bauer)

Des Bleus à l'âme (Paris: Flammarion, 1972); translated by Joanna Kilmartin as *Scars on the Soul* (New York: McGraw-Hill, 1974; London: Deutsch, 1974);

Il est des parfums, by Sagan and Guillaume Hanoteau (Paris: J. Dullis, 1973);

Un Profil perdu (Paris: Flammarion, 1974); translated by Joanna Kilmartin as *Lost Profile* (New

York: Delacorte, 1976; London: Deutsch, 1976);

Réponses: 1954-1974 (Paris: Jean-Jacques Pauvert, 1974); translated by David Macey as *Réponses: The Autobiography of Françoise Sagan* (Godalming, U.K.: Black Sheep, 1979); republished as *Night Bird: Conversations with Françoise Sagan* (New York: Clarkson Potter, 1980);

Des Yeux de soie (Paris: Flammarion, 1976); translated by Joanna Kilmartin as *Silken Eyes* (New York: Delacorte/E. Friede, 1977; London: Deutsch, 1977);

Le Lit défait (Paris: Flammarion, 1977); translated by Abigail Israel as *The Unmade Bed* (New York: Delacorte/E. Friede, 1978; Henley-on-Thames: Ellis, 1978);

Le Sang doré des Borgia, by Sagan and Jacques Quoirez (Paris: Flammarion, 1977);

Il fait beau jour et nuit (Paris: Flammarion, 1979);

Le Chien couchant (Paris: Flammarion, 1980); translated by C. J. Richards as *Salad Days* (New York: Dutton, 1984; London: Allen, 1985);

Musique de scènes (Paris: Flammarion, 1981); translated by Richards as *Incidental Music* (New York: Dutton, 1983; London: Allen, 1985);

La Femme fardée (Paris: Jean-Jacques Pauvert aux Editions Ramsay, 1981); translated by Lee Fahnestock as *The Painted Lady* (New York: Dutton, 1983; London: Allen, 1983);

Un Orage immobile (Paris: Jean-Jacques Pauvert chez Julliard, 1983); translated by Christine Donougher as *The Still Storm* (London: Allen, 1984; New York: Dutton, 1986);

Avec mon meilleur souvenir (Paris: Gallimard, 1984); translated by Donougher as *With Fondest Regards* (New York: Dutton, 1985);

De guerre lasse (Paris: Gallimard, 1985); translated by Donougher as *A Reluctant Hero* (New York: Dutton, 1987);

La Maison de Raquel Vega: Fiction d'après le tableau de Fernando Botero (Paris: Editions de la Différence, 1985);

Un Sang d'aquarelle (Paris: Gallimard, 1987);

Sarah Bernhardt: Le Rire incassable (Paris: Robert Lafont, 1987).

PLAY PRODUCTIONS: *Le Rendez-vous manqué*, ballet by Sagan and Michel Mange, Monte Carlo, January 1958;

Château en Suède, Paris, Théâtre de l'Atelier, March 1960;

Les Violons parfois, Paris, Théâtre du Gymnase, 1961;

La Robe mauve de Valentine, Paris, Théâtre des Ambassadeurs, 1963;

Bonheur, impair et passe, Paris, Théâtre Edouard VII, 1964;

Le Cheval évanoui and *L'Echarde*, Paris, Théâtre du Gymnase, 1966;

Un Piano dans l'herbe, Paris, Théâtre de l'Atelier, 15 October 1970;

Il fait beau jour et nuit, Paris, Comédie des Champs-Elysées, 1978;

L'Excès contraire, Paris, Bouffes Parisiens, 1987.

OTHER: *Mirror of Venus*, photographs by Wingate Paine, text by Sagan and Federico Fellini (New York: Random House, 1966);

Brigitte Bardot, photographs by Christian Dussart, text by Sagan (Paris: Flammarion, 1975); translated by Judith Sachs (New York: Delacorte, 1976);

Georges Sand and Alfred de Musset, *Lettres d'amour*, preface by Sagan (Paris: Hermann, 1985).

In an age of French literature where the philosophically rich fictions of Albert Camus, Jean-Paul Sartre, and André Malraux were succeeded by the formal innovations of the New Novel, the enormous success of Françoise Sagan's fragile, classic novels and the legend of her tumultuous life are anomalies. If her flamboyant, unconventional personal image has tended to overshadow her reputation as a writer, Sagan is still today a prolific, best-selling author. She has written novels, plays, short stories, screenplays, one ballet, and several nonfiction books, including two highly successful memoirs. Sagan has been a highly visible public figure in France. Since 1977 she has appeared regularly on *Apostrophes*, a popular television literary program. She has also served on the jury for the Cannes Film Festival. In 1985 Sagan was awarded the Prix de Monaco in recognition of her work as a whole.

Sagan was only seventeen years old when she wrote *Bonjour tristesse* (1954; translated, 1955). This spare, passionless first novel about a seventeen-year-old girl's careless first love affair and equally careless destruction of her father's mistress became an overnight *succès de scandale*, won the prestigious Prix des Critiques, and catapulted its young author to international fame as a postwar symbol of nihilistic youth. "She was absolutely different," said Florence Malraux, daughter of André Malraux, talking about Sagan at eighteen. "Feverishly intense, there was something very fragile, lonely, yet strong. Also, she was totally free. Students at that time didn't dare have an affair, drink, spend money or read for 10 days if they wanted. They were still children, but she was not. Somehow she knew everything; she was an adult." In its first year *Bonjour tristesse* sold more than five hundred thousand copies in France. It has since been translated into sixteen languages and continues to rank among the most popular novels in France. By the time her second novel, *Un Certain Sourire*, was published (and translated as *A Certain Smile*) in 1956, Sagan was, at twenty, to quote one critic, "more famous and infinitely richer than Voltaire had been at 80."

Sagan belongs to a generation that grew up in occupied wartime France and in the tense postwar period of political instability and realignment. The intellectual climate was one of grave reflections on the absurdity of human existence and of vague existentialist engagements. In an important sense, the spirit of disillusion which permeates Sagan's work from its beginnings is an expression of existentialism's second generation—of young French minds molded by the novels of Malraux, Camus, and, particularly, Sartre. Commenting on her literary heritage in *Réponses* (1974; translated as *Réponses: The Autobiography of Françoise Sagan*, 1979), Sagan mentions several contemporary writers who influenced her, adding, "Mais il y a un seul qui ne m'a pas trompé . . . c'est Sartre" (But there is only one who hasn't deceived me . . . that's Sartre).

If Sagan was conditioned by a Sartrean vision of a lone unbending ego choosing its patterns in an absurd universe, in her world notions of absurdity have become banal, and codes of moral consequence irrelevant. Pierre de Boisdeffre, in his *Histoire vivante de la littérature d'aujourd'hui*, articulates the difference between the generations when he states, "En 1945 les écrivains rêvaient d'être Dieu; dix ans plus tard ils ne demandaient plus qu'à plaire" (In 1945 writers dreamed of being God; ten years later they only wanted to please). What there is for Sagan—beyond the return to the classic "goût de plaire" to which Boisdeffre refers—is a serene despair and the momentary pleasures of fleeting love affairs, the only respites from the essential solitude which is the human condition. The originality of Sagan's early works lies in the fragile lucidity which permeates her heroines' voices and consciousness. As she told Leslie Garis, who interviewed her for an article published in the *New York Times Magazine* (16 November 1980), "I

wanted to make something like Racine, where people have nothing to do, they just have their feelings." Sagan depicts these feelings sparingly, with ease and precision. Indeed, the *pudeur*, or reticence and restraint, the muted tone, the simplicity of detail and absence of color—all unmistakably Sagan—are traits of the classical French style. As Marian Engel for the *New York Times Book Review* noted in an assessment of *Scars on the Soul* (the 1974 English translation of *Des Bleus à l'âme*, 1972), "She has that French essential, *measure*. No Saxon tantrums or German hurricanes for her."

The most frequent criticism of Sagan's work concerns her themes. With some notable exceptions, her world is that of the idle rich for whom sports cars, whiskey, and nightclubs provide temporary anodynes against the pain of solitude and the always deceptive illusions of love. About her decision to depict life in the bourgeois society in which she was raised, Sagan once remarked, "I don't see why I should describe peasants, workers or the Haute Couture, which I don't know. If I went to live in Gennevilliers [an industrial suburb of Paris] to try to understand, it would not only be ridiculous, it would be dishonest of me." Ironically, when she did turn her attention to working-class characters with her 1980 novel *Le Chien couchant* (translated as *Salad Days*, 1984), set in the northern mining district of France, Sagan provoked a costly and embarrassing lawsuit for plagiarism. Although she eventually won the suit brought against her by the French writer Jean Hougron, whose story "La Vieille Femme" (The Old Woman) she concedes "inspired" her, she suffered much abuse. Even her publisher, Flammarion, did not support her. Undaunted, Sagan (who once referred to herself as "un accident qui dure" [an accident which endures]) has continued to experiment with new fictional worlds, most notably in her interpretation of a painting of the Colombian artist Fernando Botero. *La Maison de Raquel Vega* (Raquel Vega's House, 1985), the first of several imaginative interpretations of paintings to be undertaken by French writers for the series Tableaux Vivants, was not only a critical success but proof of Sagan's ability to successfully conceive and portray a universe completely different from her own.

Françoise Sagan was born Françoise Quoirez, 21 June 1935, in Carjac (Lot). She was the youngest of three children of a well-to-do industrialist, Pierre Quoirez, and a protective bourgeoise mother, Marie Laubaud Quoirez. The family lived in Paris from 1935 to 1940 and moved to Saint Marcellin, near Lyons, during World War II, returning in 1945 to Paris, the city where Sagan still lives. As her sister and brother were considerably older, Sagan's childhood was spent largely alone or in the company of adults, a fact which explains in part, perhaps, her precocity. A timid, bookish child, Sagan found her first contacts with contemporaries painful. In *Réponses* she ruefully remembers being always head of the class, the unpopular teacher's favorite: "toujours premiere et ridicule" (always first and ridiculous). With adolescence came rebelliousness: skipped classes and afternoons spent in crowded, smoke-filled St. Germain des Près jazz cellars. Although she had become a recalcitrant student, she continued to be an avid reader (Proust, Stendhal, and, later, Camus) and began to write short stories and poems. Sagan passed her *baccalauréat* in 1952, but was unsuccessful in her attempt to enroll at the Sorbonne the following year. That summer, while vacationing at the family country home, Sagan wrote *Bonjour tristesse*. Upon her return to Paris, she submitted the manuscript to two publishers, Julliard and Plon. An editor at Julliard accepted the novel immediately after receiving assurance from the young author that her story was not autobiographical. Sagan's parents' reaction to the book, reported in *Réponses,* was nonplussed: "Qu'est-ce qui t'a pris d'écrire des histoires pareilles?–C'est assez bien écrit" (Whatever made you write such a story? It's rather well written). Their only apparent concern was that their daughter use a pseudonym, which Sagan derived from one of Proust's favorite authors, the Princesse de Sagan, and has used the name on all of her published works.

The plot of *Bonjour tristesse* involves a seventeen-year-old girl, Cécile, who lives in idyllic bohemian intimacy with an approving, glamorous, widowed father. Elsa, the father's current mistress (he often has new ones), has joined them on their summer holiday. Cécile clearly sees her father as her ally and the mistress as no threat to their father-daughter relationship. The summer at the beach brings a love affair with an attractive young man, Cyril, but paradise is interrupted by the arrival of Anne, an old friend of Cécile's dead mother. Cécile has just failed her exams. Although her father considers the failure unimportant, Anne makes it an issue, forcing Cécile to study. While Cécile loves and admires Anne, she is highly ambivalent about Anne's blossoming relationship with her father–they quickly dispense with Elsa and decide to marry–and outraged by

Anne's efforts to curtail her own freedom. Regardless of what Cécile sees to be the rightness of Anne's motivation–"car elle nous rendrait heureux . . . je sentais qu'elle avait raison" (because she would make us happy . . . I sensed she was right)–she is horrified by Anne's potential power to mold her life and that of her father into "êtres policiés, bien élevés" (well-bred, civilized people). Cécile decides that Anne must be eliminated so that she and her father can return to "notre vie d'antan" (our former life). She devises a plan: Cyril and Elsa pretend to be lovers; her father, jealous of this infringement of his former territory, is lured by vanity into a clandestine encounter with Elsa; the encounter is witnessed by Anne, who then dies in an automobile accident, an apparent suicide.

Sagan's devastating story of a seventeen-year-old's plot to get her own way fascinated both the critics and the public. In the eyes of many, Sagan *was* Cécile, "ce gentil petit monstre" (this charming little monster), to quote François Mauriac's famous formula, her frail, waifish image inseparable from that of her heroine. Psychological speculations abounded regarding Oedipal fantasies and mother-related adolescent anxieties, to which Sagan responded in a 1956 *Paris Review* interview, "I was astounded by their imagination and fecundity. They [the critics] saw intentions I never had." Sagan's teenage dream of seduction, sophistication, and power may be very telling as adolescent wish-fulfillment, but it was the listless logic of her heroine's attitude toward love and her ability to get away with her plan which rendered the novel truly scandalous. Reflecting many years later on the book's impact, Sagan commented, "A y réfléchir, le seul scandale était que l'héroïne couchait avec un garçon dont elle n'était pas amoureuse et que cette vilaine action n'était pas sanctionnée par le fait d'être enceinte. Elle se trouvait déniaisée, mais intacte, elle pouvait recommencer. Je crois que le scandale était là. En somme c'était un drame qui datait d'avant la pilule" (Thinking about it now, the only scandal was that the heroine slept with a boy that she wasn't in love with, and that this terrible act wasn't sanctioned by a pregnancy. If she lost her innocence, she was intact, able to begin again. I think the only scandal was there. In sum, it is a drama which dates from before the pill).

Sagan's second novel, *Un Certain Sourire,* the story of a twenty-year-old's affair with a married man old enough to be her father, delighted the critics even more than *Bonjour tristesse,* and it too became an instant best-seller. In America alone, the translations of Sagan's first two novels sold more than two million copies by 1958. If *Un Certain Sourire* is a more plausible, more subtly crafted story than *Bonjour tristesse* (Sagan says she spent two years thinking about her second book but only five weeks writing it), it resembles its predecessor in its characterizations, which, again, clearly represent Sagan's adolescent psychological universe. Both have young female first-person narrators. Present also are the figures of the seductive, urbane older man, the maternal fading beauty who is rival/friend/model to the narrator, and the bumbling or boring young lover. In the *Paris Review* interview just prior to the novel's publication, Sagan said, "I lead a character from book to book, I continue along with the same ideas. Only the angle of vision, the method, the lighting change."

Thematically, however, *Un Certain Sourire* represents different concerns. The first novel's clear-eyed disillusion with the world of adult values and its themes of adolescent solitude and will to freedom give way in the second novel to the adult discoveries that loving is frequently a solitary business and freedom a myth because one is never really master of his or her own feelings. Dominique, the heroine of *Un Certain Sourire*, is bored with her studies and boyfriend, Bertrand, when she meets Luc, Bertrand's uncle. A friendship develops with Luc and Françoise, Luc's wife. If Françoise's warm, maternal femininity, "rassurante comme la terre" (reassuring like the earth), appeals to Dominique almost as much as Luc's air of sophisticated *ennui*, Dominique's illusion that Luc's bored lassitude resembles her own–"Je n'aime que les intelligences tristes" (I only like sad intellects)–leads her to mistake simple attraction for absolute affinity. From the "violent sentiment de bonheur" (violent feeling of happiness) of the beginning of the affair to the feeling of being "assez heureuse" (happy enough) at the end, Sagan maps the itinerary of first love, with its failure, agony, and recovery. Alone at the end, Dominique smiles at herself in the mirror with calm acceptance: "J'étais une femme qui avait aimé un homme" (I was a woman who had loved a man).

Sagan's much-praised elliptical style involves setting down a set of immediate perceptions, of particular sensations with embellishment. The narrative moves along rapidly with little or no probing of characters' inner lives. In Sagan's universe, things simply are as they are. There is an easy naturalness to her voice, and she has an uncanny ability to find *le mot juste* which captures complex truth. Here is Luc, for instance, explaining to Dominique why, although he does not love his wife, he lacks the energy to love Dominique: "La base de tout, c'est ma fatigue, mon ennui. Solides bases, d'ailleurs, superbes. On peut bâtir de belles unions durables sur ces choses-là: la solitude, l'ennui. Au moins ça ne bouge pas" (At the bottom of everything is my fatigue, my boredom. Solid bases, those, superb. One can build beautiful, solid unions on these things: solitude, boredom. At least they don't move).

Many of the characteristics of Luc are said to resemble those of forty-year-old Guy Schoeller, whom Sagan married on 13 March 1958 (and from whom she was divorced in 1960). Heir to the Hachette publishing empire, Schoeller was also apparently the model for André Jolyau, the urbane theater director of *Dans un mois, dans un an* (1957; translated as *Those Without Shadows*, 1957). Sagan's third novel introduced a large cast of characters which reappear in later books. They include, in addition to Jolyau, a would-be writer, an editor, an ambitious actress, and a rich socialite. Autobiographically perhaps the most revealing of her fictional works, *Dans un mois, dans un an* is a cynical appraisal of the sophisticated, vapid world in which the young author then circulated. The novel abounds with observations such as the following description of a middle-aged editor: "Il était un vieil homme qui avait froid. Et toute la littérature ne lui servait à rien" (He was an old man who was cold. And all of literature was of no earthly good to him). Although it was another best-seller and was appreciated by certain critics (François Mauriac and André Malraux thought it the best of Sagan's novels), the book was panned by most of the press. In fact, character and plot development is so thin that the novel frequently reads like an outline. It should be noted, however, that Sagan wrote *Dans un mois, dans un an* on the heels of a nearly fatal, highly publicized accident in her sports car. *Toxique* (published and translated in 1964) is a fragment of a diary kept in 1957 while she was recovering. To alleviate her pain, she had been given morphine. Although she did not become an addict, it took nine days to relieve her of her need for it–and those nine days were rugged.

If *Dans un mois, dans un an* was, generally speaking, a critical failure, *Aimez-vous Brahms?* (1959; translated, 1960) represents Sagan at her best. The theme again is solitude, the solitude of a woman and two men caught in the eternal triangle. The youthful heroine has been replaced by a woman of thirty-nine, Paule, who divides her time between an interior-decorating business and Roger, her lover of six years. Roger is her life, and while Paule knows that he needs and wants her she also knows that he is constantly unfaithful and that he will never marry her. When twenty-five-year-old Simon, the son of a client, falls in love with her, she responds, both to assuage her own solitude and because she naturally understands the intense loneliness of the introverted youth. Paule is a Sagan heroine in the finest sense. She is sensitive, intelligent, and totally without illusions about herself or about the world and people around her. *Aimez-vous Brahms?* contains some of Sagan's finest writing. The novel in its entirety is reminiscent of Colette's *La Fin de Chéri,* and the following sentence, among others, has the ring of Proust: "Le lac du Bois de Boulogne s'étalait, glacé, devant eux, sous un soleil morne; seul un rameur sportif, un de ces hommes étranges que l'on voit chaque jour essayer de garder une forme dont personne ne peut sembler soucieux, tant leur physique est anonyme, faisait de grands efforts pour y rappeler l'été, sa rame soulevant parfois une gerbe d'eau étincelante, argentée, et presque inopportune tant l'hiver, parmi les arbres figés, s'annonçait triste" (A solitary sportive rower, one of those strange men who can be seen straining to preserve a form which no one seems to care about, so anonymous is their physique, was making mighty efforts to recall the summer, his oar occasionally raising a shower of sparkling, silver, and almost inopportune water, so sad did the winter seem among the stiffened trees).

The familiar theme of solitude runs through Sagan's first play, *Château en Suède* (Castle in Sweden, 1960). Although over the next fifteen years she was to write, direct, and produce for the theater, for film, and for television, this four-act black comedy was Sagan's greatest theatrical success. It is interesting to note that the 1959-1960 season saw the Parisian premieres of some of the great French plays of the century, including Sartre's *Les Séquestrés d'Altona* (The Condemned of Altona), Jean Genet's *Le Balcon* (The Balcony) and *Les Nègres* (The Blacks), Boris Vian's *Les Bâtisseurs d'empire* (The Empire Builders), and Jean Anouilh's *Becket ou l'honneur de Dieu* (Becket; or, The Honor of God). Sagan remembers the delight of hearing from the wings after her play's pre-

miere performance, "Et en plus elle sait écrire des pièces" (And what's more, she knows how to write plays).

The characters of *Château en Suède,* set in present-day Sweden, live in a secluded château, where they wear eighteenth-century costumes to appease the chatelaine who winces when she sees a modern suit. Sagan's gift for adroit sophisticated dialogue is perfect for the theater, and her svelte, malicious protagonists are extremely appealing. Eléanore and Sebastian van Milhem, a brother-sister duo whom Sagan brings back in her 1972 novel, *Des Bleus à l'âme,* are among the author's most likable fictional creations. Their near-incestuous intimacy is at least in part inspired by Sagan's relationship with her older brother Jacques Quoirez, who was for years her best friend and confidant. The brother-sister complicity—as in Jean Cocteau's *Les Enfants terribles* (1929) and Robert Musil's *Der Mann ohne Eigenschaften* (*The Man Without Qualities,* 1930-1933)— excludes outsiders. The result in Sagan's play is that would-be seducers are rendered either ridiculous or dead. Eléanore is married to Hugo, whose first wife, Ophelia, officially dead, is confined to a wing of the castle from which she escapes occasionally in order to find cribbage partners. Frédéric, Hugo's cousin, arrives from Stockholm and falls in love with Eléanore. After toying with him for a while, Eléanore and Sebastian set about frightening the young man to death. As soon as Frédéric is disposed of, a new victim is announced. The destruction of innocence in a rotten world, a favorite Anouilh theme, is one which Sagan evidently liked to parody, for it reappears in *Les Violons parfois* (Violins Sometimes), her second play, which was produced in 1961 and published the following year. Sagan made her debut as director with her fourth play, *Bonheur, impair et passe* (Fortune, Odd, High, produced and published in 1964). The author's many-faceted career includes a short film, *Encore un hiver* (One More Winter), which won first prize in its category at the 1979 New York Film Festival.

The disproportion between Sagan's phenomenal success and what many critics considered her limited universe and talent (Pierre de Boisdeffre wrote at one point that "ses idées restaient aussi courtes que ses cheveux" [her ideas were as short as her hair]) was widened during the 1960s when the author published a series of undistinguished novels, the worst of which was *Le Garde de cœur* (1968; translated as *The Heart-keeper,*

1968). Set in Hollywood, it is the story of a middle-aged female scriptwriter who becomes involved with a young man who enters her life as the result of an auto accident. "It is almost a joke," said Sagan, who had spent only two days in Hollywood. "The book is a complete mental picture of Hollywood." To fill in the physical facts of the southern California landscape, Sagan relied on her second husband, Minnesota-born Robert James Westhoff, a writer who translated the novel into English. Westhoff and Sagan were married in 1962. The couple, divorced in 1963, have a son, Denis.

Des Bleus à l'âme marks a radical departure from Sagan's earlier works. While it is in part a typical Sagan novel, it is also, and more importantly, a meditation on the problematics of novel-writing and encroaching middle age. The novel–brief, fragmentary, and interspersed with the author's commentaries–brings back the van Milhems, now ten years older and as charmingly "désinvoltes" (unselfconscious) as ever. So is Sagan, who wrote about herself, "J'ai trente-cinq ans, de bonnes dents, et si quelqu'un me plaît, généralement, cela marche encore" (I am thirty-five, my teeth are good, and if I feel attracted to someone, on the whole it still works). The problem is, she is no longer interested. She is also uncertain about whether to continue writing, whether the New Novelists were not perhaps right in their stress on form and technique and disavowal of classic plot.

On the first page of *Des Bleus à l'âme* Sagan speaks of "ce désaveu, cet ennui, ce profil détourné que m'inspire une existence qui jusqu'ici, et pour de fortes bonnes raisons, m'avait séduite" (the boredom, the distaste I now feel for a way of life that until now, and for very good reasons, had always attracted me). When the author bids Eléanore and Sebastian adieu on the novel's last page, she seems to be telling her readers that she is leaving behind forever a certain kind of writing as well as a way of life. Her subsequent novels, however, have not shown a marked difference either in style or substance, and none has equalled *Des Bleus à l'âme* or the early novels in quality. *Un Profil perdu* (1974; translated as *Lost Profile*, 1976) returns to the theme of a young woman and an older lover. *Le Lit défait* (1977; translated as *The Unmade Bed*, 1978) differs from other novels only in that the characters are passionately involved in their work. *La Femme fardée* (1981; translated as *The Painted Lady*, 1983), is distinguished primarily by its length and

its introductory pages, which Sagan, who rarely rewrites, says she revised eighteen times. *Un Orage immobile* (1983; translated as *The Still Storm*, 1984), set in Angoulême in 1832, is a typical Sagan novel, distinguished from others only by its historical period and male narrator. *De guerre lasse* (1985; translated as *A Reluctant Hero*, 1987), a meditation on occupied France during the early 1940s meant perhaps to be a *roman engagé*, was not successful. The following quotation from a review in *Express* captures the general response to the novel: "La politique est loin: les personnages ne se branchent guère sur Radio Londres. . . . Tout un climat bourgeois d'apathie et de mesure baigne le roman: où sont la fraîcheur et l'insolence de Françoise Sagan?" (Politics is far away: the characters don't even turn on Radio London. . . . The novel is bathed in an apathetic, measured bourgeois climate: where are Sagan's freshness and insolence?). The novel was made into a moderately successful film in 1987. Sagan's most recent work, *Un Sang d'aquarelle* (Watercolor Blood), set in Vichy France, was published in 1987, the same year that her biography, *Sarah Bernhardt: Le Rire incassable* (Sarah Bernhardt: The Unbreakable Laugh), appeared.

If Sagan's recent novels have not measured up to her early work, her two memoirs reflect the lucidity and naturalness of her best writing, and both have been extremely successful. *Réponses* (1974) is a montage of remarks culled from more than a hundred interviews over a twenty-year period. It includes the author's ideas on a wide range of subjects, from literature to love to children. Even those readers who disagree with Sagan's opinions are able to appreciate her integrity, the grace and freshness of her style, and the cool unpretentious detachment with which she views herself. For example, on her characters, whom she says certain critics have accused of futility: "Les personnages ne sont pas futiles. Ils ont en général la même attitude que moi, une attitude qui, pour beaucoup, n'est pas sérieuse. Je trouve plus agréable et même esthétique une certaine légèreté" (The characters aren't futile. In general they have the same attitude as I do, an attitude which, for many, isn't serious. I find more agreeable and even aesthetic a certain lightness).

Avec mon meilleur souvenir (1984; translated as *With Fondest Regards*, 1985) is an album of memories which have the quality of photographs. The themes are love and admiration, and Sagan's subjects, each treated in a separate essay, range from favorite activities and places–gambling, the theater, St. Tropez, and reading–to people encountered in privileged moments–Billie Holiday, Tennessee Williams, Orson Welles, Rudolf Nureyev, and Jean-Paul Sartre. Although they had had sporadic encounters over a period of twenty-five years, Sagan and Sartre did not become friends until the last year of Sartre's life. Sagan captures the tender, discreet complicity of this brief relationship when she cites Sartre's description of their conversations, like those of "deux voyageurs sur un quai de gare" (two travelers on a railroad platform). Sagan's affection and respect for her subjects and her love of things fragile and ephemeral shine in these essays as they do throughout all her work. Her "petite musique" resembles no other, and she has the ability of not taking herself too seriously. If solitude is her principal theme, her disillusion is graceful: pessimism with a certain smile.

Interviews:

Blair Fuller and Robert B. Silvers, "Françoise Sagan," in *Writers at Work: The Paris Review Interviews,* first series, edited by Malcolm Cowley (New York: Viking, 1958), pp. 301-309;

Jean-Louis Echine, "Entretien: Sagan sans clichés," *Nouvelles Littéraires* (7 April 1977): 5;

Jean-François Josselin, "Les Années Sagan," *Nouvel Observateur,* 18 March 1983, pp. 14-17.

Bibliography:

John Robert Kaiser, "Françoise Sagan," *Bulletin of Bibliography and Magazine Notes,* 30 (July-September 1973): 106-109.

References:

Leslie Garis, "Sagan: Encore Tristesse," *New York Times Magazine,* 16 November 1980, pp. 64-72, 88-103;

Françoise Giroud, "The Sagan Saga: A Continued Story," *New York Times Magazine,* 27 October 1957, pp. 16, 76;

Georges Hourdin, *Le Cas Françoise Sagan* (Paris: Cerf, 1958);

Jena Lignière, *Françoise Sagan et le succès* (Paris: Scorpion, 1957);

Judith Graves Miller, *Françoise Sagan* (Boston: Twayne, 1988);

Gerard Mourque, *Françoise Sagan* (Paris: Editions Universitaires, 1957);

Bertrand Poirot-Delpech, *Bonjour Sagan* (Paris: Herscher, 1985).

Papers:

The John Robert Kaiser Collection of Françoise Sagan, which includes several manuscripts, is at the Pennsylvania State University Library.

Michel de Saint Pierre
(12 February 1916-19 June 1987)

David O'Connell
Georgia State University

BOOKS: *Vagabondages* (Avignon: Aubanel, 1938);
Contes pour les sceptiques (Paris: Henri Lefebvre, 1945);
Ce Monde ancien (Paris: Calmann-Lévy, 1948);
Montherlant, bourreau de soi-même (Paris: Gallimard, 1949);
La Mer à boire (Paris: Calmann-Lévy, 1951);
Bernadette et Lourdes (Paris: Table Ronde, 1952); translated by Edward Fitzgerald as *Bernadette and Lourdes* (New York: Farrar, Straus & Young, 1954; London: Hutchinson, 1954);
Les Aristocrates (Paris: Table Ronde, 1954); translated by Geoffrey Sainsbury as *The Aristocrats* (London: Hutchinson, 1956; New York: Dutton, 1956);
Dieu vous garde des femmes (Paris: Denoël, 1955);
Les Ecrivains [novel] (Paris: Calmann-Lévy, 1957); translated by Peter Green as *Men of Letters* (London: Hutchinson, 1959);
Les Ecrivains [play], by Saint Pierre and Pierre de Calan (Paris: Grasset, 1959);
Les Murmures de Satan (Paris: Calmann-Lévy, 1959);
La Vie prodigieuse du curé d'Ars (Paris: Bonne Presse, 1959); translated by M. Angeline Bouchard as *The Remarkable Curé of Ars: The Life and Achievements of St. John Mary Vianney* (Garden City, N.Y.: Doubleday, 1963); definitive French-language edition (Paris: Gallimard, 1973);
Les Nouveaux Aristocrates (Paris: Calmann-Lévy, 1960); translated by Anthony and Llewela Burgess as *The New Aristocrats* (London: Gollancz, 1962; Boston: Houghton Mifflin, 1963);
La Nouvelle Race (Paris: Table Ronde, 1961);
L'Ecole de la violence (Paris: Table Ronde, 1962);
Plaidoyer pour l'amnistie (Paris: Esprit Nouveau, 1963);
Les Nouveaux Prêtres (Paris: Table Ronde, 1964); translated as *The New Priests* (Saint Louis: Herder, 1966);
Sainte Colère (Paris: Table Ronde, 1965);

Michel de Saint Pierre with his son Guillaume (photograph by Jean Mainbourg)

Ces Prêtres qui souffrent (Paris: Table Ronde, 1966);
J'étais à Fatima (Paris: Table Ronde, 1967);
Le Drame des Romanov, 2 volumes (Paris: Laffont, 1967, 1969);
La Jeunesse et l'amour (Paris: Plon, 1970);
Le Milliardaire (Paris: Grasset, 1970);
L'Accusée (Paris: Grasset, 1972);
Eglises en ruine, église en péril (Paris: Plon, 1973);
Je reviendrai sur les ailes de l'aigle (Paris: Table Ronde, 1975);
Les Fumées de Satan (Paris: Table Ronde, 1976);
Monsieur de Charette, chevalier du roi (Paris: Table Ronde, 1977);

La Passion de l'abbé Delance (Paris: Table Ronde, 1978);

Laurent (Paris: Grasset, 1980);

Docteur Erikson (Paris: Grasset, 1982);

Lettre ouverte aux assassins de l'école libre (Paris: Albin Michel, 1982);

Le Double Crime de l'impasse Salomon (Paris: Plon, 1984);

Sous le soleil de Dieu (Paris: Plon, 1984);

Les Cavaliers du Veld (Paris: Albin Michel, 1986);

La Source et la mer (Paris: Table Ronde, 1986);

Le Milieu de l'été (Paris: Albin Michel, 1987).

Michel de Saint Pierre was a widely read realist in the Balzacian tradition. His popular novels over a period of forty years sold millions of copies. At the same time, his vocal opposition to many of the changes wrought in Catholic life and ritual by the Second Vatican Council (1962-1965), and his novel on the subject, *Les Nouveaux Prêtres* (1964; translated as *The New Priests*, 1966), made him a leading spokesman for the "intégriste" movement within the Church.

Saint Pierre was born on 12 February 1916 into a rural aristocratic family with Norman roots. His parents, Antoinette and Louis de Saint Pierre (his father was a career military man who became a historian after his retirement from active service), sent him off at the age of fourteen to Saint-Jean-de-Bethune, a Catholic boarding school in Versailles. The years spent there were to play an important role in Saint Pierre's intellectual and spiritual development, even though, in terms of grades and class standing, he was hardly a brilliant student. However, it is obvious that the intensely lived atmosphere of faith built around daily attendance at mass, the enchantment of the cycle of class and holidays intimately bound up with the mystery and beauty of the Catholic liturgical year, the long hours devoted to sports as well as to study, and the camaraderie enjoyed with other boys as well as with teachers had a lasting and positive effect on him. These years affirmed his faith as a traditional Catholic and seem to have gradually revealed to him two major conclusions about himself: that as an adult he wanted to maintain his independence from outside constraint and that the best way for him to learn about the world was primarily through experience and only secondarily through books and formal learning.

Barely able to pass the state-administered *baccalauréat* at the end of his secondary studies, he nevertheless went ahead and enrolled at the Sorbonne at the age of eighteen. This much, at least, was expected of him, given his family background and social milieu. After one year, however, he passed his examinations but then dropped out. The lectures seemed moribund, and the life of a student in the Latin Quarter seemed pointless and parasitical. In September 1935, at the age of nineteen, he took a job as an unskilled worker in the shipyards at Saint-Nazaire in Brittany.

The year that Saint Pierre spent working there was also probably the most important one for French organized labor in the twentieth century, for it saw the coming to power of Léon Blum's Popular Front government of Communists, Socialists, and Radicals. French workers still received very low wages and almost no benefits, including no paid vacations. Although Saint Pierre shared the frustration and humiliation of his fellow laborers and generally supported their goals, he also took exception to many of their methods, including the general strike. As a Catholic, moreover, he was particularly angered by what he took to be the pomp and ceremony organized by the Left in imitation of Catholic ritual. The theology of Marxism, complete with its prophets (Marx and Engels), its chosen people (the working class) and clergy (party members), its construction of a satanical enemy (the bourgeois ruling class), and its promise of salvation (a materialistic paradise on earth), were concepts that he could not accept. In the summer of 1936 he therefore left Saint-Nazaire and enlisted in the navy. Later, when World War II was over and the time had come to begin seriously his career as a writer, these initial experiences of adulthood, as a student in Paris and as a worker in Saint Nazaire, would be adapted and transformed into his first novel, *Ce Monde ancien* (This Old World, 1948). Expressing himself through the character of Gilles de Lointrain, a sensitive boy in revolt against the inherited privilege of his milieu but unsure of where he fits into society without it, Saint Pierre wrote a compelling *Bildungsroman* in his first full-length literary effort.

Beginning his four years of naval service in September 1936, Saint Pierre had no way of knowing that he would not be able to return to a normal way of life until 1945 and the end of World War II. His years of prewar service, while threats and rumors of war persisted but no shots were fired, would later serve as the raw material for his second novel, *La Mer à boire* (Difficult Assignment, 1951), winner of the Grand Prix du

Roman from the Société des Gens de Lettres. The hero of the novel, Marc Van Hussel, is only a thinly disguised version of Saint Pierre. His adventures in bars and bordellos, the fights, the lovemaking, and the frustrations of young men eager for war but repeatedly disappointed when war does not come are chronicled in this novel. By the end of the work Marc has given up on his hopes of someday seeing action and has decided to desert. But before he can do so, war is declared and his wish for virile action is finally granted.

After the defeat of France, Saint Pierre went directly into the Resistance movement, where he led a clandestine life about which little is known. After the war, however, he did receive several medals and citations for his Resistance activities. Except for one brief section in his 1975 novel, *Je reviendrai sur les ailes de l'aigle* (I Shall Return on the Wings of the Eagle), in which he partially transposes his experiences through the characters Michel Cohen and Bruno Martinville, there are no other insights into this period of his life in his fiction or other writings.

From the publication of *Ce Monde ancien* to his death on 19 June 1987, Saint Pierre's personal biography and his career as a writer largely overlapped. His many novels chronicling life in twentieth-century France throughout the period of tumultuous change that has occurred since the end of World War II, but especially since the creation of the Fifth Republic, founded by Gen. Charles de Gaulle in 1958, are surely his major achievement. But this prolific writer was also active in the fields of biography and polemical essay. His major works in the realm of biography are *Bernadette et Lourdes* (1952; translated, 1954), *La Vie prodigieuse du curé d'Ars* (1959; translated as *The Remarkable Curé of Ars: The Life and Achievements of St. John Mary Vianney* (1963), and the two-volume history of the Russian czars, *Le Drame des Romanov* (1967, 1969). His notable achievements as an essayist have been: *La Nouvelle Race* (The New Race, 1961) and *L'Ecole de la violence* (The School for Violence, 1962), dealing with the problems of teenagers in revolt against society and the beginnings of juvenile delinquency in France; *Plaidoyer pour l'amnistie* (A Plea for Amnesty, 1963), an open letter to President de Gaulle asking an official pardon for the military men who had tried to overthrow him in 1961 during the Algerian war; *Sainte Colère* (Holy Anger, 1965); *Ces Prêtres qui souffrent* (These Suffering Priests, 1966); *Eglises en ruine, église en péril* (Churches in Ruin, Church in Peril, 1973); and *Les Fumées de Satan* (Satan's Smokescreen, 1976), all dealing with Saint Pierre's dissatisfaction with the changes taking place in French Catholicism as a result of Vatican II. Finally, his pamphlet *Lettre ouverte aux assassins de l'école libre* (Open Letter to the Assassins of the Private Schools, 1982), directed against French President François Mitterand and his Socialist government's proposal to nationalize France's Catholic schools by integrating them into the massive state system, was one of the major opposition texts that eventually led to the government's withdrawal of the plan and the maintenance of the educational status quo.

Saint Pierre's first great commercial success, subsequently translated into a half-dozen languages, was *Les Aristocrates* (1954; translated, 1956). The novel deals with an aristocratic family presided over by the Marquis de Maubrun, a widower living on the family estate in Burgundy. The problem of what constitutes nobility is presented early in the novel. Maubrun has married the descendant of a *maréchal*, Mousquet du Hodna, who had won his noble title of baron during the 1830s for his military exploits, raising the question of whether this type of nobility, going back only 125 years and not to the Old Regime, is acceptable or not. Saint Pierre's father wrote a great deal about his own wife's ancestor, Marshal Soult, who distinguished himself at Austerlitz with Napoleon and later served the Bourbons under the Restoration (1815-1830); like him, the brother-in-law of the Marquis de Maubrun is writing the biography of the "unknown Marshal," as the fictional Marshal du Hodna is called. Ultimately, in the novel, this "new" nobility comes to be accepted.

The line is clearly drawn, however, when a neighbor, the young Baron de Conti, dares to seek the hand of Maubrun's daughter, Daisy, in marriage. Conti has inherited his title from his father, a man who started out in life as a factory worker and who, through success in business, the accumulation of wealth, and the purchase of an estate with a title attached to it, had become a baron. He is a kind and loving young man, and Daisy does seem to love him in return. Her six brothers are divided as to whether Daisy should marry Conti, but gradually their resistance crumbles, and they try, unsuccessfully, to persuade their father to allow the marriage to take place.

Parallel to this love story runs that of Daisy's father and a young woman named Jeanne, thirty years his junior. Ironically, when the marquis declares that he wants to marry her, the children find their own bloodlines backing up on them. While they are willing to accept Daisy's marriage with the Baron de Conti (after all, he is legally a baron), they revolt at the idea of having Jeanne as their stepmother. The problems of tradition and pedigree keep getting in the way, even though the sons in certain respects are more modern than their father and better able to cope with the new, postwar economic realities.

By the end of the novel the reader gains a sense of the web of contradictions that constitute aristocratic life in France. In the last chapter one finds the marquis going over his financial accounts. He has reluctantly decided to sell his best horses and his oldest rifles in order to pay for needed repairs on the family castle (the symbol, throughout the novel, of the French aristocracy). He is willing to sacrifice whatever he must in order to preserve the castle against the ravages of time and pass it on intact to his children. Jeanne is packing her bags to leave, for the marquis has come to the realization that he cannot marry her, just as Daisy realizes that she ought not marry Conti. *Les Aristocrates* made Saint Pierre's name a household word in France. It was later made into a movie which continues to appear regularly on French television.

His next novel, *Les Ecrivains* (1957; translated as *Men of Letters*, 1959), is concerned with the generational conflict between order and tradition on the one hand and self-indulgence and novelty on the other. It deals principally with the struggle between Alexandre Damville, an established writer who greedily budgets every minute of his day in order to grind out books and articles, and his son Georges, a young man of twenty-five with literary aspirations but as yet no production. In contrast to his father's ascetic existence, Georges drinks too much, stays out too late, and wastes his time on the latest fads.

Modeled partially on Saint Pierre's cousin, the well-known writer Henry de Montherlant, Damville assumes tragic dimensions by the end of the novel. The rivalry between father and son and all that they represent is focused in the attraction that they each feel for the actress Marguerite Villère, who is starring in the great man's latest play. When Marguerite rejects the father and indicates that she would prefer the son, Alexandre suffers a stroke and dies. Having devoted his whole life to books, he seems unable to protect himself against the feelings that over-

whelm him when Marguerite prefers his son to him. Having chosen to live in his cocoon and to write for future generations, he proves himself ill-equipped to deal with everyday life once his own feelings become involved.

Although Saint Pierre evidently feels a great sympathy for his hero's sense of order, discipline, and tradition, he nonetheless disagrees with the elder Damville's tunnel vision. He seems to be saying in this novel that the writer should strive to cultivate a position midway between the unworldly asceticism of the older Damville and the trendy emptiness of his son. The real world does exist, and it offers many subjects for a good novelist. Thus, unlike the older Damville, Saint Pierre would henceforth write about life as it was being lived by his contemporaries, but like Damville, he would do so with a sense of tradition and a reverence for order.

In *Les Murmures de Satan* (Satan's Whispering, 1959) and *Les Nouveaux Aristocrates* (1960; translated as *The New Aristocrats*, 1962) one finds Saint Pierre attempting to write within the tradition of the French Catholic novel. In the first of these two works he portrays Jean Dewinter, a married layman and self-made businessman, trying to live the teachings of the Gospel in modern France. To Dewinter, the ideal is to create a Christian living unit consisting of several families grouped together and sharing expenses in an eighteenth-century manor house outside Paris. Through the character of Léo, the atheist sculptor who rents the greenhouse on the property and who regularly tells Dewinter and his followers that they are wasting their time, Saint Pierre attempts to introduce a Bernanosian dimension to the novel by having the fragmented forces of good, Dewinter and his extended family, confront the concentrated forces of evil as represented by Léo. By the end of the novel the group will be disbanded by order of the Catholic hierarchy, but for the people who have taken part in the experiment, it will have been a learning experience. Looking back on the novel, published several years before the Second Vatican Council, which gave so much power to Catholic laypersons, today's critic realizes that it stands out as a pioneering work that foreshadows many such living experiments of the 1960s and 1970s.

In *Les Nouveaux Aristocrates* the action is set in a Jesuit-run secondary school outside Paris. The hero of the novel is Denis Prullé-Rousseau, a pampered bourgeois youth who, having lost his faith, attempts to make life impossible for the school's teachers and staff. Here Saint Pierre returns to a theme that he had begun to explore in *Les Murmures de Satan*: the problem of happiness for the Christian. His conclusion is that the true Christian should not expect his faith to ensure perfect happiness in this imperfect world.

Saint Pierre's next novel, *Les Nouveaux Prêtres*, is his most important work and the one for which he is best known. The action of the novel is set in Villedieu, a fictional suburb of Paris located in the so-called red belt of industrial towns bordering Paris on the north. The parish priests in these towns, which are known for their large factories, vast government-built housing projects, and Communist-dominated municipal councils, face difficult problems which are in large part the result of the neglect shown by the Church to the needs and interests of working-class people.

The central conflict in the novel is between the forces of *progressisme* and *intégrisme* within the French Catholic Church. The progressive priests want to tear down the old parish church and hold services in a rented room in an apartment building, discard traditional clerical garb in favor of turtleneck sweaters and jeans, and work together with the local Communists to secure secular goals. In opposition to them, Saint Pierre places a more conservative priest, Paul Delance, who typifies a personal type of spirituality that one might expect to find in an earlier age. Not long after his arrival in the parish, Saint Marc, a confrontation arises between Delance and the progressive priests, Barré and Reismann. The latter, however, are extremely hardworking men, devoting long hours to helping the poor and disenfranchised, eating and drinking little, and generally living an ascetic life. The problem at the heart of the novel is thus the question as to what degree of political involvement is allowed on the part of a priest. Saint Pierre's strong anti-Communist convictions are expressed in the answer to this question, for the spirituality of Delance, simple, apolitical, and oriented toward the cult of the Virgin, is found to be more in keeping with Catholic tradition than is that of the "new priests" of the title. Thus, at the end of the novel, ecclesiastical authorities decide that Barré and Reismann have gone too far, and they are transferred to a new assignment. Barré, convinced of the rectitude of his position, accepts this rebuke in order to keep fighting within the system for his point of view. Reismann, however, the weaker of the two men, leaves the priesthood to live with a woman. The

ideal of social progress and equality has become his god. Thus, there is no longer a place for him in the Catholic Church.

This novel caused an uproar in France and was a colossal best-seller for Saint Pierre, with over four hundred thousand copies sold the first year and countless thousands sold since in the Livre de Poche series. The themes that reappear in Saint Pierre's earlier and later fiction are all expressed here: hatred of communism, reverence for the sacred nature of the priest's vocation, defense of traditional Catholic practices and beliefs, sympathy for working people who are all too often duped by Communist propaganda, and hatred of modernism (understood as the cult of the individual's interests over those of the group).

Michel de Saint Pierre changed direction in his work as a novelist in the years following the great success of *Les Nouveaux Prêtres*. It was six years before his next novel, *Le Milliardaire* (The Billionaire, 1970), appeared, and with that novel he began to see himself less as a Catholic novelist in the tradition of Mauriac and Bernanos and more as a witness to his age. The nine novels that he produced after 1970 all have a major social problem or phenomenon as their principal subject. *Le Milliardaire*, for instance, deals with the new computer age sweeping France and the consequent growth of multinational companies, while *L'Accusée* (The Guilty Woman, 1972) treats the problem of divorce and woman's rights in the French legal system, which is heavily weighted in favor of men. *Je reviendrai sur les ailes de l'aigle* deals with the situation of Jews in French society and their relationship to the state of Israel. Although a political conservative with roots in the traditionally anti-Semitic French Right, Saint Pierre is a self-styled "philosémite," and this novel offers a warmhearted endorsement of Zionism and argues for the equality of all French citizens regardless of their social origins. *La Passion de l'abbé Delance* (1978), which continues *Les Nouveaux Prêtres*, treats what Saint Pierre considers to be the continuing infiltration of Marxists and materialistic values inside the French Church, while *Laurent* (1980) deals with the problems of young people adapting to the new consumer society. Laurent, the hero of the novel, is modeled on one of Saint Pierre's five children, his son Richard, who committed suicide in a fit of despair.

Docteur Erikson (1982) takes on the French medical establishment and its refusal to use new and experimental techniques in fighting cancer, and *Le Double Crime de l'impasse Salomon* (The Double Crime in the Impasse Salomon, 1984) attacks the French judiciary, which Saint Pierre took to be too lenient toward criminals. *Les Cavaliers du Veld* (1986), a chronicle of the settlement of South Africa by French Huguenots, argues that they are entitled as much as anyone else to live in that country, while his last novel, *Le Milieu de l'été* (The Height of Summer, 1987), is a drama of religious conversion which Saint Pierre handed to his publisher the day before he died.

Although Saint Pierre cannot be ranked among the great novelists of the twentieth century, he is an accomplished writer of the second rank. Using meticulous documentation à la Balzac as the basis for his novels, he wrote books that are easy to read and highly persuasive. In an era in which many think that French academic critical practices have seriously undermined the novel, he has contributed to the maintenance of the realist strain in French literature.

Reference:

David O'Connell, "Michel de Saint Pierre and the Defense of Traditional Values," *Renascence*, 36 (Autumn-Winter 1983-1984): 88-106.

Nathalie Sarraute
(18 July 1900-)

Françoise Calin
University of Oregon

BOOKS: *Tropismes* (Paris: Denoël, 1939; revised and enlarged, Paris: Editions de Minuit, 1957); translated by Maria Jolas as *Tropisms* (New York: Braziller, 1967); republished with *The Age of Suspicion* (1967);

Portrait d'un inconnu (Paris: Robert Marin, 1948); translated by Jolas as *Portrait of a Man Unknown* (New York: Braziller, 1958; London: Calder, 1959);

Martereau (Paris: Gallimard, 1953); translated by Jolas (New York: Braziller, 1959; London: Calder, 1964);

L'Ere du soupçon (Paris: Gallimard, 1956); translated by Jolas as *The Age of Suspicion* (New York: Braziller, 1963); republished with *Tropisms* (1967);

Le Planétarium (Paris: Gallimard, 1959); translated by Jolas as *The Planetarium* (New York: Braziller, 1960; London: Calder, 1961);

Les Fruits d'or (Paris: Gallimard, 1963); translated by Jolas as *The Golden Fruits* (New York: Braziller, 1964; London: Calder, 1965);

Le Silence, suivi de Le Mensonge (Paris: Gallimard, 1967); translated by Jolas as *Silence, and The Lie* (London: Calder & Boyars, 1969);

Tropisms, and The Age of Suspicion, translated by Jolas (London: Calder & Boyars, 1967);

Entre la vie et la mort (Paris: Gallimard, 1968); translated by Jolas as *Between Life and Death* (New York: Braziller, 1969; London: Calder & Boyars, 1970); French version republished in *Théâtre* (1978);

Isma ou Ce qui s'appelle rien, suivi de Le Silence et Le Mensonge (Paris: Gallimard, 1970); republished in *Théâtre* (1978); translated by Jolas as *Izzum* in *Collected Plays of Nathalie Sarraute* (1980);

Vous les entendez? (Paris: Gallimard, 1972); translated by Jolas as *Do You Hear Them?* (New York: Braziller, 1973; London: Calder & Boyars, 1975);

"disent les imbéciles" (Paris: Gallimard, 1976); translated by Jolas as *"fools say"* (New York: Braziller, 1977; London: Calder, 1977);

Théâtre (Paris: Gallimard, 1978)—comprises *Le Silence, Le Mensonge, Isma, C'est beau,* and *Elle est là*; translated by Jolas and Barbara Wright as *Collected Plays of Nathalie Sarraute* (London: Calder, 1980; New York: Braziller, 1981);

L'Usage de la parole (Paris: Gallimard, 1980); translated by Wright as *The Use of Speech* (New York: Braziller, 1983; London: Calder, 1983);

Nathalie Sarraute (photograph copyright © Jerry Bauer)

Pour un oui ou pour un non (Paris: Gallimard, 1982);

Enfance (Paris: Gallimard, 1983); translated by Wright as *Childhood* (New York: Braziller, 1984; London: Calder, 1984);

Paul Valéry et l'enfant d'éléphant; Flaubert le précurseur (Paris: Gallimard, 1986).

PLAY PRODUCTIONS: *Le Silence* and *Le Mensonge*, Paris, Petit Odéon, 10 January 1967;

Isma ou Ce qui s'appelle rien, Paris, Espace Pierre Cardin, 5 February 1973;

C'est beau, Paris, Théâtre d'Orsay, 24 October 1975;

Elle est là, Paris, Centre Georges Pompidou, Autumn 1978; Paris, Théâtre d'Orsay, 15 January 1980;

Pour un oui ou pour un non, Paris, Petit Rond-Point, 17 February 1986.

PERIODICAL PUBLICATION: *C'est beau*, *Cahiers Renaud Barrault*, 83 (First Trimester 1973): 3-23.

Nathalie Sarraute is one of contemporary France's most important writers. In autumn 1987, at the age of eighty-seven, she was in the process of finishing her eleventh novel. The first ten have been translated into twenty-three foreign languages, including Egyptian. These books are generally designated by the term *nouveaux romans*, and, indeed, Sarraute is recognized as an initiator and one of the prime theorists of the literary current that, over the last thirty years, has decisively oriented the course of narrative fiction.

Nathalie Sarraute was born 18 July 1900 in Ivanovo-Voznessensk, Russia. Her father, Ilya Tcherniak, was a chemist; her mother, Pauline Chatounovsky Tcherniak, a writer. Her parents divorced when she was two. She lived with her mother and stepfather in Paris until age five, spending her summers at her father's home in Russia. Then her mother returned to Saint Petersburg, and Sarraute followed her, still spending her summers with her father in Switzerland and France. Traveling from one country to another, she learned French and Russian at the same time, an experience that marked the beginning of her lasting passion for languages and words. For political reasons, her father had to leave Russia and chose Paris for his exile. Sarraute joined him and his fiancée there in 1908. Originally, she was to spend only a short while in Paris and return to her mother. In fact, she stayed in Paris, "abandoned"—as her father's second wife said—by her mother. Sarraute recalls this period of her life in her 1983 memoir, *Enfance* (translated as *Childhood*, 1984).

She grew up surrounded by Russian intellectuals, immigrants to Paris, and she seems to have survived the emotional aridity of a motherless world thanks to a special relationship with her father, which she describes with subtlety and discreet emotion. It was her father who transmitted to her his passion for ideas. She remembers quarreling with him about Proust and Gide, leaving home in anger for a few days when she was seventeen after such a literary argument. They both took it for granted, from the beginning, that she would earn advanced diplomas and have a career.

Sarraute loved school and found reassuring solidity in the world presented by the French educational system. She was a good student, from the first grade to the *baccalauréat*. Meanwhile, at home, the family grew: a half sister, with whom she never developed a close relationship, and, later, a half brother, whose company she enjoyed. After attending the Lycée Fénelon (a prestigious Parisian high school), she enrolled at the Sorbonne, where she studied English and was granted a *licence* in 1920. From Paris, she went on to Oxford. She enjoyed her British experience so much that she was prepared to stay in England if her father had not protested vehemently. She returned to Paris, attended law school, and became a member of the Paris bar in 1925. Sarraute practiced law until 1940. When asked about her experience as a lawyer, she only acknowledges having learned to free herself from the classical written language and to work with oral speech patterns.

In 1925 she married one of her fellow law students: Raymond Sarraute. Literature was their common love. They read widely in three or four languages and spent a quiet, intellectual life. By the time she wrote her first book they had three daughters. Her career, one might say, began in 1932, when she sat down and produced four pages (the second sketch in her first book, *Tropismes* [1939]), which contained, in a nutshell, her obsession with the complexity of human relationships and the limitations of a language stultified by clichés.

Tropismes, when it was first published in 1939, contained a series of nineteen texts, each from one to three pages long. In 1957 a revised and expanded version with twenty-four sketches appeared. (It was translated into English in 1967.) Because names of characters and a coherent plot are conspicuous by their absence, the reader's dismay when the work first appeared is readily explicable. Only one reviewer, in a minor periodical, the *Gazette de Liège*, had the perspicacity to discern a new force in narrative fiction. As Sarraute has insisted, this first book contained all the elements that her following novels were to develop at length.

One could, in fact, take the title of Sarraute's first text and use it for her collected works. Of scientific derivation, the term *tropism* refers to the movement of an organism to–or from–its source of heat or light. An advance or a retreat in response to a foreign body, this instinctive and uncontrollable movement is for Sarraute the fundamental mechanism of all human interaction. Subject to the gaze of the Other, a person reacts, attracted to or repulsed by the speech, the smile, the conscious or unconscious desires of that Other, the interlocutor of the moment. The novelist seeks to grasp human relations not in their more dramatic manifes-

tations–the grand tradition of Love and Death–but in the banal, day-to-day meeting in a stairway or the insignificant chit-chat on a street corner.

Thus, it is a half-drunk cup of cold coffee, or some other trivial object or incident, that stirs up anguish in a character. Inevitably, human beings wish to hide these movements that upset them as soon as they fall under the influence of another. A social mask, a polite expression–these are used to veil or deny tumultuous feelings. Certain of Sarraute's characters possess the skill to see beyond the mask and the peaceful words. They unmask, disrobe, decode the truth, reveling in "sousconversations" (subconversations).

The notion of subconversation is inseparable from that of tropism. In one of the sketches in Sarraute's first book, the guests babble on happily about the latest van Gogh exhibition while the lady of the house, an anonymous "she," observes a silent "he" (husband? father? friend?–it matters little). Behind his silence, she imagines what he does not say, his irritation at their pretentious stupidity. Sarraute's text, like the woman in this tropism, scrutinizes the man's silence, seeking his unspoken words, his hidden, inner thoughts, focusing on a means of communication, another language, which does not depend on words. Critics hostile to Sarraute reproach her for presenting disembodied abstractions as characters. They seem to ignore what Proust had already called the "confidences involontaires du corps" (involuntary confessions of the body). In *Tropismes* and in all of the novels that follow, Sarraute's characters decipher the bodies of those whom they meet. Physical descriptions accumulate as so many signs in a new language, discreet signs to be read on the lips, eyes, eyebrows, and hands of one's interlocutor.

Sarraute excels at articulating the imperceptible hesitation, vibration, increase in heartbeat or rate of breathing that betray the existence of the hidden, the unspoken; both the narrator and the reader embark on a quest to find that which lies buried beneath the surface. As early as *Tropismes*, Sarraute's notion of the human tragedy is in place. A person in the presence of the Other struggles to understand that Other in order to seduce and possess. This is the situation of the man in the last tropism. Immobile, surrounded by a circle of faces that stare at him, caught in the trap of the Others, he is torn between the need to slip into their circle and become one cell in their single organism and that of fleeing in the mad hope that he can exist without them, alone but self-sufficient.

Sarraute has often stated that innovation in psychology inevitably corresponds to innovation in novelistic technique. A new language is necessary: words that will not slay the infinite mobility of sensations, words that will register the natural flow of being, words that capture what Beckett called the "innommable" (unnamable). Beginning with *Tropismes*, Sarraute and her characters pay particular attention to words. The most common cliché proves to be treacherous once one subjects it to scrutiny. Thus the novelist twists and turns familiar expressions, causing them to explode into metaphors that shock ingrained habits of speech and expose to the very bone what fascinates her: human psychology as it comes into being.

The narrator in *Portrait d'un inconnu* (1948; translated as *Portrait of a Man Unknown*, 1958) is on the lookout for human psychology as it comes into being. He turns himself into a *voyeur* in order to discern the tropisms that agitate the lives of two people brought together by daily contact and family ties. The observations of this anonymous, professionless narrator make up the novel. In this story written during World War II one finds no trace of the drama the author actually lived in Nazi-occupied France: being of Jewish extraction, she was perpetually in danger. She and her father were issued the yellow stars that the government ordered Jews to display but never wore them. Sarraute left Paris for Janvry, a quiet village in the Valley of Chevreuse where Raymond Sarraute came, bicycling, every Saturday to rejoin her and their daughters. There she sheltered Samuel Beckett and his wife when Beckett, who was in the Resistance, faced imminent arrest. Sarraute eventually had to leave this refuge when she was denounced by one of the village shopkeepers, and, hidden under various assumed names, she spent the rest of the war in a Parisian boarding school where she pretended to be one of the teachers.

As Sarraute has pointed out, it is useless to posit a bond between the events she has lived and the pages she has written. Although she uses what she has observed in friends, beyond this, she takes up only words or phrases heard here or there. As soon as the war was over, she returned to her favorite working place: a café near her Parisian apartment. Around her, as she worked, flowed bits of speech, clichés, social chit-chat—the living fount of her inspiration.

In spite of a laudatory preface by Jean-Paul Sartre, who was struck by the authenticity of the "I" in quest of human truths, *Portrait d'un inconnu* was not noticed; readers no doubt lost their way in the observations of the anonymous narrator or in the attempt to focus, in this apparently fragmented text, on the bits and pieces of story that serve as the novel's "plot." A miserly father refuses his daughter a sum of money she considers her due. Seeing that she can no longer count on him, the daughter finds a fiancé who offers her financial security—all this under the eyes of a witness, a friend and neighbor who spies on them for reasons that are not obvious. The author would protest against such a plot summary, and rightly so, because it does not tell the essential. The essential is perhaps to be found in the digressions (remarks on aesthetics, repetitive scenes) that incessantly interrupt the narrative line and disconcert the reader eager to follow the arguments between the father and the daughter.

Portrait d'un inconnu, though superficially amorphous, does have a structure. A pattern is articulated, centering on the narrator's sojourn in a city where he goes to see a painting called *Portrait d'un inconnu*. Before this visit to the museum, the narrator sought in vain to understand and explain the two people who fascinated him. After his confrontation with the portrait, he knows how to unmask the father and daughter and to communicate the complexities that govern their relationship.

Critics have pointed out that since Flaubert, when they began to hide behind their texts, novelists have liked to place at the center of their narratives an artistic creator, perhaps as a surrogate for the rejected omniscient author. Such characters abound in contemporary fiction and help the reader comprehend the nature of the creative process. They mirror the writer's work, illumine his quest, his struggle, his failure, his success. The narrator in *Portrait d'un inconnu* is one of these; an apprentice writer, he opens up to readers the journey of the artist eager to do something new.

His task is hard; he commits (in the first part of the novel) errors. His energy is dissipated in chatter as he tries to present his findings to friends before having worked them out. He discovers that literary memories slip in between himself and the people he is observing; is it possible, for example, to describe a father and his daughter without imitating Balzac? In anguish, he turns to a "specialist"–psychiatrist or professor?–who advises him to give up his quest for the new and to work at maintaining law and order, in the real world and in the world of art. This academic, conservative specialist reproaches his charge for not having named the father and daughter. He counsels him to grasp hold of concrete physical reality. The narrator is ready to obey.

He then sees the *Portrait d'un inconnu*, an anonymous painting in which the lines of the face remain vague and only the eyes appear to live. This seemingly unfinished canvas mirrors the doubts and hesitations of its creator and the "fantômes gris" (grey ghosts) that obsess the narrator. Contemplating the portrait, he realizes that all is still possible, that he can create a work shimmering with life and which does not adhere to traditional canons. He returns to his phantasms, and the second half of the novel becomes a cry of triumph whose refrain is the "Je sais maintenant" (Now I know) of an all-powerful narrator.

Portrait d'un inconnu is the story of the conquest of the imaginary, a conquest so difficult that, in the end, the exhausted narrator is defeated by one of his characters, Dumontet, who appears in the last pages of the novel. Unlike his father and daughter, he is not a "grey ghost." There is nothing unfinished about him. He has a name, a profession, and specific occupations. No subconversation is possible in his vicinity, and with him the world is indeed solid, understandable, the world the reader is used to. Was the specialist right? Must one in the end always return to Balzac and abandon the desire to innovate?

The beginning of Sarraute's next novel could make one answer in the affirmative, because the protagonist, Martereau, resembles Dumontet. Indeed, *Martereau* (1953; translated, 1959) begins where the previous work leaves off. However, the two novels follow divergent paths. *Portrait d'un inconnu* ends with the simple, solid clarity of a traditional character, Dumontet, whereas *Martereau*, conventional enough at first, in the course of the plot disintegrates into a flux of contradictory tropisms.

In this second novel, written in the first person like *Portrait d'un inconnu*, a greater number of silhouettes gravitate around the focalizing "I": an uncle, an aunt, and a cousin with whom the young narrator lives, and the family's friends, the Martereaus. To evade his taxes, the uncle asks Martereau to purchase a country house in his stead. His nephew, the narrator, hands over to Martereau the agreed-upon sum but does not mention a receipt. The suspense consists in finding out whether Martereau, who acquires the villa and immediately moves in, will return it or fleece the uncle by keeping it. "Là-dessus se branchent les tropismes," says Sarraute (From this the tropisms grow). Indeed, it is from this simple pattern that the author elaborates a myriad of suppositions and hypotheses. They include the delirious phantasms of a narrator who cannot make up his mind, tormented by the essential question: "Who is the Other?" The fact that, at the end of the novel, Martereau lets the property go in no way resolves the problem because one does not know whether he is being honest or is afraid of reprisals.

One's perception of Martereau is based entirely on the narrator's, and one of the key issues of the novel is whether or not this narrator is reliable. Convalescing at his uncle's, his only preoccupation is to observe the people around him. But whereas the narrator in *Portrait d'un inconnu* seeks only to understand the father and daughter, the narrator in *Martereau* wishes, in addition, to be loved and respected, which places him in a vulnerable position and makes him hypersensitive, ultimately a reflection of the expectations of others.

The narrator relives in his mind the moment when he delivered his uncle's money to Martereau. When Martereau put the cash in his safe, the narrator noticed how his thick fingers turned "avec précaution et fermeté la clef dans la serrure" (cautiously and firmly the key in the lock). Soon he comes to speak of "ce contentement sournois . . . de ses gros doigts replets" (the sneaking contentment . . . of his fat, satiated fingers). From a conscientious subordinate in whom he has full confidence, Martereau has become a man not to be trusted, and the narrator rushes to reveal his "discovery" to his uncle. He finishes by persuading the latter of Martereau's "crime." Everyone, including the reader, seems to forget that the real criminal may be the narrator's focalizing consciousness.

This is the same man who, from the window of his sickroom in the hospital, in a state of torpor induced by fever, "sees" Martereau leaning lovingly toward the aunt. Dream and reality are so closely fused in this scene that it is difficult for one to dissociate them. The pages immediately following mention without qualification the couple's adultery, but the reader, manipulated by the narrator's dictatorial subjectivity, must beware. The reader must also spot scenes that are depicted in detail, even though the narrator was not present when the reported action occurred. For example, he never saw the uncle talk with M. and Mme Martereau in their home. But, aware that the visit did take place, he imagines it. He indulges in reconstitutive and visionary practices so well that he produces four versions of an episode that he never witnessed. One will not know the truth concerning the encounter between the uncle and the Martereaus. Each successive version differs significantly from the preceding. From variant to variant, Martereau disintegrates a little further. He becomes, in the course of the narrator's imaginings, a mass of doubts and bitterness, a sufferer incapable of controlling his emotions. The narrator uses his mental creations to modify again and again his original estimate of Martereau. One asks in vain what is the hero's "real" nature. Sarraute leaves the reader to his incertitude; the traditional literary character, complex but knowable, explainable, is dead. Like Sarraute's previous work, *Martereau* was not well received. According to one reviewer, *Martereau* was peopled by puppets without life and who offered readers nothing.

Some of Sarraute's critical writings elucidate the theories that she put into practice in her literary works. In 1947 Sarraute published an essay, "De Dostoïevski à Kafka," in *Temps Modernes*. In 1950 a second piece appeared in the same review, "L'Ere du soupçon" ("The Age of Suspicion"). In 1956, collected with two additional articles under the title *L'Ere du soupçon*, they were received with interest in the Parisian literary world. Alain Robbe-Grillet, who published his first two novels in 1953 and 1955, recognized ideas that he was willing to endorse. When 1957 saw the appearance of Robbe-Grillet's *La Jalousie* (*Jealousy*) and the revised and enlarged edition of Sarraute's *Tropismes*, one critic from *Monde* associated them, speaking of "new novels." The term has endured.

The first essay, "De Dostoïevski à Kafka," affirms that classical psychological analysis cannot plumb the depths of the human condition. Even Proust failed, says Sarraute; he only scratched the surface of the inner chaos of human beings. Sarraute also pays tribute to Camus, Dostoyevski, and Kafka. Camus's Meursault in *L'Etranger* (*The Stranger*, 1942) does not find inside himself tears for his mother, enthusiasm for his work, love for Marie, or remorse for his crime; thus he escapes from the clichés of traditional psychology. As for Dostoyevski, it was while reading him that Sarraute had the idea for tropisms. Analyzing

Vechnyi muzh (*The Eternal Husband*, 1870), she explains that all inner strife is derived from the desire for contact with the Other. What people rigidify by using words such as *humility* or *aggressivity* is simply the energy expended to pierce the Other's mask, to disarm, control, and possess him. Dostoyevski's characters are but the bases for warring states of consciousness. Kafka's characters paradoxically resemble them by denying all emotion, sentiment, and inner movement; facing these unknowable forces at work inside man, one attitude is possible: fear and confusion.

Thus in "De Dostoïevski à Kafka" the author situates herself with references to literary tradition and examines the problems facing the contemporary novelist eager to renew psychological analysis. The essay "L'Ere du soupçon" is concerned with the reader: a reader torn between the need to find the kind of characters to which Balzac and Flaubert have accustomed him and the feeling that such characters belong to the past. Everyone knows that events no longer happen "once upon a time." The reader no longer really believes what is recounted; if he wants to believe, he consults authentic documents. The novel is a work of the imagination that proclaims its fictional nature, a subjective work in which the author presents his personal vision of the world and records his reactions (tenuous though they may be); the reader—the Other—finds it difficult to follow him.

The third article in the 1956 collection, "Conversation et sousconversation," is more technical; it concerns the texture of narrative fiction and, in particular, how to write dialogue. It is necessary, says the author, to render spoken text in a new form that will suppress any difference between dialogue and description, for it is essential not to shatter the subtlety of waves of consciousness. In pages full of wit and good humor, she condemns quotation marks, dashes, indentation, and so forth. Phrases such as "Jeanne said" and "Paul answered" are banished from the City of Books. They are as bothersome for the modern novelist as the laws of perspective were for the Cubists; and as for scenic indications and authorial commentary, which help one to interpret spoken dialogue, Sarraute advises the writer to give his reader sufficient information to put him on the right path but not to inhibit the leaps of his imagination.

To grant the reader a crucial role is to grant this role to the critic as well, and the destiny of a work of art, passed on to others, is a sub-

Jérôme Lindon of Editions de Minuit (standing in front of the doorway) and "New Novelists," 1959: (left to right) Alain Robbe-Grillet, Claude Simon, Claude Mauriac, Robert Pinget, Samuel Beckett, Nathalie Sarraute, and Claude Ollier (photos Editions de Minuit)

ject that Sarraute has often treated, and especially in the fourth essay of the collection, "Ce que voient les oiseaux" (What Birds See). How is it, she asks, that, from time to time, critics praise a work containing no literary value at all, and the public follows suit? This happens, she suggests, because there are writers who have the skill to offer the public characters and situations that correspond perfectly to current but passing tastes. The reader recognizes a familiar world and feels at ease. This pleasure does not last, however, she adds, for only a good novel warrants being reread. And a good novel should be troublesome. In order to educate her public, Sarraute wrote these theoretical essays, but her criticism reads like fiction. *L'Ere du soupçon* is sprinkled with humor, dialogue, and metaphors, and the frontier between narrative and the essay is blurred. Sarraute's next novel, *Le Planétarium* (1959; translated as *The Planetarium*, 1960), continues to speak of the art of writing, for it presents Germaine Lemaire, a fashionable woman novelist who, alone in her study, asks herself anxiously whether her work is worthy of being reread.

In contrast to the previous novels, *Le Planétarium* was acclaimed as a model of the new-fiction genre. Sarraute was no longer isolated. A photograph taken that year shows her in the company of Claude Mauriac, Claude Simon, Alain Robbe-Grillet, Samuel Beckett, Claude Ollier, and Robert Pinget. They were by then known as the Nouveaux Romanciers (New Novelists), and their books received a great deal of attention. *L'Ere du soupçon* was treated as a manifesto proclaiming the aesthetic goals of the New Novelists who, in spite of themselves, were seen as forming a literary school. Michel Butor–absent from the photograph but clearly one of them–had received the 1957 Prix Théophraste Renaudot for *La Modification*. It is true that the conservative Sorbonne had not yet added Robbe-Grillet's *La Jalousie* to its program, but foreign universities were paying attention to the New Novelists and *Le Planétarium* soon became a topic of discussion for American students of literature.

Thirty years later *Le Planétarium* remains Sarraute's most popular novel, in part, perhaps, because it appears to be more accessible. The characters all have names in this work which affords the attraction of a double plot. On the one hand, a young couple, Alain and Gisèle Guimier, are furnishing their apartment. Because it is too small, they dream of obtaining, by coaxing or by threats, the larger one belonging to their old Aunt Berthe, a widow who lives alone. On the other hand, Alain, who is at work on a doctoral thesis in art history, dreams of becoming a writer. He has been admitted to the circle of faithful admirers of Germaine Lemaire. The novel shows the young man's involvement with his family and with his intellectual friends. Beyond these narrative strands, however, the world of tropisms proliferates, more complex than ever. The family circle is particularly suited to the growth of these movements. Ever since *Tropismes*, Sarraute has written of parents obsessed with making their son or daughter a self-copy, an alter ego whose existence will preserve them from solitude. Most often Sarraute turns to the imagery of farming to concretize the relationship between adults and adolescents. Alain's father sees in his own son a soft, virgin soil that his sister, Aunt Berthe, has taken over and is cultivating as she wishes. He tries to harden the earth and to improve it by sundried "fertilizers": educational games and moral aphorisms. To defend his "works" he constructs "dikes," but his influence is not strong enough to counterbalance that of Berthe: his dikes break under the weight of her feminine "spoiling."

As usual, the tropisms are seen at work in the most banal events. At a family dinner, with father, mother, daughter, and son-in-law at the table, the son-in-law refuses the carrot salad his mother-in-law has prepared especially for him, and, at the level of the subconversation, a drama unfolds. He refuses the salad in order not to become "my son-in-law who loves carrots"–in order not be possessed. *Le Planétarium* above all chronicles an unending race in which the characters seek to capture one another. To possess the Other, his beliefs, his secrets, his suffering, his respect, his affection–this is the primary objective of each character who must fill his own void.

Images of possession are shaded with eroticism. It has been said that Sarraute's work ignores amorous or sexual passion. On the contrary, that aspect of life invades all her novels, and in *Le Planétarium* it is seen at work in the relationship of Alain's father to his daughter-in-law Gisèle. When Alain's father gazes into Gisèle's eyes his gaze caresses the "source même de la vie" (very source of life). Beneath his penetrating look, the young woman trembles, "vit plus fort" (lives more strongly), and her father-in-law is delighted to feel that she is "his thing," "his creation." These two understand each other admirably; their subconversation is rich and exempt from misunderstanding. Their discussion becomes a rendezvous in which erotic imagery reveals the extreme degree of communication that they share. Eroticism in Sarraute's work expresses the violence of the desire for total union with the Other.

The characters in *Le Planétarium* are all "écorchés vifs" (skinned alive). "Nous sommes tous un peu pareils" (We are all somewhat the same) recurs as a refrain, and the reader is all the more convinced because in this novel the narrative perspective allows him to delve into the consciousness of characters stirred up by a myriad of tropisms. An unreliable narrator no longer stands between the reader and the world described. Now a multiselective omniscience strips all minds and hearts, so that the reader does not always realize who is speaking, thinking, or imagining. But he understands that the idols are dead, that all beings are vulnerable, mobile, and complicated. He understands that a planetarium is a figment of the mind, an illusion, a petrified and therefore false representation of a cosmos ever in flight.

An important aspect of *Le Planétarium* is its commentary on the life of the popular novelist Germaine Lemaire and the life of the apprentice writer Alain Guimier. To escape the anxiety that occasionally seizes her, the first writer surrounds herself with a court of admirers who flatter her, praise her, and make her waste her time and lose her lucidity. The apprentice, in contrast, has real talent. Unlike most others, he is capable of distinguishing the subtle, complex, profound reality of life, but his intuitions dissolve in chatter and his visions are destroyed by haste and idleness. He spends too much time in literary salons. Will he ever finish his thesis? Will he ever write the story he dreams of creating? Sarraute does not say. But at the end of the novel the young man's desk has been turned around to face the wall and one should perhaps understand that Alain has decided to turn his back on the world and to face the blank page, alone, in anguish. The problems of artistic creation raised in *Le Planétarium* are the principal themes of Sarraute's next two novels: *Les Fruits d'or* (1963; translated as *The Golden*

Fruits, 1964) and *Entre la vie et la mort* (1968; translated as *Between Life and Death*, 1969).

The first of these narratives concerns the reception of a work of art; the second looks at its creator, his hopes and struggles. The first one, *Les Fruits d'or*, an analysis of critics as pitiless as it is amusing, won the International Prize for Literature in 1964–a lucid tribute to a lucid book. The hero of this novel is none other than a novel entitled *Les Fruits d'or*, a title which refers to the Judgment of Paris in Greek myth. In the name of Beauty, the critics in Sarraute's novel are ready to fight over the text written by an author named Bréhier. One knows very little about Bréhier's novel, for the critical statements about it are confusing. It may be a conventional narrative; allusions are made to romantic scenes on a lake. A few pages later, however, it appears to be characterized by a provocative modernism. One does not know whether the book is good or bad. After having enjoyed hyperbolic praise, it is soon spoken of with denigrating condescension or forgotten entirely.

Like *Le Planétarium*, *Les Fruits d'or* does not simply offer the reader a narrator to guide or deceive him. The central chapter, seventy pages long, in which well-known critics and their disciples discuss Bréhier's text, is divided into eighteen sections, each of which presents a different point of view. The commentators are, however, all anonymous, and it is impossible to identify them even by the opinions expressed. It is similarly fruitless to try to connect one conversation or scene to another. A mysterious book, anonymous subjects, an ocean of spoken or unspoken thoughts, contradictory opinions–once again the reader is plunged into uncertainty. In the midst of this uncertainty one question proves to be of crucial importance: are there aesthetic criteria, absolute values, capable of withstanding the universal flux?

Professional critics apparently answer the need to fix such standards and to guide their followers in the direction of Truth and Light. They have at their command a range of aesthetic criteria. They favor assigning works of art to distinct categories. Thus, for them, Bréhier's novel will become accessible to the public once it is fitted into a slot such as classical or symbolist. When his slot has been identified, the author will find his proper place among the "great," the "secondary," or the "minor," and his work will pass into the appropriate chapters in anthologies and school texts. The work ceases to be an end in itself; it is

a means of reaching and–as so often in Sarraute–possessing the Other.

The last chapter of *Les Fruits d'or* perhaps gives hope. Far from salons and literary circles, one reader succeeds in reading Bréhier's pages and, from the encounter, capturing his own sensations. He succeeds in holding on, in spite of the external noise that considers his obstinacy and tenacity to be stupid and intellectually weak. From this solitary confrontation between reader and text is generated the literary emotion, a strange, mysterious love. Between him and the author a bond is established, fragile but vibrant. Thus, in the space of a book, the human entity at last triumphs over its limits.

With the exception of one chapter in *Le Planétarium*, in which Germaine Lemaire has doubts about the quality of her creative spark, *Entre la vie et la mort* is the first book by Sarraute in which the central consciousness recognizes itself to be a writer and analyzes itself as such. Nonetheless, the book is not about a novelist conceived as a character in a novel. Sarraute warns readers that the attempt to organize the anecdotes recounted in *Entre la vie et la mort* in order to reconstruct the life of a hero is doomed to failure. The New Novelist Butor confessed that he found the book disconcerting. One must learn to read it, he added, to decode a new grammar. In that case the text will reveal not a coherent character as such, but the stages of a writer's vocation.

Little by little, and not in chronological order, various episodes depict the Writer facing journalists and critics, the Writer as a child discovering the sense and sound of words, the Writer flattered and paid court to, the Writer working in anguish and exaltation. The artistic vocation does not make of him a being different from others, but, on the contrary, "la substance commune" (the common substance) brought to light in Martereau, as well as in Alain Guimier, seems in his case even more porous. He absorbs with greater facility the words, intonations, smiles, and grimaces of his entourage, and his memory sets them down in order to ruminate on them better. Neither the Writer nor his work can exist without the Other, who serves as the creator's raw material and is a potential reader, one for whom the work is written, one who, by the magic of his reading, will nurture or destroy the words on the page.

In the last chapter of *Entre la vie et la mort*, recognizing himself to be vulnerable and subject to influence, the Writer forbids his double, with whom he is speaking, to listen to the public's call for "un bon style" (pretty writing) and "une belle histoire" (a pretty story). But it is difficult to resist such pressure. The book opens with a scene in which the Writer, surrounded by his admirers, tries to satisfy their curiosity. He becomes a doll or puppet, playing the role of Writer.

The Others have pressed onto his face the mask of the Artist, of the genius harassed by everyday life. Even his mother contributes to the legend, helping to rob him of his life. She tells repeatedly of his passion for words as a child, declares she knew he was predestined to be an artist, and admires blindly all his books. Those who come to visit transform his simple teapot into an exotic samovar and plead for autobiographical anecdotes in order to explicate his work. His editor, discovering what he calls a platitude, a vulgarism, in the manuscript, demands modifications and corrects the text. Novelists and critics classify him in a literary tradition, label him, compare him to other authors. In short, his life, his work, his self, become public domain and are so deformed by the Other that he can no longer recognize them. Worse still, the Others steal his time and deprive him of his privacy, indispensable for artistic creation.

Nonetheless, he succeeds occasionally in shutting himself in his room, where he strives to hear in his own depths "une présence vivante" (a living presence) that asks to be born. *Entre la vie et la mort* twice shows the Writer leaning over his pages and slipping "dans l'épaisseur de la vase" (into the depths of the slime) in order to draw out "ce qui bouge, palpite" (that which moves, palpitates) and wants to be expressed. The Writer's work and his genius consist in seizing subterranean movements, desires, and tropisms from the slime before they are hardened into masks or are conceptualized to death. In this task his tools are words. They "harponnent la petite chose tremblante" (harpoon the little trembling thing) and give it life. But words can produce texts that cease to vibrate. The Writer remembers his childhood when words obsessed and enslaved him. He knows that he must prevent them from smothering the breathing image and from seducing him by a facile harmony or elegance that would shine at the expense of what has to be expressed. Often Sarraute uses ellipsis points, so that, as she observes, the sentences breathe and remain alive.

At the time of its publication, *Entre la vie et la mort* received no great attention, perhaps because Paris was occupied by the Events of 1968

(the student and worker revolts). Unlike many other French writers, Sarraute has never been a political figure. She mentioned during an interview, referring to her student years, that she was "on the Left" but never developed the point, although the 1968 political struggle seems to have found an echo in some of the imagery in her following book, *Vous les entendez?* (1972; translated as *Do You Hear Them?*, 1973).

Vous les entendez? focuses on a family. A father and his children watch one another live, spy on one another, search for one another, flee from one another, but the novel's central concerns are again aesthetic, concentrated in a piece of sculpture, presumed to be pre-Columbian, that is reverently kept in the living room. One counterpoint to the sculpted animal, carved roughly from hard, gray rock, is the family dog whom the father, to please his children, tries to like. But his caress alternates between the dog and the statue; his desperate need to possess both life and art is observed ironically (or with affectionate amusement?) by his sons and daughters, as once again the theme of the "I" doomed to loneliness or handed over to the Others is associated with the theme of art.

In all of Sarraute's novels, scenes of departure, of breaking off, interrupt characters' lives, generating moments of drama. This motif of departure determines the basic structure of *Vous les entendez?* The novel begins with a scene in which the father and his guest are busy admiring the statue and speculating on its origin; the children, just before the action of the novel begins, have politely taken their leave and gone upstairs to bed. From this point on, separated from the children by a stairway, the father starts ruminating and his phantasms are set forth in the pages that follow.

He picks up bursts of laughter emanating from the children's room and, turning to his guest, he asks: "Vous les entendez?" Throughout the novel, what the reader "hears" are, in fact, the various interpretations made by the father of the repeated laughter that troubles his aesthetic soirée. Are his sons and daughters mocking him, his friend, and their artistic discussions? Has he raised barbarians who care only for comic strips? The father has dreamed of passing on the cultural heritage of his ancestors to these adolescents. But if the peals of laughter that he hears are mockery, then they undermine the father's life, the value of the sculptured stone, and the world of the two old friends, constructed on masterpieces from the past, collapses in ruins. The cultural tradition venerated by the father is repudiated; therefore, in despair, he comes to hate his children.

Nothing is simple in Sarraute's novels, and the father vascillates between his two loves, his children and the figurine of stone. Over and over, while conversing with his friend, the father relives his sons' and daughters' departure. To withdraw into one's own room, is that not a step in the direction of freedom? When adolescents escape the dogmatic pretentiousness of a bourgeois salon, do they not also escape the mask that their teachers strive to force on them? Their laughter would then be perhaps a cry of independence and originality, and the father, once again intoxicated with love, attributes to their laughter a quality of redemption. The laughter does not destroy Art and Beauty; it redeems them. The children have pasted onto the belly of the pre-Columbian statue a paper decoration, as others, before them, drew moustaches on the *Mona Lisa*; their rebellion, far from slaying culture, breathes into it new life. The children's revolt against good taste comes to be seen by the father as a first step in the direction of creativity. The old man, nostalgic, haunted by his own artistic sterility, envies them.

The so-called good students, those who do not laugh, absorb a simulacrum of culture but allow the most precious of gifts to dry up within themselves. The father regrets bitterly having accepted the decrees issued by the high priests of the Temple of Culture, who judged him as a schoolboy not sufficiently gifted, unworthy of following the great masters. Paralyzed in his yearning, he yielded to the temptation of silence and ever since has tried to console himself by stroking with love the statue that someone else carved. The children do not permit the past to crush them, but perhaps they go to the other extreme with their excess of casualness. Will they be able, from their walls covered with comic books, to create their own sculpture? The questions remain unanswered. At the end of the novel, the room, its door closed, keeps its secrets. *Vous les entendez?* does not prophesy the end of the world of art, nor, on the other hand, its survival in contemporary culture. Sarraute simply invites her readers, through the anxious tenderness of the father, to "hear" the sounds of their time, to listen and understand them.

During the 1970s Sarraute often spoke publicly. In 1971 her comments at the Cerisy-la-Salle colloquium devoted to the New Novel showed that the author of the first *nouveau roman*, *Tropismes*, was not ready to go as far experimentally as some of the other writers. Then, as she traveled through the United States, lecturing and serving as writer in residence on several campuses, she subtly but firmly separated herself from the fashionable Parisian circle of New New Novelists. Those who had the opportunity to observe her remember the simplicity with which she presented her work and ideas, the clarity of her explanations, and her genuine interest in students. Her husband often accompanied her, and his support was essential to her in those academic and social performances. She said once, before facing a large audience: "Je ne me suis jamais habituée à parler en public" (I have never gotten used to speaking in public). Meanwhile she was writing "*disent les imbéciles*" (1976; translated as "*fools say*," 1977), a book on the tendency that all people have to ascribe to "fools" ideas that they cannot themselves understand or accept.

This novel was not well received by the critics and has still not enjoyed the attention it deserves. Reconsidering the themes broached in *Les Fruits d'or* and *Vous les entendez?*, "*disent les imbéciles*" goes beyond aesthetic problems to the roots of human tragedy. There are no plot, no characters, but from beginning to end, there is a steadily increasing cry of alarm: freedom of thought is constantly in danger. It is endangered by the very nature of being and is perhaps only an illusion held by naive idealists.

There are several modulations of this cry of alarm in this admittedly difficult book. In one instance, a child or adolescent realizes that the family opinion concerning his grandmother–"she is sweet, isn't she?"–is meaningless. He even perceives, behind the wrinkled smile, the features of a gray-haired shrew, but the family, who has characterized and labeled her, does not allow him to undertake a quest for the "real" grandmother.

Furthermore, the bold, anxiety-ridden "I" who dreams of removing the mask forged by the words "she is sweet" is also caught up in the judgment pronounced by the others–he has an ugly chin and is "doué, certes, mais pas intelligent" (gifted, but not really bright). How is one to escape the image of oneself that one's entourage offers or shake off the weight of epithets that categorize human beings so implacably? The emptiness, the endless space that people sense in themselves is not perceived by the Other, who denies it with a word or phrase. Terms such as *good-for-nothing*, *fool, miser* smother subtly and allow the limitless, the uncertain, and the vague to be defined. *"disent les imbéciles"* alludes to well-known descriptions from Gide, Maupassant, and Dostoyevski who attempted to explain emotions, sentiments, or, for that matter, the essence of a character, using one action or gesture as a point of departure. Sarraute's text makes clear that no gesture or action can contain the total being who performs it. "I know you," "He knows me," "I know myself," "Know thyself" are centuries-old lies. Human beings do not have the capacity to know one another or to know themselves.

The same principle holds true when one is dealing with ideas. An "I"—no more identifiable than the others in the novel—strives to examine an idea—it is not said which one—that a "great thinker" has rejected, categorizing it as a "fool's idea." This narrator, an honest "I," refuses the notions of "great thinker" and "fool" and desires to seize the idea in its pristine nudity. The attempt is doomed to failure because an idea is never naked, as the central chapter of *"disent les imbéciles"* shows.

Two men sit face to face, a master and disciple who dream of communion in the world of ideas. At the very moment when their understanding appears to have attained perfection, the master makes an involuntary movement, a casual gesture which his interlocutor interprets as a sign of dismissal. The disciple is certain that his host glanced at his watch. Sensing that his gesture has been interpreted negatively, the master does all he can to dissipate the misunderstanding. He is even willing to make the ultimate concession: he reveals to his offended guest his newest idea, presented for the first time. But the idea reaches the disciple clothed in the pain he feels for having been dismissed. In a spirit of vengeance, he denigrates the new idea and refutes it pitilessly. The master, offended in turn, is reduced to calling his adversary a fool. The involuntary gesture, misinterpreted, has destroyed the idea. The book ends with a powerful and sobering chapter in which an "I" dares to criticize the ideas of a fashionable "great thinker" but is soon reduced to silence by his own dread of being included among "fools." Intellectual fascism is never far away—this is the moral of the disconcerting *"disent les imbéciles."*

Sarraute's 1980 book *L'Usage de la parole* (translated as *The Use of Speech*, 1983) is a series of sketches, each approximately fifteen pages long. Neither "great thinkers" nor "fools" speak

in this work, only anonymous passers-by–two friends drinking coffee or chatting in the park, speaking in the linguistic clichés and formulae of daily life to which, supposedly, no one pays attention. These expressions, however, provoke in the interlocutor violent reactions that he is not always able to hide, and the speaker who emits them does not do so innocently. The most harmless speech is sometimes a deadly weapon.

A quintessence of Sarraute, this book offers a totally new narrative form. A narrator descended directly from Diderot–according to Sarraute herself–addresses the reader, provokes, disturbs, or calms him. "Vous allez voir, prenez patience" (You will see; be patient). This aggressively intrusive "I" foresees the reader's reactions, verbalizes them, examines them, pretends to be surprised, and requests the reader to revise his opinion. Occasionally he pretends to yield to arguments and goes so far as to suggest that only a "hypersensitive," a neurotic person, could invent "such stories" from words as insignificant as "A très bientôt" (See you very soon) and "Ne me parlez pas de ça" (Don't talk to me about that)–forcing a smile from the recalcitrant reader.

The majority of the sketches are patterned on the same model. The narrator presents the expression to be studied: "Je ne comprends pas" (I don't understand), for example, and "perceiving" a skeptical reaction–the chosen words are too simple–he states that readers will be convinced as soon as he invents for the expressions a revealing and enlightening context. He then involves himself in a pedagogical demonstration, using two characters and their dialogue, a dialogue which he interrupts frequently in order to comment on it meticulously. His role is to render the unspoken visible, to convey the subconversation. If he fails–he "sees" the reader's head shaking "no!"– he begins again, imagining a second theatrical situation embodying the same suspect words.

Repetitive in structure, the sketches vary in their conclusions concerning the power of words. Some of them expose the vast implications hidden behind a simple "So what?" Others deplore the stifling rigidity of terms used too often. One of the best sketches, "Le Mot Amour" (The Word Love), underscores the influence of centuries of literature, social conventions, and habits of daily life on a sentiment that each lover, nevertheless, hopes to relive in a pristine state. As soon as it is born, Love is embellished with a capital *L* and encrusted with clichés and myths.

The "I" in *L'Usage de la parole*, already unmasked, invents the text before the reader's eyes. It required only one further step for the "I" to confess to being Nathalie Sarraute, a step taken in *Enfance*, whose narrator is the novelist herself in search of the little girl she was between the ages of five and eleven. The young heroine is grave, authentic, and sensitive to the extreme. She overflows with imagination; already a decoder of subconversations, the child surmises in the adults around her frightening depths that she strives not to stir up.

Tropismes and *Portrait d'un Inconnu* had opened up new paths for the novel. *Enfance* renews the autobiographical genre. It begins unexpectedly with a dialogue: the author converses with her double, who, skeptically and ironically, asks her if she truly intends to "évoquer ses souvenirs" (evoke her memories) as has been done by others so many times. Yes, answers Sarraute, precisely because to recall one's childhood without falling into sentimental clichés and stereotypical images is an impossible task, a challenge worthy of the effort. The double, the narrator's critical conscience, is ever present. Her observations interrupt the story, add nuance, and make corrections. They also illuminate the problems Sarraute encountered while writing the autobiography. Recounting memories means projecting onto the child that one was the knowledge, experience, and understanding of the adult that one has become. "Tu le sentais vraiment déjà à cet âge?" (Did you really sense this at that moment?) whispers the double, casting doubt on the child's capacity for lucidity. At other times, this demanding, intransigent voice accuses the writer of hiding the truth and of endowing the heroine with innocence that she had already lost.

Enfance, predictably, does not present a continuous story adhering to a rigorous chronology. Sometimes very brief episodes follow one another, with no effort to fill gaps or make connections. The narrative shifts, for example, from the snows of Saint Petersburg to a *pension de famille* in Meudon. "Historical" speech does not interrupt the flow of memories that (one should not be surprised) grasps most often at words, at names that memory has refused to forget. Indelible phrases resound. With "Nein, das tust du nicht" (No, you will not do it) and "Tiebia podbrossili" (They abandoned you), the little girl's life takes shape, and with it the life of a writer who, doing what they told her not to do, learned to defy literary conventions and whose "abandoned" characters wander in search of the Other who can only reject or destroy them.

Enfance is a beautiful book and one that has been widely read. However, the author has stated that it will not have a sequel. She is now working on her eleventh novel, but has "abandoned" the little girl Natasha. Not entirely, however, since in 1984 Sarraute assisted director Simone Benmussa in mounting a stage version of *Enfance* at the Théâtre du Rond-Point Renaud-Barrault. It was the first time that one of Sarraute's narratives had been adapted for the stage, but not the first time that the novelist had written drama.

Beginning with *Les Fruits d'or*, Sarraute followed the publication of each of her novels with a play. "Mon théâtre," she has noted, "continue mes romans" (My theater continues my novels), and in each play she reexamines a point raised in the preceding narrative in order to exhaust its dramatic potentialities. Thus *C'est beau* (produced in 1975, published in 1978, and translated in 1980 as *It's Beautiful*) takes up ideas set forth in *Vous les entendez?*, specifically the opposition between tradition and innovation embodied in the conflict between parents and children. Sarraute has worked with some of the most influential directors of the modern French theater—Jean-Louis Barrault, Claude Régy, and Simone Benmussa—and each in his own way has underscored the importance of tropisms in her work. One of them characterized Sarraute's theater as "scandalous," and indeed it is, because subconversation has to be expressed on stage, thus causing the characters to say what is usually left unspoken. As Sarraute has commented: "Dans mes pièces, le dialogue a quitté la surface, est descendu et s'est développé au niveau des mouvements intérieurs qui sont la substance de mes romans" (In my plays, dialogue has left the surface, has descended to the level of inner movements that are the substance of my novels).

From *Tropismes* to *Enfance*, Sarraute's work questions the world as it questions itself, thrusting back tradition, dogmas, certainties, all that which, by veiling the anguish of the human condition, would betray life and consequently the work of art. When Raymond Sarraute died in 1984 after a long illness, Sarraute found that it was difficult to go on writing without him, her first reader. But she has continued. It is useless to ask her the subject or the title of her work in progress; it is her secret until the novel appears. One can only wait, with fervor, affection, and respect.

Interviews:

Pierre Schneider, "The Novelist as Transmuter: Nathalie Sarraute Talks about her Art," *New York Times Book Review*, 9 February 1964, pp. 5, 36-37;

Bettina L. Knapp, "Interview avec Nathalie Sarraute," *Kentucky Romance Quarterly*, 14, no. 3 (1967): 283-295;

Germaine Brée, "Nathalie Sarraute," *Contemporary Literature*, 14 (Spring 1973): 137-146;

Gretchen Rous Besser, "Colloque avec Nathalie Sarraute: 22 avril 1976," *French Review*, 50 (December 1976): 284-289;

Jean-Louis de Rambures, "Nathalie Sarraute: Une Table dans un coin de bistro," in his *Comment travaillent les écrivains* (Paris: Flammarion, 1978), pp. 149-154;

Lucette Finas, "Comment j'ai écrit certains de mes livres: Entretien avec Lucette Finas," *Etudes Littéraires*, 12 (December 1979): 393-401;

Alison Finch and David Kelley, "Propos sur la technique du roman," *French Studies*, 39 (July 1985): 305-315;

Simone Benmussa, *Nathalie Sarraute: Qui êtes-vous?* (Lyons: La Manufacture, 1987).

Bibliography:

Sheila M. Bell, *Nathalie Sarraute: A Bibliography* (London: Grant & Cutler, 1982).

References:

André Allemand, *L'Œuvre romanesque de Nathalie Sarraute* (Neuchâtel: Editions à la Baconnière, 1980);

Arc, special issue on Sarraute, 95 (1984);

Gretchen Rous Besser, *Nathalie Sarraute* (Boston: Twayne, 1979);

H. A. Bouraoui, "Sarraute's Narrative Portraiture: The Artist in Search of a Voice," *Critique*, 14, no. 1 (1972): 77-89;

Celia Britton, "The Function of the Commonplace in the Novels of Nathalie Sarraute," *Language & Style*, 12 (Spring 1979): 79-90;

Britton, "The Self and Language in the Novels of Nathalie Sarraute," *Modern Language Review*, 77 (July 1982): 577-584;

Françoise Calin, "La Culture de l'Autre, dans *Vous les entendez?* de Nathalie Sarraute," *Symposium*, 28 (Winter 1974): 293-302;

Calin, *La Vie retrouvée: Etude de l'œuvre romanesque de Nathalie Sarraute* (Paris: Minard, 1976);

Ruby Cohn, "A Diminishing Difference," *Yale French Studies*, no. 27 (Spring-Summer 1961): 99-105;

Mimica Cranaki and Yvon Belaval, *Nathalie Sarraute* (Paris: Gallimard, 1965);

Elisabeth Eliez-Rüegg, *La Conscience d'autrui et la conscience des objets dans l'œuvre de Nathalie Sarraute* (Berne: Lang, 1972);

Lucette Finas, "Nathalie Sarraute et les métamorphoses du verbe," *Tel Quel*, no. 20 (Winter 1965): 68-77;

John A. Fleming, "The Imagery of Tropism in the Novels of Nathalie Sarraute," in *Image and Theme: Studies in Modern French Fiction*, edited by W. M. Frohock (Cambridge: Harvard University Press, 1969), pp. 74-98;

Jean-Luc Jaccard, *Nathalie Sarraute* (Zurich: Juris, 1967);

Ann Jefferson, "Imagery versus Description: The Problematics of Representation in the Novels of Nathalie Sarraute," *Modern Language Review*, 73 (July 1978): 513-524;

Jefferson, *The Nouveau Roman and the Poetics of Fiction* (Cambridge, U.K.: Cambridge University Press, 1981);

Roger McClure, *Sarraute: "Le Planétarium"* (London: Grant & Cutler, 1987);

Vivian Mercier, *The New Novel from Queneau to Pinget* (New York: Farrar, Straus & Giroux, 1971);

René Micha, *Nathalie Sarraute* (Paris: Editions Universitaires, 1966);

Valerie Minogue, *Nathalie Sarraute and the War of the Words* (Edinburgh: University Press, 1981);

Minogue, "Nathalie Sarraute's *Le Planétarium*: The Narrator Narrated," *Forum for Modern Language Studies*, 9 (July 1973): 217-234;

Ann Minor, "Nathalie Sarraute: *Le Planétarium*," *Yale French Studies*, no. 24 (Summer 1959): 96-100;

A. S. Newman, *Une Poésie des discours: Essai sur les romans de Nathalie Sarraute* (Geneva: Droz, 1976);

Bernard Pingaud, "Le Personnage dans l'œuvre de Nathalie Sarraute," *Preuves*, 13 (December 1963): 19-34;

Sabine Raffy, *Sarraute Romancière. Espaces intimes* (New York: Lang, 1988);

Georges Raillard, "Nathalie Sarraute et la violence du texte," *Littérature*, no. 2 (May 1971): 89-102;

Jean Ricardou and Françoise van Rossum-Guyon, eds., *Nouveau Roman: Hier, aujourd'hui*, 2 volumes (Paris: Union Générale d'Editions, 1972);

Léon S. Roudiez, "A Glance at the Vocabulary of Nathalie Sarraute," *Yale French Studies*, no. 27 (Spring/Summer 1961): 90-98;

Ruth Z. Temple, *Nathalie Sarraute* (New York: Columbia University Press, 1968);

Micheline Tison-Braun, *Nathalie Sarraute ou la recherche de l'authenticité* (Paris: Gallimard, 1971);

Helen Watson-Williams, "Etude du *Planétarium*," *Essays in French Literature*, no. 1 (November 1964): 89-104;

Watson-Williams, "Nathalie Sarraute's Golden Ap-

ples," *Essays in French Literature*, no. 3 (November 1966): 78-93;

Watson-Williams, *The Novels of Nathalie Sarraute: Towards an Aesthetic* (Amsterdam: Rodopi, 1981);

Charles G. Whiting, "Nathalie Sarraute: *Moraliste*," *French Review*, 43, no. 1 (Winter 1970): 168-174;

Christine B. Wunderli-Müller, *Le Thème du masque et les banalités dans l'œuvre de Nathalie Sarraute* (Zurich: Juris, 1970);

Gerda Zeltner, "Nathalie Sarraute et l'impossible réalisme," *Mercure de France*, 345 (August 1962): 593-608.

Albertine Sarrazin
(17 September 1937-10 July 1967)

Elissa Gelfand
Mount Holyoke College

BOOKS: *La Cavale* (Paris: Jean-Jacques Pauvert, 1965); translated by Charles Lam Markmann as *The Runaway* (New York: Grove, 1967);

L'Astragale (Paris: Jean-Jacques Pauvert, 1965); translated by Patsy Southgate as *Astragal* (New York: Grove, 1967; London: Spearman, 1968);

La Traversière (Paris: Jean-Jacques Pauvert, 1966);

Romans, lettres et poèmes (Paris: Jean-Jacques Pauvert, 1967);

Poèmes (Paris: Jean-Jacques Pauvert, 1969);

Journal de prison 1959 (Paris: Editions Sarrazin, 1972);

Le Laveur. Bibiche. L'Affaire St. Jus. La Crèche (Paris: Editions Sarrazin, 1973); republished as *Bibiche: Récits* (Montreal: Editions de La Presse, 1974); enlarged as *La Crèche; Le Laveur; Bibiche; Affaire Saint-Jus; Voyage à Tunis* (Paris: Livre de Poche, 1975);

Le Passe-peine, 1949-1967, edited by Josane Duranteau (Paris: Julliard, 1976);

Œuvres (Paris: Jean-Jacques Pauvert, 1985).

Albertine Sarrazin was the first female novel-

ist in France for whom prison was the source and substance of successful imaginative production. Her literary output of the 1960s, comparatively small because of her tragically short life, represents a radical departure from the earlier writings of women imprisoned in France: her novels' transformation of prison experience into coherent and self-sustaining fictional accounts breaks with the female tradition of confessional, apparently unshaped texts; and her resolutely affirmative assertion of authorship contrasts sharply with the apologetic stance of her imprisoned forerunners. Through her fiction, Sarrazin energetically criticizes the social conventions by which she was labeled deviant and punished. In this sense, her works reflect the more general trend in women's writing of the time toward angry or ironic rejection of gender, class, and ethnic categories. Yet, in content, Sarrazin's writing is highly conservative, because it embraces as foremost values proud individualism, romantic love, and, paradoxically, societal legitimation.

The views of Sarrazin as either rebellious or conservative emerged at the two moments she re-

Albertine Sarrazin (photograph copyright © Jerry Bauer)

ceived heightened critical attention, first in 1965, when her novels *La Cavale* (translated as *The Runaway,* 1967) and *L'Astragale* (translated as *Astragal,* 1967) appeared, then in the mid 1970s, when both prison riots and feminist activity in France brought renewed interest in her work. Initial reviews responded favorably to the multiple surprises of Sarrazin's life and work: her youth and scandalous past, her unrepentant self-assurance, her literary productivity. Journalists saw the scope of her writing as larger than the prison world, as illuminating, in the words of Robert Kanters (*Figaro Littéraire,* 11 November 1965), "toutes les prisons de la pensée et de la littérature" (all the prisons of thought and literature) as well as the highest regions of mystical love, to paraphrase Josane Duranteau (*Combat,* 7 October 1965), who later wrote a biography of Sarrazin. In the United States Gloria Steinem described her as "a symbolic figure for the younger generation in France, a kind of James Dean for the intelligent girl rebel" (*New York Times Book Review,* 9 June 1968).

The fact that *La Cavale* was accepted simultaneously by two publishers, Jean-Jacques Pauvert

and Gallimard (the latter took the book on Simone de Beauvoir's glowing recommendation), added further luster to Sarrazin's celebrity. *La Cavale* and *L'Astragale* were published almost simultaneously. Huge book sales and television appearances were followed by Sarrazin's being a finalist in competition for the Prix Théophraste Renaudot; *La Cavale* did, however, garner the Prix des Quatre Jurys in Tunisia in March 1966. The second wave of attention to Sarrazin, though broad, was more guarded. If Duranteau's 1971 biography remained dithyrambic and reviews of Sarrazin's posthumously published *Journal de prison 1959* (1972) praised the ongoing relevance of her work, along with the "spiritual purity" it evinced, many feminist critics questioned her apparent superiority complex and the harsh judgment of other women on which it rested.

Her coprisoners constituted, she wrote in her *Journal,* "la minusserie" (roughly, a confederation of nitwits). In her 1968 review Steinem had already lamented the fact that Sarrazin's work revealed "not the least concern for politics or for a change in the social order." Critical interest in Sarrazin has waned since the 1970s. But her novels, all of which are in Livre de Poche editions, are still widely read (it was estimated in 1969 that over a million people in seventeen countries had already read her prose works). Sarrazin is appreciated both by those who seek the special insight into the criminal underworld her works offer and by those who consider these imaginative renderings of prison, for all their shortcomings, unsurpassed in their subversive power and wit.

Albertine Sarrazin, first called Albertine Damien, was born in Algiers, illegitimately, to a fifteen-year-old Spanish woman who left her at the Assistance Publique. The mother she never knew haunted Sarrazin all her life: direct invocations to this adored but absent figure appear in her journals and in *La Cavale*; and more indirect insistence on her felt incompleteness, her sense of detachment from normal coordinates of human identity, marks all of Sarrazin's works. The recurrent themes of solitude, deracination, and the journey to acceptance, as well as the cyclical structure of all her novels, bespeak her quest for unity.

A French couple adopted Albertine Damien when she was eighteen months old, renamed her Anne-Marie R. . . , and brought her back to Aix-en-Provence after World War II. The adoption proved disastrous (it was revoked in 1956), particularly when the parents decided in 1952 to send

the brilliant but rebellious girl to the Bon Pasteur disciplinary school in Marseilles. Little specific material from her childhood appeared in Sarrazin's fiction until her last novel, *La Traversière* (The Crossing, 1966), bitterly exposed the tyrannical father and humiliated mother who had raised her. But for Sarrazin, her mother and father's bad marriage and failed parenting became the measure against which her own love for Julien Sarrazin, whom she married in 1959, and her successful "mothering" of books stood out.

Another incident which permanently marked Sarrazin occurred when she was ten: Sarrazin was raped by an uncle. This event, along with informing the prevalent themes of solitude and the healing quality of love, also connects to the presence of the body in Sarrazin's works, a body in which she never quite feels at ease. In 1953, as she was taking her *baccalauréat* exam in philosophy, Sarrazin escaped from the reform school to Paris, where she supported herself for five months with false identification papers and work as a prostitute; this Rimbaldian existence is recorded in her earliest journal. A prearranged reunion with a friend and lover from Bon Pasteur, Emilienne–who appears in all of Sarrazin's books as a tall, dignified coprisoner–ended in their botched armed robbery of a dress shop. Both were arrested in December 1953, and Sarrazin spent one-half of her harsh seven-year sentence in Fresnes, Doullens, and Amiens prisons, successively. Her passionate, impressionistic *Journal de Fresnes* of 1953, first published in Duranteau's biography and later collected in Sarrazin's *Le Passe-peine, 1949-1967* (Doing Time, 1949-1967; 1976), recounts her rage during this period.

Sarrazin's escape in 1957, when she was protected for eighteen months by her future husband, Julien Sarrazin, forms the narrative of her second novel, *L'Astragale*. Her relationship with Sarrazin also signaled her leaving Emilienne and her choosing heterosexual over homosexual love. Between the time she was rearrested in September 1958 until her last imprisonment ended in August 1964, Sarrazin spent a total of four and one-half years behind bars. She produced her most important writing during that period, all of which deals with her changing definition of freedom: her *Journal de prison 1959*; her grand fresco of prison life, *La Cavale*, written clandestinely during 1961-1962; and *L'Astragale*, written from April to August 1964. She also wrote several short stories based on prison anecdotes ("Le

Laveur" [The Washer], "Bibiche" [Bibiche, the title character's nickname, means "little darling"], "L'Affaire Saint-Jus" [The Story of the Blessed Brew], and "La Crèche" [The Crèche] were collected in a single volume in 1973); various poems (*Poèmes*, 1969); and a large body of correspondence (published in *Romans, lettres et poèmes* [Novels, Letters and Poems] in 1967) and illicit prison notes, or "kites" (*Biftons de prison*, 1977).

The final period of Sarrazin's life, three years of uninterrupted liberty in the south of France, produced her last novel, *La Traversière*, an account of the events surrounding the publication of *La Cavale*, and a travel diary, *Voyage à Tunis*, included in an enlarged edition of the prison stories published in 1975. In 1967, after a series of operations, she died of cardiac arrest during a kidney ablation. The circumstances of her death led Julien Sarrazin, in 1970, to bring a much-publicized and ultimately successful lawsuit against the prestigious Saint-Roch Clinic in Montpellier.

Sarrazin's fiction is inseparable from her biography. All her novels are told in the first person by the same protagonist, Anick or Anne, and Sarrazin's much-quoted phrase, "Anick, c'est moi" (Anick is myself), is more than an echo of Flaubert. It states the sole aesthetic principle to which Sarrazin subscribed, that of writing the "living truth" or, as she wrote in her *Journal de prison*, "transformer l'aspect douloureux en aspect VRAI" (transforming what is painful into what is TRUE). In this way, her conventional realistic fiction diverges from the formal experimentations characteristic of mainstream French writing of the time. It also bears little resemblance to the criminal imagination of her imprisoned colleague, Jean Genet, though some critics saw her as his female counterpart. Unlike Genet, Sarrazin neither glorifies the prison nor identifies with her sister-prisoners. If prison is the starting point for all her novels, she distances herself increasingly from it. Her focus is always herself. Her search for psychic and emotional wholeness is her constant center of interest, and writing, says Duranteau in her preface to Sarrazin's *Journal de prison*, provided the necessary "fil renoué de cette continuité de soi" (connecting thread for that continuity of self). But it is Sarrazin's unusual use of a double perspective–that of both the observed prisoner and the evaluating author–which gives her novels their complex authenticity and their stinging humor. The writer, who for Sarrazin is alive and active, watches the criminal function in the static universe of the prison, and this technique makes for an unmistakably personal voice in her fiction.

La Cavale, Sarrazin's most accomplished work, recounts five months of her life during 1961, when she was in Versailles, Compiègne, and Amiens prisons. Written over two years, it was sent secretly, in pieces, to Sarrazin's lawyer. Each chapter of this long and vivid documentary, as Sarrazin described it, evokes a scene from the daily drudgery; all that changes amid "cette matière immobile et vraie" (this matter, immovably real) are the number of cell companions and the prison's internal regimen. The novel's chronology, beginning with Anick's arrival at prison, follows prison time, which is punctuated by transfers, mail deliveries, meals, consultations with lawyers, and mindless work tasks. The characters are mediocre and interchangeable, except for three women with whom Anick feels affinities and who are drawn with sympathy and relief. In terms of the flat plane of prison life, in which Anick perfunctorily performs physical routines, nothing happens–with the exception of her failed escape attempts and her marriage to Zizi (Julien). At the novel's end, she is where she was at the outset. In contrast, all the important events occur in the intense, private domain of Anick's mind, the seat of her imaginative and affective life. The action that takes place on this mental and psychological level is her writing a book–the book that will become *La Cavale*. The immediacy of this literary device, in which the novel recounts its own invention, gives a freshness to Sarrazin's writing.

Anick's intellectual movement toward the novel's completion, along with her barren intervals of silence, constitutes the book's true structure and its dramatic tension. Superimposed on this conflict between will and inaction is a somewhat contrived religious calendar in which the completed book is "born" at Christmas and the still-imprisoned author contemplates her New Year's "gifts," the fruits of her future creativity. Though the book demystifies prison, forcing the reader to consider its overall social organization, the message of *La Cavale* is finally a personal one in which Sarrazin asserts her identity as writer, not prisoner. The title, which in slang means escape but also suggests a mythic horse, evokes the trade-off between real and imaginative freedom that structures the narrative, and it refers as well to the theme of power and powerlessness underlying Anick's identification with a fantastic beast.

The predominance accorded mental over physical prowess also highlights the importance of language in the novel, more specifically Sarrazin's belief in the superiority of her written words over the borrowed bad French and slang she speaks with other inmates. Her credo, "Le Bic, en taule, c'est mon flingue" (In the joint, my pen is my piece), combines the vulgar medium of argot with the high message of art. In his preface to Sarrazin's *Romans, lettres et poèmes*, Hervé Bazin claims that this alliance of written and spoken languages makes Sarrazin "la fille de Céline" (Louis-Ferdinand Céline's daughter). The language Sarrazin uses reflects directly the sincerity and quality of her relations with others: she reserves her loveliest passages for Julien and the women she befriends, while addressing her coprisoners, whom she deems inferior, with comic derision. This individualistic disdain, though disturbing, underlies the novel's pointed social critique. It faults criminological views, which are both normative and generalizing, for creating remedies that deaden an active human spirit.

La Cavale is Sarrazin's second-largest-selling novel (over one-half million copies by 1973). Critics almost universally responded to the book in terms of her biography: Bazin, in his preface, praised her "reporter's" qualities, seeing her work as "la seule, ayant valeur littéraire, qui ait été écrite du dedans . . . par un écrivain du Milieu" (the only one of literary value that was written from within . . . by a writer of the criminal underworld), and in his *Figaro Littéraire* review, Kanters, somewhat more metaphysically, emphasized the privileged knowledge that prisoners possess: in regard to freedom, "ils savent ce qu'ils disent, [ils] pèsent le mot" (they know what they're talking about, [they] weigh that word). Publication of the novel in English translation gave rise to somewhat more literary responses in the States, though not always favorable ones. In her review Steinem criticized it as a "long, sprawling, undisciplined book," even while she praised its "particular virtue": "It works emotionally, in spite of everything." John Updike, in the *New Yorker* (15 March 1969), characterized it as "haphazard," "the objectified diary of a precocious girl," but he also commended the "cleaner" writing, the "more complex" imagery, and the "more active" plot of the last hundred pages. Unfortunately, almost no in-depth literary studies of *La Cavale* have appeared.

The action of Sarrazin's second novel, *L'Astragale*, chronologically precedes that of *La*

Cavale. Like the previous novel, *L'Astragale* gives primacy to events in the protagonist's inner life, but here external realities are even less important than before. Because the story is set during a privileged time of freedom, Sarrazin's sixteen months of escape in 1957-1958, prison recedes, serving only as a spatial frame for Anne's circular journey toward rearrest. The heart of *L'Astragale* is a love story in which Anne and her rescuer, Julien, move toward shared recognition of their passion. Approaching Julien means breaking with her past ("un autre siècle commence"–another century is beginning), and also with Rolande (Emilienne), the lover with whom she was to reunite. Because the novel opens at the moment Anne has jumped the prison wall, breaking her astragalus, or anklebone, *L'Astragale* is also the story of her journey toward physical, as well as emotional wholeness. The narrator's body, which was virtually absent from the concentration in *La Cavale* on imaginative production, is now central to her maturation. *Astragale* is also an architectural reference to a building support, and its fracture suggests that Anne's journey toward unity will not be easy. Indeed, during this period of grace, freedom ironically proves more constricting than prison: "Ma liberté neuve m'emprisonne et me paralyse" (My new freedom imprisons and paralyzes me). Not only is Anne completely dependent on Julien, her various protectors limit her autonomy as well, and they are caricatured with the same derisive humor used for supernumeraries in *La Cavale*; the lyrical discourse reserved for Julien once again creates the mix of linguistic levels that is characteristic of Sarrazin's fiction. Also, as in *La Cavale*, the novel's apparently circular structure, in which Anne returns to prison, is subtended by another pattern of trade-off, in this case between Anne's quest for independence and her movement toward encompassing love.

L'Astragale is the most self-consciously literary of Sarrazin's novels, and, not surprisingly, it has stimulated the most thoughtful critical responses. It resembles but also distorts several novelistic subgenres. Sarrazin herself, in *La Traversière*, called *L'Astragale* a "petit roman d'amour" (little love novel), and Bazin deemed its portrayal of desire a "miracle" that makes other love stories seem "du toc" (sham). But Anne's one-sided passion and Julien's resistance undermine romantic conventions. Duranteau says in her *Combat* review that the book is a "conte de fées du monde moderne" (fairy tale of the modern world), but the story's "miracles"–Anne's plunge

from the sky and her deliverance by an idealized savior; the healing of her leg; her meeting Jean, a selfless friend–are subverted by her heavily predetermined return to prison ("La taule, c'est mon droit chemin"–I'm on a straight road to the joint). Anne Cothran, in a 1979 article in *Esprit Créateur*, shows how this ostensible "thriller" in fact twists the traditional structures of time and space to become the purely personal account of Anne's "struggle to regain control of her own life." *L'Astragale*, which has been compared to a Greek tragedy, with the lovers' separation just when they are about to be completely together, is the most tightly constructed of Sarrazin's works. But for some critics, the story's totally fictitious ending (a detective arrives while Anne is being chased in a persecution nightmare), designed to close the narrative circle, is strained. Others have judged the interweaving of Sarrazin's two narrative perspectives, that of the narrator and the character who join past with present, less effective than in her first novel. Nonetheless, *L'Astragale* has been her biggest commercial success (nearly one million copies sold by 1973), and a film adaptation with the same title was released in 1967.

Sarrazin's last novel, *La Traversière*, was her most problematic, and the uncertainties of her literary career are the substance of its narrative. Prison is all but gone, save a few retrospective references. The book encompasses the period from her release in 1963 to her completion of *La Traversière* in 1966. Thus, as in *La Cavale*, the novel recounts its own creation, but with far less detail and urgency. During those three years Sarrazin first lived in Troyes and worked as a cashier, a job whose irony is well evoked by the former thief. She then settled in Alès, where she was a reporter for the *Méridional*. In *La Traversière* the concern Sarrazin demonstrates with the difference between journalism and "real" writing–the former seems a kind of "prostitution"–stems from this experience. Though she was arrested for stealing liquor and spent four months in prison during the period covered by the novel, Sarrazin skips over this episode and concentrates instead on the time during 1964-1965 when she (the protagonist, Albertine) and Julien (called Lou in the novel) live "à trois" in the Cévennes with their faithful friend, Maurice, called Jean. Unable to bear the threesome and Jean's self-abnegation, Albertine flees; faced with an ultimatum, Lou joins her and they settle in Montpellier. She awaits and finally receives word that her first novel has been accepted for publication and goes on to confront writing anew.

Because it followed the achievement of the simultaneously published *La Cavale* and *L'Astragale*, *La Traversière* became for her that notoriously difficult enterprise, a second book. Sarrazin felt the pressure of writing to be a new form of prison. Furthermore, it was her first experience of writing while free which, as the novel relates, meant the nurturing constraints of confinement were absent. Because she felt removed from the prisoner who had narrated the earlier novels, Sarrazin wanted to experiment with new forms. She used the third-person voice in her first draft of *La Traversière*, a draft which was rejected by her publishers as "unnatural" in style. She therefore once again turned to a first-person narrator, telling Julien in a sorrowful letter, "Je ne suis bonne qu'à me raconter" (I'm only good at telling myself). She also picked up some of her earlier themes. Freedom in *La Traversière* is totally identified with writing; "Je choisis l'auteur" (I choose being an author), Albertine says authoritatively. The book's title (a *traversier* is literally a ferryboat or something that crosses over, and, in the Cévennes region, it specifically refers to steps that traverse streams) takes on multiple meanings: it signifies the paths of her life, all linked yet crisscrossed with obstacles; and the capitalized feminine form, *La Traversière*, denotes the royal road to liberty Sarrazin has chosen, writing.

In 1966 freedom was no longer imagined or temporary, as it had been when she wrote the previous novels. It was now grounded in the very outside world Sarrazin had once rejected and barely knew. Therefore, in order to assume her liberty, she also had to be readmitted to society; her acceptance as a writer would be concomitant to societal legitimation. The theme of legitimacy frames the novel, for the opening scene recalls the revocation of Albertine's adoption by her parents—her being thrust again into bastardy—and the closing evokes the author's fears that her newly won literary and social status will not last. Similarly, her adoptive mother's withdrawal of affective and financial support, evidence of her failed maternity, casts Albertine into the role of nurturer of her own literary "progeny." Legitimacy is also provided by Lou and Albertine's love, which is tested as it was in previous novels. In *La Traversière*, however, it is Albertine who controls their couple; it is she who imposes obstacles to their harmony. One senses that, having secured Lou's/Julien's love, she takes on her greatest challenge: winning the public's affection and approval. The publisher's initial rejection of *La Traversière* explains the novel's end, in which Albertine expressed deep uncertainty about her future writing.

Of Sarrazin's three novels, *La Traversière*, never translated, has received the least critical attention. Some reviewers greeted it positively as her first project explicitly addressed to a wide audience, unlike *L'Astragale*, written for Julien, and *La Cavale*, directed at herself. But Bazin's view that Sarrazin had lost the "naturalness" of her winning style was typical: "L'outil lui est tombé des mains juste au moment où il était parfaitement affûté" (Her tool fell from her hands just at the moment when it had become perfectly honed). Indeed, the novel's closing reference to her "aging" pen, a merely verbal echo of her adoptive father's opening line, "Nous sommes trop vieux" (We're too old), seems a lame construction. The disparity between the societal approval Sarrazin had ardently sought in *La Traversière* and the critical disregard the novel has met is striking.

Sarrazin's literary output also includes her extensive correspondence, which Brigitte Duc, in the introduction to *Biftons de prison*, calls Sarrazin's "bouffée vitale d'oxygène" (vital gust of oxygen), and several diaries, all of which evince an analytic talent not present in her fiction. Her *Journal de prison* is of particular note, since many of its meditative and lyrical passages are reproduced in the novels. It contains, in their most considered form, many of the principles by which the young Sarrazin lived, in particular her views on guilt as determined by society or by criminals themselves, and on the special sense of freedom the act of stealing brought her. A fragmented analogue to Sarrazin's life, the *Journal de prison* paradoxically excludes daily events; its sole focus is her emerging sexual and intellectual identities. Unlike the novels' thematic presentation of those issues, however, the *Journal de prison* evokes them, with unmatched force, through its unorthodox style. Pulsations and violent images communicate directly her intimacy with her body and her surfacing desire. Some years before the existence of a "woman's writing" was even an issue, Sarrazin's *Journal de prison*, by inscribing her "intuition et musique" (intuition and music), revealed a powerful textual internality. It was first published by Julien Sarrazin's short-lived Editions Sarrazin. Now in Livre de Poche, it is as widely read as her novels.

It is a sign of Sarrazin's ongoing popularity that virtually every page she wrote has found its way into print. Pieces never meant for publication, including prison "kites," school workbooks, childhood letters, private notebooks, and drawings, appeared as late as nine years after her death (published in *Le Passe-peine*). For an author who modestly hoped a few "crumbs" of her writing would be saved from the "shipwreck" of time, this profusion of published materials testifies to enduring public curiosity. Sarrazin's scandalous life is no doubt her initial attraction for most readers, who see it, in Steinem's words, as "proof of the indestructibility of the human spirit." As an author, she did not have the time to mature fully or to extend her inventive scope much beyond the prison. Nonetheless, her comparatively small opus not only gives sure form to her inchoate life experience; it also reveals impressive literary sophistication and originality.

Letters:

Lettres à Julien, 1958-1960, edited by Josane Duranteau (Paris: Jean-Jacques Pauvert, 1971);

Lettres de la vie littéraire, edited by Duranteau (Paris: Jean-Jacques Pauvert, 1974);

Biftons de prison (Paris: Jean-Jacques Pauvert, 1977).

Interview:

Albertine parle: Entretiens Radio avec Jean-Pierre Elkabbach (Paris: Disques Adès, 1965).

Biography:

Josane Duranteau, *Albertine Sarrazin* (Paris: Editions Sarrazin, 1971).

References:

R. Bastide, "Annick [A.S.] . . . suivi d'un texte inédit: 'Les Traversiers de la traversière,'" *Almanach Cévenol,* special issue of *Cévennes-Magazine* (1968): 37-41, 43-48;

Claude Brahimi, "Albertine, de l'enfant à l'écrivain," *Magazine Littéraire,* no. 114 (June 1976): 35-37;

Ann Cothran, "Narrative Structure as Expression of Self in Sarrazin's *L'Astragale,*" *Esprit Créateur,* 19 (Summer 1979): 13-22;

Jean-Pierre Gaubert, "Albertine Sarrazin douze ans après," *Revue du Tarn,* no. 97 (Spring 1980): 91-106;

Elissa Gelfand, "Albertine Sarrazin," in her *Imagination in Confinement: Women's Writings from French Prisons* (Ithaca: Cornell University Press, 1983), pp. 214-238;

Gelfand, "Albertine Sarrazin: The Confined Imagination," *Esprit Créateur,* 19 (Summer 1979): 47-57;

Gelfand, "Albertine Sarrazin: A Control Case for Femininity in Form," *French Review,* 51 (December 1977): 245-251;

Gelfand, "Imprisoned Women: Toward a Socio-Literary Feminist Criticism," *Yale French Studies,* no. 62 (1981): 185-203;

Gelfand, "Women Prison Authors in France: Twice Criminal," *Modern Language Studies,* 11 (Winter 1981): 57-63.

Claude Simon
(10 October 1913-   )

Doris Y. Kadish
Kent State University

BOOKS: *Le Tricheur* (Paris: Editions du Sagittaire, 1946);

La Corde raide (Paris: Editions du Sagittaire,
1947);

Gulliver (Paris: Calmann-Lévy, 1952);

Le Sacre du printemps (Paris: Calmann-Lévy,
1954);

Le Vent: Tentative de restitution d'un retable baroque
(Paris: Editions de Minuit, 1957); translated
by Richard Howard as *The Wind* (New York:
Braziller, 1959);

L'Herbe (Paris: Editions de Minuit, 1958); translated by Howard as *The Grass* (New York: Braziller, 1960; London: Cape, 1961);

La Route des Flandres (Paris: Editions de Minuit,
1960); translated by Howard as *The Flanders
Road* (New York: Braziller, 1961; London:
Cape, 1962);

Le Palace (Paris: Minuit, 1962); translated by Howard as *The Palace* (New York: Braziller,
1963; London: Cape, 1964);

Femmes, text by Simon, paintings by Joan Miró
(Paris: Maeght, 1966); Simon's text republished as *La Chevelure de Bérénice* (Paris: Editions de Minuit, 1983);

Histoire (Paris: Editions de Minuit, 1967); translated by Howard (New York: Braziller, 1968;
London: Cape, 1969);

La Bataille de Pharsale (Paris: Editions de Minuit,
1969); translated by Howard as *The Battle of
Pharsalus* (New York: Braziller, 1971; London: Cape, 1971);

Orion aveugle (Geneva: Skira, 1970); enlarged as
Les Corps conducteurs (Paris: Editions de Mi-
nuit, 1971); translated by Helen R. Lane as
Conducting Bodies (New York: Viking, 1974;
London: Calder & Boyars, 1975);

Triptyque (Paris: Editions de Minuit, 1973); translated by Lane as *Triptych* (New York: Viking,
1976; London: Calder, 1977);

Leçon de choses (Paris: Editions de Minuit, 1975);
translated by Daniel Weissbort as *The World
About Us* (Princeton, N.J.: Ontario Review
Press, 1983);

*Claude Simon in 1985, when he won the Nobel Prize for Lit-
erature (courtesy of the Swedish Academy)*

Les Géorgiques (Paris: Editions de Minuit, 1981);
translated by John Fletcher as *Georgics* (London: Calder/New York: Riverrun, 1984);

Discours de Stockholm (Paris: Editions de Minuit,
1986);

L'Invitation (Paris: Editions de Minuit, 1987).

The granting of the Nobel Prize for literature in 1985 to Claude Simon brought worldwide
attention to an author whose unique blend of
postmodernist, vividly sensorial, and broadly historical writing had already won him the recognition of many readers for at least three decades. Explaining their choice, the Nobel Academy praised

Simon for having combined the creativity of the poet and the painter and expressed a profound sense of time and the human condition. That expression, bearing on the most basic feelings of love, sorrow, passion, and pain, is the common thread linking the diverse stages in Simon's development as a novelist.

Simon is perhaps best known in connection with the group of writers, labeled the New Novelists, whose works have been published by the Editions de Minuit, under the direction of Jérôme Lindon. Like others in that group and modernists such as James Joyce, Marcel Proust, and William Faulkner, Simon calls into question the notions of causality, chronology, supremacy of plot and psychology, and subservience of description to narration. Working against tradition, he presents a fragmented treatment of time and events in which the groping movements of memory, consciousness, and writing dictate narrative development. He has described this movement as blindly moving forward "mot à mot" (word by word), comparing his efforts to those of blind Orion in the painting by Nicolas Poussin. Simon also works against tradition by presenting shadowy characters whose tangled drives and desires, manifest sporadically and incoherently during the narration, fail to form an integrated psychological entity or self. Instead of a traditional treatment of time, plot, and characters, Simon and other New Novelists promote the poetic and structural importance of description. One kind is the New Novel technique of *chosisme*, in which objects are described in such intricate material detail that their connection with human concerns becomes problematic. Other distinctive descriptive practices are colorful, impressionistic sketches of perceptions and memories; erotic evocations of people and vegetal or animal life; renderings of pictures, photographs, and other works of visual art that generate narrative episodes; and miniature reflections within the novel of the entire work, a device known as *mise en abyme*. All of these function to provide the narrative coherence that plot and psychology supplied in the traditional novel.

Simon's importance far transcends, however, an association with the New Novel, which is chiefly a deconstructive process for clearing fiction of the encumbering practices of the past. His importance must also be sought in his constructive side, in his search to answer the question of how the novel can best speak to twentieth-century readers. First and foremost, the contemporary novel should convey an intensely sen-

sorial quality, a palpable and pleasurable sense of both language and the world. Holding that writing should be as concrete as painting and that the reader should respond to the novel in terms of sense impressions rather than abstract thought, Simon produces works that are replete with the sounds, smells, textures, and colors of such seemingly banal objects as blades of grass in *L'Herbe* (1958; translated as *The Grass*, 1960), parts of a horse's body in *La Route des Flandres* (1960; translated as *The Flanders Road*, 1961), or stone walls in *Leçon de choses* (1975; translated as *The World About Us,* 1983). No wonder the phenomenologist Maurice Merleau-Ponty, in lectures given at the Collège de France in the early 1960s, used Simon's work as an illustration of how a consciousness responds to the world. From his earliest writing to his most recent, Simon explores the unexpected riches of daily sense impressions by considering the properties of objects, as in geometry one considers the properties of a figure; he fixes his mind upon a cloud, pebble, or painting until its properties have been discovered and brought into contact with the related properties of other objects.

Speaking of other artists, Simon consistently expresses his admiration for those who embody a sensorial notion of art. He frequently cites the sound of James Wait's voice at the beginning of Joseph Conrad's *The Nigger of the "Narcissus"* to show that the artist should seek for truth in the visible world and appeal to the senses, unlike the scientist whose search bears on ideas and whose appeal is to the intelligence. He admires Samuel Beckett and Alain Robbe-Grillet, not only for their precision in describing the world but because, like Gustave Flaubert, they practice a sensorial art of both the signified and the signifier, which enhances both meaning and narrative forms. Simon admires Joyce's vividly sensorial stream of consciousness and contrasting levels of speech that produce a texture of language. Faulkner and Proust stand as models because they evoke the past sensorially and enhance the importance of linguistic and narrative forms. Faulkner's noteworthy achievements are experimentation with common speech, a narrative structure based on sensorial associations, and use of proliferating, poetic sentences. Several modern artists also stand as models: Joan Miró, Robert Rauschenberg, Louise Nevelson, and the three painters Francis Bacon, Jean Dubuffet, and Paul Delvaux, whose works inspired the three narrative sequences in *Triptyque* (1973; translated as

Triptych, 1976). Simon admires their common desire to return to a basic and concrete art. How close the painter's expression of this desire can be to the writer's is evident in *Femmes* (Women, 1966), a volume with a text by Simon written to accompany a group of paintings by Miró. In addition to the common theme of women developed in the paintings and the text, Simon has mentioned that he and Miró developed common images, for example, the sand on beaches in Catalonia, or the light shining through the cloth that serves as a door in that region.

Simon's writing also transcends its association with the New Novel through its broadly historical and humanistic scope, which covers the major moments of upheaval in European history and their effects on modern man. Looking backward, Simon's narrators reconstruct historical moments through an act of imagination triggered by historical documents; some look back as far as the eighteenth century, where they discover the disarray of their aristocratic ancestors around the time of the French Revolution. The experience of earlier participants in history echoes their own in events such as World War II and the Spanish civil war. The common thread among the generations is a sense of futility in the face of the horrors of war or the pettiness of politics and a stripping away of naive illusions about the chances for meaningful social change. The resulting sense of human limitations and the cyclical nature of history is not coupled, however, with pessimism or despair. Simon's work conveys a poignant sense of the enduring value of life, even after the idealism and illusions of youth have been lost.

Simon's historical and humanistic writing differs substantially from the committed literature popular in France prior to and during World War II. Although his novels have a manifestly social and political content, Simon rejects the use of that content for political purposes and the use of the novel by André Gide, Louis Aragon, and certain writers of the absurd as a vehicle for expressing philosophical or political truths. In contrast, he praises Paul Cézanne's aesthetic approach to art, unencumbered by signposts as to the work's meaning. Simon makes a clear-cut distinction between artistically and politically revolutionary acts. Although both stem from the need to question and protest, they can only meaningfully occur in their prescribed arenas. He thus firmly rejects the notion of *engagement,* according to which the novel should further political causes such as so-

cialism; *engagement* stymies the artist's creative growth and makes him subservient to intolerant political revolutionaries.

Because there is to date no biography of Simon, any discussion of his life must be tentative. Several basic facts are known, however, either directly from comments he has made in published interviews or indirectly from his works, which he has openly declared to be largely autobiographical, especially *La Corde raide* (The Tightrope, 1947) and the novels beginning with *L'Herbe.* On 10 October 1913 Claude Eugène Henri Simon, son of Louis and Suzanne Denamiel Simon, was born in Tananarive, Madagascar, then a French possession, where his father was an officer. Because Simon was only six months old when he left there to return to Perpignan and the ancestral home of his mother's family in the southern French region of Roussillon, it is not surprising that his novels contain little in the way of exotic colonial experiences other than evocations of the fragmentary scenes on postcards that Simon's own father, like the father in *Histoire* (1967; translated, 1968), sent back to France from his travels. Nor is it surprising, because his father was killed as a cavalry officer early in World War I and Simon was raised by his mother and her family, that the paternal side, from Arbois in the Jura region of Franche-Comté—where Simon lived for part of his youth—plays less of a role in his novels than the maternal side. Notable exceptions are descriptions in *L'Herbe* of the diary and photograph of the aunt who traveled across France in 1940 and the sale of the family property in the Jura region.

After his father's death Simon was brought up in the ancient family residence under the supervision of his maternal uncle, the model for Uncle Charles in several of the novels. Simon and his second wife, Rhea Karavas (whom he married in 1978), still spend part of the year living in Salses, situated in Roussillon between Perpignan and Les Corbières, in close proximity to the location of his maternal family's vineyards and ancient home. Many biographical details connected with that location are relevant to his novels: a room in the house provided the point of departure for the opening description in *Leçon de choses;* the name L.S.M. in *Les Géorgiques* (1981; translated as *Georgics,* 1984) undoubtedly refers to Lacombe Saint-Michel, the name on the bottles from the vineyard in Salses that Simon owned until recently, where he is known as Lacombe.

His secondary studies took place in Perpignan and then at the prestigious Collège Stanislas in Paris. He successfully completed his baccalaureate studies in Paris with the final year of study being devoted not to philosophy, as he has often pointed out when questioned by critics on philosophical matters, but to mathematics. In response to family pressures, he began studies for a naval career at the Lycée Saint-Louis, but his lack of interest was manifest from the start, and he was dismissed shortly. His family then agreed to allow him to study painting, which he did for a time in Paris with André Lhote, a master of constructions that Simon characterizes as carefully designed but overly cerebral and lacking in a sense of color. Those studies were eventually abandoned because of what Simon has described as a lack of "plastic talent." Stating that he still regrets not succeeding in painting, his greatest love, he continues to make drawings and collages and to express his acute visual perceptions in his novels.

Simon's involvement in major historical events has left a profound mark on his work. After having served as a cavalryman in the 31st Dragoons at Lunéville in 1934-1935, he joined up as a volunteer in the Spanish civil war on the Republican side, acting for a time as a gunrunner. His participation was centered in Barcelona, the location of the Hotel Colon described in *Le Palace* (1962; translated as *The Palace*, 1963) and other works. He then served again as a cavalryman in the French army in 1939-1940, barely escaping death in May 1940 during the battle of the Meuse recounted in *La Route des Flandres* and other novels. Captured at Solre-le-Château near Avesnes and sent to a German prison camp in Saxony, he managed to be transferred to a POW camp in France, from which he escaped in November 1940. He then spent the remainder of the war years participating in the Resistance movement in Perpignan, in contact with Raoul Dufy and others. He painted during the day, while pursuing his literary career in the evenings. By 1941 he had completed not only *Le Tricheur* (The Cheater), which was not published until 1946, but also other works that he later destroyed.

Another decisive factor in Simon's life came later when he was bedridden for months with tuberculosis, unable to do anything but look out the window: vision and memory were all he had. Simon claims that this confinement was a turning point which enabled him to appreciate fully the simple, nonintellectual pleasures of such favorite objects as stones, which he keeps on his desk. It was then that he fully developed his enduring fascination with matter seen through a microscope. He expresses this fascination in his novels, which he produces by closeting himself daily to think and write for hours after lunch. Although he has traveled widely, including trips to Greece, the United States, and Latin America, Simon's main activity in recent years has been writing. Working steadily and peacefully, removed from the bustle of Parisian intellectual life, Simon continues to give simple but stirring expression to man's day-to-day experience. In March 1986 he claimed to be roughly halfway through another novel, tentatively entitled "Complément d'information" (Supplementary Information).

The critical reception of Simon's works over the decades has passed through various stages. During the early 1960s criticism of Simon was confined to book reviews and articles that attempted to interpret his distinctive ideas and worldview, often adopting a phenomenological approach centered on the themes of memory, perception, and imagination. In the late 1960s and throughout the 1970s full-length books on Simon began to appear; and the influence of Jean Ricardou, who focused on the formal, structural properties of Simon's use of language, was predominant. In the 1980s that influence decreased, opening the door to the application of a variety of poststructuralist, psychoanalytic, and deconstructive approaches.

Simon's novels can be divided into early, central, and recent periods. The early period, from *Le Tricheur* to *Le Vent* (1957; translated as *The Wind*, 1959), reveals an author experimenting with a variety of narrative and thematic materials, having not yet achieved the distinctive style and worldview of the later periods. The early works are strongly marked by the tone and style of Dostoyevski and Faulkner, whom Simon emulated. The influence of the Russian novelist's somber preoccupation with mystery and human frailty is especially marked in *Le Tricheur*, a haunting novel about adolescent yearnings and violence, and about adult rejection, failure, and despair. The points of view of various characters are juxtaposed in *Le Tricheur*: Louis, whose actions and feelings in running away with his child-lover, Belle, are interspersed with recollections of his past life at home and school; Catherine, Belle's mother; Gauthier, Catherine's husband and possibly Belle's father, although the suggestion of infidelity figures prominently in

Catherine's thoughts; Belle herself; and Ephraïm Rosenblaum, an outside spectator of the drama. The thoughts, memories, and sense impressions of these characters are revealed in a mixed third-person narration and interior monologue that lapses periodically into the first person. The central event is a seemingly unmotivated murder resulting from an obscure drive toward rebellion and liberation. Through parallel and converging stories about family members of different generations, the novel centers on the rebellion against conventional and hypocritical values. It also develops the themes of war, activist politics, and time.

La Corde raide is a repertoire of elements to be used in later works: the experiences of the soldier; the civil war in Spain; Spanish images such as posters, baroque architecture, tramways, and cigar boxes. *La Corde raide* also poses questions about the usefulness of art, its importance in modern times, French artistic tastes and tendencies, the artist's ability to explain or justify his art, art as evasion, and the artistically uneducated public's inability to understand modern art. The unifying thread is the narrator's search to understand why Cézanne's way of seeing the world is so unusual. *La Corde raide* comprises fourteen sections, from five to twenty-two pages each, intermingling essay and fictional or autobiographical writing. They are linked by the first-person narrative voice and the fact that the questions posed in the essays are frequently answered in the fiction: the answer to why Cézanne's way of seeing the world is so new is indirectly provided in the narrator's vivid recollections and perceptions.

Simon has characterized *Gulliver* (1952) as an unsuccessful attempt to write a conventional novel and as the only one of his works that stands apart from his steady evolution as a writer. As in conventional novels, frequent descriptions of attire and habitat suggest the psychology of typical characters: Gérard Faure, antifascist terrorist; Herzog, Jewish intellectual; Jo and Loulou de Chavannes, decadent descendants of a formerly prestigious family; Max Verdier, rich victim of metaphysical anguish. The politically motivated assassination on a Tuesday night of the de Chavannes servant, an accomplice in Loulou's scheme to extort money from Herzog, opens the novel. On the preceding night, as a lengthy flashback reveals, a complex web of events results in the murder of Bobby, Max's homosexual lover, and the suicide of Max. Further complications arise in connection with Eliane de Chavannes, Jo

and Loulou's sister and the mother of Max's child.

The family plays an important thematic role, through the grandmother's blind hypocrisy and Eliane's and Max's futile attempts to transcend the confines of her society. Psychological and visual themes are also significant: perceptual effects of wind and rain; deformation of reality because of pain; postcoital recollections of the past; visual impressions of postcards, signs, headlights, phone booths, trains, and games. The plot dwells on the irrational urge toward meaningless violence, at work in the antifascist group, the de Chavannes twins, Bobby, and Herzog's servant who, at the end, returns a kindly gesture with a hateful insult. Another important theme is disillusionment resulting from a youthful devotion to a cause. Max views his activities during the war with bitter scorn; and Bert, a journalist in love with Eliane, finally understands the ridiculousness of his role as detective in attempting to prove that Max murdered Bobby.

Le Sacre du printemps (The Rite of Spring, 1954) opens with the thoughts, perceptions, and recollections of the rebellious young Bernard Mallet, whose stepfather, a disabused veteran of the Spanish civil war, has become the target of Bernard's impetuous urge to rebel. Because the conflict between Bernard and the stepfather is central in the novel, there is some artistic justification for the switch, after the first part, to a mixture of the stepfather's first-person narration and the third-person narration of the thoughts, words, and perceptions of both Bernard and the stepfather in the rest of the novel. The novel is thematically characteristic of Simon's writing, despite its melodramatic plot: learning that Edith, the sister of a student whom he is tutoring, urgently needs money for an abortion, Bernard becomes embroiled in a violent adventure; later, learning of his stepfather's relationship with the girl, he provokes a family confrontation that ironically results in the termination of the pregnancy. The important theme is the stripping away of illusions about romantic devotion to causes. The stepfather experienced a similar "rite of spring" when as a student he devoted himself to the Spanish cause and unwittingly contributed to the meaningless violence of a fellow revolutionary's death.

Le Vent, the first of Simon's novels published by Editions de Minuit, was also the first of his works that the public associated with the New Novel and its characteristic techniques of blurring character and plot, describing nonhuman phenomena such as the wind, ignoring social and political events, and highlighting the writer's efforts to construct the novel. In *Le Vent* Antoine Montès arrives from afar to farm the lands left to him by his father, whose infidelities prior to Montès's birth provoked the permanent separation of the family; having befriended Rose, the lonely mistress of a town gypsy, and her two children, Montès finds himself embroiled in a melodramatic series of events that results in the deaths of Rose and the gypsy. The narrator is a professor whose research concerns Romanesque architecture, but whose interest is diverted to a human drama: the subtitle, *Tentative de restitution d'un retable baroque* (Attempt to Restore a Baroque Retable), highlights the narrator's attempt to restore the complex reality of Montès's life that, like the eponymous wind, represents undirected and unreasonable violence.

Because *Le Vent* is a transitional work, already displaying stylistic features perfected in the central period, it retains narrative features characteristic of the early period. Despite the hesitation surrounding events, the novel ultimately relies on a logically developed story and the resolution of enigmas to maintain the reader's interest. Montès—both as a reporter of and participant in the events—is a complex individual, who has a marked affinity with Dostoyevski's innocent Prince Myshkin: Simon has acknowledged that *Le Vent* is a remake of *The Idiot*. In a largely traditional fashion, the novel dwells on Montès's past history, physical appearance, and tragic conflict with society. Not until *L'Herbe* did Simon break decisively with the traditional psychological novel's focus on the intricate workings of an unusual character's mind.

L'Herbe is the first of the novels in Simon's central period, which is characterized by a baroque, proliferating Faulknerian style. Distinctive features of that style include such formulas as "se rappelant" (remembering), "se demandant" (wondering), "se voyant" (seeing herself); long sentences and abundant present participles; parentheses, dashes, and ellipses; the truncating of events or the fusion of present and past actions; and plays on words. Adopting a syntactical arrangement that allows words and phrases to unfold and proliferate, Simon forges sentences that are often several pages in length, containing numerous subordinate constructions set off by parentheses or dashes. The accumulation of words and phrases makes the reader conscious of the elaboration of the sentence and acts to surround assertions with an aura of doubt by proposing alterna-

tive meanings. Conjunctive constructions ("soit . . . soit . . ." [whether . . . or whether . . .]; "sans doute . . . ou peut-être" [probably . . . or perhaps . . .]; "mais peut-être même pas" [but perhaps not even that]) act to cram the sentence full of acts, images, hypotheses, and recollections, sometimes building up to a coherent picture, sometimes canceling each other out. Comparative constructions ("semblable à" [like], "comme si" [as if], "ou plutôt comme si" [or rather as if]) propose comparisons, while denying them a clearly defined meaning. Ellipses in characters' thoughts or spoken words express the ambiguous nature of language and the groping movements of memory and consciousness. Logical conjunctions that fail to establish genuine connections between propositions express a futile striving for continuity. The present participle suggests a proliferation of actions in an imaginary world.

The central period, beginning with *L'Herbe*, is also characterized by a recurring group of family members and autobiographical events that a central consciousness seeks to understand through memory, imagination, and documents from the past. *L'Herbe* is about the personal lives of Louise; her husband Georges, who turns to farming and gambling after World War II; Georges's great-aunt Marie, who dies after sacrificing her happiness to raise her brother, Pierre, to the rank of university professor; Georges's parents—Pierre, obese and taciturn, and Sabine, jealous and inebriated. The events are also personal: the aunt falls into a coma and dies; Louise's marriage crumbles, and she makes plans to leave with her lover. It is not the people or events that are important but Louise's efforts to understand them.

Uncertainty surrounds those efforts from the start, and even at the end no clear description is presented of either the aunt's death or Louise's departure, both of which are only referred to indirectly. As is suggested in the epigraph, taken from Boris Pasternak, "Personne ne fait l'histoire, on ne la voit pas, pas plus qu'on ne voit l'herbe pousser" (No one makes history, no one sees it happen, no one sees the grass grow), there is no clear perception of when, how, or why events occur. Instead, Simon describes images connected with events, for example, the T-shaped pattern of light seeping through the openings between and above the shutters in the dying aunt's room, or the sound of a train or of drops of rain. Those sounds suggest a fading out of the aunt's life and Louise's either leaving

Georges or losing hope for the future by staying with him.

Louise's decision is connected with but not strictly determined by the renunciation the aunt's life and death exemplify. She admires and respects the aunt's values to some extent, but she also rebels against her example, realizing that the aunt's life was composed of sacrifices for people such as Pierre, Sabine, and Georges, who lead futile and unhappy lives. The notion of the aunt's life, reduced to a meaningless repetition, provokes anguish in Louise, especially as she looks at some record books that she discovers in a biscuit box and at the pattern of repeated images on the box's cover.

The biscuit box also provides a *mise en abyme* or miniature version of the entire text. The woman on the cover is lying on the grass holding a box, as Louise similarly holds a box in the novel; the picture in turn portrays a miniature version of the same woman holding the same box, with the repetition of the same image going on endlessly. The series of increasingly distant images suggests the novel's retrospective perspectives: the reader looks back at the period when the narration took place and finds a narrator looking back at the ten days during which the aunt lay dying and at Louise looking back at the past life of the aunt and other members of the family. Narrative structure thus echoes the repetitive pattern of familial and historical events that Louise seeks to understand.

Simon's next novel, *La Route des Flandres*, earned him the 1960 Prix de *L'Express*. Like *L'Herbe*, it focuses on a central character's efforts to understand the past. Georges, some eight years prior to his marriage to Louise in *L'Herbe*, dwells on the enigmatic death of his distant cousin and wartime commander, de Reixach. Although he narrates some of the events to his cynical fellow prisoner Blum in a German prison camp, the central narrative situation is a night that he spends with de Reixach's young widow Corinne after the war and that culminates in her angry departure.

The novel begins with him meeting Captain de Reixach in the winter of 1939-1940 and then shifts to several days in May 1940 when two successive defeats and the deaths of de Reixach and the soldier Wack occur. Symmetrical in design, the novel also ends with the captain's death, with the important central position given to the ambush into which the squadron falls which causes its destruction. A multiplicity of seemingly unrelated episodes is recounted: the wanderings of the cavalrymen, a horse race, the trip Georges and Blum make by train to prison, the stop de Reixach and his troops make to have a drink at an inn, the recollections Georges has of his father on his farm. Simon has explained that during the final stages of writing the novel, he used colored threads and strips of paper marked with colored pencils to represent the different themes and visualize their interweaving. Gradually Georges's interest focuses on the possibility that de Reixach actually sought death in battle because of Corinne's adulterous relationship with the couple's orderly and hired hand, the jockey Iglésia. The likelihood that de Reixach wanted to die seems all the greater as Georges learns from Wack the story of another adulterous relationship involving a lame farmer, in whose barn the soldiers are billeted, and trades stories with Blum about an eighteenth-century ancestor of the de Reixachs, whose suicide is suggested visually by a stain on a family portrait resembling a bullet wound. (Simon owns the portrait he describes in the novel.) But a clear understanding of the events proves to be impossible. Iglésia and Wack may have fabricated their stories of adultery in response to Georges's and Blum's teasing. Confusion surrounds the quarrel between the lame farmer and a town official and the motive for the lame farmer's keeping his brother's wife locked up in the farmhouse. Blum takes liberties with the facts about the ancestor's having been discovered nude at the moment of his death and fails to establish whether his motive was personal jealousy or political disillusionment because of the failure of the French Revolution.

The central theme of the impossibility of understanding the past is furthered in *La Route des Flandres* by the narrative practice of calling into question the narrator's identity. The "I" who narrates and the Georges, or "he," whose actions are described, seem to be two separate characters whose voices are discordantly juxtaposed. After some fifteen pages narrated in the first person, the novel abruptly changes to the third. The similar shifts throughout the novel can be compared to the opening and closing of parentheses, with a return to the previous narrative voice occurring several pages later. "I" strives to create his subjectivity through language; but he repeatedly finds his voice and subjectivity usurped by "he," an impersonal object in his consciousness. The shifts from "I" to "he" occur at such moments of self-doubt as looking in mirrors or suffering from the effects of fatigue, alcohol, or tobacco. The opposition between "I" and "he" strips the central character of control over himself. Georges is merely a shadow of the traditional first-person narrator: as "he," he is merely an impersonal object created by the narrator "I"; as "I," he is merely an unsubstantial, verbal presence in a text.

Description, which plays a key role in *La Route des Flandres* and other novels of the central period, focuses on the key motif of horses. Air and water, whose fragmented forms merge with hoofbeats, are symbolic of the human perception of time during war. Horses on a racing field, decorated with bright colors such as coral, evoke Corinne. The cavalrymen return on four occasions to a spot where a dead horse lies decaying, its physical deterioration symbolizing the same invisible change as the growth of the grass in *L'Herbe*. Simon has described the temporal pattern formed by the repeated descriptions of the dead horse as a cloverleaf drawn by beginning at a certain point and, without lifting pencil from paper, returning to it three times. The pattern evokes the passage of time during war, the succession of words that loop back on themselves, and the novel's three-part division, with the stem of the cloverleaf formed by the introduction of themes in the "prelude." It is intended to provide the kind of immediate apprehension of the diversity of war that Simon claims to have experienced when, as he was returning on a bus from Etretat with Jérôme Lindon, a group of trees seemed to pull back revealing other trees and the entire novel came to him in a flash. He was then able to write in fourteen months what he had been thinking about for twenty years.

It is similarly through memory and imagination, in an effort to understand and reconstruct the past, that the Spanish civil war is described in *Le Palace*. The novel is divided into five parts. Part one, "Inventaire" (Inventory), begins with a description of a pigeon that the narrator observes on the balcony from inside a room, followed by a description of the room and the situation of the narrator's return to the scene of his earlier participation in the civil war. The main characters are a cynical American; two doctrinaire revolutionaries, the schoolmaster and the officer or policeman; and an Italian gunman called The Rifle. It becomes clear that the American, who deplores the use of violence to silence opposing views within the revolutionary ranks, is irrevocably alienated from the others in the group.

Part two, "Récit de l'homme-fusil" (The Rifle's Story), presents the first of a series of acts of political violence. By telling his story to the narrator and drawing a diagram, the Italian describes how he entered a restaurant, passed through a series of points from the door to a table in order to kill a man, and then retraced his movements after having committed the murder. His passage through the points is echoed in a neon sign, on which flashing neon arrows create movement, and in the epigraph, which defines revolution as "mouvement d'un mobile qui, parcourant une courbe fermée, repasse successivement par les mêmes points" (the locus of a moving body which, describing a closed curve, successively passes through the same points).

Part three, "Les Funérailles de Patrocle" (The Funeral of Patroculus), presents the assassination of the revolutionary leader Santiago. Members of a revolutionary party follow a circular path through the city in a funeral procession, carrying signs and banners that express their bewilderment about the reasons for the assassination. The circular trajectory of the procession is seen from a distance by the narrator and his companions; as they discuss its significance, the conflict between the American and the schoolmaster concerning the role of violence in furthering a revolutionary cause is heightened.

Part four, "Dans la nuit" (In The Night), presents the American's nocturnal departure, which the narrator now links to the political assassinations of the man in the restaurant and Santiago. His growing anguish about the Republican movement is indirectly expressed through a lengthy description of a cigar box. Part five, "Bureau des objets perdus" (Lost and Found), presents his further anguish in seeking to understand the facts of the American's departure and the larger meaning of revolution. Hints at the narrator's suicide or the Italian's death at the end suggest that the violence engendered by revolution will continue. As in the other novels of the central period, there is no solution to the enigmas of the past. Only the search for the solution has meaning.

A similar search is depicted in *Histoire*, winner of the 1967 Prix Médicis. The novel, whose title means either history or story, begins at night, as the narrator's perceptions of the fragmented forms and movements of a tree give rise to recollections about members of his family: the death of his mother; his father's travels through the colonial empire recorded on postcards and stamps; the death or departure of his Uncle

Charles; his grandmother's role in raising Charles's children, Corinne and Paulou.

The second chapter presents the narrator in the morning of the single day recounted in the novel, again looking at the tree and recalling the past. He remembers his wife Hélène, who either left him or committed suicide when he was leaving for Spain. Because Charles's wife also either left him or committed suicide, he abandoned his intellectual life in Paris and retired to the country, as has the narrator by returning to the house of his childhood.

Other acts recounted in *Histoire* are mundane: going to a bank to borrow money, eating in a restaurant, selling some old furniture, and the like. The narrator recalls such seemingly unrelated episodes as Corinne's provocative behavior as a young girl, de Reixach's apparent suicide in battle, and an episode of street fighting during the Spanish civil war. There is a lengthy description of a photograph depicting Uncle Charles, a painter named Van Velden, and a nude model in a studio. It becomes increasingly impossible to determine either the identity of the characters or the nature of the events–whether it was Hélène, Charles's wife, Corinne, or the artist's model who committed suicide, as is suggested by the headline about a woman jumping out of a fourth-floor window, or whether she merely left because her man was unfaithful, as is suggested by oblique references to an adulterous affair between an older man and a younger woman. The novel ends with the same poignant sense of a mysterious past and a narrator's valiant but futile efforts to understand it as the other novels of the central period.

La Bataille de Pharsale (1969; translated as *The Battle of Pharsalus*, 1971), like *Le Vent*, is a transitional work. Although certain thematic features link it to the central period, other features announce the recent period. The arrested movement of an arrow evoked in the epigraph from Paul Valéry and the discontinuous perception of a bird described in part one announce the emphasis in the new period on fragmented words and images–sun, shadow, arrow, wings, flight–which are paired and interwoven with other words and images, yet which are not meant to result in the same degree of thematic and linguistic unity evident in the central period. For example, *O*, a phoneme in the novel's first word *jaune*, appears later as a sound or letter in key words and serves to designate the narrative voice as well as to represent the circular form of the novel. That the generative process, not the story, attracts the reader's attention is characteristic of Simon's most recent period.

Part two explores the poetic qualities of seven words presented as unrelated units in a lexicon. The entry for *Bataille* describes fragmented battle scenes depicted in works of art, with no relation to a temporal context. *Machine* presents an abandoned agricultural machine that has been reduced from a functioning system to a collection of fragmented parts. Part three establishes additional new narrative patterns. The tense is the present, the narrative voice is objective, the style is simple. There are no intrusions of subjectivity, such as refrains or vituperative expressions, and virtually no parentheses, long sentences, present participles, or explicit metaphors. Simon has perfected a style that reflects the workings of language, not consciousness. According to Simon, the idea for that style came to him upon discovering New York's stark vertical lines, in contrast with the extravagant curves of baroque architecture in Europe. *La Bataille de Pharsale* closes on a distinctly optimistic note. Instead of the negative images with which the works of the central period come to an end, this novel presents the writer actively at work, not destroying but constructing, not rejecting but affirming. Reality no longer oppresses him but yields to the patterns of writing. The closing image is of sunlight progressing across the page: "La ligne de séparation entre l'ombre et le soleil coupe aux deux tiers et en oblique la feuille de papier posée devant O" (The line separating shadow and sunlight falls two-thirds of the way across the sheet of paper in front of O).

Simon also makes a transition in *La Bataille de Pharsale* by refusing to subordinate all narrative situations to one central situation. The difference between this novel and the preceding *Histoire* is striking in that both contain many of the same episodes and characters: the artist Van Velden and his model in the studio; Uncle Charles in the dimly lit office where he helps the narrator with his Latin translations; soldiers defeated in battle and fleeing in the countryside; the narrator in Greece; the narrator suffering pangs of jealousy and remorse. Not all of these are related in the narrator's memory, experience, or imagination in *La Bataille de Pharsale* as they are in *Histoire*. A radical departure from the use of a single point of view occurs when the narrator and other characters come to be designated as O–*œil* (the eye) or observer who serves as the novel's center of vision. O can be anyone, anywhere, at anytime. O is seen on a train during a trip through Italy, in Greece looking for the Pharsalus battlefield, in bed making love with the artist, in Charles's office seeking help with Latin translations. O is like a camera that enables a movie director to dwell on the artistic properties of people, places, or objects. Unity is no longer provided by memory and consciousness.

The most recent period of Simon's writing begins with the publication of *Orion aveugle* (Orion Blinded, 1970), followed by a greatly expanded version of the same text entitled *Les Corps conducteurs* (1971; translated as *Conducting Bodies*, 1974). Adopting the view that the author should exercise only limited control over the narrative process, Simon during this period has allowed generating images and words to determine the content and narrative coherence of the novel, in the absence of a preconceived narrative design. The connotative and material properties of words and images combine and send the writer down new and unexpected "sentiers de la création" (paths of creation). The author's role is to choose powerful and poetic generators that actively produce meaning. These generators transmit their electrical charge to the entire novel.

Orion aveugle, *Les Corps conducteurs*, and subsequent novels contain a multiplicity of narrative sequences, with an increasing deemphasis of the central narrative situation. Simon's goal is to consider material properties of words and things–the original title of *Les Corps conducteurs* was "Propriétés de quelques figures, géométriques ou non" (Properties of Several Geometric and Nongeometric Figures)–and then to join or superimpose those properties from one sequence to another. *Les Corps conducteurs* contains a multiplicity of episodes: a sick man moves along a street in an American city, a column of soldiers or guerrillas advances through the jungle with difficulty, a man takes a long and exhausting plane ride, a man visits a museum and a doctor's office, a writer attends an endless writers' congress in Latin America, blind Orion moves gropingly through the sky toward the sun, a man spends a night with a woman whom he has tried to reach repeatedly by phone. Although the efforts of the sick man to reach his hotel a short distance away may seem to provide the link among the various series, Simon has said that no element should be viewed as privileged or providing an anchor in reality. To dispel any realistic assumptions, he presents each series not only in its normal narrative form but also as a text (sign, book, film, and so on) read or viewed by characters in the other series.

Simon's method is perhaps more evident in *Orion aveugle* than in *Les Corps conducteurs*. The former is illustrated by a diverse collection of visual materials: works of art by Rauschenberg, Picasso, Poussin, Dubuffet, and others; anatomical drawings; geographical and commercial photographs and designs; an astrological map; and the like. Based on these visual generators, the text develops the theme of perception, culminating in the final image of an anatomical drawing of the internal parts of the eye. In *Les Corps conducteurs*, in which the visual generators disappear, the reader is less conscious of the process of generation itself and more aware of the protagonist's consciousness as the locus of perception. Since the closing visual image of the eye is replaced by an episode in which the sick man falls face down on the rug of his hotel room, an individual subjectivity seems to replace the anonymous perceptual presence in *Orion aveugle*. In the novels written after *Les Corps conducteurs*, Simon has striven increasingly to eliminate or minimize the role of this central consciousness.

In *Les Corps conducteurs* the passage among sequences is based on the sensual, textual, and thematic properties of these series. Thus the reader moves from the tubular forms of skyscrapers to the similar forms of the digestive track, from the "colonnes" (columns) in the hall where the delegates' meeting takes place or in written texts to "colons" and "côlons" (colonialists and internal organs). The text shifts from the human body, in pain or engaged in the sexual act, to political bodies, bodies of land, celestial bodies in constellations, artificial bodies of mannequins, and the like. Whatever body is at issue, certain problems arise. Remoteness from reality is common to the writers' meeting, the view of South America from a plane, and the state of intense pain. Arrested movement is common to the sick man in the street, the figure of Orion in the sky, and the colonialists or guerrillas moving through the forest. Another common theme is the fragmentation of bodies, their separation from an organic whole. In modern society, the novel suggests, man is cut off from himself and the external world. His blind and hesitant attempts to give meaning to his fragmented world correspond both to Orion's in moving through the sky and the author's in writing.

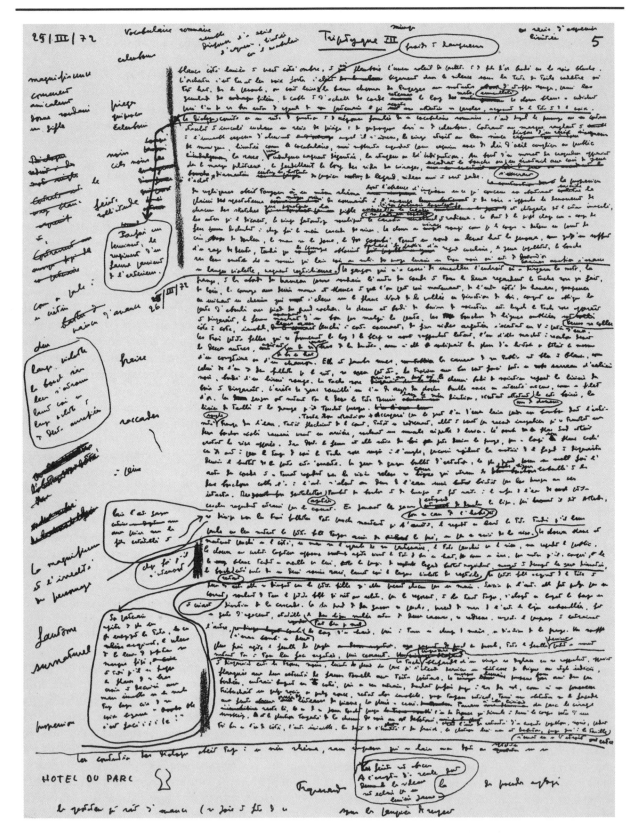

Page from the manuscript for Triptyque, *the 1973 novel in which Simon experiments with the elimination of a central narrating consciousness (by permission of Editions de Minuit)*

Triptyque, published the year Simon received an honorary degree from the University of East Anglia in Norwich, England, successfully accomplishes what the author achieved partially in *Les Corps conducteurs,* the elimination of a central consciousness and privileged narrative situation. The tripartite structure highlighted in the novel's title, which was inspired by a painting by Francis Bacon, maintains equality among the novel's various three-part arrangements. There are three sections, of which the central one is the longest; three settings (a country village, a northern industrial city, and a resort city that resembles Nice); three main types of artistic representations that link the various sequences (postcards, posters, and films); triangular images of all sorts, including geometrical figures drawn by a young boy. Within and between these tripartite arrangements, complex verbal and visual connections are formed. To combine and arrange pieces, to create a complex whole from fragmented forms—as in a puzzle, one of the novel's closing images—these are Simon's most noteworthy accomplishments in *Triptyque.*

A series of implied events underlies each sequence. In the village, a girl drowns because the woman responsible for watching her goes off to the barn to have sex with a farm worker. The two boys, who are supposed to take care of the girl during the woman's absence, are spying on the lovemaking through an opening in the wall of the barn. In the northern city, a young man deserts his bride immediately after their wedding and returns to her late that night, bloody from a drunken brawl and disheveled from having had sex with a barmaid. In the resort city, an older woman lying undressed in a hotel room enlists the assistance of two men (Lambert and Brown), undoubtedly current or former lovers, to extricate her teenage son from the police on drug charges. (Readers of Simon's other novels will identify the woman as Corinne, based on references to the de Reixach name and her aristocratic title of baroness.) In addition to the three main sequences, a circus scene featuring a clown, his companions, and a monkey is developed.

Common to these sequences is the central issue of how reality is represented. Each emphasizes angles of vision and lighting, making the reader acutely aware of who is viewing, from where, and under what perceptual conditions. Frequently, the viewer of a scene first watches and then is watched by others, as when the boys watch the lovers in the barn and are then themselves watched. Shifts also occur in the medium of the representation, as when the boys look at the world directly and then hold up to the light a filmstrip that depicts another world, or when the reader focuses on the scene in the barn and then on an engraving of a maidservant seduced in a barn. The shifts in the medium of representation are the most pronounced in the sequence of the resort city, which is presented through direct narration, as a story in a novel, described as a picture on the novel's cover, and presented in cinematographic form—as stills, transparencies, moving film, posters, and the actual filming on a set. There is no longer any separation between reality and its imaginary or artistic representation.

Another common theme in Simon is eroticism, which is treated in a new and startlingly graphic way in *Triptyque,* and in the later novel *Leçon de choses.* Explicit descriptions of genitalia and sexual acts become longer and more important as the novel progresses, especially in the story of the bridegroom and the barmaid. Closely associated with the novel's erotic theme are certain recurrent colors (pink, yellow, purple), forms (triangles, vertical lines, openings), and words such as *lips.* These colors, forms, and words are the basis of the passages from one sequence to another. Asked to comment on the graphic nature of his sexual descriptions, Simon has simply noted that they are no more or less detailed than his descriptions of trees, clouds, flowers, battles, or stones.

Leçon de choses is noteworthy because it reintroduces thematic features from Simon's central period into a work that adheres to the narrative practices of his most recent work. The result is a partial synthesis between the earlier subjective, historical vision and the later impersonal, strictly literary approach. From the latter, Simon adopts the tripartite structure used in *Triptyque,* in which the three parts are of equal importance and in which no central consciousness provides a stable narrative focus. But as in earlier novels such as *La Route des Flandres, Leçon de choses* also presents the drama of war and on several occasions adopts the first-person voice of a participant in that drama. Of the novel's seven parts—"Générique" (Generic), "Expansion," "Divertissement I" (Diversion I), "Leçon de choses" (Object Lesson), "Divertissement II," "La Charge de Reichshoffen," "Courts-circuits" (Short-circuits)—the two "divertissements" are long first-person monologues in slang that present a soldier's frantic viewpoint on war.

The soldier's viewpoint also plays a highly significant role in parts two, four, and six, in which the tripartite structure is developed by the interweaving of three narrative sequences. Their common thread is the setting of a house; it enables Simon to develop what he has called the theme and variation form of this novel. In the first sequence, two masons are demolishing a wall while remodeling a country house. The time is the present or very recent past. In the second, four cavalrymen are defending a house against the Germans during World War II. Threatened with being surrounded, they are angry about their officers' failure to order a retreat. In the third, several women, a child, and a man are walking along the cliffs near the sea; they stop on a cliff while the little girl has a snack; they watch a fisherman bring in his catch; as a subplot, one of the women, whose husband is away, meets the man later that night and commits adultery with him in a field near the country house. She becomes furious and finally runs away because he shows insensitivity to her concerns about becoming pregnant. Because of the women's old-fashioned clothing, this sequence appears to take place in the nineteenth century. Although nothing dramatic happens in any of the sequences, a sense of closure arises at the end, suggested by the decreasing light of day, the departing movement of a boat, the concluding rhythm of the sex act, and the falling down of the wall. Simon has commented that as he was finishing the book, he happened to open the dictionary to the word *chute* (fall), and realized that the whole novel consisted of variations on the diverse meanings of that word.

As in the other novels since 1970, there is no privileged sequence in *Leçon de choses*. Constant shifts occur among the three sequences, often based on passages from movement to stasis; one sequence is presented as a newspaper item or is frozen and is described as a framed representation in another sequence. It may be true that the soldiers and the workers assume a greater degree of reality than the characters in the seaside sequence, who appear more frequently as representations viewed by the other characters in calendars, books, paintings (especially impressionist paintings), and the like. Moreover, an important link between the soldiers and the workers is established at the end when it becomes apparent that the older of the two workers was one of the soldiers and thus that his point of view has special significance. That point of view becomes important only in retrospect, however,

and does not keep the reader from viewing the three sequences as equal during the reading of the novel.

The process of association in *Leçon de choses* is also characteristic of Simon's post-1970 novels. Sequences are linked through key words such as *boudin*, which at various times gives rise to associations with the impressionist painter Eugène Louis Boudin, a tightly fitting garment, rolls, the fender on a boat, and a swollen finger. Other links hinge on the two meanings of the word *voile*, sail and veil, and on the similar sounds of *ombelles* (the botanical term *umbels*) and *ombrelles* (parasols), or *mer* (sea) and *mère* (mother). The associative process used to generate the narration is highlighted in the novel's first section, "Générique," which contains a two-page description of a wall that is common to the setting of the three main narrative sequences; partial verbatim repetitions of that description occur in the novel's last section, "Courts-circuits." The second section, "Expansion," begins with the depiction of an impressionistic seascape, later identified as Monet's *Effet du soir* (Evening Effect), and continues by extending the verbal and visual associations to which the opening description gave rise. These associations provide the thematic and narrative core of the work.

The title *Leçon de choses* is a significant comment on Simon's narrative techniques as well as a reflection upon their significance. It suggests a school lesson on objective observation and refers to an elementary science textbook (*Leçons de choses*) that one soldier is reading. In the textbook he finds illustrations and a didactic text that unsuccessfully compete with things around him and fail to provide an escape from reality: the text attempts to tell, for example, how to build a house, but the soldier reaches this explanation at the moment when their shelter is crumbling. The other soldier, who talks in the two "divertissements," comes closer to providing a true "lesson of things." His lesson, like the novel's, teaches not only how to use things but also how to appreciate their properties, texture, color, sound, and smell.

A similar synthesis of Simon's central and most recent periods is accomplished on a more extensive, epic scale in *Les Géorgiques*. Although there are again three main narrative sequences that form a tripartite structure, the themes developed in those sequences are reminiscent of the central period. Each treats a participant in a major historical event: General L.S.M., who plays various military, political, and diplomatic roles before, during, and after the French Revolution; an unnamed French soldier in World War II, who retreats from Belgium during the French defeat in 1940, crosses the Meuse shortly before the bridges blow up, and escapes from a prison camp near Dresden; and an English volunteer in the Spanish civil war, designated as O, who fights on the Aragon front in 1937, is wounded by a bullet in the neck, and is chased by the police in Barcelona after the anarchist insurrection in May.

The prologue and first part of *Les Géorgiques* set a tone that is characteristic of Simon's work since 1970, with later parts developing themes from the novels of 1958-1969. The seven-page prologue introduces the generative image of the general, presented first as a character and then as a drawing. The prologue also introduces a metatextual element in reflections on the unfinished nature of the drawing and the contrast between its realistic foreground and schematic background. That metatextual element underlies the rest of the novel with its obvious allusions to novels by Proust and by Simon himself.

Part one interweaves characters, different periods in the general's life, and several different types of language to represent the general's official documents and records of daily activities; the soldier's war experiences, which he is reported to have told in a novel; O's supposedly objective reports and his naive trust in language. The style consists of the short, simple sentences characteristic of the novels since *Orion aveugle*. The interweaving of the three sequences in part one is so strong, with all three narrative figures similarly referred to as "he," that only such details as the mention of airplanes indicating the modern period and Simon's use of italics at times and of roman type at others enable the reader to distinguish one from the other.

In the rest of the novel, the themes and separate treatment of the three narrative sequences are reminiscent of earlier novels. Part two recalls *La Route des Flandres* through its focus on the hardships and reality of war. The subject is the breakdown of command during the debacle of the French defeat at the beginning of World War II and the almost total decimation of the squadron to which the soldier belonged. Part three, reminiscent of *Histoire*, introduces the narrator and establishes his link with the general; the narrator's grandmother owned a bust of the general which is the stimulus for his attempt to reconstruct the general's past life.

Part four, which recounts the hardships endured by a participant in the Spanish civil war, recalls *Le Palace*. While the participant is initially identified as O, like the "œil" or observer in *La Bataille de Pharsale,* he is later identified as George Orwell through descriptions of his English milieu. Simon has acknowledged that Orwell's *Homage to Catalonia* (1938) was the prime stimulus for this section. Three locations are described: the Aragon front, Barcelona, and England. The first is based directly on description in *Homage to Catalonia,* whereas the last is an imaginary reconstruction. The Barcelona location figures in two episodes, in chronologically reverse order: O's return after having been wounded, only to learn that he is wanted by the police; and his arrival in Spain. The return, with its focus on the frightening presence of political figures who pursue mercilessly the so-called enemies of freedom, reveals the profoundly antitotalitarian thrust of Simon's thought, while the arrival reveals Simon's critical attitude toward Orwell's omission of the basic fact that the Russians were controlling the Spanish Left. Orwell's recounting of the Spanish civil war is thus contrasted with the one Simon presents, as the two lessons about things are contrasted in *Leçon de choses*. The contrast is between an authoritative text and a hesitant one, between one that tries to imagine what happened and one that claims to know. Orwell, as an impersonal journalist, pretends to capture reality, but he too, Simon suggests, ends up writing a novel.

Part five dwells on the general's return to France after the Revolution and the hidden facts of his relationship with his family. The main fact is that L. S. M. unwittingly caused his brother's death by voting for a law whereby any aristocrat who emigrated at the time of the Revolution and who returned to France armed would receive the death penalty. Another hidden fact is that L.S.M.'s son by his first marriage removed money and valuables from the château at the time of his father's death, prompting the second wife to dispute his will and eventually regain the inheritance. Throughout this part the narrator's imagination is at work, attempting to reconstruct the truth of the general's past from the documents relating to the dispute over his will and his brother's trial for desertion. A tension is created between the legal text, which pretends to know the truth, and the novel, which seeks to discover it.

Although diverse in subject and technique, the parts of *Les Géorgiques* form a coherent thematic whole. All of them address the primary issue of the relationship between reality and literature. That relationship is central to the georgic tradition highlighted in the title's allusion to Virgil's *Georgica* and the epigraph from Rousseau's *Confessions*. Unlike Virgil, whose didactic tone encourages men to turn to working the land, Simon is concerned simply with the concrete reality of nature: the general's perceptions of his property from his château looking out over the valley, and the perceptions of the soldier and O enduring the hardships of battle. Common to all three characters is a strong sense of the rhythmic progression of the seasons and the cyclical, repetitive nature of life. The passivity of merely conforming to the cyclical nature of things, however, is contrasted with the activity of writing. Writing is Simon's response to the deterioration exemplified in history and by the advanced age of the narrator and the general. Writing means putting together the pieces of the past, as the narrator does with the pieces of the general's life and Simon does with the pieces of his former writings. It is the response to disillusionment such as that experienced by the soldier, the participant in Spain, and the general. Out of the ruins of the Revolutionary spirit and values for which L.S.M. fought, his descendant succeeds in creating new values and meaning through literature.

Simon's most recent work, *L'Invitation* (1987), reveals the same antitotalitarian viewpoint as *Les Géorgiques,* in this case directed specifically at Soviet Russia under Mikhail Gorbachev. The biographical basis for this recent work was an international writers' conference that took place in October 1986, in Frunze, at the Chinese border. *L'Invitation,* a brief narrative based on this event, adopts a sarcastic, satirical tone, directed notably against the same kind of seemingly interminable official discourses that were mocked in connection with the writers' conference in *Les Corps conducteurs.* At the same time it explores in sensorial images and metaphors the Russian landscape, culture, and language.

Despite the many twists and turns of his career, Simon has clung tenaciously to a distinctive set of themes, goals, and worldviews. As recently as his Nobel Prize acceptance speech (published as *Discours de Stockholm,* 1986), he returned to his frequently articulated belief in the novel's importance for heightening one's awareness of the material density of the world and the internal logic of language. His goal is to bring out the harmony of sounds, images, and words, as have musicians,

artists, and his favorite writers, Proust, Joyce, Faulkner, and Conrad. That he has returned continually to the same themes in pursuit of that goal and to the same episodes drawn from his own familial and historical experiences is not surprising. Those themes and episodes recur not because they are special but because they continue to produce associations for an author less concerned with literature as reproduction than as production. The memories and impressions are the same, from *Le Tricheur* to *Les Géorgiques;* what changes is the writer's encounter with language and the discoveries about the world he makes through language. As Simon said in his speech accepting the Nobel Prize: "Je fais–je produis–, donc je suis" (I make, I produce–therefore I am). Stating that the only meaning of the world is that it has none, Simon renounces the lofty goal of saying something philosophically significant and adopts instead the more modest goal of making something aesthetically harmonious. Citing Novalis, he concludes that writing tells only the story of its own production, and that the writer's mission should be less to change the world than to change man's understanding of it. Again he evokes blind Orion, whose groping movements in search of the rising sun are compared to the writer's. Because Orion is a constellation, he disappears when the sun rises. So too does the author of the novel, according to Simon. All that remains is his work.

Interviews:
Claud DuVerlie, "Entretien: Claude Simon parle," *Express,* 5 April 1962, pp. 32-33;
"Pour qui donc écrit Sartre?," *Express,* 28 May 1964, p. 33;
"Rendre la perception confuse, multiple et simultanée du monde," *Monde,* 26 April 1967, p. V;
"Tradition et révolution," *Quinzaine Littéraire* (1-15 May 1967): 12-13;
"La Fiction mot à mot," in *Nouveau Roman: Hier, aujourd'hui,* proceedings of the colloquium at the Centre Culturel International de Cerisy-la-Salle, 20-30 July 1971, 2 volumes, edited by Jean Ricardou and Françoise van Rossum-Guyon (Paris: Union Générale d'Editions, 1972), II: 73-116;
"The Crossing of the Image," *Diacritics,* 7 (December 1977): pp. 47-58;
"Un Homme traversé par le travail," *Nouvelle Critique,* 105 (1977): pp. 32-44;

DuVerlie, "The Novel as Textual Wandering: An Interview with Claude Simon," *Contemporary Literature,* 28 (September 1987): 1-13.

References:

Randi Birn, "From Sign to Saga: Dynamic Description in Two Texts by Claude Simon," *Australian Journal of French Studies,* 21 (May-August 1984): 148-160;

Joan Brandt, "History and Art in Claude Simon's *Histoire,*" *Romanic Review,* 73 (May 1982): 373-384;

Maria Minich Brewer, "An Energetics of Reading: The Intertextual in Claude Simon," *Romanic Review,* 73 (November 1982): 489-504;

Celia Britton, *Claude Simon: Writing the Visible* (Cambridge, U.K.: Cambridge University Press, 1987);

Britton, "Diversity of Discourse in Claude Simon's *Les Géorgiques,*" *French Studies,* 38 (October 1984): 423-442;

Catharine Savage Brosman, "Man's Animal Condition in Claude Simon's *La Route des Flandres,*" *Symposium,* 29 (Spring-Summer 1975): 57-68;

David Carroll, "Diachrony and Synchrony in *Histoire,*" *Modern Language Notes,* 92 (May 1977): 797-824;

Claude Simon: Analyse, théorie, proceedings of the colloquium at the Centre Culturel International de Cerisy-la-Salle, 1-8 July 1974, edited by Jean Ricardou (Paris: Union Générale d'Editions, 1975);

Critique, special issue on Simon, 37 (November 1981);

Jean H. Duffy, "*Les Géorgiques* by Claude Simon: A Work of Synthesis and Renewal," *Australian Journal of French Studies,* 21 (May-August 1984): 161-179;

Alistair B. Duncan, "La Description dans *Leçon de choses* de Claude Simon," *Littérature,* 38 (1980): 95-105;

Duncan, ed., *Claude Simon, New Directions* (Edinburgh: Scotland Academic Press, 1985);

Entretiens, special issue on Simon, 31 (1972);

Esprit Créateur, special issue on Simon, 27 (Winter 1987);

Etudes Littéraires, special issue on Simon, 9 (April 1976);

Michael Evans, "Intertextual Triptych: Reading across *La Bataille de Pharsale, La Jalousie,* and *A la recherche du temps perdu,*" *Modern Language Review,* 76 (October 1981): 839-847;

Brian Fitch, "Participe présent et procédés narratifs chez Claude Simon," in *Un Nouveau Roman,* edited by J. H. Matthews (Paris: Minard, 1964), pp. 199-216;

John Fletcher, *Claude Simon and Fiction Now* (London: Calder & Boyars, 1975);

Colette Gaudin, "Niveaux de lisibilité dans *Leçon de choses* de Claude Simon," *Romanic Review,* 68 (May 1977): 175-196;

John Gilbert, "Langage et histoire chez Claude Simon: D'*Orion aveugle* aux *Corps conducteurs,*" in *La Lecture sociocritique du texte romanesque,* edited by Graham Falconer and Henri Mitterand (Toronto: Hakkert, 1975), pp. 115-124;

Karen Gould, ed., *Orion Blinded: Essays on Claude Simon* (Lewisburg & London: Bucknell University Press, 1981);

Josette Hollenbeck, *Eléments baroques dans les romans de Claude Simon* (Paris: Pensée Universelle, 1982);

Salvador Jiménez-Fajardo, *Claude Simon* (Boston: Twayne, 1975);

François Jost, "Les Aventures du lecteur," *Poétique,* no. 29 (February 1977): 77-89;

Doris Y. Kadish, *Practices of the New Novel in Claude Simon's "L'Herbe" and "La Route des Flandres"* (Fredericton, N.B.: York Press, 1979);

Janine Anseaume Kreiter, "Perception et réflexion dans *La Route des Flandres:* Signes et sémantique," *Romanic Review,* 72 (November 1981): 489-494;

Jacqueline de Labriolle, "De Faulkner à Claude Simon," *Revue de Littérature Comparée,* 53 (July-September 1979): 358-388;

Dominique Lanceraux, "Modalités de la narration dans *La Route des Flandres,*" *Poétique,* 14 (1973): 235-249;

Morton P. Levitt, "Disillusionment and Epiphany: The Novels of Claude Simon," *Critique,* 12, no. 1 (1970): 43-71;

J. A. E. Loubère, *The Novels of Claude Simon* (Ithaca: Cornell University Press, 1975);

Loubère, "Views through the Screen: In-Site in Claude Simon," *Yale French Studies,* no. 57 (1979): 36-47;

Guy A. Newmann, *Echos et correspondances dans "Triptyque" et "Leçon de choses,"* (Lausanne: Age d'Homme, 1983);

Anthony Cheal Pugh, *Simon: Histoire* (London: Grant & Culter, 1982);

Cora Reitsma-La Brujeere, "Récit et métarécit, texte et intertexte dans *Les Géorgiques* de Claude Simon," *French Forum,* 9 (May 1984): 225-235;

Review of Contemporary Fiction, special issue on Simon, 5, no. 1 (1985);

Jean Ricardou, "La Bataille de la phrase," in his *Pour une théorie du nouveau roman* (Paris: Seuil, 1971), pp. 118-158;

Ricardou, "Un Ordre dans le débâcle," in his *Problèmes du nouveau roman* (Paris: Seuil, 1967), pp. 44-55;

Gérard Roubichou, *Lecture de "L'Herbe" de Claude Simon* (Lausanne: Age d'Homme, 1976);

Jean Rousset, "*Histoire* de Claude Simon: Les Cartes postales," *Studi di Letteratura Francese,* 8 (1982): 28-33;

Ralph William Sarkonak, *Claude Simon: Les Carrefours du texte* (Toronto: Editions Paratexte, 1986);

Jean-Luc Seylaz, "Du *Vent* à *La Route des Flandres*: La Conquête d'une forme romanesque," in *Un Nouveau Roman,* edited by J. H. Matthews (Paris: Minard, 1964), pp. 225-240;

Philip H. Solomon, "Claude Simon's *La Route des Flandres:* A Horse of a Different Colour," *Australian Journal of French Studies* 9 (May-August 1972): 190-201;

Jean Starobinski and others, *Sur Claude Simon* (Paris: Editions de Minuit, 1987);

Neal Storrs, *Liquid: A Source of Meaning and Structure in Claude Simon's "La Bataille de Pharsale"* (New York: Peter Lang, 1983);

Sub-Stance, special issue on Simon, 8 (1974);

Stuart W. Sykes, "Mise en abyme in the Novels of Claude Simon," *Forum for Modern Language Studies,* 9 (October 1973): 333-345;

Sykes, *Les Romans de Claude Simon* (Paris: Editions de Minuit, 1979);

Françoise van Rossum Guyon, "De Claude Simon à Proust: Un Exemple d'intertextualité," *Marche Romane,* 21, no. 1-2 (1971): 71-92;

van Rossum Guyon, "Ut pictura poesis: Une Lecture de *La Bataille de Pharsale," Degrés,* 1, no. 3 (1973): 91-100.

Philippe Sollers
(Philippe Joyaux)

(28 November 1936-)

Roland A. Champagne
University of Missouri at St. Louis

BOOKS: *Une Curieuse Solitude* (Paris: Seuil, 1958); translated by Richard Howard as *A Strange Solitude* (New York: Grove, 1959; London: Eyre & Spottiswoode, 1961);

Le Parc (Paris: Seuil, 1961); translated by A. M. Sheridan Smith as *The Park* (London: Calder & Boyars, 1968; New York: Red Dust, 1969);

L'Intermédiaire (Paris: Seuil, 1963);

Drame (Paris: Seuil, 1965); translated by Bruce Benderson and Ursule Molinaro as *Event* (New York: Red Dust, 1986);

Logiques (Paris: Seuil, 1968);

Nombres (Paris: Seuil, 1968);

Entretiens de Francis Ponge avec Philippe Sollers (Paris: Gallimard, 1970);

L'Ecriture et l'expérience des limites (Paris: Seuil, 1971); translated by Philip Barnard and David Hayman as *Writing and the Experience of Limits* (New York: Columbia University Press, 1983);

Lois (Paris: Seuil, 1972);

H (Paris: Seuil, 1973);

Sur le matérialisme: De l'atomisme à la dialectique révolutionnaire (Paris: Seuil, 1974);

Droga e linguaggio, by Sollers and others (Padua: Marsilio, 1976);

Paradis (Paris: Seuil, 1981);

Femmes (Paris: Gallimard, 1983);

Portrait du joueur (Paris: Gallimard, 1984);

Théorie des exceptions (Paris: Gallimard, 1986);

Le Cœur absolu (Paris: Gallimard, 1987);

Les Surprises de Fragonard (Paris: Gallimard, 1987);

Rodin, by Sollers and Alain Kirili (Paris: Gallimard, 1987).

OTHER: "Le Défi," in *Ecrire 3: "Premières Œuvres" publiées sous la direction de Jean Cayrol* (Paris: Seuil, 1957);

Francis Ponge, ou la raison à plus haut prix, edited by Sollers (Paris: Seghers, 1963);

Philippe Sollers (photograph by M. F. Plissant)

Théorie d'ensemble, edited by Sollers (Paris: Seuil, 1968);

289

"La Lutte idéologique dans l'écriture d'avant-garde," in *Littérature et idéologies*, proceedings of the Colloque de Cluny, 2-4 April 1970 (Paris: Nouvelle Critique, 1971); pp. 74ff.;

Roland Barthes, edited by Sollers (Paris: Seuil, 1971);

Artaud, edited by Sollers (Paris: Union Générale d'Editions, 1973);

Bataille, edited by Sollers (Paris: Union Générale d'Editions, 1973);

Colloque "Vers une Révolution culturelle," 2 volumes, edited by Sollers (Paris: Union Générale d'Editions, 1973);

Literatura, política y cambio, edited by Sollers (Buenos Aires: Calden, 1976);

Le Gué: Machiavel, Novalis, Marx, edited by Sollers and Alain Jouffroy (Paris: Christian Bourgois, 1977);

Alain Kirili, texts by Sollers and Donald Kuspit, edited by Sollers (Paris: Galerie Adrien Maeght, 1984).

PERIODICAL PUBLICATIONS: "Déclaration," *Tel Quel*, no. 1 (Spring 1960): 3-4;

"La Poésie, oui ou non," *Mercure de France*, 354 (May 1965): 103-108;

"Auto-portrait," *Magazine Littéraire*, no. 18 (May 1968): 38-39;

"Niveaux sémantiques d'un texte moderne," *Nouvelle Critique*, no. 12 (March 1968): 39-92;

"La Grande Méthode," *Tel Quel*, no. 34 (Summer 1968): 21-27;

"Théorie," *VH101*, no. 2 (Summer 1970): 102-109;

"Réponses," *Tel Quel*, no. 43 (Fall 1970): 71-76;

"Journal du joueur, II," *Infini*, no. 23 (Autumn 1988): 40-56.

Born 28 November 1936 in Talence, just outside of Bordeaux, Philippe Sollers was the fourth and last child of Octave Joyaux, an atheist and a bourgeois owner of a factory in the family since the mid nineteenth century, and his Catholic Parisian wife. Philippe Joyaux was an asthmatic child with ear problems and a tendency to be alone during his childhood. Subject to numerous ear operations, he developed a sensitivity for listening and what he would later call "ma propre conception du monde par l'oreille" (my own view of the world through the ear). He developed an affinity for Rabelais, became a prolific reader, learned Italian and Spanish, displayed a passion for spoken languages, and identified with Marcel Proust as a person and a writer.

Educated by Jesuits in Versailles, he learned from them to question authority and to respect method. He began writing as a teenager and adopted the pseudonym Sollers in his writing workbooks. He thus expressed his rejection of his family's bourgeois origins. The word *sollers* comes from Latin, meaning well-informed and productive, and, as his pseudonym, hid his origins and exemplified the concept of the density of language, a crucial idea during his early years with *Tel Quel* (1960-1970).

By the density or opaqueness of language, Sollers meant that language has a life of its own and does not necessarily convey its originally intended meaning. The death of Sollers's father in 1970 was a crucial event which led the author, in *H* (1973), to examine the density of his father's name and to explore its musical (Octave) and joyful (Joyaux) implications for his own identity and writing career. His novels since then (*Paradis* [Paradise, 1981]; *Femmes* [Women, 1983]; *Portrait du joueur* [Portrait of the Player, 1984]; *Le Cœur absolu* [The Absolute Heart, 1987]) have all reflected a parodic sense of self whereby he can humorously look at his presumably serious adoption of a pseudonym as a way to distance the self from the determinations of naming. Those struggles between self and language have been the subject of his creative writings. Some of his critics observe a certain vertigo in the changes of direction his narratives have undergone in the course of his career. However, the image of a spiral helps clarify the building and process of his literary vision. His career as a novelist can be understood as such a spiral proceeding through three identifiable spires to date: 1957-1958: autobiographical fiction; 1961-1972: experiments in the separation of self from language; 1973- : the reintroduction of the self as a humorous other.

The first publications of his narratives occurred when he was twenty-one years old. Although Sollers rejects his first two published narratives as part of his career as a novelist by saying that they were "neoclassical" stylistic exercises in preparation for more substantial writing, "Le Défi" (The Challenge, 1957) and *Une Curieuse Solitude* (1958; translated as *A Strange Solitude*, 1959) are important explorations of self-reflection which serve as the basis for the second stage of his narrative writing. "Le Défi" is a short story written when Sollers was nineteen. It is a first-person narrative by an adolescent who is seduced by a young woman named Claire and who then abandons her; this rejection results in her suicide. The story was praised for its psychological perception by a fellow *bordelais* and fiction writer renowned for his own psychological portrayals, François Mauriac. Louis Aragon, the former surrealist poet and novelist, extolled the story for its imaginative portrayal of dream images. These kudos were followed by a Prix Fénéon for *Une Curieuse Solitude*, which brought the Sollers narratives to the attention of Emile Henriot of the Académie Française, who hailed the author for his Proustian sensitivity. The story is also told in the first person by a teenager, this time the sixteen-year-old Felipe (Spanish for Philippe) from southwest France (the area of Bordeaux). He seduces Concha, a thirty-year-old maid, who then leaves him as he takes up serious studies in Paris. In both tales the self-centered narrator unites the themes of love and death as he retraces his sexual desire. These concerns become obsessions for Sollers in his later narratives. In these two early works the self and language are in harmony, without any struggle between them. Sollers appeared to show great promise in his mastery of neoclassical style, with a Proustian talent for psychological probing and a rich poetic verve for imaginative dream images.

The first two narratives are set in the Bordeaux of Philippe Joyaux's youth. During that period the Bordeaux metropolitan area was cosmopolitan in its assimilation of people with Italian, Spanish, Jewish, English, and South American heritages. The Joyauxes were opposed to the Vichy government of Marshal Philippe Pétain during World War II and rejected the anti-Semitic programs of the Occupation. Sollers had two sisters who married two brothers and lived in houses side by side in what he understood to be a symmetrical and conformist bourgeois life-style. The threat of bourgeois regularity haunted him. However, he admired the cosmopolitan tolerance of Bordeaux and would soon implement in his writings a breadth of literary vision that opposed a xenophobic and nationalistic tendency in French letters during the late 1950s and early 1960s. Like his father, Sollers lacked any faith until about 1979 when he converted to Catholicism, his mother's religion.

The distancing of self from language, first evident in the Sollers pseudonym, is especially characteristic of the second stage or spire in his writing. In 1960 Sollers collaborated with several others to begin editing the journal *Tel Quel* at the

Editions du Seuil. His association with Seuil lasted until 1982 and resulted in a strong current of avant-garde literature, while the *Tel Quel* group maintained Maoist political positions from 1968 to about 1975. The evolution of his critical writing with *Tel Quel* and later with the journal *Infini* at the publishing house of Denöel has been parallel to that of his creative writing.

In 1961 Sollers published *Le Parc* (translated as *The Park*, 1968), which he recognizes as the beginning of his career as a novelist. *Le Parc* received the Prix Médicis. Influenced by the French New Novel, especially the visual descriptions of Alain Robbe-Grillet, this novel does not have a tightly woven story to tell. There is a narrator who is using an orange exercise book, apparently to write what is being read. In his apartment bedroom there is a painting of a fishing port teeming with boats. Leon Roudiez, in *French Fiction Today* (1972), has pointed out that the narrator and a woman he meets are reproduced in this painting, thus creating an eidetic image, or what is called a *mise en abyme*, which the language of the novel attempts to articulate. This concern for the proximity of language and images would return with Sollers's work on Fragonard and with *Rodin*, by Sollers and Alain Kirili, both published in 1987.

The interconnections between language and painting were crucial for the early *Tel Quel* identification with structuralism and its promotion of Paul Valéry's notion of the work of art as an "enchanted structure." In *Le Parc* language creates this enchanted structure existing independently of the narrator's control as the words seem not to refer to any prior referent but to an ambiance, a park, which the words themselves create.

In 1963 Sollers published a collection of essays called *L'Intermédiaire* (The Middle Zone/The Medium), whose title refers to ambivalence as that middle ground between the opaqueness and the transparency of language. On the one hand, *Le Parc* is the first of a series of novels which exemplifies the opaqueness of words, with their refusal to adhere to meanings attributed to them in advance. On the other hand, in *L'Intérmediaire* Sollers aims at a transparency of language in his use of words to communicate his insights into Dante and into the Algerian war. Although the *Tel Quel* group's ideology proposed an agenda pointing to the density of language, Sollers would have it both ways as he also used language as a transparent vehicle when articulating his views in his essays or elucidating the Leftist program of *Tel Quel*.

Drame (1965; translated as *Event*, 1986) and *Nombres* (Numbers, 1968) continue the undermining of the novel genre with their opaque language. Both works are subtitled "roman" (novel). However, their forms subvert the traditional expectations of narrative voice, character development, and time/space parameters. Instead, *Drame* portrays the dramatic tension between a writer and the language of a work to be written. The struggle is between the writer's attempt to have language say what he wants it to say and what it says on its own. Roland Barthes, another fellow *bordelais*, praised *Drame* for its promise of precluding closure to literary works. *Drame* "ends" with the remark that the book could possibly fail to be realized. The "failure" is from the writer's point of view: the words of the book are not what the writer meant to say.

Nombres presents the debate over whether a book can ever be realized. In 1967 Sollers met Julia Kristeva, who introduced him to the subtleties of Mikhail Bakhtin's thought about the dialogic principles of intertextuality. These principles, combined with Stéphane Mallarmé's obsession with dice as the play of chance with the scientific certainty of numbers, are exemplified in *Nombres*. Its formal organization is very neat: one hundred numbered sections, divided into twenty-five sequences of four voices. The first three voices are in the imperfect tense; the fourth is in the present tense. The voices debate their own existence as a unified text and comment upon citations occurring within one of the voices. This "novel" is a theater of voices dramatizing the struggle that is part of the creative process. The complex theoretical implications of *Nombres* are presented as the perfect "deconstructive" exercise in Jacques Derrida's *La Dissémination* (1972) and as the modern Bakhtinian novel in Kristeva's *Polylogue* (1977).

The year 1968 was crucial for France and for Sollers. It was the year of the student and worker revolts in May. The invasion of Czechoslovakia by the Soviet Union occasioned a split in the *Tel Quel* editorial board over its Communist agenda. In 1968 Sollers and Kristeva were married. (They have a son, Michael.) In 1968 and 1971 Sollers produced two essay collections, *Logiques* (Logics) and *L'Ecriture et l'expérience des limites* (translated as *Writing and the Experience of Limits*, 1983). These two works include essays which explain Sollers's conception of the novel and of

the novelist. Especially notable are the essays "Le Roman et l'expérience des limites" (The Novel and the Experience of Limits), "Logique de la fiction" (Understanding Fiction), and "Littérature et totalité" (Literature and Totality). Sollers's language here is transparent in that it represents his conscious attempt to create an "ideology" uniting literature with history, politics, and philosophy. He would, however, have the novel be a voice whereby society speaks of itself, a self-reflective act whereby the writer is a transcriber of "le discours incessant, inconscient, mythique des individus" (the unceasing, unconscious, mythic discourse of individuals). The opaqueness of language in the novel can then be explained as a rejection of the existence of the author as an individual subject in favor of the vitality of language as the alembic of social consciousness.

The death of Octave Joyaux, combined with the failure of the May 1968 revolts to enact social change, filled Sollers with rage about his literary and political agenda. He began to suspect the seriousness of his prior purpose, and he rallied the *Tel Quel* group into a radical Leftist agenda, emulating what Mao had done with his cultural revolution in China. Sollers had used Chinese ideograms in *Nombres*. On the title page of *Lois* (Laws, 1972) he placed an ideogram which was a pun in Chinese for France and the Law. Once again he used the label "roman" as the subtitle in order to set up the foil for his subterfuge. His purpose in *Lois* was to "deconstruct" French culture and to implement a dialectical materialism in writing. Written in an angry and humorous tone of iconoclasm, *Lois* contains a series of accusations in colloquial French with many neologisms pointing to the failure of the French Communist party to lead France into its own cultural revolution. The humor toward sexuality and language is Rabelaisian. Various languages are used in order to question the assumption that the French have all the answers to political, cultural, historical, and philosophical issues. With a lyrical rhythm based on spoken language, Sollers developed in *Lois* a sense of humor about the French culture which he would turn on himself in *H*.

H outraged many readers because of its radical format. There is no punctuation, capitalization, or paragraph structure. It appears to be unreadable. However, it is a lyrical work, based on spoken discourse, and like James Joyce's *Finnegans Wake*, which Sollers was translating with Stephen Heath while he was writing *H*, it has a scansion that is apparent when the sentences are read aloud. The title is derived from the drug hashish, which provided Sollers with a new influence and experimental device as he wrote *H*. Once again, his Rabelaisian spirit of humor is evident as he delves into self-parody with plays on his name and that of his father. No single narrator is in control. Many voices intervene to make this novel a social record of the uncertain times following the 1968 revolts.

In 1972 Sollers led the *Tel Quel* group in a series of seminars on the works of Antonin Artaud and Georges Bataille. His active promotion of these writers, as well as of Lautréamont, Céline, and Mallarmé, was part of his agenda to make *Tel Quel* into an avant-garde forum for "literary terrorism." The visions of these writers would help to reawaken French intellectuals to the cultural stakes of a Maoist program for political change. In 1974 Sollers published *Sur le matérialisme* (On Materialism), a series of essays promoting a Leninist form of dialectical materialism which he claimed had been lost by the political compromises of the PCF (Parti Communiste Français) pursuant to the May 1968 revolts. In spring 1974 Sollers, Kristeva, Barthes, Marcelin Pleynet, and François Wahl visited Peking to see for themselves the results of Mao's revolution. Although they were fascinated by their exposure to such a radically different language and culture, the social problems of the workers and the women and the Maoist hegemonic political purges brought a certain sober tone from the returning group to the *Tel Quel* agenda. The harsh cries for Maoist revolution were attenuated, and *Tel Quel* finally ceased publishing at Editions du Seuil in October 1982, after ninety-four issues had appeared. In 1985 an interview Sollers conducted with Louis-René des Fôrets for *Tel Quel* (February 1962) was republished in book form as *Voies et détours de la fiction* (Routes and Detours of Fiction).

After his conversion to Catholicism in 1979, Sollers wrote what he considers to be his best novel, *Paradis* (1981). He emulated Joyce and Dante for their impassioned involvement of Catholicism in their epic visions. The title *Paradis* is derived from Dante's *Paradiso*, but Sollers's work purports to be a parody of the modern conception of heaven. Although this so-called novel has no punctuation, capitalization, or paragraph structure, Sollers introduced punctuation to the text when he read *Paradis* for a Belgian radio station and had it recorded on cassettes. A Paris bookstore, La Hune, broadcast the reading for passers-

by and sold the six-cassette recording to go along with the text. The novel is a series of catalogs about life in Florence and in Paris. As Sollers traveled between the two cities, he recorded information about the nature of "culture" in these two capitals of Western civilization. The work reads like a computerized data base of the most banal to the most sophisticated details, offering a parody of Christianity as inspired by the work of Joyce. Whereas Joyce provided the comic model of Christianity for Sollers, it was Dante's work, with its command of language and erudition, which inspired Sollers to portray the pathos of modern Christianity.

In the 1980s Sollers's novels have changed appreciably. Since *Femmes* (1983), they contain language which is transparent: there are a definable narrative voice, character development, intrigue, and a more traditional format with regard to sentence and paragraph structure. There is also a greater sense of self-parody concerning his literary past. This self-parody is a form of self-examination. In *Femmes*, Will, a South American Catholic journalist living in Paris, narrates his memoirs about an unmapped, erotic world belonging to women. Will refers to misunderstood intellectuals, including Sollers, Werth (Louis Althusser), and Lutz (Roland Barthes), who become pathetic victims of changing intellectual whims. *Femmes* was a success with critics and readers alike. Although some objected to what they perceived as a misogynistic tone, it is possible that Sollers's handling of the narrator is tongue-in-cheek. Many liked the catalog of the contemporary intellectual scene witnessed by Will, whose name refers to the control Sollers is exerting over language in the narrative. However, Leftist intellectuals were dismayed by what seemed to be a change in literary direction for Sollers. He appeared to be rejecting the concerns of his previous writing in order to produce a best-seller. Part of this argument comes from the rumors of the disputes between Sollers and Paul Flamand at Seuil about whether the installments of *Paradis* that appeared in *Tel Quel* during the late 1970s could attract enough readers to warrant publication of the work as a book. Sollers jumped ship by having Gallimard publish his works after 1981. Gallimard publishes a wide-ranging list in contrast to the more avant-garde Seuil.

In 1983 Sollers began to edit the avant-garde journal *Infini*, which has continued the work of *Tel Quel* in publishing texts by incisive young writers. For example, the work of Bernard-

Henri Lévy and his group of "new philosophers" has appeared in the pages of *Infini* because of its challenging melding of philosophy, history, and politics: a vision endorsed by Sollers from the beginning of *Tel Quel*. However, *Infini* has not continued the political and literary "terrorism" of *Tel Quel*.

Since *Femmes* Sollers has continued to write novels in a transparent vein. In 1984 he published *Portrait du joueur* (Portrait of the Player), and in 1987 *Le Cœur absolu* (The Absolute Heart), both of which sold well. *Le Portrait du joueur*, described by the publisher as an autobiographical essay but subtitled "roman" by Sollers, was a selection for a French book-of-the-month club. Philippe Diamant is the first-person narrator whose name returns to the family name Joyaux by way of a play on words which associates *Joyaux* with *juif* (Jew), then *joyau* (jewel), and finally *diamant* (diamond). Diamant is Sollers reliving his literary life with a sense of the comic learned from his father. The insights into the task of the writer are numerous and explain the trajectory of Sollers's writing career, still evolving. Diamant contrasts the writer's humanity with the economic pressure to produce a marketable story. Other indications of Sollers's views of himself and his narrative craft are found in *Vision à New York*, a 1981 book of interviews with David Hayman, and Sollers's essay collection *Théorie des exceptions* (Theory of Exceptions), published in 1986.

In *Le Cœur absolu* Sollers is one of the characters as well as the narrator. The title refers to a group of five friends who organize themselves into a club called Le Cœur absolu. The narrator is an aging man who feels that he is losing his attractiveness to women and his appeal as a writer to prospective readers. As the club members travel together between Paris and Venice, they discuss Sollers, his reputation, and his talents. The title suggests an idealism and a personal pathos far removed from the dialectical materialism of the politically involved Maoist of the early 1970s.

Philippe Sollers is still developing his art of writing novels. In 1986 he promised publication of a second volume of *Paradis*. Among his current interests are Judaism, filmmaking, and audiovisual technology. He is also attracted by the genius of the eighteenth-century *philosophe* Denis Diderot, who studied the interplay of nonverbal communication with technological advancements and the density of language. Like Diderot, Sollers has experimented with art criticism (*Les Surprises de Fragonard* [Fragonard's Surprises], 1987; *Rodin*, 1987). He is also exploring ways to translate his narrative vision into various media as he promotes his newly adopted motto, articulated in *Infini* (Fall 1988): "Audio, video, cogitando, ergo sum" (While thinking, I hear, I see, therefore I am).

Interviews:

Maurice Clavel, *Délivrance* (Paris: Seuil, 1977);

Edgar Faure, *Au-delà du dialogue* (Paris: Balland, 1977);

David Hayman, *Vision à New York* (Paris: Grasset & Fasquelle, 1981);

Shusi Kao, "Paradise Lost? An Interview with Philippe Sollers," *Sub-Stance*, no. 30 (1981): 31-50;

Jacques-Louis Binet, "Le Sang dit-il la vérité," *Monde*, 12-13 August 1984, V: 5.

References:

Roland Barthes, *Sollers ecrivain* (Paris: Seuil, 1979); translated, with an introduction, by Philip Thody as *Sollers Writer* (London: Athlone Press, 1987);

Roland A. Champagne, *Beyond the Structuralist Myth of Ecriture* (The Hague: Mouton, 1977);

Jacques Derrida, *La Dissémination* (Paris: Seuil, 1972);

David Hayman, Introduction to Sollers's *Writing and the Experience of Limits*, translated by Hayman and Philip Barnard (New York: Columbia University Press, 1983);

Stephen Heath, *The Nouveau Roman: A Study in the Practice of Writing* (London: Elek, 1972);

Julia Kristeva, *Polylogue* (Paris: Seuil, 1977);

Leon Roudiez, *French Fiction Today* (New Brunswick: Rutgers University Press, 1972).

Michel Tournier
(19 December 1924-)

William Cloonan
Florida State University

BOOKS: *Vendredi, ou les limbes du Pacifique* (Paris: Gallimard, 1967); translated by Norman Denny as *Friday, or The Other Island* (London: Collins, 1969; Garden City, N.Y.: Doubleday, 1969);

Le Roi des aulnes (Paris: Gallimard, 1970); translated by Barbara Bray as *The Erlking* (London: Collins, 1972); republished as *The Ogre* (Garden City, N.Y.: Doubleday, 1972);

Vendredi, ou La Vie sauvage (Paris: Flammarion, 1971); translated by Ralph Manheim as *Friday and Robinson: Life on Esperanza Island* (London: Aldus, 1972; New York: Knopf, 1972);

Les Météores (Paris: Gallimard, 1975); translated by Anne Carter as *Gemini* (London: Collins, 1981; Garden City, N.Y.: Doubleday, 1981);

Le Vent Paraclet (Paris: Gallimard, 1977);

Le Coq de bruyère (Paris: Gallimard, 1978); translated by Barbara Wright as *The Fetishist and Other Stories* (London: Collins, 1983; Garden City, N.Y.: Doubleday, 1984);

Barbedor (Paris: Gallimard, 1980);

Gaspard, Melchior et Balthazar (Paris: Gallimard, 1980); translated by Manheim as *The Four Wise Men* (London: Collins, 1982; Garden City, N.Y.: Doubleday, 1982);

Le Vol du vampire (Paris: Mercure de France, 1981);

Pierrot, ou Les Secrets de la nuit (Paris: Gallimard, 1982);

Gilles et Jeanne (Paris: Gallimard, 1983);

Les Rois mages (Paris: Gallimard, 1983);

Le Vagabond immobile (Paris: Gallimard, 1984);

La Goutte d'or (Paris: Gallimard, 1985); translated by Wright as *The Golden Droplet* (London: Collins, 1987; Garden City, N.Y.: Doubleday, 1987);

Le Tabor et le Sinaï: Essais sur l'art contemporain (Paris: Belfond, 1988).

PLAY PRODUCTION: *Le Fétichiste: Un Acte pour un homme seul*, 1974.

Michel Tournier (photograph copyright © Jerry Bauer)

OTHER: Laurent Gouvion Saint-Cyr, *Aventures et secrets du collectionneur*, introduction by Tournier (Paris: Stock, 1971);

Venise, hier et demain, photographs by Fulvia Roiter, introduction by Tournier (Paris: Editions du Chêne, 1973);

Lucien Clergue, *Mers, plages, sources et torrents, arbres*, introduction by Tournier (Paris: Editions Perceval, 1974);

Canada: Journal de voyage, photographs by Edouard Boubat, commentary by Tournier (Montreal: La Presse, 1977); republished as *Journal de voyage au Canada* (Paris: Robert Laffont, 1984);

La Famille des enfants, photograph collection, commentary by Tournier (Paris: Flammarion, 1977);

Des Clefs et des serrures, photographs edited, with commentary, by Tournier (Paris: Editions du Chêne/Hachette, 1979);

Morts et résurrections de Dieter Appelt, photographs by Dieter Appelt, introduction by Tournier (Paris: Herscher, 1981);

Vues de dos, photograph collection, commentary by Tournier (Paris: Gallimard, 1981);

Marseille, ou Le Présent incertain, photograph collection, commentary by Tournier (Paris: PUF, 1985).

Michel Tournier is a popular novelist in the finest sense of the word. He addresses topics of general interest in a prose that makes the issues he raises readily accessible to his audience. Tournier is one of the first serious French novelists to break with the tradition of *le nouveau roman*, whose penchant for stylistic complexity has marked French fiction since World War II. As Tournier puts it in his autobiographical essay, *Le Vent Paraclet* (The Holy Spirit, 1977), his aim is not to "innover dans la forme, mais de faire passer au contraire dans une forme aussi traditionnelle, préservée et rassurante que possible une matière ne possédant aucune de ces qualités" (innovate in form, but, on the contrary, to express in a traditional and reassuring fashion material that has none of these qualities).

When he received the Légion d'Honneur in 1979, an interviewer asked Tournier how a writer who claimed to be so subversive could accept this sign of bourgeois approbation. The novelist replied with a story about the twentieth-century composers Erik Satie and Maurice Ravel. It seems that Ravel turned down membership in the Légion d'Honneur. At that time Satie quipped that Ravel might well refuse this honor, but that all his music accepted it. Tournier went on to note that "Je peux accepter la Légion d'Honneur parce que toutes mes œuvres la refusent" (I can accept the Legion of Honor, because all my works reject it).

The subversive element in Tournier's writing resides less in the themes than in the treatment he accords them. He discusses questions of common concern: the shattering moral and philosophical implications of World War II, the ambiguity of sexual identity, the need to find some means of ordering experience amid the chaos of the modern world, and the role that fiction plays in the unfolding of daily life. Tournier brings to each of these questions a point of view that challenges normally held assumptions. His ability and willingness to shock is not confined to his novels. *Le Vent Paraclet* offended many by the author's apparent arrogance, but his subsequent collection of essays, *Le Vol du vampire* (The Vampire's Flight, 1981), proved equally controversial because it is a reflection on Tournier's own approach to writing in the guise of a commentary on various authors.

Michel Tournier was born on 19 December 1924 at 71 rue de la Victoire, in Paris's ninth *arrondissement*. His family was of solid bourgeois stock; his father, Alphonse Tournier, founded and directed an organization that dealt with musical copyrights. Shortly after Tournier's birth the family moved to the Parisian suburb Saint-Germain-en-Laye, where the author-to-be spent his childhood. Tournier's youth was indelibly marked by World War II. Although he was slightly too young to serve actively in the war, living close to Paris provided him with opportunities to observe the varying reactions to the German occupation. He noted the pain and suffering of the French, but also in many cases the French admiration for their German conquerors, as well as the frequently slavish adulation of Marshal Philippe Pétain and his puppet government at Vichy. After the war he was witness to the numerous distortions and fictionalizations that led to the creation of the myth of "La France résistante."

The war years were particularly painful for Tournier because he was raised in a household that had as much respect for genuine German culture as contempt for the Nazi parody of it. His family spoke German and often had spent summers in Germany. In this respect Tournier is one of the rare French writers (Jean Giraudoux is another) who appreciate the language and culture of their neighbors across the Rhine.

Tournier's postwar studies led him to what was supposed to be a brief period at the German University of Tübingen. This visit wound up lasting four years (1946-1950), during which Tournier devoted himself to the study of philosophy. When he returned to Paris, it was to prepare for the difficult French examination called the *agrégation*. In *Le Vent Paraclet* Tournier recalls that although he considered himself the finest philosopher of his generation, this opinion was not shared by his examiners, and he flunked the *agrégation*. This setback effectively ended his hopes for a university career, and for a while he drifted in the exciting intellectual world of postwar Paris. He sat in on Claude Lévi-Strauss's anthropology lectures at the Musée de l'Homme. The influence of this experience is apparent in his first published novel, *Vendredi, ou les limbes du Pacifique* (1967; translated as *Friday, or The Other Island*, 1969).

Later he worked as an editor for the Parisian publishing house, Plon, and also did translations of German works, particularly the novels of Erich Maria Remarque, whom he eventually met. He then drifted into the radio industry, where he was an announcer for Europe Numéro Un. His short story "Tristan Vox," in the collection *Le Coq de bruyère* (1978; translated as *The Fetishist and Other Stories*, 1983), displays his knowledge of the realities of the radio business, as well as the fantasies that can be engendered by the human voice. Soon television beckoned, and from 1960 to 1965 he hosted a series entitled *La Chambre noire* (The Black Box) which concerned what was to become his principal hobby, photography. This interest has led him to write many introductions to photographic collections, but to date Tournier has steadfastly refused to publish any of his own photographic work. He has, however, been active in promoting the efforts of other photographers. Tournier was one of the founders of the annual Rencontres Internationales de Photographie, which takes place in Arles. Photography figures in most of Tournier's fiction, and his ambivalent attitude toward the photographic image plays an important role in the novel *La Goutte d'or* (1985; translated as *The Golden Droplet*, 1987), as well as the short story "Les Suaires de Véronique" (Veronica's Shrouds), which appears in *Le Coq de bruyère*.

It was not until Tournier was forty-three years old that he published *Vendredi, ou les limbes du Pacifique* and began his meteoric career as a novelist. This book won him the prestigious Grand Prix du Roman de l'Académie Française. He received the Prix Goncourt for *Le Roi des aulnes* (1970; translated in 1972 and published as *The Erlking* in Great Britain and as *The Ogre* in the United States). In 1972 he accepted an invitation to join the Académie Goncourt.

Tournier, a lifelong bachelor, lives in a former rectory in the valley of the Chevreuse where he enjoys showing his occasional visitors his photographs, his cats, and his garden. Although Tournier enjoys his considerable isolation, he also likes appearing before the public. He is a frequent guest on French television talk shows, travels and lectures extensively in Germany and Africa, gives talks to French schoolchildren, and is usually available for interviews concerning his past achievements and current projects.

Tournier's public personality is as carefully sculptured as those of his fictional characters; like them he manages to be at once frank and elusive. Irony pervades his public pronouncements just as it affects the narrative perspective he brings to his novels. Tournier's comments often make him no stranger to controversy. A case in point is his suggestion, in *Le Vent Paraclet*, that Hitler could never have ordered the burning of Paris: "Comment une idée aussi sage aurait-elle pu naître dans une tête aussi mauvaise?" (How could such a fine idea have emerged from such an evil mind?). Nor is he someone whose words are meant to reassure and mollify. Tournier continually challenges *idées reçues*, yet while his touch is often light, his goals, be they to attack racism, to support freedom of sexual expression, or simply to undercut bourgeois complacency, are deadly serious. In an effort to achieve his ends, Tournier makes use of two concepts that suffuse all of his writing, but which are particularly crucial for understanding his creative works. Both have bases in his philosophical studies, and both are replete with irony. They are *le rire blanc* (white laughter) and the special meaning he gives to myth.

In *Le Vent Paraclet* Tournier notes that the "rire blanc dénonce l'aspect transitoire, relatif, d'avance de tout l'humain...; l'homme qui rit blanc vient d'entrevoir l'abîme entre les mailles desserrées des choses. Il sait tout à coup que rien n'a aucune importance. Il est la proie de l'angoisse mais se sent délivré par cela même de toute peur" (white laughter denounces the fundamentally transitory, relative nature of everything human . . . ; the man who experiences white laughter has just seen the abyss open beneath him. He knows suddenly that nothing is important. He is filled with agony, yet at the same time delivered from all fear). White laughter reflects an awareness of life's utter meaninglessness. It is precisely this intuition that many of Tournier's major characters attempt to reject by their elaborate inventions of highly structured universes.

An equally strong influence on Tournier's writing is myth. In his novels he makes frequent use of a variety of myths, but principal among them is the myth of twinship he associates with Cain and Abel. These two figures represent types of opposing but complementary personalities. Cain is the sedentary, the person who fears the complex and unforeseen; he hopes to have his life unfold in a totally predictable manner within a clearly demarcated geographic space. Abel is the nomad, the individual who, at times despite himself, becomes a wanderer and is forced to confront some of life's complexities. It is tempting yet misleading to place Tournier's characters into one or the other category. For example, Robinson of *Vendredi, ou les limbes du Pacifique* could easily be Abel and the slave Vendredi Cain. In *Le Roi des aulnes* the conveniently named Abel Tiffauges would be an Abel figure, and his friend Nestor a Cain. The globe-trotting Jean in *Les Météores* (1975; translated as *Gemini*, 1981) would be Abel and his brother Paul Cain. In spite of the neatness of this schema, it simply does not work. No single character is a Cain or an Abel; each has within himself the potential to be the other. The myth of twinship indicates for Tournier that the quest for self-fulfillment involves a struggle, not just with the beloved and despised other, but within the individual himself.

If Tournier has a literary twin, it would most likely be the eighteenth-century writer Jean-Jacques Rousseau. Both display a fondness for shocking the middle class; both profess great concern for children (Tournier is in this instance quite sincere), and both insist upon their need for solitude. A final, curious similarity is that both the Vicar of the Chevreuse and the Vicar of the Savoie were drawn to Daniel Defoe's *Robinson Crusoe*.

Vendredi is a retelling of *Robinson Crusoe*. Initially Tournier's version follows Defoe's closely. After Robinson recovers from his severe depression at being shipwrecked alone on an island he begins to create a highly structured world for himself. He tills, builds, and, from his own perspective, civilizes. The arrival of Vendredi changes everything. Robinson fails in his attempts to turn the savage into a good slave, not to mention a good citizen, and after an explosion that Vendredi inadvertently causes, their roles are reversed. Vendredi becomes the teacher, but he instructs less by word than by example. Slowly Robinson is converted to the worship of primitive nature and scorns traditional Western values. Increasingly he finds himself at one with the earth and particularly the sun, until the arrival of an English ship quickly shatters this newfound tranquility. Vendredi opts to return to England with the ship, but Robinson decides to stay on the island where the discovery of the ship's cabin boy who has deserted offsets his sorrow at the loss of Vendredi.

In the opening moments of *Vendredi, ou les limbes du Pacifique*, before the shipwreck, the ship's captain is reading Robinson's fate in the Tarot cards. He tells the young man that his sign is the *bateleur* (juggler, mountebank), and that signifies "qu'il y a en vous un organisateur. Il lutte contre un univers en désordre qu'il s'efforce de maîtriser avec des moyens de fortune" (there's in you an organizer. He struggles against a disordered universe which he tries to control by every means at hand).

This passage is crucial to the understanding of Robinson and the novel as a whole. Robinson is the first of Tournier's obsessive organizers of experience, a person whose fear of chaos is such that any structure, however farfetched, remains preferable to not being in control. Because of this mania Tournier's Robinson will order his island even more thoroughly than Defoe's did, but his every accomplishment entails certain dangers which the Tarot cards also indicate. The work of the *bateleur*, explains the ship's captain, "est illusion, son ordre est illusoire. Malheureusement il l'ignore. Le scepticisme n'est pas son fort" (is illusion, his order is illusory. Unfortunately he doesn't know that. Skepticism is not his forte). From the novel's beginning, doubts are raised concerning the degree to which Robinson's vast enterprise of organization conforms to reality. Throughout *Vendredi* he announces discoveries about the universe and his relation to it that appear to him immensely significant. For example Robinson rejects Western culture and espouses a Rousseauian return to nature; he determines that he has moved beyond normal forms of sexuality and has established a parasexual rapport with the sun, and finally he consecrates Vendredi as the ideal person upon whom he should model his life. It is the reader's task in this, as in all of Tournier's novels, to evaluate the main character's freshly minted certitudes.

The character Vendredi is seen almost entirely through Robinson's eyes. Only at the novel's end does the native boy do anything that suggests his own attitudes about the island paradise. Vendredi, one must recall, is no stranger, as is Robinson, to the tropics and an island existence. Whereas the Englishman has to adapt to a radically different way of living, Vendredi's life involves no great break with the past. He does what he does naturally, without any compulsion to examine or justify his conduct. Thus it is possible that Robinson's shock when the boy leaves with the sailors is really nothing other than the realization, however temporary, that the Vendredi he so admired was his own creation, a fiction fostered by a lonely man's need for coherence amid a frightening world.

The discovery of the cabin boy allows Robinson to avoid reflecting on such matters, and the novel ends with his being quite happy. Yet the second part of the novel's title, *les limbes du Pacifique* (The Limbo of the Pacific), furthers the suspicion that Robinson's great discoveries are fabrications. Limbo is a world between heaven and hell, reserved for children who have died without baptism. There they live in peace and harmony, freed of normal human pressures, and experience a form of existence akin to Nirvana. Robinson's island resembles limbo. It is a place set aside from life where ultimately it does not matter whether or not the structures created conform to reality.

Abel Tiffauges, the main character in *Le Roi des aulnes*, is, like Robinson, a systemizer, but the structures Abel creates have decidedly malevolent connotations. *Le Roi des aulnes* is the story of a gigantic, myopic Frenchman who is ill at ease in pre–World War II France. His one great passion, which he calls "la phorie," is the act of carrying a child on one's shoulders. Abel never sexually molests a child, but he is accused of doing just that. The outbreak of the war saves him from prison; placed in a military unit near the front, he is soon captured by the Germans and interned in a prisoner of war camp in Northern Prussia. Abel, ever in pursuit of *signes* which he believes reveal his great destiny, discovers that he loves Nazi Germany, "un pays noir et blanc" (a country of black and white), and without being completely conscious of the implications of his actions he begins to collaborate with the Nazis. Eventually he helps find boys for a *napola*, a school which turns children into SS officers. Toward the war's end a Jewish child makes Abel realize what he has been doing, and both die in an effort to escape the *napola*.

Le Roi des aulnes provoked a great deal of critical reaction, part of it quite hostile. A German critic, Jean Amery, lambasted the novel as an example of neo-Nazism (*Merkur*, 28 [1973]), and the historian Saul Friedländer, in his *Reflets du nazisme* (1982), classified it with other books and films which in his opinion glorify aspects of the Nazi experience.

The key to any understanding of *Le Roi des aulnes* is the interpretation one gives to Abel Tiffauges. Amery and Friedländer could cer-

tainly be correct if Abel were in any sense a spokesman for Tournier, or if what he did was in any sense presented in a positive light. However, neither of these possibilities is tenable.

Abel Tiffauges is a self-deluder. His muddled musings on his destiny reflect his uneasiness with the modern world and his own inability to cope in a straightforward fashion with his own difference. "La phorie" is neither good nor bad, but it is a form of emotional and sexual expression that does not fit into a heterosexual or homosexual category. Through the character of Tiffauges, Tournier develops a theme implied in *Vendredi, ou les limbes du Pacifique*, namely that Western society, by rigidly distinguishing between heterosexual and homosexual love, severely limits the ways in which human beings can express their emotions. Abel is himself a victim of this sexual stereotyping. He feels inferior and attempts to offset this sense of inadequacy by continuously proclaiming his superiority.

Tournier makes Abel's self-deception evident by showing how his main character constantly misreads all the *signes* he claims to uncover. Throughout the novel Abel compares himself to great figures from the past, such heroes as Christ, Saint Christopher, and Nestor, the Greek sage of the Trojan Wars. These analogies are frequently forced, but by insisting upon them Abel misses the most obvious analogy of all: Abel Tiffauges has remarkable similarities to Gilles de Retz. Gilles de Retz was a *compagnon* of Jeanne d'Arc. A distinguished soldier and patriot, he was a *maréchal de France* (field marshal) by the age of twenty-eight. However, his career and reputation were destroyed when, as a result of a tax audit, officials discovered that he had tortured and murdered thousands of children. The scene of these orgies was Gilles's favorite château, Tiffauges. Other analogies between Gilles and Abel appear in the course of the novel. Scholars have often identified Bluebeard, best known from the short story by Charles Perrault, with Gilles de Retz. Barbe-bleue is the horse Abel Tiffauges rides as he travels about northern Germany in search of children for the *napola*. Shortly before Gilles de Retz's arrest and execution, he was named a canon of a cathedral. Tournier parodies this event when he has Abel behaving like a bishop as he distributes an ointment to fight vitamin deficiency among his young charges. Gilles de Retz was able to survive as long as he did because of the chaotic situation that existed in war-torn Europe. In comparable fashion, Abel's story unfolds during World War II. As numerous as are the analogies between Gilles de Retz and Abel, the latter never sees any of them.

A complex series of parallels linking Abel Tiffauges, the Nazis, and the German poet and scientist Goethe serves as another indication of the main character's inability to assess properly the world about him. Throughout *Le Roi des aulnes* Abel's self-serving explanations and justifications of his conduct resemble the Third Reich's interpretation of history and its own grandiose role in it. Also, just as the Reich's alleged accomplishments are constantly contrasted with Goethe's real achievements in both art and science, Abel's own experiences are clarified by their relation to Goethe's literary works. The expression "le roi des aulnes" is the French translation of "Der Erlkönig" (The Elf King), the title of Goethe's famous ballad that Schubert subsequently set to music. In the novel German workers unearth the body of an ancient man, and a Nazi pathologist quickly dubs him "der Erlkönig," echoing a poem he considers to be "la quintessence de l'âme allemande." The doctor's association of the corpse with "the quintessence of the German soul" is somewhat startling since the ancient man was wearing a cap with a Star of David on it, but this irony is lost on the doctor and on Abel as well.

Abel Tiffauges's first job in Nazi Germany is working on an irrigation project. *Faust*, part two, the final portion of Goethe's best-known work, opens with Faust involved in a similar undertaking, but whereas Goethe's hero's positive transformation starts with this activity, Abel's enthusiasm for what he does leads him deeper into the moral and intellectual morass of the Third Reich. At the end of *Faust* the protagonist is blind, but saved, and angels bear him up to heaven. On the last page of *Le Roi des aulnes* the myopic Abel, having lost his glasses, literally cannot see, and slowly sinks into a swamp. His revelations, unlike Faust's, proved valueless since they were nothing more than the fantasies of a frightened and insecure man.

Abel's constant confusion of mystification and truth was similar to that of the Nazis. Like the masters he served, he was forever deluding himself. The demonstration of the intermingling of fiction and fact in an individual life constitutes one of the great achievements of *Le Roi des aulnes*.

While Amery's anger and Friedländer's suspicions are certainly understandable, they both fail to consider that Tournier is depicting a deeply confused person whose personality is at once a portrait and parody of the Nazi psyche. To follow Abel Tiffauges's confused odyssey is to be made aware of how the mingling of fantasy and reality can destroy not only an individual but a nation as well.

Les Météores is Tournier's most intricate novel. It features a variety of narrative perspectives, and an elaborate treatment of the themes of twinship and the need to create order out of chaos. The story begins in a Breton village, Pierres Sonnantes, where Edouard and Maria-Barbara Surin are raising their extensive family. Although they have many children, their most interesting offspring is a set of twins, Jean and Paul, whose resemblance is so perfect that they are commonly referred to as Jean-Paul. Edouard's younger brother is the ne'er-do-well Alexandre, an avowed homosexual with a visceral hatred for bourgeois, heterosexual society. He inherits one of the important family businesses, the direction of six major garbage dumps in France, and, to the general astonishment of the rest of the family, he proves extremely gifted in this line of work. While he is easily the most interesting character in the story, the lives of Jean and Paul form the novel's intellectual center. Paul considers his relationship to his brother to constitute a perfect cell of twinship; the brothers live and sleep together, and Paul is convinced that their "perfection" makes them superior to all other couples, be they heterosexual or homosexual. Jean does not share this viewpoint, and when he attempts to break away from his brother, this action precipitates a chase around the world which ends with an explosion in a tunnel linking East and West Berlin. At the novel's end Paul is alone at Pierres Sonnantes, terribly maimed, but certain that he has once again achieved union with his brother. His last word, and the word that ends the novel, is "Sublimation."

Paul is the novel's super-intellectual, a man who never doubts that the perfection and order he finds in his life conform perfectly to reality. His progress through the novel is from one certainty to another. Paul's obsession with order and his conviction that he partakes in a special destiny recalls two other benighted heroes of Tournier, Robinson Crusoe and Abel Tiffauges. All three are terrified of madness, and they attempt to control this fear by insisting upon their own uniqueness and superiority. Paul could be speaking for all three when he insists that: "Je me suis longtemps considéré comme un sur-homme. Je crois encore à une vocation hors du commun" (I have considered myself a superman for a long time. I think I have an uncommon vocation). Finally, the three of them remain convinced that they understand the nature of reality better than others. *Les Météores* destroys these sorts of delusions.

Unlike Paul, Alexandre Surin appreciates that all order is arbitrary, the creation of the human mind and nothing else. The "dandy of sewage" accepts and exploits this aspect of life by consciously championing the "artificial" over the "real," and by preferring, when the occasion presents itself, "l'idée . . . plus que la chose, et l'idée de l'idée plus que l'idée" (the idea over the thing, and the idea of the idea over the idea). Alexandre understands that society's standards are actually arbitrary laws and judgments that have been elevated to the level of objective truth, and he responds to this knowledge by concocting his own standards which reflect a purposeful deviation from anything that appears to the middle-class mind as "natural." Thus, when it comes to food he insists that he has "un faible pour le travesti alimentaire, les champignons, ce végétal déguisé en viande, la cervelle de mouton, cette viande déguisée en pulpe de fruit, l'avocat à la chair grasse comme beurre, et plus que tout j'affectionne le poisson, cette fausse chair qui n'est rien . . . sans la sauce" (a weakness for the alimentary transvestite. For mushrooms, those vegetables disguised as meat, for sheep's brains, that meat disguised as fruit pulp, for the avocado whose thick flesh resembles butter, and more than anything else I like fish whose false flesh is nothing . . . without the sauce).

Although Paul and Alexandre never talk to one another in *Les Météores*, their views are always contrasted. The sections devoted to Alexandre serve to deflate his nephew's vast intellectual pretentions by stressing that it is an act of the mind that invents the order of things that Paul takes at face value. Also, whereas Paul lives in an intellectual ivory tower and can easily hide his bizarre sexual relation with his brother and remain untouched by the political events of his lifetime, Alexandre lives very much in the world and his homosexuality provides the basis for a social critique which, while exaggerated in many respects, does condemn racial and sexual persecution. Alexandre is essentially a nihilist who creates weird situations which help him while away the time in a meaningless universe. Paul is a believer, not in God, but in some grandiose cosmic order

that places his brother and himself at the center. Alexandre dies when he wearies of the games he must play to amuse himself, when the experience of the *rire blanc* begins to become boring. Paul lives on, but only in a narrow, clearly demarcated world, one that is similar to Robinson's island, and where he can protect himself from any force or thought that threatens the fictions he has invented. At one point Paul claims that Robinson Crusoe lived in a dreamworld. Yet by the end of *Les Météores* Paul's situation is clearly worse. Alone and maimed at Pierres Sonnantes, his "sublimation" is a fancy word for despair.

Le Coq de bruyère is a collection of thirteen short stories and Tournier's one play, *Le Fétichiste: Un Acte pour un homme seul* (translated as *The Fetishist*). "Amandine ou les deux jardins" ("Amandine, or the Two Gardens") was originally written as a children's tale; "La Mère Noël" ("Mother Christmas") and "La Fugue de Petit Poucet" ("Tom Thumb Ran Away") are Christmas stories; and "Le Coq de bruyère" ("The Woodcock"), "L'Aire du muguet" ("The Lily of the Valley Rest Area"), and "Les Suaires de Véronique" have been adapted for French television. *Le Fétichiste* has been staged in Paris and Berlin. When asked why he entitled this volume *Le Coq de bruyère*, Tournier responded simply that the title story was the longest in the collection.

Le Coq de bruyère does not mark a new development in Tournier's work. The stories and the play included in the collection reflect themes he had already introduced in the three earlier novels. Obsession with order is a principal component in "La Famille Adam," "Les Suaires de Véronique," "La Fin de Robinson" ("The End of Robinson Crusoe"), "Le Nain rouge" ("The Red Dwarf"), and *Le Fétichiste*. The ambiguity of sexual identity figures in "La Mère Noël," "Amandine ou les deux jardins," "La Fugue du Petit Poucet," and "Tupic" ("Prikki"). The Cain and Abel motif is present in "La Famille Adam," ("The Adam Family"), "Le Nain rouge," and "Tristan Vox," while the role of fiction is the dominant concern in "Le Coq de bruyère," "Que ma joie demeure" ("Jesu, Joy of Man's Desiring"), and "La Jeune Fille et la mort" ("Death and the Maiden"). Together with the novel *Le Roi des aulnes*, these last two stories are the only works by Tournier with titles inspired by musical motifs. "Que ma joie demeure" refers to a cantata by J. S. Bach and "La Jeune Fille et la mort" is the title of a Schubert quartet. "L'Aire du muguet" is perhaps the most complex of the thirteen stories because it contains, in one form or another, all the themes treated in the collection.

The publication of *Gaspard, Melchior et Balthazar* (1980; translated as *The Four Wise Men*, 1982) led to a controversy over Tournier's religious beliefs. The author himself claimed that *Gaspard, Melchior et Balthazar* was his attempt to write a Christian novel and even went so far as to request an imprimatur from the bishop of Versailles. This novel certainly does mark a change of sorts in Tournier's preoccupations, but it is doubtful that the new direction leads to any form of religious orthodoxy. The novel retells the legend of the three wise men, and then adds a fourth. Gaspard, Melchior and Balthazar each set out (separately) on a quest for an answer to an important personal problem. Gaspard is black and ashamed of his skin color. Balthazar's love of art puts him at odds with the religious bigots who control his court, and Melchior is the victim of a palace revolt that has cost him his throne. They meet on the road and join together for a voyage which takes them to Bethlehem at the moment of Christ's birth. Here, each receives an answer to his problems. Gaspard sees that the infant in the manger is black; Balthazar's conscience is eased by the discovery that any depiction of the world is a tribute to the Creator; and Melchior decides to become an anchorite because he realizes that the kingdom he has really been seeking is not of this world.

The fourth king does not appear in the Gospels. Tournier says that he learned the story of the legendary fourth king, the one who came too late for Bethlehem, from the German writer Edzard Schaper. This king, Taor, is a pleasure-loving youth who sets out from his kingdom in search of a special candy (Turkish delight). His voyage lasts over thirty-three years, and transforms him from a fop to an ascetic. Taor never encounters Christ; having arrived too late for the Nativity, he manages to just miss the Last Supper, but nevertheless becomes the first person after the Apostles to taste the Eucharist.

All of Tournier's previous works treat characters terrified of complexity and in search of some means of ordering experience. *Gaspard, Melchior et Balthazar* constitutes a new stage of Tournier's thinking precisely because this novel celebrates complexity and rejects all arbitrary orderings of experience.

Gaspard, Melchior et Balthazar marks a development in Tournier's fiction. In the earlier novels his characters feared complexity and sought

elaborate, albeit simplistic ways of clarifying experience. This novel champions the complex and appreciates disorder as a part of life. The novel begins in a typical Tournier fashion with the main characters filled with confusion and even self-hatred. "Je suis noir, mais je suis roi" (I am black, but I am king) are Gaspard's initial words and the ones that open the novel. Melchior speaks in a similar vein: "Je suis roi, mais je suis pauvre" (I am a king, but I am poor), and Balthazar is tortured by the seeming contradiction between his love of physical beauty and his country's iconoclastic religious beliefs.

Tournier's earlier heroes might have opted for one pole of the contradiction over the other: blackness rather than kingship, power over poverty, or flesh instead of spirit. Such simplifications do not occur in *Gaspard, Melchior et Balthazar*, and in fact there are numerous parodies of what earlier had appeared to be insoluble dichotomies. There are, for example, references to "nomades sédentarisés" (sedentary nomads) and "voyageur sédentaire" (sedentary voyager), but here these expressions do little except suggest how life permits individuals to behave in different ways at different times. In a comparable fashion Gaspard pokes fun at any obsession with mythic prototypes when he makes the offhand remark that legends are valuable only when one cooperates with them. There is no such cooperation in this novel.

Bethlehem is the place where the three kings are freed of their anxieties. Each king comes to realize that his own instincts and ambitions are valuable, and that contradiction, far from being a fault, is the essence of divinity. This they discover in gazing at the child in the manger: "Cet Héritier du Royaume mêle des attributs incompatibles, la grandeur et la petitesse, la puissance et l'innocence, la plénitude et la pauvreté" (This Heir to the Kingdom mingles incomparable attributes, greatness and smallness, power and innocence, plenitude and poverty).

Tournier uses the three kings in *Gaspard, Melchior et Balthazar* to extend his discussion of the ordering of experience. The fourth king, Taor, serves a slightly different function. Taor set out on a quest for the silliest image of perfection, a piece of candy, and ends his journey and his life by receiving the Eucharist. In the context of this novel, the Eucharist is not just one more symbol of illusions people pursue; it is in fact the body and blood of Christ. This is the first and to date final time in Tournier's writing that the goal a character seeks has an "objective" validity. Taor's story appears to suggest that for Tournier there may exist, amid a universe of false orderings, some true, overriding structure that has the potential to give meaning to life. This is not to say, however, that this structure is embedded in any orthodox form of Christian belief. It is not, after all, Christ that Taor ultimately encounters, but a symbol of Godhead, the Eucharist, something that is at once bread and wine *and* the body and blood of Christ. The Eucharist is comprised of banal items of daily life, transformed into something holy, but without ever losing their quotidian character. As such it represents the potential of everything in the world to become sacred. This quasi-pantheistic notion seems most consistent with Tournier's constant championing of the concrete over the abstract, life over death. Christ on the Cross has no place in this novel; rather it is the message of the Eucharist, the glorification of the things of the world that Tournier highlights and with which he ends the book. To the extent that *Gaspard, Melchior et Balthazar* contains a religious message, it is a radical one that will perhaps evoke little enthusiasm from orthodox Christians of any stripe. For Tournier the good news of the Gospel was not intended to alter people's concept of heaven, but to enhance their love for the earth.

Gilles et Jeanne (1983) is a *récit* (literally a "narration," but in this instance a short novel). Originally conceived as a screenplay, the story of Gilles de Retz and his relationship to Jeanne d'Arc was transformed into a work of prose fiction. Tournier suggests that Gilles's perversion was the result of his disillusionment with French and English society's callous treatment of the Maid of Orleans. At the center of *Gilles et Jeanne* is the Cain and Abel motif, with the two protagonists as opposite sides of the same personality. Tournier stresses the ambiguity of the human personality by showing that both Gilles and Jeanne, ostensibly the Cain and Abel figures, have the potential to be the other. Their lives are paralleled and contrasted throughout the novella, with the final words of each, "Jésus, Jésus, Jésus, Jésus" (Jeanne) and "Jeanne, Jeanne, Jeanne" (Gilles), representing the ultimate choice of each character. Jeanne d'Arc opts for the spiritual whereas Gilles cannot free himself from enslavement to the physical. In this *récit* Tournier demonstrates his ability, as he did in *Le Roi des aulnes*, to do extensive historical research and provides a brilliant re-

creation of the violent era in which the gruesome events he narrates occurred.

Tournier's 1985 novel, *La Goutte d'or*, tells of a North African boy, Idriss, who leaves his homeland for France, where he hopes to find both employment and a photo of himself, taken by a blond Frenchwoman while she was traveling through the desert. "La goutte d'or" (the golden droplet) is the name of the amulet he carries to France and the slang expression for the eighteenth *arrondissement* in Paris, a section largely inhabited by immigrant workers. In Paris he meets a bizarre series of characters, notably Achille Mage, a famous director of commercials for French television. Eventually he discovers the art of Arab calligraphy and comes to appreciate the difference between the written word and the photographic image. The novel ends with Idriss attempting to drive a pneumatic drill through a store window in an effort to retrieve what he mistakes to be his lost *goutte d'or*.

Just as *Gaspard, Melchior et Balthazar*, with its suggestion of a true ordering force in the universe, appeared to mark a new direction for Tournier, *La Goutte d'or* introduces a new dimension in Tournier's work. The irony is, however, that this new direction seems to deny any claims to an objectively verifiable ordering force. Unlike Tournier's previous heroes, Idriss is not bent upon imposing his vision of himself and his world upon others. His is a work of negation; as best he can he refuses the myriad and at times contradictory images that others foist on him. The novel describes a world in which traditional distinctions between reality and illusion, truth and fiction no longer hold. Idriss's universe is one of competing fictions, where one illusion yields to another, and where the only reference point is ultimately the written word, whose function is not to separate truth from falsehood, but to chart the intersecting layers of possible meaning. On first reading, *La Goutte d'or* would seem to be a structuralist's dream since polarities abound: black versus white (skin colors), north versus south (Europe versus Africa), shifting versus stable (the desert versus the city), and so forth, but the author is only toying with his readers. *La Goutte d'or* constitutes Tournier's entrance into the world of deconstruction.

"Le Sahara, dit Idriss, j'ai appris ça en France. Chez nous y a pas de mot ça" (The Sahara, says Idriss, I learned that in France. Where I come from there is no word for that). This sentence encapsulates the pattern of creating reality out of illusions that repeats itself throughout the novel. The Sahara desert, a subject of study and romanticization among the French and for many other Westerners as well, is a concept unknown to its inhabitants. The Sahara is as much an intellectual structure as a geographical location for those who live far from it, and the meaning of the concept is made more precise through ignorance of its actual physical nature. For Idriss the Sahara is not a single place, but a constantly shifting series of designs in the sand, a world alien to permanence of any sort. The Sahara is a fixed entity only when its ambiguous, transitory qualities are denied by an act tantamount to fictionalization. Coherence and clarity emerge from this process, but at the expense of accuracy. Idriss's amazement at the European notion of the desert is enhanced when in Paris he sees photographs of Africa. In no way do they correspond to the land he knows.

In *La Goutte d'or* the greatness of Western culture is shown to reside in its ability to create stable images, and then declare these images reality. Paris is for Idriss "cette mer d'images" (this sea of images), whose principal creator/manipulator is Achille Mage. Whatever his personal failings, Mage is, by his society's standards, a genius, an individual who understands his world perfectly and who knows how to market his insight for great personal gain. When he declares that "Ce qui est certain, c'est que la pub, c'est le sommet du cinéma. A tous points de vue: technique, artistique, psychologique" (What's certain is that commercials are the high point of movies. From every viewpoint: technical, artistic, psychological), he is praising commercials as the purest form of illusion, since they do not even attempt to conform to reality. A film may try to suggest that the story is true, and that the events depicted could possibly occur in the lives of the audience. This is not the case with commercials, at least the ones that Mage creates: his evoke paradises and desires, both of which are entirely artificial, and for that reason are the most highly sought.

The notion of the Sahara made no sense to Idriss since it failed to conform to anything he would consider reality. Yet the Arab view of the world appears equally suspect and contrived to the Westerner. At the beginning and near the end of the novel there are stories that illustrate that point. In each case the Arab attitude toward hair color and sexual activity makes no sense to the Occidental mind.

East meets West under the aegis of illusion when Idriss consents to serve as a model for a clothing store which caters to the residents of "La Goutte d'or." By means of an elaborate process technicians make a mold of the boy's body. From this mold they will be able to reproduce unlimited numbers of mannequins that look like Idriss. The owner of the store, an Italian, decided that Idriss looked typically North African. He assumes that North Africans will accept eagerly images of themselves created by an Italian who lives in France. Nothing in the novel contradicts this judgment.

In *La Goutte d'or* the photographic image, associated with the West, is a tyrant that severely limits the freedom of its subjects. The image is dazzling and compelling; it provides a vision that appears more real than truth. Yet the image is always singular; it provides one powerful version of whatever it depicts. In contrast, writing can offer many versions, many levels of experience. When Idriss studies with an Arab calligrapher he learns to appreciate that words can assert some control over the often contradictory nature of events, if only by expressing each contradiction without any attempt at reconciliation.

Tournier suggests in this novel that the photographic image and the written word are the two principal formulators of experience in the modern world. The image dominates through television, films, photographs, and even cultural assumptions, but the image's power stems from its ability to simplify. The written word slows this process by reflecting the ambiguity and complexity that lie beneath the surface of the picture.

Although the written word may theoretically be able to lead to some modest control of experience, the image is the predominant force in contemporary society. The calligraphy teacher calls it "l'opium de l'Ouest" (opium of the West), but it continues to claim its victims from all cultures. Idriss becomes yet another victim of the image when he tries to drive his drill through the window in order to get what he takes to be his lost *goutte d'or*. The boy's gesture demonstrates, more than any argument can, that the immediacy of the image is infinitely more powerful than the reflection demanded by the written word.

Tournier has published no novels since the appearance of *La Goutte d'or*, but that is not to say he has been inactive. He is currently at work on a novel which deals with East German female athletes, a subject he has described as "dur" (tough). In addition he writes occasional pieces for newspapers and magazines, as well as introductions to books which, for one reason or another, interest him. His most recent substantial publication is *Le Tabor et le Sinaï* (1988), a collection of his art criticism. While these essays frequently deal with young painters and photographers who are not very well known, the book provides some valuable insights into Tournier's own concerns and hence is quite useful both to the literary critic and the student of the fine arts.

Tournier's appeal stems in part from the accessibility of his writings, but other reasons are important as well. What suffuses his fiction is a quality that might best be described as a smiling pessimism, an attitude toward life that strikes a common chord with many modern readers. Tournier's work displays few illusions about human goodness, and even less confidence in the collective progress of mankind. His books do, however, reflect a continuous amazement before the wonder of life, before the incredible privilege of being alive. There is nothing soft about this stance, and his novels provide numerous examples of the ways people destroy the gift of their own existence; yet despite these failures which his fiction documents, by dint of his art, Michel Tournier manages to convey to his readers that the pleasure they experience in his texts is a reflection of the joy inherent in life itself.

Interviews:

Penny Hueston, "An Interview with Michel Tournier," *Meanjin*, 38 (May 1978): 401-408;

Jacques Chancel, "Michel Tournier: Le Secret d'un livre est la patience," *Figaro-Dimanche*, 9 December 1979, p. 29;

J. M. de Montrémy, "Michel Tournier: 'Je me suis toujours voulu écrivain croyant,' " *Croix*, 10 November 1980, p. 8;

Roger d'Ivernois, "Michel Tournier: 'J'ai pris la plume et j'ai inventé la vérité,' " *Journal de Genève*, 9 January 1981, p. 13;

Jean-Jacques Brochier, "Qu'est-ce que c'est que la littérature? Un Entretien avec Michel Tournier," *Magazine Littéraire*, no. 179 (1982): 80-86.

References:

David Bevans, *Michel Tournier* (Amsterdam: Rodopi, 1986);

Daniel Bougnoux, "Des Métaphores à la phorie," *Critique*, 28 (June 1972): 527-543;

Arlette Bouloumié, *Michel Tournier: Le Roman mythologique* (Paris: José Corti, 1988);

André Clavel, "Un Nouveau Cynique: Tournier le jardinier," *Critique*, 33 (June-July 1977): 609-615;

William Cloonan, *Michel Tournier* (Boston: Twayne, 1985);

Cloonan, "The Spiritual Order of Michel Tournier," *Renascence*, 36 (Autumn-Winter 1983-1984): 77-87;

Cloonan, "World War II in Three Contemporary Novels," *South Atlantic Review*, 51 (May 1986): 65-75;

Colin Davis, *Michel Tournier: Philosophy and Fiction* (Oxford: Clarendon Press, 1988);

Gilles Deleuze, "Michel Tournier et le monde sans autrui," postface to Tournier's *Vendredi, ou les limbes du Pacifique* (Paris: Folio, 1969), pp. 255-281;

Marc Fumaroli, "Michel Tournier et l'esprit d'enfance," *Commentaire*, 3, no. 12 (1980): 638-643;

Salim Jay, *Idriss, Michel Tournier et les autres* (Paris: Editions de la Différence, 1986);

Phyllis Johnson and Brigitte Cazelles, "L'Orientation d'Abel Tiffauges dans *Le Roi des aulnes* de Tournier," *Rocky Mountain Review*, 29, no. 2 (1979): 166-171;

Serge Koster, *Tournier* (Paris: Henri Veyrier, 1986);

Françoise Merlillié, *Michel Tournier* (Paris: Belfond, 1988);

Susan Petit, "The Bible as Inspiration in Tournier's *Vendredi, ou les limbes du Pacifique*," *French Forum*, 9 (September 1984): 343-354;

Petit, "Fugal Structure, Nestorianism, and St. Christopher in Michel Tournier's *Le Roi des aulnes*," *Novel*, 19 (Spring 1986): 233-245;

Petit, "*Gilles et Jeanne*: Michel Tournier's *Le Roi des aulnes* Revisited," *Romanic Review*, 76 (May 1985): 308-315;

Petit, "Joachim de Fiore, the Holy Spirit, and Michel Tournier's *Les Météores*," *Modern Language Studies*, 16 (Summer 1986): 88-100;

Petit, "Salvation, the Flesh, and God in Michel Tournier's *Gaspard, Melchior et Balthazar*," *Orbis Litterarum*, 41, no. 1 (1986): 53-65;

Anthony Purdy, "*Les Météores* de Michel Tournier: Une Perspective hétérologique," *Littérature*, 40 (1980): 32-43;

Lynn Salkin Sbiroli, *Michel Tournier: La Séduction du jeu* (Geneva: Slatkine, 1987);

Roger Shattuck, "Locating Michel Tournier," in his *The Innocent Eye* (New York: Farrar, Straus & Giroux, 1984), pp. 205-218;

Sud, special issue on Tournier (Spring 1980); *Sud*, special issue on Tournier (Winter 1985-1986).

Roger Vailland

(16 October 1907-12 May 1965)

J. E. Flower
University of Exeter

BOOKS: *Drôle de jeu* (Paris: Corrêa, 1945); translated by Gerard Hopkins as *Playing with Fire* (London: Chatto & Windus, 1948); republished as *Playing for Keeps* (Boston: Houghton Mifflin, 1948);

Quelques Réflexions sur la singularité d'être français (Paris: Haumont, 1946);

Esquisse pour un portrait du vrai libertin, suivi de Entretiens de Madame Merville avec Lucrèce, Octave et Zéphyr (Paris: Haumont, 1946);

Un Homme du peuple sous la Révolution, by Vailland and Raymond Manevy (Paris: Corrêa, 1947);

Héloïse et Abélard (Paris: Corrêa, 1947);

Le Surréalisme contre la Révolution (Paris: Editions Sociales, 1948);

Les Mauvais Coups (Paris: Sagittaire, 1948); translated by Peter Wiles as *Turn of the Wheel* (London: Cape, 1962; New York: Knopf, 1962);

Bon Pied, Bon Œil (Paris: Corrêa, 1950);

Le Colonel Foster plaidera coupable (Paris: Editeurs Français Réunis, 1951);

Boroboudour: Voyage à Bali, Java et autres îles (Paris: Corrêa, 1951);

Un Jeune Homme seul (Paris: Corrêa, 1951);

Choses vues en Egypte (Paris: Editions Défense de la Paix, 1952);

Expérience du drame (Paris: Corrêa, 1953);

Beau Masque (Paris: Gallimard, 1954);

325.000 Francs (Paris: Corrêa, 1955);

Eloge du cardinal de Bernis (Paris: Fasquelle, 1956);

La Loi (Paris: Gallimard, 1957); translated by Wiles as *The Law* (London: Cape, 1958; New York: Knopf, 1958);

Monsieur Jean (Paris: Gallimard, 1959);

La Fête (Paris: Gallimard, 1960); translated by Wiles as *The Sovereigns* (London: Cape,

Roger Vailland (photograph copyright © Jerry Bauer)

1960); republished as *Fête* (New York: Knopf, 1961);

Les Liaisons dangereuses 1960: Un Film de Roger Vadim, by Vailland, Vadim, and Claude Brulé (Paris: Julliard, 1960); translated by Bernard Shir-Cliff as *Roger Vadim's "Les Liaisons dangereuses"* (New York: Ballantine, 1962);

Le Regard froid: Réflexions, esquisses, libelles, 1945-1962 (Paris: Grasset, 1963);

La Truite (Paris: Gallimard, 1964); translated by Wiles as *A Young Trout* (London: Collins, 1965); republished as *The Trout* (New York: Dutton, 1965);

Ecrits intimes (Paris: Gallimard, 1968);

Le Saint Empire (Paris: Editions de la Différence, 1978);

Chroniques des années folles à la Libération, 1928-1945 (Paris: Editions Messidor, 1984);

Chronique d'Hiroshima à Goldfinger, 1945-1965 (Paris: Editions Messidor, 1984);

La Visirova ou des Folies-Bergères jusqu'au trône (Paris: Editions Messidor, 1986).

Collection: *Œuvres complètes*, 12 volumes (Lausanne: Rencontre, 1967-1968).

MOTION PICTURE: *Les Liaisons dangereuses 1960*, screenplay by Vailland, Roger Vadim, and Claude Brulé, dialogue by Vailland, 1959.

OTHER: "Un phénomène de classe qui sert la reaction," in *Pour ou contre l'existentialisme* (Paris: Editions de l'Atlas, 1948), pp. 157-179;

Laclos par lui-même, edited, with commentary, by Vailland (Paris: Seuil, 1953).

In the spring of 1956 Roger Vailland returned to France from Moscow, where he had heard Nikita Khrushchev denounce the corruption of Stalin's regime. At once he replaced the portrait of the former Soviet leader which hung above his desk with a photograph of a flute player on the statue of Venus's throne in Rome's Thermal Museum. Such an action, trivial in itself, may nonetheless be seen as symbolic of a man whose interests were considered by many to oscillate irregularly between politics and the erotic. The fact that Vailland is difficult to define has contributed to his not being accorded a major role in the developments of French literature in the twentieth century. Yet as novelist, essayist, and, to a lesser extent, playwright and journalist, his stature is by no means negligible. His discussions and portraits of the libertine figure, his involvement with the Resistance and with the Communist party, his interest in the plastic arts, and his sure touch in most of his writing as an observer and recorder of human nature give to much of his work both complexity and vitality. In 1957 he won the Prix Goncourt for his seventh novel, *La Loi* (The Law). This, together with several other of his novels, has been widely translated. (The English translation appeared in 1958.)

Vailland was born in Acy-en-Multien (Oise) on 16 October 1907, the son of George François Vailland, a surveyor, and Geneviève Morel Vailland. Five years later his sister Geneviève was born. During his early years Vailland appears to have been surrounded and pampered by women–his mother, two grandmothers, and a maid. The general temper of his life seems to have been unostentatious but comfortable, protected, and middle class. The years of World War I were disruptive. Although officially unfit, his father volunteered for active service, during which he denounced Freemasonry for Catholicism. The rest of the family moved frequently. In 1918 they all settled for one year in Paris before moving to Rheims, where they would stay for seven years. With some contraction of time and consequent distortion, Vailland evokes this teenage period of his life in his most autobiographical novel, *Un Jeune Homme seul* (A Young Man Alone, 1951).

During these years in Rheims Vailland wrote his first poems; one, "En vélo" (Cycling), was published in a local review, the *Pampre*, in April 1923. He also met Roger Gilbert-Lecomte, Roger Meyrat, and René Daumal, and together they formed a group known as the Phrères Simplistes (Simple Brothers). Their ambitions were to express rebellion against what they saw as the mediocrity of society around them: Rheims was dull–"Reims la plate," as they called it. They indulged in mild drug abuse, referred to one another as spirits ("Anges"), and worshipped a god called Bubu. In this association lay the origins of the much more significant fringe surrealist group Le Grand Jeu (The Great Game), which published a review of the same name.

In August 1925 the Vailland family moved back to Paris but only until July of the following year, when Vailland's father bought a practice in Antibes. Vailland remained as a boarder at the Lycée Louis-le-Grand, where, if his contemporaries Robert Brasillach (*Notre avant-guerre*, 1941) and Paul Guth (*Quarante contre un*, 1947) are to be believed, he became increasingly extravagant in his behavior. His letters home (*Lettres à sa famille*, 1972) provide an interesting self-commentary during the next few years. To his mother he wrote affectionately, to his sister rather pompously, and to his father with regret at no longer having the opportunity for intellectual discussions. Demands for money were not infrequent. He continued his studies at the Sorbonne but was being increasingly tempted toward some kind of literary activity.

Le Grand Jeu ran to three published issues only, and Vailland's contributions were minimal. However, the group's impact was enough for André Breton to challenge it. He did so by publicly accusing Vailland, who had by now begun to write articles for *Paris-Midi* (including one apparently in favor of Jean Chiappe, the prefect of police), of double standards and of having no political integrity. Ironically, Vailland had already effectively broken with his Grand Jeu colleagues, but the accusations were no less hurtful.

Throughout the rest of the 1930s his life became increasingly fragmented. There are several hints in his letters of work on poems, short stories, and novels, one of which, *La Visirova ou des Folies-Bergères jusqu'au trône* (Visirova or from the Folies-Bergères right up to the Throne), was serialized in *Paris-Soir* (19 July-17 August 1933). (It was published as a book only in 1986.) Based on fact, it recounts the story of a young Russian dancer with whom the king of Albania (Thrasubie in the novel) falls in love. He persuades her to return to his country, but political developments and the return of his former mistress force him to send her back to Paris. She remains aloof, symbolically chaste, and alluring, and the story is told by her to the first-person narrator (evidently Vailland), with whom she has a chance meeting. The book was obviously written for serialization: it is loosely constructed, sentimental, and generally unconvincing in spite of some parallels to be made between Vailland's own life and Visirova's.

During this period Vailland also turned increasingly to drugs, and, unbeknownst to his parents, in May 1936 he married a nightclub singer, Andrée Blavette (Boule), whom he had met two years before. However, together with a journalist colleague, Raymond Manevy, he completed another documentary novel, *Un Homme du peuple sous la Révolution* (A Plebeian under the Revolution, 1947). As its title suggests, the political content of this story set in the 1790s is more marked than in the previous work, a reflection perhaps of a momentary enthusiasm for Léon Blum's Popular Front.

In general, Vailland's interest in politics and in the threat of fascism appears to have been low. Drugs and Blavette–"elle me consume. . . . Elle exige toute ma vie" (she devours me. . . . She

demands my entire life)–were overpoweringly strong. In 1938 he underwent his first detoxification, but at the outbreak of World War II the following year he was declared still unfit for military service. He became legal correspondent for *Paris-Soir* and after a visit to Bucharest for the paper was registered in the army reserves. Demobilized soon after the armistice with Germany, he rejoined the *Paris-Soir* team in the Southern Zone and worked with it until November 1942. His attitude to the Occupation and Resistance at this time is expressed in reference to Duc in the novel *La Fête* (1960; translated in the U.K. as *The Sovereigns*, 1960, and as *Fête* in the U.S., 1961): "Les voisins parlaient des premiers maquis, il écoutait chez eux les émissions en français de la BBC. Cela ne le concernait pas" (The neighbors would talk about the first underground movements and he would listen to the French language broadcasts of the BBC. Nothing of all that was of any concern to him).

Such an attitude was no different from the one expressed by thousands of French people for whom the full horror of the Nazi presence was not yet apparent and who could see no further than their own personal situations. In his diary in June 1942 Vailland wrote: "Tout mon bonheur, tout mon malheur, dépendent de moi et, me semble-t-il, ne dépendent que de moi; je n'ai rien à défendre que moi-même" (All my happiness and all my unhappiness are my affair, and only my affair; I have only myself to think about). Gradually, however, he came to realize how he and his compatriots had been deceived. By the end of 1942, after the invasion of the Southern Zone by the Germans, he found himself being drawn to the Resistance. Precisely how and when Vailland became involved is unclear, but by the middle of 1943 he was serving as a messenger for two networks. This was a major break with the kind of self-indulgent, precarious life he had been leading hitherto. Equally important were his successful (if only temporary) withdrawal from drugs and the death of his father ("un dur adversaire": a tough opponent) in August 1943. In the following year Vailland became cut off from his network and wrote *Drôle de jeu* (1945; translated as *Playing with Fire* [U.K.] and *Playing for Keeps* [U.S.], 1948), his first major novel and one of the best to emerge from this brief but turbulent period in French history. In 1945 it was awarded the Prix Interallié.

Vailland always claimed that *Drôle de jeu* was not simply a documentary account of the Resistance, even though there is much to recommend it in this respect. He establishes a general context but also explores the tensions and ambivalent feelings–cynicism, profiteering, corruption, betrayal, integrity, courage, ruthlessness, and so on–experienced by a representative group. He focuses in particular upon his principal character, Marat ("un promeneur solitaire," or solitary wanderer), a thinly disguised self-portrait who is finally projected as an "ideal" figure. Such concentration on his main protagonist is supported by the novel's theatrical qualities–another hallmark of all Vailland's subsequent fiction. Apart from brief and usually introductory descriptions, dialogue dominates much of the text, and the work is divided into five days ("journées") which, despite their internal division into conventional chapters, are like the acts of a play.

After Vailland's death one critic, reflecting on this period in his life, suggested that for all his apparent commitment, the Resistance had been above all else an "aventure personnelle" (personal adventure) for him. Certainly the filtering of the experience through Marat would justify this view. Marat's Resistance pseudonym is Lamballe (after the eighteenth-century libertine François Lamballe), and at the close of the novel he is furnished with new papers and hence a new identity. In personal terms, too, Vailland appears to have been searching for a new role and purpose in life for which the exorcism of his past was necessary. This purpose, he began to sense, was in communism. He applied to join the French Communist party in 1942 or early 1943 but received no response and became a member only in 1952. Certainly there was little evidence of real political activity, but more significantly his life-style hardly indicated a capacity for self-discipline.

After the war Vailland resumed his career as a journalist, working principally for *Libération* and *Action*. He also wrote several essays in which he returned obsessively to the problems of independent action and responsibility but in which he accused Catholicism, surrealism, and even existentialism of having failed to provide answers by becoming in turn merely forms of escapism for those who subscribed to them. From *Quelques Réflexions sur la singularité d'être français* (A Few Reflections on the Singularity of Being French, 1946) emerges his own preference for a key figure in his work, the "amateur" or "homme de qualité" or sovereign, of whom the Marquis de Sade was an ideal example: "L'amateur . . . ne

fait pas de profession. Il n'est pas contraint par la nécessité. . . . L'amateur n'est pas la victime, l'objet d'une passion, il n'est pas *agi*, il sait en toute occasion rester le sujet qui *agit*" (The amateur subscribes to no beliefs; he is not subject to the rules of necessity. He is neither the victim nor the object of any passion, nor is he passive. He always knows how to be the one in control). Such self-indulgent individualism was hardly likely to appeal to the Communist party, nor did his return to a life of drug addiction and alcoholism help his cause. Once again he attempted to recover, however, and he underwent another detoxification in 1947. This year also marked the beginning of his permanent separation from Blavette.

As Vailland's imaginative writing would reveal, his difficulty in freeing himself from the effects of his past was considerable. In his next novel, *Les Mauvais Coups* (1948; translated as *Turn of the Wheel*, 1962), he depicts the love-hate relationship between a couple, Milan and Roberte, complicated by the presence of a young, pure, and idealized girl, Hélène. Roberte is possessive and domineering and is based both on Blavette and Vailland's mother. She also represents Vailland's fear of losing his capacity to act (*agir*) independently. The novel contains a good deal of heavy sexual symbolism, and the whole pattern of conflicting emotions is supported by regular reference to the seasons and the natural world. At the end of the novel Roberte commits suicide but Milan is incapable of admitting her death publicly. As one critic has observed, whereas Marat is a projected ideal figure moving freely from one adventure and identity to another, Milan is a real one, trapped by circumstances and by his own inhibitions. By the end of 1948 Vailland's diaries indicate growing despair as the difficulty of resolving the tension between private life and the observed demands of political–and especially Communist–commitment became more acute. With *Bon Pied, Bon Œil* (Good Foot, Good Eye, begun in 1949 and published in 1950), he hoped, however, finally to have escaped from the constraints of what he termed bourgeois culture and to have begun to make a positive political and personal statement of his own.

In that its principal characters are Marat and Rodrigue the novel is, in a loose sense, a sequel to *Drôle de jeu*. Marat, however, has been reduced to breeding bulls and to indulging in doubtful financial transactions; above all he has chosen to be marginal ("en marge") and is tired ("fatigué"). Rodrigue, who had been uncertain and impetuous in the earlier novel, is now a political activist. (His name too evokes the qualities associated with the heroes of Corneille, a writer whom Vailland much admired.) He is imprisoned for stealing documents and while incarcerated is introduced to the history of the Convention of the revolutionary period and of Saint-Just, and he is defended by a young woman lawyer, of working-class origins, with whom he falls in love. He also comes under the influence of a fellow Communist, Albéran: "le combattant communiste, le bolchevik, un type d'homme absolument nouveau" (the Communist fighter, the Bolshevik, a totally new kind of person). But Albéran never actually appears in the novel; he remains an unseen ideal. When he leaves prison Rodrigue appears to have become converted intellectually and to have rejected "bourgeois culture," but there is no evidence of his having achieved anything. Marat remains isolated, sharing his life with Rodrigue's former wife Antoinette; Rodrigue is ready to embark on an active political life. In his diary Vailland wrote: "Je suis (ou je tends à être) un bolchevik" (I am [or I'm moving toward becoming] a Bolshevik). The process was still not complete, and his next novel, *Un Jeune Homme seul*, would take it one stage further.

In 1949 Vailland had met Elisabeth Naldi, whom he eventually married in 1954, after his divorce from Blavette, and with whom he was to share the rest of his life. Her greater political commitment and sense of purpose appear to have given Vailland increased stability, and from the early 1950s he embarked on the most politically active phase of his career. He continued to write articles for *Action* and the *Tribune des Nations*, essays, a pamphlet on the Vatican, and a play about the Korean War, *Le Colonel Foster plaidera coupable* (Colonel Foster Will Plead Guilty, 1951), an open attack on Western imperialist intervention. The play secured his entry to the Communist party, though as a work of literature it has little to recommend it.

In 1951 *Un Jeune Homme seul* was published. It is in two parts. The first, largely autobiographical, deals with the adolescence of Eugène-Marie Favart in Rheims; the second, in which the action takes place twenty years later, during the Resistance, is a projection in moral and political terms of these influences. Favart moves from isolation and indifference to action, finally helping a Resistance worker to escape from the police but being himself arrested. The novel's direction is clear;

yet Vailland avoids a simplistic political message. He explores a variety of social and moral issues as well, and while the Bolshevik figure (Madru) does reappear—and this time in action—it is the evolution of Favart within a wider context that is significant.

During the next four years Vailland was fully committed to the Communist party, involving himself in demonstrations and political meetings. The two novels from this period, *Beau Masque* (Handsome Mask, 1954) and *325.000 Francs* (1955), are both intentionally much more didactic and militant than any before or after. Both deal with specific industrial problems which impinge directly upon the lives of individuals. In *Beau Masque*—received by the Communist press as an unqualified success—the action involves the takeover of a silk-manufacturing industry in Le Clusot by an American consortium. This event brings the threat of redundancies, which is resisted in particular by the workers' leader, a young Communist divorcée, Pierrette Amable. The situation is further complicated by her relationship with Beau Masque, an Italian immigrant worker, and by the fact that the heir to the business consortium falls in love with her. Vailland explores her dilemma as she is torn between her public role and private wishes. He also analyzes with some skill the controlling family, rent internally by dissension, jealousy, rivalry, and irresponsibility, and presents too a range of differing shades of political response to the situation. As in *Drôle de jeu*, the influence of the theater is strong in *Beau Masque*. Vailland employs a five-part structure, much dialogue, and an attempted unity of place and time. He also develops his own role as narrator/observer—a technique to reappear in *325.000 Francs* and *La Truite* (1964; translated as *A Young Trout* [U.K.] and as *The Trout* [U.S.], 1965). By the close the workers announce victory, but it is achieved at a price. Beau Masque is killed and Pierrette's life is shattered for a second time. In an epilogue the narrator returns, a year later, to Le Clusot to report progress and express his own faith in the workers' revolution. But such a view is superimposed authorially: it does not emerge unequivocally from the text. Furthermore, the personal cost of political achievement and the need for the exemplary political hero to remain independent are problems that are not resolved. They do, of course, create tension, but they also point to Vailland's own lingering admiration for the amateur for whom discipline, of any sort, is naturally anathema.

The problems are no further resolved in *325.000 Francs*. In this novel the protagonist, Bernard Busard, attempts to realize his ambitions to marry Marie-Jeanne Lemercier and leave his native town of Bionnas. Busard sees the opportunity to buy a snack bar on the N7 highway and sets about raising the money by manning full-time one of the machines in the local plastics factory. He shares shifts with Le Bressan and earns his money but has his hand smashed during the last shift. No longer acceptable as the snack-bar manager, he becomes the owner of the local café, but after a rapid decline in trade he has to consider returning to the factory, where he will receive a wage increased by only a derisively small amount as the result of workers' action after his accident.

The confrontation between capitalism and work force is much less complex in this novel than in *Beau Masque*, but no more optimistic. At best, it is a novel which is militant negatively, by exposure. Three additional elements in the novel are noteworthy, of which the first is Busard's prowess as a cyclist. In chapter 1 (a kind of prologue) he is leading a local but prestigious cycle race only to fall short of the line: his failure anticipates the later one. The winner is Le Bressan, and Vailland makes much of their contrasting characters. Second is the relationship between Busard and Marie-Jeanne, which is based on a pattern of courtly love and underlines Busard's subservience. Third is the novel's structure, again dramatic but with several closely worked anticipations and echoes drawing all elements together. For example, before Busard enters the factory for the last time a cyclist passes him, skids, and falls.

In 1963 Vailland wrote in his diary that *325.000 Francs* was "le meilleur de mes romans, vrai rêve, rêve vrai, une vraie histoire qui peut être interprétée totalement par Freud, par Marx, et encore par bien d'autres, elle a toutes les faces possibles de la réalité" (my best novel, a true and exact dream, a genuine story which can be interpreted completely by reference to Freud, Marx, and many other systems. It has all the dimensions of reality possible). Herein lay the problem. His imaginative writing indicated that Vailland was still privately—or subconsciously—beset by doubt and contradictions that did not always manifest themselves in his public life. In particular, either as an exemplary working-class hero, or as a true "amateur," Busard is a failure. Yet the Left seemed convinced by the novel's power; it was seri-

alized in the Communist paper *Humanité* (December 1956 and January 1957) and was generally well received. Within six months, however, came the shock of de-Stalinization; Vailland was physically ill for two days and his whole attitude to life shaken. The Bolshevik ideal, largely modeled on Stalin, had gone and would have to be replaced by a new man "qui ne devine pas lui-même ses traits et qui ne ressemblera à rien de ce qui a encore existé" (who cannot guess himself what he looks like and who won't resemble anything that has gone before). Vailland was drained physically and mentally, and though officially he was not to leave the Communist party for another three years, he effectively broke with it from 1956 and became increasingly critical of its conservatism and lack of imagination.

In July he and Elisabeth went to Gargano in Italy. He continued to nurture an ambition to write a political novel in which there would be an outstanding and exemplary hero, but instead he embarked on *La Loi*, the novel for which, because of the Prix Goncourt, he would become best known. Set in southern Italy, it uses the game of *la legge* (the law), which provides participants with an opportunity to taunt and deride one another, as a centralizing image. Vailland explores a variety of relationships in the village of Manacore, which is ruled over by the patriarchal figure Don Cesare. His "law" prevails; he represents as well an older generation and remains aloof, finally dying stoically, indifferent to a world of new and shallow values.

Quite rightly most critics have read this aspect of the novel as a reflection of Vailland's own withdrawal, and the pages describing the various stages in Don Cesare's life could have been taken almost directly from Vailland's own diaries. The novel also explores some familiar themes: social manipulation, family tensions, the maternal relationship between a young man, Francesco, and an older woman, Donna Lucrezia. There are some fine descriptions, and features of the natural world are used to give depth to a provincialism of the most deep-rooted kind. But overall there is a sense that Vailland had set out quite deliberately to immerse himself in a novel which, at least superficially, would be quite different from the two immediately preceding ones. At the same time, by its self-contained nature and the absence of the kind of forward dynamic found in the political novels, *La Loi* does anticipate both *La Fête* and *La Truite*. Not surprisingly, while acknowledging the novel's technical competence, the Communist press saw *La Loi* as evidence of Vailland's surrender to the values of bourgeois culture.

During the next three years Vailland traveled a great deal, especially in the Middle East, writing articles for *France-Soir*. He wrote a play, *Monsieur Jean* (1959), a superficial and theatrically implausible treatment of the Don Juan theme, possibly motivated by the reception given to *La Loi*. (The title character, Jean, is finally killed by a portrait of Stalin which falls off the wall behind his desk and breaks his neck!) In 1959 Vailland adapted Laclos's novel *Les Liaisons dangereuses* (1782) for the cinema with Roger Vadim and Claude Brulé. (He had already, in 1953, written an interesting Marxist critique of the novel for the volume *Laclos par lui-même* [Laclos By Himself] which he edited.)

From his diaries during this period it would seem that political events held little or no interest for him. What appears instead to assume paramount importance is the need to achieve total self-control: "la seule souveraineté sans aliénation se borne au gouvernement de soi-même" (complete and unalloyed sovereignty must be limited to self-control). Such a preoccupation is clearly an extension of his many earlier discussions of the "amateur" or of the need for total devotion to a political cause. In *La Fête*, however, it is explored solely in terms of sexual and artistic control. The novel deals with two married couples, Duc and Léone, Jean-Marc and Lucie Lemarque. Each one of this quartet acts out a part that is strictly controlled in relation to the others and to the setting, with the result that much of the action is ritualized and almost artificial. The first three lead lives unaffected by normal material concerns, and Duc "initiates" Lucie into the same life-style, turning her from a passive to an active participant.

Without its final twist, *La Fête* would be of limited interest, one more piece of thinly veiled autobiography. But Vailland introduces a new dimension by revealing at the end of the novel (like Camus in *La Peste* [*The Plague*]) that Duc is actually writing *La Fête*. In this way Vailland too is distanced and the account of his life-style objectified. Clearly he hoped by this technique to penetrate the very process of creation and to be able to analyze the sovereignty or "singularité" of a work of art as well. As he said about a painting by his friend Pierre Soulages in 1963: "Il faut s'y enfermer" (you have to shut yourself up in it). *La Truite* was Vailland's final exploration of this same problem in writing.

Like *La Fête*, *La Truite* deals with a series of rituals, anticipated from the opening pages by the description of a bowling alley, and extended through the worlds of childhood groups, business, travel, Indian reservations, and fish-farming, from which the title is drawn. The central character, Frédérique, is the last and most complete of Vailland's pure young women. Despite marriage and several amorous adventures, she remains a virgin: "vierge magnifique, vierge royale, vierge redoutable" (magnificent, regal, and formidable virgin). No one can fully understand her quality. The only possible approach to understanding is hinted at in the description of another character, Isaac, who studies advanced mathematics in order to communicate with his adored granddaughter: "pour trouver un langage commun . . . , pour briser la clôture" (to discover a common language . . . , in order to break down the barriers). At the time of writing *La Truite* Vailland discussed in his diary various problems having to do with the adequacy of language, and he pursues this concern in *La Truite* through his acknowledged role as narrator/character. Yet a solution evades him. Writing itself–the codifying of penetration and understanding–becomes a ritual and carries with it its own potentially destructive force. Even symbols may be ultimately sterile.

La Truite clearly has links with everything Vailland had written before, but this exploration of the limits of language and fiction represents a new and potentially rich development alongside his permanent ambition to write a novel in which individual sovereignty and contingency might coexist. But already he was terminally ill with lung cancer. He decided, as a final gesture of his own sovereignty, to commit suicide on his fifty-eighth birthday. But even in this he was cheated; he died five months earlier, in May 1965.

To summarize the qualities of Vailland's work is not easy. Its mixture of several constant themes and shifting objectives, as well as its preoccupation with technical mastery and sharply observed detail, can result at best in writing that is forceful and persuasive. But the writing can also appear self-indulgent and artificial. Arguably Vailland was too much of an individualist ever to have been successful as a political writer contributing to a collective cause, yet his very individuality–even idiosyncrasy–allowed him to avoid some of the excesses of politically committed writing. As a novelist in particular his reputation is assured. His own assessment of *325.000 Francs* was certainly correct at the time, though *La Truite* is probably his most complex book and one which will stand the test of time. Having had the misfortune to write during a period when there was so much work of high quality and when major developments in ideas and in technique were abundant, Vailland will in all likelihood never be considered more than a relatively marginal writer.

Letters:

Lettres à sa famille, edited by Max Chaleil (Paris: Gallimard, 1972).

Interviews:

Marcel Mithois, "Les Secrets de l'écrivain," *Réalités*, no. 218 (March 1964): 80-88;

Madeline Chapsal, *Les Ecrivains en personne* (Paris: Julliard, 1973), pp. 303-316.

Biography:

Elisabeth Vailland, *Drôle de vie* (Paris: Lattès, 1984).

References:

René Ballet and Elisabeth Vailland, *Roger Vailland* (Paris: Seghers, 1973);

François Bott, *Les Saisons de Roger Vailland* (Paris: Grasset, 1969);

Jean-Jacques Brochier, *Roger Vailland: Tentative de description critique* (Paris: Losfeld, 1969);

Max Chaleil, ed., *Roger Vailland*, Entretiens, no. 29 (Rodez: Editions Subervié, 1970);

J. E. Flower, *Literature and the Left in France* (London: Macmillan, 1983);

Flower, *Roger Vailland: The Man and his Masks* (London: Hodder & Stoughton, 1975);

Flower, and C. H. R. Niven, Introduction to Vailland's *Un Jeune Homme seul* (London: Methuen, 1985);

Robert Gilbert-Lecomte, *Correspondance: Lettres adressées à René Daumal, Roger Vailland, René Maublanc, Pierre Minet, Véra Milanova et Jean*

Puyaubert, edited by Pierre Minet (Paris: Gallimard, 1971);

Roger Laufer, "Le Héros tragique dans les romans de Roger Vailland," *Australasian Universities Modern Languages Association*, no. 22 (November 1964): 221-232;

Jo Ann McNatt, *The Novels of Roger Vailland: The Amateur and the Professional* (New York, Frankfurt & Bern: Peter Lang, 1986);

David Nott, Introduction to Vailland's *325.000 Francs* (London: EUP, 1975; revised edition, London: Routledge, 1989);

Christian Petr, "Le Devenir écrivain de Roger Vailland (1944-1955)," 2 volumes, doctoral dissertation, Université de Paris X-Nanterre, 1986;

Petr, "Le Discours du roman réaliste," *French Review*, 57 (December 1983): 194-202;

Michel Picard, *Libertinage et tragique dans l'œuvre de Roger Vailland* (Paris: Hachette, 1972);

Picard, "Roger Vailland et le Grand Jeu," *Revue d'Histoire Littéraire de la France*, 79 (July-August 1979): 613-622;

Michel Random, *Le Grand Jeu*, 2 volumes (Paris: Denoël, 1970);

Jean Recanati, *Roger Vailland: Esquisse pour la psychanalyse d'un libertin* (Paris: Buchet-Chastel, 1971);

A. Sicard, "Réflexions sur l'œuvre de Roger Vailland," *Nouvelle Critique* (February 1966): 15-41;

Jean-Pierre Tusseau, *Roger Vailland: Un Ecrivain au service du peuple* (Paris: Debresse, 1976).

Papers:

The Médiathèque Elisabeth et Roger Vailland in Bourg-en-Bresse (Ain) has manuscripts for most of Vailland's major works and for several unpublished writings; it also includes some correspondence.

Vladimir Volkoff

(7 November 1932-)

John M. Dunaway
Mercer University

BOOKS: *L'Agent triple* (Paris: Julliard, 1962);

Métro pour l'enfer (Paris: Hachette, 1963);

Les Mousquetaires de la république (Paris: Table Ronde, 1964);

La Civilisation française, as Victor Duloup (New York: Harcourt, Brace & World, 1970);

Le Trêtre, as Lavr Divomlikoff (Paris: Robert Morel, 1972); translated by J. F. Bernard as *The Traitor* (London: Heinemann, 1974; Garden City, N.Y.: Doubleday, 1974); French edition republished under Volkoff's name (Paris: Julliard/Lausanne: Age d'Homme, 1983);

L'Enfant posthume, as Lavr Divomlikoff (Paris: Robert Morel, 1972);

Tchaikovsky: A Self-Portrait (Boston: Crescendo, 1975); translated by Volkoff as *Tchaïkovsky* (Paris: Julliard/Lausanne: Age d'Homme, 1983);

Vers une métrique française (Columbia, S.C.: French Literature Publications, 1978);

Le Retournement (Paris: Julliard, 1979); translated by Alan Sheridan as *The Turn-around* (London: Bodley Head, 1981; Garden City, N.Y.: Doubleday, 1981);

Les Humeurs de la mer, 4 volumes (Paris: Julliard/ Lausanne: Age d'Homme, 1980)–comprises *Olduvaï*, *La Leçon d'anatomie*, *Intersection*, and *Les Maîtres du temps*;

Le Complexe de Procuste (Paris: Julliard/Lausanne: Age d'Homme, 1981);

Vladimir, le soleil rouge, translated by Gérard Joulié (Paris: Julliard/Lausanne: Age d'Homme, 1981); original English version published as *Vladimir, the Russian Viking* (London: Honeyglen, 1984; Woodstock, N.Y.: Overlook, 1985);

Une Histoire surannée quelque peu (Lausanne: Age d'Homme, 1982);

Le Montage (Paris: Julliard/Lausanne: Age d'Homme, 1982); translated by Sheridan as *The Set-up: A Novel of Disinformation* (London: Bodley Head, 1984; New York: Arbor House, 1985);

Vladimir Volkoff (photograph by Jacqueline Bruller)

Le Tire-bouchon du Bon Dieu (Paris: Presses Pocket, 1982);

La Guerre des pieuvres (Paris: Presses Pocket, 1983);

L'Amour tue (Paris: Julliard/Lausanne: Age d'Homme, 1983);

Yalta (Paris: Julliard/Lausanne: Age d'Homme, 1984);

Lawrence le magnifique: Essai sur Lawrence Durrell et le roman relativiste (Paris: Julliard/Lausanne: Age d'Homme, 1984);

The Underdog Appeal: An Entertainment (Macon, Ga.: Renaissance Press, 1984);

Lecture de l'Evangile selon saint Matthieu (Paris: Julliard/Lausanne: Age d'Homme, 1985);

Le Professeur d'histoire (Paris: Julliard/Lausanne: Age d'Homme, 1985);

Nouvelles américaines (Paris: Julliard/Lausanne: Age d'Homme, 1986);

Du roi (Paris: Julliard/Lausanne: Age d'Homme, 1987);

Le Mistère de Saint Vladimir (Lausanne: Age d'Homme, 1988);

L'Interrogatoire (Paris: Fallois/Lausanne: Age d'Homme, 1988);

Vladimiriana (Lausanne: Age d'Homme, 1989);

Les Hommes du tsar (Paris: Fallois/Lausanne: Age d'Homme, 1989).

PLAY PRODUCTIONS: *L'Amour tue*, Paris, Théâtre de l'Atelier, 24 January 1983;

Yalta, Paris, Théâtre Firmin Gémier, 6 November 1984;

L'Interrogatoire, Paris, Acteurs de l'Ile-de-France, at the festival of the 13th *arrondissement*, 23 October 1987.

OTHER: "Lot's Lot," "Ministories of Life and Death," and "The White Pine Wardrobe," in *Georgia on My Mind: An Anthology of Contemporary Writers*, edited by Robert Fox (Macon, Ga.: Renaissance Press, 1983);

La Désinformation, arme de guerre, edited by Volkoff (Paris: Julliard/Lausanne: Age d'Homme, 1986).

PERIODICAL PUBLICATIONS: "Le Complexe de Rodrigue," *Commentaire*, 3 (Spring 1980): 22;

"Bâtardise et parricide," *Cahiers de la Nuit Surveillée*, no. 2 (October 1983): 41;

"Incarnation et royauté," *Commentaire*, 7 (Fall 1984): 430.

A remarkable irony of the contemporary American literary scene is the relative nonstatus of a polyglot expatriate Frenchman who makes his home in the central Georgia community of Macon. He is one of the most popular and controversial novelists in France today. His writings have won him such distinctions as the Prix Jules Verne (1963), the Prix Chateaubriand (1979), and the Grand Prix du Roman, awarded by the Académie Française (1982). He is a highly visible member of the French literati who appears often

on television talk shows, grants interviews to major dailies and magazines, and stages dramatic productions in Paris and Brussels nearly every year.

Born 7 November 1932 in Paris of White Russian parents, Nicholas and Tatiana Porokhovstchikoff Volkoff, Vladimir Volkoff grew up among Russian immigrants, shielded by his family from the culture in which they were exiled. Eventually, he was educated in French schools, taking his *licence-ès-lettres* at the Sorbonne and a doctorate in aesthetics from the University of Liège. He was an intelligence officer in the French army during the Algerian war, an assignment that was to have a profound effect on his writing. After his retirement from the army, he published several books in France before moving to the United States in 1966 to teach Russian and French at Agnes Scott College in Decatur, Georgia, retiring in 1977 to devote full time to his writing. During his years as a college professor, he continued to write; he also organized a French-language theatrical troupe (for which he served as director, writer, and actor), taught fencing, and pursued his favorite hobbies: chess, hunting, and collecting weapons. Since leaving the teaching profession, Volkoff has produced many books, ranging from novels and stories to plays, biographies, essays, and science fiction, but he is best known for his fiction.

Jean Cocteau recounts in his diary that when he first met Diaghilev, the impresario's first words to him were simply: "Etonne-moi" (Surprise me). Like Cocteau, Volkoff has a quick wit ready to respond to such a request. And like the author of *Les Enfants terribles*, thought by many to be too clever and entertaining to be a "serious" writer, Volkoff is a kind of dazzler, apparently loathing the self-consciously "serious" mode in literature. Yet in the maze of mirrors that his espionage plots resemble, one is conscious of several levels of action and meaning beyond the playfulness. Expressed repeatedly in Volkoff's fiction are the timeless themes of salvation, the problem of evil, the quest for honor, and the devotion to sacrificial duty.

L'Agent triple (The Triple Agent, 1962) was Volkoff's first novel. The protagonist is a sardonic dandy of a professor in a Jesuit college who, out of boredom rather than conviction, gets involved with a leftist political group organized to aid deserters from the Algerian war. At the same time, through a teaching colleague named Conchita, he joins a revolutionary fascist group.

The action, which revolves around the (nameless) character's role in the conflicts between the two political groups, is essentially a fable, a pretext for the author to indulge the bemused and detached mockery of his rake of a hero.

Volkoff might be called a master of intellectual science fiction. His science fiction portrays an imaginative world that is as closely related to classical myth and Western literary tradition as it is to futuristic technology and fantasy. His first novel in the science-fiction genre established the pattern.

Métro pour l'enfer (Subway to Hell, 1963) is the story of a cellist who meets his deceased girlfriend on a subway train. The girl turns out to be one of the "nécrozones" of the underworld and leads him to the nether regions via an extended subway line. Although this technologically advanced hell is ruled by a living tyrant and inhabited by living prehistoric monsters, it is peopled solely by the "nécrozones"–dead souls who are resuscitated only in a biological sense, as masses of plastic tubes and robotic accessories. An obvious recapitulation of the Dantean inferno and of the Orpheus myth, the book's portrayal of a totalitarian world is also a satire of certain tendencies Volkoff noted in the de Gaulle régime. This novel was the winner of the Prix Jules Verne.

In Volkoff's third novel, *Les Mousquetaires de la république* (The Musketeers of the Republic, 1964), he borrows freely from Alexandre Dumas's classic swashbuckler. Whereas the original musketeers were devoted servants of the queen, the Volkoff characters have a passionate need to serve, but they have no sovereign. And that is the main theme of the novel: the absence of a cause worthy of self-sacrifice. D'Artagnan chances upon a camp of Harkis (Arab soldiers who fought for the colonialist French army in Algeria). These men without a country become the cause championed by the modern-day musketeers. A story of a lost generation, *Les Mousquetaires de la république* revives the panache and bravura of another age.

Probably the best of Volkoff's work before 1979 is *Le Trêtre* (1972; translated as *The Traitor*, 1974), published under the pseudonym Lavr Divomlikoff. In an imaginative plot, Volkoff here presents the story of a secret agent whose mission is to infiltrate the Church. The story is set in an unidentified Slavic country. When told, after many years as priest in an obscure village, that his new assignment is to abjure the faith and become a fiercely atheistic university professor, he

is not sure which role reflects his own convictions. Even his devoted wife, Alona, has no suspicions of his true identity. In a note to the 1983 edition published under Volkoff's name, the author excuses himself for the untranslatable neologism he used as his title by explaining that the irreconcilable allegiances of Grigori's dual roles–"traître" (traitor) and "prêtre" (priest)–called for such a monstrous concoction. He also explains the origin of the strange pseudonym he used for this novel and for the novella *L'Enfant posthume* (The Posthumous Child, 1972): it is an anagram of his real name and a combination of the Russian words for "miraculous imprint," like that of Veronica's veil, which is a metaphor for his conception of art as bearing the image of God.

Volkoff set *L'Enfant posthume* in Canada. The English girl Rachel and her crooner friend Phil join a Montreal group on an excursion in the country, where they discover the house of a former Nazi. Having secretly become the Nazi's mistress, Rachel warns him that he must flee because of her friends' plans to denounce him to the police. In doing so, she reveals that her father was an intelligence officer who was killed by the Nazis (in a concentration camp, probably) before her birth, and that she is a Jewess. The most dramatic scene is her confrontation with the gang, to whom she declares that she alone among them has the right to condemn the Nazi, and that she pardons him. In *L'Exil est ma patrie* (Exile is My Country, 1982), a volume of interviews with Jacqueline Bruller, Volkoff comments on the metaphor of the title *L'Enfant posthume*, saying that in the modern world of rootlessness, all are posthumous children. "Symboliquement, depuis que Rousseau a mis ses enfants à l'assistance publique, tous les enfants sont à l'assistance publique. Lorsque j'ai écrit *L'Enfant posthume*, je pensais à ça" (Symbolically, ever since Rousseau gave up his children for adoption, all children have been orphaned. When I wrote *L'Enfant posthume*, that's what I had in mind).

Volkoff was not widely known in France until 1979, when he published *Le Retournement* (translated as *The Turn-around*, 1981). Winner of the Prix Chateaubriand, this book was a bestseller in France and was translated into twelve languages. Fred Zinneman was so taken with the story that he bought the movie rights to it. Had he lived to make the film, it would have doubtless aroused no small debate.

The "retournement" of the title is the startling conversion of a KGB master agent, Major

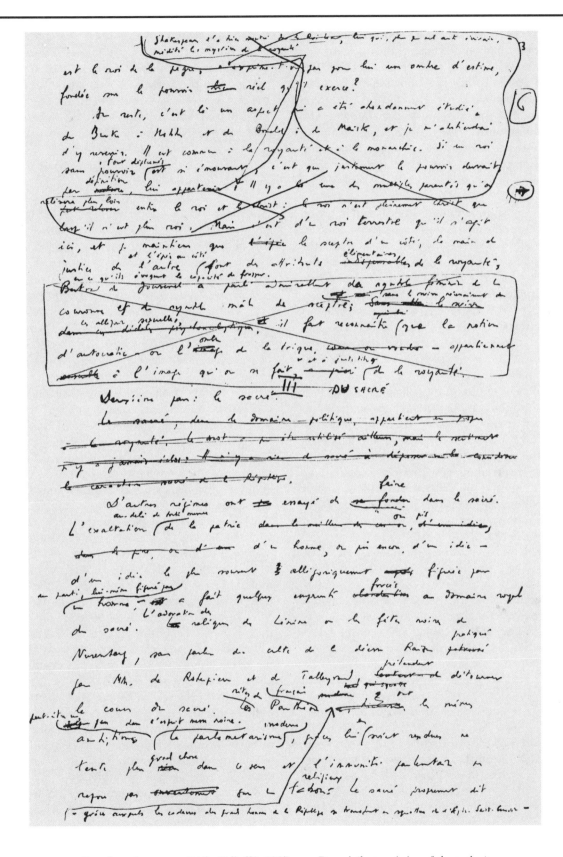

Page from the manuscript for Volkoff's 1987 essay Du roi *(by permission of the author)*

Popov, to the Christian faith. Popov, one of the most thoroughly indoctrinated products of the Communist system, is a modern-day Saul of Tarsus, and Paris is his road to Damascus. The French intelligence officer in charge of turning Popov around, Volsky, is an obscure bungler who uses his position as a way of enjoying an epicurean life-style. He stumbles upon Opération Couleuvrine, the plan he uses to convert Popov, and it works mostly in spite, rather than because, of his efforts.

The most memorable scene of the novel, which was produced as a one-act play in 1980, is Popov's confession in the Russian Orthodox Church of Saint-Serge in Paris. The rich Orthodox liturgy and the exotic beauty of the setting are admirably rendered, as well as the surprising volte-face of the character, whose confession is not only registered in heaven through the medium of the priest but also in the offices of the French intelligence services by means of a hidden tape recorder.

The disorienting plot twists and complicated strategies of the various intelligence agencies in this story are not the only challenges for the reader. In order fully to appreciate the subtleties of the dialogue, one needs considerable fluency in at least three languages: French, Russian, and English. Linguistic sophistication is also an advantage in reading other major Volkoff works, especially the multivolume *Les Humeurs de la mer* (The Moods of the Sea, 1980).

When *Le Retournement* was published, Parisian journalists and critics compared Volkoff to Ian Fleming, John le Carré, Graham Greene, and also to Feodor Dostoyevski. The rarity of a White Russian exile writing espionage novels that explored new forms of Christian witness seemed to fascinate them. And Volkoff's provocative personality made him a media success.

The year following *Le Retournement* marked the publication of Volkoff's masterpiece, the four-volume novel entitled *Les Humeurs de la mer*. His publishers proclaimed 1980 "l'année Volkoff" (the Volkoff year). Volkoff calls *Les Humeurs de la mer* a relativistic novel in the sense of Lawrence Durrell's *The Alexandria Quartet* (1962). Each volume is a coherent unit, and the four may be read in any order, although several main characters are involved in each.

The hero of the tetralogy is Colonel François Beaujeux, whose alias in the first volume, *Olduvaï*, is Frank Blok. The title of the first volume is the name of the valley in Tanzania where anthropologists found the remains of *Homo habilis*, one of the earliest known human species, described by Robert Ardrey as an aggressive being who was advanced enough to form and wield weapons. The multiplicity of perspectives in this first volume–as in two of the others–is achieved partly by the device of the work within a work. Here it is a play–also entitled *Olduvaï*–by Blok/Beaujeux that is being produced by the characters in the novel.

Most of the action of the novel, which is set in the American South during the racial unrest of the late 1960s and early 1970s, is seen through the eyes of young Arnim, who incarnates the familiar Volkovian theme of the search for the father. Readers are also introduced to Beaujeux's mysterious consort, Solange Bernard.

In *La Leçon d'anatomie* (The Anatomy Lesson), Beaujeux and Solange are living in Spain, and the colonel is trying to write a screenplay–bearing the same title as the book–recounting a decisive event in his past military career. The incident, a flashback that constitutes the majority of the book, concerns an Algerian city of which he was a kind of military governor. In the context of France's impending disengagement, Beaujeux must deal with clandestine operations, his personal opposition to the widespread use of torture in interrogations, political maneuvering from all sides, and the perplexing dilemma of the Harkis.

One of his most promising officers, Lieutenant Miloslavski, a passionately idealistic young man whom the colonel calls "L'Ange bleu" (the Blue Angel), sees Beaujeux increasingly as a demonic figure. The deepest theme of Volkoff's fiction is thus broached: the problem of evil. In what measure must he who governs use evil for the good of the governed? In an interview for *L'Exil est ma patrie* Volkoff says that what has fascinated him for years is not so much the existence of evil but its purpose and usefulness in the plan of God. "Dostoïevsky a dit: si Dieu n'existe pas, tout est permis, ma réponse est que si le diable n'existait pas, rien ne serait possible. Une certaine proportion de mal est essentielle à la forme du monde" (Dostoyevski said: if God does not exist, everything is permitted, but my reply is that if the devil did not exist, nothing would be possible. A certain proportion of evil is essential to the form of the world).

In *Intersection*, the third volume of *Les Humeurs da la mer*, the juxtaposition of multiple perspectives is not attributable to a text within the text but to the interplay of two different ontological orders. Beaujeux and Solange are watched over in this novel by their guardian angels (Petit-Michel and Grand-Michel), who comment on the action from above and recount in flashback their respective charges' pasts. Solange is actually Svetlana Bernhardt, daughter of Stalin's unscrupulous chief of Soviet literary orthodoxy. Beaujeux, one learns, was an actor before serving in military intelligence and has studied Gnosticism quite extensively. He believes that God intends to use evil against Evil in his providential design: "Le Dieu bon enchaîné par les péchés des hommes, le vrai Dieu qui n'a jamais menti, . . . le Dieu qui, pour finir, avait donné son Fils à manger au monde, ce Dieu-là, auquel François se vouait de tout son être, il n'avait pas de mal à opposer au Mal? François se laissa secouer par un soubresaut hystérique. Quelqu'un, au fond de lui, avait répondu: –Je veux être ce mal" (The good God bound by the sins of men, the true God who has never lied, . . . who ended up giving his Son to be eaten by the world, this God, to whom François was dedicating himself with all his being, had he no evil to oppose Evil? François was shaken by a sudden start of hysteria. Someone deep inside him had answered: "I wish to be that evil").

The final volume of Volkoff's tetralogy, *Les Maîtres du temps* (The Masters of Time), finds the aging Beaujeux now composing a volume of poems in which he seeks to renovate French metrics. Living in a windmill on a remote island of North Africa, he and Solange receive visits from Arnim, Miloslavski (who is about to be ordained an Orthodox priest), and Beaujeux's three brothers. Beaujeux's writing is one attempt to master time. Another is the belated decision to have a child through whom he may have a continuing legacy. The problem of Solange's age leads him to consider a rather irregular course of action, and the climax is further complicated by the arrival of two spies who have been sent to elicit the long-guarded secret of Solange's true identity.

Les Humeurs de la mer thus follows the lives and pasts of several characters, particularly Beaujeux and Solange, from the United States to France, Algeria, Spain, Czarist Russia, the Soviet Union, and even heaven. The grand themes of love, war, time and mortality, the nature of art, and the problem of evil are played out in a prose that is skillfully crafted with an eye for classical elegance and simplicity. On these four volumes, no doubt, rests Volkoff's claim to lasting literary distinction.

The 1981 essay entitled *Le Complexe de Procuste* (The Procrustes Complex) is a revealing text that deals with the characteristically modern cultural affliction of conformism, one of the favorite targets of Volkoff's satire. The myth of Procrustes, who is said to have made his victims, by chopping them off or stretching them, fit the bed to which he had strapped them, is a symbol of those who would reduce life to the drab, dull sameness of routine and habit.

The novella which immediately followed *Les Humeurs de la mer*, *Une Histoire surannée quelque peu* (A Slightly Outdated Story, 1982), is a piece of fantasy and preciosity, a vintage vampire story that will not disappoint those who favor dazzlers.

Le Montage (1982; translated as *The Set-up*, 1984) is a particularly notable entry in Volkoff's bibliography, since it won him the Grand Prix du Roman, awarded by the Académie Française. The English translation carries the subtitle, *A Novel of Disinformation*. The central character, Aleksandre Psar, the son of White Russian exiles in France, is a rather cynical, apolitical intellectual, although he is possessed with a quasimystical devotion to the land of his forbears. Profoundly moved by his father's deathbed wish that Alek would one day be able to return to Russia, he accepts the KGB's offer to recruit him as an "influence agent," in exchange for the promise that after completing his mission he will indeed be repatriated.

Psar's job becomes that of manipulating public opinion in France by subtly influencing groups of writers on both ends of the political spectrum. After thirty years of effective service, Psar is required to perform one final mission, which is designed to discredit the dissident movement. In the midst of the operation he realizes it is his own turn to be manipulated. Volkoff's portrayal of the strategies and methods of Soviet "disinformation campaigns" is chillingly authentic.

Volkoff's science-fiction novel *Le Tire-bouchon du Bon Dieu* (The Good Lord's Corkscrew, 1982) is more futuristic than the earlier *Métro pour l'enfer*. The Earth has been invaded by an aggressive form of mushrooms called Hydnes. Man has fled to other planets, reduced to a drugged, impotent, tyrannized group of three hybrid races, and the decadent totalitarian régime that remains behind enforces a wheedling racism. The young astronaut Brof, obsessed with the dream of traveling to the North Star, is the hero who attempts to save humanity. Inspired by his love for Oarilys, invisible daughter of crystals, he undertakes an interstellar journey through hyperspace, managing to exceed the speed of light by applying the Pythagorean theories of music to the spatial dimension.

Volkoff's other volume of science fiction is *La Guerre des pieuvres* (The Octopus War, 1983). In this satire of wars of decolonization (like that in Algeria), the colonized planet (Voda) is an immense drop of water inhabited by octopuses. These creatures have an insatiable hunger for information of all kinds, and they earn their livelihood by producing and selling plankton. When their need for information is not satisfied they start a revolution. The novel's two heroes, Alféo and Thor, are charged with the mission of infiltrating the octopuses, who at the end are threatened with being transformed into computers. "La SF, l'espionnage, le fantastique," remarked Volkoff in an interview for *L'Exil est ma patrie*, "sont trois procédés qui permettent de prendre conscience que le monde n'est pas vraiment ce qu'il paraît" (Science fiction, espionage, and fantasy are three ways of realizing the world is really not what it appears to be). Thus, the unusually intellectual brand of science fiction that is Volkoff's is laden with religious and philosophical insights.

In 1983 Volkoff published his comedy on the Bluebeard legend, *L'Amour tue* (Love Kills). It had been staged in Paris at the Théâtre de l'Atelier and was also performed in English at the Little Theater of Macon, Georgia. His historical tragedy, *Yalta*, was published in 1984, after having been produced in Paris and in Brussels. In the same year *Lawrence le magnifique* (Lawrence the Magnificent) appeared, an essay in which he pays tribute to Lawrence Durrell, the writer, aside from Dostoyevski, to whom he believes he owes the greatest literary influence.

Volkoff's only novel written in English, *The Underdog Appeal* (1984), is what he refers to as an experiment, or, in the words of the subtitle, *An Entertainment*. A light and carousing spoof on his own cloak-and-dagger genre, it is one of three volumes produced by Renaissance Press, a publishing house Volkoff organized to promote new writing talent in the Macon area.

Volkoff's 1985 novel, *Le Professeur d'histoire* (The History Professor), is of particular interest to American readers. Professor Frédéric Foncrest's son Joël is profoundly deracinated, for shortly after giving birth to Joël, Mme Foncrest divorces Frédéric and moves with Joël to the United States, where she remarries. The new husband adopts Joël and gives him a typical contemporary American upper-middle-class upbringing. At the age of twenty the young man crosses the Atlantic with a group of his school chums for an extended tour of the Continent, and during his stay in France he decides, largely out of curiosity, he believes, to pay his father a visit. His motivation actually runs much deeper, to the mythic search for the father, as Beaujeux calls it in *Les Maîtres du temps*. Without realizing it, Joël is obsessed with the mystery of paternity: "Cet homme est mon père.... Mais qu'est-ce que cela signifie au juste?" (This man is my father.... But what exactly does that mean?).

Joël is a tragic example of uprootedness. Having taken on the Anglo-Saxon name (Paterson with one *t*) of his adopted father, he is a product of contemporary American culture at its worst: consumeristic, materialistic, hedonistic. The reunion of father and son (*pater*/son) is a severe culture shock for Joël. He is embarrassed at Foncrest's lowly economic status: the professor does not even possess an automobile or an icemaker! Joël asks Foncrest for a loan that will enable him to pay for an abortion. The request opens up the possibility of a relationship between these two men, so intimately related and yet so foreign to one another. Foncrest reveals his own world to Joël, a world of fiercely traditional values: courtly, Christian, royalist, and Epicurean. He seems to represent everything Volkoff loves best about France.

Metaphorically speaking, the abdication of fathers is also the abdication of all those who are in authority, and it leads to the proclamation of the death of God. The proper hierarchical order of things having been overturned, it becomes the duty of adherents of the order to keep alive its memory. Thus, the father who does not wish to abdicate has the responsibility to become a history professor, conveying to his child the sacred charge of memory as faithfulness.

An unusual recent addition to Volkoff's fiction is a collection of stories that he has assembled over the years of his residence in the United States, most of them connected to the South. According to the postface, he retells these purportedly true stories just as he has heard them, changing only the names. *Nouvelles américaines* (American Stories, 1986) is thus not Volkovian fiction in the usual sense but a tribute to the culture in which he has lived for more than two decades.

Volkoff's versatility is evident in several works of nonfiction he has written over the years. *Tchaikovsky: A Self-Portrait*, published in English in 1975, is a biography of the Russian composer who was Volkoff's granduncle. Volkoff's own French translation of the book was published in 1983. *Vladimir, the Russian Viking* (1984), also written in English, is a historical biography of the patron saint of the Russian Orthodox church. The French version, translated by Gérard Joulié as *Vladimir, le soleil rouge*, had appeared three years earlier, in 1981. *Lecture de l'Evangile selon saint Matthieu*, Volkoff's commentary on the gospel of Matthew, was published in 1985. In 1987 he produced *Du roi* (On the King), an essay in which he carefully distinguishes between royalism and monarchism.

Among Volkoff's most recent publications are two that appeared in connection with his active participation in the Association Saint-Vladimir, which was organized to promote the millennial celebration of the Christianization of Russia by Volkoff's patron saint. *Le Mistère de Saint Vladimir* (1988) is a dramatization of the life, and conversion, of Saint Vladimir, done in the style of the medieval mystery plays. It was in honor of this text that Volkoff was awarded the Prix Alfred de Vigny by Paris mayor Jacques Chirac. *Vladimiriana* (1989) is a collection of Volkoff's articles on various subjects connected with the millennial observation and the mutual influence that France and Russia have had on one another because of their Christian heritage.

L'Interrogatoire (1988) is a novel about the interrogation of a German prisoner during the de-Nazification of Germany at the end of World War II. Volkoff first wrote the story as a play, which was produced in 1987 by the Acteurs de l'Ile-de-France at the festival of the 13th *arrondissement* of Paris, directed by Jean-Paul Zehnacker. The novel, however, is not an adaptation but an autonomous text; the author felt that the play had not really exhausted his subject and sought to complete the vision in the novel.

Finally, *Les Hommes du tsar* (1989) is Volkoff's latest work, a colorful historical novel set in the time of Boris Godunov, czar from 1598 to 1605, with liberal borrowings from A. K. Tolstoy and Aleksander Pushkin.

In a day and age when the literary establishment is occupied for the most part by political liberals, when the pages of the reviews and journals are filled with talk of feminism, Marxism, and deconstructionism, when many traditional aspects of French culture are being transformed by a socialist government, Vladimir Volkoff would appear to be singularly out of place. Yet he has continued, since *Le Retournement* in 1979, to enjoy a high degree of visibility in the French media, partly because of his flair for dramatics and partly because his views are so strong and so boldly stated.

For those who cherish the traditional values of French culture in its (anti-Procrustian) distinctiveness, for those who enjoy a well-written story with a beginning, middle, and end, and for those who believe that Communist influence is on the rise in contemporary Western society, Volkoff represents a clear prophetic voice. Many in the Soviet dissident community in France look upon him as a kind of French equivalent to Aleksandr Solzhenitsyn.

Volkoff's own most cherished aspiration as an artist is to be known a century hence as one of a few writers–such as Lawrence Durrell–who will have prepared the way for what he calls "le classicisme de l'an 2000" (the classicism of the year 2000).

Reference:
Jacqueline Bruller, *L'Exil est ma patrie: Entretiens* (Paris: Centurion, 1982).

Elie Wiesel
(30 September 1928-)

Jack Kolbert
Susquehanna University

See also the Nobel Peace Prize entry in *DLB Yearbook: 1986* and the Wiesel entry in *Yearbook: 1987*.

BOOKS: *Un di Velt Hot Geshvign* (Buenos Aires: Central Farbond Fun Poylishe Yidn in Argentina, 1956); revised and abridged as *La Nuit* (Paris: Editions de Minuit, 1958); *La Nuit* translated by Stella Rodway as *Night* (New York: Hill & Wang, 1960; London: MacGibbon & Kee, 1960);

L'Aube (Paris: Seuil, 1960); translated by Anne Borchardt as *Dawn* (New York: Hill & Wang, 1961); translated by Frances Frenaye (London: MacGibbon & Kee, 1961);

Le Jour (Paris: Seuil, 1961); translated by Borchardt as *The Accident* (New York: Hill & Wang, 1962);

La Ville de la chance (Paris: Seuil, 1962); translated by Stephen Becker as *The Town Beyond the Wall* (New York: Holt, Rinehart & Winston, 1964; London: Robson, 1975);

Les Portes de la forêt (Paris: Seuil, 1964); translated by Frenaye as *The Gates of the Forest* (New York: Holt, Rinehart & Winston, 1966; London: Heinemann, 1967);

Les Juifs du silence (Paris: Seuil, 1966); translated from the original Hebrew by Neal Kozodoy as *The Jews of Silence: A Personal Report on Soviet Jewry* (New York: Holt, Rinehart & Winston, 1966; London: Valentine Mitchell, 1968);

Les Chants des morts (Paris: Seuil, 1966); translated by Steven Donadio as *Legends of Our Time* (New York: Holt, Rinehart & Winston, 1968);

Zalmen ou la folie de Dieu (Paris: Seuil, 1968); translated by Nathan Edelman and adapted for the stage by Marion Wiesel as *Zalmen, or The Madness of God* (New York: Random House, 1974);

Le Mendiant de Jérusalem (Paris: Seuil, 1968); translated by Lily Edelman and Elie Wiesel as *A Beggar in Jerusalem* (New York: Random House, 1970; London: Weidenfeld & Nicolson, 1970);

Entre deux soleils (Paris: Seuil, 1970); translated by Lily Edelman and Elie Wiesel as *One Generation After* (New York: Random House, 1970; London: Weidenfeld & Nicolson, 1971);

Célébration hassidique: Portraits et légendes (Paris: Seuil, 1972); translated by Marion Wiesel as *Souls on Fire: Portraits and Legends of Hasidic Masters* (New York: Random House, 1972; London: Weidenfeld & Nicolson, 1972);

Le Serment de Kolvillàg (Paris: Seuil, 1973); translated by Marion Wiesel as *The Oath* (New York: Random House, 1973);

Ani Maamin: Un Chant perdu et retrouvé (Paris: Seuil, 1973); bilingual edition, with translation by Marion Wiesel, published as *Ani Maamin: A Song Lost and Found Again* (New York: Random House, 1973);

Célébration biblique: Portraits et légendes (Paris: Seuil, 1975); translated by Marion Wiesel as *Messengers of God: Biblical Portraits and Legends* (New York: Random House, 1976);

Un Juif aujourd'hui (Paris: Seuil, 1977); translated by Marion Wiesel as *A Jew Today* (New York: Random House, 1978);

Four Hasidic Masters and Their Struggle Against Melancholy (Notre Dame, Ind.: University of Notre Dame Press, 1978);

Le Procès de Shamgorod (tel qu'il se déroula le 25 février 1649) (Paris: Seuil, 1979); translated by Marion Wiesel as *The Trial of God (as it was held on February 25, 1649, in Shamgorod)* (New York: Random House, 1979);

Le Testament d'un poète juif assassiné (Paris: Seuil, 1980); translated by Marion Wiesel as *The Testament* (New York: Summit, 1981; London: Allen Lane, 1981);

Five Biblical Portraits (Notre Dame, Ind.: University of Notre Dame Press, 1981);

Contre la mélancolie: Célébration hassidique II (Paris: Seuil, 1981); translated by Marion Wiesel as *Somewhere a Master: Further Hasidic Portraits and Legends* (New York: Summit, 1982);

Elie Wiesel

Paroles d'étranger (Paris: Seuil, 1982);

The Golem: The Story of a Legend as Told by Elie Wiesel (New York: Summit, 1983);

Le Cinquième Fils (Paris: Grasset, 1983); translated by Marion Wiesel as *The Fifth Son* (New York: Summit, 1985);

Against Silence: The Voice and Vision of Elie Wiesel, 3 volumes, edited by Irving Abrahamson (New York: Holocaust Library, 1985);

Signes d'Exode (Paris: Grasset & Fasquelle, 1985);

Job ou Dieu dans la tempête (Paris: Grasset & Fasquelle, 1986);

Discours d'Oslo (Paris: Grasset & Fasquelle, 1987);

The Night Trilogy: Night, Dawn, The Accident (New York: Farrar, Straus & Giroux, 1987);

Le Crépuscule au loin (Paris: Grasset & Fasquelle, 1987); translated by Marion Wiesel as *Twilight* (New York: Summit Books, 1988).

OTHER: "The Holocaust as Literary Imagination," in *Dimensions of the Holocaust: Lectures at Northwestern University* (Evanston, Ill.: The University, 1977).

PERIODICAL PUBLICATIONS: "From Exile to Exile," *Nation,* 202 (25 April 1966): 494-495;

"Will Soviet Jewry Survive?," *Commentary,* 43 (February 1967): 47-52;

"Arts and Culture After the Holocaust," *Crosscurrents,* 261 (Fall 1976): 258-269;

"Why I Write: Making No Become Yes," *New York Times Book Review,* 14 April 1985, pp. 13-14.

The work of a survivor of Auschwitz and Buchenwald, Elie Wiesel's literature, most of which he wrote in French, is rooted in the horror of the Holocaust and devoted to the examination of the most fundamental moral issues. Although he has depicted events in the lives of those who outlived Hitler's gas chambers, Wiesel's novels, plays, short stories, lectures, and philosophical texts do more than serve as archives for those who suffered or perished and more than attest to the resiliency of the Jewish people. "This is what I demand for literature," Wiesel once wrote, "a moral dimension. Art for art's sake is gone. . . . Just to write a novel, that's why I survived?" Elsewhere he noted, "I have always felt that words mean responsibility. I try to use them not against the human condition but for humankind; never to create anger but to attenuate anger, not to separate people but to bring them together." In 1986 Wiesel received the Nobel Peace Prize, cited for his "commitment, which originated in the suffering of the Jewish people, [and] has been widened to embrace all oppressed people and races."

Wiesel's parents were Shlomo and Sarah Feig Wiesel. He was born Eliezer Wiesel, 30 September 1928, in Sighet, Rumania, a well-known center of Jewish culture, in the region of Transylvania. Shlomo Wiesel, a grocer and storekeeper, represented for the young Elie the spirit of learning and Hebrew education. He always encouraged his son to study Hebrew and Yiddish languages and their literatures. Wiesel's mother, Sarah, inculcated in him a respect for mysticism and faith and a fascination with the ancient teachings of the Torah and Talmud. Possibly the most influential force in the boy's life was his maternal grandfather, Dodye Feig, an old Hasid, who fired the child's imagination with tales of Hasidic inspiration. Indeed many of Wiesel's works of fiction depict an ancient storyteller who recounts similar tales to an inspired young listener.

What for Elie Wiesel was a traditional and idyllic boyhood in an orthodox Jewish family came to a dramatic end with the arrival of the Nazi armies during the spring of 1944. All of Sighet's approximately fifteen thousand Jews were arrested and deported by train to Auschwitz, Poland. Wiesel was separated by the SS guards from his mother and three sisters, Tzipora, Hilda, and Batya, although he was able to remain with his father. When Soviet troops neared Auschwitz in early 1945, these two were moved to Buchenwald. Wiesel's father perished from starvation and dysentery at Buchenwald, while his mother and Tzipora were murdered in the gas chambers of Auschwitz. Well after the liberation in 1945, Wiesel learned of the survival of his older sisters, Hilda and Batya. His best-known work, *La Nuit* (1958; translated as *Night*, 1960), was written as a memorial to his parents and his younger sister.

During his period of imprisonment in the camps, the adolescent Wiesel suffered every kind of indignity imaginable: torture, hunger, filth, intense cold, illness, and the terror that one feels when facing the constant threat of execution. These experiences are the substance of *La Nuit* and continue to reverberate in his later works.

On 11 April 1945 Wiesel was liberated at Buchenwald by the United States Third Army. His initial desire was to move to the then-British mandate of Palestine, but immigration restrictions made this impossible. To be repatriated to his native Transylvania was unthinkable. He consented to go to Belgium with hundreds of other Jewish orphans, but his train was rerouted to France at the insistence of Gen. Charles de Gaulle, who wished France to become a haven for the homeless. Initially Wiesel was sent to Normandy, where the Œuvres du Secours aux Enfants, a charitable children's aid society, provided him with nourishment and shelter. Later he

moved to Paris, where from 1948 to 1951 he studied at the Sorbonne and mastered the French language, which eventually became his preferred medium of literary expression. His principal areas were philosophy, literature, and psychology. At the same time he supported himself by working at a variety of jobs, including choir director, part-time teacher of Hebrew and the Jewish Bible, translator of Hebrew into French, and summer-camp counselor.

Under the influence of the philosopher Gustave Wahl of the Sorbonne, Wiesel studied the texts of the French classical era and those of Greco-Roman antiquity with the same dedication he had demonstrated in his boyhood analyses of the Talmud and the Hasidic texts. During his Sorbonne days, Wiesel became a journalist for the French-Jewish periodical *Arche* and was assigned to cover the early days of the State of Israel. By 1952 he was working for the Tel Aviv daily newspaper *Yediot Ahronot*. Sent to cover a story in India, Wiesel realized that he would need to learn English as well as French. Never completing his Sorbonne studies, he did acquire proficiency in English, and in 1956 he went to America to cover the United Nations for the Tel Aviv paper. He was struck by a taxicab in New York and for nearly a year was forced to remain in America, in a wheelchair. Since his French travel documents were expiring, he decided to apply for United States citizenship. Wiesel has been an American citizen since 1963, and his French books have been translated into English almost immediately following their publication in Paris. On Passover eve 1969, he married Marion Erster Rose, also a survivor of the camps; their son, Shlomo Elisha, was born in 1972. Since the early 1970s Marion Wiesel has served as the translator of her husband's books.

In 1957 Wiesel joined the staff of the *Jewish Daily Forward,* but he dreamed of writing more than the journalistic work he had been producing. As a child he had written a book (never published) about the Jewish Bible. He felt that the sincerest source of inspiration for him was his rich knowledge of old Jewish folk tales. He also felt that because he had personally witnessed the most tragic moment in human history, he should somehow recapture his experiences in durable literary form. Yet in 1945 he had taken a vow not to speak or write of his experiences in the camps for ten years. He wondered how to break his silence, how to find the right words, if indeed any existed. How could one use language, a refined and orderly system of signs developed by civilized society, to express experiences that were totally antithetical to civilization, events that were in all regards supreme manifestations of chaos and disorder? For a whole decade Wiesel pondered these questions and wondered as well whether he had the stamina to relive, even in literature, the horror of the Holocaust. In a 1984 interview in *Paris Review,* he told John S. Friedman: "I didn't want to use the wrong words. I was afraid that words might betray it [the Holocaust]. I waited. I waited. I'm still not sure that it was the wrong move, or the right move, that is, whether to choose language or silence. . . . Sometimes you don't have to speak in order to be heard, not when the message is so powerful." Ultimately, however, Wiesel realized that his message must be expressed in words.

Wiesel chose in his first major book to deal with the Holocaust. In 1954 *Yediot Ahronot* assigned him to interview the 1952 Nobel Laureate in literature, the well-known Catholic novelist François Mauriac. Mauriac, fascinated by Wiesel's memories of the Holocaust, discussed at length with him the question of Christian responsibility, even complicity, in the Holocaust. During this painful discussion Mauriac persuaded Wiesel that it was his solemn obligation to speak, to terminate his silence and write of his experiences as a witness of the concentration camps. Feeling more at home with his native Yiddish language than with his acquired French, Wiesel wrote his first book, about Auschwitz and Buchenwald, in Yiddish, calling it *Un di Velt Hot Geshvign* (And the World Remained Silent). This enormous tome (eight hundred pages in manuscript) was published initially in Buenos Aires, but its success was limited. In order to have the work accepted for publication in Paris, Wiesel drastically reduced the scope of the original to a 127-page volume, which, thanks to the intercession of Mauriac, was published in 1958 under the title *La Nuit.* The publisher was Editions de Minuit, which had become prominent for including among its authors such well-known *nouveaux romanciers* as Michel Butor. A work which has sold well since its original publication, *La Nuit* has been translated into all of the major languages. In 1960, superbly translated by Stella Rodway, it appeared in the United States and Great Britain as *Night.* The foreword, by Mauriac, adds a significant dimension to *La Nuit.* Because in this work one sees a youthful commentator describing the terror of life in the Nazi universe, many critics have compared Wiesel's book with Anne Frank's *Diary of a Young Girl* (1947), despite the fact that the two are fundamentally different in tone and subject matter. *La Nuit* is a personal record of a child's life in a world of barbed wire, starvation, and gas chambers. It recounts his innermost anxieties as he struggles to remain alive and as he clings to the last remaining vestige of his earlier life, his slowly declining father. Written in the starkest, most naked literary style, *La Nuit* seethes with powerful scenes. It is difficult to imagine a work that is more barren of literary adornment and at the same time so rich in intensity of human experience.

Once Wiesel had learned that it was possible to verbalize, at least partially, the world of the death camps, he transformed himself, in several compact, partly autobiographical novels, from a witness of death to a person who had experienced survival. Along with *Night,* the first two of these novels form Wiesel's *Night Trilogy,* published in a single volume under that title in 1987. *L'Aube* appeared in Paris in 1960 and was translated as *Dawn* in 1961. It deals with the desire of a death-camp survivor to join the underground Jewish movement just prior to the creation of the State of Israel in 1948. Having lived through the reign of terror in the camps, he now must gather enough courage to kill the enemies of the hoped-for Jewish state. One year later, in 1961, there appeared another short novel, *Le Jour* (literally, Day; freely translated into English under the title *The Accident,* in 1962), a novel about a young survivor who is hit by an automobile in New York and who considers committing suicide because of guilt from having lived through the Holocaust. After weeks of moral crisis, hovering between life and death, this young survivor realizes that his accident was not accidental, but rather an unconscious desire to do away with himself. Although he can barely endure the memories of his past, he must choose life.

In 1962 Wiesel published *La Ville de la chance* (translated as *The Town Beyond the Wall,* 1964), a novel in which he portrays a spectator who watched in silence through his windows in Sighet as the Jews of that town, his neighbors, were led through the streets toward the trains that would deport them to Auschwitz. The theme is silence, or rather the guilt of those who are silent and indifferent. Movingly, the author recaptures in the final scene the emotion of a survivor who returns to Sighet to see a similar face staring at him through a window. The novel received the Prix Rivarol in 1963.

Wiesel's subsequent volume, *Les Portes de la forêt* (1964; translated as *The Gates of the Forest*, 1966), contains his most penetrating analysis of the relationship between people suffering through the Holocaust and their God. In the novel, Gregor, a young Hungarian Jew separated from his family, survives in a camp and later fights with the partisans in the forest. After the war he seeks safety in America, but there he is devoured by the moral crisis of how the God of the Jews could have allowed his people to suffer so tragically. Accusations are interspersed with passages of remorse, but in the end Gregor chooses life, and love: "It's inhuman," one of the novel's key utterances holds, "to wall yourself up in pain and memories as if in a prison. Suffering must open us up to others. It must not cause us to reject them."

A pause in his series of semi-autobiographical novels, Wiesel's next work was a nonfictional, firsthand report on the Jews in the Soviet Union. A series of articles originally appearing in Hebrew in *Yediot Ahronot* is the basis of *Les Juifs du silence*, published in French and in English translation (as *The Jews of Silence*) in 1966. The English version of this documentary work is enriched by the historical afterword by Neal Kozodoy, who translated it from Hebrew. According to Wiesel's preface to the *Jews of Silence*: "The pages that follow are the report of a witness. Nothing more and nothing else. Their purpose is to draw attention to a problem about which no one should remain unaware." Henceforth Wiesel assumed the role of champion of the persecuted Soviet Jews. In *Les Juifs du silence* Wiesel underscores the fact that as the world remained silent during the early days of Auschwitz and Buchenwald, so too there has been silence–even among his fellow Jews–in the face of anti-Semitism in Russia.

Twenty years following his deportation from Sighet, Wiesel returned there for a visit in 1964. This visit was the basis for *Les Chants des morts*, published in 1966 in Paris and translated as *Legends of Our Time* in 1968. A loosely knit collection, it comprises philosophical essays, short stories, and autobiographical episodes. In this same vein he wrote *Entre deux soleils*, which appeared in French and in English translation (as *One Generation After*) in 1970, the twenty-fifth anniversary of Wiesel's liberation from Buchenwald.

Wiesel's next novel after *Les Portes de la forêt*, *Le Mendiant de Jérusalem* (1968; translated as *A Beggar of Jerusalem*, 1970), may be, along with *La Nuit*, his most successful literary undertaking to date. It received the Prix Médicis in Paris and was a best-seller on both sides of the Atlantic. A fictional transposition of the Israeli-Arab Six Day War of June 1967, Wiesel's novel treats the heady days of this Jewish victory as a pivotal moment in the history of his people. It is probably Wiesel's most jubilant work of fiction.

Despite the hopefulness expressed in *Le Mendiant de Jérusalem*, in a work of the same period Wiesel took up again the theme he had enunciated in *Les Juifs du silence*. But this time he chose for the first time to write a play, *Zalmen ou la folie de Dieu*, in which he dramatized his moral outrage at what was taking place in Russia. In 1968 the French version of the play was published; in 1974 the English translation, *Zalmen, or The Madness of God*, adapted for the stage by Wiesel's wife, Marion, was produced at Washington, D.C.'s Arena Stage and published in the United States Suffering from wordiness and from a not-always-successful attempt by Wiesel to blend symbolism with realism, the play nonetheless was widely viewed when public television broadcast the Arena Stage production, also in 1974. The play depicts a visit by American Jews to a small-town Russian synagogue during Yom Kippur services. The strongest character in the plot, Zalmen, is an eloquent and perceptive town idiot who serves to dramatize the plight of Soviet Jewry. Zalmen is one example of Wiesel's frequent use of the town idiot, or someone who is often wrongly perceived as mad, as a person who manifests greater insight into human destiny than those who regard themselves as rational and who refuse to see the truth as it really is.

Célébration hassidique: Portraits et légendes (1972) was Wiesel's next major work following *Le Mendiant de Jérusalem*. It received the Prix Bordin de l'Académie Française and was translated by Marion Wiesel as *Souls on Fire: Portraits and Legends of Hasidic Masters* (1972). Drawing on the heritage of Hasidic tales which he had heard from his grandfather, the author recounts a set of stories on how the Hasidic Jews lived, their relationships with their legendary rabbis, and the warmth and joy permeating the life of the Hasidic home. *Célébration hassidique* is Wiesel's finest work on this rich historical movement in Judaism. Many critics have found in this work reverberations of Camusian existentialism, especially in

Wiesel's insistence that man, despite the overwhelming odds of human destiny, must reject despair and continue to live with hope.

Of all of Wiesel's works, perhaps the most unusual is *Ani Maamin* (1973), subtitled *Un Chant perdu et retrouvé* (*A Song Lost and Found Again*) and published first in France and then in the United States in an attractive bilingual volume in 1974. Written as the libretto for a cantata by Darius Milhaud, *Ani Maamin* is a song of exaltation of the Messianic spirit in Jewish history. Composed in blank verse, the poetry is laden with tensions and rhythms that carry the reader from one crescendo to another.

One of Wiesel's most powerful novels is *Le Serment de Kolvillàg* (1973; translated as *The Oath*, 1973), an epic narrative that depicts the character type of the madman who understands more clearly than so-called people of reason the dangerous course of an insane world. The theme of silence is again central, as Azriel, a typical Wieselian character, tries to keep a young man from committing suicide by telling him a story he had been sworn (thus the "oath" of the title) never to relate to any living being: how all the Jews, except him, had been slaughtered by their gentile neighbors in the Hungarian village of Kolvillàg because they were accused of being Christ killers. Of the work Wiesel once stated, "Take *The Oath*, a novel set at the beginning of the century, about a village and a ritual murder, nothing about the Holocaust. But then on another level, it is the Holocaust—not of the Jews but of the world. That's why I called the village Kolvillàg. *Villàg* in Hungarian means world, and Kol in Hebrew means all—the entire world." *Le Serment de Kolvillàg* is in this way typical of Wiesel's novels, with the exception of *La Nuit*. As the author once noted: "I have never spoken about the Holocaust except in one book, *Night,* . . . where I tried to tell a tale directly, as though face to face with that experience." However, if one penetrates beyond Wiesel's plots, one finds the ubiquitous presence of the Holocaust. Mankind lives under the threat of renewed holocausts and in the shadow of previous ones.

With *Célébration biblique: Portraits et légendes* (1975; translated as *Messengers of God: Biblical Portraits and Legends*, 1976), Wiesel produced a volume in the same vein as *Célébration hassidique,* except that in this more recent collection of tales and legends, the main characters are not Hasidic rabbis but the patriarchs themselves. Seeking to make Abraham, Isaac, Adam, and Job more meaningful for post-Holocaust mankind Wiesel makes the patriarchs relive their own personal tragedies. Demythifying these biblical figures, the author transforms them into almost contemporary people. They are like Albert Camus's Sisyphus, who chooses perseverence and life over despair and death. The work constitutes for Wiesel a supreme reaffirmation of faith and hope.

In *Un Juif aujourd'hui* (1977; translated as *A Jew Today,* 1978), Wiesel assembled his third collection of essays, tales, fragments, and dialogues. Here he expands his concern beyond the Jewish destiny in order to include Palestinian Arabs and other oppressed peoples around the world, in South Africa, Biafra, Cambodia, Vietnam, and Bangladesh. In the late 1970s and early 1980s Wiesel wrote two English-language volumes, *Four Hasidic Masters and Their Struggle Against Melancholy* (1978) and *Five Biblical Portraits* (1981), both in the tradition of *Célébration hassidique* and *Célébration biblique.*

In 1979 Wiesel published his second play, *Le Procès de Shamgorod (tel qu'il se déroula le 25 février 1649)*, translated the same year as *The Trial of God (as it was held on February 25, 1649, in Shamgorod)*. The drama concerns a Jewish innkeeper and three Jewish troubadourlike wanderers who put God on trial for allowing the massacre of their coreligionists in a pogrom. In act two they seek an appropriate prosecutor and defense attorney. Act three presents the trial in which, with Job-like passion, Wiesel's characters accuse their God of indifference. In reality it is not God who is on trial, but rather the faith of those who would prosecute Him. The play has been performed before enthusiastic audiences by professional theaters in Paris, Oslo, and West Germany as well as by many campus groups at American universities.

Le Testament d'un poète juif assassiné (1980), a novel which received the Prix Livre-International and the Prix des Bibliothécaires, continues Wiesel's concern with the suffering of the Soviet Jews. Written as the confessional diary of a Jewish poet, Paltiel Kossover, who was murdered under the Stalin regime in 1952, the novel describes how this poet's only son, Grisha, seeks to rediscover and to comprehend the life of his father through the diary. The circumstances under which the diary was written and the way in which it comes to Grisha are important. Paltiel, imprisoned by the KGB, is told to write his autobiography. Although he never leaves the prison, the document eventually finds its way to his son. The analogy Wiesel implicitly draws between Stalin's mass murders and Hitler's is clear. The work, acclaimed with virtually unanimous applause in the Parisian press, was translated and published in English in 1981 as *The Testament*.

Wiesel's 1983 novel, *Le Cinquième Fils*, translated as *The Fifth Son* (1985), is set for the most part in New York City and portrays a son who devotes his life to unraveling the mysterious past of his parents. Eventually the young man, Ariel, learns that he had a brother, also named Ariel, who was killed by the SS during World War II. He also discovers that his father had participated in an attempt to assassinate the SS leader in his native town but that the attempt was unsuccessful. A witness relates to the young New Yorker the nightmarish experiences that his parents had endured, stressing that they are psychologically incapable of sharing these experiences with their son. Ariel departs on a trip to Europe to seek vengeance against the Nazi SS officer who had persecuted his parents and who has since assumed a mask of respectability as a high-ranking corporate executive in one of West Germany's most successful businesses. But in keeping with Wiesel's visions the vengeance does not take place.

Wiesel's most recent work, *Le Crépuscule au loin* (1987; translated as *Twilight*, 1988), may well be the most complex of his recent novels. Metaphysical in character, it deals with a problem that has ceaselessly preoccupied Wiesel: madness and sanity; the insane are those who see the truth, while the sane commit the most horrible atrocities. Set almost entirely in an institution for the insane located in upstate New York, the plot depicts a typically Wieselian character, Raphael. He searches for a long-lost friend, Pedro, who, he has reason to believe, has disappeared into the catacombs of madness. Raphael has encounters with several madmen who imagine that they are biblical personages: Cain, Adam, Abraham, even God himself. As Raphael searches for his friend he slowly, meticulously unravels the mysteries of the past—his past—and also gains greater insight into human nature, at its loftiest and basest levels of conduct. As in so many Wiesel novels, past and present are confusingly, hauntingly interlaced.

Wiesel, whose residence is in New York City, continues to write and to study ancient Hebraic texts and classics of French literature. From 1972 to 1976 he taught Judaic studies at the City University of New York. He has spoken at forums and on university campuses around the world. Since 1976 Wiesel has been an Andrew Mellon Professor in the Humanities at Boston University and commutes every week between New York and Boston.

Among the many prizes he has received are: the Grand Prix de la Littérature de la Ville de Paris; the Martin Luther King, Jr., Award; the William and Janice Epstein Fiction Award and the Frank and Ethel S. Cohen Award, both from the Jewish Book Council; the Remembrance Award; the National Jewish Book Award and the Jewish Heritage Award for excellence in literature. In 1985 he was awarded the Congressional Gold Medal of Achievement. He has also been named commander of the French Légion d'Honneur. He has received honorary doctorates from Hebrew Union College, Manhattanville College, the Jewish Theological Seminary, Yeshiva University, Bar Ilan University (Israel), Boston University, Hofstra University, Marquette University, and Yale University. He served presidents Jimmy Carter and Ronald Reagan as the chairman of the U.S. Holocaust Memorial Council.

If Wiesel had written only *La Nuit*, it would be sufficient to guarantee him a lasting place among the French writers of the post-World War II era. A tiny classic, *La Nuit* is a tautly written, tensely expressed, yet glowingly human work that ranks with such books as Vercors's *Le Silence de la mer* (*The Silence of the Sea*, 1942). But Wiesel has since written more than two dozen other works—novels, essays, short stories, chronicles, testimonies—many of which are literary works of high order. His novels, essays, and stories contain resonances of Camus, André Malraux, and, to a lesser extent, Jean-Paul Sartre and Mauriac. In his direct, relatively image-free, concise language, rich with meaning, he resembles the French classicists. Wiesel told John S. Friedman: "I reduce nine hundred pages to one hundred sixty pages. I also enjoy cutting. I do it with a masochistic pleasure although even when you cut, you don't. Writing is not like painting where you add. It is not what you put on the canvas that the reader sees. Writing is more like sculpture where you remove, you eliminate in order to make the work visible. Even those pages you remove somehow remain."

Wiesel has not remained unaffected by the bold experiments that have taken place in French narrative writing since the advent of the *nouveaux romanciers*. Some of his novels depart from traditional chronological narrative to move forward and backward in time; they also contain fragments of poetry, incantations, and often-dramatic shifts of points of view.

A compelling speaker, Wiesel leaves an indelible mark on all who have heard him. As chairman of the Nobel Committee Egel Aarvik noted in naming Wiesel recipient of the 1986 peace prize: "Elie Wiesel has emerged as one of the most spiritual leaders and guides in an age when violence, repression and racism continue to characterize the world. . . . Wiesel is a messenger to Mankind. His message is one of peace, atonement, and human dignity. His belief that the forces fighting evil in the world can be victorious is a hard-won belief."

Interviews:

Gene Koppel and Henry Kaufmann, *Elie Wiesel: A Small Measure of Victory* (Tucson: University of Arizona Press, 1974);

Harry James Cargas, *Harry James Cargas in Conversation with Elie Wiesel* (New York: Paulist Press, 1976);

John K. Roth, *A Consuming Fire: Encounters with Elie Wiesel and the Holocaust* (Atlanta: John Knox, 1979);

John S. Friedman, "The Art of Fiction LXXIX: Elie Wiesel," *Paris Review*, 26 (Spring 1984): 130-178;

Brigitte-Fanny Cohen, *Elie Wiesel–Qui êtes-vous?* (Paris: La Manufacture, 1987);

Phillipe de Saint-Chéron, *Rencontre avec Elie Wiesel* (Paris: Nouvelle Cité, 1988).

Bibliography:

Molly Abramowitz, *Elie Wiesel: A Bibliography* (Metuchen, N.J.: Scarecrow Press, 1974).

References:

Michael Berenbaum, *Vision of the Void: Theological Reflections on the Works of Elie Wiesel* (Middletown, Conn.: Wesleyan University Press, 1979);

Robert McAfee Brown, *Elie Wiesel: Messenger to All Humanity* (Notre Dame, Ind.: University of Notre Dame Press, 1983);

Brown, "The Holocaust as a Problem in Moral Choice," in *Dimensions of the Holocaust: Lectures at Northwestern University* (Evanston, Ill.: The University, 1977), pp. 47-83;

Harry James Cargas, ed., *Responses to Elie Wiesel: Critical Essays by Major Jewish and Christian Scholars* (New York: Persea Books, 1978);

Denis Diamond, "Elie Wiesel: Reconciling the Irreconcilable," *World Literature Today*, 57 (Spring 1983): 228-233;

Ted L. Estess, *Elie Wiesel* (New York: Frederick Ungar: 1980);

Ellen S. Fine, *Legacy of Night: The Literary Universe of Elie Wiesel* (Albany: State University of New York Press, 1982);

S. G. Freedman, "Bearing Witness: The Life and Work of Elie Wiesel," *New York Times Magazine*, 23 October 1983, pp. 32-36;

Joë Friedmann, *Le Rire dans l'univers tragique d'Elie Wiesel* (Paris: Nizet, 1982);

Mary Jean Green, "Witness to the Absurd; Elie Wiesel and the French Existentialists," *Renascence*, 29 (Summer 1977): 170-184;

Irving Halperin, *Messengers from the Dead* (Philadelphia: Westminster Press, 1970), pp. 65-106;

Samuel H. Joseloff, "Link and Promise: The Works of Elie Wiesel," *Southern Humanities Review*, 8 (Spring 1974): 163-170;

Lawrence Langer, *The Holocaust and the Literary Imagination* (New Haven: Yale University Press, 1975), pp. 75-89;

N. McCain, "Elie Wiesel: The Struggle to Reconcile the Reality of Evil with Faith in God," *Chronicle of Higher Education*, 13 April 1983, pp. 21-22;

Wladimir Rabi, "Elie Wiesel: Un Homme, une œuvre, un public," *Esprit*, no. 9 (1980): 79-92;

Alvin H. Rosenfeld and Irving Greenberg, eds., *Confronting the Holocaust: The Impact of Elie Wiesel* (Bloomington: Indiana University Press, 1978);

Ellen N. Stern, *Elie Wiesel: Witness for Life* (Hoboken, N.J.: Ktav, 1982).

Monique Wittig
(1935-)

Jean Duffy
University of Sheffield

BOOKS: *L'Opoponax* (Paris: Editions de Minuit, 1964); translated by Helen Weaver as *The Opoponax* (London: Owen, 1966; New York: Simon & Schuster, 1966);

Les Guérillères (Paris: Editions de Minuit, 1969); translated by David Le Vay as *The Guerrillas* (London: Owen, 1971; New York: Viking, 1971);

Le Corps lesbien (Paris: Editions de Minuit, 1973); translated by Le Vay as *The Lesbian Body* (London: Owen, 1975; New York: Morrow, 1975);

Brouillon pour un dictionnaire des amantes, by Wittig and Sande Zeig (Paris: Grasset, 1976); translated by Wittig and Zeig as *Lesbian Peoples: Material for a Dictionary* (New York: Avon, 1979; London: Virago, 1980);

Virgile, non (Paris: Editions de Minuit, 1985); translated by Le Vay and Margaret Crosland as *Across the Acheron* (London: Owen, 1987);

Le Voyage sans fin (Paris: Vlasta, 1985).

OTHER: "Paradigm," in *Homosexualities and French Literature*, edited by George Stambolian (Ithaca: Cornell University Press, 1979).

Monique Wittig (photograph copyright ©Jerry Bauer)

Monique Wittig is one of relatively few French feminist writers whose work has made an impact on both sides of the Atlantic, even though her audience has been largely restricted to radical feminist groups and progressive academic circles. Within these two groups, however, Wittig has become an important point of reference.

Belonging to a generation of French writers and theorists which distinguishes clearly between an author's private life and his or her work, Wittig has ceded very few personal details. Born in Belgium in 1935, the daughter of the Belgian poet Henri Dubois, Wittig achieved literary prominence with the 1964 publication of *L'Opoponax*, which won the Prix Médicis. Wittig's commitment to the feminist movement came to the fore in 1970 in her emergence as the spokeswoman of the newly formed Féministes Révolutionnaires, a consciousness-raising feminist association aiming to subvert the patriarchal order. Wittig was also one of a group of women who in the same year caused a stir in France by a well-chosen publicity stunt whereby they attempted to place a wreath dedicated to the wife of the unknown soldier at the soldier's tomb beneath the Arc de Triomphe. Although she now lives in the United States, Wittig has remained active in both cultures, contributing regularly to *Questions Féministes* and *Feminist Issues* and most recently staging productions of her play *Le Voyage sans fin* at Goddard College, Vermont, and the Théâtre Renaud/Barrault in Paris.

L'Opoponax (1964; translated as *The Opoponax*, 1966), Wittig's first novel, is easily her most accessible book. It belongs to a long tradition of literature on childhood and adolescence, deals with the universal experience of growing and learning, and is "realistic" in that it seeks to capture the perceptions and activities of a little girl from her first days at school until the blossoming of her infatuation with another adolescent schoolgirl. On the level of fiction, *L'Opoponax* does not radically break new ground. The situations are drawn from a familiar repertoire–the first day at school, the school trip, the play, childish superstition and persecution, fear of the dark, the child's interest in sexual difference, the schoolgirl crush.

However, recognizable though the subject and situations may be, *L'Opoponax* is far from orthodox in its approach and anticipates the subsequent thematic and technical development of Wittig's work. The child in Wittig's novel is not seen as an adult in the making; childhood is not a phase but a world in itself. Adults in *L'Opoponax* occupy a purely marginal position and generate more interest in the children when they die than they did when they were alive. Wittig's prime interest is with the child's *Lebenswelt*, the way in which he or she perceives reality and learns about it. *L'Opoponax* is a phenomenological description of childhood in which adult-specific emotions such as nostalgia and sentimentality are irrelevant and therefore excluded.

Wittig's priorities have a profound effect on the narrative structure she uses and in particular on her rejection of the pillars of the traditional novel, plot and characterization. The fact that most of Wittig's books have been published by the Editions de Minuit, the house known for publishing the Nouveaux Romanciers (New Novelists), is no accident. *L'Opoponax*, like the *nouveau roman*, challenges the synthetic and retrospective process by which multifarious sensory data are subsumed into narrative-worthy events, sequences, and, ultimately, plots. In *L'Opoponax*, the child's lack of an overview precludes anything as definite and structured as a plot. The traditional tense of fiction–the past historic–is not appropriate and is abandoned in favor of the present. For Wittig's child, details in the outside world figure only in the moment of perception and then are consigned to oblivion. Reality is reduced to discrete fragments perceived by the child and these fragments are juxtaposed in the narrative in a naive and often incongruous manner which defies sophisticated criteria such as logic and verisimilitude. Traumatic occasions are framed by descriptions of banal childish activities; death and childish games are treated in the

same neutral and unemphatic style. In short, the connections between various situations are neither causal nor logical, but chronological or associative, while the sine qua non of the traditional "story," the convention whereby certain events are seen as more momentous than others, is consistently flouted.

Characterization is subject to a similar process of leveling. There is no conventional protagonist; the distinctively sensitive or rebellious child does not interest Wittig. One character, Catherine Legrand, is, for reasons of narrative clarity and economy, elected as a token point of reference. However, she has none of the particularizing traits of the character seen in the round, no innate attributes or defects which would distinguish her from the other children. For the first half of the novel the focus is diffuse as Wittig tries to recreate at once the centripetal forces of peer pressure and companionability at work in any group of children and the infinite variety of impressions perceived by the candid childish eye. Very few of the children stand out from the others. Individual children are named, but in contrast with the paternalistic tendency of most fiction on childhood, they are throughout referred to by both given name and surname, that is, by the civil-identity tag of the schoolchild as opposed to the familiar first name often used by a traditional author for his protagonist/protégé. A child may momentarily achieve a certain notability in his or her peer group if he or she or a close relative dies, but the child's status is contingent upon that context and he or she is soon subsumed again into the group. Very occasionally one of the children is allowed to make his or her mark. Reine Dieu, a particularly impulsive and adventurous girl, makes a more lasting impression on her peers and enjoys a certain notoriety because of her unruliness. However, this unconventionality is left as a kind of absolute. No explanation is given in the text for her behavior; the reader who requires clear motivation can ultimately only supply a negative explanation and attribute it to Reine Dieu's lack of awareness of the codes of behavior which govern adult conduct. Deterministic factors, the motivational investigation of childish behavior are intellectual models imposed on the world of childhood and are therefore outside Wittig's field of interest.

The emergence of Reine Dieu as a kind of childish folklore heroine initiates a process of differentiation which in the second half of the novel culminates in the relationship between Catherine

Legrand and Valerie Borge. The relative prominence given to Valerie Borge reflects the way in which the child develops a notion of individuality through his or her awareness of the other. Valerie Borge is not studied in any depth as an individual. Her function is catalytic; she sets in motion a certain psychological mechanism which is the prelude to adulthood. She generates in Catherine Legrand feelings of preference, a personal as opposed to a group reaction which causes Catherine Legrand to focus upon one of her peers and stimulates the expression of emotions specific to herself.

The emergence of a sense of discretion and personal inclination signals the disintegration of the world of childhood in which the value-free perception of the child flits from detail to detail without conferring meaning and stress on anything in particular. It also signals the end of *L'Opoponax*. However, the cut-off point of *L'Opoponax* is the starting point for the subsequent development of Wittig's work. In *L'Opoponax*, Wittig does not venture beyond the adolescent infatuation with a member of one's own sex. By omission, she refuses to consider the process—considered to be natural—whereby affection between young girls is transferred to a heterosexual relationship.

L'Opoponax cannot be considered a feminist novel, but the seeds of a discontent with male ideology and dominance are there. Humorously but significantly, *L'Opoponax* opens with the diminutive Robert Payen encouraging his playmates to come and look at his "quequette." With gentle irony Wittig suggests the way in which the male, from a very early age, seems to consider the penis as a remarkable asset and a symbol of social status. Later in the text Wittig draws attention to the way in which historical representation has been controlled by male ideology at the expense and to the virtual exclusion of women. The description of an illustration in the history manual is the source of a neat ironic tension between the teacher's moral on Charlemagne's paternalistic equity and the children's candid recognition of an absence which denotes a male monopoly of history and representation: "Il n'y a pas de petites filles sur l'image" (There are no little girls in the picture). Finally, the fact that in the end Catherine Legrand has to resort to the words of a male poet in order to express her feelings for Valerie Borge touches on an issue which dominates not only Wittig's later work but also feminist theory and writing in general—the *décalage* between feminist awareness and the man-produced language and culture taught to girls.

The theme of language is not, however, simply an afterthought in *L'Opoponax*. It informs the entire narrative composition. The traditional mainstays of plot and character may have been abandoned but this rejection does not prevent Wittig from creating a highly coherent structure. The superficial random impressionism and the apparent anarchy of the choice of data conceal a finely graduated exploration of the theme of language, its acquisition, and the relationship between language and awareness. The novel begins at the point when Catherine Legrand has acquired a sufficient degree of linguistic competence to enter the microsociety of the classroom. She has the necessary vocabulary to express essential physical needs, a rudimentary comprehension of language which permits her to be initiated into the at first passive process of cultural assimilation. The novel comes to an end at the point when the children begin to manipulate language for their own destructive and creative purposes. By the end of the novel they have mastered language sufficiently to turn it against their teachers and to put their cultural heritage to constructive use in the expression of personal feelings. Furthermore, although objective temporal coordinates are, like everything else, subject to the fluid impressions of the children, the careful reader will realize from an early stage that the passing of time in *L'Opoponax* is charted by progress in the acquisition of linguistic skills. The novel—and the child's life—is punctuated by a variety of scholastic exercises which gauge and expand the child's linguistic competence, and Wittig records with care and sensitivity both the traumatic and exhilarating stages in this obstacle course.

From Wittig's account of the acquisition of language it is clear that the implications of post-Saussurian linguistics and structuralism have not been lost on her. Indeed, *L'Opoponax* can be viewed as a demonstration of the initiation into cultural codes to which all are subject. Wittig's discreet examination of the inextricable relationship between language and authority in this apparently innocuous first novel foreshadows her subsequent feminist attack on male-manipulated language. The classroom situation provides an ideal context for the illustration of the interdependence of linguistic competence and the possession of power. Incompetence means subordination by adults or victimization by one's peers. Language is used to command, to intimidate, to forbid, and to channel the child's perception of the world in particular directions. Conversely, rebellion involves the active manipulation of language. Thus, toward the end of the novel, the children challenge the authority of their teachers by striking and shouting slogans, while religious indoctrination is subverted by a contradictive use of language; for example, the Devil, one of the threats used to dominate the children, is recognized as being a fictional fabrication which can be undone by a negative rephrasing of hearsay about him. Perhaps the most radical form of rebellion, however, comes with the child's recognition of the possibilities of linguistic play–an unsophisticated and nonintellectualized variation on Wittig's own acute awareness of the relative and conventional, as opposed to absolute and real, nature of the relationship between word and meaning. The best illustration of this important point is undoubtedly the title of the novel: Catherine Legrand's deformation of the archaic word *opopanax* and her use of it to sum up everything that is incomprehensible to her constitutes a subversion of conventional meaning and form which anticipates Wittig's own neologistic play in later works.

Essential to any discussion of language in *L'Opoponax* is mention of the unorthodox use of narrative point of view. Although Catherine Legrand is the main point of reference in the novel, her perceptions and reflections are recounted from the point of view of an anonymous, impersonal "on" (roughly translated as "one") which corresponds to the group-based sense of identity of the child and to the way in which her perceptions are constantly filtered through and channeled by an anonymous body of cultural codes consisting of proverbs, maxims, gossip, fairy stories, and school manuals. It is only when, in the last line of the novel, Catherine Legrand finds an adequate expression for her special and personal affection for Valerie Borge, that the first person pronoun is pronounced. The fact that this "je" has been appropriated from a poet belonging to her cultural heritage bears witness both to the extent to which one's perception and expression are always adulterated by what one has been taught, as well as to the male monopoly of culture.

Critical reaction to *L'Opoponax* has been extremely good. Laudatory reviews by established writers such as Claude Simon (*Express*, 30 November-6 December 1964) set the tone while seminal essays such as Mary McCarthy's "Everybody's

Childhood" (collected in *The Writing on the Wall and Other Literary Essays*, 1970) drew attention to Wittig's radical experimentation with the novel form. The success of *L'Opoponax* can be gauged not only by the fact that it has been translated into several European languages but also by the fact that although Wittig did not produce another novel for five years, *L'Opoponax* quickly became a standard text in surveys of the literature of childhood.

On the surface Wittig's second novel, *Les Guérillères* (1969; translated, 1971), seems to constitute a radical break with the central interests of *L'Opoponax*. *Les Guérillères* is composed of a series of short prose poems evoking the customs and lifestyles of an island community of female warriors, very obviously modeled upon the mythical societies of the Lemnians and Amazons. With its wealth of allusion and its account of the wars waged on men by the women, it can be seen as an attempt to give women their own epic, to confer upon them the prominence denied them in classical epics in which, as Mandy Merck has pointed out in an essay for *Tearing the Veil* (edited by Susan Lipschitz, 1978), the Amazons are not seen as an independent force "but as the vanquished opponents of heroes credited with the establishment and protection of the Athenian State." The patriotic (and therefore divisive) aspect of the traditional epic has been eliminated in favor of a celebration of female solidarity pitted against male domination, and the catalogues of national heroes, standard set pieces in the epic, have been replaced by lists of female Christian names drawn from a wide variety of cultures and in which the mythological and the banal, the ancient and the modern are juxtaposed. These lists punctuate the work at fairly regular intervals, and their prominent position at the center of otherwise blank pages translates typographically Wittig's desire to bring to the foreground those whose names have been erased or eclipsed from historical, mythological, and literary records.

The novel is divided into two parts, the first predominantly descriptive, evoking the customs of the women, the second more eventful, recording their battles. The two parts complement each other, representing as they do two stages of female awareness. The first stage necessarily involves a reassessment of the effects of male ideology and an attack on male-centered symbolism. The most obvious and most vulnerable target is the institution of the phallus, that is, the set of associations and meanings which male-dominated culture has arbitrarily conferred upon the male organ and the pivot on which male ideology turns. The phallus, the organizing principle of political, mythological, anthropological, and psychoanalytical thinking, is undermined in the female society of *Les Guérillères*, for whom the phallus is an irrelevant notion.

As a corrective to this consecration of the penis, the women in Wittig's novel have established their own symbolism, taking the clitoris and the vulva as their main points of reference. Thus an entire section is given over to the description of the clitoris in terms which one would normally associate with the penis. In the enumeration of the features of the clitoris, Wittig ratifies the importance feminists attach to a thorough knowledge of one's own body and at the same time rectifies the process by which the clitoris has in the patriarchal society been eclipsed from discourse as a taboo subject. The attribution to the clitoris of features associated with the penis constitutes an attack on the absolute status of the phallus, a demonstration that its mystique is dependent upon the monopolization of certain words and images which can in fact be recombined to describe something quite different. It is, however, the vulva which is adopted as the principal symbol in *Les Guérillères*. Wittig's symbolic promotion of the female genitalia is no idiosyncratic whim—the vulva and in particular the image of hands held in the shape of the vulva have become an important element in feminist iconography. What is particularly interesting about Wittig's use of the symbol is the evolution it undergoes in the course of the novel. In the first half of the novel the women spend a great deal of time in what can only be described as vulva contemplation and in the elaboration of a network of similes and metaphors in which the vulva is alternately the tenor and the vehicle. This process of self-contemplation—a necessary stage since self-knowledge must precede action—gives way in the second half of the novel to direct action. By setting up a vulvacentricity to counter phallocentricity, the women are in danger of falling into the same trap as men, of imprisoning themselves within an ideology. Privileging one part of the body over the rest is not radically different from the fragmentation undergone by the female body at the hands of male poets and writers and, more seriously, this fragmentation valorizes division rather than solidarity. Thus toward the middle of the novel the women turn the criticism

they had leveled at male ideology on their own culture, subverting the metaphors and similes by which they had asserted and sublimated their own sexuality, while in the second part the mirror in which they had contemplated their private parts becomes a means of communication and a weapon. Having given female sexuality its place in discourse, they refuse to define themselves in terms of genitalia, and narcissism has given way to coordinated action.

The wars waged in the second half of the novel subvert once and for all the association of the phallus with power, strength, and aggression. The women show a ferocity which belies traditional notions of femininity. Patriarchal values have paralyzed women, shutting them in showcases, limiting their role to the bed. As they step down from their pedestals, Wittig's women, with a typical deflating disingenuousness, declare themselves to be astonished that they can move. In fact their energy and dynamism are stressed throughout the novel; this energy is channeled into a direct offensive aimed not only at men but also at the cultural structures they have created. By razing the "tall buildings" and houses they attack at once the omnipresent architectural phallic symbols and the prisons by which men have instituted possession, property, and, in particular, the household—the linchpins of the patriarchal society. Possession, as the little girls who carry home the wild birds discover, kills. The war brings about a kind of tabula rasa. The women wipe male ideology off the slate of history, and in the course of their doing so, the huge circle which punctuates the text, occupying, like the lists of female names, a whole page to itself, becomes not a symbol of the vulva but a symbolic zero, a pristine point of departure for the institution of a new society in which difference and its result—warfare—will be eliminated. Ultimate victory takes the form not of the annihilation or indeed the enslavement of man but of his conversion to a new way of looking at the world. As the women and the young converts choose together names for the elements of their world, it becomes clear that the end of the novel is a new beginning. Man is being given a second chance and the women referred to in the third person throughout the book at last have access to a communal discourse in which they can pronounce the word *nous* (we).

The act of renaming is the utopian solution to a problem which dominates Wittig's fiction: the attempt to purge language of patriarchal values and establish a discourse which will accommodate women's experiences. Language and power are seen as indissociable. The application of reductive labels such as "femelle" (female) and "nègre" (Negro) to women and blacks testifies to an attempt to negate nonmale and nonwhite cultures, the institution of difference as a means of oppression by the white male oligarchy. Wittig's retrieval of female-centered myths from a remarkable range of cultures is one form of retaliation. The rewriting of legends, fairy tales, and religious stories which form a crucial part of the cultural code and thereby condition one's view of the world is another. The biblical account of the Fall is reinterpreted as a misogynist attempt to deny women access to knowledge–an interpretation which, according to Wittig, has been corroborated in history by the outlawing of "female" wisdom and the persecution of "witches." The tale of Sleeping Beauty epitomizes the passive role assigned to women and is used to illustrate the plight of the woman who has no self-awareness; the spindle on which she inadvertently pricks her finger is a symbol of the clitoris and her hundred-year sleep an apt punishment for the woman who does not know her own body. The story of Drapaudi, who in the Hindu epic *Mahabharata* was won by a man and shared with four others, is turned upside down: Wittig's Drapaudi is the owner of five husbands and asserts her power by the application of epithets and quasi-proverbial expressions to them. Reinterpretation and reinvention are arbitrary violations of an arbitrarily instituted male culture and have the merit of exposing the assumption on which the latter is based.

The obscuration of female tradition and experience and the subordination of women are, according to Wittig, interdependent. Women have accepted enslavement simply because of the enforced ignorance in which they have been imprisoned. Man has systematically–through the manipulation of the linguistic system–destroyed the evidence that women ever occupied another status; woman's imprisonment within the prevailing linguistic code precludes the realization of alternatives. The women in *Les Guérillères* counter this negation by subverting the consecrated but arbitrary relationship between the present linguistic code and reality and by signaling the multiple aspects of reality which have not been formulated and which consequently have been eclipsed by that which has been formulated. The polyvalent symbolic zero which punctuates the text also refers to the holes, absences in the male discourse.

0 is for lacunae in Wittig's alphabet, the gaps in the apparently impenetrable patriarchal language, the intervals in which female consciousness can gain a foothold.

Wittig's promotion of the lacuna to the status of a primordial signifier suggests that her reworking of Mallarmé's "Le Cygne" (or "swan sonnet") at the end of *Les Guérillères* is not simply a pastiche. Her project is no less ambitious than his; like Mallarmé, Wittig is attempting to write the absent and to purge the language of the merely hu/man. The great register in which the women inscribe their culture is Wittig's equivalent of Mallarmé's *Livre* (that is, a *summa* of his poetic efforts, all aimed at achieving a higher reality through poetic correspondence)–a polyvalent and polyphonous text to be read not as a sequence but as a dynamic structure of infinitely recombinable units resurrecting meaning and representing the totality through multiple but highly calculated variations. The description of the great register is a kind of *mise en abyme* or miniature image for the structure of Wittig's novel, but *Les Guérillères* is no more than a blueprint for a new *Livre*, and Wittig leaves no doubt about the work to be done: "Elles disent qu'en ce qui les concerne tout est à faire à partir d'éléments embryonnaires. Elles disent qu'en premier lieu le vocabulaire de toutes les langues est à examiner, à modifier, à bouleverser de fond en comble, que chaque mot doit être passé au crible" (They say that as far as they are concerned everything has to be made starting from basic principles. They say that in the first place the vocabulary of every language is to be examined, modified, turned upside down, that every word must be screened).

Les Guérillères has not enjoyed such a wide readership as *L'Opoponax*, but–no doubt because of its "poetic" as opposed to "theoretical" character–it has successfully crossed the great divide between French and Anglo-Saxon feminism. Its exploration of cultural codes and formal originality has also generated much interest in literary-theory circles and studies of postmodernist literature.

Le Corps lesbien (1973; translated as *The Lesbian Body*, 1975) is Wittig's least approachable work, offering on the surface a picture of lesbianism which is all-consuming and violent. The shock tactics and relentless exposure of the reader to the anatomical inventory of the beloved is calculated to discourage the squeamish, those whose idealized vision of woman cannot accommodate bodily reality nor such intensity of emotion.

On one level *Le Corps lesbien* is clearly an attack on the stylized enumeration of the feminine charms found in much love poetry. Here, the enumeration of the most private bodily parts and internal organs reminds the reader again and again that woman is a creature of flesh and blood and not a combination of literary conceits. Thus in one description the romantic conceit of the quaking and dumbstruck lover is mercilessly expanded to the point where the lover's brain is moving about inside her skull and her eyes are popping, while the transformation of turtledoves, traditionally associated with young love, into monkeys is a clear reminder of the physical and animal instincts underlying romantic love.

Body awareness and the candid description of sexuality is, as Wittig illustrated in *Les Guérillères*, a central feminist issue. Here, she is clearly trying to obliterate the distinction between physical features which make of the woman a sex object and unmentionable organs which are indispensable to the functioning of that human being. Loving someone in Wittig's terms involves loving everything about that person–liver, kidney, bowels, and so forth.

The act of penetration, normally associated with the male, has become a reciprocal activity, the two "amantes" (lovers) alternately adopting active and passive roles. Lesbian sexual intercourse is seen as being both more equitable in the distribution of roles and more complete, involving as it does the entire body and not just the genitalia. As the body is explored and penetrated, it seems to explode and merge with that of the partner. It seems to be an act which gives the lovers a heightened awareness of the way in which their own and their partner's body is composed and functions. Desire and the search for the absolute are inseparable from violence and the lovers subject each other to extreme ritualistic trials where the other's body is exposed to extreme heat or cold or even buried alive. Love is not sublimated into the abstract fusion of souls; it is experienced as an intensely physical and concrete attempt to destroy the otherness of the beloved's body and fuse with it. Such fusion is, of course, never definitive; it is a process which must constantly be renewed, and the narrative of *Le Corps lesbien* charts the relentless process of body dissection and reconstitution. These dynamics of dispersal and reintegration characteristic of physical communication for Wittig stand in sharp contrast to the dislocation wrought in the speaker by the fact that to communicate verbally she has to resort to a language that is not her own, a language created by man. In Wittig's words, in the preface to the English translation: "the 'I' (Je) who writes is alien to her own writing at every word, because this 'I' (Je) uses a language alien to her." Ever ready to play with man-made language, Wittig signals this fracturing of the identity typographically by the fractured personal pronoun "j/e" which symbolizes "the exercise of a language which does not constitute m/e as a subject."

The body dominates both the textual and the fictional space, while the tense used consistently is the present, a feature which is typical of the erotic novel but perhaps even more typical of Wittig's fiction, in which traditional methods of temporal and historical measurement are rejected and the richness and potential of the here and now are stressed. However, despite the repetitiveness of the physical descriptions and the promotion of the immediate, an evolution does take place whereby the initially isolated speaker becomes by the end of the novel integrated into the society of "amantes" to which her beloved belongs and which was first perceived as an obstacle to the fulfillment of her love and a source of dangerous rivalry. *Le Corps lesbien*, like *Les Guérillères*, concludes with the establishment of a totally harmonious collectivity. The duality of the couple gives way to a generous expansion and sharing of the self and that which one holds most dear with the group. The monogamous lesbian relationship is subject to the same suspicion and jealousy as its heterosexual counterpart if it is allowed to prevail over commitment to solidarity. As the final words of the novel indicate, fulfillment must be sought through the collectivity and not through competition with it: "J/e te cherche m/a rayonnante à travers l'assemblée" (I look for you m/y radiant one through the assembly).

Le Corps lesbien is much more, however, than the happily resolved tale of love pitched against its social context. A careful reading reveals a thematic and structural similarity which suggests that it is a kind of lesbian Song of Songs. Wittig's choice of model is both irreverent and apt. Wittig's rewriting of biblical and classical sources constitutes a feminist usurpation of the Word. Her reworking of the Song of Songs, however, testifies to a profound understanding of both the spiritual and structural principles of her sources. Most recent studies of the Song of Songs have abandoned allegorical exegesis and accepted it as a frank celebration of human love and sexuality between equals. Furthermore, although it deals only with heterosexual love, it is remarkable for the fact that the female speaker is in no way afraid of taking the initiative or expressing her desire. Wittig's variation on the biblical poem may transgress some of Christianity's most fundamental taboos, but it does not alter the spirit of it. Indeed, Francis Landy's description of the Song of Songs in his *Paradoxes of Paradise* (1983) can in many respects stand as a commentary on *Le Corps lesbien*: "The lovers pursue each other across the poem, elusive but in touch, changing roles, parting and converging. Thereby they partake of a rhythm, the shared pulse that is the subject of all erotic poetry." The details of the narrative are obviously quite different in each case but the intensity of feeling and the problems encountered by each "I" in her quest to unite with the beloved are remarkably similar: the unquenchable fire of passion, the separation, the sickness and weariness of love following consummation, and the disappearance of the beloved; the hostility of the city-dwellers which the "amante" encounters in her quest. In both works the development of the relationship is inextricably bound up with the richness and beauty of the natural world, creating, in Landy's words, "a complex system of alliance between the inexpressible self and the definable universe."

Interestingly, Landy points out that in the Song of Songs the bodies of the lovers are verbally "disassembled and reconstructed" in the *wasfs* of the poem. The word *wasf* is an Arabic word meaning description which has been adopted to refer to a poem or part of a poem that describes the parts of the male and female bodies. In the Song of Songs the wasfs are set pieces which interrupt the progress of the poem and which are set off from the poem both by content and the absence of syntactic structure. *Le Corps lesbien* is similarly interrupted by lists which enumerate the parts of the lover's bodies and which are not integrated into any grammatical framework. Wittig has accentuated the formal distinction by according these catalogues a full page each and has stripped away the metaphors of the poem in the interest of total candor.

Finally, in both, it very quickly becomes apparent that traditional plot-based analysis yields nothing and that both narratives are composed through the multiplication of variations on a single paradigm as opposed to the selection and organization of different situations into a logical syntagmatic sequence. In both the Song of Songs and *Le Corps lesbien*, the author clearly has no inten-

tion of writing the story of a specific couple. By the juxtaposition of unconnected and often contrasting scenes in which love is looked at from a multitude of angles and its various combinatory possibilities are exhausted, both Wittig and the writer of the Song of Songs contrive to create representatives whose repertoire encompasses the multiple personae of love.

Le Corps lesbien has generated, predictably, a mixed reaction. Its first reviewers found it intriguing but also rebarbatively hermetic. Although it is frequently cited in feminist writing, its influence and interest have remained marginal, and mainstream criticism has tended to take a wide berth.

Brouillon pour un dictionnaire des amantes (1976; translated by the authors as *Lesbian Peoples: Material for a Dictionary*, 1979), written in collaboration with Sande Zeig, belongs to a now well-established genre, the feminist dictionary. Wittig and Zeig's project is at once very modest and extremely ambitious. It does not aim to establish a definitive new language for women; it is by its own ambition but a blueprint, a utopian lexicon which works on the now standard feminist assumption that ordinary dictionaries are both male-oriented and male-dominated. It attempts, through an idiosyncratic choice of entries, to make the reader aware of the lacunae of standard dictionaries and to eclipse those words which have distorted the history of woman. Thus the word *antenne* (antenna) has been redefined to describe a quite specific faculty located in the forehead, throat, plexus, navel, and clitoris which alerts lesbians to the possibility of relationships with other lesbians.

The general point made by Wittig and Zeig here is much more important than the facetious redefinition. The attribution to the lesbian of a faculty unknown to men stands as a kind of synecdoche for a whole world of female experience and awareness which conventional language fails to express. The appropriation of the word *antenne* is far from innocuous; it is a symbolic attack on the prevailing code. Where special female powers have been acknowledged, they have, according to most radical feminists, been misrepresented. Thus the negative associations of the word *witch* have come to epitomize in feminist circles the persecution of women. It is therefore not surprising that Wittig and Zeig offer a description which replaces the image of the malicious old hag with one of a healthy athletic figure who is at one with nature and a survivor from Amazonia. The conferral of new meanings on old words is complemented by the elimination of words whose old meanings no longer correspond to reality. One such word is *avoir* (to have), which has no place in the lesbian language, because possession–clearly seen as a divisive force–does not figure as a value in the ideal community.

The entry for *mot* (word) provides an important commentary on the principles governing the composition of the work. Wittig and Zeig have selected a linguistic least common denominator, a body of words which, under no condition, they will do without. Furthermore, an examination of the nature of the entries reveals an attempt to draw from and maintain a balance between concrete and abstract vocabulary, ordinary words and proper names–in short, to offer a linguistic cross-section. The inclusion here, as in *Les Guérillères*, of the names of historical and mythological heroines drawn from a multitude of cultures constitutes a corrective to the traditional encyclopedic dictionary. The stories of well-known figures such as Artemis, Athena, and Atalanta are rewritten from a lesbian angle, while references to "obscure" individuals, peoples, geographical locations, customs, and species give a measure of what has been omitted from standard works of reference and thereby consigned to oblivion. As the gloss on *oubli*, the word for oblivion, points out: "si vous ne voulez pas y tomber de vous-mêmes on vous y poussera" (if you do not want to fall into it yourselves, you will be pushed).

The retrieval of names and customs from a multitude of different cultures also leaves no doubt that Western supremacy is under attack. Contemporary developments in anthropology that have shown the purely relative status of Western culture have added fuel to the feminist debate and given an inkling not only of the riches of African, Eastern, and South American societies but also of the structures and patterns underlying the most "primitive" and "sophisticated" cultures. This last point is made most forcefully by the inclusion in the dictionary of entries on those goddesses and mythological figures which appear in a wide range of different cultures but under different names–an anthropological fact which could be interpreted as supporting Wittig and Zeig's claim that there was an original unified culture which has through time been fragmented. Wittig and Zeig's references draw heavily on these non-Western civilizations and societies and make it clear that lesbianism is a cross-cultural phenomenon. The kind of language they are proposing does not simply illuminate neglected areas; it

is intended to break down cultural barriers. The language of the "mères" (mothers) who shut themselves into the procreative role and make themselves the touchstone of judgment has been divisive. Any culture which makes a single biological function the main point of reference dismisses and excludes a wide range of functions and experiences. Typically Wittig and Zeig include in their *Brouillon pour un dictionnaire des amantes* references to a host of goddesses traditionally associated with motherhood or childbearing (Anahita, Anna, Artemis, Britomartis) but provide glosses which ignore this association and stress other aspects of their stories.

Responsibility for the linguistic domination of women ultimately lies with the "mères." In *Brouillon pour un dictionnaire des amantes* men are never identified as targets. They are eclipsed here as they have eclipsed women. The main aim here is to stimulate an awareness in women: specific attacks on men would be gratuitous and irrelevant. Women are urged to take responsibility for themselves and recognize that there is more to womanhood than childbearing. It is to this effect that Wittig and Zeig rewrite the history of the language, arguing that the mothers have been responsible for the destruction of an ancient tongue common to all women and for the fragmentation of female culture. In opposition to this relentless historical trend, Wittig and Zeig aim to reactivate some of these original words and to establish a universal lesbian code which will transcend geographical and cultural divisions. Indeed, the entire enterprise is founded on the same principle as *Les Guérillères:* the importance of lesbian solidarity and collective awareness.

Another feature of the standard dictionary which Wittig and Zeig attack by implication is the monopoly of male writers in providing illustrative quotations. The definitions of *Brouillon pour un dictionnaire des amantes* are illustrated primarily with quotations from women writers from all ages but in particular from contemporary feminists, the latter belonging to what Wittig and Zeig see as the "âge de gloire" (age of glory) of lesbian consciousness. To many, most of the writers cited will be unfamiliar, but this circumstance only bears out the well-rehearsed feminist argument that female writers and artists have been willfully erased from history. Furthermore, the references to a multitude of female writers in illustrating definitions and in the bibliography Wittig and Zeig provide should act as a stimulant to further reading which will complement this rough "brouillon" or draft. Quotations from well-known male writers do figure but Wittig and Zeig use them to turn the tables against men. Recognizable lines from poets such as Virgil and Charles Baudelaire appear simply as fragments which have been retrieved out of chaos while Blaise Pascal undergoes a sex change in Wittig and Zeig's hands to become one Pascale. The device is facile, even rather childish, but it does make its point. The woman's word cannot be expunged from history with impunity, for two can play at that game. The traditional definition of woman in terms of the procreative functions has been replaced by a panoramic survey of women creators whose very inclusion in the work makes this a collective rather than a coauthored venture.

The choice of the dictionary format tends to discourage an aesthetic and thematic reading. However, there are several crucial thematic strands which are developed in the course of the work and a multitude of motifs and cross-references which give the work a unity not found in the traditional dictionary. Wittig and Zeig have placed at the very center of *Brouillon pour un dictionnaire des amantes* the long entry on "histoire" and it is this entry which in a very real sense draws together all the other references. Like Wittig in her earlier works, Wittig and Zeig waste little time on antimen arguments; they are more concerned to make women react against a historical process to which they have succumbed and which has progressively reduced and degraded them. Wittig and Zeig rewrite the eleventh chapter of Genesis and the history of civilization to account for the disintegration of Amazonian society and language. The wanderings of Noah's descendants, the great tribal migrations are their sources for the description of the idyllic period when the Amazons wandered the earth. The building of Babel and tribal settlement is identified with the rise of domesticity and acquisitiveness. In the beginning, in Genesis, "the whole earth was of one language, and of one speech," but this universal tongue was shattered when the *mères*, like Noah's descendants, sought security in the construction of a city. The history of settlement and civilization is seen as a negative process of division, compartmentalization, and the source of conflict which inevitably also involved linguistic fragmentation. The open territory of the Amazons was replaced by different countries and the universal language of this golden age by a multitude of different languages using phonemes in dif-

ferent ways. Transparency and ready comprehensibility gave way to ambiguity, suspicion, and the convolutions of exegesis. Wittig and Zeig's rewriting of history and of the history of the language concentrates therefore on principle and trend as opposed to contingent historical events. History is angled in *Brouillon pour un dictionnaire des amantes* in such a way as to make women aware of their own responsibility and to suggest what Wittig and Zeig see as the only cure: a return to a collective mode of life.

The central section is not, however, a set piece to be read in isolation. The theme of history is a motif which runs through the whole book. In particular, this section needs to be read in conjunction with the entries which are given the equally important opening and concluding positions. The opening entry provides a reworking of the history of man as it is foreshadowed in Nebuchadnezzar's dream (Daniel 2: 31-45) and in Ovid's *Metamorphoses*, whereby the history of humankind is seen as a process of fragmentation and decline through the ages of gold, silver, brass, iron, and clay, which will end with the Second Coming and the establishment of a unified kingdom that will never be destroyed. For Wittig and Zeig this time of glory is to be identified with the contemporary rise of lesbian feminism, a point made most forcefully perhaps in the bibliography, where conventional publication dates have been replaced by references to this biblical schema and where Wittig and Zeig's contemporaries are duly honored as belonging to the "âge de gloire." The abandonment of the conception of history as a succession of centuries and important dates in favor of an unorthodox and irreverent interpretation of the Bible constitutes an appropriation of perhaps the most fundamental point of reference in male ideology and anticipates Wittig's approach in later works.

The final entry of *Brouillon pour un dictionnaire des amantes* stands as a pendant to the first entry and complements the entry on history. "Voyelle" (Vowel) provides the cue for the description of a hypothetical language consisting of pure but ingeniously varied sounds. It is obviously difficult to take such an abstract proposal very far, but Wittig and Zeig's ideas are not as farfetched as they seem. If one accepts contemporary linguistic theory, then language is a system by which meaning is perceived through the differentiation of related phonemes and not via a one-to-one correlation between word and referential object. What Wittig and Zeig have learned from linguistics has permitted them to tamper with the existing code in such a way as to suggest that established authoritative meanings are simply conventional, that they are in no way definitive, and that the relationship between word and meaning is a shifting one which is subject to changes in the ideological climate and in particular changes which make the lesbian woman the principal point of reference.

Brouillon pour un dictionnaire des amantes has become a familiar landmark in feminist writing and criticism in France, the United Kingdom, and the United States. A central text in the Women's Language debate, it inspired many of the entries in the massive *Feminist Dictionary* (1985) compiled by Cheris Kramarae and Paula Treichler, with the assistance of Ann Russo.

Wittig's rewriting of some of the milestones of literature continues in *Virgile, non* (1985; translated as *Across the Acheron*, 1987), a parody of Dante's *Divine Comedy* which is both very funny and deadly serious. Dante's great work provides Wittig with a framework for a catalogue of the sins committed against women by others and, more important, by themselves.

Wittig's adoption of the broad structure of the *Divine Comedy* is loose and selective. Purgatory has been eliminated and Limbo now constitutes the intermediate stage between Hell and Paradise. The strict hierarchy of the circles of Hell has been abandoned, a feature which suggests a reluctance on Wittig's part to qualify or discriminate among various crimes. For her the sins enumerated here would seem to be absolute. Wittig further adapts Dante's schema by intermingling scenes from Hell, Limbo, and Paradise, the juxtapositions of contrasting scenes accentuating the differences among the self-inflicted Hell of women who have turned themselves into men's slaves, the as yet aimless liberty of the freewheeling lesbians in Limbo, and the bliss of the paradisiacal lesbian community. In contrast too with Dante, Wittig's "âmes damnées" (damned souls) are anonymous. Dante's predominantly male sinners were nothing if not well known, drawn as they were from history and mythology. Given Wittig's view of the erasure of women's history, it is not surprising that her sinners constitute a faceless and nameless mass.

Wittig does, however, largely retain Dante's categories of sin though each is of course presented from a specifically feminist point of view. The narrator encounters the wrathful wherever she goes but this wrath has a quite specific tar-

get: what the damned called the purple plague of lesbianism, purple being the traditional color of homosexual culture. The sullen, who in Dante emit a constant moan but "speak no word intelligibly," are represented by the moronic horde of slaves who ceaselessly recite their lists of domestic chores. Gluttony is largely the sin of their persecutors but the women themselves are ready to pounce on the disgusting leftovers from the feast; in short, there is nothing they will not swallow. The narrator's conversation with one of the suicides recalls Dante's conversation with Pier della Vigna in Canto 13, but while Dante's sympathetic treatment of the character only accentuates the inexorable nature of God's justice, Wittig suggests that suicide is the logical result of man's injustice. Whereas the Church fathers viewed suicide as an extreme act of insubordination, Wittig views it as a direct consequence of the subordination of women.

Most interesting perhaps is Wittig's reworking of the notion of carnal sin. Carnal sin is not excessive passion but rather pleasureless and mechanical sex where one partner, traditionally the woman, is subordinated to the other. Female sexuality and satisfaction have been denied by both men and women and the guilt of the latter is illustrated most acutely by the theme of clitoridectomy, most frequently performed by midwives and female relatives, which figures prominently in *Virgile, non*. Wittig spares the squeamish no detail in her description of the gruesome mutilation. Furthermore, when the narrator exposes her nakedness to the wrathful women in an attempt to make them aware of the female body, their first instinct is to cut off her clitoris, to deny her sexual pleasure.

The theme of responsibility evident in Wittig's other works is central to this novel. The damned spirits are largely responsible for their situation because of their passive submission to atrocity and their lack of concern about their fate. Some indeed are such inveterate sinners that, like the damned in Dante, they rush headlong toward their punishment, or attack those who would liberate them. Women have allowed themselves to be reduced to two-dimensional images through pressure to conform to certain cultural icons, to be, as Wittig suggests, "sage comme une image" (literally, as well-behaved as a picture; idiomatically, as good as gold). Others have become subhuman, like animals led on a leash or sold in the market. Essentially, women are guilty of stupidity; even those who seem to be succeeding in a man's world and who seem to be reaping the benefits of technology fail to see that all men are ceding to them is outdated knowledge and models, that they are in fact being bought off by trinkets.

Wittig's attack in *Virgile, non* is, however, less one-sided than it is, for example, in *Brouillon pour un dictionnaire des amantes*. Her main aim is still to awaken a sense of responsibility in women but she does devote more space than ever before to quite specific male crimes. Violence, greed, and deception are specifically male sins. The battle of the sexes is an uneven one in which men resort to harassment, fouling, and the breach of treaties made in good faith by women. The demands made of women epitomize the perversity and deviousness of the male imagination; Wittig's parade of the injuries inflicted on women illustrates the multiple ways in which women of all cultures have been mutilated or disfigured in order to satisfy the prevailing male code. All the evidence suggests that woman cannot win, unless, of course, she opts out of the heterosexual situation.

The Limbo of the lesbian coterie is one alternative. The lesbians who inhabit Limbo live, as one might imagine, rather aimless, marginal lives. This is the twilight zone of the gay subculture, where much time is devoted to coy flirtation and the narcissistic flexing of admirable muscles. The self-indulgence of fashionable homosexuality contrasts sharply with the self-sacrifice of the damned heterosexual female and is treated by Wittig with a gentle, if wry, humor. The marginal status of such pockets of lesbianism is also brought out by the application of the word *bandit* to them. Their attacks on authority are simply isolated sallies into male territory, reprisals against a cruel world which has made them cruel. Their protests are not constructive, do not go beyond the level of petty crime. Ultimately, the establishment of lesbian factions on the fringe of society can only be an intermediate stage on the road to Paradise (and in this sense it could also be seen as a kind of Purgatory). It is a temporary alternative life-style, not a true solution.

The utopian world of Paradise here, as in *Les Guérillères* and *Le Corps lesbien*, is a world of lesbian solidarity. The narrator can, it would seem, be reunited with her beloved only within the context of a harmonious lesbian community. Thus, although through her long journey through Hell and Limbo the narrator was fortified by the thought of this reunion, on her arrival in Paradise she focuses not on her beloved but on the corporate harmony of the beatified: "Des mains sont serrées, des épaules sont touchées, des torses sont étreintes, des baisers sont donnés" (hands are shaken, shoulders touched, bodies embraced, kisses given). The prominence given to the heavenly host of angels is no accident: it is a knowing nod in the direction of the allegorical angel that figures prominently in the iconography of the British and American suffrage movements.

The obviously propagandist and didactic dimension of *Virgile, non* should not blind the reader to the fact that, as for Dante, the journey is a test of belief and a quest for the better which can be fulfilled only through an understanding of how the enemy works. Like the *Divine Comedy*, *Virgile, non* can be seen as a drama of the mind in which the poet examines her beliefs and her conscience and recognizes her failings. Such an interpretation helps explain the typographical layout of *Virgile, non* where the dialogue between the narrator (supposedly Wittig herself) and the guide Manastabal is placed within brackets rather than inverted commas, the brackets indicating that this is an internal dialogue in which the former rehearses her own imperfections. At the start of the journey the narrator is described as a "lesbienne de papier" (a paper lesbian); she has lived in the two-dimensional world of writing and has failed in that writing to address herself to the concrete issues of the women's movement and in particular the multiple atrocities inflicted on women. The creator of lesbian utopias must face the reality of most women before she can attain Paradise. Manastabal points out that comprehension alone permits one to go beyond historical accidents and put a stop to injustice and attacks the narrator on her simplistic and unnuanced naivete with regard to evil.

The narrator also has a lot to learn about language. That language is again a central theme is signaled very early in the novel in her fight with the robotic eagle, which has replaced Dante's eagle of justice and which falls to the ground uttering an incomprehensible jumble of clichés. This easy victory is deceptive; such clichés are simply the Aunt Sallies of ideologically corrupt language and are easily knocked down. The formulation of the offenses committed by men would also seem to be a relatively straightforward enterprise and one considered by the author to be necessary, although she recognizes that the very act of articulation is likely to provoke in men accusations of exaggeration. What is much more difficult, as the narrator finds out, is the attempt to describe the previously unnamed. Familiar abstracts such as "compassion" and "beauty" fail to describe her fellow-feeling for the damned or the sensual and highly concrete gorgeousness of Paradise. Again and again words prove to be treacherous or elusive. Her first contact with her beloved in heaven is marked by an alienating inarticulacy: the absence of appropriate words stands as a concrete barrier between them, while a poorly chosen expression is liable to precipitate her back into Hell. The careless use of language is a fault which must be purged before she gains access to heaven. Language is a minefield and her inadvertent tactical errors should alert the reader to the necessity of examining the words she or he uses. In an important, centrally placed discussion the narrator expresses a deep-felt incomprehension and frustration resulting from the discrepancy between her facility in describing Hell and her inability to find the words which will at last define and give form to Paradise. In this discrepancy, Wittig is highlighting one of the central problems in feminist theory: the *décalage* between subversive critiques which attack androcentrism and the constructive but highly problematical gynocritical attempts to establish and define a women's language.

No solution can be found in a single volume or even in the writing of a single author, but here, as in *Brouillon pour un dictionnaire des amantes*, Wittig is willing to commit herself on fundamental principles. Concrete words of the existing code fare rather better than the abstracts. Wittig stresses early on the danger of high-flying rhetoric and the relative innocuousness of the literal, and it is in the light of this lesson that one must interpret the final section with its enumeration of the names of utensils, weapons, species of birds, herbs, and fruits. Such words are acceptable and justified within the new language, for they denote with precision the basic tools and natural resources necessary to the well-being and activities of the blessed. In a parallel movement, inappropriate and unnecessary words are, as in *Brouillon pour un dictionnaire des amantes*, eliminated. Thus in direct contrast with the final centripetal canto of the *Divine Comedy*, where all the leaves of wisdom and knowledge are united in a single volume, in Wittig's Paradise language disintegrates before one's eyes and its pieces are scattered by the wind like the leaves of Virgil's Sybil. At the end of her journey the narrator is left with a single abstraction to describe the spirit of Paradise: "passion." *Passion* replaces and tran-

scends the pale *compassion* and *beauté* rejected earlier. Only *passion* can translate the intensity and harmony of the heavenly experience. This one abstraction is the keystone of Wittig's utopian language.

The thematic earnestness of *Virgile, non* is offset by a formal playfulness and irony which sugars somewhat the radical lesbian pill. As in the *Divine Comedy*, the world of *Virgile, non* is a miniature of the finite and the infinite, the realistic and the fantastic, the ancient and the contemporary. Dante's sinful city of Dis has been replaced by contemporary San Francisco, and the various episodes of the narrator's journey combine, with humor, classical allusions, and modern Americana. References to typically American phenomena such as laundrettes, gay bars, cheerleaders, jogging, tequila sunrises, the subway, and anti-Communist paranoia rub shoulders with allusions to the Acheron, the Lethe, the Phlegethon, and the story of Orpheus and the maenads. Biblical episodes are subject to a radically modern reworking. The "flaming sword" of Genesis becomes a laser beam while the narrator's ultimate test of faith combines Jacob's fight with the angel and the modern American craze for Oriental martial arts. The heavenly cohort may have names that go back to the Old Testament and the book of Enoch, but they are nonetheless motorcycling "dykes" (Wittig's term) whose full sexual apparatuses contradict the Christian and Muhammadan insistence on the sexlessness of the angels.

Of Wittig's feminist novels, *Virgile, non* is one of the most readable and immediately enjoyable, recapturing as it does some of the humor and whimsicality of *L'Opoponax*. The juxtaposition of the classics and modern America may, however, not be determined simply by humorous potential. America and women have fundamental features in common: neither of them has a long recorded history; both feel acutely the lack of a cultural tradition. In rewriting the classics, Wittig makes them the center of a new mythology.

Wittig's most recent work, a play entitled *Le Voyage sans fin* (Voyage without End, 1985), is another product of her collaboration with Zeig, an actress and mime who shared the *mise en scène* with Wittig and took the principal part in both the American and French productions. Textually a much slighter work than any of her novels, *Le Voyage sans fin* nevertheless illustrates many of the features of the earlier works. Like most of them, it is a variation on a well-known literary landmark, this time her point of departure being

Cervantes's *Don Quixote*. All of Wittig's characters, including Don Quichotte and Panza, are, predictably, female, and many allusions to female or feminized mythological and historical figures are incorporated, a little awkwardly, into this brief text. Joan of Arc, already mentioned in *Virgile, non* and a popular figure in feminist iconography, is given particular prominence as a symbol both of active female heroism and the victimization of women.

Although *Le Voyage sans fin* contains much verbal and visual humor, Wittig's Quichotte is not subject to the radically subversive irony to which Cervantes's character is exposed. Wittig's play focuses on the tension between society and the minority. Her Quichotte is the isolated feminist idealist ostracized by–significantly enough–her mother because she rejects the sedentary values of hearth and home and opts for knight-errantry and the apparently vain struggle against injustice. Quichotte's mother and sister are book-burners. They actively contribute to the suppression of knowledge and wish to control Quichotte by denying her access to her books. In contrast, Quichotte turns out to be a creative genius. Wittig's Quichotte, unlike Cervantes's, is not the product of her books but their author. In short, she is Wittig's representative in the play, a play which, like its source, aims to please and instruct though Wittig's moral is rather different.

That Quichotte is the author's representative is confirmed by several echoes of Wittig's earlier works. Quichotte, like the narrator in *Virgile, non*, is the voice of freedom and resistance to man's shackles. Her encounter with the galley slaves is reminiscent of the heroine's exposure to the damned souls in the previous work, with the crucial distinction that this time there is only praise for those whose punishment is the unjust result of their resistance to man, whether it be through a rejection of his advances, abortion, murder, or the violation of the laws of ownership. Quichotte's idealism also reiterates the utopianism of Wittig's earlier books and the island to which she has promised to take Panza is no doubt the island paradise of *Les Guérillères*. The preferability of the interfemale relationship over heterosexual commitments is restated in several partnerships. Panza, though sceptical, has abandoned husband and children to follow Quichotte. Quichotte, like the narrator in *Virgile, non* has undertaken this voyage in order to make herself worthy of her beloved Dulcina. Quichotte's second sister rejects marriage and goes to live with her

aunt (Wittig's humorous pun on the word *tante*, also a slang word for homosexual, specifies the nature of this relationship).

More clearly even than her previous work *Le Voyage sans fin* is a play about perception, affirming yet again that the view of the minority–however deviant it may seem–may well be the correct view and that madness may simply be idealism and a refusal to accept the compromises and injustices of the world as it is. Despite her many mishaps and the often comical outcomes of her adventures, Wittig's Quichotte does not allow her spirit to be broken nor her vision to be adulterated. The only real rider to her naive confidence and good will is the play's title: Quichotte's task, like that of the "guérillères," is enormous, and she will know no rest.

Thematically *Le Voyage sans fin* reads like an abstract of Wittig's dominant preoccupations. Technically, however, it is a bold enterprise. Despite the importance of the feminist message, the other elements of the stagecraft are not subordinated to the language. In its final version it remains essentially a spectacle in which gesture, movement, color, and music are given essential rather than supportive roles. As in Jean Cocteau's 1921 play *Les Mariés de la Tour Eiffel* (*The Wedding on the Eiffel Tower*), sound and image are separated, the visual image being created by a mime and a clown. (Already in *Virgile, non*, which is compared in a blurb on the book's cover to Cocteau's films, Wittig had separated typographically the principal character's vision and her commentary on it.) Wittig pushes the technique a step further than either Cocteau or her earlier text, in that sound track and stage scene do not necessarily (and in fact rarely do) coincide.

Wittig's informative "Avant-note" places the play squarely within twentieth-century experimentation in the theater. Above all she wishes to avoid what Peter Brook calls the "Deadly Theatre," where gestures and words simply complement each other and lose their autonomy in a hybrid compromise. Robert Wilson is also cited in the foreword as a guiding influence. The speedy rhythm demanded by Wittig's source material and her own desire to maintain a critical distance between the spectator and the stage world contrasts sharply with the slow motion of Wilson's plays. However, the prominence which he gives to gesture, space, and formal pattern is matched by *Le Voyage sans fin*. Furthermore, Wilson's distinction between the exterior and interior screens of perception is highly relevant here, the disjunction between the often burlesque visual images and Quichotte's idealistic pronouncements illustrating economically and with force the crucial theme that perception is relative and that the pragmatic view is limited.

The third and most important technical influence cited by Wittig is the cinema and its exploitation of the *décalage* between sound track and scene in order to convey both the external perceptions and internal voice of a character. Such a *décalage* in the theater requires of the spectators a particular effort to maintain the double focus of their attention, and in this play the discrepancy between visual and aural perceptions forces recognition that there is more to reality than what can be seen with one's own eyes and that the misadventures of the feminist Quichotte do not invalidate her internal vision.

Le Voyage sans fin is a thought-provoking rather than an intrinsically deep work. The reader has to look elsewhere for a more sustained discussion of Wittig's feminist interests. Its success is inevitably heavily dependent upon the skill of the individual mime and unfortunately in the published version Wittig has given very few specific instructions as to how the visual images should be created.

Wittig's literary work has little to offer the feminist who simply seeks equality within the male-engendered social and political hierarchy. Nor does it attempt to propose a meticulously documented historical analysis of the economical, religious, and political factors which have determined women's subordination. Wittig's prime intention is to give back to women the culture and language which have been denied them, and she has no compunction about recasting the cultural landmarks which, she would argue, man has appropriated and attributed to his gender. Wittig is unfair, unreasonable, and exclusive, but her limitations are far outweighed by the erudition and sophisticated wit which she brings to her self-imposed task of raising consciousness.

References:

Louis Barjon, "*Le Faussaire: L'Opoponax*," *Etudes*, 322 (February 1965): 232-237;

Diane Griffin Crowder, "Amazons and Mothers? Monique Wittig, Hélène Cixous and Theories of Women's Writing," *Contemporary Literature*, 24 (Summer 1983): 117-144;

Jean H. Duffy, "Language and Childhood: *L'Opoponax* by Monique Wittig," *Forum for Modern Language Studies*, 19 (October 1983): 289-300;

Duffy, "Women and Language in *Les Guérillères* by Monique Wittig," *Stanford French Review*, 7 (Winter 1983): 399-412;

Dominique Duquesne, "Essai de lecture symbolique: *Le Corps lesbien* de Wittig," *Recherches sur l'Imaginaire*, 10 (1983): 121-133;

Laura G. Durand, "Heroic Feminism as Art," *Novel*, 8 (Fall 1974): 71-78;

Marguerite Duras, "Une Œuvre éclatante," *France Observateur*, 5 November 1964, pp. 18-19;

Lynn Higgins, "Nouvelle, nouvelle autobiographie: Monique Wittig's *Le Corps lesbien*," *Sub-Stance*, 14 (1976): 160-166;

Raymond Jean, "Le 'Féminaire' de Monique Wittig," in *Pratique de la littérature* (Paris: Seuil, 1978), pp. 130-132;

Mary McCarthy, "Everybody's Childhood," in her *The Writing on the Wall and Other Literary Essays* (New York: Harcourt, Brace & World, 1970), pp. 102-112;

Erica Ostrovsky, "A Cosmogony of 0: Wittig's *Les Guérillères*," in *Twentieth Century French Fiction*, edited by George Stambolian (New Brunswick: Rutgers University Press, 1975), pp. 241-251;

C. J. Rawson, "Cannibalism and Fiction: Love and Eating in Fielding, Mailer, Genet and Wittig," *Genre*, 11 (Summer 1978): 227-313;

Marthe Rosenfeld, "Language and the Vision of a Lesbian-Feminist Utopia in Wittig's *Les Guèrillères*," *Frontiers*, 6 (Spring-Summer 1981): 6-9;

Claude Simon, "Pour Monique Wittig," *Express*, 30 November-6 December 1964, pp. 69-71;

Mary Pringle Spraggins, "Myth and Ms.: Encroachment and Liberation in Monique Wittig's *Les Guérillères*," *International Fiction Review*, 3 (January 1976): 47-51;

Vlasta, special issue on Wittig, no. 4 (1985);

Jennifer R. Waelti-Walters, "Circle Games in Monique Wittig's *Les Guérillères*," *Perspectives on Contemporary Literature*, 6 (1980): 59-64;

Hélène Vivienne Wenzel, "The Text as Body/Politics: An Appreciation of Monique Wittig's Writings in Context," *Feminist Studies*, 7 (Summer 1981): 264-287.

Books for Further Reading

The following list includes several histories of twentieth-century French literature, especially that of the middle of the century. Listed also are volumes bearing on aesthetic matters associated with French fiction of recent decades, particularly the New Novel. Additional sources, both general and specific, are listed in the major bibliographies of criticism on modern French literature. Among them, in addition to the annual *MLA International Bibliography*, are Douglas W. Alden and Richard A. Brooks, *A Critical Bibliography of French Literature*, volume 6: *The Twentieth Century*, 3 parts (Syracuse: Syracuse University Press, 1979), a work indispensable for scholars; Douglas W. Alden, and others, eds., *French XX Bibliography: Critical and Biographical Reference for the Study of French Literature Since 1885* (New York: French Institute-Alliance Française, 1949-1985; Selinsgrove, Pa.: Susquehanna University Press, 1986-), which is not annotated but lists primary works and book reviews as well as critical works; Otto Klapp, *Bibliographie der französischen Literaturwissenschaft* (Frankfurt: Klosterman, 1960-), not annotated, but very thorough and particularly good for European criticism; and the bibliography in *Revue d'Histoire Littéraire de la France*, edited by René Rancoeur (formerly a quarterly or annual section of the journal, now printed as issue number 3 of each volume), collected and enlarged in René Rancoeur, *Bibliographie de la littérature française du Moyen Age à nos jours* (Paris: Armand Colin, 1967-1981). Major collections of manuscripts from modern French writers are at the Bibliothèque Nationale in Paris, the Bibliothèque Littéraire Jacques Doucet in Paris, and the Harry Ransom Humanities Research Center at the University of Texas at Austin; however, most of the manuscripts from writers of recent decades are still held privately.

Bersani, Jacques, Michel Autrand, Jacques Lecarme, and Bruno Vercier, eds. *La Littérature en France depuis 1945*. Paris: Bordas, 1970.

Boisdeffre, Pierre de. *Histoire de la littérature de langue française, des années 1930 aux années 1980*, 2 volumes. Revised edition, Paris: Perrin, 1985.

Brée, Germaine. *Littérature française: Le XXᵉ siècle*, volume 2: *1920-1970*. Paris: Arthaud, 1975. Translated by Louise Guiney as *Twentieth-Century French Literature*. Chicago: University of Chicago Press, 1983.

Brenner, Jacques. *Histoire de la littérature française: De 1940 à nos jours*. Paris: Fayard, 1978.

Carroll, David. *The Subject in Question: The Languages of Theory and the Strategies of Fiction*. Chicago & London: University of Chicago Press, 1982.

Clerc, Jeanne-Marie. *Le Cinéma, témoin de l'imaginaire dans le roman français contemporain*. Bern: Peter Lang, 1984.

Dällenbach, Lucien. *Le Récit spéculaire: Essai sur la mise en abyme*. Paris: Seuil, 1978.

Genette, Gérard. *Figures I-III*. Paris: Seuil, 1966-1972. Selections from all three volumes translated by Alan Sheridan as *Figures of Literary Discourse*. New York: Columbia University Press, 1982. Part of *Figures III* translated by Jane E. Lewin as *Narrative Discourse: An Essay on Method*. Ithaca: Cornell University Press, 1980.

Heath, Stephen. *The Nouveau Roman: A Study in the Practice of Writing*. Philadelphia: Temple University Press, 1972.

Jefferson, Ann. *The Nouveau Roman and the Poetics of Fiction*. Cambridge, U.K. & New York: Cambridge University Press, 1980.

Mansuy, Michel, ed. *Positions et oppositions sur le roman contemporain*. Paris: Klincksieck, 1971.

Mercier, Vivian. *The New Novel from Queneau to Pinget*. New York: Farrar, Straus & Giroux, 1971.

Oppenheim, Lois, ed. *Three Decades of the French New Novel*. Translated by Lois Oppenheim and Evelyne Costa de Beauregard. Urbana: University of Illinois Press, 1986.

Pasco, Allan H. *Novel Configurations: A Study in French Fiction*. Birmingham, Ala.: Summa, 1987.

Peyre, Henri. *French Novelists of Today*. New York: Oxford University Press, 1967.

Picon, Gaëtan. *Contemporary French Literature 1945 and After*. New York: Ungar, 1974.

Poirot-Delpech, Bertrand. *Feuilletons 1972-1982: Critiques littéraires*. Paris: Gallimard, 1982.

Robert, Marthe. *Roman des origines et origines du roman*. Paris: Grasset, 1972. Translated by Sacha Rabinovitch as *Origins and the Novel*. Bloomington: Indiana University Press, 1980.

Robinson, Christopher. *French Literature in the Twentieth Century*. Newton Abbot, U.K.: David & Charles, 1980; Totowa, N.J.: Barnes & Noble, 1980.

Roudiez, Leon S. *French Fiction Today: A New Direction*. New Brunswick, N.J.: Rutgers University Press, 1972.

Sherzer, Dina. *Representation in Contemporary French Fiction*. Lincoln: University of Nebraska Press, 1986.

Stambolian, George, ed. *Twentieth-Century French Fiction: Essays for Germaine Brée*. New Brunswick, N.J.: Rutgers University Press, 1975.

Sturrock, John. *The French New Novel: Claude Simon, Michel Butor, Alain Robbe-Grillet*. London & New York: Oxford University Press, 1969.

Waugh, Patricia. *Metafiction: The Theory and Practice of Self-Conscious Fiction*. London & New York: Methuen, 1984.

Weinstein, Arnold L. *Vision and Response in Modern Fiction*. Ithaca & London: Cornell University Press, 1974.

Zéraffa, Michel. *Roman et société*. Paris: Presses Universitaires de France, 1971. Translated by Catherine Burns and Tom Burns as *Fictions: The Novel and Social Reality*. Hammondsworth, U.K. & New York: Penguin, 1976.

Contributors

Gretchen Rous Besser...*South Orange, New Jersey*
David J. Bond...*University of Saskatchewan*
Catharine Savage Brosman...*Tulane University*
Françoise Calin...*University of Oregon*
Roland A. Champagne...*University of Missouri at St. Louis*
William Cloonan...*Florida State University*
Verena Andermatt Conley...*Miami University*
Terence Dawson...*National University of Singapore*
Jean Duffy..*University of Sheffield*
John M. Dunaway..*Mercer University*
John Fletcher...*University of East Anglia*
J. E. Flower..*University of Exeter*
Elissa Gelfand...*Mount Holyoke College*
Robert M. Henkels, Jr..*Auburn University*
Tobin H. Jones...*Colorado State University*
Doris Y. Kadish...*Kent State University*
James A. Kilker...*Southern Illinois University at Carbondale*
Jack Kolbert...*Susquehanna University*
Cecile Lindsay...*University of Nevada at Reno*
Françoise Lionnet...*Northwestern University*
Bette H. Lustig...*Tufts University*
Warren F. Motte, Jr..*University of Colorado*
Carol J. Murphy...*University of Florida*
Marie Naudin...*University of Connecticut*
John T. Naughton...*Colgate University*
David O'Connell...*Georgia State University*
Gerald Prince...*University of Pennsylvania*
F. C. St. Aubyn...*University of Pittsburgh*
Marian Brown St. Onge...*Boston College*
Stephen Smith...*Central Connecticut State University*

Cumulative Index

Dictionary of Literary Biography, Volumes 1-83
Dictionary of Literary Biography Yearbook, 1980-1988
Dictionary of Literary Biography Documentary Series, Volumes 1-6

Cumulative Index

DLB before number: *Dictionary of Literary Biography,* Volumes 1-83
Y before number: *Dictionary of Literary Biography Yearbook,* 1980-1988
DS before number: *Dictionary of Literary Biography Documentary Series,* Volumes 1-6

A

C

E

G

H

I

Cumulative Index

L

N

O

P

Q

R

S

Y

Z

8052

(Continued from front endsheets)

71: *American Literary Critics and Scholars, 1880-1900*, edited by John W. Rathbun and Monica M. Grecu (1988)

72: *French Novelists, 1930-1960*, edited by Catharine Savage Brosman (1988)

73: *American Magazine Journalists, 1741-1850*, edited by Sam G. Riley (1988)

74: *American Short-Story Writers Before 1880*, edited by Bobby Ellen Kimbel, with the assistance of William E. Grant (1988)

75: *Contemporary German Fiction Writers*, Second Series, edited by Wolfgang D. Elfe and James Hardin (1988)

76: *Afro-American Writers, 1940-1955*, edited by Trudier Harris (1988)

77: *British Mystery Writers, 1920-1939*, edited by Bernard Benstock and Thomas F. Staley (1988)

78: *American Short-Story Writers, 1880-1910*, edited by Bobby Ellen Kimbel, with the assistance of William E. Grant (1988)

79: *American Magazine Journalists, 1850-1900*, edited by Sam G. Riley (1988)

80: *Restoration and Eighteenth-Century Dramatists*, First Series, edited by Paula R. Backsheider (1989)

81: *Austrian Fiction Writers, 1875-1913*, edited by James Hardin and Donald G. Daviau (1989)

82: *Chicano Writers*, First Series, edited by Francisco A. Lomelí and Carl R. Shirley (1989)

83: *French Novelists Since 1960*, edited by Catharine Savage Brosman (1989)

Documentary Series

1: *Sherwood Anderson, Willa Cather, John Dos Passos, Theodore Dreiser, F. Scott Fitzgerald, Ernest Hemingway, Sinclair Lewis*, edited by Margaret A. Van Antwerp (1982)

2: *James Gould Cozzens, James T. Farrell, William Faulkner, John O'Hara, John Steinbeck, Thomas Wolfe, Richard Wright*, edited by Margaret A. Van Antwerp (1982)

3: *Saul Bellow, Jack Kerouac, Norman Mailer, Vladimir Nabokov, John Updike, Kurt Vonnegut*, edited by Mary Bruccoli (1983)

4: *Tennessee Williams*, edited by Margaret A. Van Antwerp and Sally Johns (1984)

5: *American Transcendentalists*, edited by Joel Myerson (1988)

6: *Hardboiled Mystery Writers*, edited by Matthew J. Bruccoli and Richard Layman (1988)

Yearbooks

1980, edited by Karen L. Rood, Jean W. Ross, and Richard Ziegfeld (1981)

1981, edited by Karen L. Rood, Jean W. Ross, and Richard Ziegfeld (1982)

1982, edited by Richard Ziegfeld; associate editors: Jean W. Ross and Lynne C. Zeigler (1983)

1983, edited by Mary Bruccoli and Jean W. Ross; associate editor: Richard Ziegfeld (1984)

1984, edited by Jean W. Ross (1985)

1985, edited by Jean W. Ross (1986)

1986, edited by J. M. Brook (1987)

1987, edited by J. M. Brook (1988)

1988, edited by J. M. Brook (1989)

ST. MICHAEL'S PREP SCHOOL LIBRARY
1042 STAR RT. - ORANGE, CA. 92667